USA
BASEBALL

CONNECT WITH US!

f /USABaseball

Join the more than 200,000 fans who like us on Facebook.

🐦 @USABaseball

Over 50,000 people receive breaking news and special offers by following us on Twitter.

📷 @USABaseball

Follow us on Instagram for a behind-the-scenes look at USA Baseball's events.

OUR PASTIME'S FUTURE.

usabaseball.com

BaseBall america
2015 Directory

Editor
JOSH LEVENTHAL

Assistant Editors
BEN BADLER, J.J. COOPER, MICHAEL LANANNA, VINCE LARA-CINISOMO
JOSH NORRIS, JIM SHONERD, BILL WOODWARD

Database and Application Development
BRENT LEWIS

Photo Editor
JIM SHONERD

Design & Production
SARA HIATT MCDANIEL, LINWOOD WEBB

Programming & Technical Development
BRENT LEWIS

Cover Photo
ANDREW WOOLLEY

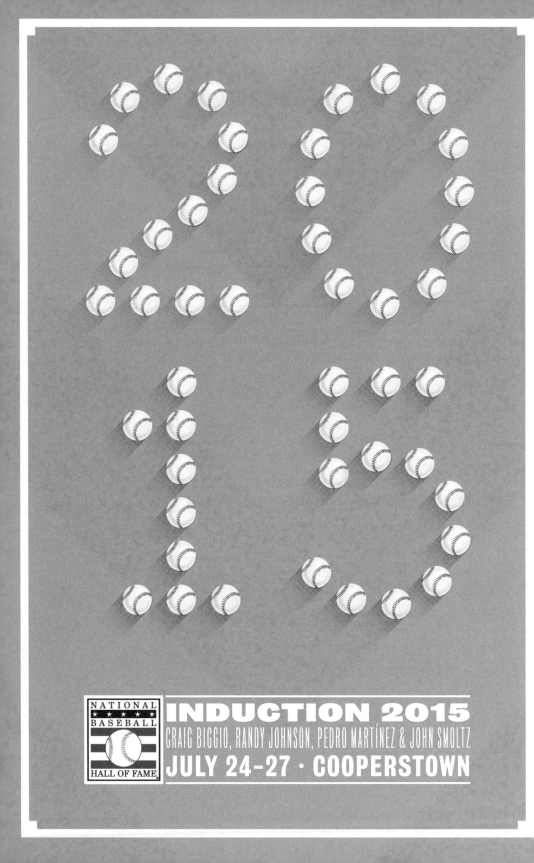

TABLE OF CONTENTS

Alex Box Stadium, Louisiana State

BB&T Ballpark, Charlotte Knights

WHAT'S NEW IN 2015

TRIPLE-A
Name Change: Oklahoma City RedHawks become Oklahoma City Dodgers.
Affiliation Changes: Albuquerque (Pacific Coast) from Dodgers to Brewers, Colorado Springs (Pacific Coast) from Rockies to Brewers, Fresno (Pacific Coast) from Giants to Astros, Oklahoma City (Pacific Coast) from Astros to Dodgers, Nashville (Pacific Coast) from Brewers to Athletics, Sacramento (Pacific Coast) from Athletics to Giants.

DOUBLE-A
Franchise Move: Biloxi Shuckers (Southern) replace Huntsville Stars.
Ballpark: Biloxi (Southern)—MGM Park
Affiliation Changes: Chattanooga (Southern) from Dodgers to Twins, New Britain (Eastern) from Twins to Rockies, Tulsa (Texas) from Rockies to Dodgers.

HIGH CLASS A
Name Changes: Daytona Cubs (Florida State) become Daytona Tortugas
Affiliation Changes: Bakersfield (California) from Reds to Mariners, Carolina (Carolina) from Indians to Braves, High Desert (California) from Mariners to Rangers, Lynchburg (Carolina) from Braves to Indians, Myrtle Beach (Carolina) from Rangers to Cubs.

LOW CLASS A
Affiliation Changes: Kane County (Midwest) from Cubs to Diamondbacks, South Bend (Midwest) from Diamondbacks to Cubs.
Name Change: South Bend Silver Hawks become South Bend Cubs.

SHORT-SEASON
Affiliation Changes: Boise (Northwest) from Cubs to Rockies, Eugene (Northwest) from Padres to Cubs, Tri-City (Northwest) from Rockies to Padres, Pulaski (Appalachian) from Mariners to Yankees.
Franchise Move: West Virginia Black Bears (New York-Penn) replace Jamestown Jammers.
Ballpark: West Virginia (New York-Penn)—West Virginia Baseball Park

ROOKIE
Affiliation: Pulaski (Appalachian) from Mariners to Yankees.
Affiliation: Kansas City rejoins the Arizona League.

TAKING FANS
OVER THE MOON
EVERY NIGHT

**LIVE LOOK-INS AND ANALYSIS ON MLB TONIGHT™
PLUS 5 LIVE GAMES EACH WEEK**

**MLB
NETWORK**

OUR NATIONAL PASTIME ALL THE TIME®

Map illustrations by Paul Trap

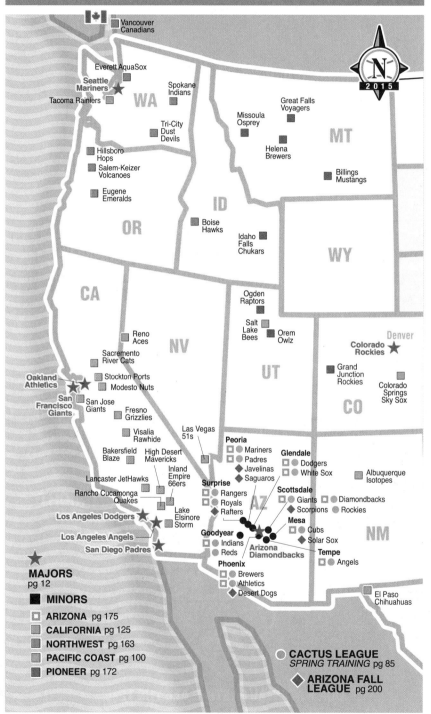

Vancouver
Canadians

Everett AquaSox

Seattle
Mariners

Tacoma Rainiers

Spokane
Indians

WA

Great Falls
Voyagers

Missoula
Osprey

MT

Tri-City
Dust
Devils

Hillsboro
Hops

Salem-Keizer
Volcanoes

Helena
Brewers

Billings
Mustangs

Eugene
Emeralds

ID

Boise
Hawks

OR

Idaho
Falls
Chukars

WY

CA

Ogden
Raptors

Reno
Aces

Salt
Lake
Bees

Orem
Owlz

Denver

Sacramento
River Cats

NV

Colorado
Rockies

Oakland
Athletics

Stockton Ports

Modesto Nuts

UT

Grand
Junction
Rockies

Colorado
Springs
Sky Sox

San
Francisco
Giants

San Jose
Giants

Fresno
Grizzlies

CO

Visalia
Rawhide

Las Vegas
51s

Peoria
□ ● Mariners
□ ● Padres
◆ Javelinas
◆ Saguaros

Bakersfield
Blaze

High Desert
Mavericks

Glendale
□ ● Dodgers
□ ● White Sox

Albuquerque
Isotopes

Lancaster JetHawks

Inland
Empire
66ers

Surprise
□ ● Rangers
□ ● Royals
◆ Rafters

Scottsdale
□ ● Giants □ ◆ Diamondbacks
◆ Scorpions ● Rockies

Rancho Cucamonga
Quakes

Lake
Elsinore
Storm

AZ

Mesa
□ ● Cubs
◆ Solar Sox

NM

Los Angeles Dodgers

Goodyear
□ ● Indians
● Reds

Los Angeles Angels

San Diego Padres

Arizona
Diamondbacks

Tempe
□ ● Angels

Phoenix
□ ● Brewers
□ ● Athletics
◆ Desert Dogs

El Paso
Chihuahuas

MAJORS
pg 12

■ MINORS

□ **ARIZONA** pg 175
■ **CALIFORNIA** pg 125
■ **NORTHWEST** pg 163
■ **PACIFIC COAST** pg 100
■ **PIONEER** pg 172

● **CACTUS LEAGUE**
SPRING TRAINING pg 85

◆ **ARIZONA FALL
LEAGUE** pg 200

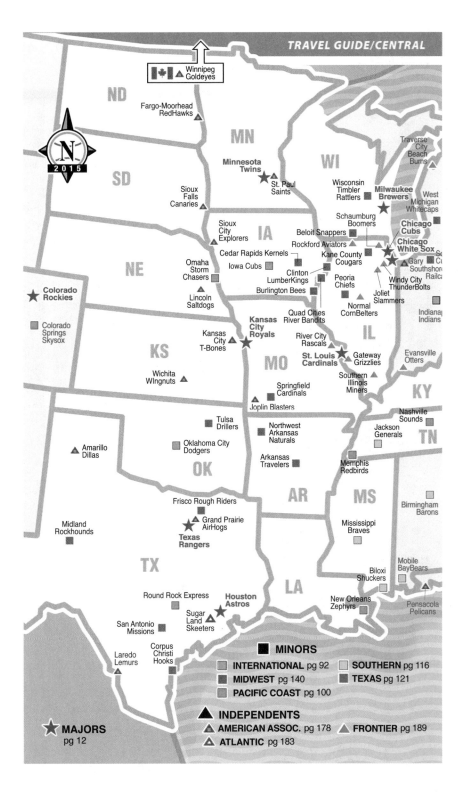

Winnipeg Goldeyes

ND

Fargo-Moorhead RedHawks

N 2015

MN

SD

Minnesota Twins

St. Paul Saints

WI

Traverse City Beach Bums

Wisconsin Timber Rattlers

Milwaukee Brewers

West Michigan Whitecaps

Sioux Falls Canaries

Sioux City Explorers

IA

Schaumburg Boomers

Beloit Snappers

Rockford Aviators

Chicago Cubs

Chicago White Sox

Cedar Rapids Kernels

Kane County Cougars

Gary Southshore

NE

Omaha Storm Chasers

Iowa Cubs

Clinton LumberKings

Peoria Chiefs

Windy City ThunderBolts

Railca

Colorado Rockies

Lincoln Saltdogs

Burlington Bees

Joliet Slammers

Colorado Springs Skysox

Quad Cities River Bandits

Normal CornBelters

Indiana Indians

Kansas City Royals

River City Rascals

IL

KS

Kansas City T-Bones

MO

St. Louis Cardinals

Gateway Grizzlies

Evansville Otters

Wichita Wingnuts

Springfield Cardinals

Southern Illinois Miners

KY

Joplin Blasters

Nashville Sounds

TN

Tulsa Drillers

Northwest Arkansas Naturals

Jackson Generals

Amarillo Dillas

Oklahoma City Dodgers

OK

Arkansas Travelers

Memphis Redbirds

AR

MS

Frisco Rough Riders

Birmingham Barons

Midland Rockhounds

Grand Prairie AirHogs

Texas Rangers

Mississippi Braves

TX

Mobile BayBears

Biloxi Shuckers

Round Rock Express

Houston Astros

LA

New Orleans Zephyrs

Pensacola Pelicans

Sugar Land Skeeters

San Antonio Missions

Corpus Christi Hooks

Laredo Lemurs

■ MINORS

■ INTERNATIONAL pg 92   □ SOUTHERN pg 116

■ MIDWEST pg 140   ■ TEXAS pg 121

□ PACIFIC COAST pg 100

▲ INDEPENDENTS

★ MAJORS pg 12

▲ AMERICAN ASSOC. pg 178   ▲ FRONTIER pg 189

▲ ATLANTIC pg 183

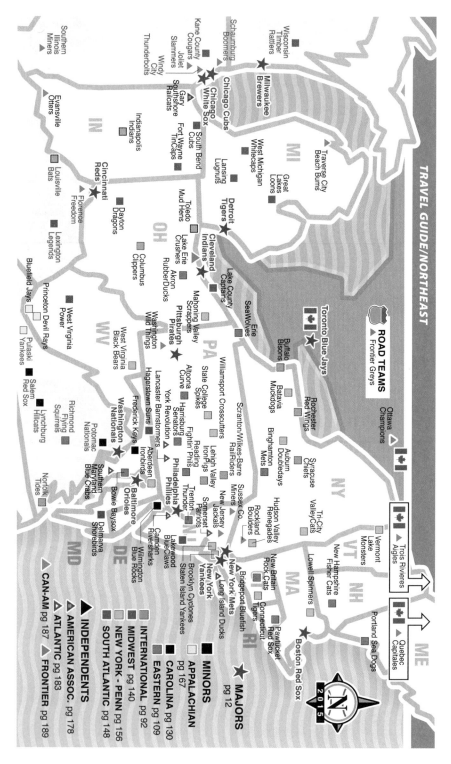

Southern Illinois Miners

Wisconsin Timber Rattlers

Schaumburg Boomers

Kane County Cougars

Joliet Slammers

Windy City Thunderbolts

Gary Southshore Railcats

Chicago White Sox

Chicago Cubs

Milwaukee Brewers

Evansville Otters

IN

Indianapolis Indians

Fort Wayne TinCaps

South Bend Cubs

Traverse City Beach Bums

Great Lakes Loons

West Michigan Whitecaps

MI

Lansing Lugnuts

Louisville Bats

Cincinnati Reds

Florence Freedom

Dayton Dragons

Toledo Mud Hens

Detroit Tigers

Lexington Legends

OH

Columbus Clippers

Akron RubberDucks

Cleveland Indians

Lake Erie Crushers

Lake County Captains

Erie SeaWolves

Bluefield Jays

Princeton Devil Rays

West Virginia Power

Mahoning Valley Scrappers

Pittsburgh Pirates

Washington Wild Things

PA

Williamsport Crosscutters

State College Spikes

Altoona Curve

Toronto Blue Jays

ROAD TEAMS
▲ Frontier Greys

Buffalo Bisons

Batavia Muckdogs

Ottawa Champions

Pulaski Yankees

Salem Red Sox

Lynchburg Hillcats

Richmond Flying Squirrels

WV

West Virginia Black Bears

Hagerstown Suns

Lancaster Barnstormers

York Revolution

Harrisburg Senators

Reading Fightin' Phils

Lehigh Valley IronPigs

Scranton/Wilkes-Barre RailRiders

Rochester Red Wings

Auburn Doubledays

Syracuse Chiefs

NY

Tri-City ValleyCats

New Hampshire Fisher Cats

Vermont Lake Monsters

Lowell Spinners

VT

NH

Trois Rivières Aigles

Quebec Capitales

Norfolk Tides

Frederick Keys

Washington Nationals

Aberdeen Ironbirds

Philadelphia Phillies

Trenton Thunder

Somerset Patriots

New Jersey Jackals

Sussex Co. Miners

Hudson Valley Renegades

Binghamton Mets

New Britain Rock Cats

Connecticut Tigers

Pawtucket Red Sox

Portland Sea Dogs

Boston Red Sox

ME

MD

DE

Potomac Nationals

Southern Maryland Blue Crabs

Bowie Baysox

Baltimore Orioles

Camden Riversharks

Delmarva Shorebirds

Wilmington Blue Rocks

Lakewood BlueClaws

Long Island Ducks

New York Yankees

Brooklyn Cyclones

Staten Island Yankees

New York Mets

Bridgeport Bluefish

Rockland Boulders

NJ

CT

MA

RI

2015

INDEPENDENTS

▲ AMERICAN ASSOC. pg 178
▲ ATLANTIC pg 183
▲ FRONTIER pg 189
▲ CAN-AM pg 187

MINORS

APPALACHIAN pg 167
CAROLINA pg 130
EASTERN pg 109
INTERNATIONAL pg 92
MIDWEST pg 140
NEW YORK - PENN pg 156
SOUTH ATLANTIC pg 148

★ MAJORS pg 12

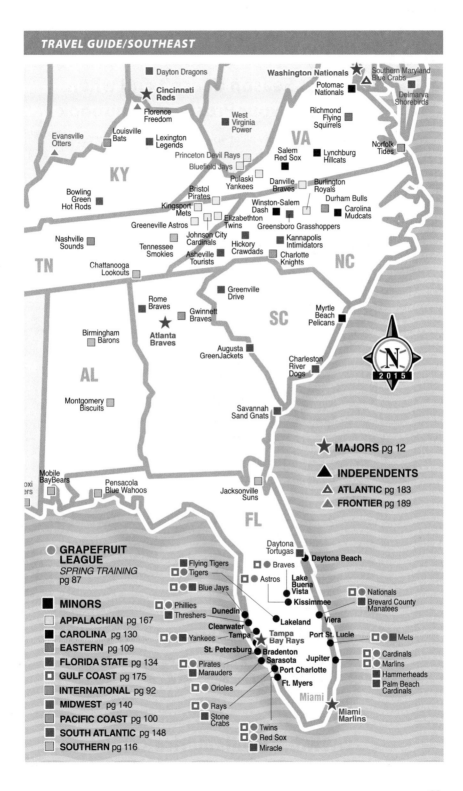

Dayton Dragons

Washington Nationals

Southern Maryland Blue Crabs

Cincinnati Reds

Potomac Nationals

Delmarva Shorebirds

Florence Freedom

Evansville Otters

Louisville Bats

Lexington Legends

West Virginia Power

Richmond Flying Squirrels

VA

Salem Red Sox

Lynchburg Hillcats

Norfolk Tides

Princeton Devil Rays

Bluefield Jays

KY

Pulaski Yankees

Danville Braves

Burlington Royals

Bowling Green Hot Rods

Bristol Pirates

Kingsport Mets

Elizabethton Twins

Winston-Salem Dash

Durham Bulls

Carolina Mudcats

Greeneville Astros

Greensboro Grasshoppers

Nashville Sounds

Johnson City Cardinals

Kannapolis Intimidators

NC

Tennessee Smokies

Asheville Tourists

Hickory Crawdads

Charlotte Knights

Chattanooga Lookouts

TN

Rome Braves

Greenville Drive

Gwinnett Braves

Myrtle Beach Pelicans

Birmingham Barons

SC

Atlanta Braves

Augusta GreenJackets

Charleston River Dogs

AL

Montgomery Biscuits

Savannah Sand Gnats

★ **MAJORS** pg 12

▲ **INDEPENDENTS**

△ **ATLANTIC** pg 183

△ **FRONTIER** pg 189

Mobile BayBears

oxi ers

Pensacola Blue Wahoos

Jacksonville Suns

FL

Daytona Tortugas

● **GRAPEFRUIT LEAGUE**
SPRING TRAINING pg 87

Flying Tigers

Tigers

Braves

Daytona Beach

Astros

Lake Buena Vista

Nationals

Brevard County Manatees

Blue Jays

Kissimmee

■ **MINORS**

☐ **APPALACHIAN** pg 167

■ **CAROLINA** pg 130

☐ **EASTERN** pg 109

■ **FLORIDA STATE** pg 134

☐ **GULF COAST** pg 175

☐ **INTERNATIONAL** pg 92

■ **MIDWEST** pg 140

☐ **PACIFIC COAST** pg 100

■ **SOUTH ATLANTIC** pg 148

☐ **SOUTHERN** pg 116

Phillies

Threshers

Dunedin

Clearwater

Yankees

Tampa
Tampa Bay Rays

St. Petersburg

Pirates

Marauders

Orioles

Rays

Stone Crabs

Lakeland

Bradenton

Sarasota

Port Charlotte

Ft. Myers

Viera

Port St. Lucie

Mets

Cardinals

Marlins

Hammerheads

Palm Beach Cardinals

Jupiter

Miami

Miami Marlins

Twins

Red Sox

Miracle

Prospect Season doesn't end when you receive your Prospect Handbook

Keep up to date on how all of your team's top prospects are progressing and find out which prospects are emerging as new stars with a subscription to *BaseballAmerica.com*. With your subscription to the Website, you will receive content you can't find anywhere else.

Get exclusive content found only online

MAJOR LEAGUES

MAJOR LEAGUE BASEBALL

Rob Manfred

Mailing Address: 245 Park Ave. New York, NY 10167.
Telephone: (212) 931-7800. **Website:** www.mlb.com.
Commissioner of Baseball: Rob Manfred.
Commissioner Emeritus: Allan H. (Bud) Selig.
President, Business/Media: Bob Bowman.
Chief Communications Officer: Pat Courtney. **Chief Legal Officer:** Dan Halem. **Chief Investment Officer:** Jonathan Mariner. **Chief Operating Officer:** Tony Petitti. **Chief Financial Officer:** Bob Starkey.

Baseball Operations

Chief Baseball Officer: Joe Torre.
Senior VP, Baseball Operations: Kim Ng, Peter Woodfork. **Senior VP, Standards/ Operations:** Joe Garagiola Jr.
Senior Director, Major League Operations: Roy Krasik. **Director, International Baseball Operations:** Chris Haydock. **Director, Baseball Operations:** Jeff Pfeifer. **Senior Manager, Minor League Operations:** Fred Seymour. **Manager, Amateur Relations:** Chuck Fox. **Manager, Latin American Game Development:** Joel Araujo. **Manager, International Baseball Operations:** Giovanni Hernandez. **Specialist, Umpire Administration:** Cathy Davis. **Specialist, International Baseball Operations:** Rebecca Seesel. **Senior Coordinator, International Baseball Operations:** Shane Barclay. **Coordinator, Major League Operations:** Gina Liento. **Coordinator, On Field Operations:** Stephen Mara, Michael Sansarran.
Coordinator, Baseball Operations: Max Thomas. **Registration Analyst:** William Clements. **Executive Assistant, Baseball Operations:** Chris Romanello. **Senior Administrative Assistant:** Llubia Reyes-Bussey.
Director, Major League Umpiring: Randy Marsh. **Director, Umpiring Development:** Rich Rieker. **Director, Umpire Medical Services:** Mark Letendre. **Director, Umpire Administration:** Matt McKendry. **Director, Instant Replay:** Justin Klemm.
Umpiring Supervisors: Cris Jones, Tom Leppard, Chuck Meriwether, Ed Montague, Steve Palermo, Charlie Reliford, Larry Young. **Umpire Evaluator:** Ed Rapuano. **Special Assistant, Umpiring:** Bruce Froemming. **Instant Replay Coordinator:** Ross Larson. **Umpire Administrator:** Raquel Wagner. **Video Coordinator:** Freddie Hernandez. **Baseball Systems:** Nancy Crofts.
Director, Dominican Operations: Rafael Perez. **Director, Arizona Fall League:** Steve Cobb. **Senior Director, Major League Scouting Bureau:** Bill Bavasi. **Assistant Director, Scouting Bureau:** Rick Oliver.

Public Relations

Telephone: (212) 931-7878. **Fax:** (212) 949-5654.
VP, Business Public Relations: Matt Bourne. **VP, Public Relations:** Mike Teevan.
Senior Director, Media Relations: John Blundell. **Director, Business Public Relations:** Jeff Heckelman, Dan Queen. **Director, Media Relations:** Donald Muller. **Manager, Business Public Relations:** Steve Arocho. **Specialist, Public Relations:** Lydia Devlin. **Specialist, Business Public Relations:** David Hochman, Jennifer Zudonyi. **Coordinator, Business Public Relations:** Sarah Leer. **Senior Administrative Assistant:** Ginger Dillon. **Official Historian:** John Thorn.

Club Relations

Senior VP, Scheduling/Club Relations: Katy Feeney. **Senior VP, Club Relations:** Phyllis Merhige.

AMERICAN LEAGUE

Year League Founded: 1901.
2015 Opening Date: April 6. **Closing Date:** Oct. 4.
Regular Season: 162 games.
Division Structure: East—Baltimore, Boston, New York, Tampa Bay, Toronto.
Central—Chicago, Cleveland, Detroit, Kansas City, Minnesota. **West**—Houston, Los Angeles, Oakland, Seattle, Texas.

Playoff Format: Two non-division winners with best records meet in one-game wildcard playoff. Wildcard winner and three division champions meet in two best-of-five Division Series. Winners meet in best-of-seven Championship Series.

All-Star Game: July 14, Great American Ballpark, Cincinnati (National League vs. American League).
Roster Limit: 25, through Aug 31, when rosters expand to 40.
Brand of Baseball: Rawlings.
Statistician: MLB Advanced Media, 75 Ninth Ave., 5th Floor, New York, NY 10011.

STADIUM INFORMATION

Team	Stadium	Dimensions			Capacity	2014 Att.
		LF	CF	RF		
Baltimore	Oriole Park at Camden Yards	333	410	318	45,971	2,464,473
Boston	Fenway Park	310	390	302	37,493	2,956,089
Chicago	U.S. Cellular Field	330	400	335	40,615	1,650,821
Cleveland	Progressive Field	325	405	325	43,345	1,437,393
Detroit	Comerica Park	345	420	330	41,782	2,917,209
Houston	Minute Maid Park	315	435	326	40,976	1,751,829
Kansas City	Kauffman Stadium	330	410	330	37,903	1,956,482
Los Angeles	Angel Stadium	333	404	333	45,050	3,095,935
Minnesota	Target Field	339	404	328	39,504	2,250,606
New York	Yankee Stadium	318	408	314	50,291	3,401,624
Oakland	O.co Coliseum	330	400	367	35,067	2,003,628
Seattle	Safeco Field	331	401	326	47,447	2,064,334
Tampa Bay	Tropicana Field	315	404	322	41,315	1,446,464
Texas	Globe Life Park in Arlington	332	400	325	49,170	2,718,733

NATIONAL LEAGUE

Year League Founded: 1876.
2015 Opening Date: April 5. **Closing Date:** Oct. 4.
Regular Season: 162 games.
Division Structure: East—Atlanta, Miami, New York, Philadelphia, Washington.
Central—Chicago, Cincinnati, Milwaukee, Pittsburgh, St. Louis. **West**—Arizona, Colorado, Los Angeles, San Diego, San Francisco.
Playoff Format: Two non-division winners with best records meet in one-game wildcard playoff. Wildcard winner and three division champions meet in two best-of-five Division Series. Winners meet in best-of-seven Championship Series.

All-Star Game: July 14, Great American Ballpark, Cincinnati. (National League vs. American League).
Roster Limit: 25, through Aug. 31 when rosters expand to 40.
Brand of Baseball: Rawlings.
Statistician: MLB Advanced Media, 75 Ninth Ave., 5th Floor, New York, NY 10011.

STADIUM INFORMATION

Team	Stadium	Dimensions			Capacity	2014 Att.
		LF	CF	RF		
Arizona	Chase Field	330	407	334	49,033	2,073,730
Atlanta	Turner Field	335	400	330	49,743	2,354,305
Chicago	Wrigley Field	355	400	353	41,160	2,652,113
Cincinnati	Great American Ball Park	328	404	325	42,319	2,476,664
Colorado	Coors Field	347	415	350	50,499	2,680,329
Los Angeles	Dodger Stadium	330	395	330	56,000	3,782,337
Miami	Marlins Park	344	422	335	37,000	1,732,283
Milwaukee	Miller Park	344	400	345	41,900	2,797,384
New York	Citi Field	335	408	330	42,200	2,148,808
Philadelphia	Citizens Bank Park	329	401	330	43,647	2,423,852
Pittsburgh	PNC Park	325	399	320	38,496	2,442,564
St. Louis	Busch Stadium	336	400	335	46,681	3,540,649
San Diego	Petco Park	336	396	322	42,685	2,195,373
San Francisco	AT&T Park	339	399	309	41,503	3,368,697
Washington	Nationals Park	336	402	335	41,888	2,579,389

Arizona Diamondbacks

Office Address: Chase Field, 401 E. Jefferson St, Phoenix, AZ 85004.
Mailing Address: P.O. Box 2095, Phoenix, AZ 85001.
Telephone: (602) 462-6500. **Fax:** (602) 462-6599. **Website:** www.dbacks.com

Ownership
Managing General Partner: Ken Kendrick. **General Partners:** Mike Chipman, Jeff Royer.

Business Operations
President/CEO: Derrick Hall. **Executive Vice President, Business Operations:** Cullen Maxey. **Special Assistants to President/CEO:** Roland Hemond, Luis Gonzalez, Randy Johnson, J.J. Putz. **Military Affairs Specialist:** Captain Jack Ensch. **Executive Assistant to President/CEO:** Brooke Mitchell. **Executive Assistant to Executive VP, Business Operations:** Katy Bernham.

Ken Kendrick

Broadcasting
VP, Broadcasting: Scott Geyer. **Senior Director, Game Operations/Multi-Media Productions:** Rob Weinheimer. **Director, Creative:** Dave Myslinski.

Corporate Partnerships/Marketing
VP, Corporate Partnerships: Judd Norris. **Director, Corporate Partnership Services:** Kerri White. **VP, Marketing:** Karina Bohn. **Director, Advertising:** Rayme Lofgren. **Manager, Hispanic/Promotions:** Jerry Romo.

Finance/Legal
Executive VP/CFO: Tom Harris. **VP, Finance:** Craig Bradley. **Director, Financial Management/Purchasing:** Jeff Jacobs. **Director, Accounting:** Chris James. **Executive Assistant to Managing General Partner/CFO:** Sandy Cox. **Senior VP/General Counsel:** Nona Lee. **Senior Director, Legal Affairs/Associate General Counsel:** Caleb Jay.

Community Affairs
VP, Corporate/Community Impact: Debbie Castaldo.

Communication/Media Relations
Director, Player/Media Relations: Casey Wilcox. **Senior Manager, Player/Media Relations:** Patrick O'Connell. **Manager, Corporate Communications:** Katie Krause. **Coordinator, Communications:** Jim Myers. **Director, Publications:** Josh Greene. **Social Media Specialist:** John Prewitt. **Team Photographer:** Jennifer Stewart.

Special Projects/Fan Experience
VP, Special Projects: Graham Rossini. **Director, Special Projects/Brand Development:** Matt Helmeid. **Director, Baseball Outreach/Development:** Jeff Rodin. **General Manager, Salt River Fields:** David Dunne.

Human Resources/Information Technology
Senior VP, Chief Human Resources/Diversity Officer: Marian Rhodes. **VP, Chief Information Officer:** Bob Zweig.

2015 SCHEDULE
Standard Game Times: 6:40 p.m.; Sun. 1:10.

APRIL		
6-8 . . . . San Francisco	25-27 . . . . .at St. Louis	7-8 . . . . .at Texas
10-12 . . . . Los Angeles (NL)	29-31 . . . . . . at Milwaukee	10-12 . . . at New York (NL)
13-15 . . . . . . at San Diego		17-19 . . . . . San Francisco
16-19 . . . at San Francisco	**JUNE**	20-22 . . . . .Miami
21-22 . . . . Texas	1-3 . . . . Atlanta	23-26 . . . . .Milwaukee
24-26 . . . . Pittsburgh	4-7 . . . . .New York (NL)	27-29 . . . . .at Seattle
27-29 . . . . .Colorado	8-10 . . at Los Angeles (NL)	31 . . . . at Houston
	12-14 . . . at San Francisco	
MAY	15-16 . . at Los Angeles (AL)	**AUGUST**
1-3 . . . at Los Angeles (NL)	17-18 . . . Los Angeles (AL)	1-2 . . . . at Houston
4-6 . . . . at Colorado	19-21 . . . . San Diego	3-6 . . . . . . at Washington
7-10 . . . . San Diego	23-25 . . . . . . at Colorado	7-9 . . . . Cincinnati
11-13 . . . . . . Washington	26-28 . . . . . at San Diego	10-12 . . . . . .Philadelphia
15-17 . . . . .at Philadelphia	29-30 . . .Los Angeles (NL)	14-16 . . . . at Atlanta
18-21 . . . . at Miami		17-19 . . . . . at Pittsburgh
22-24 . . . . . Chicago (NL)	**JULY**	20-23 . . . . . at Cincinnati
	1 . . . . . .Los Angeles (NL)	24-27 . . . . St. Louis
	2-5 . . . . .Colorado	
SEPTEMBER		
28-30 . . . . Oakland		
31 . . . . at Colorado		
1-2 . . . . at Colorado		
4-6 . . . . . .at Chicago (NL)		
7-9 . . . . . . .San Francisco		
11-13 . . . .Los Angeles (NL)		
14-16 . . . . San Diego		
18-20 . . . at San Francisco		
21-24 . at Los Angeles (NL)		
25-27 . . . . . at San Diego		
29-30 . . . . .Colorado		
OCTOBER		
1 . . . . .Colorado		
2-4 . . . . Houston		

GENERAL INFORMATION
Stadium (year opened): Chase Field (1998).
Team Colors: Sedona Red, Sonoran Sand and Black.
Player Representative: Brad Ziegler.
Home Dugout: Third Base.
Playing Surface: Grass.

Stadium Operations

VP, Facility Operations/Event Services: Russ Amaral. **Senior Director, Security:** Sean Maguire. **Director, Facility Services:** Jose Montoya. **Director, Engineering:** Jim White. **Director, Event Services:** Bryan White. **Event Coordinator:** Jeff Gomez. **Head Groundskeeper:** Grant Trenbeath.

Ticket Sales

Telephone: (602) 514-8400. **Fax:** (602) 462-4141.
Senior VP, Ticket Sales/Marketing: John Fisher. **VP, Business Analytics:** Kenny Farrell. **Senior Director, Ticket Sales:** Ryan Holmstedt.

Travel/Clubhouse

Senior Director, Team Travel/Home Clubhouse Manager: Roger Riley. **Manager, Equipment/Visiting Clubhouse:** Bob Doty.

BASEBALL OPERATIONS

Chief Baseball Officer: Tony La Russa.
Senior VP/General Manager: Dave Stewart. **Senior VP, Baseball Operations:** De Jon Watson. **Assistant GM:** Bryan Minniti. **VP/Special Assistant to GM:** Bob Gebhard. **Special Assistant to GM/Major League Scout:** Bill Bryk, Todd Greene. **Special Assistants to GM:** Barry Axelrod, Joe Carter Craig Shipley, David Duncan, Jerry Krause. **Special Assistant to VP, Latin America Operations:** Junior Noboa. **Director, Baseball Analytics/Research:** Dr. Ed Lewis. **Manager, Baseball Operations:** Sam Eaton. **Data Analyst:** John Krazit. **Major League Video Coordinator:** Allen Campbell. **Executive Assistant, Baseball Operations:** Kristyn Pierce.

Major League Staff

Manager: Chip Hale.
Coaches: Bench—Glenn Sherlock; **Pitching**—Mike Harkey; **Batting**—Turner Ward; **First Base**—Dave McKay; **Third Base**—Andy Green; **Bullpen**—Mel Stottlemyre, Jr; **Assistant Hitting**—Mark Grace; **Coach/Translator**—Ariel Prieto.

Tony La Russa

Medical/Training

Club Physician: Dr. Gary Waslewski. **Head Trainer:** Ken Crenshaw. **Assistant Trainer:** Ryan DiPanfilo. **Strength/ Conditioning Coordinator:** Nate Shaw. **Manual/Performance Therapist:** Neil Rampe.

Player Development

Telephone: (602) 462-6500. **Fax:** (602) 462-6425.
Director, Player Development: Mike Bell. **Assistant to Player Development:** TJ Lasita. **Senior Coordinator, Minor League Administration:** Shawn Marette. **Coordinators:** Tony Perezchica (field/infield), Dan Carlson (pitching), Chris Cron (hitting), Joel Youngblood (outfield/baserunning), Bill Plummer (catching), Hatuey Mendoza (Latin American Operations), Wilfredo Tejada (Dominican field), Brad Arnsberg (rehab pitching), Andrew Hauser (medical), Paul Porter (assistant medical), Vaughn Robinson (strength), Kyle Torgerson (manual performance), Jim Currigan (video), Bob Bensinger (complex).

Farm System

Class	Club (League)	Manager	Hitting Coach	Pitching Coach
Triple-A	Reno (PCL)	Phil Nevin	Greg Gross	Mike Parrott
Double-A	Mobile (SL)	Robby Hammock	Jason Camilli	Wellington Cepeda
High A	Visalia (CAL)	JR House	Jonathan Matthews	Gil Heredia
Low A	Kane County (MWL)	Mark Grudzielanek	Vince Harrison	Doug Bochtler
Short-season	Hillsboro (NWL)	Shelley Duncan	Javier Colina	Doug Drabek
Rookie	Missoula (PIO)	Joe Mather	Tack Wilson	Jeff Bajenaru
Rookie	Diamondbacks (AZL)	Mike Benjamin	Jacob Cruz	Larry Pardo

Scouting

Telephone: (602) 462-6500. **Fax:** (602) 462-6425.
Director, Scouting: Deric Ladnier.
Director, Pacific Rim Operations: Mack Hayashi. **Special Assistant, Pacific Rim Operations:** Jim Marshall. **Assistant Director, Scouting:** Brendan Domaracki. **Special Assistant/Coordinator, Pro Scouting:** Mike Russell. **Major League Scout:** Mike Piatnik (Winter Haven, FL). **Pro Scouts:** Mike Brown (Naples, FL), Bob Cummings (Oak Lawn, IL), Clay Daniel (Jacksonville, FL), Jeff Gardner (Costa Mesa, CA), Ben Johnson (Litchfield Park, AZ), Brad Kelley (Scottsdale, AZ), Bill Gayton (San Diego, CA), Pat Murtaugh (West Lafayette, IN), Tom Romenesko (Santee, CA), Wade Taylor (Oviedo, FL), John Vander Wal (Grand Rapids, MI). **Part-Time Scout—Mexico:** Derek Bryant. **Independent Leagues, Coordinator:** Chris Carminucci (Southbury, CT).
Regional Supervisors: Spencer Graham (Gresham, OR), Greg Lonigro (Connellsville, PA), Steve McAllister (Chillicothe, IL), Howard McCullough (Greenville, NC), Frankie Thon Jr (Miami, FL). **Scouting Supervisor:** James Merriweather III. **Area Scouts:** John Bartsch (Rocklin, CA), Nathan Birtwell (Nashville, TN), Kerry Jenkins (Birmingham, AL) Hal Kurtzman (Lake Balboa, CA), TR Lewis (Marietta, GA), Joe Mason (Millbrook, AL), Rick Matsko (Davidsville, PA), Jeff Mousser (Huntington Beach, CA), Rusty Pendergrass (Missouri City, MO), Donnie Reynolds (Portland, OR), Joe Robinson (St Louis, MO), Tony Piazza (Springfield, MO), JR Salinas (Dallas, TX), Mike Serbalik (Clifton Park, NY), Rick Short (Peoria, IL), Doyle Wilson (Phoenix, AZ), George Swain (Wilmington, NC), Frank Damas (Miami Lakes, FL), Luke Wrenn (Lakeland, FL). **Part-Time Scouts:** Doug Mathieson (Aldergrove, BC), Homer Newlin (Tallahassee, FL), Steve Oleschuk (Verdun, QC).
International Scouting Supervisor: Luis Baez (Santo Domingo, DR). **International Scouts:** Dominican Republic— Gabriel Berroa, José Ortiz, Rafael Mateo; Panama—José Díaz Perez; Nicaragua—Julio Sanchez; Colombia—Luis Gonzalez; Venezuela—Andres Garcia, Alfonso Mora.

Atlanta Braves

Office Address: 755 Hank Aaron Dr., Atlanta, GA 30315.
Mailing Address: PO Box 4064, Atlanta, GA 30302.
Telephone: (404) 522-7630. **Website:** www.braves.com.

Ownership
Operated/Owned By: Liberty Media.
Chairman/CEO: Terry McGuirk. **Chairman Emeritus:** Bill Bartholomay. **President:** John Schuerholz. **Senior Vice President:** Henry Aaron.

BUSINESS OPERATIONS
Executive VP, Business Operations: Mike Plant. **Senior VP/General Counsel:** Greg Heller.

Finance
Senior VP/Chief Financial Officer: Chip Moore.

Marketing/Sales
Executive VP, Sales/Marketing: Derek Schiller. **VP, Marketing:** Gus Eurton. **VP, Ticket Sales:** Paul Adams. **VP, Corporate Sales:** Jim Allen.

Media Relations/Public Relations
Telephone: (404) 614-1556. **Fax:** (404) 614-1391.
Director, Media Relations: Brad Hainje. **Director, Public Relations:** Beth Marshall.
Publications Manager: Andy Pressley, Kelly Barnes. **Media Relations Manager:** Adrienne Midgley.

Terry McGuirk

Stadium Operations
VP, Stadium Operations/Security: Larry Bowman. **Field Director:** Ed Mangan. **Director, Game Entertainment:** Scott Cunningham. **PA Announcer:** Casey Motter. **Official Scorers:** Mike Stamus, Jack Wilkinson.

Ticketing
Telephone: (404) 577-9100. **Fax:** (404) 614-2480. **Email:** ticketsales@braves.com.
Director, Ticket Operations: Anthony Esposito.

Travel/Clubhouse
Traveling Secretary: Chris Van Zant Visiting Clubhouse Manager: John Holland.

2015 SCHEDULE
Standard Game Times: 7:10 p.m.; Fri. 7:35; Sun. 1:35.

APRIL
6-8 . . . . at Miami
10-12 . . . . . .New York (NL)
13-15 . . . . .Miami
17-19 . . . . at Toronto
21-23 . . . at New York (NL)
24-26 . . . at Philadelphia
27-29 . . . . . . Washington
30 . . . . Cincinnati

MAY
1-3 . . . . Cincinnati
4-6 . . . . .Philadelphia
8-10 . . . . . at Washington
11-13 . . . . . at Cincinnati
15-17 . . . . at Miami
19-20 . . . . . .Tampa Bay

21-24 . . . . .Milwaukee
25-27 . . at Los Angeles (NL)
28-31 . . . . at San Francisco

JUNE
1-3 . . . . at Arizona
5-7 . . . . Pittsburgh
8-11 . . . . San Diego
12-14 . . at New York (NL)
15-16 . . . . at Boston
17-18 . . . . Boston
19-21 . . . . . .New York (NL)
23-25 . . . . . at Washington
26-28 . . . . . at Pittsburgh
30 . . . . Washington

JULY
1-2 . . . . .Washington

3-5 . . . . .Philadelphia
6-8 . . . . at Milwaukee
9-12 . . . . at Colorado
17-19 . . . . . Chicago (NL)
20-22 . . . .Los Angeles (NL)
24-26 . . . . .at St. Louis
27-29 . . . . .at Baltimore
30-31 . . . . at Philadelphia

AUGUST
1-2 . . . . . . at Philadelphia
3-5 . . . . San Francisco
6-9 . . . . .Miami
11-12 . . . . . . at Tampa Bay
14-16 . . . . .Arizona
17-19 . . . . . at San Diego
20-23 . . . .at Chicago (NL)

24-26 . . . . .Colorado
28-30 . . . . .New York (AL)
31 . . . . .Miami

SEPTEMBER
1-2 . . . . .Miami
3-6 . . . . . . at Washington
7-9 . . . . . at Philadelphia
10-13 . . . .New York (NL)
15-17 . . . . .Toronto
18-20 . . . . . .Philadelphia
21-23 . . . at New York (NL)
25-27 . . . . at Miami
29-30 . . . . . . Washington

OCTOBER
1 . . . . Washington
2-4 . . . . St. Louis

GENERAL INFORMATION
Stadium (year opened):
Turner Field (1997).
Team Colors: Red, white and blue.

Player Representative: Unavailable.
Home Dugout: First Base.
Playing Surface: Grass.

BASEBALL OPERATIONS

John Hart

Telephone: (404) 522-7630. **Fax:** (404) 614-3308.
President, Baseball Operations: John Hart.
Assistant GM/Director, Pro Scouting: John Coppolella. **Director, Baseball Operations:** Billy Ryan.
Assistant Director, Pro Scouting/Analytics: Matt Grabowski. **Executive Assistants:** Chris Rice, Eli Jimenez.

Major League Staff
Manager: Fredi Gonzalez.
Coaches: Bench—Carlos Tosca; **Pitching**—Roger McDowell; **Hitting**—Kevin Seitzer; **Assistant Hitting Coach**—Jose Castro; **First Base**—Terry Pendleton; **Third Base**—Bo Porter; **Bullpen Coach**—Eddie Perez; **Bullpen Catcher**—Alan Butts; **Assistant Coach**—Horacio Ramirez.

Medical/Training
Head Team Physician: Dr. Xavier Duralde.
Trainer: Jeff Porter. **Assistant Trainer:** Jim Lovell.
Director, Strength/Conditioning: Rick Slate. **Major League Strength/Conditioning Coach:** Phil Falco.

Player Development
Telephone: (404) 522-7630. **Fax:** (404) 614-1350.
Director, Player Development: Dave Trembley. **Assistant Director, Player Development:** Jonathan Schuerholz. **Manager, Minor League Administration:** Ron Knight. **Assistant, Player Development:** A.J. Scola.
Senior Advisors, Player Development: Lee Elia, Lebi Ochoa.
Pitching Coordinator: Rich Dubee. **Hitting Coordinator:** Ronnie Ortegon. **Roving Coordinators:** Joe Breeden (catching), Bobby Mitchell (outfield/baserunning), Luis Lopez (infield), Chris Dayton (assistant strength/conditioning). **Minor League Equipment Manager:** Jeff Pink.

Farm System

Class	Club (League)	Manager	Hitting Coach	Pitching Coach
Triple-A	Gwinnett (IL)	Brian Snitker	John Moses	Marty Reed
Double-A	Mississippi (SL)	Aaron Holbert	Garey Ingram	Dennis Lewallyn
High A	Carolina (CL)	Luis Salazar	Carlos Mendez	Derrick Lewis
Low A	Rome (SAL)	Randy Ingle	Bobby Moore	Gabe Luckett
Rookie	Danville (APP)	Rocket Wheeler	Ivan Cruz	Dan Meyer
Rookie	Braves (GCL)	Robinson Cancel	Rick Albert	William Martinez
Rookie	Braves (DSL)	Francisco Santiesteban	Tommy Herrera	Mike Alvarez

Scouting
Telephone: (404) 522-7630. **Fax:** (404) 614-1350.
Special Assistants to GM: Gordon Blakeley (Newnan, GA), Roy Clark (Marietta, GA), Tony Demacio (Virginia Beach, VA), Chad MacDonald (Arlington, TX), Rick Williams (Tampa, FL). **Major League Scouts:** Matt Carroll (Erdenheim, PA), Dennis Haren (San Diego, CA), Dave Holliday (Bixby, OK), Brad Sloan (Brimfield, IL). **Professional Scouts:** Rod Gilbreath (Lilburn, GA), Lloyd Merritt (Myrtle Beach, SC), John Stewart (Granville, NY), Pat Shortt (South Hempstead, NY), Rick Arnold (Spring Mills, PA) .
Director, Scouting: Brian Bridges. **Manager, Scouting Operations:** Dixie Keller.
National Crosscheckers: Tom Battista (Westlake Village, CA), Sean Rooney (Apex, NC), Deron Rombach (Arlington, TX). **Regional Crosscheckers: West**—Tom Davis (Ripon, CA). **Southern Supervisor:** Reed Dunn (Nashville, TN).
Area Scouts: Kevin Barry (Kinmundy, IL), Billy Best (Holly Spings, NC), Bill Bliss (Phoenix, AZ), Hugh Buchanan (Snellville, GA), Justin Clark (Marrietta, GA), Dan Cox (Huntington Beach, CA), Nate Dion (Edmond, OK), Brett Evert (Salem, OR), Ralph Garr (Richmond, TX), Gene Kerns (Hagerstown, MD), Chris Knabenshue (Fort Collins, CO), Kevin Martin (Los Angeles, CA), Greg Morhardt (South Windsor, CT), Rick Sellers (Remus, MI), Don Thomas (Geismar, LA), Terry C. Tripp (Norris, IL), Darin Vaughan (Kingwood, TX). **Part-Time Scouts:** Dick Adams (Lincoln, CA), Stu Cann (Bradley, IL), Dewayne Kitts (Moncks Corner, SC), Abraham Martinez (Santa Isabel, PR).
Director, International Operations: Marc Russo. **Director, Latin American Operations:** Mike Silvestri. **Assistant Director, Latin American Operations:** Rolando Petit.
International Coordinators: Central American Supervisor—Luis Ortiz (San Antonio, TX); **Eastern Rim**—Phil Dale (Victoria, Australia).
International Area Supervisors: Matias Laureano (Dominican Republic), Hiroyuki Oya (Japan), Rolando Petit (Venezuela), Manuel Samaniego (Mexico). **Part-Time Scouts:** Nehomar Caldera (Venezuela), Jeremy Chou (Taiwan), Carlos Garcia Roque (Colombia), Raul Gonzalez (Panama), Remmy Hernandez (Dominican Republic), Hyun-Sung Kim (South Korea), Dargello Lodowica (Curacao), Nestor Perez (Spain), Carlos Rodriguez (Venezuela), Jefferson Romero D'Lima (Venezuela), Miguel Theran (Colombia), Marvin Throneberry (Nicaragua), Carlos Torres (Venezuela).

Baltimore Orioles

Office Address: 333 W Camden St., Baltimore, MD 21201.
Telephone: (888) 848-BIRD. **Fax:** (410) 547-6272.
E-mail Address: birdmail@orioles.com. **Website:** www.orioles.com.

Ownership
Operated By: The Baltimore Orioles Limited Partnership Inc.
Chairman/CEO: Peter Angelos.

BUSINESS OPERATIONS
Executive Vice President: John Angelos. **VP/Special Liaison to Chairman:** Lou Kousouris.
General Legal Counsel: Russell Smouse. **Director, Human Resources:** Lisa Tolson. **Director, Information Systems:** James Kline.

Finance
Executive VP/CFO: Robert Ames. **VP, Finance:** Michael D. Hoppes, CPA.

Public Relations/Communications
Telephone: (410) 547-6150. **Fax:** (410) 547-6272.
VP, Communications/Marketing: Greg Bader. **Director, Public Relations:** Kristen Hudak. **Manager, Media Relations:** Jim Misudek. **Coordinator, Public Relations/New Media:** Amanda Sarver. **Public Relations Assistant:** Chris Martrich. **Director, Promotions/Community Relations:** Kristen Schultz.

Peter Angelos

Ballpark Operations
Director, Ballpark Operations: Kevin Cummings. **Head Groundskeeper:** Nicole McFadyen.
PA Announcer: Ryan Wagner. **Official Scorers:** Jim Henneman, Marc Jacobson, Ryan Eigenbrode.

Ticketing
Telephone: (888) 848-BIRD. **Fax:** (410) 547-6270.
VP, Ticketing/Fan Services: Neil Aloise. **Assistant Director, Sales:** Mark Hromalik.

Travel/Clubhouse
Director, Team Travel: Kevin Buck.
Equipment Manager (Home): Chris Guth. **Equipment Manager (Road):** Fred Tyler.

2015 SCHEDULE
Standard Game Times: 7:05 p.m; Sun. 1:35

APRIL
6-8 . . . . at Tampa Bay
10-12 . . . . .Toronto
13-15 . . . . .New York (AL)
17-20 . . . . at Boston
21-23 . . . . at Toronto
24-26 . . . . Boston
27-29 . . . . . . Chicago (AL)

MAY
1-3 . . . . .Tampa Bay
5-6 . . . . . at New York (NL)
7-10 . . . . at New York (AL)
11-13 . . . . .Toronto
15-17 . . . Los Angeles (AL)
19-21 . . . . Seattle
22-24 . . . . at Miami

25-27 . . . . Houston
29-31 . . . . . . .Tampa Bay

JUNE
1-4 . . . . at Houston
5-7 . . . . .at Cleveland
9-11 . . . . Boston
12-14 . . . . .New York (AL)
15-16 . . . . . . .Philadelphia
17-18 . . . . .at Philadelphia
19-21 . . . . .at Toronto
23-25 . . . . at Boston
26-28 . . . . Cleveland
29-30 . . . . Texas

JULY
1-2 . . . . Texas
3-5 . . . . . .at Chicago (AL)

6-8 . . . . at Minnesota
10-12 . . . . . .Washington
17-19 . . . . at Detroit
21-23 . . . at New York (AL)
24-26 . . . . . at Tampa Bay
27-29 . . . . Atlanta
30-31 . . . . Detroit

AUGUST
1-2 . . . . Detroit
3-5 . . . . .at Oakland
7-9 . . . at Los Angeles (AL)
10-12 . . . . .at Seattle
14-17 . . . . Oakland
18-19 . . . . .New York (NL)
20-23 . . . . . . .Minnesota
24-27 . . . . .at Kansas City

28-30 . . . . .at Texas
31 . . . . .Tampa Bay

SEPTEMBER
1-2 . . . . .Tampa Bay
4-6 . . . . at Toronto
7-9 . . . . . at New York (AL)
11-13 . . . . Kansas City
14-16 . . . . Boston
17-20 . . . . at Tampa Bay
21-23 . . . . . at Washington
25-27 . . . . at Boston
28-30 . . . . .Toronto

OCTOBER
1 . . . . .Toronto
2-4 . . . . . . .New York (AL)

GENERAL INFORMATION
Stadium (year opened): Oriole Park at Camden Yards (1992).
Team Colors: Orange, black and white.

Player Representative: Darren O'Day.
Home Dugout: First Base.
Playing Surface: Grass.

BASEBALL OPERATIONS

Telephone: (410) 547-6107. **Fax:** (410) 547-6271.
Executive VP, Baseball Operations: Dan Duquette.
VP, Baseball Operations: Brady Anderson. **Special Assistant to Executive VP, Baseball Operations:** Lee Thomas. **Director, Baseball Operations:** Tripp Norton. **Director, Major League Administration:** Ned Rice. **Assistant Director, Major League Administration:** Bill Wilkes. **Director, Player Personnel:** John Stockstill. **Assistant Director, Player Personnel:** Mike Snyder. **Director, Baseball Analytics:** Sarah Gelles. **Coordinator, Baseball Operations:** Pat DiGregory. **Coordinator, Video:** Michael Silverman. **Coordinator, Advance Scouting:** Ben Werthan. **Coordinator, Pro Scouting:** Matt Koizim.

Dan Duquette

Major League Staff

Manager: Buck Showalter.
Coaches: Bench—John Russell; **Pitching**—Dave Wallace; **Hitting**—Scott Coolbaugh; **Assistant Hitting**—Einar Diaz; **First Base**—Wayne Kirby; **Third Base**—Bobby Dickerson; **Bullpen**—Dom Chiti.

Medical/Training

Club Physician: Dr. William Goldiner. **Club Physician, Orthopedics:** Dr. Michael Jacobs. **Head Athletic Trainer:** Richie Bancells. **Assistant Athletic Trainers:** Brian Ebel, Chris Correnti. **Strength/Conditioning Coaches:** Joe Hogarty, Ryo Naito.

Player Development

Telephone: (410) 547-6120. **Fax:** (410) 547-6298.
Director, Player Development: Brian Graham. **Director, Minor League Operations:** Kent Qualls. **Coordinator, Minor League Administration:** J. Maria Arellano. **Coordinator, Player Development:** Cale Cox. **Director, Pitching Development:** Rick Peterson. **Coordinator, Minor League Hitting:** Jeff Manto. **Organizational Hitting Instructor/Evaluator:** Terry Crowley. **Coordinator, Minor League Catching:** Don Werner. **Coordinator, Minor League Infield:** Kevin Bradshaw. **Roving Instructor, Outfield/Baserunning/Strength:** Scott Beerer.
Medical Coordinator: Dave Walker. **Latin American Medical Coordinator:** Manny Lopez. **Coordinator, Strength/Conditioning—Sarasota:** Ryan Driscoll. **Coordinator, Minor League Rehab Pitching:** Scott McGregor. **Minor League Equipment Manager:** Jake Parker. **Pitching Administrator, Florida/DSL:** Dave Schmidt. **Administrator, Sarasota Operations:** Len Johnston.

Farm System

Class	Club (League)	Manager	Hitting Coach	Pitching Coach
Triple-A	Norfolk (IL)	Ron Johnson	Sean Berry	Mike Griffin
Double-A	Bowie (EL)	Gary Kendall	Paco Figueroa	Alan Mills
High A	Frederick (CL)	Orlando Gomez	Unavailable	Kennie Steenstra
Low A	Delmarva (SAL)	Ryan Minor	Howie Clark	Blaine Beatty
Short-season	Aberdeen (NYP)	Luis Pujols	Scott Thomas	Justin Lord
Rookie	Orioles (GCL)	Matt Merullo	Milt May	Wilson Alvarez
Rookie	Orioles (DSL)	Elvis Morel	Ramon Caraballo	Dionis Pascual
Rookie	Orioles (DSL2)	Nelson Norman	Beny Adames	Robert Perez

Scouting

Telephone: (410) 547-6212. **Fax:** 410-547-6928.
Director, Amateur Scouting: Gary Rajsich.
Scouting Administrator: Brad Ciolek. **Special Assistant to the GM/Scouting:** Danny Haas (Fort Myers, FL). **National Crosschecker Supervisor:** Matt Haas (Cincinnati, OH). **West Coast Supervisor:** David Blume (Elk Grove, CA). **Midwest Supervisor:** Jim Richardson (Marlow, OK). **Upper Midwest Supervisor:** Ernie Jacobs (Wichita, KS).
Area Scouts: Dean Albany (Baltimore, MD), Mike Boulanger (Broken Arrow, OK), Kelvin Colon (Miami, FL), Adrian Dorsey (Nashville, TN), Thom Dreier (The Woodlands, TX), Dan Durst (Rockford, IL), Kirk Fredriksson (Torrington, CT), John Gillette (Gilbert, AZ), Ken Guthrie (Sanger, TX), David Jennings (Spanish Fort, AL), Arthur McConnehead (Atlanta, GA), Rich Morales (Blacksburg, VA), Mark Ralston (Carlsbad, CA), Jeff Stevens (Walnut Creek, CA), Jim Thrift (Sarasota, FL), Brandon Verley (White Salmon, WA), Scott Walter (Manhattan Beach, CA).
Special Assignment Scouts: Wayne Britton (Waynesboro, VA), Dave Machemer (Stevensville, MI). **Major League Scouts:** Dave Engle (San Diego, CA), Jim Howard (Clifton Park, NY), Bruce Kison (Bradenton, FL). **Professional Scouts:** Todd Frohwirth (Waukesha, WI).
Executive Director, International Recruiting: Fred Ferreira. **Director, Baseball Operations for the Dominican Republic:** Nelson Norman. **Academy Director, Dominican Republic:** Felipe Rojas Alou. **International Scouts:** Joel Bradley, Enrique Constante, Calvin Maduro, Brett Ward.

Boston Red Sox

Office Address: Fenway Park, 4 Yawkey Way, Boston, MA 02215.
Telephone: (617) 226-6000. **Fax:** (617) 226-6416. **Website:** www.redsox.com

Ownership
Principal Owner: John Henry. **Chairman:** Thomas C. Werner. **President, Fenway Sports Group:** Michael Gordon.
President/CEO: Larry Lucchino. **Vice Chairmen:** David Ginsberg, Phillip H. Morse. **Executive Vice President,
Corporate Strategy/General Counsel:** Ed Weiss.

BUSINESS OPERATIONS
Executive VP/Chief Operating Officer: Sam Kennedy. **Executive VP, Business Affairs:**
Jonathan Gilula. **Executive VP/Senior Advisor to the President/CEO:** Charles Steinberg.
Senior VP, Fenway Affairs: Larry Cancro. **VP/Corporate Strategy/Special Counsel:** David
Beeston. **Financial Advisor to the President/CEO:** Jeff White. **Senior Advisor, Baseball
Projects:** Jeremy Kapstein. **VP, Business Development:** Tim Zue.

Finance
Senior VP/CFO: Steve Fitch. **VP/Controller:** Mark Solitro.

Human Resources/Information Technology
Senior VP, Human Resources: Amy Waryas. **VP, Information Technology:** Brian Shield.

Sales/Corporate Partnerships/Marketing
Senior VP, Corporate Partnerships: Troup Parkinson. **VP, Client Services:** Marcell
Bhangoo. **Senior VP, Marketing/Brand Development:** Adam Grossman.

Larry Lucchino

Public Affairs/Media
Senior Director, Public Affairs: Pam Kenn. **Director, Media Relations:** Kevin Gregg.

Legal
Senior VP/Assistant General Counsel: Jennifer Flynn. **Senior VP/Special Counsel:** David Friedman. **VP/Club
Counsel:** Elaine Weddington Steward.

Foundation
Honorary Chairman: Tim Wakefield. **Executive Director:** Gena Borson.

Ballpark Operations
VP, Fan Services/Entertainment: Sarah McKenna. **VP, Ballpark Operations:** Pete Nesbit. **Senior Director, Florida
Business Operations:** Katie Haas.

Ticketing/Sales
Senior VP, Ticketing/Fenway Enterprises: Ron Bumgarner. **VP, Ticketing:** Richard Beaton. **VP, Fenway Enterprises:**
Carrie Campbell. **VP/Ticket Sales:** William Droste.

2015 SCHEDULE
Standard Game Times: 7:10 p.m.; Sun. 1:35

APRIL			
6 . . . . at Philadelphia	22-24 . . . . Los Angeles (AL)	3-5. . . . . Houston	28-30 . . . . at New York (NL)
8-9. . . . . at Philadelphia	25-27 . . . . . . at Minnesota	7-8. . . . . .Miami	31 . . . . .New York (AL)
10-12 . . . . at New York (AL)	28-31 . . . . .at Texas	10-12 . . . . . .New York (AL)	
13-15 . . . . . . .Washington		17-20 . . at Los Angeles (AL)	SEPTEMBER
17-20 . . . . Baltimore	JUNE	21-23 . . . . at Houston	1-2. . . . . . . .New York (AL)
21-23 . . . . . at Tampa Bay	1-4. . . . . .Minnesota	24-26 . . . . Detroit	4-6. . . . . .Philadelphia
24-26 . . . . . .at Baltimore	5-7. . . . . Oakland	27-30 . . . . . Chicago (AL)	7-9. . . . . .Toronto
27-29 . . . . .Toronto	9-11 . . . . . . .at Baltimore	31 . . . . .Tampa Bay	11-13 . . . . . . at Tampa Bay
	12-14 . . . . .Toronto		14-16 . . . . . . .at Baltimore
MAY	15-16 . . . . Atlanta	AUGUST	18-20 . . . . . . at Toronto
1-3. . . . . . .New York (AL)	17-18 . . . . at Atlanta	1-2. . . . . .Tampa Bay	21-24 . . . . .Tampa Bay
4-6. . . . . . . .Tampa Bay	19-21 . . . . .at Kansas City	4-6. . . . . at New York (AL)	25-27 . . . . Baltimore
8-10 . . . . at Toronto	23-25 . . . . Baltimore	7-9. . . . . at Detroit	28-30 . . . . at New York (AL)
11-13 . . . . .at Oakland	26-28 . . . . . at Tampa Bay	11-12 . . . . at Miami	
14-17 . . . . .at Seattle	29-30 . . . . at Toronto	14-16 . . . . Seattle	OCTOBER
19-21 . . . . Texas		17-19 . . . . Cleveland	1 . . . . at New York (AL)
	JULY	20-23 . . . . . . Kansas City	2-4. . . . . .at Cleveland
	1-2. . . . . at Toronto	24-26 . . . . .at Chicago (AL)	

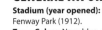

GENERAL INFORMATION
Stadium (year opened):
Fenway Park (1912).
Team Colors: Navy blue, red and white.

Player Representative: Unavailable.
Home Dugout: First Base.
Playing Surface: Grass.

BASEBALL OPERATIONS

Executive VP/General Manager: Ben Cherington.
Senior VP/Assistant GM: Mike Hazen, Brian O'Halloran. **Senior VP, Player Personnel:**
Allard Baird. **VP, Amateur/International Scouting:** Amiel Sawdaye. **VP, Baseball
Administration:** Raquel Ferreira.
Traveling Secretary: Jack McCormick. **Director, Major League Operations:** Zack Scott.
Senior Baseball Analyst: Tom Tippett. **Baseball Operations Analysts:** Greg Rybarczyk,
Joe McDonald. **Assistant Director, Major League Operations:** Mike Murov. **Coordinator,
Baseball Operations:** Mike Regan. **Coordinator, Baseball Systems Development:** Shawn
O'Rourke. **Executive Assistant:** Erin Cox. **Senior Advisor:** Bill James. **Special Assistants to
GM:** Pedro Martinez, Jason Varitek.

Ben Cherington

Major League Staff

Manager: John Farrell.
Coaches: Bench—Torey Lovullo; Pitching—Juan Nieves; Hitting—Chili Davis; First Base—Arnie Beyeler; Third
Base—Brian Butterfield; Bullpen—Dana LeVangie; Assistant Hitting Coach—Victor Rodriguez; Bullpen Catcher—Mani
Martinez. **Major League Staff Assistant:** Adrian Lorenzo. **BP Thrower:** Matt Noone.

Sports Medicine Service

Director, Sports Medicine Service: Dan Dyrek. **Medical Director:** Dr. Larry Ronan. **Head Team Orthopedist:** Dr.
Peter Asnis. **Head Athletic Trainer:** Rick Jameyson. **Assistant Trainers:** Brad Pearson, Masai Takahashi. **Strength/
Conditioning Coach:** Pat Sandora. **Massage Therapists:** Russell Nua, Shinichiro Uchikubo. **Physical Therapist:** Ray
Mattfeld. **Head Minor League Physician:** Brian Busconi. **Director, Behavioral Health Program:** Dr. Richard Ginsburg.
Mental Skills Coaches: Bob Tewksbury, Laz Gutierrez, Justin Su'a.

Player Development

Director, Player Development: Ben Crockett.
Assistant Director, Player Development: Brian Abraham. **Assistant Director, Florida Baseball Operations:** Ethan
Faggett. **Minor League Equipment Manager:** Mike Stelmach. **Field Coordinator:** David Howard. **Latin American
Pitching Coordinator/GCL Pitching Coach:** Goose Gregson. **Minor League Medical Coordinator:** Paul Buchheit.
Latin Medical Coordinator: Mauricio Elizondo. **Strength/Conditioning Coordinator:** Mike Roose. **Physical Therapist/
Clinical Educator:** Jason Bartley. **Roving Instructors:** Andy Fox (infield), Chad Epperson (catching), Tim Hyers (hitting),
Ralph Treuel (pitching), George Lombard (outfield/baserunning).

Farm System

Class	Club (League)	Manager	Hitting Coach	Pitching Coach
Triple-A	Pawtucket (IL)	Kevin Boles	Rich Gedman	Bob Kipper
Double-A	Portland (EL)	Billy McMillon	Kevin Walker	David Joppie
High A	Salem (CL)	Carlos Febles	Paul Abbott	Jon Nunnally
Low A	Greenville (SAL)	Darren Fenster	Nelson Paulino	Walter Miranda
Short-season	Lowell (NYP)	Joe Oliver	Iggy Suarez	Lance Carter
Rookie	Red Sox (GCL)	Tom Kotchman	Junor Zamora	Dick Such
Rookie	Red Sox (DSL)	Jose Zapata	Wilton Veras	Amaury Telemaco

Scouting

Director, Professional Scouting: Jared Porter. **Director, Amateur Scouting:** Mike Rikard. **Director, International
Scouting:** Eddie Romero.
Assistant Director, Professional/International Scouting: Gus Quattlebaum. **Assistant Director, Amateur
Scouting:** Steve Sanders. **Assistant Director, Player Personnel:** Jared Banner. **Advance Scouting Assistant:** Harrison
Slutsky. **Assistant, Amateur/International Scouting:** Justin Horowitz. **Special Assistants, Player Personnel:** Eddie
Bane, Mark Wasinger. **Global Crosschecker:** Paul Fryer. **Special Assignment Scouts:** Dave Klipstein, Steve Peck.
Major League Advance Scout: Steve Langone. **Major League Scouts:** Jaymie Bane, Bob Hamelin. **Pro Scouts:** Brian
Bannister, Nate Field, Gary Hughes, John Lombardo, Matt Mahoney, Joe McDonald, Anthony Turco, Les Walrond.
Crosscheckers: John Booher, Fred Petersen, Jim Robinson, Quincy Boyd, Dan Madsen.
Area Scouts: Jon Adkins (Houston, TX), Chris Calciano (Millville, DE), Tim Collinsworth (McKinney, TX), Raymond
Fagnant (East Granby, CT), Todd Gold, (Raleigh, NC), Stephen Hargett, (Jacksonville, FL), Blair Henry (Loves Park, IL), Tom
Kotchman (Seminole, FL), Josh Labandeira, (Fresno, CA), Chris Mears (Norman, OK), Brian Moehler (Marietta, GA), Edgar
Perez (Vega Baja, PR), Chris Pritchett (Vancouver, BC), John Pyle (Lexington, KY), Willie Romay (Miami Springs, FL), Demond
Smith (Elk Grove, CA), Danny Watkins (Daphne, AL), Vaughn Williams (Gilbert, AZ), Jim Woodward (Claremont, CA). **Part-
Time Scouts:** Buzz Bowers, Rob English, Tim Martin, Jay Oliver, Keith Prager, Dick Sorkin, Adam Stern, Terry Sullivan.
International Crosschecker/Coordinator, Latin American Scouting: Todd Claus. **International Crosschecker:**
Rolando Pino. **Coordinator, Pacific Rim Scouting:** Jon Deeble. **Director, Dominican Academy:** Jesus Alou. **Assistant
Director, Dominican Academy:** Javier Hernandez. **Dominican Republic Scouting Supervisor:** Manny Nanita.
International Area Supervisor/Dominican Republic Crosschecker: Victor Rodriguez, Jr. **Coordinator, Venezuela
Scouting/Venezuela Scout:** Manny Padron.
International Scouts: Jonathan Cruz (Dominican Republic), Angel Escobar (Venezuela), Falevi Franco (Panama),
Steve Fish (Australia), Cris Garibaldo (Panama), Ernesto Gomez (Venezuela), Toshi Kato (Japan), John Kim (Korea),
Louie Lin (Taiwan), Carlos Lugo (Dominican Republic), Wilder Lobo (Venezuela), Pedro Machado (Brazil), Ramon Mora
(Venezuela), Rafael Mendoza (Nicaragua), Dennis Neuman (Aruba/Curacao), Francisco Polanco (Dominican Republic),
Santiago Prada (Colombia), Alex Requena (Venezuela), Lenin Rodriguez (Venezuela), Rene Saggiadi (Europe), David
Tapia (Mexico), Sotero Torres (Mexico).

Chicago Cubs

Office Address: Wrigley Field, 1060 W. Addison St., Chicago, IL 60613.
Telephone: (773) 404-2827. **Website:** www.cubs.com.

Ownership
Chairman: Tom Ricketts. **Board of Directors:** Laura Ricketts, Pete Ricketts, Todd Ricketts and Tribune Company.

BUSINESS OPERATIONS

Tom Ricketts

President, Business Operations: Crane Kenney. **Executive VP, Community Affairs/ General Counsel:** Michael Lufrano. **Senior VP, Strategy/Development:** Alex Sugarman. **Senior VP/CFO:** Jon Greifenkamp. **VP, Sales/Partnerships:** Colin Faulkner. **VP, Ballpark Operations:** Carl Rice. **VP, Human Resources:** Bryan Robinson. **VP, Communications/ Community:** Julian Green. **VP, General Counsel:** Lydia Wahlke. **Senior Advisor, Business Operations:** Mark McGuire. **Executive Assistant to the Chairman:** Lorraine Swiatly. **Executive Coordinator, Business Operations:** Sarah Poontong.

Ballpark Operations
Senior Director, Wrigley Field Event Operations: Matt Kenny. **Director, Fan Experiences:** Jahaan Blake. **Director, Security/Safety Operations:** James Reynolds. **Assistant Director, Guest Services:** Hannah Basinger. **Assistant Director, Event Operations/Security:** Derek Crawford. **Head Groundskeeper:** Roger Baird. **Public Address Announcer:** Andrew Belleson. **Organist:** Gary Pressy.

Marketing/Communications
Senior Director, Marketing: Alison Miller. **Assistant Director, Organizational Communications:** Lindsay Bago. **Manager, Communications:** Kevin Saghy. **Coordinator, Public Relations:** Alyson Cohen.

Corporate Partnerships
Senior Director, Corporate Partnerships: Allen Hermeling. **Assistant Director, Corporate Partnerships Sales Operations:** Brian O'Connor. **Controller:** Melissa Shields. **Director, Procurement/Sourcing:** Patrick Meenan.

Information Technology/Human Resources
Senior Director, Information Technology: Andrew McIntyre. **Assistant Director, Human Resources:** Rachel O'Connell. **HR Manager, Ballpark Operations:** Danielle Alexa. **HR Manager, Organization/Staffing:** Marisol Widmayer..

Legal/Community Affairs
Counsel: Mike Feldman. **Director, Community Affairs:** Connie Falcone.

Ticket Sales/Service/Operations
Director, Ticket Sales: Andy Blackburn. **Director, Ticket Service:** Brian Garza. **Director, Ticket Operations:** Cale Vennum.

2015 SCHEDULE
Standard Game Times: 7:05 p.m.; Sun. 1:20

APRIL			
5 . . . . St. Louis	22-24 . . . . at Arizona	3-5. . . . . .Miami	25-27 . . . . at San Francisco
7-8 . . . . St. Louis	25-27 . . . . . . .Washington	6-8 . . . . St. Louis	28-30 . . at Los Angeles (NL)
10-12 . . . . . . at Colorado	29-31 . . . . . . Kansas City	10-12 . . . . . Chicago (AL)	31 . . . . Cincinnati
13-15 . . . . Cincinnati		17-19 . . . . at Atlanta	
17-19 . . . . . . San Diego	**JUNE**	20-22 . . . . . at Cincinnati	**SEPTEMBER**
20-23 . . . . . at Pittsburgh	1-3 . . . . at Miami	24-26 . . . . . .Philadelphia	1-2 . . . . Cincinnati
24-26 . . . . . at Cincinnati	4-7 . . . . . . at Washington	27-29 . . . . .Colorado	4-6 . . . . .Arizona
27-29 . . . . Pittsburgh	9-10 . . . . at Detroit	30-31 . . . . . at Milwaukee	7-9 . . . . .at St. Louis
	11-14 . . . . Cincinnati		10-13 . . . . . at Philadelphia
MAY	15-16 . . . . Cleveland	**AUGUST**	15-17 . . . . . . at Pittsburgh
1-3 . . . . .Milwaukee	17-18 . . . . .at Cleveland	1-2 . . . . at Milwaukee	18-20 . . . . St. Louis
4-7 . . . . .at St. Louis	19-21 . . . . . at Minnesota	3-5 . . . . at Pittsburgh	21-23 . . . . . . .Milwaukee
8-10 . . . . . . at Milwaukee	22-25 . . . .Los Angeles (NL)	6-9 . . . . San Francisco	25-27 . . . . .Pittsburgh
11-14 . . . . . .New York (NL)	26-28 . . . . . . .at St. Louis	11-13 . . . . . . .Milwaukee	29-30 . . . . . at Cincinnati
15-17 . . . . Pittsburgh	30 . . . . . at New York (NL)	14-16 . . .at Chicago (AL)	
19-21 . . . . . at San Diego		18-19 . . . . Detroit	**OCTOBER**
	JULY	20-23 . . . . Atlanta	1 . . . . at Cincinnati
	1-2. . . .at New York (NL)		2-4. . . . . . . at Milwaukee

GENERAL INFORMATION
Stadium (year opened): Wrigley Field (1914). **Team Colors:** Royal blue, red and white.

Player Representative: Unavailable. **Home Dugout:** Third Base. **Playing Surface:** Grass.

BASEBALL OPERATIONS

Theo Epstein

Telephone: (773) 404-2827. **Fax:** (773) 404-4147.
President, Baseball Operations: Theo Epstein.
Executive VP/General Manager: Jed Hoyer. **Assistant GMs:** Randy Bush, Shiraz Rehman.
Special Assistant to GM/Director, International Scouting: Louis Eljaua. **Special Assistant to GM/Director, Video/Advance Scouting:** Kyle Evans. **Special Assistant to President/GM:** Tim Wilken. **Director, Baseball Operations:** Scott Harris. **Director, Research/Development:** Chris Moore. **Traveling Secretary:** Vijay Tekchandani. **Executive Assistant to President/GM:** Hayley DeWitte. **Analyst, Research/Development:** Jeremy Greenhouse.
Assistant to the GM: Jeff Greenberg. **Coordinator, Major League Video/Pacific Rim Liaison:** Naoto Masamoto. **Coordinator, Advance Scouting:** Nate Halm. **Coordinator, Advance Scouting:** Tommy Hottovy. **Coordinator, Player Development/Scouting Video:** Mitch Duggins. **Baseball Systems Architect:** Ryan Kruse. **Analyst, Research/Development:** Chris Jones. **Assistant, Research/Development:** Sean Ahmed. **Assistant, Baseball Operations:** Greg Davey. **Special Assistants to President/GM:** Ryan Dempster, Ted Lilly, Kerry Wood.

Major League Staff
Manager: Joe Maddon.
Coaches: Bench—Dave Martinez; **Pitching**—Chris Bosio; **Hitting**—John Mallee; **Assistant Hitting**—Eric Hinske; **Third Base**—Gary Jones; **First Base**—Brandon Hyde; **Bullpen**—Lester Strode; **Quality Assurance Coach**—Henry Blanco; **Catching Coach**—Mike Borzello; **Staff Assistant** – Franklin Font; **Bullpen Catcher**—Chad Noble.

Medical/Training
Team Physician: Dr. Stephen Adams. **Team Orthopedist:** Dr. Stephen Gryzlo. **Director, Medical Administration:** Mark O'Neal. **Head Athletic Trainer:** P.J. Mainville. **Assistant Athletic Trainers:** Ed Halbur, Matt Johnson.

Media Relations
Director, Media Relations: Peter Chase. **Assistant Director, Media Relations:** Jason Carr. **Coordinator, Media Relations:** Safdar Khan. **Assistant, Media Relations:** Alex Wilcox.

Player Development
Telephone: (773) 404-4035. **Fax:** (773) 404-4147.
Senior VP, Scouting/Player Development: Jason McLeod. **Director, Player Development:** Jaron Madison. **Assistant Director, Player Development/International Scouting:** Alex Suarez. **Assistant Director, Minor League Operations:** Bobby Basham. **Coordinator, Minor League Administration:** Derrick Fong. **Assistant, Player Development/International Scouting:** Kenny Socorro. **Director, Mental Skills Program:** Josh Lifrak. **Coordinator, Mental Skills Program:** Darnell McDonald. **Field Coordinator:** Tim Cossins. **Coordinators:** Derek Johnson (pitching), Anthony Iapoce (hitting), Doug Dascenzo (outfield/baserunning), Jose Flores (infield), Dave Keller (Latin American field), Tom Beyers (assistant hitting), Mike Mason (assistant pitching), Rick Tronerud (rehab pitching). **Coordinator, Minor League Athletic Training:** Nick Frangella. **Assistant Coordinator, Minor League Athletic Training:** Chuck Baughman.

Farm System

Class	Club (League)	Manager	Hitting Coach	Pitching Coach
Triple-A	Iowa (PCL)	Marty Pevey	Brian Harper	Mike Cather
Double-A	Tennessee (SL)	Buddy Bailey	Desi Wilson	Storm Davis
High A	Myrtle Beach (CL)	Mark Johnson	Mariano Duncan	David Rosario
Low A	South Bend (MWL)	Jimmy Gonzalez	Jesus Feliciano	Brian Lawrence
Short-season	Eugene (NWL)	Gary Van Tol	Ricardo Medina	Anderson Tavarez
Rookie	Cubs (AZL)	Carmelo Martinez	Oscar Bernard	Ron Villone
Rookie	Cubs (DSL)	Juan Cabreja	Claudio Almonte	Armando Gabino
Rookie	Cubs (VSL)	Pedro Gonzalez	Franklin Blanco	Eduardo Villacis

Scouting
Director, Amateur Scouting: Matt Dorey (Seattle, WA). **Assistant Director, Amateur Scouting:** Lukas McKnight (Libertyville, IL). **Director, Professional Scouting:** Joe Bohringer (Western Springs, IL). **Coordinator, Pro Scouting:** Andrew Bassett (Chicago, IL). **Major League Scouts:** Terry Kennedy (Chandler, AZ), Jason Karegeannes (De Pere, WI), Adam Wogan (Brooklyn, NY). **Pro Scouts:** Billy Blitzer (Brooklyn, NY), Steve Boros (Kingwood, TX), Jake Ciarrachi (Chicago, IL), Jason Cooper (Kirkland, WA), Denny Henderson (Orange, CA), Steve Hinton (Mather, CA), Mark Kiefer (Hunt, TX), Ken Kravec (Sarasota, FL), Bob Lofrano (Woodland Hills, CA), Mark Servais (LaCrosse, WI), Keith Stohr (Viera, FL). **Amateur Scouting Assistant:** Shane Farrell (Chicago, IL). **Pro/Amateur Scout:** Jason Parks (Scottsdale, AZ).
National Supervisors: Sam Hughes (Atlanta, GA), Ron Tostenson (El Dorado Hills, CA). **Crosscheckers: Southeast**—Bobby Filotei (Mobile, AL); **Central**—Trey Forkerway (Houston, TX); **West**—Mark Adair (Irvine, CA); **Midwest/Northeast**—Tim Adkins (Hungtington, WV). **Area Scouts:** Daniel Carte (Morgantown, WV), Tom Clark (Lake City, FL), Chris Clemons (Robinson, TX), Ramser Correa (Caguas, PR), Jim Crawford (Madison, MS), Kevin Ellis (Houston, TX), Al Geddes (Canby, OR), Greg Hopkins (Camas, WA), John Koronka (Clermont, FL), Alex Levitt (Nashville, TN), Keith Lockhart (Dacula, GA), Alex Lontayo (Chula Vista, CA), Steve McFarland (Scottsdale, AZ), Tom Myers (Santa Barbara, CA), Ty Nichols (Broken Arrow, OK), Luis Raffan (Miami, FL), Keith Ryman (Jefferson City, TN), Eric Servais (Minneapolis, MN), Matt Sherman (Kingston, MA), Billy Swoope (Norfolk, VA), Gabe Zappin (Walnut Creek, CA), Stan Zielinski (Winfield, IL).
International Crosschecker: Paul Weaver (Phoenix, AZ). **Coordinator, Pacific Rim Scouting:** Min Kyu Sung. **International Scouting Supervisor:** Hector Ortega (Venezuela), Jose Serra (Dominican Republic). **International Scouts:** Brent Phelan (Australia), Manny Esquivia (Colombia), Cirilo Cumberbatch (Panama), Gian Guzman (Dominican Republic), Sergio Hernandez (Mexico), Julio Figueroa (Venezuela).

Chicago White Sox

Office Address: U.S. Cellular, Field, 333 W. 35th St., Chicago, IL 60616.
Telephone: (312) 674-1000. **Fax:** (312) 674-5116. **Website:** www.whitesox.com and orgullosox.com.

Ownership
Chairman: Jerry Reinsdorf. **Vice Chairman:** Eddie Einhorn.
Board of Directors: Robert Judelson, Judd Malkin, Robert Mazer, Allan Muchin, Jay Pinsky, Lee Stern, Burton Ury, Charles Walsh.
Special Assistant to Chairman: Dennis Gilbert. **Assistant to Chairman:** Barb Reincke. **Coordinator, Administration/Investor Relations:** Katie Hermle.

BUSINESS OPERATIONS
Senior Executive Vice President: Howard Pizer.
Senior Director, Information Services: Don Brown. **Senior Director, Human Resources:** Moira Foy. **Senior Coordinator, Human Resources:** Leslie Gaggiano.

Finance
Senior VP, Administration/Finance: Tim Buzard. **Senior Director, Finance:** Bill Waters.
Accounting Manager: Chris Taylor.

Marketing/Sales
Senior VP, Sales/Marketing: Brooks Boyer. **Senior Director, Business Development/Broadcasting:** Bob Grim. **Director, Game Presentation:** Cris Quintana. **Senior Manager, Scoreboard Operations/Production:** Jeff Szynal. **Senior Manager, Game Presentation:** Amy Sheridan. **Manager, Game Operations:** Dan Mielke. **Senior Coordinator, Graphic Apparel/Design:** Lauren Markiewicz.

Jerry Reinsdorf

Director, Corporate Partnerships Sales Development: George McDoniel. **Director, Corporate Partnerships Activation:** Gail Tucker. **Manager, Corporate Partnerships Development:** Jeff Floerke. **Coordinators, Corporate Partnership Activation:** Arden Reed, Kat Claeys.
Senior Director, Ticket Sales: Tom Sheridan. **Manager, Premium Seating Sales:** Rob Boaz.

Media Relations/Public Relations
Telephone: (312) 674-5300. **Fax:** (312) 674-5116.
Senior VP, Communications: Scott Reifert.
Director, Media Relations: Bob Beghtol. **Director, Public Relations:** Sheena Quinn. **Manager, Media Relations:** Ray Garcia. **Manager, Public Relations:** Julianne Bartosz. **Coordinators, Media Relations/Services:** Joe Roti, Megan Golden.
Senior Director, Community Relations/Executive Director, CWS Charities: Christine O'Reilly. **Managers, Community Relations:** Sarah Marten, Lauren Pesqueda. **Director, Youth Baseball Initiatives:** Kevin Coe.
Director, Digital Communications: Brad Boron. **Director, Advertising/Design Services:** Gareth Breunlin. **Manager, Online Communications:** Dakin Dugaw.

2015 SCHEDULE
Standard Game Times: 7:10 p.m.; Sun. 1:10.

APRIL			
6 . . . . .at Kansas City	22-24 . . . . . . .Minnesota	3-5. . . . . Baltimore	27-30 . . . . Seattle
8-9. . . . . . .at Kansas City	25-27 . . . . at Toronto	6-9. . . . . .Toronto	**SEPTEMBER**
10-12 . . . . . . .Minnesota	29-31 . . . . at Houston	10-12 . . . . .at Chicago (NL)	1-3. . . . . at Minnesota
14-15 . . . . . .at Cleveland		17-19 . . . . Kansas City	4-6. . . . . . .at Kansas City
17-19 . . . . at Detroit	**JUNE**	21-22 . . . . St. Louis	7-9. . . . . Cleveland
20-22 . . . . Cleveland	2-4. . . . . .at Texas	23-26 . . . . .at Cleveland	11-13 . . . . .Minnesota
23-26 . . . . . . Kansas City	5-7. . . . . Detroit	27-30 . . . . at Boston	14-17 . . . . Oakland
27-29 . . . .at Baltimore	8-10 . . . . Houston	31 . . . . . . .New York (AL)	18-20 . . . . . .at Cleveland
30 . . . . . . at Minnesota	12-14 . . . . . at Tampa Bay		21-23 . . . . at Detroit
	15-16 . . . . . at Pittsburgh	**AUGUST**	24-27 . . . .at New York (AL)
MAY	17-18 . . . . Pittsburgh	1-2. . . . . . .New York (AL)	29-30 . . . . . . Kansas City
1-3. . . . . . . at Minnesota	19-21 . . . . Texas	3-5. . . . . .Tampa Bay	
5-7. . . . . Detroit	22-24 . . . . . at Minnesota	7-9. . . . . . .at Kansas City	**OCTOBER**
8-10 . . . . Cincinnati	25-28 . . . . at Detroit	10-12 . . . . Los Angeles (AL)	1 . . . . Kansas City
11-13 . . . . . at Milwaukee	30 . . . . .at St. Louis	14-16 . . . . . . Chicago (NL)	2-4. . . . . Detroit
15-17 . . . . . . .at Oakland		17-20 . . at Los Angeles (AL)	
18-21 . . . . Cleveland	**JULY**	21-23 . . . . .at Seattle	
	1 . . . . .at St. Louis	24-26 . . . . Boston	

GENERAL INFORMATION
Stadium (year opened):   **Player Representative:** Tyler Flowers.
U.S. Cellular Field (1991).   **Home Dugout:** Third Base.
Team Colors: Black, white and silver.   **Playing Surface:** Grass.

Stadium Operations
Senior VP, Stadium Operations: Terry Savarise. **Senior Director, Park Operations:** Greg Hopwood. **Senior Director, Guest Services/Diamond Suite Operations:** Julie Taylor. **Head Groundskeeper:** Roger Bossard. **PA Announcer:** Gene Honda. **Official Scorers:** Bob Rosenberg, Don Friske.

Ticketing
Telephone: (312) 674-1000. **Fax:** (312) 674-5102.
Director, Ticket Operations: Mike Mazza. **Manager, Ticket Accounting Administration:** Ken Wisz.

Travel/Clubhouse
Director, Team Travel: Ed Cassin.
Manager, White Sox Clubhouse: Vince Fresso. **Manager, Visiting Clubhouse:** Gabe Morell. **Manager, Umpires Clubhouse:** Joe McNamara Jr.

BASEBALL OPERATIONS

Rick Hahn

Executive Vice President: Ken Williams.
Senior VP/General Manager: Rick Hahn.
VP/Assistant GM: Buddy Bell. **Assistant to GM:** Jeremy Haber. **Special Assistants:** Bill Scherrer, Dave Yoakum, Marco Paddy.
Major League Advance Scout: Bryan Little. **Executive Assistant to GM:** Nancy Nesnidal. **Senior Director, Baseball Operations:** Dan Fabian. **Assistant Director, Baseball Operations:** Daniel Zien. **Coordinator, Baseball Information:** Dan Strittmatter.

Major League Staff
Manager: Robin Ventura.
Coaches: Bench—Mark Parent; **Pitching**—Don Cooper; **Batting**—Todd Steverson; **First Base**—Daryl Boston; **Third Base**—Joe McEwing; Bullpen—Bobby Thigpen. **Assistant Hitting Coach:** Harold Baines.

Medical/Training
Senior Team Physician: Dr. Charles Bush-Joseph. **Head Athletic Trainer:** Herm Schneider. **Assistant Athletic Trainer:** Brian Ball. **Director, Strength/Conditioning:** Allen Thomas.

Player Development
Senior Director, Minor League Operations: Grace Guerrero Zwit. **Director, Player Development:** Nick Capra. **Assistant Director, Player Development/Scouting:** Del Matthews. **Senior Coordinator, Minor League Administration:** Kathy Potoski. **Coordinator, Latin American Operations:** Arturo Perez. **Manager, Clubhouse/Equipment:** Dan Flood.
Minor League Field Coordinator: Kirk Champion. **Pitching Coordinator:** Curt Hasler. **Hitting Instructor:** Tim Laker. **Hitting Coordinator:** Vance Law. **Instructors:** Doug Sisson (outfield/baserunning), Everado Magallanes (infield), John Orton (catching), Dale Torborg (conditioning coordinator). **Minor League Medical/Rehabilitation Coordinator:** Scott Takao. **Physical Therapist, Brett Walker. Coaching Assistants:** Jerry Hairston, Chet DiEmidio, Anthony Santiago. **Dominican Republic Academy/Field Coordinator:** Rafael Santana.

Farm System

Class	Club (League)	Manager	Hitting Coach	Pitching Coach
Triple-A	Charlotte (IL)	Joel Skinner	Andy Tomberlin	Richard Dotson
Double-A	Birmingham (SL)	Julio Vinas	Jaime Dismuke	Britt Burns
High A	Winston-Salem (CL)	Tim Esmay	Charlie Poe	J.R. Perdew
Low A	Kannapolis (SAL)	Tommy Thompson	Robert Sasser	Jose Bautista
Rookie	Great Falls (PIO)	Cole Armstrong	Greg Briley	Brian Drahman
Rookie	White Sox (AZL)	Mike Gellinger	Gary Ward	Felipe Lira
Rookie	White Sox (DSL)	Julio Valdez	Angel Gonzalez	Leo Hernandez

Scouting
Telephone: (312) 674-1000. **Fax:** (312) 674-5105.
Director, Amateur Scouting: Doug Laumann (Florence, KY).
Assistant Director, Scouting/Player Development: Nick Hostetler (Hebron, KY). **National Crosscheckers:** Nathan Durst (Sycamore, IL), Ed Pebley (Brigham City, UT). **Regional Crosscheckers: East**—Joe Siers (Wesley Chapel, FL), **Midwest**—Mike Shirley (Anderson, IN), **West**—Derek Valenzuela (Temecula, CA).
Advisor to Baseball Department: Larry Monroe (Schaumburg, IL).
Area Scouts: Mike Baker (Santa Ana, CA), Kevin Burrell (Sharpsburg, GA), Robbie Cummings (Portland, OR), Ryan Dorsey (Dallas, TX), Abe Fernandez (Ft. Mill, SC), Joel Grampietro (Revere, MA), Garret Guest (Frankfort, IL), Phil Gulley (Morehead, KY), Warren Hughes (Mobile, AL), JJ Lally (Denison, IA), George Kachigian (Coronado, CA), John Kazanas (Phoenix, AZ), Steve Nichols (Mount Dora, FL), Glenn Murdock (Livonia, MI), Jose Ortega (Fort Lauderdale, FL), Clay Overcash (Oologan, OK), Keith Staab (College Station, TX), Noah St. Urbain (Stockton, CA), Adam Virchis (Modesto, CA), Chris Walker (Houston, TX), Gary Woods (Solvang, CA).
Pro Scouts: Bruce Benedict (Atlanta, GA), Kevin Bootay (Sacramento, CA), Joe Butler (Long Beach, CA), Chris Lein (Jacksonville, FL), Alan Regier (Gilbert, AZ), Daraka Shaheed (Vallejo, CA), Keith Staab (College Station, TX), John Tumminia (Newburgh, NY), Bill Young (Scottsdale, AZ).
International Scouts: Amador Arias (Venezuela), Marino DeLeon (Dominican Republic), Robinson Garces (Venezuela), Tomas Herrera (Mexico), Miguel Peguero (Dominican Republic), Guillermo Peralta (Dominican Republic), Omar Sanchez (Venezuela), Fermin Ubri (Dominican Republic).

Cincinnati Reds

Office Address: 100 Joe Nuxhall Way, Cincinnati, OH 45202.
Telephone: (513) 765-7000. **Fax:** (513) 765-7342.
Website: www.reds.com.

Ownership

Operated by: The Cincinnati Reds LLC.
President/CEO: Robert H. Castellini. **Chairman:** W. Joseph Williams Jr. **Vice Chairman/Treasurer:** Thomas L. Williams. **COO:** Phillip J. Castellini. **Executive Assistant to COO:** Diana Busam. **Secretary:** Christopher L. Fister.

BUSINESS OPERATIONS

Bob Castellini

Senior Vice President, Business Operations: Karen Forgus. **Business Operations Assistant/Speakers Bureau:** Emily Mahle. **Business Operations Assistant:** Alex Heekin. **Senior Advisor, Business Operations:** Joe Morgan.

Finance/Administration

VP, Finance/CFO: Doug Healy. **VP/General Counsel:** James Marx. **Controller:** Bentley Viator. **Assistant to General Counsel/CFO:** Teena Schweier. **Director, Human Resources:** Garry McGuire. **Senior Manager, Human Resources:** Allison Stortz. **VP, Technology:** Brian Keys.

Sales/Ticketing

VP, Corporate Sales: Bill Reinberger. **Director, Sponsorship Development:** Dave Collins. **VP, Ticketing/Business Development:** Aaron Eisel. **Senior Director, Ticket Sales/Service:** Mark Schueler. **Director, Premium Sales/Service:** Chris Bausano. **Director, Client Services:** Craig Warman. **Senior Director, Ticket Operations:** John O'Brien. **Assistant Director, Ticket Operations:** Ken Ayer. **Season Ticket Manager:** Bev Bonavita. **Director, Group Sales/Service:** Shannon Senger. **Director, Season Sales/Retention:** Patrick Montague.

Media Relations

Director, Media Relations: Rob Butcher. **Assistant Director, Media Relations:** Larry Herms. **Assistant Director, Media Relations/Digital Content:** Jamie Ramsey.

Communications/Marketing

VP, Communications/Marketing: Ralph Mitchell. **Director, Digital Media:** Lisa Braun. **Director, Marketing:** Audra Sordyl. **Senior Manager, Communications/Web Content:** Jarrod Rollins. **Public Relations Manager:** Michael Anderson. **Promotional Purchasing/Broadcasting Administration:** Lori Watt. **Communications Coordinator:** Brendan Hader. **Senior Director, Productions/Creative:** Adam Lane. **Director, Creative Operations:** Jansen Dell. **Senior Manager, Entertainment/Productions:** Jami Itiavkase. **Senior Director, Promo Events/Player Relations:** Zach Bonkowski. **Director, Promo Events/Player Relations:** Corey Hawthorne.

2015 SCHEDULE

Standard Game Times: 7:10 p.m.; Sun. 1:10

APRIL
6 . . . . Pittsburgh
8-9 . . . . Pittsburgh
10-12 . . . . St. Louis
13-15 . . . . at Chicago (NL)
17-19 . . . . . . at St. Louis
20-23 . . . . at Milwaukee
24-26 . . . . . Chicago (NL)
27-29 . . . . Milwaukee
30 . . . . at Atlanta

MAY
1-3 . . . . at Atlanta
5-7 . . . . at Pittsburgh
8-10 . . . . . at Chicago (AL)
11-13 . . . . Atlanta
14-17 . . . . . San Francisco
19-20 . . . . at Kansas City

22-24 . . . . . . at Cleveland
25-27 . . . . Colorado
29-31 . . . . . Washington

JUNE
2-4 . . . . . at Philadelphia
5-7 . . . . San Diego
8-10 . . . . . . Philadelphia
11-14 . . . . at Chicago (NL)
15-16 . . . . at Detroit
17-18 . . . . Detroit
19-21 . . . . Miami
23-25 . . . . . at Pittsburgh
26-28 . . at New York (NL)
29-30 . . . . . . Minnesota

JULY
1 . . . . Minnesota

3-5 . . . . Milwaukee
6-8 . . . . . at Washington
9-12 . . . . at Miami
17-19 . . . . . . Cleveland
20-22 . . . . . Chicago (NL)
24-26 . . . . at Colorado
27-29 . . . . . at St. Louis
30-31 . . . . . . Pittsburgh

AUGUST
1-2 . . . . Pittsburgh
4-6 . . . . St. Louis
7-9 . . . . at Arizona
10-12 . . . at San Diego
13-16 . . at Los Angeles (NL)
18-19 . . . . . Kansas City
20-23 . . . . Arizona
25-27 . . . Los Angeles (NL)

28-30 . . . . . at Milwaukee
31 . . . . . . at Chicago (NL)

SEPTEMBER
1-2 . . . . . at Chicago (NL)
4-6 . . . . Milwaukee
7-9 . . . . Pittsburgh
10-13 . . . . St. Louis
14-16 . . . at San Francisco
18-20 . . . . at Milwaukee
21-23 . . . . . . at St. Louis
24-27 . . . . New York (NL)
29-30 . . . . Chicago (NL)

OCTOBER
1 . . . . Chicago (NL)
2-4 . . . . . . at Pittsburgh

GENERAL INFORMATION

Stadium (year opened):
Great American Ball Park (2003).
Home Dugout: First Base.

Player Representative: Mike Leake.
Playing Surface: Grass.
Team Colors: Red, white and black.

Community Relations

Executive Director, Community Fund: Charley Frank. **Director, Community Relations:** Lindsey Lander. **Executive Director, Reds Hall of Fame:** Rick Walls. **Operations Manager/Chief Curator, Reds Hall of Fame:** Chris Eckes.

Ballpark Operations

VP, Ballpark Operations: Tim O'Connell. **Senior Director, Ballpark Operations:** Sean Brown. **Director, Ballpark Administration:** Colleen Rodenberg. **Ballpark Operations Superintendent:** Bob Harrison. **Guest Relations Manager:** Jan Koshover. **Manager, Technology Business Center:** Chris Campbell. **Director, Safety/Security:** Kerry Rowland. **Chief Engineer:** Roger Smith. **Assistant Chief Engineer:** Gary Goddard. **Head Groundskeeper:** Doug Gallant. **Assistant Head Groundskeeper:** Derrik Grubbs. **Grounds Supervisor:** Robbie Dworkin. Manager, Reds Clubhouse/Equipment: Rick Stowe. Visiting Clubhouse Manager: Mark Stowe. Reds Clubhouse Assistant: Josh Stewart.

BASEBALL OPERATIONS

President, Baseball Operations/General Manager: Walt Jocketty. **Executive Assistant to GM:** Melissa Hill.

Walt Jocketty

VP, Baseball Operations/Assistant GM: Dick Williams. **VP/Special Assistant:** Jerry Walker. **Special Assistants:** Miguel Cairo, Eric Davis, Mario Soto. **Senior Director, Baseball Operations:** Nick Krall. **Senior Director, Baseball Analytics:** Sam Grossman. **Manager, Baseball Systems Development:** Brett Elkins. **Manager, Video Scouting:** Rob Coughlin. **Manager, Baseball Operations:** Eric Lee. **Baseball Operations Analyst:** Bo Thompson.

Medical/Training

Medical Director: Dr. Timothy Kremchek. **Head Athletic Trainer:** Paul Lessard. **Assistant Athletic Trainers:** Steve Baumann, Tomas Vera. **Stength/Conditioning Coordinator:** Sean Marohn.

Major League Staff

Manager: Bryan Price.

Coaches: Bench—Jay Bell; **Hitting**—Don Long; **Pitching**—Jeff Pico; **First Base**—Billy Hatcher; **Third Base**—Jim Riggleman; **Bullpen**—Mack Jenkins; **Catching**—Mike Stefanski; **Coach**—Freddie Benavides. **Special Assistants:** Jeff Schugel, Kevin Towers.

Player Development

Director, Player Development: Jeff Graupe. **Director, Minor League Administration:** Lois Hudson. **Arizona Operations Manager:** Mike Saverino. **Assistant to Arizona Operations Manager:** Charlie Rodriguez. **Minor League Video Coordinator:** Mike Persichilli. **Minor League Equipment Manager:** Jonathan Snyder. **Minor League Clubhouse Assistant:** John Bryk. **Field Coordinator:** Bill Doran. **Latin America Field Coordinator:** Joel Noboa. **Coordinators:** Ryan Jackson (hitting), Mark Riggins (pitching), Darren Bragg (outfield/baserunning), Richard Stark (medical), Patrick Serbus (athletic training). **Director, Dominican Republic Academy:** Juan Peralta. **Physical Therapist/Rehab Coordinator:** Brad Epstein.

Farm System

Class	Club (League)	Manager	Hitting Coach	Pitching Coach
Triple-A	Louisville (IL)	Delino DeShields	Tony Jaramillo	Ted Power
Double-A	Pensacola (SL)	Pat Kelly	Alex Pelaez	Jeff Fassero
High A	Daytona (FSL)	Eli Marrero	Kevin Mahar	Tony Fossas
Low A	Dayton (MWL)	Jose Miguel Nieves	Luis Bolivar	Tom Browning
Rookie	Billings (PIO)	Dick Schofield	Jolbert Cabrera	Derrin Ebert
Rookie	Reds (AZL)	Ray Martinez	Travis Dawkins	Elmer Dessens
Rookie	Reds 1 (DSL)	Jose Castro	Fleming Baez	Luis Montano
Rookie	Reds 2 (DSL)	Luis Saturria	Cristobal Rodriguez	Luis Andujar

Scouting

Senior Director, Pro Scouting: Terry Reynolds. **Senior Director, Amateur Scouting:** Chris Buckley. **Assistant Director, Amateur Scouting:** Paul Pierson. **Special Assistants:** Cam Bonifay, J. Harrison, Marty Maier, John Morris, Jeff Schugel, Mike Squires, Jeff Taylor, Kevin Towers. **Major League Scout:** Shawn Pender. **Professional Scouts:** Will Harford, Bruce Manno, Jeff Morris, Jonathan Reynolds, Steve Roadcap.

Crosscheckers: Jeff Barton (Gilbert, AZ), Bill Byckowski (Ontario, Canada), Jerry Flowers (Cypress, TX), Mark McKnight (Tega Cay, SC), Mark Snipp (Humble, TX). **Scouting Supervisors:** Tony Arias (Miami Lakes, FL), Rich Bordi (Rohnert Park, CA), Jeff Brookens (Chambersburg, PA), John Ceprini, Dan Cholowsky, Rex De La Nuez (Burbank, CA), Byron Ewing (Haslet, TX), Rick Ingalls (Long Beach, CA), Ben Jones (Alexandria, LA), Joe Katuska (Cincinnati, OH), Mike Keenan (Manhattan, KS), Brad Meador (Cincinnati, OH), Mike Misuraca (Murrieta, CA), John Poloni (Tarpon Springs, FL), Lee Seras (Flanders, NJ), Perry Smith (Charlotte, NC), Andy Stack (Hartford, WI), Greg Zunino (Cape Coral, FL). **Scouts:** Nick Carrier (Hemlock, NY), Dave Dawson (Santa Clarita, CA), Jim Grief (Paducah, KY), Bill Killian (Stanwood, MI), Denny Nagel (Cincinnati, OH), Lou Snipp (Humble, TX), Marlon Styles (Cincinnati, OH), Mike Wallace (Escondido, CA), John Walsh (Windsor, CT), Roger Weberg (Bemidji, MN).

Director, International Scouting: Tony Arias. **Assistant Director, International Scouting:** Miguel Machado. **Director, Global Scouting:** Jim Stoeckel. **Scouting Coordinator, Dominican Republic:** Enmanuel Cartagena. **Scouting Administrator, Venezuela:** Jose Fuentes.

International Scouts: Edward Bens (Dominican Republic), Geronimo Blanco (Colombia), San Mateo Garcia (Dominican Republic), Eury Luis Haslen (Dominican Republic), Victor Nova (Dominican Republic), Gary Peralta (Dominican Republic), Jose Valdelamar (Colombia).

Cleveland Indians

Office Address: Progressive Field, 2401 Ontario St., Cleveland, OH 44115.
Telephone: (216) 420-4200. **Fax:** (216) 420-4396.
Website: www.indians.com.

Ownership
Owner: Larry Dolan. **Chairman/Chief Executive Officer:** Paul Dolan.

BUSINESS OPERATIONS
President: Mark Shapiro.
Senior Vice President, Strategy/Business Analytics: Andrew Miller. **Executive Administrative Assistant:** Marlene Lehky. **Executive VP, Business:** Dennis Lehman. **Executive VP, Sales/Marketing:** Brian Barren. **Executive Administrative Assistant, Business:** Dru Kosik.

Corporate Partnerships/Finance
Senior Director, Corporate Partnership: Ted Baugh. **Manager, Corporate Partnership Services:** Sam Zelasko. **Partnership Manager:** Bryan Hoffart. **Account Executives, Corporate Partnerships:** Dominic Polito, Penny Forster, Julie Weaver, Raphael Collins. **Administrative Assistant:** Kim Scott.
VP, Finance/CFO: Ken Stefanov. **VP/General Counsel:** Joe Znidarsic. **Controller:** Sarah Taylor. **Senior Director, Planning, Analysis/Reporting:** Rich Dorffer. **Manager, Accounting:** Karen Menzing. **Manager, Payroll Accounting/Services:** Mary Forkapa. **Concessions Accounting Manager:** Diane Turner.

Larry Dolan

Human Resources
VP, Human Resources/Chief Diversity Officer: Sara Lehrke. **Assistant Director, Talent Acquisition:** Mailynh Vu. **Assistant Director, Talent Development/Engagement:** Jennifer Gibson.

Marketing
VP, Marketing/Brand Management: Alex King. **Assistant Director, Brand Management:** Nicole Schmidt.

Communications/Baseball Information
Telephone: (216) 420-4380. **Fax:** (216) 420-4430.
Senior VP, Public Affairs: Bob DiBiasio. **Senior Director, Communications:** Curtis Danburg. **Director, Baseball Information:** Bart Swain. **Assistant Director, Communications:** Anne Keegan. **Assistant Director, Baseball Information:** Court Berry-Tripp. **Coordinator, Communications:** Joel Hammond. **Team Photographer:** Dan Mendlik.

Ballpark Operations
VP, Ballpark Operations: Jim Folk. **Senior Director, Ballpark Operations:** Jerry Crabb. **Senior Director, Facility Operations:** Seth Cooper. **Head Groundskeeper:** Brandon Koehnke. **Manager, Game Day Staff:** Renee

2015 SCHEDULE
Standard Game Times: 7:05 p.m.; Sun. 1:05.

APRIL			
6 . . . . at Houston	22-24 . . . . Cincinnati	3-5 . . . . at Pittsburgh	28-30 . . . . Los Angeles (AL)
8-9 . . . . at Houston	25-27 . . . . Texas	6-9 . . . . Houston	31 . . . . at Toronto
10-12 . . . . Detroit	28-31 . . . . .at Seattle	10-12 . . . . Oakland	
14-15 . . . . . . Chicago (AL)		17-19 . . . . . at Cincinnati	SEPTEMBER
17-19 . . . . at Minnesota	JUNE	21-22 . . . . . at Milwaukee	1-2 . . . . at Toronto
20-22 . . . .at Chicago (AL)	2-4 . . . . . . .at Kansas City	23-26 . . . . . Chicago (AL)	4-6 . . . . at Detroit
24-26 . . . . at Detroit	5-7 . . . . Baltimore	27-29 . . . . . Kansas City	7-9 . . . . . .at Chicago (AL)
27-29 . . . . . . Kansas City	9-11 . . . . Seattle	30-31 . . . . . . .at Oakland	10-13 . . . . Detroit
30 . . . . .Toronto	12-14 . . . . at Detroit		14-17 . . . . . . Kansas City
	15-16 . . . .at Chicago (NL)	AUGUST	18-20 . . . . . Chicago (AL)
MAY	17-18 . . . . . Chicago (NL)	1-2 . . . . .at Oakland	22-24 . . . . . at Minnesota
1-3 . . . . .Toronto	19-21 . . . . . . .Tampa Bay	3-5 . . . . at Los Angeles (AL)	25-27 . . . .at Kansas City
5-7 . . . . . . .at Kansas City	22-24 . . . . Detroit	7-9 . . . . .Minnesota	28-30 . . . . .Minnesota
8-10 . . . . .Minnesota	26-28 . . . . . .at Baltimore	11-13 . . . . . .New York (AL)	
12-14 . . . . St. Louis	29-30 . . . . . at Tampa Bay	14-16 . . . . . at Minnesota	OCTOBER
15-17 . . . . .at Texas		17-19 . . . . . . at Boston	1 . . . . .Minnesota
18-21 . . . . .at Chicago (AL)	JULY	20-23 . . . . at New York (AL)	2-4 . . . . Boston
	1-2 . . . . at Tampa Bay	25-26 . . . . . . .Milwaukee	

GENERAL INFORMATION
Stadium (year opened):
Progressive Field (1994).
Team Colors: Navy blue, red and silver.

Player Representative: Corey Kluber.
Home Dugout: Third Base.
Playing Surface: Grass.

VanLaningham. **Manager, Ballpark Operations:** Steve Walters. **Manager, Security:** Omar Jufko. **Manager, Arizona Operations:** Ryan Lantz.

Information Systems
Senior VP, Technology/Chief Information Officer: Neil Weiss. **Director, Software Development:** Matt Tagliaferri. **Director, Infrastructure/Operations:** Whitney Kuszmaul.

Ticketing
Telephone: (216) 420-4487. **Fax:** (216) 420-4481.
Director, Ticket Services: Andrea Jirousek. **Ticket Services Manager:** Shedrick Taylor. **Ticket Operations Manager:** Nate Thompson. **Ticket Office Manager:** Jennifer McGee. **Ticket Services Coordinator:** Tamara Bell.

Team Operations/Clubhouse
Director, Team Travel: Mike Seghi. **Home Clubhouse Manager:** Tony Amato. **Assistant Home Clubhouse Manager:** Marty Bokovitz. **Manager, Video Operations:** Bob Chester. **Visiting Clubhouse Manager:** Willie Jenks. **Manager, Arizona Clubhouse:** Fletcher Wilkes.

BASEBALL OPERATIONS

Chris Antonetti

Telephone: (216) 420-4200. **Fax:** (216) 420-4321.
Executive VP/General Manager: Chris Antonetti.
VP, Baseball Operations/Assistant GM: Mike Chernoff. **Director, Baseball Administration:** Wendy Hoppel. **Director, Baseball Operations:** Derek Falvey. **Director, Baseball Analytics:** Keith Woolner. **Executive Administrative Assistant:** Marlene Lehky. **Sports Psychologist:** Dr. Charles Maher. **Performance Coach:** Ceci Clark. **Assistant Directors, Baseball Operations:** Matt Forman, Victor Wang. **Senior Baseball Analyst:** Sky Andrecheck.

Major League Staff
Manager: Terry Francona.
Coaches: Bench—Brad Mills; **Pitching**—Mickey Callaway; **Hitting**—Ty Van Burkleo; **First Base**—Sandy Alomar Jr.; **Third Base**—Mike Sarbaugh; **Bullpen**—Jason Bere; **Assistant Hitting Coach**—Matt Quatraro. **Assistants, Major League Staff:** Armando Camacaro, Ricky Pacione. **Replay Coordinator:** Gregg Langbehn.

Medical/Training
Head Team Physician: Dr. Mark Schickendantz. **Senior Director, Medical Services:** Lonnie Soloff. **Head Athletic Trainer:** James Quinlan. **Assistant Athletic Trainers:** Jeff Desjardins, Michael Salazar. **Strength/Conditioning Coach:** Joe Kessler.

Player Development
Telephone: (216) 420-4308. **Fax:** (216) 420-4321.
VP, Player Personnel: Ross Atkins. **Director, Player Development:** Carter Hawkins. **Assistant Director, Player Development:** Eric Binder. **Administrative Assistant:** Nilda Taffanelli. **Advisors:** Johnny Goryl, Tim Tolman. **Special Assistants:** Tim Belcher, Edwin Rodriguez. **Director, Latin America Operations:** Ramon Pena. **Field Coordinator:** Tom Wiedenbauer. **Coordinators:** Ruben Niebla (pitching), Jim Rickon (hitting), Scooter Tucker (catching), Todd Kubacki (strength/conditioning), Thomas Albert (rehab), Julio Rangel (lower level pitching), Ken Knutson (pitching programs/rehab). **Advisor, Latin America:** Minnie Mendoza. **Latin America Strength/Conditioning Coordinator:** Nelson Perez.

Farm System

Class	Club	Manager	Hitting Coach	Pitching Coach
Triple-A	Columbus (IL)	Chris Tremie	Rouglas Odor	Carl Willis
Double-A	Akron (EL)	David Wallace	Tony Mansolino	Jeff Harris
High A	Lynchburg (CL)	Mark Budzinski	Unavailable	Tony Arnold
Low A	Lake County (MWL)	Shaun Larkin	Unavailable	Steve Karsay
Short-season	Mahoning Valley (NYP)	Travis Fryman	Larry Day	Greg Hibbard
Rookie	Indians (AZL)	Anthony Medrano	Junior Betances	Rigo Beltran
Rookie	Indians (DSL)	Jose Mejia	Danny Bautista	Jesus Sanchez

Scouting
Senior Director, Scouting Operations: John Mirabelli.
Special Assistants to the GM: Steve Lubratich, Dave Malpass, Don Poplin. **Director, Amateur Scouting:** Brad Grant. **Director, Pro Scouting:** Paul Gillispie. **Assistant Director, Amateur Scouting:** Scott Barnsby. **Assistant Director, Pro Scouting:** Victor Wang. **Advance Scouting Coordinator:** Alex Eckelman. **Assistants, Amateur Scouting:** Mike Kanen, Clint Longenecker. **Assistant Director, International Scouting:** Jason Lynn. **International Crosschecker:** Koby Perez. **Latin America Crosschecker/South Florida Area Scout:** Juan Alvarez. **Major League Advance Scout:** Jim Cuthbert (Breinigsville, PA). **Pro Scouts:** Mike Calitri (Tampa, FL), Doug Carpenter (North Palm Beach, FL), Chris Gale (Austin, TX), Trey Hendricks (Cleveland, OH), Dave Miller (Wilmington, NC), Brent Urcheck (Philadelphia, PA). **National Crosschecker/Advisor Scouting Personnel:** Bo Hughes (Sherman Oaks, CA). **Advance Scouting Intern:** Aaron Klinec.
West Coast Crosschecker/Scout Advisor: Paul Cogan (Rocklin, CA). **Regional Crosscheckers:** Mark Allen (Lake Kiowa, TX), Kevin Cullen (Frisco, TX), Scott Meaney (Apex, NC). **Area Scouts:** Steve Abney (Lawrence, KS), Chuck Bartlett (Starkville, MS), CT Bradford (Stamford, CT), Mike Bradford (Pensacola, FL), Conor Glassey (Woodinville, WA), Jon Heuerman (Chandler, AZ), Blaze Lambert (Azle, TX), Don Lyle (Sacramento, CA), Bob Mayer (Somerset, PA), Junie Melendez (North Ridgeville, OH), Carlos Muniz (San Pedro, CA), Les Pajari (Angora, MN), Ryan Perry (Keller, TX), Jason Smith (Long Beach, CA), Mike Soper (Tampa, FL), Brad Tyler (Bishop, GA), Kyle Van Hook (Brenham, TX). **Part-Time Scouts:** Bob Malkmus (Union, NJ), Bill Schudlich (Dearborn, MI), Adam Stahl (Ballwin, MO), Jose Trujillo (Bayamon, PR).

Colorado Rockies

Office Address: 2001 Blake St., Denver, CO 80205.
Telephone: (303) 292-0200. **Fax:** (303) 312-2116.
Website: www.coloradorockies.com.

Ownership

Operated by: Colorado Rockies Baseball Club Ltd.
Owner/General Partner: Charles K. Monfort. **Owner/Chairman/Chief Executive Officer:** Richard L. Monfort.
Executive Assistant to the Owner/General Partner: Patricia Penfold. **Executive Assistant to the Owner/Chairman/Chief Executive Officer:** Terry Douglass.

BUSINESS OPERATIONS

Executive Vice President/Chief Operating Officer: Greg Feasel. **Assistant to Executive VP/Chief Operating Officer:** Kim Olson. **VP, Human Resources:** Elizabeth Stecklein.

Finance

Executive VP/CFO/General Counsel: Hal Roth. **VP, Finance:** Michael Kent. **Senior Director, Purchasing:** Gary Lawrence. **Coordinator, Purchasing:** Gloria Giraldi. **Senior Director, Accounting:** Phil Emerson. **Accountants:** Joel Binfet, Laine Campbell. **Payroll Administrator:** Juli Daedelow.

Sales

VP, Corporate Sales: Walker Monfort. **Assistant to VP, Corporate Sales:** Nicole Ortiz. **Assistant Director, Corporate Sales:** Kari Anderson. **Account Executives:** Dan Lentz, Nate VanderWal. **VP Community/Retail Operations:** James P. Kellogg. **Director, Retail Operations:** Aaron Heinrich. **Director, Promotions/Special Events:** Jason Fleming. **Director, In-Game Entertainment/Broadcasting:** Kent Krosbakken.

Marketing/Communications

Telephone: (303) 312-2325. **Fax:** (303) 312-2319.
VP, Marketing/Communications: Jill Campbell. **Supervisor, Advertising/Marketing:** Sarah Topf. **Assistant Director, Digital Media/Publications:** Julian Valentin. **Coordinator, Marketing/Communications:** Erin Shneider. **Director, Communications:** Unavailable. **Assistant Director, Communications:** Nick Piburn. **Manager, Communications:** Matt Whewell.

Ballpark Operations

VP, Ballpark Operations: Kevin Kahn. **Senior Director, Food Service Operations/Development:** Albert Valdes. **Senior Director, Guest Services:** Steven Burke. **Head Groundskeeper:** Mark Razum. **Assistant Head Groundskeeper:** James Sowl. **Senior Director, Engineering/Facilities:** James Wiener. **Director, Engineering:** Randy Carlill. **Director, Facilities:** Oly Olsen.

Richard Monfort

2015 SCHEDULE

Standard Game Times: 6:40 p.m.; Sat. 6:10; Sun. 1:10.

APRIL		
6-8 . . . . at Milwaukee	25-27 . . . . . at Cincinnati	7-8 . . . . . Los Angeles (AL)	28-30 . . . . . at Pittsburgh
10-12 . . . . . Chicago (NL)	29-31 . . . . . at Philadelphia	9-12 . . . . Atlanta	31 . . . . Arizona
13-15 . . . at San Francisco		17-19 . . . . . at San Diego	
17-19 . . at Los Angeles (NL)	JUNE	20-22 . . . . Texas	SEPTEMBER
20-23 . . . . San Diego	1-3 . . . . . Los Angeles (NL)	24-26 . . . . . . Cincinnati	1-2 . . . . Arizona
24-26 . . . . . San Francisco	5-7 . . . . Miami	27-29 . . . . at Chicago (NL)	3-6 . . . . San Francisco
27-29 . . . . at Arizona	8-10 . . . . St. Louis	30-31 . . . . at St. Louis	7-9 . . . . at San Diego
	11-14 . . . . at Miami		11-13 . . . . at Seattle
MAY	15-16 . . . . . . at Houston	AUGUST	14-16 . . at Los Angeles (NL)
1-3 . . . . . . at San Diego	17-18 . . . . Houston	1-2 . . . . at St. Louis	18-20 . . . . San Diego
4-6 . . . . Arizona	19-21 . . . . Milwaukee	3-5 . . . . Seattle	21-24 . . . . Pittsburgh
8-10 . . . . . Los Angeles (NL)	23-25 . . . . Arizona	7-9 . . . . . . at Washington	25-27 . . . Los Angeles (NL)
12-13 . . at Los Angeles (AL)	26-28 . . . at San Francisco	10-13 . . . at New York (NL)	29-30 . . . . at Arizona
14-17 . . at Los Angeles (NL)	29-30 . . . . at Oakland	14-16 . . . . San Diego	
18-21 . . . . . . Philadelphia		18-20 . . . . . . Washington	OCTOBER
22-24 . . . . . San Francisco	JULY	21-23 . . . . . New York (NL)	1 . . . . at Arizona
	1 . . . . at Oakland	24-26 . . . . at Atlanta	2-4 . . . . . at San Francisco
	2-5 . . . . at Arizona		

GENERAL INFORMATION

Stadium (year opened): Coors Field (1995).
Team Colors: Purple, black and silver.

Player Representative: Unavailable.
Home Dugout: First Base.
Playing Surface: Grass.

Senior Director, Information Systems: Bill Stephani.
Official Scorers: Dave Einspahr, Dave Plati. Public Address Announcer: Reed Saunders.

Ticketing

Telephone: (303) 762-5437, (800) 388-7625. Fax: (303) 312-2115.
VP, Ticket Operations/Sales/Services: Sue Ann McClaren. Senior Director, Ticket Services/Finance/Technology: Kent Hakes. Assistant Director, Ticket Operations: Kevin Flood. Senior Director, Season Tickets/Renewals/Business Strategy: Jeff Benner. Assistant Director, Season Tickets: Farrah Magee. Senior Director, Groups/Outbound Sales/ Suites: Matt Haddad. Manager, Suites/Party Facilities: Traci Abeyta. Senior Account Executive: Todd Thomas.

Travel/Clubhouse

Director, Major League Operations: Paul Egins. Director, Clubhouse Operations: Alan Bossart.

BASEBALL OPERATIONS

Senior VP/General Manager: Jeff Bridich.
Assistant to Senior VP/GM: Adele Armagost. Assistant GM, Baseball Operations/ Assistant General Counsel: Zack Rosenthal. Assistant GM/Player Personnel: Jon Weil. Manager, Baseball Administration: Domenic DiRicco. Coordinator, Baseball Operations/ Staff Counsel: Matt Obernauer. Coordinator, Baseball Analytics: Trevor Patch. Special Assistant to the GM: Danny Montgomery.

Major League Staff

Manager: Walt Weiss.
Coaches: Bench—Tom Runnells; Pitching—Steve Foster; Hitting—Blake Doyle; Third Base—Stu Cole; First Base —Eric Young, Sr.; Bullpen—Darren Holmes; Catching/Defensive Coordinator—Rene Lachemann; Bullpen Catcher—Pat Burgess; Director, Physical Performance—Gabe Bauer; Video—Brian Jones.

Jeff Bridich

Medical/Training

Senior Director, Medical Operations/Special Projects: Tom Probst. Medical Director: Dr. Thomas Noonan. Club Physicians: Dr. Allen Schreiber, Dr. Douglas Wyland. Head Trainer: Keith Dugger. Assistant Athletic Trainer: Scott Gehret.

Player Development

Assistant Director, Player Development: Zach Wilson. Management, Player Development: Chris Forbes. Coordinator, Minor League Operations: Jesse Stender. Director, Pitching Operations: Mark Wiley. Head Pitching Coordinator: Doug Linton. Assistant Pitching Coordinator: Bob Apodaca. Hitting Coordinator: Duane Espy. Catching Coordinator: Mark Strittmatter.
Latin America Field Coordinator: Edison Lora. Head Rehabilitation Coordinator: Scott Murayama. Assistant Rehabilitation Coordinator: Andy Stover. Physical Performance Coordinators: Brian Buck, Mike Jasperson. Cultural Development Coordinator: Josh Rosenthal. Cultural Development Teacher: Angel Amparo. Peak Performance Coordinator: Andy McKay. Equipment Manager: Jerry Bass.

Farm System

Class	Club (League)	Manager	Hitting Coach	Pitching Coach
Triple-A	Albuquerque (PCL)	Glenallen Hill	Dave Hajek	Darryl Scott
Double-A	New Britain (EL)	Darin Everson	Jeff Salazar	Dave Burba
High A	Modesto (CAL)	Fred Ocasio	Drew Saylor	Brandon Emmanuel
Low A	Asheville (SAL)	Warren Schaeffer	Mike Devereaux	Mark Brewer
Short-season	Boise (NWL)	Frank Gonzales	Andy Gonzalez	Doug Jones
Rookie	Grand Junction (PIO)	Anthony Sanders	Lee Stevens	Ryan Kibler
Rookie	Rockies (DSL)	Mauricio Gonzalez	Eugenio Jose	Edison Lora

Scouting

VP, Scouting: Bill Schmidt.
Senior Director, Scouting Operations: Marc Gustafson. Special Assistant, GM: Danny Montgomery. Assistant Scouting Director: Damon Iannelli. Special Assistant, Scouting: Rick Mathews. Assistant, Scouting/Field Operations: Sterling Monfort. Assistant, Scouting/Baseball Operations: Irma Castaneda.
Advance Scouts: Chris Warren, Joe Little. Special Assistant, Player Personnel: Ty Coslow (Louisville, KY).
Major League Scouts: Steve Fleming (Louisa, VA), Will George (Woolwich Township, NJ), Jack Gillis (Sarasota, FL), Mark Germann (Atkins, IA), Joe Housey (Hollywood, FL), Mike Paul (Tucson, AZ).
Professional Scout: John Corbin (Hollywood, FL). Part-Time Professional Scout: Jim Pransky (Davenport, IA).
National Crosscheckers: Mike Ericson (Phoenix, AZ), Jay Matthews (Concord, NC).
Area Scouts: Julio Campos (Guaynabo, PR) John Cedarburg (Fort Myers, FL), Scott Corman (Lexington, KY), Jordan Czarniecki (Nashville, TN), Jeff Edwards (Missouri City, TX), Scott Alves (Phoenix, AZ), Mike Garlatti (Edison, NJ), Brett Baldwin (Kansas City, MO), Matt Hattabaugh (Westminster, CA), Darin Holcomb (Seattle, WA), Jon Lukens (Dana Point, CA), Alan Matthews (Atlanta, GA), Jesse Retzlaff (Dallas, TX), Rafeal Reyes (Miami, FL), Ed Santa (Powell, OH), Gary Wilson (Sacramento, CA), Zack Zulli (Hammond, LA) Part-Time Scouts: Norm DeBriyn (Fayetteville, AR), Dave McQueen (Bossier City, LA), Greg Pullia (Plymouth, MA).
VP, International Scouting/Player Development: Rolando Fernandez. Manager, Dominican Operations: Jhonathan Leyba. Supervisor, Venezuelan Scouting: Orlando Medina. International Scouts: Phil Allen (Australia), Martin Cabrera (Dominican Republic), Carlos Gomez (Venezuela), Frank Roa (Dominican Republic), Josher Suarez (Venezuela). Part-Time International Scouts: Rogers Figueroa (Colombia), Marius Loupadiere (Panama).

Detroit Tigers

Office Address: 2100 Woodward Ave, Detroit, MI 48201.
Telephone: (313) 471-2000. **Fax:** (313) 471-2138. **Website:** www.tigers.com

Ownership

Operated By: Detroit Tigers Inc. **Owner:** Michael Ilitch.
President/CEO/General Manager: David Dombrowski.
Special Assistants to President: Al Kaline, Willie Horton. **Special Assistants to the General Manager:** Jim Leyland, Dick Egan, Alan Trammell. **Executive Assistant to President/CEO/GM:** Marty Lyon. **Senior VP:** Jim Devellano.

BUSINESS OPERATIONS

Mike Ilitch

Executive Vice President, Business Operations: Duane McLean.
Executive Assistant to Executive VP, Business Operations: Peggy Thompson.

Finance/Administration

VP/CFO: Stephen Quinn.
Senior Director, Finance: Kelli Kollman. **Director, Purchasing/Supplier Diversity:** DeAndre Berry. **Accounting Manager:** Sheila Robine.
Financial Analyst: Kristin Jorgensen. **Accounts Payable Coordinator:** Debbi Sword. **Administrative Assistant:** Tracy Rice.
Senior Director, Human Resources: Karen Gruca. **Director, Payroll Administration:** Maureen Kraatz. **Associate Counsel:** Amy Peterson. **Internal Audit Manager:** Candice Lentz.

Public/Community Affairs

VP, Community/Public Affairs: Elaine Lewis.
Director, Tigers Foundation: Jordan Field. **Manager, Player Relations:** Sam Abrams. **Manager, Community Affairs:** Alexandrea Thrubis. **Community Affairs Coordinator:** Garnet Conerway. **Administrative Assistants:** Audrey Zielinski/Donna Bernardo.

Sales/Marketing

VP, Corporate Partnerships: Steve Harms.
Director, Corporate Sales: Steve Cleary. **Senior Director, Corporate Sales:** Kurt Buhler. **Corporate Sales Managers:** Soula Burns, John Wolski. **Sponsorship Services Manager:** Angelita Hernandez. **Sponsorship Services Coordinator:** Sjonne Mitchell, Ellyn Yurgalite.
VP, Marketing: Ellen Hill Zeringue.
Director, Marketing: Ron Wade. **Marketing Coordinator:** Mac Slavin. **Marketing/Promotions Coordinator:** Angela Perez. **Director, Promotions/Special Events:** Eli Bayles. **Promotions Coordinator:** Haley Kolff. **Director, Broadcasting/In-Game Entertainment:** Stan Fracker. **VP, Ticket/Suite Sales:** Scot Pett.

2015 SCHEDULE

Standard Game Times: 7:08 p.m.; Sun. 1:08.

APRIL
6	Minnesota
8-9	Minnesota
10-12	at Cleveland
13-15	at Pittsburgh
17-19	Chicago (AL)
20-23	New York (AL)
24-26	Cleveland
27-29	at Minnesota
30	at Kansas City

MAY
1-3	at Kansas City
5-7	at Chicago (AL)
8-10	Kansas City
12-14	Minnesota
15-17	at St. Louis
18-20	Milwaukee
21-24	Houston
25-27	at Oakland
28-31	at Los Angeles (AL)

JUNE
2-4	Oakland
5-7	at Chicago (AL)
9-10	Chicago (NL)
12-14	Cleveland
15-16	Cincinnati
17-18	at Cincinnati
19-21	at New York (AL)
22-24	at Cleveland
25-28	Chicago (AL)
30	Pittsburgh

JULY
1-2	Pittsburgh
3-5	Toronto
6-8	at Seattle
9-12	at Minnesota
17-19	Baltimore
20-23	Seattle
24-26	at Boston
27-29	at Tampa Bay
30-31	at Baltimore

AUGUST
1-2	at Baltimore
4-6	Kansas City
7-9	Boston
10-12	at Kansas City
14-16	at Houston

SEPTEMBER
18-19	at Chicago (NL)
20-23	Texas
25-27	Los Angeles (AL)
28-30	at Toronto
1-3	at Kansas City
4-6	Cleveland
7-9	Tampa Bay
10-13	at Cleveland
14-16	at Minnesota
18-20	Kansas City
21-23	Chicago (AL)
25-27	Minnesota
28-30	at Texas

OCTOBER
2-4	at Chicago (AL)

GENERAL INFORMATION

Stadium (year opened): Comerica Park (2000).
Team Colors: Navy blue, orange and white.

Player Representative: Alex Avila.
Home Dugout: Third Base.
Playing Surface: Grass.

Media Relations/Communications
Telephone: (313) 471-2114. **Fax:** (313) 471-2138.
VP, Communications: Ron Colangelo. **Director, Baseball Media Relations:** Aileen Villarreal. **Manager, Baseball Media Relations:** Chad Crunk.

BASEBALL OPERATIONS
Telephone: (313) 471-2000. **Fax:** (313) 471-2099.
General Manager: David Dombrowski.
VP/Assistant GM: Al Avila. **VP/Legal Counsel:** John Westhoff. **VP, Player Personnel:** Scott Reid. **VP, Amateur Scouting/Special Assistant:** David Chadd. **Special Assistant:** Dick Egan. **Director, Baseball Operations:** Mike Smith. **Statistical Analysis Coordinator:** Sam Menzin. **Executive Assistant to President/GM:** Marty Lyon. **Executive Assistant:** Eileen Surma.

Dave Dombrowski

Major League Staff
Manager: Brad Ausmus.
Coaches: Pitching—Jeff Jones; **Batting**—Wally Joyner; **First Base**—Omar Vizquel; **Third Base**—Dave Clark; **Bullpen**—Mick Billmeyer; **Bench**—Gene Lamont; **Assistant Hitting**—David Newhan.

Medical/Training
Director, Medical Services/Head Athletic Trainer: Kevin Rand. **Assistant Athletic Trainers:** Matt Rankin, Doug Teter. **Strength/Conditioning Coordinator:** Chris Walter. **Assistant Strength/Conditioning:** Kyle Bergman. **Team Physicians:** Dr. Michael Workings, Dr. Stephen Lemos, Dr. Louis Saco (Florida). **Coordinator, Medical Services:** Gwen Keating.

Player Development
Director, Minor League Operations: Dan Lunetta. **Director, Player Development:** Dave Owen. **Director, Minor League/Scouting Administration:** Cheryl Evans. **Director, Latin American Player Development:** Manny Crespo. **Coordinator, Minor League Operations:** Avi Becher. **Coordinator, International Player Programs:** Sharon Lockwood. **ESL/Cultural Assimilation Instructor:** Alberto Gonzalez. **Administrative Assistant, Minor League Operations:** Marilyn Acevedo. **Minor League Field Coordinator:** Bill Dancy. **Minor League Medical Coordinator:** Corey Tremble. **Minor League Strength/Conditioning Coordinator:** Steve Chase. **International Medical Coordinator:** Steve Melendez. Minor League Video Operations Assistant: RJ Burgess.
Roving Instructors: Bruce Fields (hitting), Scott Fletcher (infield), AJ Sager (pitching), Joe DePastino (catching), Gene Roof (outfield/baserunning), Brian Peterson (performance enhancement), Robert "Ghost" Frutchey (minor league clubhouse manager), Bo Bianco (assistant minor league clubhouse manager).

Farm System
Class	Club	Manager	Hitting Coach	Pitching Coach
Triple-A	Toledo (IL)	Larry Parrish	Leon Durham	Mike Maroth
Double-A	Erie (EL)	Lance Parrish	Gerald Perry	Mike Henneman
High A	Lakeland (FSL)	Dave Huppert	Nelson Santovenia	Jorge Cordova
Low A	West Michigan (MWL)	Andrew Graham	Phil Clark	Mark Johnson
Short-season	Connecticut (NYP)	Mike Rabelo	Scott Dwyer	Carlos Chantres
Rookie	Tigers (GCL)	Basilio Cabrera	Edgar Alfonzo	Jaime Garcia

Scouting
Telephone: (863) 413-4103. **Fax:** (863) 413-1954.
VP, Amateur Scouting/Special Assistant to GM: David Chadd.
Director, Amateur Scouting: Scott Pleis. **Assistant, Amateur Scouting:** Clayton Zoellner.
Director, Pro Scouting: Scott Bream. **Major League Scouts:** Jim Olander (Vail, AZ), Dave Littlefield (Sewickley, PA), Bruce Tanner (New Castle, PA), Jeff Wetherby (Wesley Chapel, FL).
National Crosscheckers: Ray Crone (Cedar Hill, TX), Tim Hallgren (Cape Girardeau, MO). **Regional Crosscheckers: East**—James Orr (Orlando, FL); **Central**—Tim Grieve (New Braunfels, TX); **Midwest**—Mike Hankins (Lee's Summit, MO); **West**—Marti Wolever (Scottsdale, AZ).
Area Scouts: Nick Avila (Pembroke Pines, FL), Bryson Barber (Pensacola, FL), Grant Brittain (Hickory, NC), Bill Buck (Manassas, VA), Scott Cerny (Rocklin, CA), Murray Cook (Orlando, FL), Tim Grieve (New Braunfels, TX), Garrett Guest (Lockport, IL), Ryan Johnson (Oregon City, OR), Matt Lea (Austin, TX), Tim McWilliam (San Diego, CA), Marty Miller (Chicago, IL), Tom Osowski (Franklin, WI), Steve Pack (San Marcos, CA), Brian Reid (Gilbert, AZ), Jim Rough (Sharpsburg, GA), Chris Wimmer (Yukon, OK), Harold Zonder (Louisville, KY).
Director, International Operations: Tom Moore. **Director, Latin American Player Development:** Manny Crespo. **Director, Latin American Scouting:** Miguel Garcia. **Coordinator, Pacific Rim:** Kevin Hooker. **Director, Dominican Republic Operations:** Ramon Perez. **Director, Dominican Academy:** Oliver Arias. **Venezuelan Scouting Supervisor:** Alejandro Rodriguez. **Venezuelan Academy Administrator:** Oscar Garcia. **Scouting Assistant, International Operations:** Eric Nieto.

Houston Astros

Office Address: Minute Maid Park, Union Station, 501 Crawford, Suite 400, Houston, TX 77002.
Mailing Address: PO Box 288, Houston, TX 77001.
Telephone: (713) 259-8000. **Fax:** (713) 259-8981.
Email Address: fanfeedback@astros.mlb.com. **Website:** www.astros.com.

Ownership
Owner/Chairman: Jim Crane.

BUSINESS OPERATIONS
President, Business Operations: Reid Ryan. **Executive Advisor:** Nolan Ryan. **Executive Assistant:** Eileen Colgin.

Jim Crane

Senior VP, Broadcasting/Alumni Relations: Jamie Hildreth. **Senior VP, Business Operations:** Marcel Braithwaite. **Senior VP, Corporate Partnerships:** Matt Brand. **Senior VP, Ticket Sales/Strategy:** Jason Howard. **Senior VP, Finance:** Jonathan Germer. **Senior VP, Marketing/Communications:** Anita Sehgal. **Executive Director, Astros Foundation/Community Relations:** Twila Carter. **VP, Media Relations:** Gene Dias. **VP, Stadium Operations:** Bobby Forrest. **VP, Finance:** Doug Seckel. **VP, Foundation Development:** Marian Harper. **VP, Strategy/Analytics:** Michael Dillon. **VP, Human Resources:** Vivian Mora. **General Counsel:** Giles Kibbe. **Director, Business Development:** Samir Mayur.

Media Relations/Community Relations
Telephone: (713) 259-8900. **Fax:** (713) 259-8025.

Managers, Media Relations: Steve Grande, Dena Propis. **Coordinators, Media Relations:** Jake Holtrop, Chris Peixoto. **Manager, Broadcasting:** Ginny Gotcher. **Coordinator, Community Relations:** Rachel Bubier. **Business Development, Astros Foundation:** Steve Muraco. **Director, Urban Youth Academy:** Daryl Wade.

Marketing/Analytics
Director, Brand Engagement: Christie Miller. **Director, Business Strategy/Analytics:** Jay Verrill. **Director, Ballpark Entertainment:** Chris E. Garcia. **Director, Creative Services:** Chris David Garcia. **Manager, Media Strategy/Marketing:** Ryan Smith. **Senior Manager, Marketing Entertainment:** Kyle Hamsher. **Manager, Promotions/Events:** Brianna Carbonell. **Manager, Social Media:** Amanda Rykoff.

Corporate Partnerships
Senior Director, Corporate Partnerships: Creighton Kahoalii. **Director, Activation/Strategy:** Jacqueline Uram. **Account Executives, Corporate Sponsorships:** Keshia Dupas, Matt Richardson, Jeff Stewart.

Events/Human Resources
Director, Special Events/Tours: Jonathan Sterchy. **Director, Special Event/Live Entertainment/Sales:** Stephanie Stegall. **Assistant Director, Special Events:** Allison White. **Manager, Special Events Operations:** Cara Lewanda. **Director, Safety:** Lowell Matheny. **Managers, HR:** Chanda Lawdermilk, Edna Chan, Jennifer Springs.

2015 SCHEDULE
Standard Game Times: 7:10 p.m.; Sat. 6:10; Sun. 1:10.

APRIL
6 . . . . Cleveland
8-9 . . . . Cleveland
10-12 . . . . .at Texas
13-15 . . . . Oakland
17-19 . . . . Los Angeles (AL)
20-22 . . . . .at Seattle
24-26 . . . . at Oakland
27-29 . . . . . . at San Diego
30 . . . . Seattle

MAY
1-3 . . . . Seattle
4-6 . . . . Texas
7-10 . . . at Los Angeles (AL)
12-13 . . . . .San Francisco
14-17 . . . . .Toronto
18-20 . . . . Oakland

21-24 . . . . at Detroit
25-27 . . . . . . .at Baltimore
29-31 . . . . . Chicago (AL)

JUNE
1-4 . . . . Baltimore
5-7 . . . . at Toronto
8-10 . . . .at Chicago (AL)
12-14 . . . . Seattle
15-16 . . . . .Colorado
17-18 . . . . . at Colorado
19-21 . . . . .at Seattle
22-24 . . at Los Angeles (AL)
25-28 . . . .New York (AL)
29-30 . . . . . . Kansas City

JULY
1 . . . . Kansas City

3-5 . . . . at Boston
6-9 . . . . .at Cleveland
10-12 . . . . at Tampa Bay
17-19 . . . . Texas
21-23 . . . . Boston
24-26 . . . . .at Kansas City
28-30 . . . . Los Angeles (AL)
31 . . . . Arizona

AUGUST
1-2 . . . . Arizona
3-5 . . . . .at Texas
6-9 . . . . .at Oakland
11-12 . . . . at San Francisco
14-16 . . . . Detroit
17-20 . . . . .Tampa Bay
21-23 . . . .Los Angeles (NL)
24-26 . . . . at New York (AL)

28-30 . . . . . at Minnesota
31 . . . . Seattle

SEPTEMBER
1-2 . . . . Seattle
4-6 . . . . .Minnesota
7-9 . . . . .at Oakland
11-13 . . at Los Angeles (AL)
14-17 . . . . .at Texas
18-20 . . . . Oakland
21-23 . . . .Los Angeles (AL)
25-27 . . . . Texas
28-30 . . . . .at Seattle

OCTOBER
2-4 . . . . at Arizona

GENERAL INFORMATION

Stadium (year opened):
Minute Maid Park (2000).
Team Colors: Navy and orange.

Player Representative: Unavailable.
Home Dugout: First Base.
Playing Surface: Grass.

Stadium Operations

Director, Stadium Operations: Dave McKenzie. **Director, Security/Parking:** Ben Williams. **Director, Engineering:** Philip Pizzo. **Senior Director, Major League Field Operations:** Dan Bergstrom. **Director, Guest Services:** Michael Kenny.

Ticketing

Senior Director, Ticket Operations/Strategy: Brooke Ellenberger. **Senior Director, Group Sales/Inside Sales:** P.J. Keene. **Director, Box Office Operations:** Bill Cannon. **Director, Premium Sales/Service:** Clay Kowalski. **Director, Season Ticket Services:** Alan Latkovic. **Director, Season Ticket Sales:** Duane Haring.

BASEBALL OPERATIONS

General Manager: Jeff Luhnow. **Assistant GM:** David Stearns. **Special Assistants:** Craig Biggio, Roger Clemens, Enos Cabell. **Baseball Operations Manager:** Brandon Taubman. **Coordinator, Baseball Operations:** Pete Putila. **Director, Decision Sciences:** Sig Mejdal. **Analyst:** Mike Fast. **Mathematical Modeler:** Colin Wyers. **Senior Technical Architect:** Ryan Hallahan. **Analytics Developer:** Darren DeFreeuw. **Coordinator, International Operations:** Eve Rosenbaum.

Major League Staff

Manager: A.J. Hinch.
Coaches: Bench—Trey Hillman; **Pitching**—Brent Strom; **Hitting**—Dave Hudgens; **First Base**—Rich Dauer; **Third Base**—Gary Pettis; **Bullpen**—Craig Bjornson; **Assistant Hitting Coach**—Alan Zinter; **Bullpen Catcher**—Javier Bracamonte.

Team Operations/Clubhouse

Jeff Luhnow

Manager, Team Operations: Dan O'Neill. **Coordinator, Advance Information:** Tom Koch-Weser. **Assistant, Advance Scouting:** Matt Hogan. **Clubhouse Manager:** Carl Schneider. **Visiting Clubhouse Manager:** Steve Perry. **Video Coordinator/Analyst:** Evan Stackpole.

Medical/Training

Medical Director: Dr. David Lintner. **Team Physicians:** Dr. Thomas Mehlhoff, Dr. James Muntz, Dr. Pat McCulloch. **Medical Risk Manager/Analyst:** Bill Firkus. **Head Trainer:** Nate Lucero. **Strength/Conditioning Coach:** Jacob Beiting.

Player Development

Telephone: (713) 259-8920. **Fax:** (713) 259-8600.
Director, Player Development: Quinton McCracken. **Assistant Director, Player Development:** Allen Rowin. **Director, Florida Operations:** Jay Edminston. **Assistant, Player Development:** Armando Velasco. **Field Coordinator:** Paul Runge. **Minor League Coordinators:** Jamey Snodgrass (medical), Brendan Verner (strength/conditioning), Daniel Roberts (rehab), Jeff Albert (hitting), Dyar Miller (pitching), Doug White (pitching rover), Ralph Dickenson (hitting rover). **Development Specialists:** Jeff Murphy (Triple-A), Tom Lawless (Double-A), Ramon Vazquez (High A), Tim Garland (Low A). **Rehab Coach:** MIke Burns. **Infield Instructor:** Adam Everett. **Catching Instructor:** Mark Bailey. **GCL Pitching Advisor:** Gary Ruby. **Special Assignment Coach:** Morgan Ensberg. **GCL Coach:** Wladimir Sutil. **DSL Outfield Specialist:** Melvi Ortega. **DSL Camp Coordinator:** Johan Maya. **Latin America Development Specialist/Pitching Coordinator:** Erick Abreu. **DSL Hitting Specialist:** Rene Rojas. **DSL Catching Specialist:** Carlos Lugo.

Farm System

Class	Club	Manager	Hitting Coach	Pitching Coach
Triple-A	Fresno (PCL)	Tony DeFrancesco	Leon Roberts	Arthur "Ace" Adams
Double-A	Corpus Christi (TL)	Rodney Linares	Dan Radison	Doug Brocail
High A	Lancaster (CAL)	Omar Lopez	Darryl Robinson	Don Alexander
Low A	Quad Cities (SAL)	Josh Bonifay	Joel Chimelis	Dave Borkowski
Short-season	Tri-City (NYP)	Ed Romero	Russ Steinhorn	Chris Holt
Rookie	Greeneville (APP)	Lamarr Rogers	Cesar Cedeno	Josh Miller
Rookie	Astros (GCL)	Marty Malloy	Vinny Lopez	Hector Mercado
Rookie	Astros 1 (DSL)	Charlie Romero	Luis Mateo	Erick Abreu
Rookie	Astros 2 (DSL)	Neder Horta	Sixto Ortega	Carlos Gonzalez

Scouting

Telephone: (713) 259-8928. **Fax:** (713) 315-5550.
Director, Amateur Scouting: Mike Elias. **Director, Pro Scouting:** Kevin Goldstein. **Coordinator, Amateur Scouting:** Paul Cusick. **Pro Scouts:** Charles Aliano (Land O' Lakes, FL), Hank Allen (Upper Marlboro, MD), Alex Jacobs (Lakeland, FL), Jason Lefkowitz (Dallas, TX), Spike Lundberg (Murrieta, CA), Tim Moore (Greeneville, NC), Paul Ricciarini (Pittsfield, MA), Tom Shafer (Lockport, IL), Will Sharp (Athens, GA), Aaron Tassano (Glendale, AZ), Chris Young (Georgetown, TX). **Senior Scouting Advisor:** Charlie Gonzalez (Davie, FL). **Regional Supervisors: Midwest**—Ralph Bratton (Dripping Springs, TX); **East**—JD Alleva (Charlotte, NC); **West**—Kris Gross (Newport Beach, CA); **FL/PR/NE**— Evan Brannon. **Area Scouts:** Tim Bittner (Mechanicsville, VA), Bryan Byrne (Walnut Creek, CA), Brad Budzinski (Huntington Beach, CA), Tim Costic (Stevenson Ranch, CA), Justin Cryer (Oxford, MS), Gavin Dickey (Atlanta, GA), Paul Gale (Keizer, OR), Noel Gonzales (Houston, TX), Troy Hoerner (Middleton, WI), John Martin (Tampa, FL), Mark Ross (Tucson, AZ), Bobby St. Pierre (Port Washington, NY), Jim Stevenson (Tulsa, OK), Nick Venuto (Newton Falls, OH). **Senior Advising Scout:** Bob King (La Mesa, CA). **Part-Time Scouts:** Joey Sola (Caguas, PR), Robert Gutierrez (Miami Gardens, FL), Ross Smith (Valdosta, GA). **Director, International:** Oz Ocampo (New York, NY). **International Development Coordinator:** Carlos Alfonso (Naples, FL). **Latin American Development Advisor:** Julio Linares. **Supervisor, Latin American Operations:** Caridad Cabrera. **International Scouts: Venezuela**—Oscar Alvarado, Daniel Acuna, Jose Palacios; **Dominican Republic**—Roman Ocumarez, Rene Rojas, Francis Mojica, Jose Lima, Leocadio Guevara, David Brito; **Panama**—Carlos Gonzalez; **Colombia**— Neder Horta; **Curacao/Aruba**—Quincy Martina; **Mexico**—Raul Lopez, Ruben Amaro Sr.

Kansas City Royals

Office Address: One Royal Way, Kansas City, MO 64129.
Mailing Address: PO Box 419969, Kansas City, MO 64141.
Telephone: (816) 921-8000. **Fax:** (816) 924-0347. **Website:** www.royals.com.

Ownership
Operated By: Kansas City Royals Baseball Club, Inc.
Chairman/CEO: David Glass. **President:** Dan Glass. **Board of Directors:** Ruth Glass, Don Glass, Dayna Martz, Julia Irene Kauffman.

BUSINESS OPERATIONS

David Glass

Senior Vice President, Business Operations: Kevin Uhlich. **Executive Administrative Assistant:** Cindy Hamilton. **Director, Royals Hall of Fame:** Curt Nelson. **Director, Authentic Merchandise Sales:** Justin Villarreal.

Finance/Administration
VP, Finance/Administration: David Laverentz. **Director, Finance:** Adam Tyhurst. **Director, Human Resources:** Johnna Meyer. **Director, Risk Management:** Patrick Fleischmann. **Director Payroll:** Jodi Parsons. **Senior Director, Information Systems:** Brian Himstedt. **Senior Director, Ticket Operations:** Anthony Blue. **Director, Ticket Operations:** Chris Darr.

Communications/Broadcasting
VP, Communications/Broadcasting: Mike Swanson. **Assistant Director, Communications:** Mike Cummings. **Coordinator, Media Relations/Alumni:** Dina Blevins. **Coordinator, Communications/Broadcasting:** Colby Curry.

Publicity/Community Relations
VP, Community Affairs/Publicity: Toby Cook. **Senior Director, Community Relations:** Ben Aken. **Senior Director, Publicity:** Lora Grosshans. **Director, Royals Charities:** Marie Dispenza. **Director, Community Outreach:** Betty Kaegel.

Ballpark Operations
VP, Ballpark Operations/Development: Bob Rice. **Senior Director, Groundskeeping/Landscaping:** Trevor Vance. **Senior Director, Stadium Engineering:** Todd Burrow. **Director, Ballpark Services:** Johnny Williams. **Director, Event Operations:** Isaac Riffel. **Director, Guest Services/Experience:** Anthony Mozzicato.

Marketing/Business Development
VP, Marketing/Business Development: Michael Bucek. **Senior Director, Event Presentation/Production:** Don Costante. **Director, Event Presentation/Production:** Steven Funke. **Director, Marketing/Advertising:** Brad Zollars. **Director, Digital/Social Media:** Erin Sleddens. **Senior Director, Corporate Partnerships/Broadcast Sales:** Jason Booker. **Senior Director, Client Services:** Michele Kammerer. **Senior Director, Sales/Service:** Steve Shiffman. **Director, Sales/Service:** Scott Wadsworth.

2015 SCHEDULE
Standard Game Times: 7:10 p.m.; Sat. 6:10; Sun. 1:10.

APRIL		JULY	
6 . . . . Chicago (AL)	19-20 . . . . Cincinnati	1 . . . . at Houston	20-23 . . . . at Boston
8-9 . . . . Chicago (AL)	22-24 . . . . St. Louis	2-5 . . . . Minnesota	24-27 . . . . Baltimore
10-12 . . at Los Angeles (AL)	25-27 . . . . at New York (AL)	6-9 . . . . Tampa Bay	28-30 . . . . . at Tampa Bay
13 . . . . at Minnesota	29-31 . . . . .at Chicago (NL)	10-12 . . . . Toronto	
15-16 . . . . . . at Minnesota		17-19 . . . . .at Chicago (AL)	SEPTEMBER
17-19 . . . . Oakland	JUNE	20-22 . . . . Pittsburgh	1-3 . . . . Detroit
20-22 . . . . Minnesota	2-4 . . . . Cleveland	24-26 . . . . Houston	4-6 . . . . Chicago (AL)
23-26 . . . . .at Chicago (AL)	5-7 . . . . Texas	27-29 . . . . . . .at Cleveland	7-9 . . . . Minnesota
27-29 . . . . .at Cleveland	8-10 . . . . . . at Minnesota	30-31 . . . . at Toronto	11-13 . . . . . .at Baltimore
30 . . . . Detroit	12-14 . . . . . .at St. Louis		14-17 . . . . . .at Cleveland
	15-16 . . . . . at Milwaukee		18-20 . . . . at Detroit
MAY	17-18 . . . . Milwaukee	AUGUST	22-24 . . . . Seattle
1-3 . . . . Detroit	19-21 . . . . Boston	1-2 . . . . at Toronto	25-27 . . . . Cleveland
5-7 . . . . Cleveland	22-24 . . . . .at Seattle	4-6 . . . . at Detroit	29-30 . . . . .at Chicago (AL)
8-10 . . . . . . at Detroit	26-28 . . . . . . .at Oakland	7-9 . . . . Chicago (AL)	
11-14 . . . . .at Texas	29-30 . . . . . . at Houston	10-12 . . . . Detroit	OCTOBER
15-17 . . . . .New York (AL)		13-16 . . . . Los Angeles (AL)	1 . . . . .at Chicago (AL)
		18-19 . . . . . at Cincinnati	2-4 . . . . at Minnesota

GENERAL INFORMATION
Stadium (year opened): Ewing M. Kauffman Stadium (1973). **Team Colors:** Royal blue and white.

Player Representative: Unavailable. **Home Dugout:** First Base. **Playing Surface:** Grass.

BASEBALL OPERATIONS

Telephone: (816) 921-8000. **Fax:** (816) 924-0347.
Senior VP, Baseball Operations/General Manager: Dayton Moore.
VP, Baseball Operations/Assistant GM: Dean Taylor. **VP/Assistant GM, Player Personnel:** J.J. Picollo. **VP/Assistant GM, International Operations:** Rene Francisco. **VP, Baseball Operations:** George Brett. **Assistant GM, Baseball Administration:** Jin Wong. **Assistant GM, Baseball Operations:** Scott Sharp. **Senior Advisor to GM, Scouting/Player Development:** Mike Arbuckle. **Director, Baseball Operations/Analytics:** Mike Groopman.
Director, Baseball Administration: Kyle Vena. **Director, Baseball Analytics/Player Personnel:** John Williams. **Director, Baseball Analytics/Research Science:** Daniel Mack. **Senior Advisors:** Art Stewart, Donnie Williams. **Advisor:** Rafael Belliard. **Special Assistants to GM:** Louie Medina, Pat Jones, Mike Toomey, Mike Pazik, Jim Fregosi, Jr., Tim Conroy. **Special Assistant to Baseball Operations:** Mike Sweeney. **Executive Assistant to the GM:** Emily Penning. **Assistant to Analytics:** Guy Stevens. **Baseball Operations Assistant:** Phil Stringer. **Systems Architect:** Harper Weaver.

Dayton Moore

Travel/Clubhouse

Senior Director, Clubhouse Operations/Team Travel: Jeff Davenport. **Assistant Equipment Manager:** Patrick Gorman. **Visiting Clubhouse Manager:** Chuck Hawke. **Video Coordinator:** Mark Topping.

Major League Staff

Manager: Ned Yost.
Coaches: Bench—Don Wakamatsu; **Pitching**—Dave Eiland; **Hitting**—Dale Sveum; **First Base**—Rusty Kuntz; **Third Base**—Mike Jirschele; **Bullpen**—Doug Henry; **Coach**—Pedro Grifol; **Replay/Advance Scouting Coordinator**—Bill Duplissea; **Bullpen Catcher**—Cody Clark.

Medical/Training

Team Physician: Dr. Vincent Key. **Head Athletic Trainer:** Nick Kenney. **Assistant Athletic Trainer:** Kyle Turner. **Strength/Conditioning:** Ryan Stoneberg. **Physical Therapist:** Jeff Blum.

Player Development

Telephone: (816) 921-8000. **Fax:** (816) 924-0347.
Director, Minor League Operations: Ronnie Richardson.
Baseball Operations Assistant/Player Development: Chris Getz. **Minor League/Amateur Video Coordinator:** Nick Relic. **Senior Coordinator:** Chino Cadahia. **Senior Pitching Advisor:** Bill Fischer. **Special Assistant, Player Development:** John Wathan, Harry Spilman. **Advisor to Player Development/Hitting:** Bill Springman. **Coordinators:** Larry Carter (pitching), Terry Bradshaw (hitting), Rafael Belliard (infield), Milt Thompson (bunting/baserunning), Chris DeLucia (medical), Tony Medina (Latin America Medical), Garrett Sherrill (strength/conditioning), Luis Perez (Latin America strength/conditioning), Justin Hahn (rehab), Jeff Diskin (cultural development), Freddy Sandoval (mental skills).

Farm System

Class	Club (League)	Manager	Hitting Coach	Pitching Coach
Triple-A	Omaha (PCL)	Brian Poldberg	Tommy Gregg	Al Nipper
Double-A	Northwest Arkansas (TL)	Vance Wilson	Brandon Moore	Jim Brower
High A	Wilmington (CL)	Brian Buchanan	Abraham Nunez	Steve Luebber
Low A	Lexington (SAL)	Omar Ramirez	Damon Hollins	Carlos Reyes
Rookie	Idaho Falls (PIO)	Justin Gemoll	Andre David	Jeff Suppan
Rookie	Burlington (APP)	Scott Thorman	Jesus Azuaje	Carlos Martinez
Rookie	Royals (AZL)	Darryl Kennedy	Nelson Liriano	Mark Davis
Rookie	Royals (DSL)	Jose Gualdron	Onil Joseph	Gustavo Martinez

Scouting

Telephone: (816) 921-8000. **Fax:** (816) 924-0347.
Director, Scouting: Lonnie Goldberg. **Director, Pro Scouting:** Gene Watson.
Manager, Scouting Operations: Linda Smith. **Assistant to Amateur Scouting:** Jack Monahan.
Professional Scouts: Dennis Cardoza (Munds Park, AZ), Mike Pazik (Bethesda, MD), Tony Tijerina (Newark Valley, NY); Jon Williams (Imperial, MO), Ron Toenjes (Georgetown, TX), Mitch Webster (Kansas City, MO), Alec Zumwalt (Winston-Salem, NC). **National Supervisors:** Paul Gibson (Center Moriches, NY), Junior Vizcaino (Raleigh, NC). **Regional Supervisors: Midwest**—Gregg Miller (Meeker, OK), **Southeast**—Gregg Kilby (Tampa, FL), **West**—Dan Ontiveros (Laguna Niguel, CA), **Northeast**—Keith Connolly (Fair Haven, NJ). **Area Supervisors:** Rich Amaral (Huntington Beach, CA), Jim Buckley (Tampa, FL), Travis Ezi (New Orleans, LA), Casey Fahy (Apex, NC), Jim Farr (Williamsburg, VA), Mike Farrell (Indianapolis, IN), Bobby Gandolfo (King of Prussia, PA), Sean Gibbs (Canton, GA), Colin Gonzales (Dana Point, CA), Buddy Gouldsmith (Reno, NV), Josh Hallgren (Vancouver, WA), Chad Lee (Norman, OK), Justin Lehr (The Woodlands, TX), Scott Melvin (Quincy, IL), Alex Mesa (Miami, FL), Ken Munoz (Scottsdale, AZ), Matt Price (Overland Park, KS).
Part-Time Scouts: Kirk Barclay (Wyoming, ON), Eric Briggs (Bolivar, MO), Rick Clendenin (Clendenin, WV), Louis Collier (Chicago, IL), Corey Eckstein (Abbotsford, BC), Brian Hiler (Cincinnati, OH), Jerry Lafferty (Kansas City, MO), Brittan Motley (Grandview, MO), Chad Raley (Baton Rouge, LA), Johnny Ramos (Carolina, PR).
Latin America Supervisor: Orlando Estevez. **International Scouts:** Neil Burke (Australia), Richard Castro (Venezuela), Alberto Garcia (Venezuela) Juan Indriago (Venezuela), Jose Gualdron (Venezuela), Joelvis Gonzalez (Venezuela), Edson Kelly (Aruba), Juan Lopez (Nicaragua), Nathan Miller (Taiwan), Rafael Miranda (Colombia), Fausto Morel (Dominican Republic), Ricardo Ortiz (Panama), Edis Perez (Dominican Republic), Rafael Vasquez (Dominican Republic), Franco Wawoe (Curacao).

Los Angeles Angels

Office Address: 2000 Gene Autry Way, Anaheim, CA 92806.
Mailing Address: 2000 Gene Autry Way, Anaheim, CA 92803.
Telephone: (714) 940-2000. **Fax:** (714) 940-2205.
Website: www.angels.com.

Ownership
Owner: Arte Moreno. **Chairman:** Dennis Kuhl. **President:** John Carpino.

BUSINESS OPERATIONS

Arte Moreno

Chief Financial Officer: Bill Beverage. **Senior Vice President, Finance/Administration:** Molly Jolly. **Director, Legal Affairs/Risk Management:** Alex Winsberg. **Controller:** Cris Lacoste. **Accountants:** Lorelei Schlitz, Kylie McManus, Jennifer Whynott. **Financial Analyst:** Jennifer Jeanblanc. **Accounting Assistant:** Linda Chubak. **Payroll Assistant:** Alison Kelso. **Benefits Manager:** Cecilia Schneider.

Director, Human Resources: Deborah Johnston. **Human Resources Generalist:** Brittany Johnson. **Human Resources Representative:** Mayra Trinidad. **Staffing Analyst:** Kristin Machuca. **Director, Information Services:** Al Castro. **Senior Network Engineer:** Neil Fariss. **Senior Desktop Support Analyst:** David Yun. **Technology Integration Specialist:** Paramjit 'Tiny' Singh.

Corporate Sales
VP, Sales: Neil Viserto. **Senior Director, Business Development:** Mike Fach. **Senior Corporate Account Executives:** Nicole Provansal, Rick Turner. **Corporate Account Executive:** Drew Zinser. **Sponsorship Services Managers:** Maria Dinh, Bobby Kowan. **Sponsorship Services Coordinators:** Rosanne Tarrant, Vanessa Vega. **Sponsorship Research Analyst:** Michael Sylvan.

Marketing/Entertainment
VP, Marketing/Ticket Sales: Robert Alvarado. **Marketing Managers:** John Rozak, Kevin Shaw, Ryan Vance. **Marketing Coordinator/Graphic Designer:** Jeff Lee. **Social Media Coordinator:** Tara Nicodemo. **Marketing Associate:** Alex Tinyo. **Director, Entertainment/Production:** Peter Bull. **Producer, Video Operations:** David Tsuruda. **Associate Producer:** Danny Pitts. **Entertainment Coordinator:** Emily Cabrera.

Public/Media Relations/Communications
Telephone: (714) 940-2014. **Fax:** (714) 940-2205.
VP, Communications: Tim Mead. **Director, Communications:** Eric Kay. **Media Relations Representative:** Adam Chodzko. **Communications Assistant:** Matt Birch. **Senior Director, Community Relations:** Jenny Price. **Community Relations Coordinator:** Chrissy Vaughn. **Team Photographer:** Matt Brown. **Photo Editor:** Robert Huskey.

2015 SCHEDULE
Standard Game Times: 7:05 p.m.; Sun. 12:35.

APRIL		
6-8 . . . . .at Seattle		
10-12 . . . . . . Kansas City		
13-15 . . . . .at Texas		
17-19 . . . . . . at Houston		
20-23 . . . . Oakland		
24-26 . . . . Texas		
28-30 . . . . . . .at Oakland		

MAY		
1-3 . . . . . at San Francisco		
4-6 . . . . Seattle		
7-10 . . . . Houston		
12-13 . . . . .Colorado		
15-17 . . . . . .at Baltimore		
18-21 . . . . at Toronto		
22-24 . . . . at Boston		

25-27 . . . . San Diego
28-31 . . . . Detroit

JUNE
1-3 . . . . .Tampa Bay
5-7 . . . . . at New York (AL)
9-11 . . . . . . at Tampa Bay
12-14 . . . . Oakland
15-16 . . . . .Arizona
17-18 . . . . at Arizona
19-21 . . . . . . .at Oakland
22-24 . . . . Houston
26-28 . . . . Seattle
29-30 . . . . .New York (AL)

JULY
1 . . . . .New York (AL)

3-5 . . . . .at Texas
7-8 . . . . at Colorado
9-12 . . . . .at Seattle
17-20 . . . . Boston
21-23 . . . . . . .Minnesota
24-26 . . . . Texas
28-30 . . . . . . at Houston
31 . . . . at Los Angeles (NL)

AUGUST
1-2 . . . at Los Angeles (NL)
3-5 . . . . Cleveland
7-9 . . . . Baltimore
10-12 . . . . .at Chicago (AL)
13-16 . . . . . .at Kansas City
17-20 . . . . . Chicago (AL)
21-23 . . . . .Toronto

25-27 . . . . at Detroit
28-30 . . . . . .at Cleveland
31 . . . . .at Oakland

SEPTEMBER		
1-2 . . . . .at Oakland		
4-6 . . . . Texas		
7-9 . . . . .Los Angeles (NL)		
11-13 . . . . Houston		
14-16 . . . . .at Seattle		
17-20 . . . . . . at Minnesota		
21-23 . . . . . . at Houston		
25-27 . . . . Seattle		
28-30 . . . . Oakland		

OCTOBER		
1-4 . . . . .at Texas		

GENERAL INFORMATION
Stadium (year opened):
Angel Stadium of Anaheim (1966).
Team Colors: Red, dark red, blue and silver.

Player Representative: C.J. Wilson.
Home Dugout: Third Base.
Playing Surface: Grass.

Ballpark Operations/Facilities

Senior Director, Ballpark Operations: Brian Sanders. **Director, Ballpark Operations:** Sam Maida. **Event Manager:** Calvin Ching. **Security Manager:** Mark Macias. **Field/Ground Maintenance Manager:** Barney Lopas. **Turf Grass Manager:** Greg Laesch. **Receptionists:** Margie Walsh, Marty Valles.
Director, Facility Services: Mike McKay. **Purchasing Manager:** Suzanne Peters. **Asset Coordinator:** Daniel Angulo. **Manager, Facility Maintenance:** Steve Preston. **Custodial Supervisors:** Nathan Bautista, Ray Nells. **Custodial Shift Supervisor:** Pedro Del Castillo. **Office Assistant:** Jose Padilla.

Ticketing

Director, Ticketing Operations: Sheila Brazelton. **Manager, Ticket Office:** Susan Weiss. **Event Sales/Service Manager:** Courtney Wallace. **Director, Ticket Services:** Johnny Mendez. **Director, Ticket Sales/Services:** Tom DeTemple. **Manager, Ticket Sales:** Josh Hunhoff. **Manager, Client Services:** Justin Hallenbeck.

Travel/Clubhouse

Clubhouse Manager: Keith Tarter. **Assistant Clubhouse Manager:** Shane Demmitt. **Visiting Clubhouse Manager:** Brian 'Bubba' Harkins. **Senior Video Coordinator:** Diego Lopez. **Video Coordinator:** Ruben Montano. **Traveling Secretary:** Tom Taylor.

BASEBALL OPERATIONS

General Manager: Jerry Dipoto.
Assistant GM, Baseball Operations: Matt Klentak. **Assistant GM, Player Development/Scouting:** Scott Servais. **Special Advisor:** Bill Stoneman. **Special Assistants to GM:** Tim Bogar, Tim Huff, Marcel Lachemann. **Director, Baseball Operations:** Justin Hollander. **Manager, Major League Operations:** Jonathan Strangio. **Coordinator, Scouting:** Nate Horowitz. **Coordinator, Advance Scouting:** Jeremy Zoll. **Baseball Administration Coordinator:** Kathy Mair.

Jerry Dipoto

Major League Staff

Manager: Mike Scioscia. **Coaches: Bench**—Dino Ebel; **Pitching**—Mike Butcher; **Batting**—Don Baylor; **First Base**—Alfredo Griffin; **Third Base**—Gary DiSarcina; **Bullpen**—Steve Soliz; **Bullpen Catcher**—Tom Gregorio; **Assistant Hitting**—Dave Hansen; **Major League Player Information**—Rico Brogna.

Medical/Training

Team Physician: Dr. Craig Milhouse. **Team Orthopedists:** Dr. Robert Grumet, Dr. Michael Shepard. **Head Athletic Trainer:** Adam Nevala. **Assistant Athletic Trainer:** Rick Smith. **Strength/Conditioning Coach:** T.J. Harrington.

Player Development

Director, Player Development: Bobby Scales.
Assistant Director, Player Development: Mike LaCassa. **Minor League Equipment Manager, Arizona:** Brett Crane. **Field Coordinator:** Mike Micucci. **Roving Instructors:** Paul Sorrento (Hitting), Jim Eppard (Assistant Hitting), Bill Lachemann (Catching/Special Assignment), Tyrone Boykin (Outfield/Baserunning/Bunting), Jim Gott (Pitching), Kernan Ronan (Rehab Pitching), Keith Johnson (Infield), Pete Harnisch (Special Assignment Pitching), Bobby Knoop (Special Assignment Infield), Geoff Hostetter (Training Coordinator), Al Sandoval (Strength/Conditioning), Eric Munson (Rehab).

Farm System

Class	Club	Manager	Hitting Coach	Pitching Coach
Triple-A	Salt Lake (PCL)	Dave Anderson	Johnny Narron	Erik Bennett
Double-A	Arkansas (TL)	Bill Richardson	Tom Tornincasa	Pat Rice
High A	Inland Empire (CAL)	Denny Hocking	Brenton Del Chiaro	Matt Wise
Low A	Burlington (MWL)	Chad Tracy	Ryan Barba	Ethan Katz
Rookie	Orem (PIO)	Dave Stapleton	Buck Coats	John Slusarz
Rookie	Angels (AZL)	Elio Sarmiento	Brian Betancourth	Jairo Cuevas
Rookie	Angels (DSL)	Carson Vitale	Anel De Los Santos	Hector Astacio

Scouting

Director, Pro Scouting: Hal Morris.
Major League/Special Assignment Scout: Timothy Schmidt (San Bernardino, CA). **Professional Scouts:** Jeff Cirillo (Medina, WA), Chris Fetter (Carmel, IN), Travis Ice (Lawrence, KS), Kevin Jarvis (Franklin, TN), Mike Koplove (Philadelphia, PA), Tim McIntosh (Stockton, CA), Ken Stauffer (Katy, TX), Gary Varsho (Chili, WI), Bobby Williams (Sarasota, FL).
Director, Amateur Scouting: Ric Wilson.
National Crosscheckers: Jeff Malinoff (Lopez, WA). **Regional Supervisors: Northeast**—Jason Baker (Lynchburg, VA); **Southeast**—Chris McAlpin (Moultrie, GA); **Northern Midwest**—Joel Murrie (Evergreen, CO); **Southern Midwest**—Kevin Ham (Cypress, TX); **Northwest**—Scott Richardson (Sacramento, CA); **Southwest**—Jayson Durocher (Phoenix, AZ).
Area Scouts: Don Archer (Canada), Jared Barnes (South Bend, IN), John Burden (Fairfield, OH), Drew Chadd (Wichita, KS), Tim Corcoran (LaVerne, CA), Ben Diggins (Newport Beach, CA), Jason Ellison (Issaquah, WA), Nick Gorneault (Springfield, MA), John Gracio (Mesa, AZ), Chad Hermansen (Henderson, NV), Todd Hogan (Dublin, GA), Ryan Leahy (Beverly, MA), Brandon McArthur (Kennesaw, GA), Ralph Reyes (Miami, FL), Omar Rodriguez (Puerto Rico), Rudy Vasquez (San Antonio, TX), Rob Wilfong (San Dimas, CA), J.T. Zink (Hoover, AL).
Director, International Scouting: Carlos Gomez.
International Scouting Supervisors: Marlon Urdaneta (Venezuela), Alfredo Ulloa (Dominican Republic).
International Scouts: Jochy Cabrera (Dominican Republic), Domingo Garcia (Dominican Republic), Carlos Ramirez (Venezuela), Franciso Tejeda (Dominican Republic), Mauro Zerpa (Venezuela).

Los Angeles Dodgers

Office Address: 1000 Elysian Park Ave., Los Angeles, CA 90012.
Telephone: (323) 224-1500. **Fax:** (323) 224-1269. **Website:** www.dodgers.com.

Ownership/Executive Office

Chairman: Mark Walter.
Partner: Earvin 'Magic' Johnson, Peter Guber, Todd Boehly, Robert 'Bobby' Patton, Jr.
President/CEO: Stan Kasten. **Special Advisors to Chairman:** Tommy Lasorda, Sandy Koufax, Don Newcombe.
Senior Advisor to President/CEO: Ned Colletti. **Special Assistants to President/CEO:** Vance Lovelace, Rick Ragazzo.

BUSINESS OPERATIONS

Executive Vice President: Bob Wolfe. **Executive VP/Chief Marketing Officer:** Lon Rosen.
CFO: Tucker Kain. **Senior VP/General Counsel:** Sam Fernandez. **Senior VP, Planning/
Development:** Janet Marie Smith. **Senior VP, Corporate Partnerships:** Michael Young.
Senior VP, Stadium Operations: Steve Ethier. **Controller:** Eric Hernandez. **Director, Finance:**
Gregory Buonaccorsi.

Mark Walter

Sales/Partnership

VP, Ticket Sales: David Siegel. **Senior Director, Partnership Administration:** Jenny
Oh. **Senior Director, Corporate Partnerships:** Lorenzo Sciarrino. **Director, Season Sales:**
David Kirkpatrick. **Director, Partnership Sales Administration:** Paige Kirkpatrick. **Director,
Premium Sales/Services:** Antonio Morici.

Marketing/Broadcasting

VP, Marketing/Broadcasting: Erik Braverman. **Director, Advertising/Promotions:** Shelley
Wagner. **Director, Production:** Greg Taylor. **Director, Graphic Design:** Ross Yoshida. **Director, Broadcast Engineering:**
Tom Darin.

Human Resources/Legal

Senior Director, Human Resources: Leonor Romero. **Senior Counsel:** Chad Gunderson.

Communications/Community Affairs

Director, Public Relations: Joe Jareck. **Assistant Director, Public Relations:** Yvonne Carrasco. **Director, Digital/
Print Content:** Jon Weisman. **Senior Director, External Affairs/Community Relations:** Naomi Rodriguez.

Information Technology/Stadium Operations/Security

VP, Information Technology: Ralph Esquibel. **VP, Security/Guest Services:** Shahram Ariane. **Director, Facilities:**
David Edford. **Assistant Director, Turf/Grounds:** Eric Hansen.

Ticketing

Telephone: (323) 224-1471. **Fax:** (323) 224-2609.
VP, Ticket Operations: Billy Hunter. **VP, Ticket Development:** Seth Bluman.

2015 SCHEDULE

Standard Game Times: 7:10 p.m.; Sun. 1:10

APRIL		
6-8 . . . . San Diego	25-27 . . . . Atlanta	6-9 . . . . .Philadelphia	28-30 . . . . . Chicago (NL)
10-12 . . . . at Arizona	29-31 . . . . .at St. Louis	10-12 . . . . .Milwaukee	31 . . . . .San Francisco
13-15 . . . . Seattle		17-19 . . . . . at Washington	
17-19 . . . . Colorado	**JUNE**	20-22 . . . . at Atlanta	**SEPTEMBER**
21-23 . . . . at San Francisco	1-3 . . . . at Colorado	23-26 . . . .at New York (NL)	1-2 . . . . .San Francisco
24-26 . . . . . at San Diego	4-7 . . . . St. Louis	28-29 . . . . Oakland	3-6 . . . . at San Diego
27-29 . . . . .San Francisco	8-10 . . . . .Arizona	31 . . . . . Los Angeles (AL)	7-9 . . . . at Los Angeles (AL)
	12-14 . . . . . at San Diego		11-13 . . . . at Arizona
MAY	15-16 . . . . .at Texas	**AUGUST**	14-16 . . . . .Colorado
1-3 . . . . .Arizona	17-18 . . . . Texas	1-2 . . . . . Los Angeles (AL)	18-20 . . . . .Pittsburgh
4-7 . . . . at Milwaukee	19-21 . . . . .San Francisco	4-6 . . . . . . at Philadelphia	21-24 . . . . .Arizona
8-10 . . . . . . at Colorado	22-25 . . . . .at Chicago (NL)	7-9 . . . . at Pittsburgh	25-27 . . . . . at Colorado
11-13 . . . . .Miami	26-28 . . . . at Miami	10-12 . . . . . .Washington	28-30 . . . . . at San Francisco
14-17 . . . . .Colorado	29-30 . . . . at Arizona	13-16 . . . . Cincinnati	
19-21 . . . . at San Francisco		18-19 . . . . .at Oakland	**OCTOBER**
22-24 . . . . San Diego	**JULY**	21-23 . . . . at Houston	1 . . . . at San Francisco
	1 . . . . at Arizona	25-27 . . . . . . at Cincinnati	2-4 . . . . San Diego
	3-5 . . . . . . .New York (NL)		

GENERAL INFORMATION

Stadium (year opened):
Dodger Stadium (1962).
Team Colors: Dodger blue and white.

Player Representative: Zack Greinke.
Home Dugout: Third Base.
Playing Surface: Grass

BASEBALL OPERATIONS

Telephone: (323) 224-1500. **Fax:** (323) 224-1463.
President, Baseball Operations: Andrew Friedman.
General Manager: Farhan Zaidi. **Senior VP, Baseball Operations:** Josh Byrnes. **Senior Scouting Advisor:** Ralph Avila. **Director, Baseball Operations:** Alex Tamin. **Director, Baseball Administration:** Ellen Harrigan. **Director, Team Travel:** Scott Akasaki. **Advisor, Team Travel:** Billy DeLury. **Senior Advisor, Baseball Operations:** Gerry Hunsicker. **Special Assistant:** Pat Corrales. **Major League Video Coordinator:** John Pratt. **Manager, Baseball Research/Contracts:** Matt Marks. **Coordinator, Baseball Operations:** Jordan Peikin. **Assistant, Baseball Operations/Analysis:** Emilee Fragapane.

Farhan Zaidi

Major League Staff

Manager: Don Mattingly.
Coaches: Bench—Tim Wallach; **Pitching**—Rick Honeycutt; **Hitting**—Mark McGwire; **First Base**—Davey Lopes; **Third Base**—Lorenzo Bundy; **Bullpen**—Chuck Crim. **Assistant Pitching Coach:** Ken Howell. **Assistant Hitting Coach:** John Valentin. **Catching Instructor:** Steve Yeager. **Bullpen Catchers:** Rob Flippo, Steve Cilladi.

Medical/Training

VP, Medical Services: Stan Conte. **Assistant Athletic Trainer:** Nancy Flynn. **Strength/Conditioning Coaches:** Brandon McDaniel, Chris Dunaway. **Physical Therapist:** Steve Smith. **Massage Therapist:** Yosuke Nakajima. **Head Team Physician:** Dr. Neal ElAttrache.

Player Development

Telephone: (323) 224-1500. **Fax:** (323) 224-1359.
Director, Player Development: Gabe Kapler.
Assistant Director, Player Development: Nick Francona. **Senior Advisors to Player Development:** Gene Clines, Charlie Hough. **Director, International/Minor League Relations:** Joseph Reaves. **Senior Manager, Player Development:** Chris Madden. **Manager, Minor League Administration:** Adriana Urzua. **Field Coordinator:** Clayton McCullough. **Coordinators:** Damon Mashore (hitting), Rick Knapp (pitching), Brady Clark (outfield/baserunning), Juan Castro (infield), Travis Barbary (catching), Todd Takayoshi (assistant hitting), Kremlin Martinez (assistant pitching). **Roving Baserunning Instructor:** Maury Wills. **Special Advisor, Latin America:** Ramon Martinez. **Latin America Field Coordinator:** Bruce Hurst. **Coordinator, Minor League Medical/Rehab:** Nick Conte. **Rehab Strength/Conditioning Coordinator:** Brian Stoneberg. **Rehab Athletic Trainer:** Kevin Orloski. **International Medical Coordinator:** Wilkin Perez. **Manager, Baseball Operations, Glendale:** Juan Rodriguez. **Assistant, Baseball Operations:** Matt McGrath. **Coordinator, Minor League Video:** Matt Lawrence.

Farm System

Class	Club (League)	Manager	Hitting Coach	Pitching Coach
Triple-A	Oklahoma City (PCL)	Damon Berryhill	Franklin Stubbs	Scott Radinsky
Double-A	Tulsa (TL)	Razor Shines	Shawn Wooten	Matt Herges
High A	Rancho Cucamonga (CAL)	P.J. Forbes	Mike Eylward	Bill Simas
Low A	Great Lakes (MWL)	Bill Haselman	Jay Gibbons	Glenn Dishman
Rookie	Ogden (PIO)	John Shoemaker	Darryl Brinkley	Bobby Cuellar
Rookie	Dodgers (AZL)	Jack McDowell	Aaron Bates	Greg Sabat
Rookie	Dodgers (DSL)	Pedro Mega	Freddy Tiburcio	Roberto Giron

Scouting

VP, Amateur/International Scouting: David Finley.
Director, Amateur Scouting: Billy Gasparino. **National Crosschecker:** John Green (Tucson, AZ). **Special Advisor to Scouting Director/National Crosschecker:** Gib Bodet (San Clemente, CA). **Pitching Crosschecker:** Jack Cressend. **East Regional Supervisor:** Manny Estrada (Longwood, FL). **Midwest Regional Supervisor:** Gary Nickels (Naperville, IL). **West Regional Supervisor:** Brian Stephenson (Fullerton, CA). **Manager, Scouting/Travel Administration:** Jane Capobianco. **Scouting Coordinator:** Jonah Rosenthal. **Coordinator, Video Scouting:** Angelo Nicolosi.
Area Scouts: Clint Bowers (Kingwood, TX), Adrian Casanova (Miami, FL), Bobby Darwin (Corona, CA), Rich Delucia (Reading, PA), Scott Hennessey (Ponte Verde, FL), Josh Herzenberg (Dallas, TX), Orsino Hill (Sacramento, CA), Henry Jones (Vancouver, WA), Lon Joyce (Spartanburg, SC), Jeffrey Lachman (Los Angeles, CA), Marty Lamb (Nicholasville, KY), Scott Little (Jackson, MO), Trey Magnuson (Missoula, MT), Dennis Moeller (Simi Valley, CA), Matthew Paul (Biloxi, MS), Clair Rierson (Wake Forest, NC), Chet Sergo (Plano, IL), Dustin Yount (Phoenix, AZ). **Part Time Scouts:** Luis Faccio, George Genovese, Artie Harris. **Director, Player Personnel:** Galen Carr. **Advance Scouts:** Willie Fraser, Gary Pellant. **Professional Scouts:** Josh Bard, Peter Bergeron, Greg Booker, Lou Colletti, Scott Groot, Toney Howell, Bill Latham, Ron Mahay, Tydus Meadows, Steve Pope, John Sanders, Chris Smith, Matt Smith. **Special Assistants, Player Personnel:** Aaron Sele, Jose Vizcaino. **Special Assistant, Pro Scouting/Player Development:** Jeff Pickler. **Senior Manager, Pro Scouting:** Alex Slater. **Assistant, Baseball Operations:** Kyle Esecson.
VP, International Scouting: Bob Engle. **Senior Manager, International Scouting Operations:** Hidenori Sueyoshi. **Manager, International Scouting:** Roman Barinas. **Special Advisor, International Player Performance:** Rafael Colon. **Supervisor, Dominican Republic:** Franklin Taveras. **Coordinator, Pacific Rim:** Pat Kelly. **Coordinator, Latin America:** Patrick Guerrero. **Coordinator, Venezuela:** Pedro Avila. **Coordinator, Europe:** Doug Skiles. **Special Assignment, Latin America:** Mike Tosar. **International Scouts:** Rolando Chirino (Curacao), Elvio Jimenez (Dominican), Manelik Pimentel (Dominican), Marco Mazzieri (Italy), Isao O'Jimi (Japan), Byung-Hwan An (Korea), Mike Brito (Mexico), Nemesio Porras (Nicaragua), Jamey Storvick (Pacific Rim), Luis Molina (Panama), Juan Garcia-Puig (Spain), Jose Briceno (Venezuela), Francisco Cartaya (Venezuela), Camilo Pascual (Venezuela), Oswaldo Villalobos (Venezuela).

Miami Marlins

Office Address: Marlins Park, 501 Marlins Way, Miami, FL 33125
Telephone: (305) 480-1300. **Fax:** (305) 480-3012.
Website: www.marlins.com.

Ownership
Owner/CEO: Jeffrey H. Loria. **Vice Chairman:** Joel A. **Mael. President:** David P. Samson. **Special Assistants to the Owner:** Bill Beck, Jack McKeon. **Special Assistants to the President:** Jeff Conine, Andre Dawson, Tony Perez.

BUSINESS OPERATIONS

Executive Vice President/Chief Financial Officer: Michel Bussiere. **Executive VP, Operations/Events:** Claude Delorme.
Executive Assistant to Owner/Vice Chairman/President: Beth McConville. **Executive Assistant to the Executive VP/CFO:** Lisa Milk. **Executive Assistant to the Executive VP, Operations/Events:** Teresita Garcia.

Administration
VP, Human Resources: Ana Hernández. **Manager, Human Resources:** Michelle Casanova. **Administrative Coordinator, Human Resources:** Giselle Lopez. **Director, Risk Management:** Fred Espinoza.

Finance
Jeffrey Loria

Senior VP, Finance: Susan Jaison. **Administrator, Payroll:** Carolina Calderon. **Assistant, Payroll:** Edgar Perez. **Staff Accountant:** Michael Mullane. **Coordinators, Accounts Payable:** Nick Kautz, Anthony Paneque. **Coordinator, Accounting:** John Cantalupo. **Assistant, Accounting:** Mary Horton, Jose Paez.

Marketing
Senior VP, Marketing/Event Booking: Sean Flynn. **Director, Multicultural Marketing:** Juan Martinez. **Director, Marketing/Promotions:** Matthew Britten. **Manager, Multicultural Marketing:** Darling Jarquin. **Manager, Marketing:** Boris Menier. **Supervisor, Promotions:** Rafael Capdevila.

Legal
Senior VP/General Counsel: Derek Jackson. **Associate Counsel:** Ashwin Krishnan. **Executive Assistant, Legal:** Sade Diaz.

Sales/Ticketing
Senior VP, Corporate Partnerships: Brendan Cunningham. **VP, Business Development:** Dale Hendricks. **Director, Corporate Partnerships:** Michael Meyers. **VP, Sales/Service:** Ryan McCoy. **Director, Ticket Operations:** Mardi Dilger.

Game Presentation/Events/Ballpark Operations
Senior Director, Game Presentation/Events: Larry Blocker. **Director, Engineering:** Randolph Cousar. **Assistant**

2015 SCHEDULE
Standard Game Times: 7:10 p.m.; Sun. 1:10

APRIL
6-8 . . . . Atlanta
10-12 . . . . .Tampa Bay
13-15 . . . . at Atlanta
16-19 . . . .at New York (NL)
21-23 . . . . . at Philadelphia
24-26 . . . . . . .Washington
27-29 . . . . . .New York (NL)

MAY
1-3 . . . . .Philadelphia
4-6 . . . . at Washington
7-10 . . . . . at San Francisco
11-13 . . at Los Angeles (NL)
15-17 . . . . .Atlanta
18-21 . . . . .Arizona
22-24 . . . . Baltimore

25-27 . . . . . at Pittsburgh
29-31 . . . .at New York (NL)

JUNE
1-3 . . . . Chicago (NL)
5-7 . . . . at Colorado
8-10 . . . . at Toronto
11-14 . . . . .Colorado
15-16 . . . . . .New York (AL)
17-18 . . . at New York (AL)
19-21 . . . . . . at Cincinnati
23-25 . . . . St. Louis
26-28 . . . Los Angeles (NL)
30 . . . . San Francisco

JULY
1-2 . . . . San Francisco
3-5 . . . . . .at Chicago (NL)

7-8 . . . . at Boston
9-12 . . . . Cincinnati
17-19 . . . . .at Philadelphia
20-22 . . . . at Arizona
23-26 . . . . . at San Diego
28-30 . . . . . .Washington
31 . . . . San Diego

AUGUST
1-2 . . . . San Diego
3-5 . . . . . .New York (NL)
6-9 . . . . at Atlanta
11-12 . . . . Boston
14-16 . . . . . . .at St. Louis
17-19 . . . . .at Milwaukee
20-23 . . . . . .Philadelphia
24-27 . . . . Pittsburgh

28-30 . . . . . at Washington
31 . . . . at Atlanta

SEPTEMBER
1-2 . . . . at Atlanta
4-6 . . . . . . .New York (NL)
7-9 . . . . .Milwaukee
11-13 . . . . . . .Washington
14-16 . . . .at New York (NL)
17-20 . . . . at Washington
22-24 . . . . . .Philadelphia
25-27 . . . . Atlanta
29-30 . . . . . at Tampa Bay

OCTOBER
1 . . . . at Tampa Bay
2-4 . . . . . . at Philadelphia

GENERAL INFORMATION
Stadium (year opened): Marlins Park (2012).
Team Colors: Red-Orange, Yellow, Blue, Black, White.

Player Representative: Steve Cishek.
Home Dugout: Third Base.
Playing Surface: Grass.

Director, Engineering: Chad Messina. **VP, Facilities:** Jeffrey King. **Senior Director, Ballpark Operations:** Michael Hurt. **Director, Parking:** Michael McKeon. **Director, Game Services:** Antonio Torres-Roman.

Communications/Media Relations
Senior VP, Communications/Broadcasting: P.J. Loyello. **Senior Director, Communications:** Matt Roebuck. **Manager, Baseball Information:** Marty Sewell. **Supervisor, Baseball Information:** Joe Vieira. **Manager, Communications:** Jon Erik Alvarez. **Coordinator, Communications:** Maria Armella. **Director, Broadcasting:** Emmanuel Muñoz. **Coordinator, Broadcasting:** Kyle Sielaff. **Senior Director, Community Outreach:** Angela Smith. **Director, Creative Services:** Alfred Hernandez. **VP/Executive Director, Marlins Foundation:** Alfredo Mesa. **Director, Marlins Foundation:** Alan Alvarez.

Travel/Clubhouse
Director, Team Travel: Manny Colon. **Equipment Manager:** John Silverman. **Visiting Clubhouse Manager:** Rock Hughes. **Assistant Clubhouse Manager:** Michael Diaz. **Assistant, Clubhouse Attendant/Umpires Room:** Lou Asalone.

BASEBALL OPERATIONS
Telephone: (305) 480-1300. **Fax:** (305) 480-3032.
President, Baseball Operations: Michael Hill. **VP/General Manager:** Dan Jennings.
Executive Assistant to the President, Baseball Operations/VP/GM: Nancy Berry.
VP/Assistant GM: Mike Berger. **VP, Player Personnel:** Craig Weissmann. **Senior Advisor to Player Personnel:** Orrin Freeman. **Director, Baseball Operations:** Dan Noffsinger. **Director, Team Travel:** Manny Colon. **Video Coaching Coordinator:** Cullen McRae.

Michael Hill

Major League Staff
Manager: Mike Redmond.
Coaches: Bench—Rob Leary; **Pitching**—Chuck Hernandez; **Hitting**—Frank Menechino; **First Base/Infield**—Perry Hill; **Third Base**—Brett Butler; **Bullpen**—Reid Cornelius; **Bullpen Coordinator**—Jeff Urgelles.

Medical/Training
Head Trainer: Sean Cunningham. **Assistant Trainers:** Mike Kozak, Dustin Luepker. **Strength/Conditioning Coach:** Ty Hill. **Team Psychologist:** Robert Seifer.

Player Development
VP, Player Development: Marty Scott. **Director, Player Development:** Brian Chattin. **Assistant Director, Player Development/International Operations:** Marc Lippman. **Senior Advisor, Player Development:** Tommy Thompson. **Assistant Director, Player Development:** Brett West. **Minor League Video Coordinator:** Dan Budreika.
Field Coordinator: John Pierson. **Pitching Coordinator:** Charlie Corbell. **Assistant Pitching Coordinator:** Jeff Schwarz. **Assistant Hitting Coordinator:** Andy Barkett. **Infield Coordinator:** Jorge Hernandez. **Outfield/Baserunning Coordinator:** Frank Moore. **Catching Coordinator:** Bobby Ramos. **Training/Rehab Coordinator:** Gene Basham. **Strength/Conditioning Coordinator:** Mark Brennan. **Rehab Pitching Coordinator:** Wayne Rosenthal. **Minor League Equipment/Clubhouse Manager:** Mark Brown.

Farm System

Class	Club (League)	Manager	Hitting Coach	Pitching Coach
Triple-A	New Orleans (PCL)	Andy Haines	Damon Minor	John Duffy
Double-A	Jacksonville (SL)	Dave Berg	Rich Arena	Derek Botelho
High A	Jupiter (FSL)	Brian Schneider	Corey Hart	Joe Coleman
Low A	Greensboro (SAL)	Kevin Randel	Unavailable	Jeremy Powell
Short-season	Batavia (NYP)	Angel Espada	Rigoberto Silverio	Brendan Sagara
Rookie	Marlins (GCL)	Julio Bruno	Daniel Santin	Manny Olivera

Scouting
Telephone: (561) 630-1816.
VP, Scouting: Stan Meek.
Assistant Director, Scouting Administration: Gregg Leonard. **Assistant Director, Amateur Scouting:** Michael Youngberg.
Director, Pro Scouting: Jeff McAvoy. **Assistant Director, Pro Scouting:** David Keller. **Advance Scout:** Mike Goff (Mobile, AL). **Special Assignment Scout:** Dominic Viola (Holly Springs, NC). **Professional Scouts:** Pierre Arsenault (Pierrefonds, QC), Matt Kinzer (Fort Wayne, IN), Benny Latino (Hammond, LA), Joe Moeller (San Clemente, CA), Dave Roberts (Fort Worth, TX), Phil Rossi (Jessup, PA), Mickey White (Sarasota, FL).
National Crosschecker: David Crowson (College Station, TX). **Regional Supervisors: Southeast**—Mike Cadahia (Miami, FL); **Northeast**—Carmen Carcone (Woodstock, GA); **Central**—Steve Taylor (Shawnee, OK); **West**—Scott Goldby (Yuba City, CA); **Canada**—Steve Payne (Barrington, RI). **Area Scouts:** Eric Brock (Indianapolis, IN), Christian Castorri (Dacula, GA), Robby Corsaro (Victorville, CA), Dave Dangler (Tampa, FL), Matt Gaski (Columbus, OH), John Hughes (Walnut Creek, CA), Brian Kraft (Bixby, OK), Laz Llanes (Miami, FL), Joel Matthews (Concord, NC), Tim McDonnell (Westminster, CA), Bob Oldis (Iowa City, Iowa), Gabe Sandy (Damascus, OR), Scott Stanley (Peoria, AZ), Ryan Wardinsky (The Woodlands, TX), Mark Willoughby (Hammond, LA), Nick Zumsande (Fairfax, IA).
Director, International Operations: Albert Gonzalez. **International Supervisors:** Sandy Nin (Santo Domingo, Dominican Republic), Wilmer Castillo (Maracay, VZ). **International Scouts:** Hugo Aquero (Dominican Republic), Carlos Avila (Venezuela), Luis Cordoba (Panama), Edgarluis J Fuentes (Venezuela), Alvaro Julio (Colombia), Alix Martinez (Dominican Republic), Domingo Ortega (Dominican Republic), Robin Ordonez (Venezuela).

Milwaukee Brewers

Office Address: Miller Park, One Brewers Way, Milwaukee, WI 53214.
Telephone: (414) 902-4400. **Fax:** (414) 902-4053.
Website: www.brewers.com.

Ownership
Operated By: Milwaukee Brewers Baseball Club.
Chairman/Principal Owner: Mark Attanasio.

BUSINESS OPERATIONS
Chief Operating Officer: Rick Schlesinger. **Executive Vice President, Finance/Administration:** Bob Quinn. **VP, General Counsel:** Marti Wronski. **VP, Business Operations:** Teddy Werner. **Executive Assistant:** Adela Reeve. **Executive Assistant, Ownership Group:** Samantha Ernest. **Executive Assistant/Paralegal:** Kate Rock.

Finance/Accounting
VP/Controller: Joe Zidanic. **Accounting Director:** Vicki Wise. **Payroll Manager:** Vickie Gowan. **VP, Human Resources/Office Management:** Sally Andrist.
VP, Technology/Information Systems: Nick Watson. **Director, Network Services:** Corey Kmichik. **Manager, Infrastructure/Information Security:** Adam Bauer. **Manager, Baseball Systems Development:** Josh Krowiorz.

Marketing/Corporate Sponsorships

Mark Attanasio

VP, Corporate Marketing: Tom Hecht. **Senior Director, Corporate Marketing:** Andrew Pauls. **Director, Corporate Marketing:** Jed Justman. **VP, Consumer Marketing:** Jim Bathey. **Senior Director, Merchandise Branding:** Jill Aronoff. **Senior Director, Marketing:** Kathy Schwab. **Director, Suite Services:** Kristin Miller. **Coordinator, Marketing/Promotions:** Brittany Luznicky.
VP, Broadcasting/Entertainment: Aleta Mercer. **Director, Audio/Video Productions:** Deron Anderson. **Manager, Entertainment/Broadcasting:** Tim Shea. **Coordinators, Audio/Video Production:** Cory Wilson, Matt Morell.

Media Relations/Communications
VP, Communications: Tyler Barnes. **Senior Director, Media Relations:** Mike Vassallo. **Director, New Media:** Caitlin Moyer. **Senior Manager, Media Relations:** Ken Spindler. **Manager, Media Relations:** Zach Weber. **Publications Assistant:** Robbin Barnes. **Senior Director, Community Relations:** Katina Shaw. **Director, Alumni Relations:** Dave Nelson. **Coordinator, Community Relations:** Erica Bowring. **Executive Director, Brewers Community Foundation:** Cecelia Gore.

Stadium Operations
VP, Stadium Operations: Bob Hallas. **Director, Grounds:** Michael Boettcher. **Manager, Warehouse:** John Weyer. **VP, Brewers Enterprises:** Jason Hartlund. **Director, Brewers Enterprises:** Tai Pauls. **Manager, Event Services:** Matt Lehmann. **Senior Manager, Guest Relations:** Jennacy Cruz. **Receptionists:** Jody McBee, Susan Ramsdell.

2015 SCHEDULE
Standard Game Times: 7:10 p.m.; Sun. 1:10.

APRIL		JUNE (cont.)		AUGUST (cont.)		SEPTEMBER (cont.)

APRIL
6-8 . . . . Colorado
10-12 . . . . Pittsburgh
13 . . . . at St. Louis
15-16 . . . . . . at St. Louis
17-19 . . . . . at Pittsburgh
20-23 . . . . Cincinnati
24-26 . . . . St. Louis
27-29 . . . . . at Cincinnati

MAY
1-3 . . . . . . at Chicago (NL)
4-7 . . . . . Los Angeles (NL)
8-10 . . . . . . Chicago (NL)
11-13 . . . . . Chicago (AL)
15-17 . . . at New York (NL)
18-20 . . . . at Detroit

21-24 . . . . at Atlanta
25-27 . . . . . San Francisco
29-31 . . . . Arizona

JUNE
1-3 . . . . at St. Louis
5-7 . . . . . . at Minnesota
8-10 . . . . . . at Pittsburgh
11-14 . . . . . . Washington
15-16 . . . . . . Kansas City
17-18 . . . . at Kansas City
19-21 . . . . . . at Colorado
23-25 . . . . New York (NL)
26-28 . . . . Minnesota
29-30 . . . . at Philadelphia

JULY
1-2 . . . . . at Philadelphia

3-5 . . . . at Cincinnati
6-8 . . . . Atlanta
10-12 . . at Los Angeles (NL)
17-19 . . . . Pittsburgh
21-22 . . . . Cleveland
23-26 . . . . at Arizona
27-29 . . . at San Francisco
30-31 . . . . . Chicago (NL)

AUGUST
1-2 . . . . Chicago (NL)
3-6 . . . . San Diego
7-9 . . . . St. Louis
11-13 . . . . at Chicago (NL)
14-16 . . . . . . Philadelphia
17-19 . . . . Miami
21-23 . . . . at Washington

25-26 . . . . . at Cleveland
28-30 . . . . Cincinnati

SEPTEMBER
1-3 . . . . Pittsburgh
4-6 . . . . at Cincinnati
7-9 . . . . at Miami
10-13 . . . . . at Pittsburgh
15-17 . . . . St. Louis
18-20 . . . . Cincinnati
21-23 . . . at Chicago (NL)
24-27 . . . . . . at St. Louis
29-30 . . . . . at San Diego

OCTOBER
1 . . . . at San Diego
2-4 . . . . Chicago (NL)

GENERAL INFORMATION
Stadium (year opened): Miller Park (2001).
Team Colors: Navy blue, gold and white.
Player Representative: Unavailable.
Home Dugout: First Base.
Playing Surface: Grass.

Ticketing

Telephone: (414) 902-4000. **Fax:** (414) 902-4056.
Senior Director, Ticket Operations: Regis Bane. **Senior Director, Ticket Sales:** Billy Friess. **Senior Group Ticket Sales Specialist:** Chris Barlow. **Administrative Assistant:** Irene Bolton.

BASEBALL OPERATIONS

Telephone: (414) 902-4400. **Fax:** (414) 902-4515.
President, Baseball Operations/General Manager: Doug Melvin.
VP/Assistant GM: Gord Ash. **Special Assistant to GM/Pro Scouting/Player Personnel:** Dick Groch. **Special Assistant to GM:** Craig Counsell.
Senior Director, Baseball Operations: Tom Flanagan. **Director, Video Scouting/Baseball Research for Pro Scouting:** Karl Mueller. **Manager, Advance Scouting/Baseball Research:** Scott Campbell. **Manager/Coaching Assistant/Digital Media Coordinator:** Joe Crawford.
Senior Administrator, Baseball Operations: Barb Stark. **Senior Director, Team Travel:** Dan Larrea.

Doug Melvin

Major League Staff

Manager: Ron Roenicke.
Coaches: Bench—Jerry Narron; **Pitching**—Rick Kranitz; **Hitting**—Darnell Coles; **First Base**—Mike Guerrero; **Third Base**—Ed Sedar; **Bullpen**—Lee Tunnell; **Outfield Coach**—John Shelby.

Medical/Training

Head Team Physician: Dr. William Raasch. **Head Athletic Trainer:** Dan Wright. **Assistant Athletic Trainer:** Dave Yeager. **Strength/Conditioning Specialist:** Josh Seligman. **Director, Medical Operations:** Roger Caplinger.

Player Development

Special Assistant to GM/Director, Player Development/Training Center: Reid Nichols (Phoenix, AZ). **Special Assistant to GM/Baseball Operations:** Dan O'Brien.
Director, Minor League Business Operations: Scott Martens. **Manager, Administration/Player Development:** Mark Mueller. **Assistant to Director, Staff/Player Development:** Tony Diggs. **Coordinator, Arizona Complex/Video Operations:** Matt Kerls. **Field/Catching Coordinator:** Charlie Greene. **Coordinators:** Frank Neville (athletic training), Rick Tomlin (pitching), Jeremy Reed (hitting), Bob Miscik (infield), Mark Dewey (assistant pitching coordinator). **Special Instructor, Player Development:** Don Money.

Farm System

Class	Club (League)	Manager	Coach	Pitching Coach
Triple-A	Colorado Springs (PCL)	Rick Sweet	Bob Skube	Fred Dabney
Double-A	Biloxi (SL)	Carlos Subero	Sandy Guerrero	Chris Hook
High A	Brevard County (FSL)	Joe Ayrault	Ned Yost IV	David Chavarria
Low A	Wisconsin (MWL)	Matt Erickson	Chuckie Caufield	Gary Lucas
Rookie	Helena (PIO)	Tony Diggs	Jason Dubois	Rolando Valles
Rookie	Brewers (AZL)	Nestor Corredor	Al LeBoeuf	Steve Cline
Rookie	Brewers (DSL)	Jose Pena	Luis De Los Santos	Geraldo Obispo

Scouting

Telephone: (414) 902-4400. **Fax:** (414) 902-4059.
VP, Amateur Scouting/Special Assistant to the GM: Ray Montgomery.
Director, Professional Scouting: Zack Minasian. **Assistant Director, Amateur Scouting:** Tod Johnson. **Manager, Administration/Amateur Scouting:** Amanda Kropp. **Assistant, Pro Scouting:** Ben McDonough.
Southwest National Supervisor: Joe Ferrone (Grosse Pointe, MI). **Midwest National Supervisor:** Steve Riha (Houston, TX). **National Pitching Supervisor:** Jim Rooney (Berwyn, IL). **Regional Supervisors:** Corey Rodriguez (Palo Verdes Estates, CA), Doug Reynolds (Tallahassee, FL), Tim McIlvaine (Nashville, TN).
Pro Scouts: Lary Aaron (Fayetteville, GA), Brad Del Barba (Fort Mitchell, KY), Bryan Gale (Wayne, PA), Joe Kowal (Yardley, PA), Cory Melvin (Tampa, FL), Ben McLure (Hummelstown, PA), Tom Mooney (Pittsfield, MA), Andy Pratt (Peoria, AZ), Marv Thompson (West Jordan, UT), Ryan Thompson (Scottsdale, AZ), Derek Watson (Milwaukee, WI), Tom Wheeler (Martinez, CA), Leon Wurth (Paducah, KY).
Area Scouts: Drew Anderson (Waite Park, MN), Josh Belovsky (Orange, CA), KJ Hendricks (Arlington, TX), Manolo Hernandez (Puerto Rico), Dan Huston (Westlake Village, CA), Harvey Kuenn, Jr (New Berlin, WI), Jay Lapp (London, Ontario, Canada), Justin McCray (Davis, CA), Mark Muzzi (Grand Prairie, TX), Dan Nellum (Crofton, MD), Scott Nichols (Richland, MS), Brian Sankey (The Hills, TX), Jeff Scholzen (Santa Clara, UT), John T. Shelby III (Tampa, FL), Jeff Simpson (Nashville, TN), Steve Smith (Kennesaw, GA), Charles Sullivan (Weston, FL), Shawn Whalen (Vancouver, WA), Steffan Wilson (Wayne, PA). **Junior Scout:** Carlos Dominguez (Raleigh, NC).
Part-Time Scouts: Ted Brzenk (Waukesha, WI), Richard Colpaert (Shelby Township, MI), Don Fontana (Pittsburgh, PA), Joe Hodges (Rockwood, TN), Ernie Rogers (Chesapeake, VA), JP Roy (Saint Nicolas, Quebec, Canada), Lee Seid (Las Vegas, NV), Brad Stoll (Lawrence, KS), Nathan Trosky (Carmel, CA).
Director, Latin America Operations/Scouting: Eduardo Brizuela (Pembroke Pines, FL). **Director, Latin America Scouting:** Manny Batista (Vega Alta, PR). **Latin America Scout Supervisors:** Eduardo Sanchez (Dominican Republic), Fernando Veracierto (Venezuela). **Latin America Scouts:** Julio De La Cruz (Dominican Republic), Reinaldo Hidalgo (Venezuela), Alcides Melendez (Venezuela), Jose Morales (Dominican Republic), Clifford Nuitter (Central America), Edgar Suarez (Venezuela).

Minnesota Twins

Office Address: Target Field, 1 Twins Way, Minneapolis, MN 55403.
Telephone: (612) 659-3400. **Fax:** 612-659-4025. **Website:** www.twinsbaseball.com.

Ownership
Operated By: The Minnesota Twins.
Chief Executive Officer: Jim Pohlad.
Executive Board: Jim Pohlad, Bob Pohlad, Bill Pohlad, Dave St. Peter.

BUSINESS OPERATIONS
President, Minnesota Twins: Dave St. Peter. **Executive Vice President, Business Development:** Laura Day. **Executive VP, Business Administration/CFO:** Kip Elliott. **Special Assistant to the President/GM:** Bill Smith. **Director, Ballpark Development/Planning:** Dan Starkey. **Executive Assistants:** Danielle Berg, Joan Boeser, Lynette Gittins.

Jim Pohlad

Human Resources/Finance/Technology
VP, Human Resources/Diversity: Raenell Dorn. **Director, Payroll:** Lori Beasley. **Director, Benefits:** Leticia Silva. **Human Resources Generalist:** Holly Corbin. **Senior Director, Finance:** Andy Weinstein. **Senior Manager, Ticket Accounting:** Jerry McLaughlin. **Senior Manager, Accounting:** Lori Windschitl. **Senior Manager, Financial Planning/Analysis:** Mike Kramer. **Senior Director, Procurement:** Bud Hanley. **Manager, Procurement:** Mike Sather.
VP, Technology: John Avenson. **Senior Director, Technology:** Wade Navratil.

Marketing
VP, Brand Marketing: Nancy O'Brien. **Senior Manager, Marketing/Promotions Manager:** Julie Okland. **Director, Diversity Marketing:** Miguel Ramos. **Senior Manager, Twins Productions:** Sam Henschen. **Manager, Creative Services:** Matt Semke.

Corporate Partnerships
Senior Director, Corporate Partnership: Jeff Jurgella. **Senior Account Executives:** Doug Beck, Karen Cleary, Jordan Woodcroft, Chad Jackson. **Manager, Client Services:** Amelia Johnson. **Coordinators, Corporate Client Services:** Brittany Kennedy, Ann Kincaid, Joe Morin, Kayleen Tecker.

Communications
Telephone: (612) 659-3471. **Fax:** (612) 659-4029.
Director, Baseball Communications/Player Relations: Dustin Morse. **Senior Manager, Baseball Information:** Mitch Hestad. **Manager, Publications/Content:** Mike Kennedy. **Coordinator/Senior Director, Corporate Communications/Broadcasting:** Kevin Smith. **Baseball Communications Assistant:** Cori Frankenberg.

Community Relations
Senior Director, Community Affairs: Bryan Donaldson. **Manager, Community Relations:** Stephanie Johnson.

2015 SCHEDULE
Standard Game Times: 7:10 p.m.; Sun 1:10.

APRIL		
6 . . . . at Detroit	19-20 . . . . . . at Pittsburgh	
8-9 . . . . at Detroit	22-24 . . . . .at Chicago (AL)	
10-12 . . . . .at Chicago (AL)	25-27 . . . . Boston	
13 . . . . Kansas City	29-31 . . . . .Toronto	
15-16 . . . . . . Kansas City		
17-19 . . . . Cleveland	**JUNE**	
20-22 . . . .at Kansas City	1-4 . . . . at Boston	
24-26 . . . . . .at Seattle	5-7 . . . . .Milwaukee	
27-29 . . . . Detroit	8-10 . . . . Kansas City	
30 . . . . Chicago (AL)	12-14 . . . . .at Texas	
	15-16 . . . . . . .at St. Louis	
MAY	17-18 . . . . St. Louis	
1-3 . . . . Chicago (AL)	19-21 . . . . . . Chicago (NL)	
4-7 . . . . Oakland	22-24 . . . . . Chicago (AL)	
8-10 . . . . . . .at Cleveland	26-28 . . . . .at Milwaukee	
12-14 . . . . . . at Detroit	29-30 . . . . . at Cincinnati	
15-17 . . . . . . .Tampa Bay		

JULY		
1 . . . . at Cincinnati	20-23 . . . . . .at Baltimore	
2-5 . . . . . . .at Kansas City	25-27 . . . . at Tampa Bay	
6-8 . . . . Baltimore	28-30 . . . . Houston	
9-12 . . . . Detroit		
17-19 . . . . . . .at Oakland	**SEPTEMBER**	
21-23 . . at Los Angeles (AL)	1-3 . . . . Chicago (AL)	
24-26 . . . . . .New York (AL)	4-6 . . . . at Houston	
28-29 . . . . Pittsburgh	7-9 . . . . . . .at Kansas City	
30-31 . . . . Seattle	11-13 . . . . .at Chicago (AL)	
	14-16 . . . . Detroit	
AUGUST	17-20 . . . Los Angeles (AL)	
1-2 . . . . Seattle	22-24 . . . . Cleveland	
3-6 . . . . at Toronto	25-27 . . . . at Detroit	
7-9 . . . . .at Cleveland	28-30 . . . . . .at Cleveland	
11-13 . . . . Texas		
14-16 . . . . Cleveland	**OCTOBER**	
17-19 . . . .at New York (AL)	1 . . . . .at Cleveland	
	2-4 . . . . Kansas City	

GENERAL INFORMATION
Stadium (year opened): Target Field (2010).   **Home Dugout:** First Base.
Team Colors: Red, navy blue and white.   **Playing Surface:** Four-way blend
Player Representative: Glen Perkins.   of Kentucky Bluegrass.

Manager, Community Programs: Josh Ortiz. **Coordinator, Community Relations:** Gloria Westerdahl.

Ticketing/Events
   Telephone: 1-800-33-TWINS. **Fax:** (612) 659-4030.
   VP, Ticket Sales/Service: Mike Clough. **Director, Suite/Premium Seat Sales/Service:** Scott O'Connell. **Director, Season Sales/Service:** Eric Hudson. **VP, Ticket Operations:** Paul Froehle. **Director, Box Office:** Mike Stiles. **Director, Target Field Events/Tours:** David Christie.

Ballpark Operations
   Senior VP, Operations: Matt Hoy. **Senior Director, Ballpark Operations:** Dave Horsman. **Senior Director, Facilities:** Gary Glawe. **Director, Guest Services:** Patrick Forsland. **Head Groundskeeper:** Larry DiVito. **Manager, Grounds:** Al Kuehner. **Manager, Field Maintenance:** Jared Alley. **Senior Manager, Ballpark Maintenance:** Dana Minion. **Senior Manager, Ballpark Operations:** John McEvoy. **Senior Manager, Premium Services:** Jeffrey Kroll. **Manager, Building Security:** Jeff Reardon. **Manager, Event Security:** Dick Dugan. **PA Announcer:** Adam Abrams.

BASEBALL OPERATIONS

Terry Ryan

   Executive VP/General Manager: Terry Ryan.
   VP, Player Personnel: Mike Radcliff. **VP/Assistant GM:** Rob Antony. **Special Assistant:** Tom Kelly. **Manager, Major League Administration/Baseball Research:** Jack Goin. **Administrative Assistant to the GM:** Lizz Downey. **Director, Team Travel:** Mike Herman. **Developer, Baseball Systems:** Jeremy Raadt. **Baseball Operations Assistant:** Nick Beauchamp. **Coordinator, Baseball Research:** Andrew Ettel.

Major League Staff
   Manager: Paul Molitor.
   Coaches: Bench—Joe Vavra; **Pitching**—Neil Allen; **Hitting**—Tom Brunansky; **First Base**—Butch Davis; **Third Base**—Gene Glynn; **Bullpen**—Eddie Guardado; **Assistant Hitting**—Rudy Hernandez. **Equipment Manager:** Rod McCormick. **Visitors Clubhouse:** Jason Lizakowski. **Director, Major League Video:** Sean Harlin.

Medical/Training
   Club Physicians: Dr. John Steubs, Dr. Vijay Eyunni, Dr. Tom Jetzer, Dr. Jon Hallberg, Dr. Diane Dahm, Dr. Amy Beacom, Dr. Pearce McCarty, Dr. Rick Aberman. **Head Trainer:** Dave Pruemer. **Assistant Trainers:** Tony Leo, Lanning Tucker. **Strength/Conditioning Coach:** Perry Castellano.

Player Development
   Telephone: (612) 659-3480. **Fax:** (612) 659-4026.
   Director, Minor League Operations: Brad Steil.
   Senior Manager, Minor League Administration: Kate Townley. **Senior Manager, Florida Operations:** Brian Maloney. **Assistant, Florida/International Operations:** Rafael Yanez. **Minor League Coordinators:** Joel Lepel (field), Eric Rasmussen (pitching), Sam Perlozzo (infield/baserunning), Erik Beiser (strength/conditioning), Jose Marzan (Latin American Operations), David Jeffrey (Video).

Farm System

Class	Club (League)	Manager	Coach	Pitching Coach
Triple-A	Rochester (IL)	Mike Quade	Tim Doherty	Marty Mason
Double-A	Chattanooga (SL)	Doug Mientkiewicz	Chad Allen	Stu Cliburn
High A	Fort Myers (FSL)	Jeff Smith	Jim Dwyer	Ivan Arteaga
Low A	Cedar Rapids (MWL)	Jake Mauer	Tommy Watkins	Henry Bonilla
Rookie	Elizabethton (APP)	Ray Smith	Jeff Reed	Luis Ramirez
Rookie	Twins (GCL)	Ramon Borrego	Riccardo Ingram	Virgil Vasquez
Rookie	Twins (DSL)	Jimmy Alvarez	Ramon Nivar	Manuel Santana
Rookie	Twins (VSL)	Asdrubal Estrada	Unavailable	Unavailable

Scouting
   Telephone: (612) 659-3491. **Fax:** (612) 659-4026.
   Director, Scouting: Deron Johnson.
   Coordinator, Professional Scouting: Vern Followell. **Senior Manager, Scouting/International Administration:** Amanda Daley. **Administrative Assistant to Scouting:** Brittany Minder.
   Major League Scouts: Ken Compton, Wayne Krivsky. **Pro Scouts:** Larry Corrigan, Bill Harford, Bob Hegman, Mike Larson, Bill Mele, Bill Milos, Earl Winn. **Special Assignment Scout:** Earl Frishman.
   National Crosschecker: Tim O'Neil. **Scouting Supervisors: East**—Mark Quimuyog; **West**—Sean Johnson; **Southeast**—Billy Corrigan; **Midwest**—Mike Ruth. **Area Scouts:** Trevor Brown (WA), Taylor Cameron (CA), JR DiMercurio (KS), Brett Dowdy (FL), Marty Esposito (TX), John Leavitt (CA), Jeff Pohl (IN), Jack Powell (GA), Greg Runser (TX), Alan Sandberg (TN), Elliott Strankman (CA), Ricky Taylor (NC), Freddie Thon (FL), Jay Weitzel (PA), Ted Williams (AZ), John Wilson (NJ), Mark Wilson (MN).
   Coordinator, International Scouting: Howard Norsetter. **Coordinator, Latin American Scouting:** Fred Guerrero.
   International Scouts—Full-Time: Cary Broder (Taiwan), Glenn Godwin (Europe, Africa), David Kim (Pacific Rim), Luis Lajara (Dominican Republic), Jose Leon (Supervisor-Venezuela, Panama), Manuel Luciano (Dominican Republic), Marlon Nava (Venezuela), Eduardo Soriano (Dominican Republic). **International Scouts—Part-Time:** Hector Barrios (Panama), Gavin Bennett (South Africa), John Cortese (Italy), Andy Johnson (Europe), Juan Padilla (Venezuela), Franklin Parra (Venezuela), Yan-Yu "Kenny" Su (Taiwan), Koji Takahashi (Japan), Pablo Torres (Venezuela), Lester Victoria (Curacao), Troy Williams (Germany).

New York Mets

Office Address: Citi Field, 126th Street, Flushing, NY 11368.
Telephone: (718) 507-6387. **Fax:** (718) 507-6395.
Website: www.mets.com. **Twitter:** @mets.

Ownership
Operated By: Sterling Mets LP.
Chairman/Chief Executive Officer: Fred Wilpon. **President:** Saul Katz. **Chief Operating Officer:** Jeff Wilpon.

BUSINESS OPERATIONS
Executive VP/Chief Revenue Officer: Lou DePaoli. **Executive Director, Business Intelligence/Analytics:** John Morris.

Legal/Human Resources
Executive VP/Chief Legal Officer: David Cohen. **VP/Deputy General Counsel:** Neal Kaplan. **Senior Counsel:** James Denniston. **VP, Human Resources:** Holly Lindvall.

Finance
CFO: Mark Peskin. **VP/Controller:** Len Labita. **Assistant Controller/Director:** John Ventimiglia.

Marketing/Communications/Sales
Senior VP, Corporate Sales/Services: Paul Asencio. **Senior VP, Marketing/Communications:** David Newman. **VP, Corporate Partnerships Sales/Services:** Wes Engram. **Executive Director, Corporate Sales:** Matthew Soloff. **Executive Director, Marketing Productions:** Tim Gunkel. **Senior Director, Marketing:** Mark Fine. **Senior Director, Broadcasting:** Lorraine Hamilton.

Fred Wilpon

Media Relations
Telephone: (718) 565-4330. **Fax:** (718) 639-3619.
VP, Media Relations: Jay Horwitz. **Executive Director, Communications:** Harold Kaufman. **Senior Director, Media Relations:** Shannon Forde.

Ticketing
Telephone: (718) 507-8499. **Fax:** (718) 507-6369.
VP, Ticket Sales/Services: Chris Zaber. **Senior Director, Group Sales:** Kirk King. **Senior Director, Season Ticket Account Services:** Jamie Ozure. **Executive Director, Ticket Sales:** Katie Mahon. **Senior Director, Premium/Ticket Sales:** Brian Towers.

Venue Services/Operations/Technology
Senior VP, Venue Services/Operations: Mike Landeen. **VP, Metropolitan Hospitality:** Heather Collamore. **VP, Ballpark Operations:** Sue Lucchi. **VP, Technology:** Tom Festa. **Executive Director, Venue Services:** Paul Schwartz.

2015 SCHEDULE
Standard Game Times: 7:10 p.m.; Sun. 1:10.

APRIL
6 . . . . at Washington
8-9 . . . . . . at Washington
10-12 . . . . at Atlanta
13-15 . . . . . .Philadelphia
16-19 . . . . .Miami
21-23 . . . . Atlanta
24-26 . . . at New York (AL)
27-29 . . . . at Miami
30 . . . . Washington

MAY
1-3 . . . . Washington
5-6 . . . . Baltimore
8-10 . . . . . at Philadelphia
11-14 . . . .at Chicago (NL)
15-17 . . . . . .Milwaukee
18-21 . . . . St. Louis

22-24 . . . . . at Pittsburgh
25-27 . . . . . .Philadelphia
29-31 . . . . .Miami

JUNE
1-3 . . . . at San Diego
4-7 . . . . at Arizona
9-11 . . . . . .San Francisco
12-14 . . . . Atlanta
15-16 . . . . .Toronto
17-18 . . . . at Toronto
19-21 . . . . at Atlanta
23-25 . . . . . at Milwaukee
26-28 . . . . Cincinnati
30 . . . . Chicago (NL)

JULY
1-2 . . . . Chicago (NL)

3-5 . . . . at Los Angeles (NL)
6-8 . . . . . . at San Francisco
10-12 . . . . Arizona
17-19 . . . . . .at St. Louis
20-22 . . . . at Washington
23-26 . . . .Los Angeles (NL)
28-30 . . . . San Diego
31 . . . . Washington

AUGUST
1-2 . . . . Washington
3-5 . . . . at Miami
7-9 . . . . . . at Tampa Bay
10-13 . . . . .Colorado
14-16 . . . . Pittsburgh
18-19 . . . . . .at Baltimore
21-23 . . . . . . at Colorado
24-27 . . . . . at Philadelphia

28-30 . . . . Boston
31 . . . . .Philadelphia

SEPTEMBER
1-2 . . . . .Philadelphia
4-6 . . . . at Miami
7-9 . . . . . at Washington
10-13 . . . . at Atlanta
14-16 . . . . .Miami
18-20 . . . . .New York (AL)
21-23 . . . . Atlanta
24-27 . . . . . at Cincinnati
29-30 . . . . at Philadelphia

OCTOBER
1 . . . . at Philadelphia
2-4 . . . . Washington

GENERAL INFORMATION
Stadium (year opened): Citi Field (2009).
Team Colors: Blue and orange.
Player Representative: Unavailable.
Home Dugout: First Base.
Playing Surface: Grass.

Executive Director, Guest Experience: Chris Brown. **Senior Director, Building Operations:** Peter Cassano.

Travel/Clubhouse
    Clubhouse Manager: Kevin Kierst. **Assistant Equipment Manager:** Dave Berni. **Visiting Clubhouse Manager:** Tony Carullo. **Director, Team Travel:** Brian Small.

BASEBALL OPERATIONS
Telephone: (718) 803-4013, (718) 565-4339. **Fax:** (718) 507-6391.
General Manager: Sandy Alderson.
VP/Assistant GM: John Ricco. **Special Assistant to GM:** J.P. Ricciardi. **Executive Assistant to GM:** June Napoli. **Director, Baseball Operations:** Adam Fisher. **Manager, Baseball Research/Development:** TJ Barra. **Coordinator, Baseball Systems Development:** Joe Lefkowitz. **Coordinator, Baseball Operations:** Jeffrey Lebow. **Assistant, Advance Scouting/ Replay Coordinator:** Jim Kelly. **Manager, Player Relations:** Donovan Mitchell.

Sandy Alderson

Major League Staff
    Manager: Terry Collins.
    Coaches: Bench—Bob Geren; **Pitching**—Dan Warthen; **Batting**—Kevin Long; **Assistant Batting**—Pat Roessler; **First Base**—Tom Goodwin; **Third Base**—Tim Teufel; **Bullpen**—Ricky Bones.

Medical/Training
    Medical Director: Dr. David Altchek. **Physician:** Dr. Struan Coleman. **Trainer:** Ray Ramirez. **Assistant Trainer:** Brian Chicklo. **Strength/Conditioning Coordinator:** Dustin Clarke. **Physical Therapist:** John Zajac. **Massage Therapist:** Yoshihiro Nishio.

Player Development
    Telephone: (718) 565-4302. **Fax:** (718) 205-7920.
    VP, Scouting/Player Development: Paul DePodesta.
    Director, Player Development: Dick Scott. **Director, Minor League Operations:** Ian Levin. **Manager, St. Lucie Operations:** Ronny Reyes. **Equipment/Operations Manager:** John Mullin. **Coordinator, Minor League/International Operations:** Jennifer Wolf. **Director, Latin American Operations:** Juan Henderson. **International Field Coordinator:** Rafael Landestoy. **International Catching Instructor:** Ozzie Virgil.
    Instruction/Infield Coordinator: Kevin Morgan. **Hitting Coordinator:** Lamar Johnson. **Short-Season Hitting Coordinator:** Ryan Ellis. **Full Season Pitching Coordinator:** Ron Romanick. **Short-Season Pitching Coordinator:** Miguel Valdes. **Catching Coordinator:** Bob Natal. **Outfield Coordinator:** Benny Distefano. **Rehab Pitching Coordinator:** Jon Debus. **Athletic Training Coordinator:** Mike Herbst. **Rehab/Physical Therapist Coordinator:** Dave Pearson. **Strength/Conditioning Coordinator:** Jason Craig. **Senior Advisor:** Guy Conti. **Special Instructors:** Bobby Floyd, Edgardo Alfonso.

Farm System

Class	Club	Manager	Hitting Coach	Pitching Coach
Triple-A	Las Vegas (PCL)	Wally Backman	Jack Voigt	Frank Viola
Double-A	Binghamton (EL)	Pedro Lopez	Luis Natera	Glenn Abbott
High A	St. Lucie (FSL)	Luis Rojas	Joel Fuentes	Phil Regan
Low A	Savannah (SAL)	Jose Leger	Val Pascucci	Marc Valdes
Short-season	Brooklyn (NYP)	Tom Gamboa	Unavailable	Tom Signore
Rookie	Kingsport (APP)	Luis Rivera	Yunir Garcia	Jonathan Hurst
Rookie	Mets (GCL)	Jose Carreno	Ender Chavez	Royce Ring
Rookie	Mets 1 (DSL)	Manny Martinez	Alberto Castillo	Benjamin Marte
Rookie	Mets 2 (DSL)	David Davalillo	P. Reyes	Francisco Martinez

Scouting
    Telephone: (718) 565-4311. **Fax:** (718) 205-7920.
    Director, Amateur Scouting: Tommy Tanous. **Assistant Scouting Director:** Marc Tramuta (Fredonia, NY). **Assistant, Amateur Scouting:** Bryan Hayes. **Regional Supervisors: Southeast**—Steve Barningham (Land O'Lakes, FL), **West**— Doug Thurman (San Jose, CA), **Northeast**—Marlin McPhail (Irmo, SC), **Midwest**—Mac Seibert (Cantonment, FL). **Area Supervisors:** Cesar Aranguren (Clermont, FL), Jim Blueberg (Carson City, NV), Jet Butler (Jackson, MS), Ray Corbett (College Station, TX), Jarrett England (Murfreesboro, TN), John Hendricks (Clemmons, NC), Tyler Holmes (Forest Park, IL), Tommy Jackson (Birmingham, AL), Jim Reeves (Camas, WA), Kevin Roberson (Scottsdale, AZ), Justin Schwartz (Oklahoma City, OK), Max Semler (Allen, TX), Jim Thompson (Philadelphia, PA), Andrew Toussaint (Los Angeles, CA), Jon Updike (Sorrento, FL).
    Director, Pro Scouting: Jim D'Aloia. **Professional Scouts:** Bryn Alderson (New York, NY), Mack Babitt (Richmond, CA), Conor Brooks (Plymouth, MA), Thomas Clark (Shrewsbury, MA), Tim Fortugno (Elk Grove, CA), Roland Johnson (Newington, CT), Ashley Lawson (Athens, TN), Shaun McNamara (Worcester, MA), Art Pontarelli (Lincoln, RI), Roy Smith (Chicago, IL), Rudy Terrasas (Santa Fe, TX).
    Director, International Scouting: Chris Becerra (Ventura, CA). **International Supervisors:** Gerardo Cabrera (Dominican Republic), Hector Rincones (Venezuela). **Crosscheckers:** Hilario Soriano (Dominican Republic), Harold Herrera (Colombia). **International Scouts:** Modesto Abreu (Dominican Republic), Marciano Alvarez (Dominican Republic), Fernando Encarnacion (Dominican Republic), Robert Espejo (Venezuela), Gabriel Low (Mexico), Nestor Moreno (Venezuela), Daurys Nin (Dominican Republic), Ismael Perez (Venezuela), Carlos Perez (Venezuela), Sendly Reina (Curacao), Andrew Sallee (Europe). **Video Coordinators:** Anthony Samboy, Anderson Tavares.

New York Yankees

Office Address: Yankee Stadium, One East 161st St., Bronx, NY 10451.
Telephone: (718) 293-4300. **Fax:** (718) 293-8431.
Website: www.yankees.com, www.yankeesbeisbol.com. **Twitter:** @Yankees, @YankeesPR, @LosYankees.

Ownership
Managing General Partner/Co-Chairperson: Harold Z. (Hal) Steinbrenner. **General Partner/Co-Chairperson:** Henry G. (Hank) Steinbrenner. **General Partner/Vice Chairperson:** Jennifer Steinbrenner Swindal. **General Partner/Vice Chairperson:** Jessica Steinbrenner. **Vice Chairperson:** Joan Steinbrenner. **Executive Vice President/Chief International Officer:** Felix Lopez.

BUSINESS OPERATIONS
President: Randy Levine, Esq.
Chief Operating Officer/General Counsel: Lonn A. Trost, Esq.
Senior VP, Strategic Ventures: Marty Greenspun. **Senior VP, Chief Security Officer:** Sonny Hight. **Senior VP, Yankee Global Enterprises/Chief Financial Officer:** Anthony Bruno. **Senior VP, Corporate/Community Relations:** Brian E. Smith. **Senior VP, Corporate Sales/Sponsorship:** Michael Tusiani. **Senior VP, Marketing:** Deborah Tymon. **VP/Chief Financial Officer, Accounting:** Robert B. Brown. **Chief Financial Officer/VP, Financial Operations:** Scott M. Krug. **Deputy General Counsel/VP, Legal Affairs:** Alan Chang. **Controller:** Derrick Baio. **VP, Stadium Operations:** Doug Behar. **VP, Chief Information Officer:** Mike Lane.

Harold Steinbrenner

Communications/Media Relations
Telephone: (718) 579-4460. **Fax:** (718) 293-8414.
Executive Director, Communications/Media Relations: Jason Zillo. **Assistant Director, Baseball Information/Public Communications:** Michael Margolis. **Manager, Baseball Information:** Lauren Moran. **Manager, Communications/Media Relations, Yankee Stadium Events:** Kenny Leandry. **Senior Coordinator, Media Services:** Alexandra Trochanowski. **Assistant, Communications/Media Relations:** Kaitlyn Brennan. **Administrative Assistant, Media Relations:** Dolores Hernandez. **Japanese Media Advisor:** Yoshiki Sato.

Ticket Operations
Telephone: (718) 293-6000.
VP, Ticket Sales/Service/Operations: Kevin Dart. **Senior Director, Ticket Operations:** Irfan Kirimca.

2015 SCHEDULE
Standard Game Times: 7:05 p.m.; Sat.-Sun. 1:05.

APRIL			
6 . . . . .Toronto	22-24 . . . . Texas	3-5 . . . . .Tampa Bay	24-26 . . . . Houston
8-9 . . . . .Toronto	25-27 . . . . . . Kansas City	7-9 . . . . Oakland	28-30 . . . . at Atlanta
10-12 . . . . Boston	28-31 . . . . . .at Oakland	10-12 . . . . . at Boston	31 . . . . at Boston
13-15 . . . .at Baltimore		17-19 . . . . Seattle	
17-19 . . . . at Tampa Bay	JUNE	21-23 . . . . Baltimore	SEPTEMBER
20-23 . . . . at Detroit	1-3 . . . . .at Seattle	24-26 . . . . at Minnesota	1-2 . . . . at Boston
24-26 . . . . .New York (NL)	5-7 . . . . Los Angeles (AL)	27-30 . . . . .at Texas	4-6 . . . . .Tampa Bay
27-29 . . . . . . .Tampa Bay	9-10 . . . . . . .Washington	31 . . . . . .at Chicago (AL)	7-9 . . . . Baltimore
	12-14 . . . . . .at Baltimore		10-13 . . . . .Toronto
MAY	15-16 . . . . . . at Miami	AUGUST	14-16 . . . . . at Tampa Bay
1-3 . . . . at Boston	17-18 . . . . .Miami	1-2. . . . . . .at Chicago (AL)	18-20 . . at New York (NL)
4-6. . . . . at Toronto	19-21 . . . . Detroit	4-6 . . . . Boston	21-23 . . . . at Toronto
7-10 . . . . Baltimore	22-24 . . . . . .Philadelphia	7-9 . . . . .Toronto	24-27 . . . . . Chicago (AL)
11-14 . . . . . at Tampa Bay	25-28 . . . . . . at Houston	11-13 . . . . . .at Cleveland	28-30 . . . . Boston
15-17 . . . . . Kansas City	29-30 . . at Los Angeles (AL)	14-16 . . . . at Toronto	OCTOBER
19-20 . . . . . at Washington	JULY	17-19 . . . . . . .Minnesota	1 . . . . Boston
	1 . . . . . at Los Angeles (AL)	20-23 . . . . Cleveland	2-4 . . . . .at Baltimore

GENERAL INFORMATION
Stadium (year opened): Yankee Stadium (2009).
Team Colors: Navy blue and white.
Player Representative: Unavailable.
Home Dugout: First Base.
Playing Surface: Grass.

BASEBALL OPERATIONS

Senior VP/General Manager: Brian Cashman.
Senior VP/Assistant GM: Jean Afterman, Esq. **Senior VP, Special Advisor:** Gene Michael.
VP/Assistant GM: Billy Eppler. **Assistant GM:** Michael Fishman. **Special Advisors:** Yogi Berra,
Reggie Jackson. **Director, Team Travel/Player Services:** Ben Tuliebitz. **Coordinator, Baseball
Operations:** Stephen Swindal Jr. **Assistants, Baseball Operations:** Timothy Choi, Matt Ferry.
Major League Systems Architect: Brian Nicosia. **Senior Web Director:** Nick Eby. **Analysts,
Baseball Operations:** David Grabiner, Jim Logue.

Brian Cashman

Major League Staff

Manager: Joe Girardi.
Coaches: Bench— Rob Thomson; **Pitching**—Larry Rothschild; **Hitting**—Jeff Pentland;
Assistant Hitting—Alan Cockrell; **First Base**—Tony Pena; **Third Base**—Joe Espada;
Bullpen—Gary Tuck; **Bullpen Catcher**—Roman Rodriguez.

Medical/Training

Team Physician, New York: Dr. Christopher Ahmad.
Senior Advisor, Orthopedics: Stuart Hershon, M.D. **Head Athletic Trainer:** Steve Donohue. **Assistant Athletic
Trainer:** Mark Littlefield. **Physical Therapist/Assistant Athletic Trainer:** Michael Schuk.

Player Development

Vice President, Player Development: Gary Denbo.
Director, Performance Science: John Kremer. **Director, Minor League Operations:** Eric Schmitt. **Assistant
Director, Minor League Operations Development:** Hadi Raad. **Enterprise Solutions Engineer:** Rob Owens.
Director, Pitching: Gil Patterson. **Pitching Instructor:** Nardi Contreras. **Field Coordinator:** Jody Reed. **Hitting
Coordinator:** James Rowson. **Pitching Coordinator:** Danny Borrell. **Infield Coordinator:** Carlos Mendoza. **Outfield/
Baserunning Coordinator:** Reggie Willits. **Catching Coordinator:** Josh Paul. **Assistant Field Coordinator:** Luis Sojo.
Rehab Pitching Instructors: Greg Pavlick, Miguel Bonilla. **Position Player Rehab Instructors:** Tom Nieto, Leonel
Vinas. **Interpreter:** Kyle Lee. **Video Coordinator, Player Development:** Adam Hunt. **Education Coordinator:** Yunior
Tabares. **Analysts, Baseball Operations:** Scott Benecke, Dan Greenlee. **Assistant, Player Development/Amateur
Scouting:** David Longley. **Medical Coordinator, Preventative Programs:** Mike Wickland. **Head Athletic Trainer,
Player Development:** Tim Lentych. **Strength/Conditioning Coordinator:** Mike Kicia. **Assistant Head Athletic
Trainer:** Greg Spratt.

Farm System

Class	Club (League)	Manager	Hitting Coach	Pitching Coach
Triple-A	Scranton/WB (IL)	Dave Miley	Marcus Thames	Scott Aldred
Double-A	Trenton (EL)	Al Pedrique	PJ Pilittere	Jose Rosado
High A	Tampa (FSL)	Dave Bialas	Tom Slater	Tommy Phelps
Low A	Charleston (SAL)	Luis Dorante	Greg Colbrunn	Tim Norton
Short-season	Staten Island (NYP)	Patrick Osborn	Ty Hawkins	Butch Henry
Rookie	Pulaski	Tony Franklin	Edwar Gonzalez	Justin Pope
Rookie	Yankees I (GCL)	Julio Mosquera	Caonabo Cosme	Elvys Quezada
Rookie	Yankees II (GCL)	Mark Bombard	Jason Brown	Unavailable
Rookie	Yankees I (DSL)	Raul Dominguez	Roy Gomez	Gerardo Casadiego
Rookie	Yankees II (DSL)	Sonder Encarnacion	Edwin Beard	Gabriel Tatis

Scouting

VP, Domestic Amateur Scouting: Damon Oppenheimer.
Assistant Director, Domestic Amateur Scouting: Ben McIntyre. **Director, Professional Scouting:** Kevin
Reese. **Manager, Professional Scouting:** Steve Martone. **Video Coordinator, Amateur Scouting:** Mitch Colahan.
Professional Scouts: Joe Caro, Kendall Carter, Matt Daley, Jay Darnell, Jeff Datz, Dave DeFreitas, Brandon Duckworth,
Bill Emslie, Abe Flores, Dan Giese, Drew Henson, Jalal Leach, Tim Naehring, Greg Orr, Dennis Twombley, Tom Wilson.
Special Assignment Scouts: Eric Chavez, Jim Hendry. **Pitching Analyst:** Scott Lovekamp. **Amateur Scouting,
National Crosscheckers:** Brian Barber, Tim Kelly, Jeff Patterson, D.J. Svihlik.
Area Scouts: Troy Afenir (Escondido, CA), Denis Boucher (Montreal), Jeff Deardorff (Minneola, FL), Bobby DeJardin
(San Clemente, CA), Phil Geisler (Half Moon Bay, CA), Mike Gibbons (Liberty Township, OH), Billy Godwin (Emerald Isle,
NC), Matt Hyde (Canton, MA), Dave Keith (Anaheim, CA), Mike Kmetko (Phoenix, AZ), Steve Lemke (Geneva, IL), Mike
Leuzinger (Canton, TX), Carlos Marti (Miramar, FL), Ronnie Merrill (Tampa, FL), Darryl Monroe (Decatur, GA), Bill Pintard
(Carpinteria, CA), Cesar Presbott (Bronx, NY), Matt Ranson (Topeka, KS), Brian Rhees (Live Oak, TX), Stewart Smothers
(Springfield, VA), Mike Thurman (West Linn, OR), Mike Wagner (Nashville, TN).
Director, International Player Development: Pat McMahon. **Director, International Scouting:** Donny Rowland.
Assistant Director, International Operations: Alex Cotto. **Assistant Director, International Player Development:**
Mario Garza. **Head Trainer, International Operations:** Alfonso Malaguti. **Director, Latin Baseball Academy:** Joel
Lithgow. **Coordinator, Cultural Development:** Hector Gonzalez. **Video Coordinator, International Operations:** Taylor
Emmanuels. **International Crosschecker:** Dennis Woody. **International Crosschecker/Coordinator/Pacific Rim:** Steve
Wilson. **Supervisors, Latin American:** Ricardo Finol, Victor Mata. **Supervisor, Dominican Republic:** Raymon Sanchez.
Dominican Republic Scouts: Miguel Bentiez, Esteban Castillo, Raymi Dicent, Arturo Pena, Juan Rosario, Jose Sabino.
Venezuela Scouts: Alan Atacho, Darwin Bracho, Roney Calderon, Jose Gavidia, Borman Landaeta, Cesar Suarez.
Mexico Scouts: Leobardo Figueroa, Lee Sigman, Humberto Soto. **International Scouts:** Jae Sung Lee (South Korea),
Hensley Josephina (Curacao), Carlos Levy (Panama), Edgard Rodriguez (Nicaragua), Luis Sierra (Colombia), John
Wadsworth (Australia)..

Oakland Athletics

Office Address: 7000 Coliseum Way, Oakland, CA 94621.
Telephone: (510) 638-4900. **Fax:** (510) 562-1633. **Website:** www.oaklandathletics.com.

Ownership
Owner/Managing Partner: Lew Wolff.

BUSINESS OPERATIONS
President: Michael Crowley. **Vice-President, Venue Development:** Keith Wolff. **Executive Assistant:** Carolyn Jones. **General Counsel:** Neil Kraetsch. **Assistant General Counsel:** Ryan Horning.

Lew Wolff

Finance/Administration
Vice President, Finance: Paul Wong. **Senior Director, Finance:** Kasey Jarcik. **Accounting Manager:** Ling Ding. **Payroll Manager:** Rose Dancil. **Senior Accountant, Accounts Payable:** Isabelle Mahaffey. **Director, Human Resources:** Kim Kubo. **Human Resources Assistant:** Erica Sahli. **Director, Information Technology:** Nathan Hayes. **IT Manager:** David Frieberg. **Desktop Administrator:** Chris Jio. **Office Services Coordinator:** Tina Jimenez. **Executive Offices Receptionist:** Maggie Baptist.

Sales/Marketing
VP, Sales/Marketing: Jim Leahey. **Assistant, Sales/Marketing:** Elizabeth Staub. **Senior Director, Marketing:** Troy Smith. **Senior Manager, Digital Marketing:** Travis LoDolce. **Advertising Assistant:** Laiken Whitters. **Creative Services Manager:** Mike Ono. **Senior Director, Corporate Partnerships:** Steve Pastorino. **Director, Partnership Services:** Franklin Lowe. **Senior Account Manager, Corporate Partnerships:** Jill Golden. **Corporate Account Managers:** Jessica Smith, Tim Sommer. **Corporate Partnership Assistant:** Evan Twomey. **Senior Manager, Promotion/Events:** Heather Rajeski. **Special Events Coordinator:** Sandy Karbel.

Public Relations/Communications
VP, Communications/Broadcasting: Ken Pries. **Baseball Information Manager:** Mike Selleck. **Manager, Player/Media Relations:** Adam Loberstein. **Media Services Manager:** Debbie Gallas. **Coordinator, Media Relations/Broadcasting:** Zak Basch. **Team Photographer:** Michael Zagaris. **Director, Community Relations:** Detra Paige. **Coordinator, Community Relations:** Melissa Guzman. **Community Relations Assistant:** Amanda Young. **Manager, Authentication:** Erik Farrell. **Senior Director, Multimedia Services:** David Don. **Director, Entertainment/Production:** Matt Shelton. **Multimedia Services Manager:** Jon Martin. **Public Address Announcer:** Dick Callahan.

Stadium Operations
VP, Stadium Operations: David Rinetti. **Senior Director, Stadium Operations:** Paul La Veau. **Senior Manager, Stadium Operations Events:** Kristy Ledbetter. **Stadium Services Manager:** Randy Duran. **Guest Services Manager:**

2015 SCHEDULE
Standard Game Times: 7:05 p.m.; Sat./Sun. 1:05.

APRIL			
6-9 . . . . Texas	25-27 . . . . Detroit	2-5 . . . . Seattle	24-26 . . . . .at Seattle
10-12 . . . . Seattle	28-31 . . . . . New York (AL)	7-9 . . . . . at New York (AL)	28-30 . . . . at Arizona
13-15 . . . . . . at Houston		10-12 . . . . . .at Cleveland	31 . . . . . Los Angeles (AL)
17-19 . . . . . .at Kansas City	JUNE	17-19 . . . . . . .Minnesota	
20-23 . . at Los Angeles (AL)	2-4 . . . . at Detroit	21-23 . . . . .Toronto	SEPTEMBER
24-26 . . . . Houston	5-7 . . . . at Boston	24-26 . . . . at San Francisco	1-2 . . . . . Los Angeles (AL)
28-30 . . . Los Angeles (AL)	9-11 . . . . Texas	28-29 . . at Los Angeles (NL)	4-6 . . . . Seattle
	12-14 . . at Los Angeles (AL)	30-31 . . . . Cleveland	7-9 . . . . Houston
MAY	15-16 . . . . . at San Diego		11-13 . . . . .at Texas
1-3 . . . . .at Texas	17-18 . . . . San Diego	AUGUST	14-17 . . . . .at Chicago (AL)
4-7 . . . . at Minnesota	19-21 . . . . Los Angeles (AL)	1-2 . . . . Cleveland	18-20 . . . . . . at Houston
8-10 . . . . .at Seattle	23-25 . . . . .at Texas	3-5 . . . . Baltimore	22-24 . . . . Texas
11-13 . . . . Boston	26-28 . . . . . Kansas City	6-9 . . . . Houston	25-27 . . . . . San Francisco
15-17 . . . . . Chicago (AL)	29-30 . . . . .Colorado	11-13 . . . . at Toronto	28-30 . . at Los Angeles (AL)
18-20 . . . . . at Houston		14-17 . . . . . . .at Baltimore	
21-24 . . . . . at Tampa Bay	JULY	18-19 . . . Los Angeles (NL)	OCTOBER
	1 . . . . .Colorado	21-23 . . . . . . .Tampa Bay	2-4 . . . . .at Seattle

GENERAL INFORMATION
Stadium (year opened): O.co Coliseum (1968).
Team Colors: Kelly green and gold.
Player Representative: Unavailable.
Home Dugout: Third Base.
Playing Surface: Grass.

Elisabeth Aydelotte. **Stadium Operations Manager:** Matt Van Norton.

Ticket Sales/Operations/Services
Executive Director, Ticket Sales/Operations: Steve Fanelli. **Senior Director, Ticket Services:** Josh Ziegenbusch. **Director, Ticket Operations:** David Adame. **Ticket Services Manager:** Catherine Glazier. **Premium Services Manager:** Michael Neis. **Premium Services Coordinator:** Marco Ruidiaz. **Ticket Operations Manager:** Anuj Patel. **Season Ticket Retention Coordinator:** Tamara Burnett. **Box Office Coordinator:** Patricia Heagy. **Director, Ticket Sales:** Brian DiTucci. **Manager, Group Sales:** Josh Feinberg. **Manager, Season Ticket Sales:** Aaron Dragomir. **Manager, Inside Sales:** David Nosti.

Travel/Clubhouse
Director, Team Travel: Mickey Morabito. **Equipment Manager:** Steve Vucinich. **Visiting Clubhouse Manager:** Mike Thalblum. **Assistant Equipment Manager:** Brian Davis. **Umpire/Clubhouse Assistant:** Matt Weiss. **Arizona Clubhouse Manager:** James Gibson. **Arizona Assistant Clubhouse Managers:** Thomas Miller, Chad Yaconetti.

BASEBALL OPERATIONS
VP/General Manager: Billy Beane.
Assistant GM: David Forst. **Assistant GM:** Dan Kantrovitz. **Director, Pro Scouting/Baseball Development:** Dan Feinstein. **Director, Player Personnel:** Billy Owens. **Special Assistants to GM:** Grady Fuson, Chris Pittaro. **Executive Assistant:** Betty Shinoda. **Director, Baseball Administration:** Pamela Pitts. **Video Coordinator:** Adam Rhoden. **Special Assistant to Baseball Operations:** Scott Hatteberg. **Architect Baseball Systems:** Rob Naberhaus. **Baseball Operations Analyst:** Michael Schatz.

Billy Beane

Major League Staff
Manager: Bob Melvin.
Coaches: Bench—Mike Aldrete; **Pitching**—Curt Young; **Batting**—Darren Bush; **First Base**—Tye Waller; **Third Base**—Mike Gallego; **Bullpen**—Scott Emerson; **Assistant Hitting/Catching Coach**—Marcus Jensen.

Medical/Training
Head Athletic Trainer: Nick Paparesta. **Assistant Athletic Trainers:** Walt Horn, Brian Schulman. **Strength/Conditioning Coach:** Michael Henriques. **Major League Massage Therapist:** Ozzie Lyles. **Team Physicians:** Dr. Allan Pont, Dr. Elliott Schwartz. **Team Orthopedist:** Dr. Jon Dickinson. **Associate Team Orthopedist:** Dr. Will Workman. **Arizona Team Physicians:** Dr. Fred Dicke, Dr. Doug Freedberg.

Player Development
Telephone: (510) 638-4900. **Fax:** (510) 563-2376.
Director, Player Development: Keith Lieppman. **Director, Minor League Operations:** Ted Polakowski. **Administrative Assistant, Player Development:** Nancy Moriuchi. **Minor League Roving Instructors:** Juan Navarrete (infield): Garvin Alston (pitching), Greg Sparks (hitting). **Minor League Video Coordinator:** Mark Smith. **Minor League Medical Coordinator:** Jeff Collins. **Coordinator, Medical Services:** Larry Davis. **Minor League Strength/Conditioning Coordinator:** Josh Cuffe. **Minor League Strength/Conditioning Assistant Coordinator:** Sean Doran. **Special Instructor, Pitching/Rehabilitation:** Craig Lefferts. **Minor League Rehabilitation Coordinator:** Nate Brooks.

Farm System

Class	Club (League)	Manager	Coach	Pitching Coach
Triple-A	Nashville (PCL)	Steve Scarsone	Webster Garrison	Don Schulze
Double-A	Midland (TL)	Ryan Christenson	Eric Martins	John Wasdin
High A	Stockton (CAL)	Rick Magnante	Brian McArn	Rick Rodriguez
Low A	Beloit (MWL)	Fran Riordan	Lloyd Turner	Steve Connelly
Short-season	Vermont (NYP)	Aaron Nieckula	Tommy Everidge	Carlos Chavez
Rookie	Athletics (AZL)	Ruben Escalera	Juan Dilone	Unavailable
Rookie	Athletics (DSL)	Carlos Casimiro	Rahdames Perez	Gabriel Ozuna

Scouting
Telephone: (510) 638-4900. **Fax:** (510) 563-2376.
Director, Scouting: Eric Kubota (Rocklin, CA).
Assistant Director, Scouting: Michael Holmes (Winston Salem, NC). **Director, Pro Scouting/Baseball Development:** Dan Feinstein (Lafayette, CA). **Scouting Assistant:** Ben Lowry (Berkeley, CA). **West Coast Supervisor:** Scott Kidd (Folsom, CA). **Midwest Supervisor:** Ron Marigny (Cypress, TX). **East Coast Supervisor:** Marc Sauer (Tampa, FL). **Northeast Supervisor:** Pat Portugal (Wake Forest, NC). **Pro Scouts:** Jeff Bittiger (Saylorsburg, PA), Dan Freed (Lexington, IL), John McLaren (Peoria, AZ), Will Schock (Oakland, CA), Steve Sharpe (Kansas City, MO), Tom Thomas (Phoenix, AZ), Mike Ziegler (Orlando, FL). **Area Scouts:** Neil Avent (Greensboro, NC), Yancy Ayres (Topeka, KS), Armann Brown (Houston, TX), Jermaine Clark (Discovery Bay, CA), Jim Coffman (Portland, OR), Ruben Escalera (Carolina, PR), Matt Higginson (Burlington, ON), Craig Conklin (Malibu, CA), Kevin Mello (Chicago, IL), Kelcey Mucker (Baton Rouge, LA), Trevor Ryan (Escondido, CA), Trevor Schaffer (Belleair, FL), Rich Sparks (Sterling Heights, MI), Jemel Spearman (Lithonia, GA), JT Stotts (Moorpark, CA), Ron Vaughn (Windsor, CT).
Director, Latin American Operations: Raymond Abreu (Santo Domingo, DR). **Coordinator, Latin American Scouting:** Julio Franco (Carrizal, VZ). **International Scouts:** Ruben Barradas (Venezuela), Juan Carlos De La Cruz (Dominican Republic), Angel Eusebio (Dominican Republic), Andri Garcia (Venezuela), Adam Hislop (Taiwan), Lewis Kim (South Korea), Pablo Marmol (Dominican Republic), Juan Mosquera (Panama), Tito Quintero (Colombia), Amaurys Reyes (Dominican Republic), Oswaldo Troconis (Venezuela), Juan Villanueva (Venezuela).

Philadelphia Phillies

Office Address: Citizens Bank Park, One Citizens Bank Way, Philadelphia, PA 19148.
Telephone: (215) 463-6000. **Website:** www.phillies.com.

Ownership
Operated By: The Phillies.
President: Pat Gillick. **Chairman:** David Montgomery. **Chairman Emeritus:** Bill Giles.

BUSINESS OPERATIONS
Vice President/General Counsel: Rick Strouse. **VP, Phillies Enterprises:** Richard Deats.
VP, Employee/Customer Services: Kathy Killian. **Director, Ballpark Enterprises/Business
Development:** Joe Giles. **Director, Information Systems:** Brian Lamoreaux. **Director,
Employee Benefits/Services:** JoAnn Marano.

David Montgomery

Ballpark Operations
Senior VP, Administration/Operations: Michael Stiles. **Director, Operations/Facility:**
Mike DiMuzio. **Director, Operations/Events:** Eric Tobin. **Director, Operations/Security:** Sal
DeAngelis. **Manager, Concessions Development:** Bruce Leith. **Head Groundskeeper:** Mike
Boekholder. **PA Announcer:** Dan Baker. **Official Scorers:** Jay Dunn, Mike Maconi.

Communications
Telephone: (215) 463-6000. **Fax:** (215) 389-3050.
VP, Communications: Bonnie Clark. **Director, Baseball Communications:** Greg Casterioto.
Coordinator, Baseball Communications: Craig Hughner. **Communications Assistant:** Deanna Sabec. **Baseball
Communications Assistant:** Chris Ware.

Finance
VP/CFO: John Nickolas. **Director, Payroll Services:** Karen Wright.

Marketing/Promotions
Senior VP, Marketing/Sales: David Buck. **Manager, Client Services/Alumni Relations:** Debbie Nocito. **Director,
Corporate Partnerships:** Rob MacPherson. **Director, Advertising Sales:** Brian Mahoney. **Director, Corporate Sales:**
Scott Nickle. **Manager, Advertising Sales:** Tom Sullivan.
VP, Marketing Programs/Events: Kurt Funk.. **Director, Entertainment:** Chris Long. **Manager, Broadcasting:** Rob
Brooks. **Manager, Advertising/Internet Services:** Jo-Anne Levy-Lamoreaux.

Sales/Tickets
Telephone: (215) 463-1000. **Fax:** (215) 463-9878.
VP, Sales/Ticket Operations: John Weber. **Director, Ticket Department:** Dan Goroff. **Director, Ticket Technology/
Development:** Chris Pohl. **Director, Season Ticket Sales:** Derek Schuster. **Manager, Suite Sales/Services:** Tom
Mashek. **Director, Ticket Services/Intern Program:** Phil Feather. **Manager, Season Ticket Services:** Mike Holdren.

2015 SCHEDULE
Standard Game Times: 7:05 p.m.; Sun. 1:35

APRIL		
6 . . . . Boston	22-24 . . . . . at Washington	3-5 . . . . at Atlanta	28-30 . . . . San Diego
8-9 . . . . Boston	25-27 . . . . at New York (NL)	6-9 . . . . at Los Angeles (NL)	31 . . . . . . at New York (NL)
10-12 . . . . . . .Washington	29-31 . . . . .Colorado	10-12 . . . . at San Francisco	
13-15 . . . at New York (NL)		17-19 . . . . .Miami	SEPTEMBER
16-19 . . . . . at Washington	JUNE	20-22 . . . . . . .Tampa Bay	1-2. . . . . .at New York (NL)
21-23 . . . . .Miami	2-4 . . . . Cincinnati	24-26 . . . . .at Chicago (NL)	4-6. . . . . at Boston
24-26 . . . . Atlanta	5-7 . . . . San Francisco	28-29 . . . . at Toronto	7-9 . . . . Atlanta
27-30 . . . . .at St. Louis	8-10 . . . . . . at Cincinnati	30-31 . . . . Atlanta	10-13 . . . . . Chicago (NL)
	12-14 . . . . . . at Pittsburgh		14-16 . . . . . . .Washington
MAY	15-16 . . . . . . .at Baltimore	AUGUST	18-20 . . . . at Atlanta
1-3 . . . . at Miami	17-18 . . . . Baltimore	1-2. . . . . Atlanta	22-24 . . . . at Miami
4-6. . . . . at Atlanta	19-21 . . . . St. Louis	4-6. . . . . .Los Angeles (NL)	25-27 . . . . . at Washington
8-10 . . . . . .New York (NL)	22-24 . . . at New York (AL)	7-9. . . . . . . at San Diego	29-30 . . . . .New York (NL)
11-14 . . . . Pittsburgh	26-28 . . . . . . .Washington	10-12 . . . . . . at Arizona	
15-17 . . . . . . .Arizona	29-30 . . . . . . .Milwaukee	14-16 . . . . . at Milwaukee	OCTOBER
18-21 . . . . . . at Colorado		18-19 . . . . .Toronto	1 . . . . .New York (NL)
	JULY	20-23 . . . . .at Miami	2-4. . . . . .Miami
	1-2 . . . . .Milwaukee	24-27 . . . . .New York (NL)	

GENERAL INFORMATION
Stadium (year opened): Citizens
Bank Park (2004).
Team Colors: Red, white and blue.

Player Representative: Unavailable.
Home Dugout: First Base.
Playing Surface: Natural Grass.

Travel/Clubhouse
Director, Team Travel/Clubhouse Services: Frank Coppenbarger.
Manager, Visiting Clubhouse: Kevin Steinhour. **Manager, Home Clubhouse:** Phil Sheridan. **Manager, Equipment/ Umpire Services:** Dan O'Rourke.

BASEBALL OPERATIONS
Senior VP/General Manager: Ruben Amaro Jr.
Senior Advisor to the President/GM: Pat Gillick. **Assistant GM:** Scott Proefrock. **Assistant GM, Player Personnel:** Benny Looper. **Senior Advisor to GM:** Dallas Green. **Senior Advisor to GM:** Charlie Manuel. **Special Assistants to GM:** Bart Braun, Charley Kerfeld. **Special Special Assistant, Baseball Operations:** Ed Wade. **Director, Baseball Administration:** Susan Ingersoll Papaneri. **Director, Professional Scouting:** Mike Ondo. **Baseball Information Analyst:** Jay McLaughlin. **Manager, Baseball Analytics:** Scott Freedman. **Administrative Assistant, Baseball Operations:** Adele MacDonald. **Baseball Operations Representative:** Chris Cashman.

Ruben Amaro Jr.

Major League Staff
Manager: Ryne Sandberg.
Coaches: Bench—Larry Bowa; **Pitching**—Bob McClure; **Hitting**—Steve Henderson; **First Base**—Juan Samuel; **Third Base**—Pete Mackanin; **Assistant Hitting**—John Mizerock; **Bullpen**—Rod Nichols; **Bullpen Catcher**—Jesus Tiamo.

Medical/Training
Director, Medical Services: Dr. Michael Ciccotti. **Head Athletic Trainer:** Scott Sheridan. **Assistant Athletic Trainers:** Shawn Fcasni, Chris Mudd. **Strength/Conditioning Coordinator:** Paul Fournier. **Employee Assistance Professional:** Dickie Noles.

Player Development
Telephone: (215) 463-6000. **Fax:** (215) 755-9324.
Assistant GM, Player Personnel: Benny Looper. **Director, Player Development:** Joe Jordan.
Director, Minor League Operations: Lee McDaniel. **Assistant Director, Player Development:** Steve Noworyta. **Special Assistant, Player Personnel:** Jorge Velandia. **Director, Florida Operations/GM. Clearwater Threshers:** John Timberlake. **Assistant Director, Minor League Operations/Florida Operations:** Joe Cynar. **Coordinator, International Operations:** Ray Robles.
Field Coordinator: Doug Mansolino. **Senior Advisor, Player Development:** Mike Compton. **Assistant Field Coordinator/Hitting:** Andy Tracy. **Pitching Coordinator:** Rafael Chaves. **Roving Pitching Coach:** Carlos Arroyo. **Infield Coordinator:** Chris Truby. **Outfield/Baserunning:** Andy Abad. **Catching:** Ernie Whitt. **Athletic Trainer coordinator:** James Ready. **Strength/Conditioning Coordinator:** Jason Meredith.

Farm System

Class	Club (League)	Manager	Hitting Coach	Pitching Coach
Triple-A	Lehigh Valley (IL)	Dave Brundage	Sal Rende	Ray Burris
Double-A	Reading (EL)	Dusty Wathan	Frank Cacciatore	Dave Lundquist
High A	Clearwater (FSL)	Greg legg	Rob Ducey	Steve Schrenk
Low A	Lakewood (SAL)	Shawn Williams	Nelson Prada	Aaron Fultz
Short-season	Williamsport (NYP)	Pat Borders	Eddie Dennis	Les Lancaster
Rookie	Clearwater (GCL)	Roly deArmas	Rafael DeLima	Brian Sweeney
Rookie	Phillies (DSL)	Manny Amador	Cristino Henriquez	Alex Concepcion
Rookie	Phillies (VSL)	Trino Aguilar	Silverino Navas	Les Straker

Scouting
Director, Amateur Scouting: Johnny Almaraz (San Antonio, TX).
Director, Amateur Scouting Administration: Rob Holiday (Philadelphia, PA). **Coordinators, Scouting:** Mike Ledna (Arlington Heights, IL), Bill Moore (Alta Loma, CA).
Regional Supervisors: Gene Schall (Mid-Atlantic/Harleysville, PA), Eric Valent (Southeast/Wernersville, PA), Scott Trcka (Central/Hobart, IN), Darrell Conner (West/Riverside, CA).
Area Scouts: Alex Agostino (Quebec), Shane Bowers (La Verne, CA), Steve Cohen (Spring, TX), Joey Davis (Rocklin, CA), Mike Garcia (Moreno Valley, CA), Brad Holland (Gilbert, AZ), Aaron Jersild (Alpharetta, GA), Brian Kohlscheen (Norman, OK), Alan Marr (Sarasota, FL), Timi Moni (Nashville, TN), Paul Murphy (Wilmington, DE), Demerius Pittman (Corona, CA), Paul Scott (Rockwall, TX), David Seifert (Paw Paw, IL), Mike Stauffer (Brandon, MS).
Director International Scouting: Sal Agostinelli (Kings Park, NY). **International Scouts:** Norman Anciani (Panama), Rafael Alvarez (Venezuela), Franklin Felida (Dominican Republic), Gene Grimaldi (Antilles), Tomas Herrera (Mexico), Andres Hiraldo (Dominican Republic), Gregory Manuel (Aruba), Jesus Mendez (Venezuela), Jairo Morelos (Colombia), Romulo Oliveros (Venezuela), Bernardo Perez (Dominican Republic), Philip Riccobono (Korea), Carlos Salas (Dominican Republic), Claudio Scerrato (Italy), Darryn Smith (South Africa), Ebert Valazuez (Venezuela).
Director, Major League Scouting: Gordon Lakey (Barker, TX). **Special Assignment Scouts:** Howie Frieling (Apex, NC), Dave Hollins (Orchard Park, NY), Craig Colbert (Portland, OR). **Professional Scouts:** Sonny Bowers (Hewitt, TX), Steve Jongewaard (Napa, CA), Jesse Levis (Fort Washington, PA), Jon Mercurio (Coraopolis, PA), Roy Tanner (Palatka , FL), Del Unser (Scottsdale, AZ), Dan Wright (Cave Springs, AR).

Pittsburgh Pirates

Office Address: PNC Park at North Shore, 115 Federal St., Pittsburgh, PA, 15212.
Mailing Address: PO Box 7000, Pittsburgh, PA 15212.
Telephone: (412) 323-5000. **Fax:** (412) 325-4412. **Website:** www.pirates.com. **Twitter:** @Pirates.

Ownership
Chairman of the Board: Robert Nutting.
Board of Directors: Donald Beaver, Eric Mauck, G. Ogden Nutting, Robert Nutting, William Nutting, Duane Wittman.

BUSINESS OPERATIONS
President: Frank Coonelly. **Vice President/General Counsel:** Bryan Stroh.

Frank Coonelly

Communications
VP, Communications/Broadcasting: Brian Warecki. **Director, Baseball Communications:** Jim Trdinich. **Director, Broadcasting:** Marc Garda. **Director, Media Relations:** Dan Hart. **Manager, Business Communications/Social Media:** Terry Rodgers.

Community Relations
Senior VP, Community/Public Affairs: Patty Paytas. **Director, Community Relations:** Michelle Mejia. **Manager, Diversity Initiatives:** Chaz Kellem. **Manager, Pirates Charities:** Jackie Hunter.

Marketing
Senior Director, Marketing/Special Events: Brian Chiera. **Director, Alumni Affairs/Promotions/Licensing:** Joe Billetdeaux. **Director, Advertising/Creative Services:** Kiley Cauvel. **Director, Special Events/Game Presentation:** Christine Serkoch. **Director, PNC Park Events:** Ann Elder.

Corporate Sponsorships
Senior Director, Corporate Sponsorship Sales/Service: Aaron Cohn.

Stadium Operations
Executive VP/General Manager, PNC Park: Dennis DaPra. **Senior Director, Ballpark Operations:** Chris Hunter. **Senior Director, Security/Contract Services:** Jeff Podobnik. **Senior Director, Florida Operations:** Trevor Gooby. **Director, Field Operations:** Manny Lopez.

Finance/Administration/Information Technology
Executive VP/CFO: Jim Plake. **Senior Director, IT:** Terry Zeigler. **Director, Employee Services:** Patti Mistick. **Senior Director, Business Analytics:** Jim Alexander.

Ticketing
Telephone: (800) 289-2827.

2015 SCHEDULE
Standard Game Times: 7:05 p.m.; Sun. 1:35.

APRIL
6	at Cincinnati
8-9	at Cincinnati
10-12	at Milwaukee
13-15	Detroit
17-19	Milwaukee
20-23	Chicago (NL)
24-26	at Arizona
27-29	at Chicago (NL)

MAY
1-3	at St. Louis
5-7	Cincinnati
8-10	St. Louis
11-14	at Phillies
15-17	at Chicago (NL)
19-20	Minnesota
22-24	New York (NL)
25-27	Miami
28-31	at San Diego

JUNE
1-3	at San Francisco
5-7	at Atlanta
8-10	Milwaukee
12-14	Philadelphia
15-16	Chicago (AL)
17-18	at Chicago (AL)
19-21	at Washington
23-25	Cincinnati
26-28	Atlanta
30	at Detroit

JULY
1-2	at Detroit
3-5	Cleveland
6-8	San Diego
9-12	St. Louis
17-19	at Milwaukee
20-22	at Kansas City
23-26	Washington
28-29	at Minnesota
30-31	at Cincinnati

AUGUST
1-2	at Cincinnati
3-5	Chicago (NL)
7-9	Los Angeles (NL)
11-13	at St. Louis
14-16	at New York (NL)
17-19	Arizona
20-23	San Francisco
24-27	at Miami
28-30	Colorado

SEPTEMBER
1-3	at Milwaukee
4-6	at St. Louis
7-9	at Cincinnati
10-13	Milwaukee
15-17	Chicago (NL)
18-20	at Los Angeles (NL)
21-24	at Colorado
25-27	at Chicago (NL)
28-30	St. Louis

OCTOBER
2-4	Cincinnati

GENERAL INFORMATION
Stadium (year opened): PNC Park (2001).
Team Colors: Black and gold.
Player Representative: Neil Walker.
Home Dugout: Third Base.
Playing Surface: Grass.

Director, Suite Sales/Service: Terri Smith. Director, New Business Development: Nick McNeill. Director, Season Ticket Service/Retention: Jim Popovich. Director, Ticket Operations: Andrew Bragman.

BASEBALL OPERATIONS

Executive VP/General Manager: Neal Huntington.
Assistant GMs: Greg Smith, Kyle Stark. **Director, Player Personnel:** Tyrone Brooks.
Director, Baseball Operations: Kevan Graves. **Director, Baseball Systems Development:** Dan Fox. **Special Assistants to GM:** Jim Benedict, Marc DelPiano, Jax Robertson, Doug Strange. **Major League Scouts:** Mike Basso, Bob Minor, Steve Williams. **Pro Scouts:** Mike Baker, Ricky Bennett, Carlos Berroa, Jim Dedrick, Mal Fichman, Ron Hopkins, John Kosciak, Alvin Rittman, Gary Robinson, Lewis Shaw. **Senior Advisor, Baseball Operations:** Grady Little. **Special Assistants to Baseball Operations:** Jamey Carroll, Kevin Young. **Coordinator, Baseball Operations:** Alex Langsam. **Baseball Operations Assistant:** Will Lawton. **Quantitative Analyst:** Mike Fitzgerald. **Data Architect:** Josh Smith. **Video Coordinator:** Kevin Roach. **Video Advance Scout:** Joe Hultzen.

Neal Huntington

Major League Staff

Manager: Clint Hurdle.
Coaches: Pitching—Ray Searage; **Hitting**—Jeff Branson; **First Base**—Nick Leyva; **Third Base**—Rick Sofield; **Bullpen**—Euclides Rojas; **Coach**—David Jauss; **Coach**—Jeff Livesey; **Coach**—Brad Fischer.

Medical/Training

Medical Director: Dr. Patrick DeMeo. **Team Physician:** Dr. Edward Snell. **Head Major League Athletic Trainer:** Todd Tomczyk. **Assistant Major League Athletic Trainer:** Ben Potenziano. **Head Major League Strength/Conditioning Coach:** Brendon Huttmann. **Physical Therapist/Rehab Coordinator:** Jeremiah Randall.

Player Development

Director, Minor League Operations: Larry Broadway.
Coordinator, Baseball Administration: Diane DePasquale. **Coordinator, Minor League Operations:** Brian Selman. **Coordinator, Instruction:** Frank Kremblas. **Quality Assurance/Camp Coordinator:** Dave Turgeon. **Outfield/Baserunning Coordinator:** Kimera Bartee. **Pitching Coordinator:** Scott Mitchell. **Assistant Pitching Coordinator:** Tom Filer. **Latin American Pitching Coordinator:** Amaury Telemaco. **Infield Coordinator:** Gary Green. **Hitting Coordinator:** Larry Sutton.
Senior Advisor, Latin American Operations: Luis Silverio. **Senior Advisor, Player Development:** Woody Huyke. **Senior Advisor, Player Development:** Mike Lum. **Dominican Academy Coordinator:** Gera Alvarez. **Athletic Training Coordinator:** Carl Randolph. **Sport Performance Coordinator:** Carlo Alvarez. **Strength/Conditioning Specialists:** Joe Hughes, Kiyoshi Momose. **Director, Mental Conditioning:** Bernie Holliday. **Mental Conditioning Coordinator:** Tyson Holt. **Mental Conditioning Assistant Coordinator:** Hector Morales. **Coordinator, Personal/Professional Development:** Jon Hammermeister. **Minor League Equipment Manager:** Pat Hagerty.

Farm System

Class	Club (League)	Manager	Hitting Coach	Pitching Coach
Triple-A	Indianapolis (IL)	Dean Treanor	Butch Wynegar	Stan Kyles
Double-A	Altoona (EL)	Tom Prince	Kevin Riggs	Justin Meccage
High A	Bradenton (FSL)	Michael Ryan	Ryan Long	Scott Elarton
Low A	West Virginia (SAL)	Brian Esposito	Keoni De Renne	Mark DiFelice
Short-season	West Virginia (NYP)	Wyatt Toregas	Jonathan Prieto	Tom Filer
Rookie	Bristol (APP)	Edgar Varela	Austin McClune	Jeff Johnson
Rookie	Bradenton (GCL)	Milver Reyes	Kory DeHaan	Elvin Nina
Rookie	Pirates 1 (DSL)	Mendy Lopez	Osiel Flores	Dan Urbina

Scouting

Fax: (412) 325-4414.
Director, Amateur Scouting: Joe Delli Carri.
Coordinator, Amateur Scouting: Jim Asher. **National Supervisors:** Jack Bowen (Bethel Park, PA), Jimmy Lester (Columbus, GA), Matt Ruebel (Oklahoma City, OK). **Regional Supervisors:** Jesse Flores (Sacramento, CA), Rodney Henderson (Lexington, KY), Everett Russell (Thibodaux, LA), Greg Schilz (Washington D.C.).
Area Supervisors: Rick Allen (Agoura Hills, CA), Matt Bimeal (Olathe, KS), Trevor Haley (Temperance, MI), Sean Heffernan (Florence, SC), Phil Huttmann, (McKinney, TX), Jerry Jordan (Kingsport, TN), Max Kwan (Kent, WA) Darren Mazeroski (Panama City Beach, FL), Nick Presto (Palm Beach Gardens, FL), Dan Radcliff (Palmyra, VA), Mike Sansoe (Walnut Creek, CA), Steve Skrinar (Framingham, MA), Tyler Stohr (Houston,TX), Brian Tracy (Yorba Linda, CA), Derrick Van Dusen (Phoenix, AZ), Anthony Wycklendt (Brookfield, WI). **Part-Time Scout:** Enrique Hernandez (Puerto Rico).
Director, Latin American Scouting: Rene Gayo.
International Scouts: Fu-Chun Chiang (Korea, Taiwan), Orlando Covo (Colombia), Tom Gillespie (Europe), Tony Harris (Australia), Nelson Llenas (Dominican Republic), Juan Mercado (Dominican Repuplic), Rodolfo Petit (Venezuela), Victor Santana (Dominican Republic), Cristino Valdez (Dominican Republic), Jesus Chino Valdez (Mexico). **Part-Time International Scouts:** John Akel (Ecuador), Esteban Alvarez (Dominican Republic), Pablo Csorgi (Venezuela), Denny Diaz (Dominican Republic), Eugene Helder (Aruba), Jhoan Hidalgo (Venezuela), Jose Lavagnino (Mexico), Javier Magdaleno (Venezuela), Yeferson Mercado (Dominican Republic), Juan Morales (Venezuela), Robinson Ortega (Colombia), Jose Ortiz (Dominican Republic), Jose Pineda (Panama), Juan Pinto (Mexico), Cesar Saba (Dominican Republic), Cristobal Santoya (Colombia), Leon Taylor (Jamaica), Jesus Valdez (Mexico) Marc Van Zanten (Netherlands Antilles).

St. Louis Cardinals

Office Address: 700 Clark Street, St. Louis MO 63102.
Telephone: (314) 345-9600. **Fax:** (314) 345-9523. **Website:** www.cardinals.com.

Ownership
Operated By: St. Louis Cardinals, LLC.
Chairman/Chief Executive Officer: William DeWitt, Jr.
President: Bill DeWitt III.
Senior Administrative Assistant to Chairman: Grace Kell. **Senior Administrative Assistant to President:** Julie Laningham.

BUSINESS OPERATIONS

Finance
Fax: (314) 345-9520.
Senior VP/Chief Financial Officer: Brad Wood. **Director, Finance:** Rex Carter. **Director, Human Resources:** Ann Seeney.
VP, Event Services/Merchandising: Vicki Bryant. **Director, Special Events:** Julia Row.

Marketing/Sales/Community Relations
Fax: (314) 345-9529.
Senior VP, Sales/Marketing: Dan Farrell. **Administrative Assistant, VP Sales/Marketing:** Gail Ruhling. **VP, Corporate Marketing/Stadium Entertainment:** Thane van Breusegen.
Director, Scoreboard Operations/Fan Entertainment/Senior Account Executive: Tony Simokaitis. **Director, Publications:** Steve Zesch.
VP, Community Relations/Executive Director, Cardinals Care: Michael Hall.
Administrative Assistant: Bonnie Parres.

Bill DeWitt III

Communications
Fax: (314) 345-9530.
VP, Communications: Ron Watermon. **Director, Communications:** Brian Bartow. **Manager, Communications:** Melody Yount. **Manager, Photography:** Taka Yanagimoto. **Communications Specialist:** Chris Tunno. **Coordinator, Communications:** Lindsey Weber. **Administrative Assistant, Communications:** Marybeth Rae. **PA Announcer:** John Ulett. **Official Scorers:** Gary Muller, Jeff Durbin, Mike Smith.

Stadium Operations
Fax: (314) 345-9535.
VP, Stadium Operations: Joe Abernathy. **Administrative Assistant:** Hope Baker. **Director, Security/Special Services:** Joe Walsh. **Director, Stadium Operations/Guest Services:** Mike Ball. **Director Facility, Security/Stadium**

2015 SCHEDULE
Standard Game Times: 7:15 p.m.; Sun. 1:15.

APRIL			
5 . . . . . . .at Chicago (NL)	22-24 . . . . .at Kansas City	2-5. . . . . San Diego	28-30 . . . . at San Francisco
7-8. . . . . .at Chicago (NL)	25-27 . . . . .Arizona	6-8. . . . . .at Chicago (NL)	31 . . . . .Washington
10-12 . . . . . . at Cincinnati	29-31 . . . .Los Angeles (NL)	9-12 . . . . . . at Pittsburgh	
13 . . . . .Milwaukee		17-19 . . . . .New York (NL)	**SEPTEMBER**
15-16 . . . . . .Milwaukee	**JUNE**	21-22 . . . .at Chicago (AL)	1-2. . . . . .Washington
17-19 . . . . Cincinnati	1-3. . . . . .Milwaukee	24-26 . . . . Atlanta	4-6. . . . . .Pittsburgh
21-23 . . . . at Washington	4-7. . . . at Los Angeles (NL)	27-29 . . . . Cincinnati	7-9. . . . . . . Chicago (NL)
24-26 . . . . . at Milwaukee	8-10 . . . . at Colorado	30-31 . . . . .Colorado	10-12 . . . . . . at Cincinnati
27-30 . . . . . .Philadelphia	12-14 . . . . . . Kansas City		15-17 . . . . . at Milwaukee
	15-16 . . . . . . .Minnesota	**AUGUST**	18-20 . . . .at Chicago (NL)
MAY	17-18 . . . . . at Minnesota	1-2. . . . . .Colorado	21-23 . . . . Cincinnati
1-3. . . . . Pittsburgh	19-21 . . .at Philadelphia	4-6. . . . . . . at Cincinnati	24-27 . . . . .Milwaukee
4-7. . . . . . . Chicago (NL)	23-25 . . . . at Miami	7-9. . . . . . . at Milwaukee	28-30 . . . . . . at Pittsburgh
8-10 . . . . . . at Pittsburgh	26-28 . . . . . Chicago (NL)	11-13 . . . . .Pittsburgh	
12-14 . . . . . .at Cleveland	30 . . . . Chicago (AL)	14-16 . . . . .Miami	**OCTOBER**
15-17 . . . . Detroit		17-19 . . . . .San Francisco	2-4. . . . . at Atlanta
18-21 . . . .at New York (NL)	**JULY**	21-23 . . . . at San Diego	
	1 . . . . Chicago (AL)	24-27 . . . . at Arizona	

GENERAL INFORMATION
Stadium (year opened): Busch Stadium (2006). **Team Colors:** Red and white.
Player Representative: Jon Jay. **Home Dugout:** First Base. **Playing Surface:** Grass.

Operations: Hosei Maruyama. **Head Groundskeeper:** Bill Findley.

Ticketing
Fax: (314) 345-9522.
VP, Ticket Sales/Service: Joe Strohm.

Travel/Clubhouse
Fax: (314) 345-9523.
Traveling Secretary: C.J. Cherre. **Equipment Manager:** Rip Rowan. **Assistant Equipment Manager:** Ernie Moore. **Visiting Clubhouse Manger:** Jerry Risch. **Video Coordinator:** Chad Blair.

BASEBALL OPERATIONS
Senior VP/General Manager: John Mozeliak.
Assistant GM: Mike Girsch. **Senior Executive Assistant:** Linda Brauer. **Senior Special Assistant to GM:** Mike Jorgensen. **Special Assistant to GM:** Cal Eldred, Ryan Franklin, Willie McGee. **Director, Player Personnel:** Matt Slater. **Director, Major League Administration:** Judy Carpenter-Barada. **Director, Baseball Administration:** John Vuch. **Manager, Baseball Information:** Jeremy Cohen. **Quantitative Analysts:** Matt Bayer, Patrick Casanta, Dane Sorensen.

John Mozeliak

Major League Staff
Telephone: (314) 345-9600.
Manager: Mike Matheny.
Coaches: Bench—David Bell; **Pitching**—Derek Lilliquist; **Hitting**—John Mabry; **Assistant Hitting Instructor**—Bill Mueller; **First Base**—Chris Maloney; **Third Base**—Jose Oquendo; **Bullpen**—Blaise Ilsley; **Bullpen Catchers**—Jamie Pogue, Kleininger Teran.

Medical/Training
Head Team Physician: Dr. Michael Milne. **Head Trainer:** Greg Hauck. **Assistant Trainer:** Chris Conroy. **Assistant Trainer/Rehabilitation Coordinator:** Adam Olsen. **Strength/Conditioning Coach:** Pete Prinzi.

Player Development
Director, Player Development: Gary LaRocque.
Baseball Operations Coordinator/Player Development: Tony Ferreira. **Special Assistant, Player Development:** Gaylen Pitts. **Minor League Field Coordinator:** Mark DeJohn.
Coordinators: Tim Leveque (pitching), Derrick May (hitting), Ron Warner (roving infield), Luis Aguayo (Latin America coordinator), Paul Davis (pitching coach/coordinator, pitching analytics/rehab), George Greer (offensive strategist), Barry Weinberg (senior medical advisor), David Meyer (minor league medical/rehab), Rachel Balkovec (strength/conditioning). **Minor League Equipment Manager:** Dave Vondarhaar.

Farm System

Class	Club (League)	Manager	Hitting Coach	Pitching Coach
Triple-A	Memphis (PCL)	Ron Warner	Mark Budaska	Bryan Eversgerd
Double-A	Springfield (TL)	Mike Shildt	Erik Pappas	Randy Niemann
High A	Palm Beach (FSL)	Dann Bilardello	Roger LaFrancois	Ace Adams
Low A	Peoria (MWL)	Joe Kruzel	Jobel Jimenez	Jason Simontacchi
Short-season	State College (NYP)	Oliver Marmol	Ramon Ortiz	Dernier Orozco
Rookie	Johnson City (APP)	Johnny Rodriguez	Roberto Espinoza	Paul Davis
Rookie	Cardinals (GCL)	Steve Turco	Kleininger Teran	Darwin Marrero
Rookie	Cardinals (DSL)	Fray Peniche	Unavailable	John Matos

Scouting
Fax: (314) 345-9519.
Director, Scouting: Chris Correa.
Coordinator, Baseball Operations/Scouting: Jared Odom. **Special Assistant to Amateur Scouting:** Mike Roberts.
Professional Scouts: Nick Brannon (Huntersville, NC), Patrick Elkins (Baltimore, MD), Jeff Ishii (Chino, CA), Mike Jorgensen (Fenton, MO), Marty Keough (Scottsdale, AZ), Deric McKamey (Bluffton, OH), Ricky Meinhold (Tampa, FL), Joe Rigoli (Parsippany, NJ), Kerry Robinson (Ballwin, MO).
Crosscheckers: Joe Almaraz (San Antonio, TX), Fernando Arango (Davie, FL), Brian Hopkins (Holly Springs, NC), Jeremy Schied (Temecula, CA), Roger Smith (Eastman, GA), Jamal Strong (Surprise, AZ), Matt Swanson (Round Rock, TX).
Area Scouts: Matt Blood (Durham, NC), Nicholas Brannon (Baton Rouge, LA), Jason Bryans (Windsor, Ontario), Dominic "Ty" Boyles (Atlanta, GA), Mike Dibiase (Tampa, FL), Rob Fidler (Seattle, WA), Mike Garciaparra (Orange, CA), Ralph Garr Jr. (Houston, TX), Dirk Kinney (Kansas City, MO), Aaron Krawiec (Gilbert, AZ), Aaron Looper (Shawnee, OK), Tom Lipari (Omaha, NE), Marcus McBeth (Chandler, AZ), Sean Moran (Levittown, PA), Zach Mortimer (Sacramento, CA), Jared Odom (St. Louis, MO), Charles Peterson (Memphis, TN), Juan Ramos (Carolina, PR).
Part-Time Scouts: Todd Stein (St. Louis, MO), Steve Walsh (St. Louis, MO).
Director, International Operations: Moises Rodriguez. **Assistant Director, International Scouting:** Luis Morales.
International Crosschecker: Cesar Geronimo, Jr. **Scouting Supervisor, Dominican Republic:** Angel Ovalles.
Administrator, Dominican Republic Operations: Aaron Rodriguez. **International Scouts:** Omar Rogers (Dominican Republic), Jean Carlos Alvarez (Dominican Republic), Ezequiel Sepulveda (Dominican Republic), Braly Guzman (Dominican Republic), Adel Granadillo (Venezuela), Estuar Ruiz (Venezuela), Carlos Balcazar (Colombia), Crysthiam Blanco (Nicaragua), Jose Gonzalez (Venezuela), Damaso Espino (Panama), Ramon Garcia (Mexico).

San Diego Padres

Office Address: Petco Park, 100 Park Blvd, San Diego, CA 92101.
Mailing Address: PO Box 122000, San Diego, CA 92112.
Telephone: (619) 795-5000. **E-mail address:** comments@padres.com. **Website:** www.padres.com.
Twitter: @padres. **Facebook:** www.facebook.com/padres. **Instagram:** www.instagram.com/padres

Ownership
Operated By: Padres LP. **Executive Chairman:** Ron Fowler. **President/CEO:** Mike Dee.

BUSINESS OPERATIONS

Ron Fowler

Executive Vice President, Business Administration/General Counsel: Erik Greupner.
Senior Director, Business Analytics: Ryan Gustafson. Associate General Counsel: Caroline Perry.

Finance/Administration/Information Technology/Human Resources
Senior VP/CFO: Ronda Sedillo. **Director, Accounting:** Todd Bollman. **Director, Information Technology:** Ray Chan. **Director, Human Resources:** Sara Greenspan.

Community Relations/Military Affairs
Telephone: (619) 795-5265. **Fax:** (619) 795-5266.
VP, Community Relations: Sue Botos. **Director, Military Affairs:** Michael Berenston.
Military Affairs Advisor: J.J. Quinn. **Manager, Community Affairs/Padres Foundation:** Nhu Tran. **Manager, Latino Affairs:** Alex Montoya. **Managers, Community Relations:** Veronica Nogueira, Christina Papasedero.

Entertainment/Marketing/Communications/Creative Services
Senior VP/Chief Marketing Officer: Wayne Partello. **Senior Director, Game Day Presentation:** Matt Coy. **Director, Marketing/Brand Activation:** Katie Jackson. **Director, Content:** Jesse Agler. **Director, Entertainment/Production:** Erik Meyer. **Director, Production:** Brendan Nieto. **Director, Communications:** Shana Wilson.
Manager, Advertising: Nicole Miller. **Manager, Community Marketing:** Darryl Mendoza. **Manager, Fan Programs Technology:** Alex Williams. **Manager, In-Park Entertainment:** Mike Grace. **Manager, Entertainment/Production Engineer:** Hendrik Jaehn. **Manager, Media Relations:** Josh Ishoo. **Manager, Content:** Nicky Patriarca. **Coordinator, Media Relations:** Patrick Kurish. **Multimedia Producer:** Seth Foster.

Ballpark Operations/Hospitality
VP, Chief Hospitality Officer: Scott Marshall. **VP, Ballpark Operations/GM, Petco Park:** Mark Guglielmo. **VP, Petco Park Events:** Jeremy Horowitz. **Senior Director, Ballpark Operations:** Nick Capo. **Director, Security:** John Leas. **Director, Event Operations:** Ken Kawachi. **Director, Field Operations:** Luke Yoder. **Director, Guest Services:** Kameron Durham. **Manager, Security/Transportation:** Matt Kennedy. **Official Scorers:** Jack Murray, Bill Zavestoski.

2015 SCHEDULE

Standard Game Times: 7:10 p.m.; Sat. 5:40; Sun. 1:10

APRIL
6-8 . . . . at Los Angeles (NL)
9-12 . . . . San Francisco
13-15 . . . . Arizona
17-19 . . . . .at Chicago (NL)
20-23 . . . . . . at Colorado
24-26 . . . Los Angeles (NL)
27-29 . . . . Houston

MAY
1-3 . . . . Colorado
4-6 . . . . . at San Francisco
7-10 . . . . at Arizona
12-13 . . . . .at Seattle
14-17 . . . . . . Washington
19-21 . . . . Chicago (NL)
22-24 . . at Los Angeles (NL)

25-27 . . at Los Angeles (AL)
28-31 . . . . Pittsburgh

JUNE
1-3 . . . . New York (NL)
5-7 . . . . . . at Cincinnati
8-11 . . . . at Atlanta
12-14 . . . Los Angeles (NL)
15-16 . . . . Oakland
17-18 . . . . . . .at Oakland
19-21 . . . . . at Arizona
23-25 . . . at San Francisco
26-28 . . . . Arizona
30 . . . . Seattle

JULY
1 . . . . Seattle
2-5 . . . . .at St. Louis

6-8 . . . . at Pittsburgh
10-12 . . . . .at Texas
17-19 . . . . Colorado
20-22 . . . . . San Francisco
23-26 . . . . Miami
28-30 . . . . at New York (NL)
31 . . . . at Miami

AUGUST
1-2 . . . . at Miami
3-6 . . . . at Milwaukee
7-9 . . . . Philadelphia
10-12 . . . . Cincinnati
14-16 . . . . . . at Colorado
17-19 . . . . Atlanta
21-23 . . . . St. Louis
25-27 . . . . . at Washington

28-30 . . . . . at Philadelphia
31 . . . . Texas

SEPTEMBER
1-2 . . . . Texas
3-6 . . . . Los Angeles (NL)
7-9 . . . . Colorado
11-13 . . . . at San Francisco
14-16 . . . . at Arizona
18-20 . . . . . . at Colorado
22-24 . . . . . . San Francisco
25-27 . . . . Arizona
29-30 . . . . Milwaukee

OCTOBER
1 . . . . Milwaukee
2-4 . . . . at Los Angeles (NL)

GENERAL INFORMATION
Stadium (year opened): Petco Park (2004).
Team Colors: Blue, white, tan and gray

Player Representative: Tyson Ross.
Home Dugout: First Base.
Playing Surface: Grass.

Ticketing
Telephone: (619) 795-5500. **Fax:** (619) 795-5034.
VP, Ticket Sales: Eric McKenzie. **Senior Director, Business Development:** Gordon Cooke. **Director, Ticket Operations:** Jim Kiersnowski. **Director, Partnership Services:** Danielle Sergeant. **Director, Membership Services:** Sindi Schug. **Assistant Director, Ticket Vault Operations:** Jeff Brown.

Travel/Clubhouse
Director, Team Travel/Equipment Manager: Brian Prilaman . **Assistant Equipment Manager/Umpire Room Attendant:** Tony Petricca. **Assistant to Equipment Manager:** Spencer Dallin. **Visiting Clubhouse Manager:** David Bacharach.

BASEBALL OPERATIONS

Telephone: (619) 795-5077. **Fax:** (619) 795-5361.
Executive VP/General Manager: AJ Preller.
VP/Assistant GM: Fred Uhlman Jr. **VP, Scouting Operations:** Don Welke. **Senior Advisor to GM/Director, Pro Scouting:** Logan White. **Assistant GM:** Josh Stein. **Senior Advisor/ Special Assignment Scout:** Randy Smith. **Director, Baseball Operations:** Nick Ennis. **Director, Team Travel/Equipment Manager:** Brian Prilaman. **Architect, Baseball Systems:** Wells Oliver. **Developer, Baseball Systems:** Brian McBurney. **Advance Scout, Major League:** Ben Sestanovich. **Video Coordinator, Clubhouse:** Mike Tompkins. **Executive Assistant:** Julie Myers.

A.J. Preller

Major League Staff
Manager: Bud Black.
Coaches: Bench—Dave Roberts; **Pitching**—Darren Balsley; **Hitting**—Mark Kotsay; **Assistant Hitting**—Alonzo Powell; **First Base**—Jose Valentin; **Third Base**—Glenn Hoffman; **Bullpen**—Willie Blair.

Medical/Training
Club Physician: Scripps Clinic Medical Staff. **Head Athletic Trainer:** Todd Hutcheson. **Assistant Athletic Trainer:** Paul Navarro. **Massage Therapist:** Philip Kerr. **Strength/Conditioning Coach:** Brett McCabe.

Player Development
Telephone: (619) 795-5343. **Fax:** (619) 795-5036.
Director, Player Development: Sam Geaney.
Manager, Minor Leagues Operations: Warren Miller. **Equipment Manager, Player Development:** Zach Nelson. **Coordinator, Dominican Republic Operations:** Cesar Rizik. **Assistant Administrator, Dominican Republic Operations:** Jesus Negrette. **Roving Instructors:** Luis Ortiz (Field/Hitting Coordinator), Mark Prior (Pitching Coordinator), Eddie Rodriguez (Infield Coordinator), Tarrik Brock (Outfield/Baserunning Coordinator), Ryley Westman (Catching Coordinator), Eric Junge (Minor League Pitching Instructor), Gorman Heimueller (Roving Pitching Instructor), Evaristo Lantigua (Coordinator, Latin American Instruction), Joseph Tarantino (Medical Coordinator), Jordan Wolf (Strength/Conditioning Coordinator), Ryan Bitzel (Rehab Coordinator).

Farm System

Class	Farm Club (League)	Manager	Hitting Coach	Pitching Coach
Triple-A	El Paso (PCL)	Pat Murphy	Jody Davis	Bronswell Patrick
Double-A	San Antonio (TL)	Jamie Quirk	Morgan Burkhart	Jimmy Jones
High A	Lake Elsinore (CAL)	Michael Collins	Rod Barajas	Glendon Rusch
Low A	Fort Wayne (MWL)	Francisco Morales	Unavailable	Burt Hooton
Short-season	Tri-City (NWL)	Unavailable	Unavailable	Nelson Cruz
Rookie	Padres (AZL)	Anthony Contreras	Carlos Sosa	Ben Fritz
Rookie	Padres (DSL)	Evaristo Lantigua	Julio Ramirez	Mel Rojas

Scouting
Director, Scouting: Mark Conner (Hendersonville, TN). **Director, International Scouting:** Chris Kemp. **Assistant to Director, Scouting:** Eddie Ciafardini (San Diego, CA). **Video Coordinator, Scouting/Player Development:** Matt Schaffner (Peoria, AZ). **National Crosscheckers:** Sean Campbell (San Diego, CA), Kurt Kemp (Peachtree City, GA). **Amateur Crosschecker:** Rob St. Julien (Scott, LA)
Supervisors: Pete DeYoung (Carlsbad, CA), Tim Holt (Allen, TX), Chipw Lawrence (Palmetto, FL), Andrew Salvo (Pace, FL). **Amateur Scouts:** Stephen Baker (Houston, TX), Justin Baughman (Portland, OR), Willie Bosque (Winter Garden, FL), Jim Bretz (South Windsor, CT), Tom Burns (Harrisburg, PA), Jeff Curtis (Arlington, TX), Lane Decker (Piedmont, OK), Josh Emmerick (Oceanside, CA), Chris Kelly (Sarasota, FL), Dave Lottsfeldt (Denver, CO), Brent Mayne (Costa Mesa, CA), Steve Moritz (Kennesaw, GA), Sam Ray (San Francisco, CA), Jeff Stewart (Normal, IL), Tyler Stubblefield (Acworth, GA), Matt Thomas (Nashville, TN). **Part-Time Scouts:** Willie Ronda (Las Lomas Rio Piedras, PR), Murray Zuk (Souris, Manitoba).
Special Assignment Scouts: Senior Advisor/Special Assignment Scout: Randy Smith (Phoenix, AZ). **Professional Scouts:** Steve Lyons (San Antonio, TX), Chris Bourjos (Scottsdale, AZ), Jim Elliott (Winston-Salem, NC), Al Hargesheimer (Arlington Heights, IL), Mark Merila (Minneapolis, MN), Dominic Scavone (Palm Harbor, FL), Mike Venafro (Fort Myers, FL). **Coordinator, Latin American Scouting:** Felix Feliz. **Supervisor, Venezuela:** Yfrain Linares. **International Supervisor:** Trevor Schumm. **International Crosschecker:** Chip Lawrence. **International Scouts:** Antonio Alejos (Venezuela), Milton Croes (Aruba), Marcial Del Valle (Colombia), Emenejildo Diaz (Dominican Republic), Elvin Jarquin (Nicaragua), Martin Jose (Dominican Republic), Victor Magdaleno (Venezuela), Ricardo Montenegro (Panama), Luis Prieto (Venezuela), Ysrael Rojas (Dominican Republic), Jose Salado (Dominican Republic). **Part-time Scouts:** Andres Cabadias (Colombia), Ryan Drees (Japan), Hoon NamGung (South Korea), Damian Shanahan (Australia).

San Francisco Giants

Office Address: AT&T Park, 24 Willie Mays Plaza, San Francisco, CA 94107.
Telephone: (415) 972-2000. **Fax:** (415) 947-2800. **Website:** sfgiants.com, sfgigantes.com.

Ownership
Operated by: San Francisco Baseball Associates L.P.

BUSINESS OPERATIONS

President/Chief Executive Officer: Laurence M. Baer. **Special Assistant:** Willie Mays.
Senior Advisor: Willie McCovey.

Finance
Senior Vice President Finance: Lisa Pantages. **Senior VP/Chief Information Officer:** Bill Schlough. **Senior Director, Information Technology:** Ken Logan.

Human Resources/Legal
Chief People Officer: Leilani Gayles. **VP, Human Resources:** Joyce Thomas. **Senior VP/General Counsel:** Jack F. Bair. **VP/Deputy General Counsel:** Elizabeth R. Murphy.

Communications
Telephone: (415) 972-2445. **Fax:** (415) 947-2800.

Laurence M. Baer

Senior VP, Communications/Senior Advisor to the CEO: Staci Slaughter. **Senior Director, Broadcast Services:** Maria Jacinto. **Senior Director, Media Relations:** Jim Moorehead. **Director, Baseball Information:** Matt Chisholm. **Manager, Hispanic Marketing/Media Relations:** Erwin Higueros. **Coordinator, Baseball Information/Media Relations:** Liam Connolly. **Media Relations Assistant:** Megan Nelson. **VP, Public Affairs/Community Relations:** Shana Daum. **VP, Creative Services/Visual Identity:** Nancy Donati. **Director, Photography/Archives:** Missy Mikulecky.

Business Operations
Senior VP, Business Operations: Mario Alioto. **Managing VP, Sponsorship/New Business Development:** Jason Pearl. **VP, Special Events/Marketing Activation:** Danny Dann. **Director, Promotions/Event Production:** Valerie McGuire. **Director, Sponsorship Sales:** Bill Lawrence. **VP, Retail Operations:** Dave Martinez.

Ticketing
Telephone: (415) 972-2000. **Fax:** (415) 972-2500.
Managing VP, Ticket Sales/Services: Russ Stanley. **VP, Sales:** Jeff Tucker.
VP, Strategic Revenue Services: Jerry Drobny. **Senior Director, Ticket Services:** Devin Lutes. **VP, Client Relations:** Annemarie Hastings.

Marketing
Senior VP, Marketing: Tom McDonald. **Senior Director, SFG Productions/Entertainment:** Chris Gargano. **Director/Executive Producer:** Keith Macri. **PA Announcer:** Renel Brooks-Moon.

2015 SCHEDULE
Standard Game Times: 7:15 p.m.; Sun. 1:05

APRIL	JUNE	AUGUST	SEPTEMBER
6-8. . . . . at Arizona	1-3. . . . . Pittsburgh	1-2. . . . . .at Texas	1-2. . . . at Los Angeles (NL)
9-12 . . . . . . at San Diego	5-7. . . . . . at Philadelphia	3-5. . . . . at Atlanta	3-6. . . . . at Colorado
13-15 . . . . .Colorado	9-11 . . . . . at New York (NL)	6-9. . . . . . .at Chicago (NL)	7-9. . . . . at Arizona
16-19 . . . . .Arizona	12-14 . . . . .Arizona	11-12 . . . . Houston	11-13 . . . . San Diego
21-23 . . . Los Angeles (NL)	15-16 . . . . Seattle	13-16 . . . . . .Washington	14-16 . . . . Cincinnati
24-26 . . . . . . at Colorado	17-18 . . . . .at Seattle	17-19 . . . . . . .at St. Louis	18-20 . . . . Arizona
27-29 . . at Los Angeles (NL)	19-21 . . at Los Angeles (NL)	20-23 . . . . . at Pittsburgh	22-24 . . . . . at San Diego
	23-25 . . . . San Diego	25-27 . . . . . Chicago (NL)	25-27 . . . . .at Oakland
MAY	26-28 . . . . .Colorado		28-30 . . . .Los Angeles (NL)
1-3. . . . . Los Angeles (AL)	30 . . . . at Miami	6-8. . . . . . .New York (NL)	
4-6. . . . . San Diego		10-12 . . . . . .Philadelphia	OCTOBER
7-10 . . . . .Miami	JULY	17-19 . . . . at Arizona	1 . . . . . . .Los Angeles (NL)
12-13 . . . . . . at Houston	1-2. . . . . at Miami	20-22 . . . . . at San Diego	2-4. . . . . .Colorado
14-17 . . . . . at Cincinnati	3-5. . . . . . at Washington	24-26 . . . . Oakland	
19-21 . . . Los Angeles (NL)	25-27 . . . . . at Milwaukee	27-29 . . . . . .Milwaukee	28-30 . . . . St. Louis
22-24 . . . . . . at Colorado	28-31 . . . . Atlanta	31 . . . . .at Texas	31 . . . . at Los Angeles (NL)

GENERAL INFORMATION
Stadium (year opened): AT&T Park (2000).
Team Colors: Black, orange and cream.

Player Representative: Matt Cain.
Home Dugout: Third Base.
Playing Surface: Grass.

Facilities

Senior VP, Administration: Alfonso Felder. **Senior VP, Ballpark Operations:** Jorge Costa. **VP, Ballpark Operations:** Gene Telucci. **Senior Director, Security:** Tinie Roberson. **VP, Guest Services:** Rick Mears. **Director, Field Operations:** Greg Elliott.

BASEBALL OPERATIONS

Telephone: (415) 972-1922. **Fax:** (415) 947-2929.
Senior VP/General Manager: Brian R. Sabean. **Exec Assistant to GM:** Karen Sweeney.
VP/Assistant GM, Player Personnel: Dick Tidrow. **VP/Assistant GM:** Bobby Evans. **Special Assistant to GM:** Felipe Alou. **VP, Pro Scouting/Player Evaluation:** Jeremy Shelley. **Senior Advisor, Baseball Operations:** Tony Siegle. **Senior Director, Minor League Operations/ Quantitative Analysis:** Yeshayah Goldfarb. **Senior Advisor, Home Clubhouse:** Miguel Murphy. **Senior Director, Team Travel/Home Clubhouse Manager:** Bret Alexander. **Senior Director, Arizona Baseball Operations/Major League Equipment Manager:** Alan Lee. **Coordinator, Organizational Travel:** Mike Scardino. **Coordinators, Video Coaching System:** Danny Martin, Yo Miyamoto. **Home Clubhouse Assistants:** Brandon Evans, David Lowenstein.

Brian Sabean

Major League Staff

Manager: Bruce Bochy.
Coaches: Bench—Ron Wotus; **Pitching**—Dave Righetti; **Hitting**—Hensley Meulens/Joe Lefebvre; **First Base**—Bill Hayes; **Third Base**—Roberto Kelly; **Bullpen**—Mark Gardner.
Bullpen Catchers: Eli Whiteside, Taira Uematsu. **Assistant Coach/Video Replay Analyst:** Shawon Dunston. **Batting Practice Pitcher/Video Replay Analyst:** Chad Chop.

Medical/Training

Team Physicians: Dr. Robert Murray, Dr. Ken Akizuki, Dr. Anthony Saglimbeni. **Head Trainer:** Dave Groeschner. **Assistant Trainers:** Anthony Reyes, Eric Ortega. **Strength/Conditioning Coach:** Carl Kochan. **Assistant Strength/ Conditioning Coach:** Geoff Head. **Coordinator, Medical Administration:** Chrissy Yuen.

Player Development

Director, Player Development: Shane Turner. **Coordinator, Instruction/Minor League Hitting:** Steve Decker. **Coordinator, Minor League Pitching:** Bert Bradley. **Senior Consultant, Player Personnel:** Jack Hiatt. **Special Assistants, Player Development:** Joe Amalfitano, Jim Davenport, Fred Stanley. **Minor League Coach:** Tom Trebelhorn. **Minor League Roving Instructors:** Gary Davenport (infield), Lee Smith (pitching), Jeff Tackett (catching), Kirt Manwaring (catching). **Senior Manager, Player Personnel Administration:** Clara Ho. **Coordinator, Minor League Operations:** Eric Flemming. **Coordinator, Arizona Minor League Operations:** Gabriel Alvarez.

Farm System

Class	Farm Club (League)	Manager	Hitting Coach	Pitching Coach
Triple-A	Sacramento (PCL)	Bob Mariano	Andy Skeels	Dwight Bernard
Double-A	Richmond (EL)	Jose Alguacil	Ken Joyce	Steve Kline
High A	San Jose (CAL)	Russ Morman	Lipso Nava	Michael Couchee
Low A	Augusta (SAL)	Nestor Rojas	Todd Linden	Jerry Cram
Short-season	Salem-Keizer (NWL)	Kyle Haines	Ricky Ward	Matt Yourkin
Rookie	Giants (AZL)	Henry Cotto	Billy Horton	Larry McCall
Rookie	Giants (DSL)	Carlos Valderrama	Juan Parra	Marcos Aguasvivas

Scouting

Telephone: (415) 972-2360. **Fax:** (415) 947-2929.
VP/Assistant GM, Scouting/International Operations: John Barr (Haddonfield, NJ).
Coordinator, Scouting Administration: Adam Nieting. **Scouting Assistant:** Jose Bonilla. **Senior Advisors, Scouting:** Ed Creech (Moultrie, GA), Lee Elder (Ocean Springs, MS), John Flannery (Austin, TX), Doug Mapson (Chandler, AZ), Matt Nerland (San Francisco, CA), Paul Turco Sr. (Sarasota, FL). **Special Assignment Scouts:** Joe Bochy (Plant City, FL), Pat Burrell (Scottsdale, AZ), Tom Korenek (Houston, TX), Darren Wittcke (Sherwood, OR). **Advance Scouts:** Steve Balboni (Berkeley Heights, NJ), Keith Champion (Ballwin, MO). **Major League Scouts:** Brian Johnson (Detroit, MI), Michael Kendall (Rancho Palos Verde, CA), Glenn Tufts (Bridgewater, MA), Paul Turco Jr (Chicago, IL), Tom Zimmer (Seminole, FL). **Senior Consultants, Scouting:** Dick Cole (Costa Mesa, CA).
Supervisors: Midwest—Arnold Brathwaite (Grand Prairie, TX); **Northeast**—John Castleberry (High Point, NC); **Southeast**—Mike Metcalf (Sarasota, FL); **West**—Joe Strain (Englewood, CO). **Area Scouts: Northeast**—Ray Callari (Cote Saint Luc, Quebec), Kevin Christman (Noblesville, IN), John DiCarlo (Glenwood, NJ), Mark O'Sullivan (Hartford, MA), Donnie Suttles (Marion, NC); **Southeast**—Jose Alou (Boynton Beach, FL), Jim Gabella (Deltona, FL), Andrew Jefferson (Atlanta, GA), Jeff Wood (Birmingham, AL); **Midwest**—Todd Coryell (Aurora, IL), James Mouton (Missouri City, TX), Daniel Murray (Prairie Village, KS), Todd Thomas (Dallas, TX), Hugh Walker (Jonesboro, AR); **West**—Brad Cameron (Los Alamitos, CA), Chuck Fick (Newbury Park, CA), Chuck Hensley Jr. (Mesa, AZ), Keith Snider (Stockton, CA), Matt Woodward (Camas, WA). **West Coast Video/Area Scout:** Colin Sabean (San Francisco, CA). **Part-Time Scouts:** Bob Barth (Williamstown, NJ), Jorge Posada Sr. (Rio Piedras, PR), Tim Rock (Orlando, FL).
Director, Dominican Operations: Pablo Peguero. **Coordinator, Pacific Rim Scouting:** John Cox (Yucaipa, CA). **International Crosschecker:** Joe Salermo (Hallandale Beach, FL). **Latin America Crosschecker:** Junior Roman (San Sebastian, PR). **Venezuela Supervisor:** Ciro Villalobos. **Assistant Director, Dominican Operations:** Felix Peguero. **International Scouts:** Jonathan Arraiz (Venezuela), Jonathan Bautista (Dominican Republic), Rogelio Castillo (Panama), Phillip Elhage (Curacao/Bonaire/Aruba), Gabriel Elias (Dominican Republic), Edgar Fernandez (Venezuela), Jeff Kusumoto (Japan), Juan Marquez (Venezuela), Daniel Mavarez (Colombia), Oscar Montero (Venezuela), Sandy Moreno (Nicaragua), Ruddy Moretta (Dominican Republic), Jim Patterson (Australia), Luis Pena (Mexico), Jesus Stephens (Dominican Republic).

Seattle Mariners

Office Address: 1250 First Ave. South, Seattle, WA 98134.
Mailing Address: PO Box 4100, Seattle, WA 98194.
Telephone: (206) 346-4000. **Fax:** (206) 346-4400. **Website:** www.mariners.com.

Ownership
Board of Directors: Minoru Arakawa, John Ellis, Buck Ferguson, Chris Larson, Howard Lincoln, Wayne Perry, Frank Shrontz.
Chair/CEO: Howard Lincoln.
President/Chief Operating Officer: Kevin Mather.

BUSINESS OPERATIONS

Finance
Senior VP, Finance: Tim Kornegay. **Controller:** Greg Massey. **Senior VP, Human Resources:** Marianne Short.

Corporate Business/Marketing
Executive VP, Business/Operations: Bob Aylward. **VP, Corporate Business/Community Relations:** Joe Chard. **Senior Director, Corporate Business:** Ingrid Russell-Narcisse. **Senior Director, Community Relations:** Gina Hasson. **Manager, Community Programs:** Sean Grindley. **VP, Marketing:** Kevin Martinez. **Senior Director, Marketing:** Gregg Greene.

Sales
VP, Sales: Frances Traisman. **Director, Ticket Sales:** Cory Carbary. **Director, Group Business Development:** Bob Hellinger.

Howard Lincoln

Baseball Information/Communications
Telephone: (206) 346-4000. **Fax:** (206) 346-4400.
Senior VP, Communications: Randy Adamack.
Senior Director, Baseball Information: Tim Hevly. **Assistant Director, Baseball Information:** Jeff Evans. **Manager, Baseball Information:** Kelly Munro. **Manager, Baseball Information:** Fernando Alcala.
Director, Public Information: Rebecca Hale. **Director, Graphic Design:** Carl Morton.

Ticketing
Telephone: (206) 346-4001. **Fax:** (206) 346-4100.
Senior Director, Ticketing/Parking Operations: Malcolm Rogel. **Director, Ticket Services:** Jennifer Sweigert.

Stadium Operations
VP, Ballpark Operations: Joe Myhra. **Senior Director, Safeco Field Operations:** Tony Pereira. **Director, Engineering/Maintenance:** Ryan van Maarth. **Director, Events:** Alisia Anderson. **VP, Information Services:** Dave Curry. **Director, Information Systems:** Oliver Roy. **Director, Database/Applications:** Justin Stolmeier. **Director,**

2015 SCHEDULE
Standard Game Times: 7:10 p.m.; Sun. 1:10.

APRIL
6-8 . . . . . Los Angeles (AL)
10-12 . . . . .at Oakland
13-15 . . at Los Angeles (NL)
17-19 . . . . Texas
20-22 . . . . Houston
24-26 . . . . .Minnesota
27-29 . . . . .at Texas
30 . . . . at Houston

MAY
1-3 . . . . at Houston
4-6 . . . . at Los Angeles (AL)
8-10 . . . . Oakland
12-13 . . . . San Diego
14-17 . . . . Boston
19-21 . . . . . . .at Baltimore

22-24 . . . . at Toronto
25-27 . . . . . . at Tampa Bay
28-31 . . . . Cleveland

JUNE
1-3 . . . . .New York (AL)
4-7 . . . . .Tampa Bay
9-11 . . . . .at Cleveland
12-14 . . . . at Houston
15-16 . . . . at San Francisco
17-18 . . . . .San Francisco
19-21 . . . . Houston
22-24 . . . . Kansas City
26-28 . . at Los Angeles (AL)
30 . . . . at San Diego

JULY
1 . . . . at San Diego

2-5 . . . . .at Oakland
6-8 . . . . Detroit
9-12 . . . . .Los Angeles (AL)
17-19 . . . . at New York (AL)
20-23 . . . . at Detroit
24-26 . . . . .Toronto
27-29 . . . . .Arizona
30-31 . . . . . at Minnesota

AUGUST
1-2 . . . . at Minnesota
3-5 . . . . at Colorado
7-9 . . . . Texas
10-12 . . . . Baltimore
14-16 . . . . . . at Boston
17-19 . . . . .at Texas
21-23 . . . . . Chicago (AL)

24-26 . . . . Oakland
27-30 . . . .at Chicago (AL)
31 . . . . at Houston

SEPTEMBER
1-2 . . . . at Houston
4-6 . . . . .at Oakland
7-10 . . . . Texas
11-13 . . . . .Colorado
14-16 . . . . Los Angeles (AL)
18-20 . . . . .at Texas
22-24 . . . . . .at Kansas City
25-27 . . at Los Angeles (AL)
28-30 . . . . Houston

OCTOBER
2-4 . . . . Oakland

GENERAL INFORMATION
Stadium (year opened): Safeco Field (1999).
Team Colors: Northwest green, silver and navy blue.
Player Representative: Charlie Furbush.
Home Dugout: First Base.
Playing Surface: Grass.

Procurement: Norma Cantu. **Head Groundskeeper:** Bob Christofferson. **Assistant Head Groundskeepers:** Tim Wilson, Leo Liebert. **PA Announcer:** Tom Hutyler. **Official Scorer:** Eric Radovich.

Merchandising
Senior Director, Merchandise: Jim LaShell. **Director, Retail Merchandising:** Julie McGillivray.

Travel/Clubhouse
Director, Team Travel: Ron Spellecy.
Clubhouse Manager: Ryan Stiles. **Visiting Clubhouse Manager:** Ted Walsh. **Video Coordinator:** Jimmy Hartley. **Assistant Video Coordinator:** Craig Manning.

BASEBALL OPERATIONS

Jack Zduriencik

Executive VP/General Manager: Jack Zduriencik.
Assistant GM: Jeff Kingston. **Special Assistants:** Roger Hansen, Ken Madeja, Joe McIlvaine, Ted Simmons, Pete Vuckovich. **Manager, Baseball Operations:** Caleb Peiffer. **Administrator, Baseball Operations:** Debbie Larsen.

Major League Staff
Manager: Lloyd McClendon.
Coaches: Bench—Trent Jewett; **Pitching**—Rick Waits; **Hitting**—Howard Johnson; **First Base**—Chris Woodward; **Third Base**—Rich Donnelly; **Assistant Hitting/Outfield Coach**—Andy Van Slyke; **Bullpen**—Mike Rojas; **Bullpen Catcher**—Jason Phillips.

Medical/Training
Medical Director: Dr. Edward Khalfayan. **Club Physician:** Dr. Mitchel Storey. **Head Trainer:** Rick Griffin. **Assistant Trainers:** Rob Nodine, Matt Toth, Yoshi Nakazawa. **Strength/Conditioning:** James Clifford, Chad Uihlein.

Player Development
Telephone: (206) 346-4316. **Fax:** (206) 346-4300.
Director, Player Development: Chris Gwynn. **Administrator, Minor League Operations:** Jan Plein. **Assistant, Minor League Operations:** Jack Mosimann. **Coordinator, Minor League Instruction:** Jack Howell. **Coordinator, Athletic Trainers:** James Southard. **Latin Athletic Trainer Coordinator:** Javier Alvidrez. **Assistant Athletic Trainer:** Ben Fraser. **Rehab Pitching Coordinator:** Gary Wheelock. **Performance Specialist Coordinator:** Rob Fumagalli. **Roving Instructors:** Terry Clark (pitching), Dan Wilson (catching), Lee May Jr. (hitting), Jim Pankovits (infield), Brant Brown (outfield), Daren Brown (bunting/baserunning), Alvin Davis (special assignment), Jose Moreno (Latin America field), Nasusel Cabrera (Latin America pitching).

Farm System

Class	Club (League)	Manager	Hitting Coach	Pitching Coach
Triple-A	Tacoma (PCL)	Pat Listach	Cory Snyder	Jaime Navarro
Double-A	Jackson (SL)	James Horner	Roy Howell	Lance Painter
High A	Bakersfield (CAL)	Eddie Menchaca	Max Venable	Andrew Lorraine
Low A	Clinton (MWL)	Scott Steinmann	Mike Kinkade	Cibney Bello
Short-season	Everett (NWL)	Rob Mummau	Mike Davis	Jason Blanton
Rookie	Peoria (AZL)	Darrin Garner	Andy Bottin	Rich Dorman
Rookie	Mariners (DSL)	Jose Umbria	Jose Guillen	Danielin Acevedo
Rookie	Mariners (VSL)	Russell Vasquez	Selwyn Langaigne	Carlos Hernandez

Scouting
Telephone: (206) 346-4314. **Fax:** (206) 346-4300.
Director, Professional Scouting: Tom Allison. **Pro Scouting Assistant:** Jordan Bley. **Director, Amateur Scouting:** Tom McNamara. **Assistant Scouting Director/Senior National Crosschecker:** Mark Lummus. **Scouting Administrator:** Hallie Larson. **Amateur Scouting Assistant:** Ken Wade. **Amateur Analyst:** Anthony Aloisi.
Major League Scouts: Micah Franklin (Gilbert, AZ), Roger Hansen (Stanwood, WA), Lee MacPhail (Shaker Heights, OH), Ken Madeja (Novi, MI), Bill Masse (Manchester, CT), Joe McIlvaine (Newtown Square, PA), John McMichen (Tampa, FL), Joe Nelson (West Palm Beach, FL), Joe Nigro (Staten Island, NY), Duane Shaffer (Goodyear, AZ), Ted Simmons (Chesterfield, MO), Ross Vecchio (Canonsburg, PA), Pete Vuckovich (Johnstown, PA), Woody Woodward (Palm Coast, FL).
Amateur Scouts/Territorial Supervisors: West—Jeremy Booth (Katy, TX), **Midwest**—Jesse Kapellusch (Emporia, KS), **Canada**—Brian Nichols (Taunton, MA), **Northeast**—Alex Smith (Abingdon, MD); **Southeast**—Garrett Ball (Atlanta, GA); **East Coast**—Devitt Moore (Durham, NC).
Area Supervisors: Joe Barbera (Elliott City, MD), Jay Catalano (Nashville, TN), Ben Collman (Austin, TX), Dustin Evans (Atlanta, GA), Dennis Gonsalves (Torrance, CA), Ryan Holmes (Simi Valley, CA), John Hughes (Thiells, NY), Steve Markovich (Highlands, NJ), Mike Moriarty (Marlton, NJ), Rob Mummau (Palm Harbor, FL), Dana Papasedero (Chelan, WA), Gary Patchett (Murrieta, CA), Chris Pelekoudas (Mesa, AZ), Stacey Pettis (Antioch, CA), Myron Pines (Garden Grove, CA) Tony Russo (Montgomery, IL), Jeff Sakamoto (Tualatin, OR), Rafael Santo Domingo (Puerto Rico), Noel Sevilla (Miami, FL), Bob Steinkamp (Beatrice, NE), John Wiedenbauer (Ormond Beach, FL). **International Scouting Director:** Tim Kissner (Kirkland, WA). **Supervisor, Dominican Republic:** Eddy Toledo (Santo Domingo, DR). **Coordinator, Pacific Rim/Mexico:** Ted Heid (Glendale, AZ). **Administrative Director, Dominican Operations:** Martin Valerio (Santo Domingo, Dominican Republic). **Coordinator, Venezuelan Operations:** Emilio Carrasquel (Barquisimeto, Venezuela). **International Crosschecker:** Scott Hunter (Mt. Laurel, NJ). **Canada/Europe Coordinator:** Wayne Norton. **International Scouts:** Tristan Loetzsch (QLD, Australia), Manabu Noto (Saitama, Japan).

Tampa Bay Rays

Office Address: Tropicana Field, One Tropicana Drive, St. Petersburg, FL 33705.
Telephone: (727) 825-3137. **Fax:** (727) 825-3111. **Website:** www.raysbaseball.com.

Ownership
Principal Owner: Stuart Sternberg.
President: Brian Auld.

BUSINESS OPERATIONS

Senior Vice President, Administration/General Counsel: John Higgins. **Senior VP:** Mark Fernandez. **Senior VP, Strategy/Development:** Melanie Lenz. **VP, Strategy/Development:** William Walsh. **VP, Human Resources/Administration:** Bill Wiener, Jr. **VP, IT:** Juan Ramirez. **Senior Director, Human Resources:** Jennifer Tran. **Senior Director, Guest Relations:** Cass Halpin.

Finance
VP, Finance: Rob Gagliardi. **Controller:** Patrick Smith. **Director, Financial Planning/Analysis:** Jason Gray

Marketing/Community Relations
VP, Branding/Fan Experience: Darcy Raymond. **Director, Marketing:** Carey Cox. **Director, Promotions:** Stephon Thomas. **Senior Director, Community Relations:** Suzanne Luecke.

Stuart Sternberg

Communications/Broadcasting
Phone: (727) 825-3242.
VP, Communications: Rick Vaughn. **Senior Director, Communications:** Dave Haller. **Senior Director, Broadcasting:** Larry McCabe.

Corporate Partnerships
VP, Corporate Partnerships: Josh Bullock. **Director, Corporate Partnership Services:** Devin O'Connell.

Ticket Sales
Phone: (888) FAN-RAYS. **VP, Sales/Service:** Brian Richeson. **Senior Director, Season Ticket Sales/Service:** Jeff Tanzer. **Director, Ticket Operations:** Robert Bennett. **Assistant Director, Ticket Operations:** Ken Mallory.

Stadium Operations
VP, Operations/Facilities: Rick Nafe. **Senior Director, Stadium Operations:** Scott Kelyman, Tom Karac. **Director, Stadium Operations:** Chris Raineri. **Head Groundskeeper:** Dan Moeller.

Travel/Clubhouse
Director, Team Travel/Clubhouse Operations: Chris Westmoreland. **Manager, Home Clubhouse:** Jose Fernandez. **Manager, Visitor Clubhouse:** Guy Gallagher. **Video Coordinator:** Chris Fernandez.

2015 SCHEDULE
Standard Game Times: 7:10 p.m.; Sun. 1:40.

APRIL
6-8 . . . . Baltimore
10-12 . . . . at Miami
13-16 . . . . at Toronto
17-19 . . . . . New York (AL)
21-23 . . . . Boston
24-26 . . . . .Toronto
27-29 . . . . at New York (AL)

MAY
1-3 . . . . .at Baltimore
4-6 . . . . at Boston
7-10 . . . . Texas
11-14 . . . . . New York (AL)
15-17 . . . . . at Minnesota
19-20 . . . . at Atlanta
21-24 . . . . Oakland

25-27 . . . . Seattle
29-31 . . . . . .at Baltimore

JUNE
1-3 . . . at Los Angeles (AL)
4-7 . . . . .at Seattle
9-11 . . . . .Los Angeles (AL)
12-14 . . . . . . Chicago (AL)
15-16 . . . . . . Washington
17-18 . . . . . at Washington
19-21 . . . . . . .at Cleveland
22-24 . . . . .Toronto
26-28 . . . . Boston
29-30 . . . . Cleveland

JULY
1-2 . . . . Cleveland
3-5 . . . . . at New York (AL)

7-9 . . . . . . .at Kansas City
10-12 . . . . Houston
17-19 . . . . at Toronto
20-22 . . . . at Philadelphia
24-26 . . . . Baltimore
27-29 . . . . Detroit
31 . . . . at Boston

AUGUST
1-2 . . . . at Boston
3-5 . . . . . .at Chicago (AL)
7-9 . . . . . .New York (NL)
11-12 . . . . Atlanta
14-16 . . . . .at Texas
17-20 . . . . . . at Houston
21-23 . . . . . . .at Oakland
25-27 . . . . . . .Minnesota

28-30 . . . . . . Kansas City
31 . . . . .at Baltimore

SEPTEMBER
1-2 . . . . .at Baltimore
4-6 . . . . . at New York (AL)
7-9 . . . . at Detroit
11-13 . . . . Boston
14-16 . . . . . .New York (AL)
17-20 . . . . Baltimore
21-24 . . . . at Boston
25-27 . . . . . . at Toronto
29-30 . . . . .Miami

OCTOBER
1 . . . . .Miami
2-4 . . . . .Toronto

GENERAL INFORMATION
Stadium (year opened): Tropicana Field (1998).
Team Colors: Dark blue, light blue, yellow.
Player Representative: Matt Moore.
Home Dugout: First Base.
Playing Surface: AstroTurf Game Day Grass 3D-60 H.

BASEBALL OPERATIONS

President, Baseball Operations: Matt Silverman.
VPs, Baseball Operations: Chaim Bloom, Erik Neander. **Director, Major League Administration:** Sandy Dengler. **Director, Baseball Research/Development:** James Click. **Architect, Baseball Systems:** Brian Plexico. **Developer, Baseball Systems:** Bradley Ankrom. **Special Advisor, Baseball Operations:** George Hendrick. **Analytics Developer, Baseball Systems:** Michael Vanger. **Coordinator, Baseball Research/Development:** Peter Bendix. **Analysts, Baseball Research/Development:** Joshua Kalk, Shawn Hoffman, Jonathan Erlichman. **Coordinator, Baseball Operations:** Graham Tyler. **Video Coordinator, Baseball Operations:** Ryan Bristow. **Assistant, Baseball Research/Development:** Adam Esquer. **Assistant, Baseball Operations:** Andrew Ball.

Matthew Silverman

Major League Staff
Manager: Kevin Cash.
Coaches: Bench—Tom Foley; **Pitching**—Jim Hickey; **Hitting**—Derek Shelton; **First Base**—Rocco Baldelli; **Third Base**—Charlie Montoyo; **Bullpen**—Stan Boroski; **Hitting/Catching**—Jamie Nelson.

Medical/Training
Medical Director: Dr. James Andrews. **Medical Team Physician:** Dr. Michael Reilly. **Orthopedic Team Physician:** Dr. Koco Eaton. **Head Athletic Trainer:** Ron Porterfield. **Assistant Athletic Trainers:** Paul Harker, Mark Vinson. **Strength/Conditioning Coach:** Kevin Barr.

Player Development
Telephone: (727) 825-3267. **Fax:** (727) 825-3493.
Director, Minor League Operations: Mitch Lukevics.
Assistant Director, Minor League Operations: Jeff McLerran. **Administrator, International/Minor League Operations:** Giovanna Rodriguez. **Field Coordinators:** Jim Hoff, Bill Evers. **Minor League Coordinators:** Skeeter Barnes (outfield/baserunning), Dick Bosman (pitching), Steve Livesey (hitting), Paul Hoover (catching), Chad Mottola (hitting), Dewey Robinson (pitching), Jorge Moncada (pitching), Joe Benge (medical), Joel Smith (rehabilitation), Chris Tomashoff (Latin American medical), Jairo De La Rosa (Latin American Cultural), Trung Cao (strength/conditioning). **Equipment Manager:** Tim McKechney. **Assistant Equipment Manager:** Shane Rossetti. **Assistant, International/Minor League Operations:** Alex Zampier.

Farm System

Class	Club (League)	Manager	Hitting Coach	Pitching Coach
Triple-A	Durham (IL)	Jared Sandberg	Dave Myers	Kyle Snyder
Double-A	Montgomery (SL)	Brady Williams	Ozzie Timmons	R.C. Lichtenstein
High A	Charlotte (FSL)	Michael Johns	Joe Szekely	Steve Watson
Low A	Bowling Green (MWL)	Reinaldo Ruiz	Dan Dement	Bill Moloney
Short-season	Hudson Valley (NYP)	Tim Parenton	Manny Castillo	Brian Reith
Rookie	Princeton (APP)	Danny Sheaffer	Craig Albernaz	Jose Gonzalez
Rookie	Rays (GCL)	Jim Morrison	Wuarnner Rincones	Marty DeMerritt
Rookie	Rays (DSL)	Julio Zorrilla	Arturo DeFreites	Roberto Yil
Rookie	Rays (VSL)	German Melendez	Alejandro Freire	Edgar Ramos

Scouting
Director, Scouting: R.J. Harrison (Phoenix, AZ).
Assistant Director, Amateur Scouting: Rob Metzler. **Assistant, Amateur Scouting:** Tim Steggall. **Administrator, Scouting:** Samantha Bireley. **Director, Pro Scouting:** Matt Arnold. **Special Assignment Scouts:** Todd Donovan (East Lyme, CT), Oneri Fleita (Niles, IL), Bobby Heck (Windemere, FL), Mike Juhl (Indian Train, NC), Fred Repke (Carson City, NV).
Major League Scouts: Bob Cluck (San Diego, CA). **Pro Scouts:** Michael Brown (Chandler, AZ), Ken Califano (Aberdeen, MD), Jason Cole (Austin, TX), Brent Gates (Grand Rapids, MI), Jason Grey (Mesa, AZ), Matt Hahn (Tampa, FL), Kevin Ibach (Geneva, IL), Ryan Isaac (New York, NY), Brian Keegan (Matthews, NC).
National Crosschecker: Chuck Ricci (Williamsburg, VA). **Eastern Regional Supervisor:** Jeff Cornell (Lee's Summit, MO). **Western Regional Supervisor:** Jake Wilson (Ramona, CA). **Scout Supervisors:** Tim Alexander (Jamesville, NY), James Bonnici (Auburn Hills, MI), Rickey Drexler (New Iberia, LA), Kevin Elfering (Wesley Chapel, FL), J.D. Elliby (Mansfield, TX), Brett Foley (Chicago, IL), Ryan Henderson (Gilbert, AZ), Brian Hickman (Fort Mill, SC), Milt Hill (Cumming, GA), Alan Hull (Culver City, CA), Jamie Jones (Poway, CA), Paul Kirsch (Wilsonville, OR), Pat Murphy (Marble Falls, TX), Greg Whitworth (Los Angeles, CA), Lou Wieben (Little Ferry, NJ). **Part-Time Area Scouts:** Brian Compton (Cypress, CA), Tom Couston (Sarasota, FL), Jose Hernandez (Miami, FL), Gil Martinez (San Juan, PR), Graig Merritt (Pitts Meadow, Canada), Casey Onaga (Honolulu, HI), Ethan Purser (Tampa, FL), Jack Sharp (Dallas, TX), Donald Turley (Spring, TX).
Director, International Scouting: Carlos Rodriguez (Tampa, FL). **Coordinator, International Operations:** Patrick Walters (Tampa, FL). **International Crosschecker:** Steve Miller (Tampa, FL). **Coordinator, South American Operations:** Ronnie Blanco. **Consultant, International Operations:** John Gilmore. **Coordinator, Colombia:** Angel Contreras. **Scouting Supervisor, Mexico:** Eddie Diaz. **Scouting Supervisor, Dominican Republic:** Danny Santana. **Scouting Supervisor, Venezuela:** Marlon Roche. **International Scouts:** Aaron Acosta (Mexico), Guillermo Armenta (Mexico), William Bergolla (Venezuela), Orlando Cabrera (Brazil), Juan Francisco Castillo (Venezuela), Alfredo Celestin (Dominican Republic), Adriano De Souza (Brazil), Francisco Gamez (Mexico), Mario Gonzalez (Venezuela), Keith Hsu (Taiwan), Chairon Isenia (Curacao), Grimaldo Martinez (Mexico), Eric Ramirez (Dominican Republic), Miguel Richardson (Dominican Republic), Victor Torres (Dominican Republic), Tateki Uchibori (Japan), Euclides Vargas (Venezuela), Jiri Vitt (Czech Republic), Ulli Wermuth (Germany), Gustavo Zapata (Panama).

Texas Rangers

Office Address: 1000 Ballpark Way, Arlington, TX 76011. **Mailing Address:** P.O. Box 90111, Arlington, TX 76011. **Telephone:** (817) 273-5222. **Fax:** (817) 273-5110. **Website:** www.texasrangers.com.

Ownership
Co-Chairman: Ray C. Davis, Bob R. Simpson. **Chairman, Ownership Committee:** Neil Leibman.

BUSINESS OPERATIONS

Ray Davis

Executive Vice President, Business Partnerships/Development: Joe Januszewski. **Executive VP, Business Operations:** Rob Matwick. **Executive VP/CFO:** Kellie Fischer. **Executive VP, Communications:** John Blake. **Executive VP, Entertainment/Productions:** Chuck Morgan. **Executive Assistant to Co-Chairman:** Keli West. **Executive Assistant to Business Operations/Finance:** Gabrielle Stokes. **Executive Assistant to Business Partnerships/Development:** Courtney Rowell. **Manager, Ownership Concierge Services:** Amy Beam.

Finance/Accounting
VP/Controller: Starr Gulledge. **Assistant Controller:** Brian Thompson.

Human Resources/Legal/Information Technology
Senior VP, Human Resources/Risk Management: Terry Turner. **Associate Counsel:** Kate Cassidy. **Director, Human Resources:** Mercedes Riley. **VP, Information Technology:** Mike Bullock.

Ballpark/Event Operations
VP, Security/Parking: Blake Miller. **Assistant VP, Customer Service:** Donnie Pordash. **Director, Parking/Security:** Mike Smith.

Communications/Community Relations
Assistant VP, Broadcasting/Communications: Angie Swint. **Assistant VP, Player Relations:** Taunee Paur Taylor. **Senior Director, Media Relations:** Rich Rice. **Director, Social Media:** Kaylan Eastepp. **Manager, Player Relations:** Rebecca Starkey. **Manager, Photography:** Kelly Gavin. **Manager, Media Relations:** Brian SanFilippo. **Manager, Broadcast Operations:** Madison Pelletier. **Coordinator, Communications:** Kate Munson. **VP, Community Outreach/ Executive Director, Foundation:** Karin Morris. **Assistant VP, Community Outreach:** Breon Dennis.

Facilities
VP, Ballpark Operations: Sean Decker. **Senior Director, Maintenance:** Mike Call. **Senior Director, Facility Operations:** Duane Arber. **Director, Grounds:** Dennis Klein. **Director, Complex Grounds:** Steve Ballard.

Marketing/Game Presentation
VP, Marketing: Becky Kimbro. **Director, Creative Media Services:** Jerod Couch. **Senior Director, Game Entertainment/Productions:** Chris DeRuyscher.

2015 SCHEDULE
Standard Game Times: 7:05 p.m.; Sun. 2:05.

APRIL			
6-9 . . . . .at Oakland	25-27 . . . . . . .at Cleveland	3-5 . . . . . Los Angeles (AL)	25-27 . . . . .Toronto
10-12 . . . . Houston	28-31 . . . . Boston	7-8 . . . . .Arizona	28-30 . . . . Baltimore
13-15 . . . . Los Angeles (AL)		10-12 . . . . San Diego	31 . . . . at San Diego
17-19 . . . . .at Seattle	**JUNE**	17-19 . . . . . . at Houston	
21-22 . . . . at Arizona	2-4 . . . . Chicago (AL)	20-22 . . . . . at Colorado	**SEPTEMBER**
24-26 . . at Los Angeles (AL)	5-7 . . . . . .at Kansas City	24-26 . . at Los Angeles (AL)	1-2 . . . . at San Diego
27-29 . . . . Seattle	9-11 . . . . .at Oakland	27-30 . . . . .New York (AL)	4-6 . . . . at Los Angeles (AL)
	12-14 . . . . .Minnesota	31 . . . . San Francisco	7-10 . . . . .at Seattle
	15-16 . . . .Los Angeles (NL)		11-13 . . . . Oakland
MAY	17-18 . . at Los Angeles (NL)	**AUGUST**	14-17 . . . . Houston
1-3 . . . . Oakland	19-21 . . . . .at Chicago (AL)	1-2 . . . . San Francisco	18-20 . . . . Seattle
4-6 . . . . at Houston	23-25 . . . . Oakland	3-5 . . . . Houston	22-24 . . . . . . .at Oakland
7-10 . . . . . . at Tampa Bay	26-28 . . . . . at Toronto	7-9 . . . . .at Seattle	25-27 . . . . . at Houston
11-14 . . . . . . Kansas City	29-30 . . . . . .at Baltimore	11-13 . . . . . at Minnesota	28-30 . . . . Detroit
15-17 . . . . Cleveland		14-16 . . . . . . .Tampa Bay	
19-21 . . . . at Boston	**JULY**	17-19 . . . . Seattle	**OCTOBER**
22-24 . . . . at New York (AL)	1-2 . . . . .at Baltimore	20-23 . . . . at Detroit	1-4 . . . . . Los Angeles (AL)

GENERAL INFORMATION
Stadium (year opened): Globe Life Park in Arlington (1994). **Team Colors:** Royal blue and red.

Player Representative: Derek Holland. **Home Dugout:** First Base. **Playing Surface:** Grass.

Sponsorship/Tickets

Senior VP, Partnerships/Client Service: Jim Cochrane. **Senior Director, Media Sales:** Wade Howell. **Senior VP, Ticket Sales/Service:** Paige Farragut. **Senior Director, Ticket Services:** Mike Lentz.

BASEBALL OPERATIONS

Telephone: (817) 273-5222. **Fax:** (817) 273-5285.
President, Baseball Operations/General Manager: Jon Daniels.
Assistant GM: Thad Levine. **Special Assistants to the GM:** Tom Giordano, Greg Maddux, Darren Oliver, Ivan Rodriguez, Michael Young. **Director, Baseball Operations:** Matt Vinnola. **Executive Assistant to President, Baseball Operations/GM:** Barbara Pappenfus. **Major League Special Assistant:** Scott Littlefield. **Special Assistant, Major League Scout:** Greg Smith.

Jon Daniels

Major League Staff

Manager: Jeff Banister.
Coaches: Bench—Steve Buechele; **Pitching**—Mike Maddux; **Hitting**—Dave Magadan; **First Base**—Hector Ortiz, Jr.; **Third Base**—Tony Beasley; **Coach**—Jayce Tingler; **Bullpen**—Andy Hawkins; **Assistant Hitting Coach**—Bobby Jones.

Medical/Training

Team Physician: Dr. Keith Meister. **Team Internist:** Dr. David Hunter.
Spine Consultant: Dr. Andrew Dossett. **Senior Director, Medical Operations:** Jamie Reed. **Head Trainer:** Kevin Harmon. **Assistant Trainers:** Matt Lucero, TJ Nakagawa. **Director, Strength/Conditioning:** Jose Vazquez.

Player Development

Telephone: (817) 436-5999. **Fax:** (817) 273-5285.
Senior Director, Player Development: Mike Daly.
Manager, Minor League/International Operations: Paul Kruger. **Special Assistant, Player Development:** Mark Connor. **Field Coordinator:** Casey Candaele. **Pitching Coordinator:** Danny Clark. **Coordinators:** Josue Perez (hitting), Dwayne Murphy (assistant hitting/Outfield), Chris Briones (catching), Juan Lopez (assistant catching), Keith Comstock (rehab pitching), Bruce Hines (baserunning), Brian Dayett (special assignment coach), Napoleon Pichardo (strength/conditioning), Dale Gilbert (medical), Jeff Bodenhamer (rehab). **Assistant, Arizona Operations:** Stosh Hoover. **Minor League Equipment Manager:** Chris Ackerman.

Farm System

Class	Club (League)	Manager	Coach	Pitching Coach
Triple-A	Round Rock (PCL)	Jason Wood	Justin Mashore	Brad Holman
Double-A	Frisco (TL)	Joe Mikulik	Jason Hart	Jeff Andrews
High A	High Desert (CAL)	Jason Wood	Justin Mashore	Brad Holman
Low A	Hickory (SAL)	Corey Ragsdale	Francisco Matos	Oscar Marin
Short-season	Spokane (NWL)	Tim Hulett	Rick Down	Jose Jaimes
Rookie	Rangers (AZL)	Kenny Holmberg	Kenny Hook	Joey Seaver
Rookie	Rangers (DSL)	Aaron Levin	Guillermo Mercedes	Henderson Lugo

Scouting

Senior Director, Amateur Scouting: Kip Fagg. **Senior Director, Player Personnel:** Josh Boyd. **Director, International Scouting:** Gil Kim.
Manager, Amateur Scouting: Matt Klotsche. **Major League Scouts:** Russ Ardolina (Rockville, MD), Keith Boeck (Chandler, AZ). **Pro Scouts:** Mike Anderson (Austin, TX), Scot Engler (Montgomery, IL), Jay Eddings (Plano, TX), Ross Fenstermaker (Granite Bay, CA), Mike Grouse (Lubbock,TX), Todd Walther (Hurst, TX).
National Crosschecker: Clarence Johns (Atlanta, GA). **Special Assistant to the General Manager:** James Keller (Sacramento, CA). **West Coast Crosschecker:** Casey Harvie (Lake Stevens, WA). **Midwest Crosschecker:** Randy Taylor (Katy, TX). **Eastern Crosschecker:** Ryan Coe (Acworth, GA). **Southeast Crosschecker:** Brian Williams (Cincinnati, OH). **Special Assignment Crosschecker:** Jake Krug (Flower Mound, TX). **Area Scouts:** Doug Banks (Scottsdale, AZ), Brett Campbell (Orlando, FL), Roger Coryell (Ypsilanti, MI), Bobby Crook (Fort Worth, TX), Steve Flores (Temecula, CA), Jonathan George (North Huntingdon, PA), Todd Guggiana (Long Beach, CA), Jay Heafner (Charlotte, NC), Bob Laurie (Plano, TX), Gary McGraw (Gaston, OR), Michael Medici (Danville, IN), Butch Metzger (Sacramento, CA), Brian Morrison (Birmingham, AL), Joel Ronda (Guaynabo, Puerto Rico), Takeshi Sakurayama (Manchester, CT), Dustin Smith (Olathe, KS), Cliff Terracuso (Jupiter, FL), Derrick Tucker (Kennesaw, GA). **Part-Time Scouts:** Chris Collias (Oak Park, MI), Buzzie Keller (Seguin, TX), Rick Schroeder (Phoenix, AZ), James Vilade (Frisco, TX).
Senior Advisor, Pacific Rim Operations: Jim Colborn. **Coordinator, Pacific Rim Operations:** Joe Furukawa (Japan). **Director, Latin America Scouting:** Rafic Saab. **Latin America Supervisor:** Roberto Aquino. **Dominican Program Coordinator/Scout:** Danilo Troncosco. **Manager, Pacific Rim Operations:** Curtis Jung. **Assistant, International Operations:** Tyler Jeske. **Latin America Crosschecker:** Chu Halabi (Aruba).
DR Complex Administrator: Marlenis Alejo. **International Scouts:** Rafael Belen (Dominican Republic), Willy Espinal (Dominican Republic), Jose Felomina (Curacao), Jose Fernandez (Florida), Jhonny Gomez (Venezuela), Carlos Gonzalez (Venezuela), Jung-Hua Liu (Taiwan), Rodolfo Rosario (Dominican Republic), Joel Ronda (Puerto Rico), Hamilton Sarabia (Colombia), Eduardo Thomas (Panama), Manuel Velez (Mexico), Hajime Watabe (Japan).

Toronto Blue Jays

Office/Mailing Address: 1 Blue Jays Way, Suite 3200, Toronto, Ontario M5V 1J1.
Telephone: (416) 341-1000. **Fax:** (416) 341-1245. **Website:** www.bluejays.com.

Ownership
Operated by: Toronto Blue Jays Baseball Club. **Principal Owner:** Rogers Communications Inc.

BUSINESS OPERATIONS

Paul Beeston

Chairman, Toronto Blue Jays: Edward Rogers. **Vice Chairman, Rogers Communications:** Phil Lind. **President, Rogers Media:** Keith Pelley. **President/CEO, Toronto Blue Jays/Rogers Centre:** Paul Beeston. **Consultants:** Howard Starkman, Cito Gaston.

Finance/Administration
Senior VP, Business Operations: Stephen R. Brooks. **Executive Assistant:** Donna Kuzoff. **Senior Director, Finance:** Lynda Kolody. **Director, Payroll/Benefits:** Brenda Dimmer. **Director, Risk Management:** Suzanne Joncas. **Senior Manager:** Ciaran Keegan. **Accounting Manager:** Tanya Proctor. **Financial Business Manager:** Leslie Galant-Gardiner. **Manager, Revenue Reporting/Analysis:** Craig Whitmore. **Manager, Stadium Payroll:** Sharon Dykstra. **Manager, Ticket Receipts/Vault Services:** Joseph Roach.
Manager, Human Resources: Matthew Dusureault. **Senior Manager, Information Technology:** Anthony Miranda. **VP, Business Affairs/Legal Counsel:** Matthew Shuber. **Director, Business Affairs:** Jessica Fingerhut. **Executive Assistant, Business Affairs:** Suey Lau.

Marketing/Community Relations
VP, Marketing/Merchandising: Anthony Partipilo. **Executive Assistant, Marketing:** Maria Cresswell. **Director, Game Entertainment/Promotions:** Marnie Starkman. **Manager, Community Marketing/Player Relations:** Holly Gentemann. **Manager, Direct Marketing:** Sherry Oosterhuis. **Manager, Promotions/Fan Activation:** Michelle Seniuk. **Manager, Social Marketing:** Rob Jack. **Manager, Special Events:** Kristy-Leigh Boone. **Manager, Stadium Entertainment:** Daniel Joseph. **VP, Corporate Partnerships:** Mark Ditmars. **Directors, Corporate Partnership/Business Development:** John Griffin, David O'Reilly. **Director, Marketing Services:** Natalie Agro. **Senior Manager, Corporate Partnerships/Business Development:** Mark Palmer. **Senior Managers, Marketing Services:** Honsing Leung, Manpreet Pandha.

Communications
VP, Communications: Jay Stenhouse. **Manager, Baseball Information:** Mal Romanin. **Coordinator, Baseball Information:** Erik Grosman. **Coordinator, Communications:** Sue Mallabon.

Stadium Operations
VP, Stadium Operations/Security: Mario Coutinho. **Executive Assistant:** June Sym. **Director, Guest Experience:** Carmen Day. **Manager, Event Services:** Julie Minott. **Manager, Game Operations:** Karyn Gottschalk.

2015 SCHEDULE
Standard Game Times: 7:07 p.m.; Sat/Sun: 1:07

APRIL
6 . . . . . . at New York (AL)
8-9 . . . . . at New York (AL)
10-12 . . . . . . .at Baltimore
13-16 . . . . . . .Tampa Bay
17-19 . . . . Atlanta
21-23 . . . . Baltimore
24-26 . . . . at Tampa Bay
27-29 . . . . . . at Boston
30 . . . . .at Cleveland

MAY
1-3 . . . . .at Cleveland
4-6 . . . . . . .New York (AL)
8-10 . . . . Boston
11-13 . . . . . .at Baltimore
14-17 . . . . at Houston
18-21 . . . . Los Angeles (AL)

22-24 . . . . Seattle
25-27 . . . . . Chicago (AL)
29-31 . . . . . at Minnesota

JUNE
1-3 . . . . . . at Washington
5-7 . . . . Houston
8-10 . . . . .Miami
12-14 . . . . . . at Boston
15-16 . . . at New York (NL)
17-18 . . . .New York (NL)
19-21 . . . . Baltimore
22-24 . . . . . at Tampa Bay
26-28 . . . . Texas
29-30 . . . . Boston

JULY
1-2 . . . . Boston

3-5 . . . . at Detroit
6-9 . . . . . .at Chicago (AL)
10-12 . . . . . .at Kansas City
17-19 . . . . . . .Tampa Bay
21-23 . . . . . . .at Oakland
24-26 . . . . . . .at Seattle
28-29 . . . . . .Philadelphia
30-31 . . . . . Kansas City

AUGUST
1-2 . . . . Kansas City
3-6 . . . . .Minnesota
7-9 . . . . . at New York (AL)
11-13 . . . . Oakland
14-16 . . . . .New York (AL)
18-19 . . . . .at Philadelphia
21-23 . . at Los Angeles (AL)
25-27 . . . . .at Texas

28-30 . . . . Detroit
31 . . . . Cleveland

SEPTEMBER
1-2 . . . . Cleveland
4-6 . . . . Baltimore
7-9 . . . . at Boston
10-13 . . . at New York (AL)
15-17 . . . . at Atlanta
18-20 . . . . Boston
21-23 . . . . .New York (AL)
25-27 . . . . . . .Tampa Bay
28-30 . . . . . .at Baltimore

OCTOBER
1 . . . . .at Baltimore
2-4 . . . . at Tampa Bay

GENERAL INFORMATION
Stadium (year opened): Rogers Centre (1989).
Team Colors: Blue and white.

Player Representative: Unavailable.
Home Dugout: Third Base.
Playing Surface: AstroTurf 3DXtreme 60 Product.

Ticket Operations
Director, Ticket Operations: Justin Hay. **Director, Ticket Services:** Sheila Stella. **Manager, Box Office:** Christina Dodge.

Ticket Sales/Service
VP, Ticket Sales/Service: Jason Diplock. **Executive Assistant:** Stacey Jackson. **Director, Luxury Suite Sales/Service:** Michael Hook. **Manager, Group Sales:** Ryan Gustavel. **Manager, Season Ticket Services:** Erik Bobson. **Manager, Ticket Sales:** John Santana.

Travel/Clubhouse
Director, Team Travel/Clubhouse Operations: Mike Shaw. **Equipment Manager:** Jeff Ross. **Clubhouse Manager:** Kevin Malloy. **Visiting Clubhouse Manager:** Len Frejlich. **Video Operations:** Robert Baumander. **Major League Advance Scouting Coordinator:** Ryan Mittleman. **Director, Team Employee Assistance Program:** Ray Karesky. **Coordinator, Advance Scouting/Video:** Harry Einbinder.

BASEBALL OPERATIONS

Alex Anthopoulos

Senior VP, Baseball Operations/General Manager: Alex Anthopoulos.
VP, Baseball Operations/Assistant GM: Tony LaCava. **Assistant GM:** Andrew Tinnish. **Special Assistant to the GM:** Dana Brown. **Special Assistants to Organization:** Roberto Alomar, George Bell, Carlos Delgado, Pat Hentgen, Paul Quantrill. **Manager, Major League Administration:** Heather Connolly. **Manager, Baseball Research/Development:** Joe Sheehan. **Baseball Operations Analyst:** Jason Pare. **Executive Assistant to GM:** Anna Coppola.

Major League Staff
Manager: John Gibbons.
Coaches: Bench—DeMarlo Hale; **Pitching—**Pete Walker; **Hitting—**Brook Jacoby; **First Base—**Tim Leiper; **Third Base—**Luis Rivera; **Bullpen—**Dane Johnson; Assistant Hitting—Eric Owens. **Bullpen Catcher:** Alex Andreopoulos, Jesus Figueroa.

Medical/Training
Medical Advisor: Dr. Bernie Gosevitz. **Consulting Physician:** Dr. Ron Taylor. **Consulting Team Physicians:** Dr. Irv Feferman, Dr. Noah Forman. **Head Trainer:** George Poulis. **Assistant Trainer:** Mike Frostad. **Strength/Conditioning Coordinator:** Chris Joyner.

Player Development
Telephone: (727) 734-8007. **Fax:** (727) 734-8162.
Director, Minor League Operations: Charlie Wilson. **Minor League Field Coordinator:** Doug Davis. **Senior Advisor:** Rich Miller. **Senior Pitching Advisor:** Rick Langford. **Rehab Pitching Coach:** Darold Knowles. **Coordinators:** Mike Barnett (hitting), Mike Mordecai (instruction), Tim Raines (outfield/baserunning), Sal Fasano (pitching), Donovan Santas (strength/conditioning). **Roving Infield Coach:** Danny Solano. **Roving Hitting Instructor:** Steve Springer. **Athletic Training/Rehab Coordinator:** Jeff Stevenson. **Assitant Athletic Training/Rehab Coordinator:** Jose Ministral. **Consultant:** Sandy Alomar Sr. **Equipment Coordinator:** Billy Wardlow. **Player Development Assistant:** Megan Evans, Mike Nielsen. **Assistant, Latin American Administration:** Blake Bentley. **Administrative Assistant:** Kim Marsh.

Farm System

Class	Club (League)	Manager	Hitting Coach	Pitching Coach
Triple-A	Buffalo (IL)	Gary Allenson	Richie Hebner	Randy St. Claire
Double-A	New Hampshire (EL)	Bobby Meacham	Stubby Clapp	Bob Stanley
High A	Dunedin (FSL)	Omar Malave	John Tamargo Jr.	Vince Horsman
Low A	Lansing (MWL)	Ken Huckaby	Kenny Graham	Jeff Ware
Short-season	Vancouver (NWL)	John Schneider	Dave Pano	Jim Czajkowski
Rookie	Bluefield (APP)	Dennis Holmberg	Aaron Mathews	Antonio Caceres
Rookie	Blue Jays (GCL)	Cesar Martin	Paul Elliott	Willie Collazo
Rookie	Blue Jays (DSL)	Jose Mateo	Carlos Villalobos	Rafael Lazo

Scouting
Director, Professional Scouting: Perry Minasian. **Director, Amateur Scouting:** Brian Parker.
Special Assistant, Amateur Scouting: Chuck LaMar. **Coordinator, Professional Scouting:** David Haynes. **Special Assignment Scout:** Russ Bove. **Major League Scouts:** Jim Beattie, Sal Butera, Ed Lynch, Jim Skaalen. **Senior Advisor/Professional Scout:** Mel Didier. **Professional Crosscheckers:** Kevin Briand, Dean Decillis, Dan Evans, Jon Lalonde. **Professional Scouts:** Matt Anderson, Jon Bunnell, Steve Connelly, Kimball Crossley, Bob Fontaine, Kevin Fox, Bryan Lambe, Ted Lekas, Nick Manno, Brad Matthews, David May Jr. **Crosscheckers:** Blake Crosby, Blake Davis, C.J. Ebarb, Mike Mangan, Tim Rooney, Paul Tinnell. **Area Scouts:** Mike Alberts (Leominster, MA), Joey Aversa (Fountain Valley, CA), Coulson Barbiche (Columbus, OH), Matt Bishoff (Tampa, FL), Dallas Black (Conway, AZ), Darold Brown (Elk Grove, CA), Ryan Fox (Yakima, WA), Pete Holmes (Phoenix, AZ), Jeff Johnson (Indianapolis, IN), Brian Johnston (Baton Rouge, LA), Chris Kline (Tarboro, NC), Randy Kramer (Aptos, CA), Jim Lentine (San Clemente, CA), Nate Murrie (Bowling Green, KY), Don Norris (Gainesville, FL), Matt O'Brien (Clermont, FL), Wes Penick (Clive, IA), Bud Smith (Lakewood, CA), Mike Tidick (Statesboro, GA), Gerald Turner (Bedford, TX), Doug Witt (Brooklyn, MD). **Special Assistant, Latin American Operations:** Ismael Cruz. **Director, Dominican Republic:** Jose Rosario. **Director, Venezuela:** Luis Marquez. **Canada Scouts:** Don Cowan (Delta, BC), Jamie Lehman (Syracuse, NY). **International Scouts:** Jairo Castillo (San Pedro, DR), Lionel Chattelle (Wiesbaden, Germany), Jose Contreras (Oriente, VZ), Alexis de la Cruz (Santo Domingo, DR), Luciano del Rosario (Bani, DR), Enrique Falcon (Cartagena, COL), Juan Garcia (Oriente, VZ), Lorenzo Perez (Manoguayabo, DR), Francisco Plasencia (Turmero, VZ), Henry Sandoval (Culiacan, VZ), Daniel Sotelo (Managua, Nicaragua), Marino Tejada (Santo Domingo, DR), Alex Zapata (Panama City, Panama).

Washington Nationals

Office Address: 1500 South Capitol Street SE, Washington, DC 20003.
Telephone: (202) 640-7000. **Fax:** (202) 547-0025.
Website: www.nationals.com.

Ownership
Managing Principal Owner: Theodore Lerner.
Principal Owners: Annette Lerner, Mark Lerner, Marla Lerner Tanenbaum, Debra Lerner Cohen, Robert Tanenbaum, Edward Cohen, Judy Lenkin Lerner.

BUSINESS OPERATIONS

Ted Lerner

Chief Operating Officer, Lerner Sports: Alan Gottlieb. **Chief Revenue/Marketing Officer:** Valerie Camillo. **Chief Financial Officer:** Lori Creasy. **Senior Vice President:** Elise Holman.

Ballpark Enterprises
VP, Ballpark Enterprises: Catherine Silver. **Senior Director, Ballpark Enterprises:** Maggie Gessner. **Director, Ballpark Enterprises Operations:** Lisa Marie Czop.

Legal
Senior VP/General Counsel: Damon T. Jones. **Deputy General Counsel:** Amy Inlander Minniti.

Human Resources
VP, Human Resources: Alexa Herndon. **Director, Benefits:** Stephanie Giroux. **Director, Human Resources:** Steve Reed.

Communications
VP, Communications: Jennifer Giglio. **Senior Director, Baseball Communications:** Amanda Comak. **Senior Manager, Corporate Communications:** Alexandra Schauffler. **Manager, Baseball Communications:** Kyle Brostowitz. **Coordinator, Communications:** Carly Rolfe.

Community Relations
VP, Community Engagement: Gregory McCarthy. **Senior Director, Community Relations:** Shawn Bertani.

Marketing/Broadcasting
VP, Marketing/Broadcasting: John Guagliano. **Executive Director, Production/Entertainment/Promotions:** Jacqueline Coleman. **Director, Production/Operations:** Dave Lundin. **Manager, Promotions/Events:** Amanda Hauge.

Ticketing/Sales
VP, Ticket Sales, Service/Operations: David McElwee. **Senior Director, Ticket Operations:** Tom Jackson. **Director, Ticket Services/Sales Development:** Ben Cobleigh. **Senior Account Executive, Membership Sales:** Kevin Nawrocki. **Manager, Group Sales:** Brian Beck. **Manager, Sales Development:** Brandon Lapetina.

2015 SCHEDULE
Standard Game Times: 7:05 p.m.; Sun. 1:35

APRIL
6 . . . . .New York (NL)
8-9 . . . . . . .New York (NL)
10-12 . . . . . at Philadelphia
13-15 . . . . at Boston
16-19 . . . . .Philadelphia
21-23 . . . . St. Louis
24-26 . . . . at Miami
27-29 . . . . . . at Atlanta
30 . . . . . at New York (NL)

MAY
1-3. . . . . at New York (NL)
4-6. . . : . . . . .Miami
8-10 . . . . Atlanta
11-13 . . . . at Arizona
14-17 . . . . at San Diego
19-20 . . . . .New York (AL)

22-24 . . . . . .Philadelphia
25-27 . . . . .at Chicago (NL)
29-31 . . . . . . at Cincinnati

JUNE
1-3. . . . . .Toronto
4-7. . . . . . . Chicago (NL)
9-10 . . . at New York (AL)
11-14 . . . . . at Milwaukee
15-16 . . . . . at Tampa Bay
17-18 . . . . .Tampa Bay
19-21 . . . . . . Pittsburgh
23-25 . . . . Atlanta
26-28 . . . at Philadelphia
30 . . . . at Atlanta

JULY
1-2. . . . . at Atlanta

3-5 . . . . .Giants
6-8. . . . . Cincinnati
10-12 . . . . . . at Baltimore
17-19 . . . Los Angeles (NL)
20-22 . . . . .New York (NL)
23-26 . . . . at Pittsburgh
28-30 . . . . at Miami
31 . . . . . at New York (NL)

AUGUST
1-2. . . . . at New York (NL)
3-6. . . . . .Arizona
7-9. . . . . .Colorado
10-12 . . at Los Angeles (NL)
13-16 . . . at San Francisco
18-20 . . . . . at Colorado
21-23 . . . . . . .Milwaukee
25-27 . . . . San Diego

28-30 . . . . .Miami
31 . . . . at St. Louis

SEPTEMBER
1-2. . . . . at St. Louis
3-6. . . . . Atlanta
7-9. . . . . . .New York (NL)
11-13 . . . . at Miami
14-16 . . . . at Philadelphia
17-20 . . . . .Miami
21-23 . . . . Baltimore
25-27 . . . . . .Philadelphia
29-30 . . . . at Atlanta

OCTOBER
1 . . . . at Atlanta
2-4. . . . . at New York (NL)

GENERAL INFORMATION
Stadium (year opened): Nationals Park (2008).
Team Colors: Red, white and blue.

Player Representative: Unavailable.
Home Dugout: First Base.
Playing Surface: Grass.

Ballpark Operations
VP, Ballpark Operations: Frank Gambino.
Executive Director, Ballpark Operations/Guest Experience: Jonathan Stahl. Director, Event Operations: Billy Langenstein. Director, Security: Stewart Branam. Head Groundskeeper: John Turnour.

BASEBALL OPERATIONS

General Manager/President, Baseball Operations: Mike Rizzo.
Assistant GM/VP, Baseball Operations: Bob Miller. Assistant GM/VP, Finance: Ted Towne. Assistant GM/Director, Baseball Operations: Adam Cromie. Senior Advisor to GM: Phillip Rizzo. Special Assistant to the GM/Major League Administration: Harolyn Cardozo. VP, Clubhouse Operations/Team Travel: Rob McDonald. Assistant, Clubhouse/Team Travel: Ryan Wiebe. Director, Baseball Research/Development: Sam Mondry-Cohen.
Manager, Baseball Research/Development: Michael DeBartolo. Analyst, Baseball Research/Development: Lee Mendelowitz, Josh Weinstock. Assistant, Baseball Operations: John Wulf. Coordinator, Advance Scouting/Video: Erick Dalton. Assistant, Advance Scouting/Video: Christopher Rosenbaum. Clubhouse/Equipment Manager: Mike Wallace. Visiting Clubhouse Manager: Matt Rosenthal. Equipment Coordinator: Dan Wallin. Clubhouse Assistants: Andrew Melnick, Darwin Beacham.

Mike Rizzo

Major League Staff
Manager: Matt Williams.
Coaches: Bench—Randy Knorr; Pitching—Steve McCatty; Hitting—Rick Schu; First Base—Tony Tarasco; Third Base—Bob Henley; Bullpen—Matt LeCroy; Defensive Coordination/Advance Coach: Mark Weidemaier.

Medical/Training
Medical Director/Head Team Physician: Dr. Wiemi Douoguih.
Head Athletic Trainer: Lee Kuntz. Assistant Athletic Trainer: Steve Gober. Strength/Conditioning Coach: John Philbin. Assistant, Strength/Conditioning Coach: Matt Eiden. Medical Staff Assistant: John Hsu. Team Physician/Internist: Dr. Dennis Cullen. Team Physician, Florida: Dr. Bruce Thomas.

Player Development
Assistant GM/VP, Player Development/Pro Scouting: Doug Harris.
VP, Player Personnel: Bob Boone. Director, Player Development: Mark Scialabba. Assistant Director, Minor League Operations: Ryan Thomas. Assistant, Player Development: JJ Estevez. Director, Florida Operations: Thomas Bell. Senior Manager, Florida Operations: Jonathan Tosches.
Field Coordinators: Jeff Garber, Tommy Shields. Hitting Coordinator: Troy Gingrich. Pitching Coordinator: Paul Menhart. Catching Coordinator: Michael Barrett. Outfield/Baserunning Coordinator: Gary Thurman. Coordinator, Instruction: Gary Cathcart. Rehabilitation Pitching Coordinator: Mark Grater. Medical/Rehabilitation Coordinator: Jon Kotredes. Strength/Conditioning Coordinator: Landon Brandes. Life Skills Coordinator: Rick Ankiel. Minor League Equipment Coordinator: Calvin Minasian. Senior Advisor, Player Development: Spin Williams.

Farm System

Class	Club	Manager	Hitting Coach	Pitching Coach
Triple-A	Syracuse (IL)	Billy Gardner Jr.	Joe Dillon	Bob Milacki
Double-A	Harrisburg (EL)	Brian Daubach	Mark Harris	Chris Michalak
High A	Potomac (CL)	Tripp Keister	Brian Rupp	Franklin Bravo
Low A	Hagerstown (SAL)	Patrick Anderson	Luis Ordaz	Sam Narron
Short-season	Auburn (NYP)	Gary Cathcart	Amaury Garcia	Tim Redding
Rookie	Nationals (GCL)	Michael Barrett	Jorge Mejia	Micheal Tejera
Rookie	Nationals (DSL)	Sandy Martinez	Jose Herrera	Pablo Frias

Scouting
Assistant GM/VP, Scouting Operations: Kris Kline.
Assistant Director, Scouting Operations: Eddie Longosz. Director, Player Procurement: Kasey McKeon. Director, International Scouting/Special Assistant to GM: Bill Singer. Special Assistants to GM: Steve Arnieri, Chuck Cottier, Mike Cubbage, Mike Daughtry, Bob Johnson, Ron Rizzi, Jay Robertson, Bob Schaefer, Terry Wetzel.
Professional Scout: Aron Weston. Special Assistant to GM/National Crosschecker, East: Jeff Zona. National Supervisor: Mark Baca. National Crosschecker, Midwest: Jimmy Gonzales. National Crosschecker, West: Fred Costello.
Area Supervisors: Ray Blanco (Miami, FL), Justin Bloxom (Lexington, KY), Brian Cleary (Cincinnati, OH), Paul Faulk (Myrtle Beach, SC), Ben Gallo (Encinitas, CA) Ed Gustafson (Denton, TX), Buddy Hernandez (Windermere, FL), Brandon Larson (San Antonio, TX), Steve Leavitt (Huntington Beach, CA), John Malzone (Needham, MA), Alex Morales (Wellington, FL), Bobby Myrick (Colonial Heights, VA), Scott Ramsay (Mount Vernon, OR), Eric Robinson (Acworth, GA), Mitch Sokol (Phoenix, AZ), Everett Stull (Elk Grove, CA), Tyler Wilt (Willis, TX).
Director, Latin American Operations: Johnny DiPuglia.
Director, Academy Operations: Fausto Severino. Administrator, Dominican Republic Academy: Alex Rodriguez. Assistant, International Scouting: Taisuke Sato. Dominican Republic Scouting Supervisor: Moises De La Mota. Venezuela Scouting Supervisor: German Robles. Coordinator, Pacific Rim: Marty Brown.
International Scouts: Modesto Ulloa (Dominican Republic), Carlos Ulloa (Dominican Republic). Part-Time International Scouts: Pablo Arias (Dominican Republic), Virgilio De Leon (Dominican Republic), Juan Munoz (Venezuela), Salvador Donadelli (Venezuela), Eduardo Rosario (Venezuela), Ronald Morillo (Venezuela), Caryl Van Zanten (Curacao), Miguel Ruiz (Panama), Eduardo Cabrera (Colombia).

MEDIA
INFORMATION

LOCAL MEDIA INFORMATION

AMERICAN LEAGUE

BALTIMORE ORIOLES
Radio Announcers: Joe Angel, Fred Manfra. **Flagship Station:** WJZ-FM 105.7 The Fan.
TV Announcers: Mike Bordick, Jim Hunter, Jim Palmer, Gary Thorne. **Flagship Station:** Mid-Atlantic Sports Network (MASN).

BOSTON RED SOX
Radio Announcers: Joe Castiglione, Dave O'Brien. **Flagship Station:** WEEI (93.7 FM/850 AM).
TV Announcers: Don Orsillo, Jerry Remy. **Flagship Station:** New England Sports Network (regional cable).

CHICAGO WHITE SOX
Radio Announcers: Ed Farmer, Darrin Jackson, Chris Rongey (pre/post). **Flagship Station:** WSCR The Score 670-AM.
TV Announcers: Ken Harrelson, Steve Stone. **Flagship Stations:** WGN TV-9, WCIU-TV, Comcast SportsNet Chicago (regional cable).

CLEVELAND INDIANS
Radio Announcers: Tom Hamilton, Jim Rosenhaus. **Flagship Station:** WTAM 1100-AM.
TV Announcers: Rick Manning, Matt Underwood. **Flagship Station:** SportsTime Ohio.

DETROIT TIGERS
Radio Announcers: Dan Dickerson, Jim Price. **Flagship Station:** WXYT 97.1 FM and AM 1270.
TV Announcers: Rod Allen, Mario Impemba. **Flagship Station:** FOX Sports Detroit (regional cable).

HOUSTON ASTROS
Radio Announcers: Steve Sparks, Robert Ford. **Spanish:** Alex Trevino, Francisco Romero. **Flagship Stations:** KBME 790-AM, KLAT 1010-AM (Spanish).
TV Announcers: Bill Brown, Alan Ashby, Geoff Blum. **Flagship Station:** ROOT Sports Houston.

KANSAS CITY ROYALS
Radio Announcers: Denny Matthews, Steve Physioc, Steve Stewart. **Kansas City affiliate:** KCSP 610-AM.
TV Announcers: Ryan Lefebvre, Rex Hudler, Joel Goldberg. **Flagship Station:** FOX Sports Kansas City.

LOS ANGELES ANGELS
Radio Announcers: Terry Smith, Mark Langston. **Flagship Station:** AM 830, 1330 KWKW (Spanish).
TV Announcers: Victor Rojas, Mark Gubicza. **Spanish TV Announcers:** Jose Mota, Amaury Pi-Gonzalez. **Flagship TV Station:** Fox Sports West (regional cable).

MINNESOTA TWINS
Radio Announcers: Cory Provus, Dan Gladden. **Radio Network Studio Host:** Kris Atteberry. **Radio Engineer:** Kyle Hammer. **Spanish Radio Play-by-Play:** Alfonso Fernandez. **Spanish Radio Analyst:** Tony Oliva. **Flagship Station:** 1500 ESPN.
TV Announcers: Bert Blyleven, Dick Bremer. **Flagship Station:** Fox Sports North.

NEW YORK YANKEES
Radio Announcers: John Sterling, Suzyn Waldman. **Flagship Station:** WFAN 660-AM, WADO 1280-AM. **Spanish Radio Announcers:** Francisco Rivera, Rickie Ricardo.
TV Announcers: David Cone, Jack Curry, John Flaherty, Michael Kay, Al Leiter, Bob Lorenz, Meredith Marakovits, Paul O'Neill, Ken Singleton. **Flagship Station:** YES Network (Yankees Entertainment & Sports).

OAKLAND A'S
Radio Announcers: Vince Cotroneo, Ken Korach. **Flagship Station:** KGMZ 95.7 The Game, FM.
TV Announcers: Ray Fosse, Glen Kuiper. **Flagship Stations:** Comcast Sports Net California.

SEATTLE MARINERS
Radio Announcers: Rick Rizzs, Aaron Goldsmith. **Flagship Station:** KOMO 1000-AM.
TV Announcers: Mike Blowers, Dave Sims. **Flagship Station:** FOX Sports Net Northwest.

TAMPA BAY RAYS
Radio Announcers: Andy Freed, Dave Wills. **Flagship Station:** Sports Animal WDAE 620 AM.
TV Announcers: Brian Anderson, Dewayne Staats, Todd Kalas. **Flagship Station:** Sun Sports.

TEXAS RANGERS
Radio Announcers: Eric Nadel, Matt Hicks; Spanish-Eleno Ornelas, Jose Guzman. **Flagship Station:** 105.3 The Fan FM, KZMP 1540 AM (Spanish). **TV Announcers:** Steve Busby, Tom Grieve, Mark McLemore, Emily Jones; **Spanish**-Victor Villalba. **Flagship Stations:** FOX Sports Southwest (regional cable), Time Warner (Spanish).

TORONTO BLUE JAYS
Radio Announcers: Jerry Howarth, Joe Siddal, Mike Wilner. **Flagship Station:** SportsNet Radio Fan 590-AM.
TV Announcers: Buck Martinez, Pat Tabler. **Flagship Station:** Rogers Sportsnet.

NATIONAL LEAGUE

ARIZONA DIMAONDBACKS
Radio Announcers: Greg Schulte, Tom Candiotti, Jeff Munn, Rodrigo Lopez (Spanish), Oscar Soria (Spanish), Richard Saenz (Spanish). **Flagship Stations:** Arizona Sports 98.7 FM & KSUN Radio Fiesta 1400 AM (Spanish).
TV Announcers: Steve Berthiaume, Bob Brenly, Luis Gonzalez, Joe Garagiola Sr. **Flagship Stations:** FOX Sports Arizona (regional cable).

ATLANTA BRAVES
Radio Announcers: Jim Powell, Don Sutton. **Flagship Stations:** WCNN-AM 680, The Fan (93.7 FM), WYAY-FM (106.7).
TV Announcers: Chip Caray, Joe Simpson. **Flagship Stations:** FOX Sports South/SportSouth (regional cable).

CHICAGO CUBS
Radio Announcers: Pat Hughes, Ron Coomer. **Flagship Station:** WGN 720-AM.
TV Announcers: Len Kasper, Jim Deshaies. **Flagship Stations:** WGN Channel 9 (national cable), Comcast SportsNet Chicago (regional cable), WCIU-TV Channel 26.

CINCINNATI REDS
Radio Announcers: Marty Brennaman, Thom Brennaman, Jeff Brantley, Jim Kelch, Chris Welsh, Doug Flynn.
Flagship Station: WLW 700-AM.
TV Announcers: Chris Welsh, Thom Brennaman, Jeff Brantley. **Flagship Station:** Fox Sports Ohio (regional cable).

COLORADO ROCKIES
Radio Announcers: Jack Corrigan, Jerry Schemmel. **Flagship Station:** KOA 850-AM.
TV Announcers: Drew Goodman, George Frazier, Jeff Huson.

LOS ANGELES DODGERS
Radio Announcers: Vin Scully, Rick Monday, Charley Steiner, Nomar Garciaparra. **Spanish:** Jaime Jarrín, Fernando Valenzuela, Pepe Yñiguez. **Flagship Stations:** AM570 Fox Sports LA, KTNQ 1020-AM (Spanish).
TV Announcers: Vin Scully, Charley Steiner, Orel Hershiser, Nomar Garciaparra, Alanna Rizzo, John Hartung, Jerry Hairston, Jr. **Spanish:** Jorge Jarrin, Manny Mota. **Flagship Stations:** SportsNet LA (regional cable).

MIAMI MARLINS
Radio Announcers: Dave Van Horne, Glenn Geffner. **Flagship Stations:** WINZ 940-AM, WAQI 710-AM (Spanish).
Spanish Radio Announcers: Felo Ramirez, Yiky Quintana.
TV Announcers: Tommy Hutton, Rich Waltz, Jeff Conine, Craig Minervini, Preston Wilson. **Spanish TV Announcers:** Raul Striker Jr. **Flagship Stations:** FSN Florida (regional cable).

MILWAUKEE BREWERS
Radio Announcers: Bob Uecker, Joe Black. **Flagship Station:** WTMJ 620-AM.
TV Announcers: Bill Schroeder, Brian Anderson. **Flagship Station:** Fox Sports Net North.

NEW YORK METS
Radio Announcers: Howie Rose, Josh Lewin. **Flagship Station:** WOR 710-AM.
TV Announcers: Gary Cohen, Keith Hernandez, Ron Darling, Steve Gelbs. **Flagship Stations:** Sports Net New York (regional cable), PIX11-TV.

PHILADELPHIA PHILLIES
Radio Announcers: Larry Andersen, Scott Franzke, Jim Jackson. **Flagship Stations:** WPHT 1210-AM.
TV Announcers: Tom McCarthy. **Flagship Stations:** WPHL PHL17, Comcast SportsNet (regional cable).

PITTSBURGH PIRATES
Radio Announcers: Steve Blass, Greg Brown, Tim Neverett, Bob Walk, John Wehner. **Flagship Station:** Sports Radio 93.7 FM The Fan.
TV Announcers: Steve Blass, Greg Brown, Tim Neverett, Bob Walk, John Wehner. **Flagship Station:** ROOT SPORTS (regional cable).

ST. LOUIS CARDINALS
Radio Announcers: Mike Shannon, John Rooney. **Flagship Station:** KMOX 1120 AM.
TV Announcers: Rick Horton, Al Hrabosky, Dan McLaughlin. **Flagship Stations:** Fox Sports Midwest.

SAN DIEGO PADRES
Radio Announcers: Ted Leitner, Bob Scanlan. **Flagship Stations:** The Mighty 1090-AM/ESPN 1700-AM.
TV Announcers: Dick Enberg, Mark Grant and Jesse Agler. **Flagship Station:** Fox Sports San Diego. **Spanish Announcers:** Eduardo Ortega, Carlos Hernandez

SAN FRANCISCO GIANTS
Radio Announcers: Mike Krukow, Duane Kuiper, Jon Miller, Dave Flemming.
Spanish: Tito Fuentes, Erwin Higueros. **Flagship Station:** KNBR 680-AM (English); ESPN Deportes-860AM (Spanish).
TV Announcers: CSN Bay Area-Mike Krukow, Duane Kuiper; KNTV-NBC 11—Jon Miller, Mike Krukow. **Flagship Stations:** KNTV-NBC 11, CSN Bay Area (regional cable).

WASHINGTON NATIONALS
Radio Announcers: Charlie Slowes, Dave Jageler. **Flagship Station:** WJFK 106.7 FM.
TV Announcers: Bob Carpenter, FP Santangelo. **Flagship Station:** Mid-Atlantic Sports Network (MASN).

NATIONAL MEDIA INFORMATION

BASEBALL STATISTICS

ELIAS SPORTS BUREAU INC. NATIONAL MEDIA BASEBALL STATISTICS
Official Major League Statistician
Mailing Address: 500 Fifth Ave., Suite 2140, New York, NY 10110. Telephone: (212) 869-1530. Fax: (212) 354-0980.
Website: www.esb.com.
President: Seymour Siwoff.
Executive Vice President: Steve Hirdt. Vice President: Peter Hirdt. Data Processing Manager: Chris Thorn.

MLB ADVANCED MEDIA Official Minor League Statistician
Mailing Address: 75 Ninth Ave., New York, NY 10011. Telephone: (212) 485-3444. Fax: (212) 485-3456. Website: MiLB.com.
Director, Stats Operations: Chris Lentine. Senior Manager, Stats: Shawn Geraghty.
Senior Supervisors, Stats: Jason Rigatti, Ian Schwartz. Stats Supervisors: Lawrence Fischer, Kelvin Lee. Stats Coordinators: Jake Fox, Dominic French.

MiLB.com Official Website of Minor League Baseball
Mailing Address: 75 Ninth Ave, New York, NY 10011. Telephone: (212) 485-3444. Fax: (212) 485-3456. Website: MiLB.com.
Director, Minor League Club Initiatives: Nathan Blackmon. Managing Producer, MiLB.com: Brendon Desrochers. Club Producers: Dan Marinis, Danny Wild. Columnist: Ben Hill.

STATS LLC
Mailing Address: 2775 Shermer Road, Northbrook, IL 60062. Telephone: (847) 583-2100. Fax: (847) 470-9140.
Website: www.stats.com. Email: sales@stats.com. Twitter: @STATSBiznews; @STATS_MLB
CEO: Gary Walrath.
Chief Operating Officer: Robert Schur. EVP, Global Sales/Marketing: Greg Kirkorsky. EVP, Pro Analytics: Bill Squadron. SVP, Products: Jim Corelis. VP, Marketing: Kirsten Porter. Director, Marketing/Communications: Nick Stamm. Assistant Vice President, Sports Operations: Allan Spear. Manager, Baseball Operations: Jeff Chernow.

TELEVISION NETWORKS

ESPN/ESPN2
Mailing Address, ESPN Connecticut: ESPN Plaza, Bristol, CT 06010.
Telephone: (860) 766-2000. Fax: (860) 766-2213. Mailing Address, ESPN New York Executive Offices: 77 W 66th St, New York, NY, 10023. Telephone: (212) 456-7777. Fax: (212) 456-2930.
Executive Chairman, ESPN, Inc.: George Bodenheimer.
President: John Skipper. Executive VP, Administration: Ed Durso. Executive VP, Programming/Production: John Wildhack. Executive VP, Program Scheduling/Development: Norby Williamson. Executive VP, News/Talent/ Content Operations: Steve Anderson. Senior VP/Executive Producer, Production: Jed Drake. Senior VP Production/ Remote Events: Mark Gross. Senior VP Programming Acquisitions: Burke Magnus. VP, Production: Mike McQuade. Coordinating Producer, Baseball Tonight: Fernando Lopez. Senior Publicist, Communications: Kristen Hudak (Kristen.M.Hudak@espn.com).

FOX SPORTS/FOX SPORTS 1
Mailing Address, Los Angeles: Fox Network Center, Building 101, Fifth floor, 10201 West Pico Blvd., Los Angeles, CA 90035. Telephone: (310) 369-6000. Fax: (310) 969-6700. Mailing Address, New York: 1211 Avenue of the Americas, 20th Floor, New York, NY 10036. Telephone: (212) 556-2500. Fax: (212) 354-6902. Website: www.foxsports. com.
President/COO: Eric Shanks. Executive Vice President/Executive Producer: John Entz. General Manager/ COO, FOX Sports 1: David Nathanson. Executive VP, News: Scott Ackerson. Executive VP, Field Operations/ Engineering: Ed Delaney. Executive VP/Creative Director: Gary Hartley. Executive VP, Programming/Research: Bill Wanger. Senior VP, Production: Jack Simmons. VP, Production: Judy Boyd. VP, Field Operations/Engineering: Mike Davies. Coordinating Producer, MLB on FOX: Pete Macheska. Game Director, MLB on FOX: Bill Webb. Senior VP, Communications/Media Relations: Lou D'Ermilio. VP, Communications: Dan Bell. Director, Communications: Ileana Pena. Manager: Eddie Motl. Publicist: Valerie Krebs.

MLB NETWORK
Mailing Address: One MLB Network Plaza, Secaucus, NJ 07094. Telephone: (201) 520-6400. President: Rob McGlarry. Executive VP, Advertising/Sales: Bill Morningstar.
Senior VP, Production: Dave Patterson. Senior VP, Marketing/Promotion: Mary Beck. Senior VP, Finance/ Administration: Tony Santomauro. Senior VP, Operations/Engineering: Susan Stone. VP, Production: Mike Santini. VP, Programming: Andy Butters. VP, Engineering/IT: Mark Haden. VP, Distribution/Affiliate Sales/Marketing: Brent Fisher. VP, Studio/Broadcast Operations: Bob Mincieli. VP, Creative Services: Chris Mallory. VP, Business Public Relations, Major League Baseball: Matt Bourne. Director, Media Relations, MLB Network: Lorraine Fisher. Specialist, Media Relations, MLB Network: Lou Barricelli.

OTHER TELEVISION NETWORKS

CBS SPORTS
Mailing Address: 51 W 52nd St., New York, NY 10019. **Telephone:** (212) 975-5230. **Fax:** (212) 975-4063.
Chairman: Sean McManus. **President:** David Berson. **Executive VP, Programming:** Rob Correa. **Executive Producer/VP, Production:** Harold Bryant. **Senior VP, Communications:** Jennifer Sabatelle.

CNN SPORTS
Mailing Address: One CNN Center, Atlanta, GA 30303. **Telephone:** (404) 878-1600. **Fax:** (404) 878-0011.
Vice President, Production: Jeffrey Green.

HBO SPORTS
Mailing Address: 1100 Avenue of the Americas, New York, NY 10036. **Telephone:** (212) 512-1000. **Fax:** (212) 512-1751. **President, HBO Sports:** Ken Hershman.

ROGERS SPORTSNET (Canada)
Mailing Address: 9 Channel Nine Court, Toronto, ON M1S 4B5. **Telephone:** (416) 332-5600. **Fax:** (416) 332-5629.
Website: www.sportsnet.ca.
President, Rogers Media: Keith Pelley. **President, Rogers Sportsnet:** Scott Moore. **Director, Communications/Promotions:** Dave Rashford.

THE SPORTS NETWORK (Canada)
Mailing Address: 9 Channel Nine Court, Toronto, ON M1S 4B5. **Telephone:** (416) 384-5000. **Fax:** (416) 332-4337.
Website: www.tsn.ca.

RADIO NETWORKS

ESPN RADIO
Address: ESPN Plaza, 935 Middle St., Bristol, CT 06010. **Telephone:** (860) 766-2000, (800) 999-9985. **Fax:** (860) 766-4505. **Website:** http://espn.go.com/espnradio.
GM, ESPN Radio Network: Mo Davenport. **Vice President, Network Content:** David Roberts. **Vice President, Deportes Programming/Business Initiatives:** Freddy Rolon. **Senior Director, Radio Programming/Digital Audio Content:** Peter Gianesini. **Director Affiliate Relations:** Jeff Martindale. **Executive Producer II:** John Martin.

SIRIUS XM SATELLITE RADIO
Mailing Address: 1500 Eckington Place NE, Washington, DC 20002. **Telephone:** (202) 380-4000. **Fax:** 202-380-4500.
Hotline: (866) 652-6696. **E-Mail Address:** mlb@siriusxm.com. **Website:** www.siriusxm.com.
President/Chief Content Officer: Scott Greenstein. **Senior VP, Sports:** Steve Cohen. **VP, Sports:** Brian Hamilton.
Director, MLB programming: Chris Eno. **Senior Director, Communications/Sports Programming:** Andrew Fitzpatrick.

SPORTS BYLINE USA
Mailing Address: 300 Broadway, Suite 8, San Francisco, CA 94133. **Telephone:** (415) 434-8300. **Guest Line:** (800) 358-4457. **Studio Line:** (800) 878-7529. **Fax:** (415) 391-2569. **E-Mail Address:** editor@sportsbyline.com. **Website:** www.sportsbyline.com. **President:** Darren Peck. **Executive Producer:** Ira Hankin.

YAHOO SPORTS RADIO
Mailing Address: 5353 West Alabama St., **Suite 415, Houston, TX 77056. Telephone:** (800) 224-2004. **Fax:** (713) 479-5333. **Website:** www.yahoosportsradio.com.

GENERAL INFORMATION

SCOUTING

MAJOR LEAGUE BASEBALL SCOUTING BUREAU

Mailing Address: 3500 Porsche Way, Suite 100, Ontario, CA 91764. **Telephone:** (909) 980-1881. **Fax:** (909) 980-7794. **Year Founded:** 1974.

Senior Director: Bill Bavasi. **Assistant Director:** Rick Oliver. **Office Coordinator:** Debbie Keedy. **Supervisor, Scouting Operations:** Adam Cali.

Scouts: Andy Campbell (Gilbert, AZ), Rodney Davis (Los Angeles, CA), Dan Dixon (Temecula, CA), Brad Fidler (Douglassville, PA), Sean Gamble (Sauk Rapids, MN), Rusty Gerhardt (New London, TX), Chris Heidt (Rockford, IL), Don Kohler (Asbury, NJ), Johnny Martinez (St Louis, MO), Paul Mirocke (Land O Lakes, FL), Carl Moesche (Gresham, OR), Tim Osborne (Woodstock, GA), Gary Randall (Rock Hill, SC), Kevin Saucier (Pensacola, FL), Harry Shelton (Ocoee, FL), Craig Smajstrla (Pearland, TX), Robin Wallace (Newburyport, MA), Jim Walton (Shattuck, OK).

Supervisor, Canada: Walt Burrows (Brentwood Bay, BC).

Canadian Scouts: Jason Chee-Aloy (Toronto), Ken Lenihan (Bedford, Nova Scotia), Jasmin Roy (Longueuil, Quebec), Bob Smyth (Ladysmith, BC), Tony Wylie (Anchorage, AK).

Supervisor, Latin America, Puerto Rico: Pepito Centeno (Cidra, PR). **Latin American Scouts:** Franco Frias (Dominican Republic), Raul Gomez (Dominican Republic), Luis Perez (Venezuela), Julio Cordido (Venezuela).

Video Technicians: Jabari Barnett (Phoenix, AZ), Matt Barnicle (Long Beach, CA), Wayne Mathis (Cuero, TX), Felvin Veloz (Dominican Republic), Christie Wood (Raleigh, NC).

PROFESSIONAL BASEBALL SCOUTS FOUNDATION

Mailing Address: 5010 N Parkway Calabasas, Suite 201, Calabasas, CA 91302. **Telephone:** (818) 224-3906 / Fax (818) 267-5516. **Email:** cindy.pbsf@yahoo.com. **Website:** www.pbsfonline.com.

Chairman: Dennis J. Gilbert.

Executive Director: Cindy Picerni.

Board of Directors: Bill "Chief" Gayton, Pat Gillick, Derrick Hall, Roland Hemond, Gary Hughes, Jeff Idelson, Dan Jennings, JJ Lally, Tommy Lasorda, Frank Marcos, Roberta Mazur, Harry Minor, Bob Nightengale, Damon Oppenheimer, Tracy Ringolsby, John Scotti, Dale Sutherland, Kevin Towers, Dave Yoakum, John Young.

SCOUT OF THE YEAR FOUNDATION

Mailing Address: PO Box 211585, West Palm Beach, FL 33421. **Telephone:** (561) 798-5897, (561) 818-4329. **E-Mail Address:** bertmazur@aol.com.

President: Roberta Mazur. **Vice President:** Tracy Ringolsby. **Treasurer:** Ron Mazur II.

Board of Advisers: Pat Gillick, Roland Hemond, Gary Hughes, Tommy Lasorda.

Scout of the Year Program Advisory Board: Tony DeMacio, Joe Klein, Roland Hemond, Gary Hughes, Dan Jennings, Linda Pereira.

UMPIRES

JIM EVANS ACADEMY

Mailing Address: 200 South Wilcox St., #508, Castle Rock, CO 80104. **Telephone:** (303) 290-7411. **E-Mail Address:** jim@umpireacademy.com. **Website:** www.umpireacademy.com.

Operator: Jim Evans.

THE UMPIRE SCHOOL

Mailing Address: PO Box A, St. Petersburg, FL, 33731-1950. **Telephone:** (877) 799-UMPS. **Fax:** (727) 456-1745. **Email:** info@therightcall.net. **Website:** www.therightcall.net.

Director: Dusty Dellinger. **Chief of Instruction:** Mike Felt. **Curriculum Coordinator:** Larry Reveal. **Lead Rules Instructor:** Jorge Bauza. **Classroom Instructor:** Brian Sinclair. **Field Leaders:** Tyler Funneman, Mark Lollo, Darren Spagnardi. **Medical Coordinator:** Mark Stubblefield. **Administrator:** Andy Shultz.

PROFESSIONAL BASEBALL UMPIRE CORP

Street Address: 9550 16th Street North, St Petersburg, FL 33716. **Mailing Address:** PO Box A, St. Petersburg, FL 33731-1950.

Telephone: (727) 822-6937. **Fax:** (727) 821-5819.

President/CEO: Pat O'Conner. **Secretary/VP, Legal Affairs/General Counsel:** D. Scott Poley. **Director, PBUC:** Dusty Dellinger. **Chief, Instruction/PBUC Evaluator:** Mike Felt. **Field Evaluators/Instructors:** Jorge Bauza, Tyler Funneman, Larry Reveal, Darren Spagnardi, Brian Sinclair and Mark Lollo. **Medical Coordinator:** Mark Stubblefield. **Special Assistant, PBUC:** Lillian Patterson.

WENDELSTEDT UMPIRE SCHOOL

Mailing Address: PO Box 1079 Albion, MI, 49224. **Telephone:** 800-818-1690. **Fax:** 888-881-9801.

Email Address: admin@umpireschool.com. **Website:** www.umpireschool.com.

WORLD UMPIRES ASSOCIATION

Year Founded: 2000.

President: Joe West. **Vice President:** Fielden Culbreth. **Secretary/Treasurer:** Jim Reynolds.

Governing Board: Dan Bellino, Sam Holbrook, Dan Iassogna, Bill Miller, Tim Timmons, Bill Welke.

Labor Counsel: Brian Lam. **Administrator:** Phil Janssen.

TRAINERS

PROFESSIONAL BASEBALL ATHLETIC TRAINERS SOCIETY

Mailing Address: 1201 Peachtree St, 400 Colony Square, Suite 1750, Atlanta, GA 30361. **Telephone:** (404) 875-4000, ext 1. **Fax:** (404) 892-8560. **E-Mail Address:** rmallernee@mallernee-branch.com. **Website:** www.pbats.com.
Year Founded: 1983.
President: Mark O'Neal (Chicago Cubs). **Secretary:** Ron Porterfield (Tampa Bay Rays). **Treasurer:** Tom Probst (Colorado Rockies). **American League Head Athletic Trainer Representative:** Nick Kenney (Kansas City Royals). **American League Assistant Athletic Trainer Representative:** Rob Nodine (Seattle Mariners). **National League Head Athletic Trainer Representative:** Keith Dugger (Colorado Rockies). **National League Assistant Athletic Trainer Representative:** Mike Kozak (Miami Marlins). **Immediate Past President:** Richie Bancells (Baltimore Orioles). **General Counsel:** Rollin Mallernee II.

MUSEUMS

BABE RUTH BIRTHPLACE

Office Address: 216 Emory St, Baltimore, MD 21230. **Telephone:** (410) 727-1539. **Fax:** (410) 727-1652. **E-Mail Address:** info@baberuthmuseum.org . **Website:** www.baberuthmuseum.com.
Year Founded: 1973.
Executive Director: Mike Gibbons. **Curator:** Amanda Peacock. **Communications:** John Hein
Fall/Winter Hours: Museum open Tuesday-Sunday: 10 am to 5 pm Closed: New Year's Day, Thanksgiving and Christmas.
Spring/Summer Hours: Museum open Monday-Sunday: 10 am to 5 pm **Open until 7 on Oriole Night Game Days

CANADIAN BASEBALL HALL OF FAME AND MUSEUM

Museum Address: 386 Church St., St. Marys, Ontario N4X 1C2. **Mailing Address:** PO Box 1838, St Marys, Ontario N4X 1C2. **Telephone:** (519) 284-1838. **Fax:** (519) 284-1234. **E-Mail Address:** baseball@baseballhalloffame.ca. **Website:** www.baseballhalloffame.ca.
Year Founded: 1983.
Director, Operations: Scott Crawford.
Hours: May-weekends only; 10:30-4 pm (June 1-August 31-Monday-Saturday); 10:30-4 pm (Sunday, noon-4pm; Sept 1-Oct 10, Thursday-Saturday; Sunday noon-4.

FIELD OF DREAMS MOVIE SITE

Address: 28995 Lansing Rd, Dyersville, IA 52040. **Mailing Address:** PO BOX 300, Dyersville, IA. **52040. Telephone:** (563) 875-8404; (888) 875-8404. **Fax:** (888) 519-2254.
E-Mail Address: info@fodmoviesite.com. **Website:** www.fodmoviesite.com.
Year Founded: 1989. **Gift Shop Office/Business Manager:** Betty Boeckenstedt.
Hours: April-November, 9 am-6 pm

WORLD OF LITTLE LEAGUE: PETER J. McGOVERN MUSEUM AND OFFICIAL STORE

Office Address: 525 Route 15, South Williamsport, PA 17702. **Mailing Address:** PO Box 3485, Williamsport, PA 17701. **Telephone:** (570) 326-3607. **Fax:** (570) 326-2267. **E-Mail Address:** museum@littleleague.org. **Website:** www. LittleLeagueMuseum.org. **Facebook:** LittleLeagueMuseum
Year Founded: 1982.
Vice President/Executive Director: Lance Van Auken. **Director, Public Programming/Outreach:** Janice Ogurcak. **Curator:** Adam Thompson.
Museum Hours: Open 9 am to 5 pm, Monday-Sunday. **Closed:** Easter, Thanksgiving, Dec 24, 25, 31 and New Year's Day.

LOUISVILLE SLUGGER MUSEUM AND FACTORY

Office Address: 800 W. Main St., Louisville, KY 40202.
Telephone: (502) 588-7228, (877) 775-8443. **Fax:** (502) 585-1179. **Website:** www.sluggermuseum.com.
Year Founded: 1996.
Executive Director: Anne Jewell.
Museum Hours: Jan 1-June 30/Aug 10-Dec 31, Mon-Sat 9 am-5 pm, Sun 11 am-5 pm. July 1-Aug. 9-Sun-Thurs 9 am-6 pm, Fri-Sat 9 am-8 pm. **Closed:** Thanksgiving/Christmas Day.

NATIONAL BASEBALL HALL OF FAME AND MUSEUM

Address: 25 Main St., Cooperstown, NY 13326. **Telephone:** (888) 425-5633, (607) 547-7200. **Fax:** (607) 547-2044. **E-Mail Address:** info@baseballhalloffame.org. **Website:** www.baseballhall.org.
Year Founded: 1939.
Chairman: Jane Forbes Clark. **Vice Chairman:** Joe Morgan. **President:** Jeff Idelson.
Museum Hours: Open daily, year-round, closed only Thanksgiving, Christmas and New Year's Day. 9 am-5 pm Summer hours, 9 am-9 pm (Memorial Day weekend through the day before Labor Day.)
2015 Hall of Fame Induction Weekend: July 24-27, Cooperstown, NY.

NEGRO LEAGUES BASEBALL MUSEUM

Mailing Address: 1616 E 18th St, Kansas City, MO 64108. **Telephone:** (816) 221-1920. **Fax:** (816) 221-8424. **E-Mail Address:** bkendrick@nlbm.com. **Website:** www.nlbm.com.
Year Founded: 1990.
President: Bob Kendrick. **Executive Director Emeritus:** Don Motley.
Museum Hours: Tues-Sat 9 am-6 pm; Sun noon-6 pm.

NOLAN RYAN FOUNDATION AND EXHIBIT CENTER
Mailing Address: 2925 South Bypass 35, Alvin, TX 77511. Telephone: (281) 388-1134. FAX: (281) 388-1135. Website: www.nolanryanfoundation.org.
Hours: Mon.-Fri. 9 am-4 pm The exhibit is closed Saturdays and Sundays.

RESEARCH

SOCIETY FOR AMERICAN BASEBALL RESEARCH
Mailing Address: 4455 East Camelback Rd, Suite D-140, Phoenix, AZ 85018. Telephone: (800) 969-7227. Fax: (602) 595-5690. Website: www.sabr.org.
Year Founded: 1971.
President: Vince Gennaro. Vice President: Bill Nowlin. Secretary: Todd Lebowitz. Treasurer: F.X. Flinn. Directors: Ty Waterman, Chris Dial, Emily Hawks, Leslie Heaphy. Executive Director: Marc Appleman. Web Content Editor/Producer: Jacob Pomrenke.

ALUMNI ASSOCIATION

MAJOR LEAGUE BASEBALL PLAYERS ALUMNI ASSOCIATION
Mailing Address: 1631 Mesa Ave, Copper Building, Suite D, Colorado Springs, CO 80906. Telephone: (719) 477-1870. Fax: (719) 477-1875. E-Mail Address: postoffice@mlbpaa.com. Website: www.baseballalumni.com. Facebook: facebook.com/majorleaguebaseballplayersalumniassociation. Twitter: @MLBPAA.
Chief Executive Officer: Dan Foster (dan@mlbpaa.com). Chief Operating Officer: Geoffrey Hixson (geoff@mlbpaa.com). Vice President, Operations: Mike Groll (mikeg@mlbpaa.com). Director, Communications: Nikki Warner (nikki@mlbpaa.com). Director, Development: Elaine Riebow (elaine@mlbpaa.com). Director, Membership: Kate Hutchinson (Kate@mlbpaa.com). Director, Memorabilia: Greg Thomas (greg@mlbpaa.com). Special Events Coordinator: Rene Vizcarra (Rene@mlbpaa.com). Special Events Coordinator: Eric Kronebusch (eric@mlbpaa.com). Public Relations Assistant: Rachel Levitsky (Rachel@mlbpaa.com). Database Administrator: Chris Burkeen (cburkeen@mlbpaa.com)

MAJOR LEAGUE ALUMNI MARKETING
Chief Executive Officer: Dan Foster (dan@mlbpaa.com). Chief Operating Officer: Geoffrey Hixson (geoff@mlbpaa.com). Vice President, Legends Entertainment Group: Chris Torgusen (chris@mlbpaa.com). Vice President of Operations: Mike Groll (mikeg@mlbpaa.com). Director, Administration: Mary Russell Baucom (maryrussell@mlbpaa.com). Marketing Coordinator, Legends Entertainment Group: Ryan Thomas (rthomas@mlbpaa.com). Director of New Business Development: Pete Kelly (pete@mlbpaa.com). Memorabilia Coordinator: Matt Tissi (mtissi@mlbpaa.com). Account Executive: Jennifer Gulino (Jennifer@mlbpaa.com). Memorabilia Coordinator: Chris Spomer (cspomer@mlbpaa.com). Sales Manager: Kyle Matthews (kyle@mlbpaa.com). Sales Manager: Amy Wagner (Amy@mlbpaa.com).

MINOR LEAGUE BASEBALL ALUMNI ASSOCIATION
Mailing Address: PO Box A, St. Petersburg, FL 33731-1950. Telephone: (727) 822-6937. Fax: (727) 821-5819. E-Mail Address: alumni@MiLB.com. Website: www.milb.com.

BASEBALL ASSISTANCE TEAM (B.A.T.)
Mailing Address: 245 Park Ave, 31st Floor, New York, NY 10167.
Telephone: (212) 931-7822, Fax: (212) 949-5433. Website: www.baseballassistanceteam.com.
Year Founded: 1986. To Make a Donation: (866) 605-4594.
President: Randy Winn.
Vice President: Bob Watson.
Board of Directors: Sal Bando, Dick Freeman, Steve Garvey, Luis Gonzalez, Adam Jones, Mark Letendre, Alan Nahmias, Christine O'Reilly, Staci Slaughter, Gary Thorne, Bob Watson, Greg Wilcox, Randy Winn.
Director: Erik Nilsen. Secretary: Thomas Ostertag. Treasurer: Scott Stamp. Advisor: Laurel Prieb. Consultant: Sam McDowell. Consultant: Dr. Genoveva Javier. Consultant: Benny Ayala. Operations: Vladimir Cruz, Michelle Fucich.

MINISTRY

BASEBALL CHAPEL
Mailing Address: PO Box 302, Springfield, PA 19064. Telephone: (610) 999-3600.
E-Mail Address: office@baseballchapel.org. Website: www.baseballchapel.org.
Year Founded: 1973.
President: Vince Nauss.
Hispanic Ministry: Cali Magallanes, Gio Llerena. Director, Ministry Operations: Rob Crose.
Board of Directors: Don Christensen, Greg Groh, Dave Howard, Vince Nauss, Bill Sampen, Walt Wiley.

CATHOLIC ATHLETES FOR CHRIST
Mailing Address: 3703 Cameron Mills Road, Alexandria, VA 22305. Telephone: (703) 239-3070.
E-Mail Address: info@catholicathletesforchrist.org. Website: www.catholicathletesforchrist.org.
Year Founded: 2006.
President: Ray McKenna.
MLB Ministry Coordinator: Kevin O'Malley.
MLB Athlete Advisory Board Members: Mike Sweeney (Chairman), Jeff Suppan (Vice Chairman), Sal Bando, David Eckstein, Terry Kennedy, Jack McKeon, Darrell Miller, Mike Piazza, Vinny Rottino, Craig Stammen.

TRADE/EMPLOYMENT

BASEBALL WINTER MEETINGS
Mailing Address: PO Box A, St. Petersburg, FL 33731. **Telephone:** (727) 822-6937. **Fax:** (727) 821-5819. **E-Mail Address:** BaseballWinterMeetings@milb.com. **Website:** www.baseballwintermeetings.com.
2015 Convention: Dec 7-10, Gaylord Opryland Resort & Convention Center, Nashville, Tenn.

BASEBALL TRADE SHOW
Mailing Address: PO Box A, St. Petersburg, FL 33731-1950. **Telephone:** (866) 926-6452. **Fax:** (727) 683-9865. **E-Mail Address:** TradeShow@MiLB.com. **Website:** www.BaseballTradeShow.com.
2015 Show: Dec. 8-10, Gaylord Opryland Resort & Convention Center, Nashville, Tenn.

PROFESSIONAL BASEBALL EMPLOYMENT OPPORTUNITIES
Mailing Address: PO Box A, St Petersburg, FL 33731-1950. **Telephone:** 866-WE-R-PBEO. **Fax:** 727-821-5819. **Website:** www.PBEO.com. **Email:** info@PBEO.com. **Contact:** Mark Labban, Manager, Business Development.

BASEBALL CARD MANUFACTURERS

PANINI AMERICA INC.
Mailing Address: Panini America, 5325 FAA Blvd., Suite 100, Irving TX 75061. Telephone: (817) 662-5300, (800) 852-8833. **Website:** www.paniniamerica.net. Email: RM_Marketing@paniniamerica.net. **Marketing Manager:** Scott Prusha.

GRANDSTAND CARDS
Mailing Address: 22647 Ventura Blvd., #192, Woodland Hills, CA 91364. **Telephone:** (818) 992-5642. **Fax:** (818) 348-9122. **E-Mail Address:** gscards1@pacbell.net.

BRANDT SPORTS MARKETING (FORMERLY MULTIAD SPORTS)
Mailing Address: 8914 N. Prairie Pointe Ct., Peoria, IL 61615. **Telephone:** (800) 720-9740. **Fax:** (563) 386-4817. **Website:** http://www.brandtco.com/sports.
Contact: Jim Dougas, jim.douglas@brandtco.com. **Phone:** 309-215-9243. **Fax:** 563-386-4817.
Contact: Dave Mateer, dave.mateer@brandtco.com. **Phone:** 309-215-9248. **Fax:** 563-386-4817.

TOPPS
Mailing Address: One Whitehall St., New York, NY 10004. **Telephone:** (212) 376-0300. **Fax:** (212) 376-0573. **Website:** www.topps.com.

UPPER DECK
Mailing Address: 2251 Rutherford Rd., Carlsbad, CA 92008. **Telephone:** (800) 873-7332. **Fax:** (760) 929-6548.
E-Mail Address: customer_service@upperdeck.com. **Website:** www.upperdeck.com.

SPRING TRAINING

CACTUS LEAGUE

For spring training schedules, see page 240

ARIZONA DIAMONDBACKS

Major League
   Complex Address: Salt River Fields at Talking Stick, 7555 North Pima Road, Scottsdale, AZ 85256. **Telephone:** (480) 270-5000. **Seating Capacity:** 11,000 (7,000 fixed seats, 4,000 lawn seats). **Location:** From Loop-101, use exit 44 (Indian Bend Road) and proceed west for approximately one-half mile; turn right at Pima Road to travel north and proceed one-quarter mile; three entrances to Salt River Fields will be available on the right-hand side.

Minor League
   Complex Address: Same as major league club.

CHICAGO CUBS

Major League
   Complex Address: Cubs Park, 2330 West Rio Salado Parkway, Mesa, AZ 85201. **Telephone:** (480) 668-0500. **Seating Capacity:** 15,000.
   Location: on the land of the former Riverview Golf Course, bordered by the 101 and 202 interchange in Mesa.

Minor League
   Complex Address: Same as major league club.

CHICAGO WHITE SOX

Major League
   Complex Address: Camelback Ranch-Glendale, 10710 West Camelback Road, Phoenix, AZ 85037. **Telephone:** (623) 302-5000. **Seating Capacity:** 13,000.
   Hotel Address: Comfort Suites Glendale, 9824 W Camelback Rd, Glendale, AZ 85305. **Telephone:** (623) 271-9005. **Hotel Address:** Renaissance Glendale Hotel & Spa, 9495 W Coyotes Blvd, Glendale, AZ 85305. **Telephone:** 629-937-3700.

Minor League
   Complex/Hotel Address: Same as major league club.

CINCINNATI REDS

Major League
   Complex Address: Cincinnati Reds Player Development Complex, 3125 S Wood Blvd, Goodyear, AZ 85338. **Telephone:** (623) 932-6590. **Ballpark Address:** Goodyear Ballpark, 1933 S Ballpark Way, Goodyear, AZ 85338. **Telephone:** (623) 882-3120.
   Hotel Address: Marriott Residence Inn, 7350 N Zanjero Blvd, Glendale, AZ 85305. **Telephone:** (623) 772-8900. **Fax:** (623) 772-8905.

Minor League
   Complex/Hotel Address: Same as major league club.

CLEVELAND INDIANS

   Complex Address: Cleveland Indians Player Development Complex 2601 S Wood Blvd, Goodyear, AZ 85338; Goodyear Ballpark 1933 S Ballpark Way, AZ 85338. **Telephone:** (623) 882-3120.
   Location: From Downtown Phoenix/East Valley: West on I-10 to Exit 127, Bullard Avenue and proceed south

(left off exit), Bullard Avenue turns into West Lower Buckeye Road. Turn left on to Wood Blvd.
   Hotel Address: (Media) Hampton Inn and Suites, 2000 N Litchfield Rd, Goodyear, AZ 85395. **Telephone:** (623) 536-1313. **Hotel Address:** Holiday Inn Express, 1313 N Litchfield Rd, Goodyear, AZ 85395. **Telephone:** (623) 535-1313. **Hotel Address:** TownePlace Suites, 13971 West Celebrate Life Way, Goodyear, AZ 85338. **Telephone:** (623) 535-5009. **Hotel Address:** Residence Inn by Marriott, 2020 N Litchfield Rd, Goodyear, AZ 85395. **Telephone:** (623) 866-1313.

Minor League
   Complex Address: Same as major league club.

COLORADO ROCKIES

Major League
   Complex Address: Salt River Fields at Talking Stick, 7555 North Pima Rd, Scottsdale, AZ 85258. **Telephone:** (480) 270-5800. **Seating Capacity:** 11,000 (7,000 fixed seats, 4,000 lawn seats). **Location:** From Loop-101, use exit 44 (Indian Bend Road) and proceed west for approximately one-half mile; turn right at Pima Road to travel north and proceed one-quarter mile; three entrances to Salt River Fields will be available on the right-hand side. **Visiting Team Hotel:** The Scottsdale Plaza Resort, 7200 North Scottsdale Road, Scottsdale, AZ 85253. **Telephone:** (480) 948-5000. **Fax:** (480) 951-5100.

Minor League
   Complex/Hotel Address: Same as major league club.

KANSAS CITY ROYALS

Major League
   Complex Address: Surprise Stadium, 15850 North Bullard Ave, Surprise, AZ 85374. **Telephone:** (623) 222-2000. **Seating Capacity:** 10,700. **Location:** I-10 West to Route 101 North, 101 North to Bell Road, left on Bell for five miles, stadium on left.
   Hotel Address: Wigwam Resort, 300 East Wigwam Blvd, Litchfield Park, Arizona 85340. **Telephone:** (623) 935-3811.

Minor League
   Complex Address: Same as major league club. **Hotel Address:** Comfort Hotel and Suites, 13337 W Grand Ave, Surprise, AZ 85374. **Telephone:** (623) 583-3500.

LOS ANGELES ANGELS

Major League
   Complex Address: Tempe Diablo Stadium, 2200 West Alameda Drive, Tempe, AZ 85282. **Telephone:** (480) 858-7500. **Fax:** (480) 438-7583. **Seating Capacity:** 9,558. **Location:** I-10 to exit 153B (48th Street), south one mile on 48th Street to Alameda Drive, left on Alameda.

Minor League
   Complex Address: Tempe Diablo Minor League Complex, 2225 W Westcourt Way, Tempe, AZ 85282. **Telephone:** (480) 858-7558.
   Hotel Address: Sheraton Phoenix Airport, 1600 South 52nd Street, Tempe, AZ 85281. **Telephone:** (480) 967-6600.

LOS ANGELES DODGERS

Major League
   Complex Address: Camelback Ranch, 10710 West Camelback Rd, Phoenix, AZ 85037. **Seating Capacity:** 13,000, plus standing room.
   Location: I-10 or I-17 to Loop 101 West or North, Take Exit 5, Camelback Road West to ballpark. **Telephone:** (623) 302-5000. **Hotel:** Unavailable.

Minor League
   Complex/Hotel Address: Same as major league club.

MILWAUKEE BREWERS

Major League
   Complex Address: Maryvale Baseball Park, 3600 N 51st Ave, Phoenix, AZ 85031. **Telephone:** (623) 245-5555. **Seating Capacity:** 9,000. **Location:** I-10 to 51st Ave, north on 51st Ave
   Hotel Address: Unavailable.

Minor League
   Complex Address: Maryvale Baseball Complex, 3805 N 53rd Ave, Phoenix, AZ 85031. **Telephone:** (623) 245-5600. **Hotel Address:** Unavailable.

OAKLAND A'S

Major League
   Complex Address: Hohokam Stadium, 1235 North Center Street, Mesa, AZ 85201. **Telephone:** (480) 644-4451. **Seating Capacity:** 10,000.
   Hotel Address: Unavailable.

Minor League
   Complex Address: Same as major league club.

SAN DIEGO PADRES

Major League
   Complex Address: Peoria Sports Complex, 8131 West Paradise Lane, Peoria, AZ 85382. **Telephone:** (623) 773-8700. **Fax:** (623) 486-7154. **Seating Capacity:** 12,000.
   Location: I-17 to Bell Road exit, west on Bell to 83rd Ave Hotel Address: La Quinta Inn & Suites (623) 487-1900, 16321 N 83rd Avenue, Peoria, AZ 85382.

Minor League
   Complex/Hotel: Country Inn and Suites (623) 879-9000, 20221 N 29th Avenue, Phoenix, AZ 85027.

SAN FRANCISCO GIANTS

Major League
   Complex Address: Scottsdale Stadium, 7408 East Osborn Rd, Scottsdale, AZ 85251. **Telephone:** (480) 990-7972. **Fax:** (480) 990-2643. **Seating Capacity:** 11,500. **Location:** Scottsdale Road to Osborne Road, east on Osborne for A 1/2 mile. **Hotel Address:** Hilton Garden Inn Scottsdale Old Town, 7324 East Indian School Rd, Scottsdale, AZ 85251. **Telephone:** (480) 481-0400.

Minor League
   Complex Address: Giants Minor League Complex 8045 E Camelback Road, Scottsdale, AZ 85251. **Telephone:** (480) 990-0052. **Fax:** (480) 990-2349.

SEATTLE MARINERS

Major League
   Complex Address: Peoria Sports Complex, 8131 West Paradise Lane, Peoria, AZ 85382. **Telephone:** (623) 776-4800. **Fax:** (623) 776-4829. **Seating Capacity:** 12,000. **Location:** I-17 to Bell Road exit, west on Bell to 83rd Ave
   Hotel Address: La Quinta Inn & Suites, 16321 N 83rd Ave, Peoria, AZ 85382. **Telephone:** (623) 487-1900.

Minor League
   Complex Address: Peoria Sports Complex (1993), 15707 N 83rd Ave, Peoria, AZ 85382. **Telephone:** (623) 776-4800. **Fax:** (623) 776-4828. **Hotel Address:** Hampton Inn, 8408 W Paradise Lane, Peoria, AZ 85382. **Telephone:** (623) 486-9918.

TEXAS RANGERS

Major League
   Complex Address: Surprise Stadium, 15754 North Bullard Ave, Surprise, AZ 85374. **Telephone:** (623) 266-8100. **Seating Capacity:** 10,714. **Location:** I-10 West to Route 101 North, 101 North to Bell Road, left at Bell for seven miles, stadium on left. **Hotel Address:** Residence Inn Surprise, 16418 N Bullard Ave, Surprise, AZ 85374. **Telephone:** (623) 249-6333.

Minor League
   Complex Address: Same as major league club. **Hotel Address:** Holiday Inn Express and Suites Surprise, 16549 North Bullard Ave, Surprise AZ 85374. **Telephone:** (800) 939-4249.

GRAPEFRUIT LEAGUE

For spring training schedules, see page 240

ATLANTA BRAVES

Major League
   Stadium Address: Champion Stadium at ESPN Wide World of Sports Complex, 700 S Victory Way, Kissimmee, FL 34747. **Telephone:** (407) 939-1500.
   Seating Capacity: 9,500. **Location:** I-4 to exit 25B (Highway 192 West), follow signs to Magic Kingdom/Wide World of Sports Complex, right on Victory Way.
   Hotel Address: World Center Marriott, World Center Drive, Orlando, FL 32821. **Telephone:** (407) 239-4200.

Minor League
   Complex Address: Same as major league club. **Telephone:** (407) 939-2232. **Fax:** (407) 939-2225.
   Hotel Address: Marriot Village at Lake Buena Vista, 8623 Vineland Ave, Orlando, FL 32821. **Telephone:** (407) 938-9001.

BALTIMORE ORIOLES

Major League
   Complex Address: Ed Smith Stadium, 2700 12th Street, Sarasota, FL 34237. **Telephone:** (941) 893-6300. **Fax:** (941) 893-6377. **Seating Capacity:** 7,500. **Location:** I-75 to exit 210, West on Fruitville Road, right on Tuttle Avenue. **Hotel Address:** Residence Inn, 1040 University Blvd, Sarasota, FL 34234. **Telephone:** (941) 358-1468.

Minor League
   Complex Address: Buck O'Neil Baseball Complex at Twin Lakes Park, 6700 Clark Rd, Sarasota, FL 34241. **Telephone:** (941) 923-1996. **Hotel Address:** Days Inn, 5774 Clark Rd, Sarasota, FL 34233. **Telephone:** (941) 921-7812. **Hotel Address:** AmericInn, 5931 Fruitville Rd, Sarasota, FL 34232. **Telephone:** (941) 342-8778.

BOSTON RED SOX

Major League
   Complex Address: JetBlue Park at Fenway South, 11500 Fenway South Drive, Fort Myers, FL 33913.
   Telephone: (239) 334-4700. **Directions:** From the North: Take I-75 South to Exit 131 (Daniels Parkway); Make a left off the exit and go east for approximately two miles; JetBlue Park will be on your left. **From the South:** Take I-75 North to Exit 131 (Daniels Parkway); Make a right off exit and go east for approximately two miles; JetBlue Park will be on your left.

Minor League
   Complex/Hotel Address: Fenway South, 11500 Fenway South Drive, Fort Myers, FL 33913.

DETROIT TIGERS

Major League
   Complex Address: Joker Marchant Stadium, 2301 Lakeland Hills Blvd, Lakeland, FL 33805. **Telephone:** (863) 686-8075. **Seating Capacity:** 9,000. **Location:** I-4 to exit 33 (Lakeland Hills Boulevard).

Minor League
   Complex Address: Tigertown, 2125 N Lake Ave, Lakeland, FL 33805. **Telephone:** (863) 686-8075.

HOUSTON ASTROS

Major League
   Complex Address: Osceola County Stadium, 631 Heritage Park Way, Kissimmee, FL 34744. **Telephone:** (321) 697-3200. **Fax:** (321) 697-3197. **Seating Capacity:** 5,300. **Location:** From Florida Turnpike South, take exit 244, west on US 192, right on Bill Beck Blvd. **Hotel Address:** Embassy Suites Orlando-Lake Buena Vista South, 4955 Kyngs Heath Rd, Kissimmee, FL 34746. **Telephone:** (407) 597-4000.

Minor League
   Complex Information: Same as Major League club. **Hotel Address:** Holiday Inn Main Gate East, 5711 W Irlo Bronson Memorial Hwy, Kissimmee, FL 34746. **Telephone:** (407) 396-4222.

MIAMI MARLINS

Major League
   Complex Address: Roger Dean Stadium, 4751 Main Street, Jupiter, FL 33458. **Telephone:** (561) 775-1818. **Telephone:** (561) 799-1346. **Seating Capacity:** 7,000. **Location:** I-95 to exit 83, east on Donald Ross Road for one mile to Central Blvd, left at light, follow Central Boulevard to circle and take Main Street to Roger Dean Stadium. **Hotel Address:** Palm Beach Gardens Marriott, 4000 RCA Boulevard, Palm Beach Gardens, FL 33410. **Telephone:** (561) 622-8888. **Fax:** (561) 622-0052.

Minor League
   Complex/Hotel Address: Same as major league club.

MINNESOTA TWINS

Major League
   Complex Address: Centurylink Sports Complex/Hammond Stadium, 14100 Six Mile Cypress Parkway, Fort Myers, FL 33912. **Telephone:** (239) 533-7610. **Seating Capacity:** 8,100. **Location:** Exit 21 off I-75, west on Daniels Parkway, left on Six Mile Cypress Parkway. **Hotel Address:** Four Points by Sheraton, 13600 Treeline Avenue South, Ft. Myers, FL 33913. **Telephone:** (800) 338-9467.

Minor League
   Complex/Hotel Address: Same as major league club.

NEW YORK METS

Major League
   Complex Address: Tradition Field, 525 NW Peacock Blvd, Port St. Lucie, FL 34986. **Telephone:** (772) 871-2100. **Seating Capacity:** 7,000. **Location:** Exit 121C (St Lucie West Blvd) off I-95, east 1/4 mile, left onto NW Peacock. **Hotel Address:** Hilton Hotel, 8542 Commerce Centre Drive, Port St. Lucie, FL 34986. **Telephone:** (772) 871-6850.

Minor League
   Complex Address: Same as major league club. **Hotel Address:** Main Stay Suites, 8501 Champions Way, Port St. Lucie, FL 34986. **Telephone:** (772) 460-8882.

NEW YORK YANKEES

Major League

Complex Address: George M. Steinbrenner Field, One Steinbrenner Dr., Tampa, FL 33614. **Telephone:** (813) 875-7753. **Seating Capacity:** 11,076. **Hotel:** Unavailable.

Minor League

Complex Address: Yankees Player Development/ Scouting Complex, 3102 N Himes Ave, Tampa, FL 33607. **Telephone:** (813) 875-7569. **Hotel:** Unavailable.

PHILADELPHIA PHILLIES

Major League

Complex Address: Bright House Networks Field, 601 N. Old Coachman Rd, Clearwater, FL 33765. **Telephone:** (727) 467-4457. **Fax:** (727) 712-4498. **Seating Capacity:** 8,500. **Location:** Route 60 West, right on Old Coachman Road, ballpark on right after Drew Street. **Hotel Address:** Holiday Inn Express, 2580 Gulf to Bay Blvd, Clearwater, FL 33765. **Telephone:** (727) 797-6300. **Hotel Address:** La Quinta Inn, 21338 US 19 North, Clearwater, FL 33765. **Telephone:** (727) 799-1565.

Minor League

Complex Address: Carpenter Complex, 651 N Old Coachman Rd, Clearwater, FL 33765. **Telephone:** (727) 799-0503. **Fax:** (727) 726-1793. **Hotel Addresses:** Hampton Inn, 21030 US Highway 19 North, Clearwater, FL 34625. **Telephone:** (727) 797-8173. **Hotel Address:** Econolodge, 21252 US Hwy 19, Clearwater, FL 34625. **Telephone:** (727) 799-1569.

PITTSBURGH PIRATES

Major League

Stadium Address: McKechnie Field, 17th Ave West and Ninth Street West, Bradenton, FL 34205. **Seating Capacity:** 8,500. **Location:** US 41 to 17th Ave, west to 9th Street. **Telephone:** (941) 747-3031. **Fax:** (941) 747-9549.

Minor League

Complex: Pirate City, 1701 27th St E, Bradenton, FL 34208.

ST. LOUIS CARDINALS

Major League

Complex Address: Roger Dean Stadium, 4795 University Dr., **Jupiter, FL 33458. Telephone:** (561) 775-1818. **Fax:** (561) 799-1380. **Seating Capacity:** 6,864. **Location:** I-95 to exit 58, east on Donald Ross Road for 1/4 mile. **Hotel Address:** Embassy Suites, 4350 PGA Blvd, Palm Beach Gardens, FL 33410. **Telephone:** (561) 622-1000.

Minor League

Complex: Same as major league club. **Hotel:** Double Tree Palm Beach Gardens. **Telephone:** (561) 622-2260.

TAMPA BAY RAYS

Major League

Stadium Address: Charlotte Sports Park, 2300 El Jobean Road, Port Charlotte, FL 33948. **Telephone:** (941) 235-5025. **Seating Capacity:** 6,823 (5,028 fixed seats). **Location:** I-75 to US-17 to US-41, turn left onto El Jobean Rd. **Hotel Address:** None.

Minor League

Complex/Hotel Address: None.

TORONTO BLUE JAYS

Major League

Stadium Address: Florida Auto Exchange Stadium, 373 Douglas Ave, Dunedin, FL 34698. **Telephone:** (727) 733-0429. **Seating Capacity:** 5,509. **Location:** US 19 North to Sunset Point; west on Sunset Point to Douglas Avenue; north on Douglas to Stadium; ballpark is on the southeast corner of Douglas and Beltrees.

Minor League

Complex Address: Bobby Mattick Training Center at Englebert Complex, 1700 Solon Ave, Dunedin, FL 34698. **Telephone: (727) 733-9302. Hotel Address:** Clarion Inn & Suites, 20967 US Highway 19 North Clearwater, FL 33765. **Telephone:** (727) 799-1181.

WASHINGTON NATIONALS

Major League

Complex Address: Space Coast Stadium, 5800 Stadium Pkwy, Viera, FL 32940. **Telephone:** (321) 633-9200. **Seating Capacity:** 8,100. **Location:** I-95 southbound to Fiske Blvd (exit 74), south on Fiske/Stadium Parkway to stadium; I-95 northbound to State Road #509/Wickham Road (exit 73), left off exit, right on Lake Andrew Drive; turn right on Stadium Parkway, stadium is 1/2 mile on left. **Hotel Address:** Hampton Inn, 130 Sheriff Drive, Viera, FL. **Telephone:** (321) 255-6868.

Minor League

Complex Address: Carl Barger Complex, 5600 Stadium Pkwy, Viera, FL 32940. **Telephone:** (321) 633-8119. **Hotel:** Same as major league club.

MINOR
LEAGUES

MINOR LEAGUE BASEBALL

THE NATIONAL ASSOCIATION OF PROFESSIONAL BASEBALL LEAGUES

MINOR LEAGUE BASEBALL ™

Street Address: 9550 16th St. North, St. Petersburg, FL 33716. **Mailing Address:** PO Box A, St. Petersburg, FL 33731-1950. **Telephone:** (727) 822-6937. **Fax:** (727) 821-5819. **Fax/Marketing:** (727) 894-4227. **Fax/Licensing:** (727) 825-3785. **President/CEO:** Pat O'Conner.

Vice President: Stan Brand. **Chief Operating Officer:** Brian Earle. **Chief Marketing Officer/President, MiLB Enterprises:** Michael Hand. **Senior VP, Legal Affairs/General Counsel:** Scott Poley. **Special Counsel:** George Yund. **VP, Finance:** Sean Brown. **VP, Baseball/Business Operations:** Tim Brunswick. **VP, Marketing Strategy:** Kurt Hunzeker. **VP, National/Regional Sales:** Rod Meadows. **Director, Information Technology:** Rob Colamarino. **Director, Security/Facility Operations:** Earnell Lucas. **Director, Licensing:** Sandie Hebert. **Director, Business Development:** Scott Kravchuk. **Director, Communications:** Jeff Lantz. **Assistant Director, Legal Affairs:** Louis Brown. **Manager, Baseball Operations/Executive Assistant to the President:** Mary Wooters.

Pat O'Conner

AFFILIATED MEMBERS/COUNCIL OF LEAGUE PRESIDENTS

Triple-A

League	President	Telephone	Fax Number
International	Randy Mobley	(614) 791-9300	(614) 791-9009
Mexican	Plinio Escalante	011-52-555-557-1007	011-52-555-395-2454
Pacific Coast	Branch Rickey	(512) 310-2900	(512) 310-8300

Double-A

League	President	Telephone	Fax Number
Eastern	Joe McEacharn	(207) 761-2700	(207) 761-7064
Southern	Lori Webb	(770) 321-0400	(770) 321-0037
Texas	Tom Kayser	(210) 545-5297	(210) 545-5298

High Class A

League	President	Telephone	Fax Number
California	Charlie Blaney	(805) 985-8585	(805) 985-8580
Carolina	John Hopkins	(336) 691-9030	(336) 464-2737
Florida State	Chuck Murphy	(386) 252-7479	(386) 252-7495

Low Class A

League	President	Telephone	Fax Number
Midwest	Dick Nussbaum	(574) 231-3000	(574) 231-3000
South Atlantic	Eric Krupa	(727) 538-4270	(727) 499-6853

Short-Season

League	President	Telephone	Fax Number
New York-Penn	Ben Hayes	(727) 289-7112	(727) 683-9691
Northwest	Mike Ellis	(406) 541-9301	(406) 543-9463

Rookie Advanced

League	President	Telephone	Fax Number
Appalachian	Lee Landers	(704) 252-2656	Unavailable
Pioneer	Jim McCurdy	(509) 456-7615	(509) 456-0136

Rookie

League	President	Telephone	Fax Number
Arizona	Bob Richmond	(208) 429-1511	(208) 429-1525
Dominican Summer	Orlando Diaz	(809) 532-3619	(809) 532-3619
Gulf Coast	Operated by MiLB	(727) 456-1734	(727) 821-5819
Venezuela Summer	Franklin Moreno	011-58-241-823-8101	011-58-241-823-8101

NATIONAL ASSOCIATION BOARD OF TRUSTEES

TRIPLE-A
At-large: Ken Young (Norfolk). **International League:** Ken Schnacke (Columbus). **Pacific Coast League:** Sam Bernabe, Chairman (Iowa). **Mexican League:** Cuauhtemoc Rodriguez (Quintana Roo).

DOUBLE-A
Eastern League: Joe Finley (Trenton). **Southern League:** Stan Logan (Birmingham). **Texas League:** Reid Ryan (Corpus Christi).

CLASS A
California League: Tom Volpe (Stockton). **Carolina League:** Chuck Greenberg (Myrtle Beach). **Florida State League:** Ken Carson, Secretary (Dunedin). **Midwest League:** Tom Dickson (Lansing). **South Atlantic League:** Chip Moore (Rome).

SHORT-SEASON
New York-Penn League: Marv Goldklang (Hudson Valley). **Northwest League:** Bobby Brett (Spokane).

ROOKIE
Appalachian League: Mitch Lukevics (Princeton). **Pioneer League:** Dave Elmore, (Idaho Falls). **Gulf Coast League:** Bill Smith (Twins).

PROFESSIONAL BASEBALL PROMOTION CORP.
President/CEO: Pat O'Conner.
Senior Vice President, Legal Affairs/General Counsel: Scott Poley.
Chief Marketing Officer/President, MiLB Enterprises: Michael Hand. **VP, Baseball/Business Operations:** Tim Brunswick. **Chief Operating Officer:** Brian Earle. **VP, National/Regional Sales:** Rod Meadows. **VP, Finance:** Sean Brown. **Director, Information Technology:** Rob Colamarino. **Director, Licensing:** Sandie Hebert. **Director, Business Development:** Scott Kravchuk. **Director, Security/Facility Operations:** Earnell Lucas. **Manager, Human Resources:** Amber Kukulya. **Senior Assistant Director, Event Services:** Kelly Butler. **Assistant Director, Licensing:** Carrie Adams. **Assistant Director, Legal Affairs:** Louis Brown. **Assistant Director, Accounting:** James Dispanet. **Assistant Director, Business Development:** Courtney Jantz. **Senior Manager, Corporate Communications:** Mary Marandi. **Assistant Director, Account Services:** Heather Raburn.
Associate Counsel: Robert Fountain. **Manager, Business Development:** Mark Labban. **Contract Manager/Legal Assistant:** Jeannette Machicote. **Manager, Sales/Account Services:** Gabe Rendon. **Manager, Trade Show Services:** Eileen Sahin-Murphy. **Manager, Baseball/Business Operations:** Andy Shultz. **Manager, Baseball Operations/ Executive Assistant to President:** Mary Wooters. **Graphic Designer:** Ashley Allphin. **Staff Accountant:** Michelle Heystek. **Research Coordinator:** Cory Bernstine. **Executive Assistant, Marketing:** Michelle Jurado. **Coordinator, Licensing/Contracts:** Jessica Merrick. **Coordinator, E-Commerce/Business Services:** Jill Philippi. **Coordinator, Trademarks/Intellectual Properties:** Jess Vera.

PROFESSIONAL BASEBALL UMPIRE CORP.
President/CEO: Pat O'Conner.
Secretary/Vice President, Legal Affairs/General Counsel: Scott Poley.
Director, PBUC: Dusty Dellinger. **Chief, Instruction/PBUC Evaluator:** Mike Felt. **Field Evaluators/Instructors:** Jorge Bauza, Tyler Funneman, Mark Lollo, Larry Reveal, Brian Sinclair, Darren Spagnardi. **Medical Coordinator:** Mark Stubblefield. **Special Assistant, PBUC:** Lillian Patterson.

GENERAL INFORMATION

			Regular Season		All-Star Games	
	Teams	Games	Opening Day	Closing Day	Date	Host
International	14	144	April 9	Sept. 7	*July 15	Omaha
Pacific Coast	16	144	April 9	Sept. 7	*July 15	Omaha
Eastern	12	142	April 9	Sept. 7	July 15	Portland
Southern	10	140	April 9	Sept. 7	June 23	Montgomery
Texas	8	140	April 9	Sept. 7	June 30	Corpus Christi
California	10	140	April 9	Sept. 7	#June 23	R. Cucamonga
Carolina	8	140	April 9	Sept. 7	#June 23	R. Cucamonga
Florida State	12	140	April 9	Sept. 6	June 20	St. Lucie
Midwest	16	140	April 9	Sept. 7	June 16	Peoria
South Atlantic	14	140	April 9	Sept. 7	June 23	Asheville
New York-Penn	14	76	June 19	Sept. 7	Aug. 18	Aberdeen
Northwest	8	76	June 18	Sept. 6	^Aug. 4	Spokane
Appalachian	10	68	June 23	Sept. 1	None	
Pioneer	8	76	June 16	Sept. 4	^Aug. 4	Spokane
Arizona	13	56	June 20	Aug. 29	None	
Gulf Coast	16	60	June 22	Aug. 29	None	

*Triple-A All-Star Game. #California League vs. Carolina League. ^Northwest League vs. Pioneer League.

INTERNATIONAL LEAGUE

Address: 55 South High St., Suite 202, Dublin, Ohio 43017.
Telephone: (614) 791-9300. **Fax:** (614) 791-9009.
E-Mail Address: office@ilbaseball.com. **Website:** www.ilbaseball.com.
Years League Active: 1884-
President/Treasurer: Randy Mobley.
Vice Presidents: Dave Rosenfield, Tex Simone. **Assistant to the President:** Chris Sprague.
Corporate Secretary: Max Schumacher.
Directors: Don Beaver (Charlotte), Rob Crain (Scranton/Wilkes-Barre), Joe Finley (Lehigh Valley), George Habel (Durham), North Johnson (Gwinnett), Joe Napoli (Toledo), Bob Rich Jr. (Buffalo), Dave Rosenfield (Norfolk), Ken Schnacke (Columbus), Max Schumacher (Indianapolis), Naomi Silver (Rochester), Bill Dutch (Syracuse), Mike Tamburro (Pawtucket), Gary Ulmer (Louisville).
Office Manager: Gretchen Addison.
Division Structure: North—Buffalo, Lehigh Valley, Pawtucket, Rochester, Scranton/Wilkes-Barre, Syracuse. West—Columbus, Indianapolis, Louisville, Toledo. South—Charlotte, Durham, Gwinnett, Norfolk.
Regular Season: 144 games. **2015 Opening Date:** April 9. **Closing Date:** Sept 7.
All-Star Game: July 15 at Omaha (IL vs Pacific Coast League).

Randy Mobley

Playoff Format: South winner meets West winner in best of five series; wild card (non-division winner with best winning percentage) meets North winner in best of five series. Winners meet in best-of-five series for Governors' Cup championship.
Triple-A Championship Game: Sept. 22 at El Paso (IL vs Pacific Coast League).
Roster Limit: 25. **Player Eligibility:** No restrictions.
Official Baseball: Rawlings ROM-INT.
Umpires: Joey Amaral (Baltimore, MD), Jonathan Bailey (Lithia Springs, GA), Sean Barber (Lakeland, FL), Toby Basner (Snellville, GA), Joe Born (Lafayette, IN), Seth Buckminster (Fort Worth, TX), Jon Byrne (Charlotte, NC), Brian BeBrauwere (Hummelstown, PA), Clint Fagan (Tomball, TX), Ian Fazio (Springfield, MO), Jeff Gosney (Lakeland, FL), Max Guyll (Fort Wayne,IN), Adam Hamari (Marquette, MI), Tom Honec (Harrisonburg, VA), Nic Lentz (Holland, MI), Ben May (Racine, WI), Derek Mollica (Lake Worth, FL), David Soucy (Bluffton, SC), Carlos Torres (Acarigua, Venezuela), John Tumpane (Chicago, IL), Chris Vines (Canton, GA), Jansen Visconti (Latrobe, PA), Chad Whitson (Dublin, OH).

STADIUM INFORMATION

Club	Stadium	Opened	Dimensions LF	CF	RF	Capacity	2014 Att.
Buffalo	Coca-Cola Field	1988	325	404	325	18,025	535,275
Charlotte	BB&T Ballpark	2015	325	400	315	10,002	687,715
Columbus	Huntington Park	2009	325	400	318	10,100	628,980
Durham	Durham Bulls Athletic Park	1995	305	400	327	10,000	533,033
Gwinnett	Coolray Field	2009	335	400	335	10,427	303,959
Indianapolis	Victory Field	1996	320	402	320	14,500	660,289
Lehigh Valley	Coca-Cola Park	2008	336	400	325	10,000	614,888
Louisville	Louisville Slugger Field	2000	325	400	340	13,131	567,256
Norfolk	Harbor Park	1993	333	400	318	12,067	358,147
Pawtucket	McCoy Stadium	1946	325	400	325	10,031	515,665
Rochester	Frontier Field	1997	335	402	325	10,840	422,454
Scranton/WB	PNC Field	2013	330	408	330	10,000	401,618
Syracuse	NBT Bank Stadium	1997	330	400	330	11,671	247,046
Toledo	Fifth Third Field	2002	320	408	315	10,300	545,265

BUFFALO BISONS

Address: Coca-Cola Field, One James D Griffin Plaza, Buffalo, NY 14203.
Telephone: (716) 846-2000. **Fax:** (716) 852-6530.
E-Mail Address: info@bisons.com. **Website:** www.bisons.com.
Affiliation (2nd year): Toronto Blue Jays (2013).
Years in League: 1886-90, 1912-70, 1998-

OWNERSHIP/MANAGEMENT

Operated By: Rich Products Corp. **Principal Owner/President:** Robert Rich Jr.
President, Rich Entertainment Group: Melinda Rich. **Vice President/Chief Operating Officer, Rich Entertainment Group:** Joseph Segarra. **President, Rich Baseball Operations:** Jon Dandes. **VP/General Manager:** Mike Buczkowski. **VP/Secretary:** William Gisel. **Corporate Counsel:** Jill Bond, William Grieshober. **Director, Sales:** Anthony Sprague.

Director, Stadium Operations: Tom Sciarrino. Controller: Kevin Parkinson. Senior Accountants: Rita Clark. Accountants: Amy Delaney, Tori Dwyer. Director, Ticket Operations: Mike Poreda. Director, Public Relations: Brad Bisbing. Director, Entertainment/Marketing Services: Matt La Sota. Creative Services/Website Marketing Coordinator: Ashley Beamish. Group Sales Manager: Geoff Lundquist.

Sales Coordinators: Rachel Osucha, Mike Simoncelli. Account Executives: Jeffrey Erbes, Mark Gordon, Jim Harrington, Nick Iacona, Robert Kates, Geoff Lundquist, Burt Mirti, Frank Mooney, Beth Potozniak. Ticket Sales Representatives: Nicholas Iacona. Coordinator, Merchandise Coordinator: Victoria Rebmann. Manager, Office Services: Margaret Russo. Executive Assistant: Tina Lesher. Community Relations: Gail Hodges. Director, Food Services: Robert Free. General Manager, Pettibones Grille: Sean Regan. Food Service Operations Supervisor: Curt Anderson. Head Groundskeeper: Chad Laurie. Chief Engineer: Pat Chella. Home Clubhouse/Baseball Operations Coordinator: Scott Lesher. Visiting Clubhouse Manager: Steve Morris.

FIELD STAFF
Manager: Gary Allenson. Hitting Coach: Richie Hebner. Pitching Coach: Randy St. Claire. Athletic Trainer: Voon Chong. Strength/Conditioning Coach: Armando Gutierrez Jason Dowse.

GAME INFORMATION
Radio Announcers: Ben Wagner, Duke McGuire. No of Games Broadcast: 144. Flagship Station: WWKB-1520.
PA Announcer: Jerry Reo, Tom Burns. Official Scorers: Kevin Lester, Jon Dare.
Stadium Name: Coca-Cola Field. Location: From north, take I-190 to Elm Street exit, left onto Swan Street; From east, take I-190 West to exit 51 (Route 33) to end, exit at Oak Street, right onto Swan Street; From west, take I-190 East, exit 53 to I-90 North, exit at Elm Street, left onto Swan Street. Standard Game Times: 7:05 pm, Sun 1:05. Ticket Price Range: $6-13.
Visiting Club Hotel: Adams Mark, 120 Church St, Buffalo, NY 14202. Telephone: (716) 845-5100. Visiting Club Hotel: Hyatt, 2 Fountain Plaza, Buffalo, NY 14202. Telephone: (716) 856-1234.

CHARLOTTE KNIGHTS

Address: BB&T Ballpark 324 S. Mint St., Charlotte, NC 28202.
Telephone: (704) 274-8300. Fax: 704-274-8330.
E-Mail Address: knights@charlotteknights.com. Website: www.charlotteknights.com.
Affiliation (first year): Chicago White Sox (1999). Years in League: 1993-

OWNERSHIP/MANAGEMENT
Operated by: Knights Baseball, LLC. Principal Owners: Don Beaver, Bill Allen.
Executive Vice President/Chief Operating Officer: Dan Rajkowski. General Manager, Baseball Operations: Scotty Brown. VP, Marketing: Mark Smith. VP, Sales: Chris Semmens. Director, Special Programs/Events: Julie Clark. Director, PR/Media Relations: Tommy Viola. Director, Broadcasting/Team Travel: Matt Swierad. Business Manager: Michael Sanger. Director, Stadium Operations: Mark McKinnon. Facility Manager: Tom Gorter. Merchandise Manager: Karen Schieber. Director, Ticket Sales/Hospitality: Sean Owens. Director, Ticket Operations: Matt Millward. Director, Community/Team Relations: Lindsey Roycraft. Video Director: David Ruckman. Creative Director: Bill Walker. Corporate Sales Executives: Jeremy Auker, Rob Koebel. Corporate Sales Representative: Tommy Henry.
Senior Account Executive: Brett Butler. Season Ticket Sales Representatives: Brandon T. Batts, David Burns, Ian Holmes, Daniel Nobles. Group Sales Representatives: Kathryn Bobel, J.J. Briceno, Kevin Hughes. Ticket Sales Associate: Jonathan English. Special Events Manager: Katherine Anderson. Premium Services Manager: Bess LaMay. Head Groundskeeper: Eddie Busque. Stadium Operations Associate: Nick Braun. Front Desk Receptionist: Ashley Warshauer.

FIELD STAFF
Manager: Joel Skinner. Hitting Coach: Andy Tomberlin. Pitching Coach: Richard Dotson. Coach: Ryan Newman. Trainer: Scott Johnson. Strength Coach: Chad Efron.

GAME INFORMATION
Radio Announcers: Matt Swierad, Mike Pacheco. No. of Games Broadcast: 144. Flagship Station: ESPN 730 AM.
PA Announcer: Official Scorers: Jerry Bowers, Dave Friedman, Karl Lyles, David McDowell. Stadium Name: BB&T Ballpark Location: Exit 10 off I 77. Ticket Price Range: $8-$19.
Visiting Club Hotel: Doubletree by Hilton Charlotte, 895 W. Trade St., Charlotte, NC 28202.

COLUMBUS CLIPPERS

Address: 330 Huntington Park Lane, Columbus, OH 43215.
Telephone: (614) 462-5250. Fax: (614) 462-3271. Tickets: (614) 462-2757.
E-Mail Address: info@clippersbaseball.com. Website: www.clippersbaseball.com.
Affiliation (first year): Cleveland Indians (2009). Years in League: 1955-70, 1977-

OWNERSHIP/MANAGEMENT
Operated By: Columbus Baseball Team Inc. Principal Owner: CBT Inc. Board of Directors: Steven Francis, Tom Fries, Wayne Harer, Thomas Katzenmeyer, David Leland, Cathy Lyttle, Gary Schaeffer, Jeffrey Sopp, McCullough Williams.
President/General Manager: Ken Schnacke. Assistant GM: Mark Warren. Director, Ballpark Operations: Steve

Dalin. **Assistant Director, Ballpark Operations:** Tom Rinto. **Director, Ticket Operations:** Scott Ziegler. **Assistant Director, Ticket Operations:** Eddie Langhenry. **Assistant Directors, Ticket Sales:** Kevin Daniels, Ashley Ramirez. **Director, Marketing/Sales:** Mark Galuska. **Assistant Director, Marketing:** Emily Poynter. **Assistant Directors, Sales:** Kaycie Jacobs, Chelsea Gilman.

Director, Promotions/In-Game Entertainment: Seth Rhodes. **Assistant Director, Promotions/Mascots:** Steve Kuilder. **Director, Communications/Media/Historian:** Joe Santry. **Assistant Director, Media Relations/Statistics:** Anthony Slosser. **Director, Social Media/Website Communication:** Josh Samuels. **Directors, Broadcasting:** Ryan Mitchell, Scott Leo. **Director, Merchandising:** Krista Oberlander. **Assistant Director, Merchandising:** Robin Vlah. **Director, Group Sales:** Ben Keller. **Assistant Directors, Group Sales:** Kevin Smith, Robert Freese. **Director, Multimedia:** Josh Glenn. **Assistant Director, Multimedia:** Yoshi Ando. **Director, Finance/Administration:** Bonnie Badgley. **Executive Assistant to the President/GM:** Ashley Held.

Office Manager: Melissa Schrader. **Director, Sponsor Relationships:** Joyce Martin. **Director, Event Planning:** Micki Shier. **Assistant Director, Event Planning/Catering/Suites:** Shannon O'Boyle. **Director, Clubhouse Operations:** George Robinson. **Clubhouse Manager:** Matt Pruzinsky. **Ballpark Superintendent:** Gary Delozier. **Head Groundskeeper:** Wes Ganobcik. **Assistant Groundskeeper:** Nick Roe.

FIELD STAFF

Field Manager: Chris Tremie. **Pitching Coach:** Carl Willis. **Hitting Coach:** Rouglas Odor. **Trainer:** Chad Wolfe. **Strength/Conditioning Coach:** Ed Subel.

GAME INFORMATION

Radio Announcers: Ryan Mitchell, Scott Leo. **No of Games Broadcast:** 144. **Flagship Station:** WMNI 920 AM.

PA Announcer: Matt Leininger. **Official Scorer:** Jim Habermehl, Ray Thomas, Ty Debevoise and Paul Pennell.

Stadium Name: Huntington Park. **Location:** From north: South on I-71 to I-670 west, exit at Neil Avenue, turn left at intersection onto Neil Avenue; From south: North on I-71, exit at Front Street (#100A), turn left at intersection onto Front Street, turn left onto Nationwide Blvd; From east: West on I-70, exit at Fourth Street, continue on Fulton Street to Front Street, turn right onto Front Street, turn left onto Nationwide Blvd; From west: East on I-70, exit at Fourth Street, continue on Fulton Street to Front Street, turn right onto Front Street, turn left onto Nationwide Blvd. **Ticket Price Range:** $4-20.

Visiting Club Hotel: Crowne Plaza, 33 East Nationwide Blvd, Columbus, OH 43215. **Telephone:** (877) 348-2424. **Visiting Club Hotel:** Drury Hotels Columbus Convention Center, 88 East Nationwide Blvd, Columbus, OH 43215. **Telephone:** (614) 221-7008. **Visiting Club Hotel:** Hyatt Regency Downtown, 350 North High Street, Columbus, OH 43215. **Telephone:** (614) 463-1234.

DURHAM BULLS

Office Address: 409 Blackwell St, Durham, NC 27701. **Mailing Address:** PO Box 507, Durham, NC 27702.

Telephone: (919) 687-6500. **Fax:** (919) 687-6560.

Website: www.durhambulls.com. **Twitter:** @DurhamBulls.

Affiliation (first year): Tampa Bay Rays (1998). **Years in League:** 1998-2015.

OWNERSHIP/MANAGEMENT

Operated By: Capitol Broadcasting Company, Inc.

President/CEO: Jim Goodmon. **Vice President:** George Habel.

General Manager: Mike Birling. **Director, Corporate Partnerships:** Chip Allen. **Director, Marketing:** Scott Carter. **Director, Ticket Sales/Service:** Peter Wallace. **Director, Promotions:** Krista Boyd. **Manager, Multimedia:** Walmer Medina. **Manager, Corporate Partnerships:** Morgan Weber.

Account Executives, Sponsorship: Nick Bavin, Patrick Kinas, Jenn Paonessa. **Coordinator, Mascot/Community Relations:** Nicholas Tennant. **Coordinator, Media Relations:** Matt Sutor. **Director, Ticket Operations:** Tim Seaton. **Manager, Premium Ticket Sales:** Eli Starkey. **Assistant Manager, Premium Ticket Sales:** Tim Campbell. **Premium Ticket Sales Associates:** Cassie Fowler, Colin Phibbs, Phillip Sims. **Manager, Group Sales:** Brian Simorka. **Assistant Manager, Group Sales:** Andrew Ferrier. **Group Sales Consultants:** Michele Fox, Evan Gross, Leslie Lambert, Melanie Rumfelt. **Director, Special Events:** Erin Anderson. **Director, Baseball Tournaments:** Lee Folger. **Director, Merchandise/Team Travel:** Bryan Wilson. **Director, Stadium Operations:** Josh Nance.

Head Groundskeeper, DBAP: Scott Strickland. **Head Groundskeeper, DAP:** Cameron Brendle. **Manager, Business:** Rhonda Carlile. **Supervisor, Accounting:** Theresa Stocking. **Accountant/Receptionist:** NaTasha Jessup. **Manager, Home Clubhouse:** Colin Saunders. **Manager, Visiting/Umpires Clubhouses:** Aaron Kuehner. **Team Ambassador:** Bill Law.

FIELD STAFF

Manager: Jared Sandberg. **Hitting Coach:** Dave Myers. **Pitching Coach:** Kyle Snyder. **Trainer:** Mike Sandoval. **Strength/Conditioning:** Bryan King.

GAME INFORMATION

Broadcasters: Patrick Kinas, Ken Tanner. **No. of Games Broadcast:** 144. **Flagship Stations:** 620 AM, 99.9 FM.

PA Announcer: Tony Riggsbee. **Official Scorer:** Brent Belvin.

Stadium Name: Durham Bulls Athletic Park. **Location:** From Raleigh, I-40 West to Highway 147 North, exit 12B to Willard, two blocks on Willard to stadium; From I-85, Gregson Street exit to downtown, left on Chapel Hill Street, right on Mangum Street. **Standard Game Times:** 7:05 pm, Sunday 5:05. **Ticket Price Range:** $6-14.

Visiting Club Hotel: Hilton Durham Near Duke University; 3800 Hillsborough Road, Durham, NC 27705. **Telephone:** (919) 383-8033.

GWINNETT BRAVES

Office Address: 2500 Buford Drive, Lawrenceville, GA 30043. **Mailing Address:** P.O. Box 490310, Lawrenceville, GA 30049.
Telephone: (678) 277-0300. **Fax:** (678) 277-0338.
E-Mail Address: gwinnettinfo@braves.com. **Website:** www.gwinnettbraves.com.
Affiliation (first year): Atlanta Braves (1966). **Years in League:** 1884, 1915-17, 1954-64, 1966-

OWNERSHIP/MANAGEMENT

General Manager: North Johnson. **Assistant GM:** Shari Massengill.
Office Manager: Tyra Williams. **Corporate Partnerships Manager:** Ande Sadtler. **Corporate Partnerships Manager:** Koby Hearn. **Corporate Partnerships Coordinator:** Aaron Morrison. **Ticket Sales Manager:** Tyler Graham. **Assistant Ticket Sales Manager:** Jerry Pennington. **Ticket Operations Manager:** Crystal Tanner. **Ticket Operations Coordinator:** Julian Perez-Dowdy. **Account Executives:** Alden Treadway, Mitch Weiler, Jason Wright. **Media Relations Manager:** Dave Lezotte. **Marketing/Promotions Manager:** Brandon Apter. **Community Relations Coordinator:** Alison Atkins. **Creative Services Manager:** Andrea Roa. **Creative Services Coordinator:** Casey Comeaux. **Stadium Operations Manager:** Ryan Stoltenberg. **Stadium Operations Coordinator:** Jonathan Blair. **Facilities Maintenance Manager:** Gary Hoopaugh. **Sports Turf Manager:** Chris Ball. **Clubhouse Manager:** Nick Dixon

FIELD STAFF

Manager: Brian Snitker. **Pitching Coach:** Marty Reed. **Hitting Coach:** John Moses. **Trainer:** Mike Graus.

GAME INFORMATION

Radio Announcer: Tony Schiavone. **No. of Games Broadcast:** 144. **Flagship Station:** Unavailable.
PA Announcer: Kevin Kraus. **Official Scorers:** Guy Curtright, Jon Schwartz, Frank Barnett, Tim Gaines.
Stadium Name: Coolray Field. **Location:** I-85 (at Exit 115, State Road 20 West) and I-985 (at Exit 4), follow signs to park. **Ticket Price Range:** $6-40.
Visiting Club Hotel: Courtyard by Marriott Buford/Mall of Georgia, 1405 Mall of Georgia Boulevard, Buford, GA 30519. **Telephone:** (678) 215-8007.

INDIANAPOLIS INDIANS

Address: 501 W Maryland Street, Indianapolis, IN 46225.
Telephone: (317) 269-3542. **Fax:** (317) 269-3541.
E-Mail Address: indians@IndyIndians.com. **Website:** www.indyindians.com.
Affiliation (first year): Pittsburgh Pirates (2005). **Years in League:** 1963, 1998-

OWNERSHIP/MANAGEMENT

Operated By: Indians Inc. **President/Chairman of the Board:** Max Schumacher.
Vice President, Baseball/Administrative Affairs: Cal Burleson. **General Manager:** Randy Lewandowski. **VP, Corporate Affairs:** Bruce Schumacher. **Director, Business Operations:** Brad Morris. **Director, Broadcasting:** Howard Kellman. **Director, Corporate Sales/Marketing:** Joel Zawacki. **Director, Merchandising:** Mark Schumacher. **Director, Facilities:** Tim Hughes. **Director, Tickets/Operations:** Matt Guay. **Senior Manager, Marketing/Communications:** Jon Glesing. **Senior Manager, Ticket/Premium Services:** Kerry Vick.
Office Manager: Julie Rumschlag. **Manager, Community Relations/Promotions:** Brian McLaughlin. **Manager, Telecast/Productions:** Scott Templin. **Manager, Partnership Activation:** Drew Donovan. **Manager, Marketing:** Kim Stoebick. **Manager, Creative Services:** Adam Pintar. **Manager, IT:** Sean Couse. **Manager, Stadium Maintenance:** Allan Danehy. **Manager, Operations:** Andrew Jackson. **Manager, Facilities:** Matt Rapp. **Manager, Ticket Sales:** Chad Bohm. **Manager, Ticket Services:** Bryan Spisak. **Coordinator, Communications:** Brian Bosma. **Coordinator, Community Relations/Promotions:** Chelsea Lowman. **Coordinator, Media Relations:** Chris Robinson. **Coordinator, Partnership Activation:** Kylie Iadicicco. **Sponsorship Sales Account Executives:** Chris Inderstrodt, Chandler Prince, Christina Toler.
Graphic/Web Designer: Whitney Alderson. **Senior Ticket Sales Executives:** Ryan Barrett, Jonathan Howard. **Ticket Sales Executives:** Nathan Butler, Noelle Cook, Ty Eaton, Garrett Rosh. **Administrative Assistant:** Sarah McKinney. **Operations Support:** Ricky Floyd. **Operations Support:** Sandra Johnson. **Head Groundskeeper:** Joey Stevenson. **Community Relations Assistant:** Sarah Palya . **Marketing/Sponsorship Assistant:** Erika Loomer. **Mascot Assistant:** Jevin Fluegel. **Business Operations Assistant:** Tawne Bucherl. **Stadium Operations Assistant:** Eddie Acheson. **Video Production Assistant:** Brock Workman. **Premium Services/Event Operations Assistant:** Taylor Kempf. **Ticket Services Assistants:** Andrew Calangelo, Christina Ferguson, Matthew Goode, Sam Pille, Michael Rodgers, Britney Wilczynski. **Grounds Assistant:** Andrew Dunn, Andrew Raes.

FIELD STAFF

Manager: Dean Treanor. **Hitting Coach:** Butch Wynegar. **Pitching Coach:** Stan Kyles. **Trainer:** Bryan Housand. **Strength/Conditioning Coach:** Ricky White.

GAME INFORMATION

Radio Announcers: Howard Kellman, Will Flemming. **No. of Games Broadcast:** 144. **Flagship Station:** WNDE 1260-AM.
PA Announcer: David Pygman. **Official Scorers:** Bill McAfee, Bill Potter, Kim Rogers, Ed Holdaway.
Stadium Name: Victory Field. **Location:** I-70 to West Street exit, north on West Street to ballpark; I-65 to Martin Luther

King and West Street exit, south on West Street to ballpark. **Standard Game Times:** 7:05 pm; 1:35 (Wed/Sun), 7:15 (Fri). **Ticket Price Range:** $10-16.
   Visiting Club Hotel: Comfort Suites City Centre 515 S. West Street, Indianapolis, IN 46225. **Telephone:** 317-631-9000.

LEHIGH VALLEY IRONPIGS

   Address: 1050 IronPigs Way, Allentown, PA 18109.
   Telephone: (610) 841-7447. **Fax:** (610) 841-1509.
   E-Mail Address: info@ironpigsbaseball.com. **Website:** www.ironpigsbaseball.com.
   Affiliation (first year): Philadelphia Phillies (2008). **Years in League:** 2008-

OWNERSHIP/MANAGEMENT
   Ownership: LV Baseball LP. **President/General Manager:** Kurt Landes.
   Assistant GM: Howard Scharf. **Director, Media Relations:** Matt Provence. **Director, New Media:** Jon Schaeffer. **Director, Community Relations:** Dana DeFilippo. **Manager, Community Relations:** Hannah Ishida. **Director, Merchandise:** Rob Cvetan. **Director, Ticket Sales:** Scott Evans. **Director, Group Sales:** Don Wilson. **Director, Marketing:** Ron Rushe. **Marketing Services Managers:** Courtney Novotnak, Amanda Stout. **Director, Creative Services:** Terrance Breen. **Manager, Creative Services:** Justin Vrona. **Director, Promotions:** Lindsey Knupp. **Director, Special Events:** Mary Nixon. **Director, Concessions/Catering:** Alex Rivera. **Manager, Concessions:** Brock Hartranft. **Manager, Catering:** Steve Agosti. **Executive Chef:** Jerry Rogers. **Controller:** Deb Landes. **Manager, Finance:** Michelle Perl.
   Director, Stadium Operations: Jason Kiesel. **Stadium Operations Managers:** Ryan Beck, Kyle Walbert. **Managers, Sponsorship:** Chris Kobela, Gary Nevolis. **Manager, Ticket Operations:** Brittany Balonis. **Ticket Representatives:** Kristen Alford, Steve Carhart, Andrew Klein, Bryan Soulard Rory Muth. **Manager, Group Sales:** Brad Ludwig. **Group Reps:** Liz DiBerardino, Ryan Hines, Nick Wootsick. **Director, Field Operations:** Ryan Hills. **Receptionist:** Pat Golden.

FIELD STAFF
   Manager: Dave Brundage. **Hitting Coach:** Sal Rende. **Pitching Coach:** Ray Burris. **Coach:** Mickey Morandini. **Trainers:** Jon May. **Strength/Conditioning:** Dong Lien.

GAME INFORMATION
   Radio Announcers: Matt Provence, Jon Schaeffer. **No. of Games Broadcast:** 144. **Flagship Radio Station:** ESPN 1240/1320 AM. **Television Station:** TV2. **Television Announcers:** Mike Zambelli, Steve Degler, Matt Provence, Doug Heater. **No. Games Televised:** 72 (all home games).
   PA Announcer: Unavailable. **Official Scorers:** Mike Falk, Jack Logic, David Sheriff, Dick Shute.
   Stadium Name: Coca-Cola Park. **Location:** Take US 22 to exit for Airport Road South, head south, make right on American Parkway, left into stadium. **Standard Game Times:** 7:05 pm, Sat 6:35, Sun 1:35.

LOUISVILLE BATS

   Address: 401 E Main St, Louisville, KY 40202.
   Telephone: (502) 212-2287. **Fax:** (502) 515-2255.
   E-Mail Address: info@batsbaseball.com. **Website:** www.batsbaseball.com.
   Affiliation (first year): Cincinnati Reds (2000). **Years in League:** 1998.

OWNERSHIP/MANAGEMENT
   Chairman: Stuart and Jerry Katzoff (MC Sports)
   Board of Directors: Dan Ulmer Jr., Edward Glasscock, Gary Ulmer, Kenny Huber, Steve Trager, Michael Brown. **President/CEO:** Gary Ulmer. **Senior VP:** Greg Galiette.
   VP, Business Operations: James Breeding. **VP, Operations/Technology:** Scott Shoemaker. **Director, Baseball Operations:** Josh Hargreaves. **Controller:** Michele Anderson. **Director, Ticket Operations:** Brian Knight. **Director, Media/Public Relations:** Chadwick Fischer. **Media Relations Assistant:** Ryan Ritchey. **Director, Group Sales:** Bryan McBride. **Director, Broadcasting:** Matt Andrews. **Director, Corporate Suites:** Malcolm Jollie. **Assistant Director, Stadium Operations:** Nathan Renfrow. **Director, Online Media/Design:** Tony Brown. **Director, Sponsorships:** Sarah Nordman. **Senior Account Executives:** Hal Norwood, Evan Patrick, Michael Harmon, Brad Wagner, Kevin Gamm. **Assistant Director, Ticket Operations:** Andrew Siers. **Groundskeeper:** Tom Nielsen. **Clubhouse Manager:** Derrick Jewell.

FIELD STAFF
   Manager: Delino DeShields. **Hitting Coach:** Tony Jaramillo. **Pitching Coach:** Ted Power. **Trainer:** Jimmy Mattocks.

GAME INFORMATION
   Radio Announcers: Matt Andrews, Nick Curran. **No. of Games Broadcast:** 144. **Flagship Station:** WKRD 790-AM. **PA Announcer:** Charles Gazaway. **Official Scorer:** Nick Evans. **Organist:** Bob Ramsey. **Stadium Name:** Louisville Slugger Field.
   Location: I-64 and I-71 to I-65 South/North to Brook Street exit, right on Market Street, left on Jackson Street; stadium on Main Street between Jackson and Preston.
   Ticket Price Range: $7-11. **Visiting Club Hotel:** Galt House Hotel, 140 North Fourth Street, Louisville, KY 40202. **Telephone:** (502) 589-5200.

NORFOLK TIDES

Address: 150 Park Ave, Norfolk, VA 23510.
Telephone: (757) 622-2222. **Fax:** (757) 624-9090.
E-Mail Address: receptionist@norfolktides.com. **Website:** www.norfolktides.com.
Affiliation (first year): Baltimore Orioles (2007). **Years in League:** 1969-

OWNERSHIP/MANAGEMENT

Operated By: Tides Baseball Club Inc. **President:** Ken Young. **General Manager:** Joe Gregory. **Executive Vice President/Senior Advisor to the President:** Dave Rosenfield.

Assistant GM: Ben Giancola. **Director, Media Relations:** Ian Locke. **Director, Community Relations:** Heather McKeating. **Director, Ticket Operations:** Gretchen Todd. **Director, Group Sales:** John Muszkewycz. **Director, Premium Services:** Stephanie Hierstein. **Director, Stadium Operations:** Mike Zeman. **Business Manager:** Andrew Garrelts. **Director, Business Development/Gameday Experience:** Mike Watkins. **Corporate Sponsorships/Promotions:** Jonathan Mensink, John Rogerson. **Manager, Merchandising:** Ann Marie Piddisi. **Assistant Director, Stadium Operations:** Mike Cardwell. **Assistant to the Director, Tickets:** Sze Fong. **Administrative Assistant:** Lisa Blocker. **Group Sales Representatives:** Taylor Gustafson, Jordyn Surratt.

Head Groundskeeper: Kenny Magner. **Assistant Groundskeeper:** Derek Trueblood. **Home Clubhouse Manager:** Kevin Casey. **Visiting Clubhouse Manager:** Mark Bunge. **Media Relations Assistant:** Kori Burcher. **Community Relations Assistant:** Chase Davenport.

FIELD STAFF

Manager: Ron Johnson. **Hitting Coach:** Sean Berry. **Pitching Coach:** Mike Griffin. **Coach:** Luis Hernandez. **Field Coach:** Jose Hernandez.

GAME INFORMATION

Radio Announcers: Pete Michaud, Dave Rosenfield. **No. of Games Broadcast:** 144. **Flagship Station:** ESPN 94.1 FM. **PA Announcer:** Jack Ankerson. **Official Scorers:** Mike Holtzclaw, Dave Lewis.

Stadium Name: Harbor Park. **Location:** Exit 9, 11A or 11B off I-264, adjacent to the Elizabeth River in downtown Norfolk. **Standard Game Times:** 6:35 pm during weekdays in April & May, 7:05 pm, Sun 1:05 pm (first half of season) , 6:05 pm (second half of season). **Ticket Price Range:** $11-14.

Visiting Club Hotel: Sheraton Waterside, 777 Waterside Dr, Norfolk, VA 23510. **Telephone:** (757) 622-6664.

PAWTUCKET RED SOX

Office Address: One Ben Mondor Way, Pawtucket, RI 02860. **Mailing Address:** PO Box 2365, Pawtucket, RI 02861.
Telephone: (401) 724-7300. **Fax:** (401) 724-2140.
E-Mail Address: info@pawsox.com. **Website:** www.pawsox.com.
Affiliation (first year): Boston Red Sox (1973). **Years in League:** 1973-

OWNERSHIP/MANAGEMENT

Operated by: Pawtucket Red Sox Baseball Club, Inc.

President: Mike Tamburro. **Vice President/General Manager:** Lou Schwechheimer. **VP/Chief Operating Officer:** Matt White. **VP, Sales/Marketing:** Michael Gwynn. **VP, Stadium Operations:** Mick Tedesco. **VP, Public Relations:** Bill Wanless. **Director, Community Relations:** Jeff Bradley. **Director, Merchandising/Concessions:** Eric Petterson. **Director, Media Creation:** Kevin Galligan. **Director, Ticket Sales:** John Wilson. **Director, Warehouse Operations:** Dave Johnson. **Director, Hospitality:** Lauren Dincecco. **Account Executives:** Tom Linehan, Sam Sousa, Mike Lyons, Geoff Sinnott, Brian Airoldi. **Field Superintendant:** Matt McKinnon. **Director, Security:** Rick Medeiros. **Director, Clubhouse Operations:** Carl Goodreau. **Executive Chef:** Ken Bowdish.

FIELD STAFF

Manager: Kevin Boles. **Hitting Coach:** Dave Joppie. **Pitching Coach:** Unavailable. **Coach:** Bruce Crabbe. **Trainer:** Jon Jochim.

GAME INFORMATION

Radio Announcers: Jeff Levering and Josh Maurer. **No. of Games Broadcast:** 144. **Flagship Station:** WHJJ 920-AM. **PA Announcers:** Jim Martin, Scott Fraser. **Official Scorer:** Bruce Guindon.

Stadium Name: McCoy Stadium. **Location:** From north, 95 South to exit 2A in Massachusetts (Newport Ave), follow Newport Ave for 2 miles, right on Columbus Ave, follow one mile, stadium on right; From south, 95 North to exit 28 (School Street), right at bottom of exit ramp, through two sets of lights, left onto Pond Street, right on Columbus Ave, stadium entrance on left; From west (Worcester), 295 North to 95 South and follow directions from north; From east (Fall River), 195 West to 95 North and follow directions from south. **Standard Game Times:** 7 pm, Sat 6, Sun 1. **Ticket Price Range:** $5-11.

Visiting Club Hotel: Wyndham Garden Providence, 220 India Street, Providence, RI 02903. **Telephone:** (401) 272-5577.

ROCHESTER RED WINGS

Address: One Morrie Silver Way, Rochester, NY 14608.
Telephone: (585) 454-1001. **Fax:** (585) 454-1056.
E-Mail: info@redwingsbaseball.com. **Website:** RedWingsBaseball.com.
Affiliation (first year): Minnesota Twins (2003). **Years in League:** 1885-89, 1891-92, 1895-present

OWNERSHIP/MANAGEMENT

Operated by: Rochester Community Baseball, Inc. **President/CEO/COO:** Naomi Silver.
Chairman: Gary Larder. **General Manager:** Dan Mason. **Assistant GM:** Will Rumbold. **Controller:** Christina Duquin. **Director, Human Resources:** Paula LoVerde. **Manager, Ticket Office:** Dave Welker. **Manager, Executive Services:** Marcia DeHond. **Director, Communications:** Tim Doohan. **Director, Corporate Development:** Nick Sciarratta. **Director, Group Sales/Promotions:** Bob Craig. **Assistant Director, Group Sales:** Derek Swanson. **Senior Director, Sales:** Matt Cipro. **Director, Ticket Operations:** Rob Dermody. **Assistant Director, Ticket Operations:** Eric Friedman. **Director, Video Production:** John Blotzer. **Director, Merchandising:** Kathy Bills.
Head Groundskeeper: Gene P Buonomo. **Assistant Groundskeeper:** Geno Buonomo. **Receptionist/Administrative Assistant:** Gini Darden. **GM, Food/Beverage:** Jeff Dodge. **Business Manager, Food/Beverage:** Dave Bills. **Manager, Concessions:** Jeff DeSantis. **Director, Catering:** Courtney Trawitz. **Sales Manager, Catering:** Steve Gonzalez. **Executive Chef:** Dan Shea. **Manager, Warehouse:** Rob Burgett.

FIELD STAFF

Manager: Mike Quade. **Hitting Coach:** Tim Doherty. **Pitching Coach:** Marty Mason. **Trainer:** Larry Bennese.

GAME INFORMATION

Radio Announcer: Josh Whetzel. **No. of Games Broadcast:** 144. **Flagship Stations:** WHTK 1280-AM, WYSL 1040-AM.
PA Announcers: Kevin Spears, Rocky Perrotta. **Official Scorers:** Warren Kozireski, Brendan Harrington.
Stadium Name: Frontier Field. **Location:** I-490 East to exit 12 (Brown/Broad Street) and follow signs; I-490 West to exit 14 (Plymouth Ave) and follow signs. **Standard Game Times:** 7:05 pm, Sun 1:05. **Ticket Price Range:** $8-12.
Visiting Club Hotel: Rochester Plaza, 70 State St, Rochester, NY 14608. **Telephone:** (585) 546-3450.

SCRANTON/WILKES-BARRE RAILRIDERS

Address: 235 Montage Mountain Rd., Moosic, PA 18507.
Telephone: (570) 969-2255. **Fax:** (570) 963-6564.
E-Mail Address: info@swbrailriders.com. **Website:** www.railriders.com
Affiliation (first year): New York Yankees (2007). **Years in League:** 1989- OWNERSHIP/MANAGEMENT

OWNERSHIP/MANAGEMENT

Owned by: SWB Yankees, LLC. **Operated by:** SWB Yankees, LLC.
Interim General Manager: Jeremy Ruby. **Executive VP, Business Operations:** Paul Chilek. **VP, Marketing/Corporate Services:** Katie Beekman. **VP, Baseball Operations:** Curt Camoni. **VP, Partnerships:** Mike Trudnak.
Director, Media Relations/Broadcasting: John Sadak. **Assistant Director, Media Relations/Broadcasting:** Darren Headrick. **Director, Gameday Operations:** William Steiner. **Corporate Partnerships Executive:** Josh Dilts. **Director, Special Events/Graphic Design:** Kristina Knight. **Director, Community Relations:** Rachel Mark. **Corporate Services Manager:** Lindsey Graham. **Corporate Services/Analytics Manager:** Karen Luciano. **Video/Website Manager:** Victor Sweet. **Director, Marketing/Promotions:** Barry Snyder. **Director, Ticket Operations:** Felicia Adamus. **Assistant Ticket Operations Manager:** Bryant Guilmette. **Director, Ticket Sales:** Robert McLane. **Regional Corporate Sales Managers:** Giovanni Fricchione, Alyssa Novick, Mike Poplaski. **Regional Group Sales Managers:** Morgan Andreas, Mike Harvey, Matt LaFrennie. **Senior Inside Sales Representative:** Kelly Cusick. **Inside Sales Representative:** Amanda Lance. **Specialty Sales Coordinator:** Calvin Santiago. **Director, Field Operations:** Steve Horne. **Director, Ballpark Operations:** Joe Villano. **Receptionist/Office Manager:** Maggie Rowlands.

FIELD STAFF

Manager: Dave Miley. **Hitting Coach:** Marcus Thames. **Pitching Coach:** Scott Aldred. **Defensive Coach:** Justin Tordi. **Trainer:** Darren London. **Strength Coach:** Lee Tressel.

GAME INFORMATION

Radio Announcers: John Sadak, Darren Headrick. **No. of Games Broadcast:** 144. **Flagship Stations:** 100.7 FM, 1340 WYCK-AM, 1400 WICK-AM, 1440 WCDL-AM, 106.7 FM. **TV Announcer:** John Sadak. **No. of Games Broadcast:** Home—20. **Flagship Station:** WQMY-TV.
PA Announcer: Unavailable. **Official Scorers:** Dave Lauriha, John Errico.
Stadium Name: PNC Field. **Location:** Exit 182 off Interstate 18; stadium is on Montage Mountain Road. **Standard Game Times:** 6:35 pm (April/May) 7:05 pm (June-August), Sun 1:05 pm. **Ticket Price Range:** $7-$12.
Visiting Club Hotel: Radisson Lackawanna Station. **Telephone:** (570) 342-8300.

SYRACUSE CHIEFS

Address: One Tex Simone Dr, Syracuse, NY 13208.
Telephone: (315) 474-7833. Fax: (315) 474-2658.
E-Mail Address: baseball@syracusechiefs.com. Website: www.syracusechiefs.com.
Affiliation (first year): Washington Nationals (2009). Years in League: 1885-89, 1891-92, 1894-1901, 1918, 1920-27, 1934-55, 1961-

OWNERSHIP/MANAGEMENT

Operated by: Community Owned Baseball Club of Central New York, Inc.
Chairman: Robert Julian, Esq. President: William Dutch. First Executive Vice President: Paul Solomon.
General Manager: Jason Smorol. Assistant GM: Jason Horbal. Director, Sales/Marketing: Kathleen McCormick. Director, Finance: Frank Santoro. Assistant Director, Finance: Joseph Persia. Director, Group Sales/Graphic Design Coordinator: Brandon Massey. Director, Broadcasting/Public Relations: Jason Benetti. Assistant Director, Broadcasting/Public Relations: Kevin Brown. Director, Ticket Sales: Greg Dietz. Director, Multimedia Production: Anthony Cianchetta. Manager, Corporate Sales: Julie Cardinali. Manager, Luxury Suites/Guest Relations: Erin Stancick. Manager, Community Relations/Social Media: Jeffrey Irizarry. Head Groundskeeper: John Stewart. Team Historian: Ron Gersbacher.

FIELD STAFF

Manager: Billy Gardner, Jr. Hitting Coach: Joe Dillon. Pitching Coach: Paul Menhart. Trainer: Jeff Allred. Strength Coordinator: Brett Henry.

GAME INFORMATION

Radio Announcers: Jason Benetti/Kevin Brown. No. of Games Broadcast: 144. Flagship Station: The Score 1260 AM. PA Announcers: Nick Aversa, Roger Mirabito. Official Scorer: Dom Leo.
Stadium Name: NBT Bank Stadium. Location: New York State Thruway to exit 36 (I-81 South), to 7th North Street exit, left on 7th North, right on Hiawatha Boulevard. Standard Game Times: 7 pm, Sun 2pm. Ticket Price Range: $5-12.
Visiting Club Hotel: Crowne Plaza Syracuse, 701 E Genesee St, Syracuse, NY 13210. Telephone: (315) 479-7000.

TOLEDO MUD HENS

Address: 406 Washington St., Toledo, OH 43604.
Telephone: (419) 725-4367. Fax: (419) 725-4368.
E-Mail Address: mudhens@mudhens.com. Website: www.mudhens.com.
Affiliation (first year): Detroit Tigers (1987). Years in League: 1889, 1965-

OWNERSHIP/MANAGEMENT

Operated By: Toledo Mud Hens Baseball Club, Inc.
Chairman of the Board: Michael Miller. Vice President: David Huey. Secretary/Treasurer: Charles Bracken. President/General Manager: Joseph Napoli. Chief Marketing Officer: Kim McBroom. Assistant GM/Director, Corporate Partnerships: Neil Neukam. Assistant GM, Ticket Sales/Operations: Erik Ibsen. Assistant GM, Food/Beverage: Craig Nelson. CFO: Brian Leverenz. Manager, Promotions: Michael Keedy. Communications Director: Andi Roman.
Director, Ticket Sales/Services: Thomas Townley. Accounting: Sheri Kelly, Tom Mitchell. Manager, Gameday Operations: Greg Setola. Corporate Sales Associate: Ed Sintic. Director, Ticket Sales/Services: Thom Townley. Season Ticket/Group Sales Associates: Frank Kristie, Kyle Moll, Phil Bargardi, Chad Huffman, John Manzoian, Becky Fitts, McKay Phillips. Manager, Digital Communications: Nathan Steinmetz. Game Plan Advisor: Colleen Rerucha. Special Events Coordinator: Emily Croll. Director, Broadcast Services: Greg Tye. Graphic Designer: Dan Royer. Director, Merchandise & Licensing: Craig Katz. Manager, Swamp Shop: Stephanie Miller. Manager, Office Manager: Carol Hamilton. Executive Assistant: Tracy Evans. Turf Manager: Jake Tyler. Clubhouse Manager: Joe Sarkisian. Team Historian: John Husman.

FIELD STAFF

Manager: Larry Parrish. Coach: Leon Durham. Pitching Coach: Mike Maroth. Trainer: Chris McDonald.

GAME INFORMATION

Radio Announcer: Jim Weber. No. of Games Broadcast: 144. Flagship Station: WCWA 1230 AM. TV Announcers: Jim Weber, Matt Melzak. No. of Games Broadcast: 72 (all home games). TV Flagship: Buckeye Cable Sports Network (BCSN).
PA Announcer: Unavailable. Official Scorers: Jeff Businger, Ron Kleinfelter, Guy Lammers, John Malkoski Jr.
Stadium Name: Fifth Third Field. Location: From Ohio Turnpike 80/90, exit 54 (4A) to I-75 North, follow I-75 North to exit 201-B, left onto Erie Street, right onto Washington Street; From Detroit, I-75 South to exit 202-A, right onto Washington Street; From Dayton, I-75 North to exit 201-B, left onto Erie Street, right on Washington Street; From Ann Arbor, Route 23 South to I-475 East, I-475 east to I-75 South, I-75 South to exit 202-A, right onto Washington Street.
Ticket Price Range: $10.
Visiting Club Hotel: Park Inn, 101 North Summit, Toledo, OH 43604. Telephone: (419) 241-3000.

PACIFIC COAST LEAGUE

PACIFIC COAST LEAGUE

Address: One Chisholm Trail, Suite 4200, Round Rock, Texas 78681.
Telephone: (512) 310-2900. **Fax:** (512) 310-8300.
E-Mail Address: office@pclbaseball.com. **Website:** www.pclbaseball.com.
President: Branch B. Rickey.

Vice President: Don Logan (Las Vegas).
Directors: Don Beaver (New Orleans), Sam Bernabe (Iowa), John Pontius John Mozeliak (Memphis), Chris Cummings (Fresno), Dave Elmore (Colorado Springs), Aaron Artman (Tacoma), Don Logan (Las Vegas), Chris Almendarez (Round Rock), Marc Amicone (Salt Lake), Gary Green (Omaha), Art Matin Larry Freedman (Oklahoma), Josh Hunt (El Paso), Jeff Savage (Sacramento), John Traub (Albuquerque), Frank Ward (Nashville), Stuart Katzoff Herb Simon (Reno).

Director, Business: Melanie Fiore. **Director, Baseball Operations:** Dwight Hall. **Media/Operations Assistant:** Andrew Cockrum.

Division Structure: American Conference—Northern: Colorado Springs, Iowa, Omaha, Oklahoma City. Southern: Memphis, Nashville, New Orleans, Round Rock. **Pacific Conference**—Northern: Fresno, Reno, Sacramento, Tacoma. **Southern:** Albuquerque, El Paso, Las Vegas, Salt Lake.

Regular Season: 144 games. **2015 Opening Date:** April 9. **Closing Date:** Sept 7.
All-Star Game: July 15 at Omaha (PCL vs International League).

Playoff Format: Pacific Conference/Northern winner meets Southern winner, and American Conference/Northern winner meets Southern winner in best-of-five semifinal series. Winners meet in best-of-five series for league championship.

Triple-A Championship Game: Sept 22 at El Paso (PCL vs International League).

Roster Limit: 24. **Player Eligibility Rule:** No restrictions. **Brand of Baseball:** Rawlings ROM.

Umpires: Nick Bailey (Big Spring, TX), Jordan Baker (Shawnee, OK), Lance Barrett (Fort Worth, TX), Ryan Blakney (Wenatchee, WA), Cory Blaser (Westminster, CO), Blake Davis (Englewood, CO), Jordan Ferrell (Clarksville, TN), Spencer Flynn, (Plymouth, MN Forney, TX), Hal Gibson (Marysville, WA), Brian Hertzog (Lake Stevens, WA), Patrick Hoberg (Urbandale, IA), Joel Hospodka (Omaha, NE), Kolin Kline (Arvada, CO), Shaun Lampe (Phoenix, AZ Dubuque, IA), Patrick Mahoney (Pittsburg, CA), Brandon Misun (Edmond, OK), Gabriel Morales (Livermore, CA), Jeffrey Morrow (Fenton, MO) Michael Muchlinski (Ephrata, WA), Alex Ortiz (Los Angeles, CA), Marcus Pattillo (Jonesboro, AR), Daniel Reyburn (Franklin, TN), Mark Ripperger (Carlsbad, CA), Stuart Scheurwater (Regina, Saskatchewan, Canada), Adam Schwarz (Riverside Nuevo, CA), Chris Segal (Burke, VA), Gregory Stanzak (Phoenix, AZ Tulsa, OK), Quinn Wolcott (Puyallup, WA), Thomas Woodring (Boulder, Las Vegas, NV); Ramon De Jesus (Santo Domingo, DR), Travis Eggert (Pine, AZ), Chris Gonzalez (San Jose, CA); Ryan Goodman (Encino, CA), Brandon Henson (Gowrie, IA), Anthony Johnson (McComb, MS), Nicholas Mahrley (Phoenix, AZ) Thomas Newsom (King, NC), Robert Ortiz (Hopkinsville, KY), Alberto Ruiz (Las Vegas, NV).

Branch Rickey

STADIUM INFORMATION

Club	Stadium	Opened	Dimensions LF	CF	RF	Capacity	2014 Att.
Albuquerque	Isotopes Park	2003	340	400	340	13,279	564,625
Colorado Springs	Security Service Field	1988	350	410	350	8,400	350,374
El Paso	Southwest University Park	2014	322	406	322	9,650	560,997
Fresno	Chukchansi Park	2002	324	402	335	12,500	467,862
Iowa	Principal Park	1992	335	400	335	11,000	492,060
Las Vegas	Cashman Field	1983	328	433	328	9,334	329,429
Memphis	AutoZone Park	2000	319	400	322	14,500	381,429
*Nashville	First Tennessee Park	2015	327	400	327	10,000	321,042
New Orleans	Zephyr Field	1997	325	400	325	10,000	348,796
Oklahoma City	Chickasaw Bricktown Ballpark	1998	325	400	325	9,000	429,190
Omaha	Werner Park	2011	310	402	315	9,023	393,946
Reno	Aces Ballpark	2009	339	410	340	9,100	379,439
Round Rock	Dell Diamond	2000	330	405	325	8,722	595,700
Sacramento	Raley Field	2000	330	405	325	14,014	607,839
Salt Lake	Salt Lake Smith's Ballpark	1994	345	420	315	15,411	470,565
Tacoma	Cheney Stadium	1960	325	425	325	7,200	305,446

* Team played at Greer Stadium in 2014

ALBUQUERQUE ISOTOPES

Address: 1601 Avenida Cesar Chavez SE, Albuquerque, NM 87106.
Telephone: (505) 924-2255. **Fax:** (505) 242-8899.
E-Mail Address: info@abqisotopes.com. **Website:** www.abqisotopes.com.
Affiliation (first year): Colorado Rockies (2015). **Years in League:** 1972-2000, 2003-

OWNERSHIP/MANAGEMENT

President: Ken Young. **Vice President/Secretary/Treasurer:** Emmett Hammond. **VP/GM :** John Traub. **VP, Corporate Development:** Nick LoBue.

Assistant GM, Business Operation: Chrissy Baines. **Assistant GM, Sales/Marketing:** Adam Beggs. **Director, Stadium Operations:** Bobby Atencio. **Director, Retail Operations:** Kara Hayes. **Baseball Information Manager:** Lee VanHorn. **Box Office/Administration Manager:** Mark Otero. **Community Relations Manager:** Samantha Nicolson. **Season Tickets/Group Sales Manager:** Jason Buchta. **Marketing/Promotions Manager:** Kasen Dudley. **Game Production Manager:** Kris Shepard. **Suite Relations Manager:** Paul Hartenberger. **Stadium Operations Manager:** Nick Orn. **Travel Coordinator/Home Clubhouse Manager:** Ryan Maxwell. **Visiting Clubhouse Manager:** Joe Tatro. **Broadcaster:** Josh Suchon.

Graphic Services/Social Media Manager: Jason Grohoske. **Corporate Sales Executive:** Dylan Storm. **Ticket Sales Executives:** Bryan Pruitt, Aaron Robinson, Malcolm Smith, Scott Cilke, Terry Clark. **Director, Accounting/Human Resources:** Cynthia DiFrancesco. **Retail Operations Assistant:** Michael Malgieri. **Director, Field Operations:** Casey Griffin. **Assistant Groundskeeper:** Clint Belau. **Front Office Assistant:** Margaret Harris. **GM, Ovations Foodservices:** Patrick Queeney. **Catering Manager, Ovations Foodservices:** Amanda Baca. **Concession Manager, Ovations Foodservices:** Matt Butler. **Head Chef:** Mario D'Elia Scott Eastburn.

FIELD STAFF

Manager: Glenallen Hill. **Hitting Coach:** Dave Hajek. **Pitching Coach:** Darryl Scott.

GAME INFORMATION

Radio Announcer: Josh Suchon. **No. of Games Broadcast:** 144. **Flagship Station:** KNML 610-AM.
PA Announcer: Stu Walker. **Official Scorers:** Gary Herron.
Stadium Name: Isotopes Park. **Location:** From 1-25, exit east on Avenida Cesar Chavez SE to University Boulevard; From I-40, exit south on University Boulevard SE to Avenida Cesar Chavez. **Standard Game Times:** 7:05 pm, Sun 6:05. **Ticket Price Range:** $7-$25.
Visiting Club Hotel: Sheraton Albuquerque Airport Hotel, 2910 Yale Blvd SE, Albuquerque, NM 87106. **Telephone:** (505) 843-7000.

COLORADO SPRINGS SKY SOX

Address: 4385 Tutt Blvd., Colorado Springs, CO 80922.
Telephone: (719) 597-1449. **Fax:** (719) 597-2491.
E-Mail address: info@skysox.com. **Website:** www.skysox.com.
Affiliation (first year): Milwaukee Brewers (2015). **Years in League:** 1988-

OWNERSHIP/MANAGEMENT

Operated By: Colorado Springs Sky Sox Inc.
Principal Owner: David Elmore.
President/General Manager: Tony Ensor. **Director, Public Relations:** Nick Dobreff. **Assistant GM/Senior Director, Corporate Sales:** Chris Phillips. **Senior Director, Ticketing:** Whitney Shellem. **Senior Director, Group Sales:** Keith Hodges. **Director, Broadcasting:** Dan Karcher. **Director, Accounting:** Kelly Hanlon. **Senior Director, Marketing/Promotions:** Jon Eddy. **Vice President, Field Operations:** Steve DeLeon. **Manager, Merchandise/Social Media:** Nicole Tropp. **Manager, Promotions/Graphics:** Phil George. **Manager, Stadium Operations:** Eric Martin. **Manager, Corporate Sales:** Drew Trujillo. **Director, Group Sales:** Jim Rice. **Manager, Community Relations/Ticketing:** Alyce Bofferding. **Manager, Group Sales:** Kevin Soto. **Manager, Ticketing:** Jake Cooke. **Event Manager:** Brien Smith. **GM, Diamond Creations:** Don Giuliano. **Executive Chef:** Chris Evans.
Receptionist: Marianne Paine. **Home Clubhouse Manager:** Ricky Grima. **Visiting Clubhouse Manager:** Steve Martin.

FIELD STAFF

Manager: Rick Sweet. **Coach:** Bob Skube. **Pitching Coach:** Fred Dabney.

GAME INFORMATION

Radio Announcer: Dan Karcher. **No. of Games Broadcast:** 144. **Flagship Station:** AM 1300 The Animal.
PA Announcer: Josh Howe. **Official Scorer:** Marty Grantz, Rich Wastler.
Stadium Name: Security Service Field. **Location:** I-25 South to Woodmen Road exit, east on Woodmen to Powers Blvd., **right on Powers to Barnes Road. Standard Game Times:** 7:05 pm, Sat 6:05, Sun 1:35. **Ticket Price Range:** $5-13.
Visiting Club Hotel: Hilton Garden Inn, 1810 Briargate Parkway, Colorado Springs, CO 80920. **Telephone:** (719) 598-6866.

EL PASO CHIHUAHUAS

Address: 1 Ballpark Plaza, El Paso, TX 79901.
Telephone: (915) 533-2273. **Fax:** (915) 242-2031.
E-Mail Address: info@epchihuahuas.com. **Website:** www.epchihuahuas.com.
Affiliation (first year): San Diego Padres (2014). **Years in League:** 2014-

OWNERSHIP/MANAGEMENT

Owner/Chairman of the Board: Paul Foster. **Owner/CEO/Vice Chairman:** Josh Hunt. **Owners:** Alejandra de la Vega

Foster, Woody Hunt.
President: Alan Ledford. **General Manager:** Brad Taylor.
Head Groundskeeper: Andy Beggs. **Director, Finance/Administration:** Pamela De La O. **Director, Ballpark Operations:** Douglas Galeano. **Manager, Broadcasting/Media Relations:** Tim Hagerty. **Manager, Retail Operations:** Unavailable. **Account Executive, Ticket Sales:** Dana Argo, Ryan Knox, Primo Martinez, Nick Seckerson, Ryan Veinotte. **Manager, Ticket Operations:** Rebecca Jacobsen. **Director, Corporate Partnerships:** Becky Lee. **Senior Account Executive, Ticket Sales:** Colby Miller. **Director, Marketing Communications:** Angela Olivas. **Director, Ticket Sales:** Nathan Reilly. **Account Executive, Corporate Partnerships:** Judge Scott. **Manager, Database/Special Projects:** Jon Staub. **Manager, Promotions:** Tori Stein. **Account Executive, Group Sales:** AJ Barbalace. **Special Events/Military Groups Coordinator:** Monica Castillo. **Director, Guest Services/Baseball Operations:** Lizette Espinosa. **Facilities Supervisor/Operations:** Will Forney. **Administrative Assistant:** Denise Gaytan.
Mascot/Entertainment Coordinator: Grant Gorham. **Manager, Video/Digital Production:** Juan Gutierrez. **Accounting Assistant:** Heather Hagerty. **Account Services Executive, Corporate Partnerships:** Ashley Hermosillo. **Promotions/Game Entertainment:** Andy Imfeld. **Assistant Head Groundskeeping Supervisor:** Nate Jones. **Senior Account Executive, Group Sales:** Brittany Morgan, Yari Marte Natal. **Operations/Event Sales/Service Representative:** David Meza. **Baseball Operations Assistant:** Mike Raymundo. **Account Services Executive, Ticket Sales:** Nick Seckerson.

FIELD STAFF
Manager: Pat Murphy. **Hitting Coach:** Jody Davis. **Pitching Coach:** Bronswell Patrick. **Trainers:** Nathan Stewart, Isak Yoon.

GAME INFORMATION
Radio Announcer: Tim Hagerty. **No. of Games Broadcast:** 144. **Flagship Station:** ESPN 600 AM El Paso. **PA Announcer:** Unavailable. **Official Scorer:** Bernie Ricono.
Stadium Name: Southwest University Park. **Standard Game Times:** 7:05 pm, Sun 1:05. **Ticket Price Range:** $5-10.50. **Visiting Club Hotel:** Hilton Garden Inn.

FRESNO GRIZZLIES

Address: 1800 Tulare St, Fresno, CA 93721.
Telephone: (559) 320-4487. **Fax:** (559) 264-0795.
E-Mail Address: info@fresnogrizzlies.com. **Website:** www.FresnoGrizzlies.com.
Affiliation (first year): Houston Astros (2015). **Years in League:** 1998-

OWNERSHIP/MANAGEMENT
Operated By: Fresno Baseball Club, LLC.
President: Chris Cummings. **Executive Vice President:** Derek Franks. **VP, Revenue:** Jerry James. **Director, Marketing:** Sam Hansen. **Director, Operations:** Joe Castillo. **Director, Sales:** Andrew Milios. **Director, Stadium Maintenance:** Harvey Kawasaki. **Community Fund Director:** Whitney Campbell. **Director, Corporate Sales:** Andrew Melrose. **Director, Human Resources:** Ashley Tennell.
Communications/Marketing Manager: Ryan Young. **Ticket Sales Manager:** Cody Holden. **Entertainment Manager:** Nick Haas. **Guest Relations Manager:** Steve Sodini. **Inside Sales Manager/Account Executive:** Andrew Hacnik. **Stadium Maintenance Manager:** Ira Calvin. **Merchandise Manager:** Lalonnie Calderon. **Premium Seating Sales Manager:** Jon Stockton. **Assistant Ticket Sales Manager:** Brian Boden. **Finance Manager:** Monica DeLacerda. **Baseball Operations Coordinator:** Chris Wilson. **Entertainment/Mascot Coordinator:** Troy Simeon. **Partnership Activation Coordinator:** Camille Moultrie. **Ticket Sales Coordinator:** Eric Moreno. **Corporate Partnership Executive:** Kyle Esty. **Corporate Partnership Executive:** Ray Ortiz. **Group Sales Account Executive:** Kyle Kleiman. **Staff Accountant:** Landon Hollman. **Communications/Marketing Assistant:** Mayra Alvarez. **Community Fund Assistant:** Chris Ortiz. Ticket Sales Assistant: Kendra Coy. Administrative Assistant: Yanet Richardson. Head Groundskeeper: David Jacinto.

FIELD STAFF
Manager: Tony DeFrancesco. **Hitting Coach:** Leon Roberts. **Pitching Coach:** Arthur "Ace" Adams. **Athletic Trainer:** Bryan Baca. **Strength/Conditioning Coach:** Trey Wiedman.

GAME INFORMATION
Radio Announcer: Doug Greenwald. **No. of Games Broadcast:** 144. **Flagship Radio Station:** 1430 AM KYNO. **Flagship TV Station:** ABC 30.1.
Stadium Name: Chukchansi Park. **Location:** 1800 Tulare St, Fresno, CA 93721. **Directions:** From 99 North, take Fresno Street exit, left on Fresno Street, left on Inyo or Tulare to stadium; From 99 South, take Fresno Street exit, left on Fresno Street, right on Broadway to H Street; From 41 North, take Van Ness exit toward Fresno, left on Van Ness, left on Inyo or Tulare, stadium is straight ahead; From 41 South, take Tulare exit, stadium is located at Tulare and H Streets, or take Van Ness exit, right on Van Ness, left on Inyo or Tulare, stadium is straight ahead. **Ticket Price Range:** $9-19.
Visiting Club Hotel: University Square Hotel of Fresno (4961 North Cedar Avenue, Fresno, CA 93726). **Telephone:** (559) 224-4200.

IOWA CUBS

Address: One Line Drive, Des Moines IA 50309.
Telephone: (515) 243-6111. **Fax:** (515) 243-5152.
Website: www.iowacubs.com
Affiliation (first year): Chicago Cubs (1981). **Years in League:** 1969-

OWNERSHIP/MANAGEMENT

Operated By: Raccoon Baseball Inc.
Chairman/Principal Owner: Michael Gartner. **Executive Vice President:** Michael Giudicessi. **President/General Manager:** Sam Bernabe. **Shareholder:** Mike Gartner. **Executive VP/Assistant GM:** Nate Teut. **VP/CFO:** Sue Tollefson. **VP/Director, Broadcast Operations:** Deene Ehlis. **Director, Media Relations:** Randy Wehofer. **Director, Communications:** Scott Sailor. **Director, Multimedia Arts:** Justin Walters. **Director, Ticket Operations:** Kenny Houser. **Director, Luxury Suites:** Brent Conkel. **Assistant Ticket Manager:** Aaron Roland. **Director, Stadium Operations:** Jeff Tilley. **Manager, Stadium Operations:** Nic Peters, Andrew Quillin. **Corporate Relations:** Red Hollis, Eric Hammes, Brianne Westlake. **Head Groundskeeper:** Chris Schlosser. **Director, Merchandise:** Shelby Heimbuch. **Director, Special Events:** KC Routos. **Accountant:** Lori Auten. Director, Information Technology: Ryan Clutter. Landscape Coordinator: Shari Kramer.

FIELD STAFF

Manager: Marty Pevey. **Hitting Coach:** Brian Harper. **Pitching Coach:** Mike Cather. **Athletic Trainer:** Scott Barringer. **Strength/Conditioning:** Ryan Clausen.

GAME INFORMATION

Radio Announcers: Deene Ehlis, Randy Wehofer. **No. of Games Broadcast:** 144. **Flagship Station:** AM 940 KPSZ.
PA Announcers: Aaron Johnson, Mark Pierce, Corey Coon, Rick Stageman, Joe Hammen. **Official Scorers:** Jayme Adam, Michael Pecina, James Hilchen, Steve Mohr.
Stadium Name: Principal Park. **Location:** I- 80 or I-35 to I-235, to Third Street exit, south on Third Street, left on Line Drive. **Standard Game Times:** 7:05 pm, Sun 1:05. **Ticket Price Range:** $4-14.
Visiting Club Hotel: Renaissance Savery Hotel, 401 Locust Street, Des Moines IA 50309. **Telephone:** (515) 244-2151

LAS VEGAS 51S

Address: 850 Las Vegas Blvd North, Las Vegas, NV 89101.
Telephone: (702) 943-7200. **Fax:** (702) 943-7214.
E-Mail Address: info@lv51.com. **Website:** www.lv51.com.
Affiliation (first year): New York Mets (2013). **Years in League:** 1983-

OWNERSHIP/MANAGEMENT

Operated By: Summerlin Las Vegas Baseball Club LLC.
President/COO: Don Logan. **General Manager/VP of Sales/Marketing:** Chuck Johnson. **VP, Ticket Operations:** Mike Rodriguez. **VP, Operations/Security:** Nick Fitzenreider. **Director, Sponsorships:** James Jensen. **Chief Financial Officer:** Tim Colbert. **Senior Accountant/Analyst:** Scott Montes. **Director, Broadcasting:** Russ Langer. **Director, Ticket Sales:** Erik Eisenberg. **Director, Community Relations/Customer Service:** Melissa Harkavy. **Sponsorship Services Manager/Travel Coordinator:** William Graham. **Business Development:** Larry Brown. **Media Relations Director:** Jim Gemma. **Ticket Operations Assistant:** Michelle Taggart. **Administrative Assistants:** Jan Dillard, Pat Dressel. **Account Executives, Ticket Sales:** Bryan Frey, TJ Thedinga. **Retail Operations Manager:** Jason Weber. **Operations Manager:** Chip Vespe.

FIELD STAFF

Manager: Wally Backman. **Hitting Coach:** Jack Voigt. **Pitching Coach:** Frank Viola. **Athletic Trainer:** Joe Golia. **Strength/Conditioning Coach:** Jon Cioffi.

GAME INFORMATION

Radio Announcer: Russ Langer. **No. of Games Broadcast:** 144. **Flagship Station:** Sports 920 (AM) The Game.
PA Announcer: Dan Bickmore. **Official Scorers:** Peter Legner, Mark Wasik.
Stadium Name: Cashman Field. **Location:** I-15 to US 95 exit (downtown), east to Las Vegas Boulevard North exit, one-half mile north to stadium. **Standard Game Time:** 7:05 pm. **Ticket Price Range:** $11-14.
Visiting Club Hotel: Golden Nugget Hotel & Casino, 129 Fremont Street, Las Vegas, NV 89101. **Telephone:** (702) 385-7111.

MEMPHIS REDBIRDS

Office Address: 175 Toyota Plaza, Suite 300, Memphis, TN 38103. **Stadium Address:** 200 Union Ave, Memphis, TN 38103.
Telephone: (901) 721-6000. **Fax:** (901) 842-1222.
Website: www.memphisredbirds.com.
Affiliation (first year): St. Louis Cardinals (1998). **Years in League:** 1998-

OWNERSHIP/MANAGEMENT

Ownership: St. Louis Cardinals.
General Manager: Craig Unger. **Director, Corporate Sales:** Kelly Lackey. **Director, Operations:** Mark Anderson. **Coordinator, Operations:** Kevin Rooney. **Ticket Operations Manager:** Travis Trumitch. **Season Ticket Sales Manager:** S.J. Tucker. **Director, Media Relations:** Michael Whitty. **Corporate Sales Executive:** Michael Hunter. **Corporate Sales Coordinator:** Lauren Thomas. **Accounting Manager:** Cindy Neal. **Assistant Groundskeeper:** Brian Bowe. **Maintenance Technician:** Spencer Shields. **Community Relations Coordinator:** Isaiah Bell.

FIELD STAFF

Manager: Mike Shildt. **Hitting Coach:** Mark Budaska. **Pitching Coach:** Bryan Eversgerd. **Trainer:** Jeremy Clipperton.

GAME INFORMATION

Radio Announcer: Steve Selby. **No. of Games Broadcast:** 144. **Flagship Station:** WHBQ 560-AM.
PA Announcer: Unavailable. **Official Scorer:** J.J. Guinozzo, Eric Opperman.
Stadium Name: AutoZone Park. **Location:** North on I-240, exit at Union Avenue West, one and half mile to park.
Standard Game Times: 7:05 pm, Sat 6:05, Sun 1:35. **Ticket Price Range:** $6-23.
Visiting Club Hotel: Sleep Inn at Court Square, 40 N Front, Memphis, TN 38103. **Telephone:** (901) 522-9700.

NASHVILLE SOUNDS

Address: 401 Jackson Street, Nashville, TN 37219.
Telephone: (615) 690-HITS Fax: (615) 256-5684.
E-Mail address: info@nashvillesounds.com. **Website:** www.nashvillesounds.com.
Affiliation (first year): Oakland Athletics (2015). **Years in League:** 1998-

OWNERSHIP/MANAGEMENT

Operated By: MFP Baseball. **Owners:** Frank Ward, Masahiro Honzawa. **Chief Operating Officer:** Garry Arthur.
Senior VP, Operations: Doug Scopel. **Senior VP, Corporate/Premium Partnerships:** Jason Franke. **Senior VP, Fan Experience:** Brandon Yerger. **VP, Stadium Operations:** James Rozzoni.
Director, Accounting: Barb Walker. **Director, Multimedia Productions:** Brett Ausbrooks. **Director, Entertainment:** Mary Hegley. **Director, Guest Services:** Amy Schoch. **Director, Ticket Operations:** Chris Sprunger. **Senior Manager, Premium Sales:** Chris Day. **Senior Manager, Group Sales:** Justin Webster. **Managers, Group Sales:** Justin Fenlon, Tim Nemes, Rebecca Woolard. **Manager, Community Relations/Mascot Coordinator:** Buddy Yelton. **Manager, Merchandise:** Katie Ward. **Manager, Community Relations:** Dani Ward. **Manager, Stadium Operations:** Chad Green. **Assistant Manager, Stadium Operations:** Jeremy Wells. **Manager, Media Relations:** Grant Braden. **Manager, Corporate Partnerships Activation:** Andi Grindley. **Manager, Corporate Partnerships Activation:** Danielle Gaw.
Manager, Advertising: Ryan Madar. **Manager, Creative Services:** Alex Wassel. **Manager, Ticket Operations:** Leon McCathen. **Manager, Premium Sales:** Rob Koch. **Manager, Premium Sales:** Jilian Brake. **Manager, Premium Sales:** Eric Sundvold. **Manager, Premium Services:** Marcus Plumb. **Head Groundskeeper:** Thomas Trotter. **Assistant Groundskeeper:** Patrick Barnaby. **Clubhouse Managers:** Matt Gallant, Patrick King. **Executive Assistant:** Jane Nicholson.

FIELD STAFF

Manager: Steve Scarsone. **Hitting Coach:** Webster Garrison. **Pitching Coach:** Don Schulze. **Trainer:** Brad LaRosa. **Strength/Conditioning Coach:** Terence Brannic.

GAME INFORMATION

Radio Announcer: Jeff Hem. **No. of Games Broadcast:** 144. **Flagship Station:** Unavailable.
PA Announcers: Unavailable. **Official Scorers:** Eric Jones, Trevor Garrett, Kyle Parkinson.
Stadium Name: First Tennessee Park. **Location:** I-65 to exit 85 (Rosa L Parks Blvd) and head south; Turn left on Jefferson St, then turn right onto 5th Ave North, then turn left on Jackson St. **Standard Game Times:** 7:05 pm, Sat 6:35, Sun 2:05 (April-June 21), 6:35 (June 28-Sept). **Ticket Price Range:** $7-26.
Visiting Club Hotel: Unavailable.

NEW ORLEANS ZEPHYRS

Address: 6000 Airline Dr, Metairie, LA 70003.
Telephone: (504) 734-5155. **Fax:** (504) 734-5118.
E-Mail Address: zephyrs@zephyrsbaseball.com. **Website:** www.zephyrsbaseball.com.
Affiliation (first year): Miami Marlins (2009). **Years in League:** 1998-

OWNERSHIP/MANAGEMENT

Managing Partner/President: Don Beaver.

Minority Owner/Vice President/General Counsel: Walter Leger. **Executive Director/General Manager:** Mike Schline. **VP, Sales/Marketing/Community Relations:** Jeff Booker.

Director, Broadcasting/Team Travel: Tim Grubbs.

Color Analyst/Speakers Bureau: Ron Swoboda. **Director, Media Relations:** Dave Sachs. **Director, Promotions/Community Relations:** Brandon Puls. **Director, Ticket Operations:** Kathy Kaleta. **Assistant, Community Relations/Promotions:** Rachel Whitley. **Director, Finance/Accounting:** Donna Light. **Director, Stadium Operations:** Jose Avila. **Assistant, Stadium Operations:** Timmy Hinds. **Director, Group Sales:** Alex Sides. **Director, Clubhouse:** Brett Herbert. **Group Outings Coordinators:** Jonathan Christensen, Daniel Straney, Hunter Whitfield, Lindsey Roll. **Marketing:** Sarah Wasser. **Head Groundskeeper:** Thomas Marks. **Maintenance Coordinator:** Craig Shaffer. **Receptionist:** Susan Radkovich.

FIELD STAFF

Manager: Andy Haines. **Hitting Coach:** Damon Minor. **Pitching Coach:** Charlie Corbell. **Trainer:** Chris Olson.

GAME INFORMATION

Radio Announcers: Tim Grubbs, Ron Swoboda. **No. of Games Broadcast:** 144. **Flagship Station:** WMTI 106.1 FM. **PA Announcer:** Doug Moreau. **Official Scorer:** JL Vangilder.

Stadium Name: Zephyr Field. **Location:** I-10 West toward Baton Rouge, exit at Clearview Pkwy (exit 226) and continues south, right on Airline Drive (US 61 North) for 1 mile, stadium on left; From airport, take Airline Drive (US 61) east for 4 miles, stadium on right. **Standard Game Times:** 7 pm, Sat 6, Sun 2 (April-May), 6 (June-Sept). **Ticket Price Range:** $6-10.

Visiting Club Hotel: Sheraton Four Points, 6401 Veterans Memorial Blvd, Metairie, LA 70003. **Telephone:** (504) 885-5700.

OKLAHOMA CITY DODGERS

Address: 2 S Mickey Mantle Dr., Oklahoma City, OK 73104.
Telephone: (405) 218-1000. **Fax:** (405) 218-1001.
E-Mail Address: info@okcdodgers.com. **Website:** www.okcdodgers.com.
Affiliation (first year): Los Angeles Dodgers (2015). **Years in League:** 1963-1968, 1998-

OWNERSHIP/MANAGEMENT

Operated By: MB OKC LLC. **Principal Owner:** Mandalay Baseball. **President/General Manager:** Michael Byrnes. **Senior Vice President:** Jenna Byrnes.

Director, Ticket Operations/Project Development: Armando Reyes. **Director, Finance/Accounting:** Jon Shaw. **Director, Corporate Partnerships:** Matt Taylor. **Director, Operations:** Mitch Stubenhofer. **Director, Facility Operations:** Harlan Budde. **Director, Media Relations/Broadcasting:** Alex Freedman. **Director, Entertainment:** Shannon Landers. **Director, Food/Beverage:** Travis Johnson. **Manager, Sponsor Services:** Jennifer Van Tuyl. **Office Manager:** Travis Hunter. **Head Groundskeeper:** Monte McCoy.

FIELD STAFF

Manager: Damon Berryhill. **Hitting Coach:** Franklin Stubbs. **Pitching Coach:** Scott Radinsky. **Coach:** Johnny Washington. **Athletic Trainer:** Greg Harrel. **Strength/Conditioning Coach:** Travis Smith.

GAME INFORMATION

Radio Announcer: Alex Freedman No. **of Games Broadcast:** 144. **Station:** KGHM-AM 1340 (www.1340thegame.com). **PA Announcer:** Tom Travis. **Official Scorers:** Jim Byers, Ryan McGhee, Rich Tortorelli.

Stadium Name: Chicasaw Bricktown Ballpark. **Location:** Bricktown area in downtown Oklahoma City, near interchange of I-235 and I-40, off I-235 take Sheridan exit to Bricktown; off I-40 take Shields exit, north to Bricktown. **Standard Game Times:** 7:05 pm, Sun 2:05 (April-May, Sept.), 6:05 (June-Aug). **Ticket Price Range:** $8-20.

Visiting Club Hotel: Courtyard Oklahoma City Downtown 2 West Reno Ave., Oklahoma City, OK 73102. **Phone:** (405) 232-2290.

OMAHA STORM CHASERS

Address: Werner Park, 12356 Ballpark Way, Papillion, NE 68046
Administrative Office Phone: (402) 734-2550. **Ticket Office Phone:** (402) 738-5100. **Fax:** (402) 734-7166
E-mail Address: info@omahastormchasers.com. **Website:** www.omahastormchasers.com.
Affiliation (first year): Kansas City Royals (1969). **Years in League:** 1998-

OWNERSHIP/MANAGEMENT

Operated by Alliance Baseball Managing Partners: Gary Green, Larry Botel, Eric Foss, Brian Callaghan, Stephen Alepa, Alan Stein, Peter Huff. **Chief Executive Officer:** Gary Green. **President/General Manager:** Martie Cordaro. **Assistant GM:** Laurie Schlender. **Assistant GM, Operations:** Andrea Stava.

Business Manager: Meredith Daniels. Director, Broadcasting: Mark Nasser. Director, Business Development: Dave Endress. Director, Ticket Sales: Sean Olson. Director, Ballpark Operations: Brett Myers. Broadcaster/Director, Baseball Operations: Brett Pollock. Corporate Sales Manager: Danny Dunbar. Corporate Sales Executive: Jason Kinney. Client Services Manager: Kaci Long. Marketing & Promotions Manager: Rob Sternberg. Group Sales Manager: Alex Beck. Senior Group Sales Executives: Ryan Worthen, Alex Jerden, Lauren Teer. Ticket Operations Manager: Zach Daw. Media Relations Manager: Andrew Mitchell. Manager, Production/Design: Adam McLaughlin.

Special Events Coordinator: Shawn Fitzpatrick. Community Relations Manager: Megan Burdek. Community Relations Assistant: Taylor Edmonds. All-Star Game/Special Projects: Madison Rozell. Ballpark Operations Assistant: Matt Owen. Head Groundskeeper: Noah Diercks. Assistant Groundskeeper: Adam Basinger. Front Office Assistant: Donna Kostal.

FIELD STAFF

Manager: Brian Poldberg. Hitting Coach: Tommy Gregg. Pitching Coach: Al Nipper. Athletic Trainer: Dave Iannicca. Strength Coach: Joe Greany

GAME INFORMATION

Radio Announcers: Mark Nasser, Brett Pollock. No. of Games Broadcast: 144. Flagship Station: KZOT-AM 1180. PA Announcer: Craig Evans. Official Scorers: Frank Adkisson, Steve Pivovar, Ryan White. Stadium Name: Werner Park. Location: Highway 370, just east of I-80 (exit 439). Standard Game Times: 6:35 pm (April-May), 7:05 (June-Sept), Fri/Sat 7:05, Sun 2:05.

Visiting Club Hotel: Courtyard Omaha La Vista, 12560 Westport Parkway, La Vista, NE 68128. Telephone: (402) 339-4900. Fax: (402) 339-4901.

RENO ACES

Address: 250 Evans Ave, Reno, NV 89501.
Telephone: (775) 334-4700. Fax: (775) 334-4701.
Website: www.renoaces.com.
Affiliation (first year): Arizona Diamondbacks (2009). Years in League: 2009-

OWNERSHIP/MANAGEMENT

President/Managing Partner: Stuart Katzoff.

Partners: Jerry Katzoff, Herb Simon, Steve Simon. Chief Financial Officer: Kevin Bower. General Counsel: Brett Beecham. Executive Vice President/Chief Operating Officer: Eric Edelstein. Assistant General Manager: Andrew Daugherty. Director of Finance: Chris Gelfuso. Vice President, Ticket Sales: Todd Pund. Vice President, Ballpark Operations: Tara O'Connor. Director, Freight House Operations: Jason Yount. Vice President, Community/Corporate Impact: Rick Parr. Director, Broadcasting: Ryan Radtke. Manager, Communications: Chad Seely. Senior Manager of Marketing/Promotions: Audrey Hill. Coordinator, Graphic Design/Entertainment: Dominic Mascola.

Director, Business Development: Brian Moss. Manager, Marketing Partnerships: Emily Jaenson. Account Executive, Corporate Sponsorships: Niko Saladis. Manager, Ticket Operations: Sarah Bliss. Ticket Office Supervisor: Liz Bell. Manager, Group Sales: Kris Morrow. Account Executives, Outside Sales: Jeff Turner, Malcolm Chapman & Jack Maloney. Account Executives, Group Sales: Lorenzo Taormina, Nick Gassner, Edgar Montoya, David Woodard. Manager, Grounds: Eric Blanton. Assistant Groundskeeper: Lane Pickle. Coordinator, Operations: Kyle Titus. Manager, Facilities: Mark Link. Assistant, Facilities: Miguel Paredes. Director, Merchandise: Chris Sundvold. Retail Buyer: Stacey Little. Senior Staff Accountant: Melinda Jessee. Junior Staff Accountant: Jacquie Menicucci. Human Resources/Payroll: Shawn Force. Staff Accountant: Joe Valenti.

FIELD STAFF

Manager: Phil Nevin. Hitting Coach: Greg Gross. Pitching Coach: Mike Parrott. Coach: Luis Urueta. Athletic Trainer: Joe Metz. Strength/Conditioning Coordinator: Mike Schofield.

GAME INFORMATION

Radio Announcer: Ryan Radtke. No. of Games Broadcast: 144. Flagship Station: Fox Sports 630 AM. PA Announcer: Unavailable. Official Scorer: Billy Lee, Nick Saccomanno, Katie Rihn, Gregg Zive. Stadium Name: Aces Ballpark. Location: From Carson City (south of Reno): 395 North to I-80 West, Exit 14 (Wells Ave.), left on Wells, right at Kuenzli St., ballpark on right; From East, I-80 West to exit 14 (Wells Ave.), left on Wells, right on Kuenzli, right at East 2nd St.; From West, I-80 East to Exit 13 (Virginia St.), right on Virginia, left on Second, ballpark on left; From North, 395 South to I-80 West, Exit 14 (Wells Ave.), left on Wells, right on Kuenzli. Standard Game Times: 7:05 pm, 6:35, 1:05. Ticket Price Range: $7-30.

Visiting Club Hotel: Silver Legacy Resort Casino. Telephone: 775-325-7401.

ROUND ROCK EXPRESS

Address: 3400 East Palm Valley Blvd, Round Rock, TX 78665.
Telephone: (512) 255-2255. Fax: (512) 255-1558.
E-Mail Address: info@rrexpress.com. Website: www.roundrockexpress.com.
Affiliation (first year): Texas Rangers (2011). Year in League: 2005-

OWNERSHIP/MANAGEMENT

Operated By: Ryan Sanders Baseball, LP. **Principal Owners:** Nolan Ryan, Don Sanders. **Owners:** Reese Ryan (CEO), Reid Ryan, Brad Sanders, Bret Sanders, Jay Miller, Eddie Maloney. **Chief Operating Officer, Ryan Sanders Baseball:** JJ Gottsch. **Executive Assistant, Ryan Sanders Baseball:** Debbie Bowman.

President: Jay Miller. **General Manager:** Chris Almendarez.

Assistant GM, Baseball Operations: Tim Jackson. **Senior Vice President, Marketing:** Laura Fragoso. **VP, Corporate Sales:** Henry Green. **VP, Ticket Sales:** Gary Franke. **VP, Business Development:** Gregg Miller. **VP, Administration/Accounting:** Debbie Coughlin.

Senior Director, Stadium Operations: David Powers. **Senior Director, United Heritage Center:** Scott Allen. **Senior Director, Ticket Operations:** Ross Scott. **Director, Broadcasting:** Mike Capps. **Director, Communications:** Jill Cacic. **Director, Ballpark Entertainment:** Steve Richards. **Director, Stadium Maintenance:** Aurelio Martinez. **Retail Manager:** Debbie Goodman. **Community Relations Coordinator:** Cassidy MacQuarrie. **Client Services:** Zach Pustka. **IT Manager:** Sam Isham.

Stadium Maintenance Manager: Corey Woods. **Manager, Ticket Sales:** Stuart Scally. **Dell Account Manager:** Julia Benavides, Account Executives: Drew Maulsby, Melissa Schmalbach. **Head Groundskeeper:** Garrett Reddehase. **Clubhouse Manager:** Kenny Bufton. **Maintenance Staff:** Raymond Alemon, Ofelia Gonzalez. **Office Manager:** Wendy Abrahamsen.

FIELD STAFF

Manager: Jason Woods. **Hitting Coach:** Justin Mashore. **Pitching Coach:** Brad Holman. **Trainer:** Jason Roberts. **Strength Coach:** Ric Mabie.

GAME INFORMATION

Radio Announcers: Mike Capps. **No. of Games Broadcast:** 144. **Flagship Station:** The Horn 104.9 FM.
PA Announcer: Glen Norman. **Official Scorer:** Tommy Tate.
Stadium Name: Dell Diamond. **Location:** US Highway 79, 3.5 miles east of Interstate 35 (exit 253) or 1.5 miles west of Texas Tollway 130. **Standard Game Times:** 7:05 pm, 6:05, 1:05. **Ticket Price Range:** $7-$14.
Visiting Club Hotel: Hilton Garden Inn, 2310 North IH-35, Round Rock, TX 78681. **Telephone:** (512) 341-8200.

SACRAMENTO RIVER CATS

Address: 400 Ballpark Drive, West Sacramento, CA 95691.
Telephone: (916) 376-4700. **Fax:** (916) 376-4710.
E-Mail Address: reception@rivercats.com. **Website:** www.rivercats.com.
Affiliation (First Year): San Francisco Giants (2015). **Years in League:** 1903, 1909-11, 1918-60, 1974-76, 2000-

OWNERSHIP/MANAGEMENT

Majority Owner/CEO: Susan Savage. **President:** Jeff Savage. **General Manager:** Chip Maxson. **Senior Director, Human Resources:** Grace Bailey. **Director, Corporate Partnerships:** Greg Coletti. **Manager, Corporate Partnerships:** Ross Richards. **Coordinator, Partnership Activation:** Barbara Turpen. **Director, Stadium Operations, Events & Entertainment:** Ryan Von Sossan. **Director, Marketing:** Erin O'Donnell. **Manager, Marketing:** Emily Williams. **Manager, Entertainment/Promotions:** Dane Lund. **Community Relations Coordinator:** Mike Osborn. **Coordinator, Multimedia/Graphic Design:** Mike Villarreal. **Graphic Designer:** Ann Frazier. **Mascot Coordinator:** Lee Warner. **Public Relations Assistant/New Media Editor:** Daniel Emmons. **Manager, Merchandise:** Rose Holland. **Assistant Manager, On Deck Shop:** Erin Kilby. **Coordinator, Website/Research:** Brent Savage.

Head Groundskeeper: Chris Shastid. **Coordinator, Grounds:** Marcello Clamar. **Landscaper:** Rafael Quiroz. **Facility Engineer:** Mike Gossen. **Operations Lead:** Russ Casselberry. **Director, Ticket Operations:** John Krivacic. **Ticket Operations Assistant:** Khimberly Marshall. **Senior Director, Ticket Sales:** Adam English. **Senior Manager, Inside Sales:** Jordan Cannon. **Membership/Suite Coordinator:** Alicia Stefani. **Senior Corporate Account Executive:** John Watts. **Corporate Account Executives:** Cooper Farrer, Andrew Dean, Jon Choi, DuMaurier Jordan, Michael Stewart. **Senior Group Events Account Executive:** Joey Van Cleave. **Group Events Account Executives:** Michele Bello, Eddie Eixenberger, Alejandro Lacayo, Alexandria Harbowy, Cara Paganini, Andrea Rodriguez. **Inside Sales Representative:** Amanda Holland. **Controller:** Maddie Strika. **Executive Assistant:** Kimberly Morales. **Accounting Assistant:** Michelle Agurto. **Receptionist:** Leah Larot.

FIELD STAFF

Manager: Bob Mariano. **Hitting Coach:** Andy Skeels. **Pitching Coach:** Dwight Bernard. **Athletic Trainer:** James Petra. **Strength Coach:** Brad Lawson. **Clubhouse Manager:** Pablo Lopez.

GAME INFORMATION

Radio Broadcaster: Johnny Doskow. **No. of Games Broadcast:** 144.
PA Announcer: Greg Lawson. **Official Scorers:** Brian Berger, Ryan Bjork, Mark Honbo.
Stadium Name: Raley Field. **Location:** I-5 to Business-80 West, exit at Jefferson Boulevard. **Standard Game Time:** 7:05 pm. **Ticket Price Range:** $9-65.
Visiting Club Hotel: Holiday Inn Capitol Plaza.

SALT LAKE BEES

Address: 77 W 1300 South, Salt Lake City, UT 84115.
Telephone: (801) 325-2337. **Fax:** (801) 485-6818.
E-Mail Address: info@slbees.com. **Website:** www.slbees.com.
Affiliation (first year): Los Angeles Angels (2001). **Years in League:** 1915-25, 1958-65, 1970-84, 1994-.

OWNERSHIP/MANAGEMENT

Operated by: Larry H Miller Baseball Inc. **Principal Owner:** Gail Miller.
CEO, Larry H Miller Group of Companies: Greg Miller. **President, Miller Sports Properties:** Steve Miller. **Chief Operating Officer:** Jim Olson. **Chief Revenue Officer:** Don Stirling. **Vice President/General Manager:** Marc Amicone. **Senior VP, Corporate Partnerships:** Chris Baum. **Senior VP, Marketing:** Craig Sanders. **Senior VP, Ticket Sales:** Clay Jensen. **General Counsel:** Robert Tingey. **Senior VP, Communications:** Frank Zang.
Director, Broadcasting: Steve Klauke. **VP, Corporate Partnerships:** Greg Tanner. **Director, Game Operations:** Renata Hadden. **Director, Ticket Sales/Services:** Brad Jacoway. **Director, Corporate Partnerships:** Brian Prutch. **Director, Marketing:** Kevin Dalton. **Box Office Manager:** Laura Russell. **Communications Manager:** Kraig Williams. **Ticket/Group Sales Manager:** Collin Forbes. **VP, Public Safety:** Jim Bell. **VP, Food Services:** Mark Stedman. **Director, Food Services:** Dave Dalton. **Youth Programs Coordinator:** Nate Martinez. **Clubhouse Manager:** Eli Rice.

FIELD STAFF

Manager: Dave Anderson. **Hitting Coach:** Johnny Narron. **Pitching Coach:** Erik Bennett. **Trainer:** Brian Reinker.

GAME INFORMATION

Radio Announcer: Steve Klauke. **No. of Games Broadcast:** 144. **Flagship Station:** 1280 AM.
PA Announcer: Jeff Reeves. **Official Scorers:** Howard Nakagama, Troy Rowley, Steve Hansen.
Stadium Name: Smith's Ballpark. **Location:** I-15 North/South to 1300 South exit, east to ballpark at West Temple.
Standard Game Times: 6:35 (April-May), 7:05 (June-Sept), Sun 1:05. **Ticket Price Range:** $8-24.
Visiting Club Hotel: Sheraton City Centre, 150 W 500 South, Salt Lake City, UT 84101. **Telephone:** (801) 401-2000.

TACOMA RAINIERS

Address: 2502 South Tyler St, Tacoma, WA 98405.
Telephone: (253) 752-7707. **Fax:** (253) 752-7135. **Website:** www.tacomarainiers.com.
Affiliation: Seattle Mariners (1995). **Years in League:** 1960-

OWNERSHIP/MANAGEMENT

Owners: The Baseball Club of Tacoma. **President:** Aaron Artman.
Director, Administration/Assistant to the President: Patti Stacy. **Vice President, Business Development:** Jim Flavin. **VP, Ticket Sales:** Shane Santman. **Controller:** Brian Coombe. **Senior Director, Ballpark Operations:** Ryan Schutt. **Creative Director:** Tony Canepa. **Director, Marketing/Media Development:** Ben Spradling. **Director, Partner Development:** Julia Falvey. **Director, Baseball Operations/Merchandise:** Ashley Schutt. **Director, Ticket Operations:** Cameron Badgett. **Manager, Corporate Partner Services:** Betsy Hechtner. **Manager, Stadium Operations:** Nick Cherniske.
Manager, Suite Services/Events: Taryn Duncan. **Corporate Sales Managers:** Andrew Barry, Ben Nelson, Tim O'Hollaren, Tyler Olsson, Patrick Hilsabeck, Brian Sinclair. **Coordinator, Box Office:** Necia Borba. **Coordinator, Event Sales:** Byron Pullen. **Coordinator, Corporate Partner Services:** Meghan Granito. **Group Event Coordinators:** Chris Aubertin, Caitlin Calnan, Haley Harshaw, Skylan Morris. **Accounting:** Elise Schorr. **Head Groundskeeper:** David Schutt. **Receptionist:** Taylor Barham. **Home Clubhouse Manager:** Shane Hickenbottom.

FIELD STAFF

Manager: Pat Listach. **Hitting Coach:** Cory Snyder. **Pitching Coach:** Jamie Navarro. **Trainers:** Tom Newberg, Tyler Moos. **Performance Coach:** Will Lindholm.

GAME INFORMATION

Radio Broadcaster: Mike Curto. **No. of Games Broadcast:** 144. **Flagship Station:** KHHO 850-AM.
PA Announcer: Unavailable. **Official Scorers:** Kevin Kalal, Gary Brooks, Michael Jessee.
Stadium Name: Cheney Stadium. **Location:** From I-5, take exit 132 (Highway 16 West) for 1.2 miles to 19th Street East exit, merge right onto 19th Street, right onto Clay Huntington Way and follow into the parking lot of the ballpark.
Standard Game Times: 7:05, Sun 1:35. **Ticket Price Range:** $7.50-$25.50.
Visiting Club Hotel: Hotel Murano, 1320 Broadway Plaza, Tacoma, WA 98402. **Telephone:** (253) 238-8000.

EASTERN LEAGUE

Address: 30 Danforth St, Suite 208, Portland, ME 04101.
Telephone: (207) 761-2700. **Fax:** (207) 761-7064.
E-Mail Address: elpb@easternleague.com. **Website:** www.easternleague.com.
Years League Active: 1923-

President/Treasurer: Joe McEacharn.

Vice President/Secretary: Charlie Eshbach. **VP:** Chuck Domino. **Assistant to President:** Bill Rosario. **Directors:** Ken Babby (Akron), Rick Brenner (New Hampshire), Lou DiBella (Richmond), Josh Solomon (New Britain), Charlie Eshbach (Portland), Joe Finley (Trenton), Bob Lozinak (Altoona), Art Matin (Erie), Michael Reinsdorf (Harrisburg), Brian Shallcross (Bowie), Craig Stein (Reading), Mike Urda (Binghamton).

Division Structure: Eastern—Binghamton, New Britain, New Hampshire, Portland, Reading, Trenton. Western—Akron, Altoona, Bowie, Erie, Harrisburg, Richmond.

Regular Season: 142 games. **2015 Opening Date:** April 9. **Closing Date:** Sept 7.

All-Star Game: July 15 at Portland.

Playoff Format: Top two teams in each division meet in best-of-five series. Winners meet in best-of-five series for league championship.

Roster Limit: 25. **Player Eligibility Rule:** No restrictions.

Brand of Baseball: Rawlings.

Joe McEacharn

Umpires: John Bacon (Sherrodsville, OH), Ryan Clark (McDonough, GA), Paul Clemons (Oxford, KS), Doug Del Bello (Hamburg, NY), Blake Felix (Fort Worth, TX), Eric Gillam (Roscoe, IL), John Libka (Ft. Gratiot, MI), Dan Merzel (Philadelphia, PA), Roberto Moreno (Cumana, VZ), Brian Peterson (Manchester, NJ), Charlie Ramos (Battle Creek, MI), Jeremie Rehak (Monroeville, PA), Sean Ryan (Waunakee, WI), Jorge Teran (Barquisimeto, VZ), Chris Tipton (Kissimmee, FL), Alex Tosi (Lake Villa, IL), Junior Valentine (Maryville, TN), Ryan Wills (Fredericksburg, VA).

STADIUM INFORMATION

Club	Stadium	Opened	Dimensions LF	CF	RF	Capacity	2014 Att.
Akron	Canal Park	1997	331	400	337	7,630	350,704
Altoona	Peoples Natural Gas Field	1999	325	405	325	7,210	275,823
Binghamton	NYSEG Stadium	1992	330	400	330	6,012	171,279
Bowie	Prince George's Stadium	1994	309	405	309	10,000	248,630
Erie	Jerry Uht Park	1995	317	400	328	6,000	209,299
Harrisburg	Metro Bank Park	1987	325	400	325	6,300	273,645
New Britain	New Britain Stadium	1996	330	400	330	6,146	302,865
New Hampshire	Northeast Delta Dental Stadium	2005	326	400	306	6,500	340,299
Portland	Hadlock Field	1994	315	400	330	7,368	359,427
Reading	FirstEnergy Stadium	1951	330	400	330	9,000	394,458
Richmond	The Diamond	1985	330	402	330	9,560	418,147
Trenton	Arm & Hammer Park	1994	330	407	330	6,150	361,369

AKRON RUBBERDUCKS

Address: 300 S Main St, Akron, OH 44308.
Telephone: (330) 253-5151. **Fax:** (330) 253-3300.
E-Mail Address: information@akronrubberducks.com. **Website:** www.akronrubberducks.com.
Affiliation (first year): Cleveland Indians (1989). **Years in League:** 1989-

OWNERSHIP/MANAGEMENT

Operated By: Akron Baseball, LLC. **Principal Owner:** Ken Babby.

General Manager/COO: Jim Pfander. **Assistant GM:** Scott Riley. **Controller:** Leslie Wenzlawsh. **Assistant, Finance:** Sean Flowerday. **Coordinator, Promotions:** Christina Urycki. **Director, Public/Media Relations:** Adam Liberman. **Director, Broadcasting/Baseball Information:** Dave Wilson. **Manager, Merchandise:** Joe Lande. **Manager, Creative Services:** Unavailable. **Director, Stadium Operations:** Adam Horner. **Head Groundskeeper:** Chris Walsh. **Assistant Director, Ballpark Operations:** Taylor Englebaugh. **Director, Food/Beverage:** Brian Manning. **Assistant Director, Food/Beverage:** Colin Tulley. **Manager, Suites/Picnics:** Sam Dankoff. **Office Manager:** Missy Dies.

Manager, Community Relations/Special Events: Brock Cline. **Box Office Manager:** Pete Nugent. **Director, Ticketing:** Brian Flenner. **Assistant Director, Ticketing:** Jeremy Heit. **Senior Group Sales Manager:** Mitch Cromes. **Ticket Sales Executives:** Dee Shilling, Craig Wilson, Mark Carlozzi, Jenna Reed. **Director, Corporate Partnerships:** Brent DeCoster. **Sponsorship Sales Coordinator:** Juli Donlen. **Graphic Designer:** Taylor Myers. **Director, Player Facilities:** Shad Gross.

FIELD STAFF

Manager: Dave Wallace. **Hitting Coach:** Rouglas Odor. **Pitching Coach:** Jeff Harris. **Trainer:** Jeremy Heller. **Strength/Conditioning Coach:** Jake Sankal.

GAME INFORMATION

Radio Announcers: Jim Clark, Dave Wilson. **No of Games Broadcast:** 142. **Flagship Station:** Fox Sports Radio 1350-AM.

PA Announcer: Lenoard Grabowski. **Official Scorer:** Tom Giffen.

Stadium Name: Canal Park. **Location:** From I-76 East or I-77 South, exit onto Route 59 East, exit at Exchange/Cedar, right onto Cedar, left at Main Street; From I-76 West or I-77 North, exit at Main Street/Downtown, follow exit onto Broadway Street, left onto Exchange Street, right at Main Street. **Standard Game Time:** 6:35 (April-May); 7:05 pm (June-Sept), Sun 2:05. **Ticket Price Range:** $5-9.

Visiting Club Hotel: Radisson Akron-Fairlawn. **Telephone:** (330) 666-9300.

ALTOONA CURVE

Address: Peoples Natural Gas Field, 1000 Park Avenue, Altoona, PA 16602.
Telephone: (814) 943-5400. **Fax:** (814) 942-9132.
E-Mail Address: frontoffice@altoonacurve.com. **Website:** www.altoonacurve.com
Affiliation (first year): Pittsburgh Pirates (1999). **Years in League:** 1999-

OWNERSHIP/MANAGEMENT

Operated By: Lozinak Professional Baseball. **Managing Members:** Bob and Joan Lozinak.
COO: David Lozinak. **CFO:** Mike Lozinak. **Chief Administrative Officer:** Steve Lozinak. **General Manager:** Rob Egan. **Senior Advisor:** Sal Baglieri. **Assistant GM:** Mike Passanisi. **Director, Finance:** Mary Lamb. **Director, Ticket Operations:** Corey Homan. **Director, Merchandising:** Claire Hoover. **Director, Ballpark Operations:** Doug Mattern.

Head Groundskeeper: Ben Young. **Manager, Concessions:** Glenn McComas. **Assistant Manager, Concessions:** Michelle Anna. **Director, Creative Services:** Mark Milligan. **Manager, Community Relations/Special Events:** Emily Rosencrants. **Development/Operations:** Tim Lozinak. **Sponsorship Sales Account Executive:** Adam Erikson. **Mascot Development/Marketing:** Isaiah Arpino. **Box Office Manager:** Steffan Langguth. **Senior Associate, Ticketing:** Nathan Bowen. **Associates, Ticketing:** Luke Johnson, Jess Knott. **Administrative Assistant:** Donna Harpster.

FIELD STAFF

Manager: Tom Prince. **Hitting Coach:** Kevin Riggs. **Pitching Coach:** Justin Meccage. **Trainer:** Dru Scott. **Strength/Conditioning:** Furey Leva.

GAME INFORMATION

Radio Announcers: Mike Passanisi. **No. of Games Broadcast:** 142. **Flagship Station:** WVAM 1430-AM.
PA Announcer: Rich DeLeo. **Official Scorers:** Ted Beam, Dick Wagner.
Stadium Name: Peoples Natural Gas Field. **Location:** Located just off the Frankstown Road Exit off I-99. **Standard Game Times:** 7pm, 6:30 (April-May); Sat 6, Sun 6. **Ticket Price Range:** $5-12.
Visiting Club Hotel: Unavailable.

BINGHAMTON METS

Office Address: 211 Henry St., Binghamton, NY 13901. **Mailing Address:** PO Box 598, Binghamton, NY 13902.
Telephone: (607) 723-6387. **Fax:** (607) 723-7779.
E-Mail Address: bmets@bmets.com. **Website:** www.bmets.com.
Affiliation (first year): New York Mets (1992). **Years in League:** 1923-37, 1940-63, 1966-68, 1992-

OWNERSHIP/MANAGEMENT

President: Michael Urda. **Board of Directors:** Michael Urda, Bill Maines, David Maines, George Scherer. **General Manager:** Jim Weed. **Assistant GM/Director, Marketing:** Heith Tracy.

Director, Stadium Operations: Richard Tylicki. **Director, Broadcasting/Media Relations:** Tim Heiman. **Director, Video Production:** Joe Campione. **Director, Community Relations:** Connor Gates. **Box Office Manager:** Joe Pascarella. **Sports Turf Manager:** EJ Folli. **Office Manager, Senior Accountant:** Karen Micalizzi. **Scholastic Programs Coordinator:** Lou Ferarro. **Special Events Coordinators:** Connor Gates, Erica Folli, Bobby Urda. **Merchandise Manager:** Lisa Shattuck. **Account Executive:** Eddie Saunders. **Official Scorer:** Steve Kraly. **Public Address Announcers:** Chris Schmidt, Roger Neel.

FIELD STAFF

Manager: Pedro Lopez. **Coach:** Luis Natera. **Pitching Coach:** Glenn Abbott.

GAME INFORMATION

Radio Announcer: Tim Heiman. **No. of Games Broadcast:** 142. **Flagship Station:** WNBF 1290-AM.
PA Announcer: Chris Schmidt. **Official Scorer:** Steve Kraly.
Stadium Name: NYSEG Stadium. **Location:** I-81 to exit 4S (Binghamton), Route 11 exit to Henry Street. **Standard Game Times:** 6:35, 7:05 (Fri-Sat), 1:05 (Day Games). **Ticket Price Range:** $7-22.
Visiting Club Hotel: Best Western, 569 Harry L Drive, Johnson City, NY 13790. **Telephone:** (607) 729-9194.

BOWIE BAYSOX

Address: Prince George's Stadium, 4101 NE Crain Hwy, Bowie, MD 20716.
Telephone: (301) 805-6000. **Fax:** (301) 464-4911.
E-Mail Address: info@baysox.com. **Website:** www.baysox.com.
Affiliation (first year): Baltimore Orioles (1993). **Years in League:** 1993-

OWNERSHIP/MANAGEMENT
Owned By: Bowie Baysox Baseball Club LLC.
President: Ken Young. **General Manager:** Brian Shallcross. **Assistant GM:** Phil Wrye. **Director, Marketing:** Brandan Kaiser. **Director, Field/Facility Operations:** Matt Parrott. **Director, Ticket Operations:** Charlene Fewer. **Director, Sponsorships:** Matt McLaughlin. **Promotions Manager:** Chris Rogers. **Communications Manager:** Matt Wilson. **Sponsorship Account Manager:** Adam Pohl. **Group Events Managers:** Jake Seils, Ted Elsasser, Ashley Nalley. **Box Office Manager:** Landon Ferrell. **Community Programs Manager:** Joe Miller. **Director, Video Production:** Elizabeth Moir. **Stadium Operations Manager:** Austin Ingersoll. **Assistant Head Groundskeeper:** Andrew Lawing. **Director, Gameday Personnel:** Darlene Mingioli. **Clubhouse Manager:** Andy Maalouf. **Bookkeeper:** Carol Terwilliger.

FIELD STAFF
Manager: Gary Kendall. **Coach:** Paco Figueroa. **Pitching Coach:** Alan Mills.

GAME INFORMATION
Radio Announcer: Adam Pohl. **No. of Games Broadcast:** 142. **Flagship Station:** www.1430wnav.com.
PA Announcer: Adrienne Roberson. **Official Scorers:** Peter O'Reilly, Carl Smith, Ted Black, Herb Martinson.
Stadium Name: Prince George's Stadium. **Location:** 1/4 mile south of US 50/Route 301 Interchange in Bowie.
Standard Game Times: 6:35 pm (Apr-Jun) 7:05 pm (Jul-Sep), Sat 6:35 pm, Sun 2:05 pm. **Ticket Price Range:** $7-17.
Visiting Club Hotel: Best Western Annapolis, 2520 Riva Rd, Annapolis, MD 21401. **Telephone:** (410) 224-2800.

ERIE SEAWOLVES

Address: 110 E 10th St, Erie, PA 16501.
Telephone: (814) 456-1300. **Fax:** (814) 456-7520.
E-Mail Address: seawolves@seawolves.com. **Website:** www.seawolves.com.
Affiliation (first year): Detroit Tigers (2001). **Years in League:** 1999-

OWNERSHIP/MANAGEMENT
Principal Owners: Mandalay Baseball Properties, LLC. **President:** Greg Coleman.
Assistant GM, Communications: Greg Gania. **Assistant GM, Sales:** Mark Pirrello. **Director, Accounting/Finance:** Amy McArdle. **Account Executive:** Megan Allen. **Director, Corporate Sales:** Kevin Forte. **Director, Group Sales:** Dan Torf. **Ticket Operations Manager:** Nick Marckel. **Director, Food/Beverage (Pro Sports Catering):** Trevor Parnell. **Assistant Director, Food/Beverage (Pro Sports Catering):** Danielle Tenfelde.

FIELD STAFF
Manager: Lance Parrish. **Coach:** Gerald Perry. **Pitching Coach:** Mike Henneman. **Trainer:** T.J. Saunders.

GAME INFORMATION
Radio Announcer: Greg Gania. **No. of Games Broadcast:** 142. **Flagship Station:** Fox Sports Radio WFNN 1330-AM.
PA Announcer: Bob Shreve. **Official Scorer:** Les Caldwell.
Stadium Name: Jerry Uht Park. **Location:** US 79 North to East 12th Street exit, left on State Street, right on 10th Street.
Standard Game Times: 7:05 pm, 6:35 (April-May), Sun 1:35. **Ticket Price Range:** $9-14.
Visiting Club Hotel: Clarion Lake Erie, 2800 West 8th St., Erie, PA 16505. **Telephone:** (814) 833-1116.

HARRISBURG SENATORS

Office Address: Metro Bank Park, City Island, Harrisburg, PA 17101. **Mailing Address:** PO Box 15757, Harrisburg, PA 17105.
Telephone: (717) 231-4444. **Fax:** (717) 231-4445.
E-Mail address: information@senatorsbaseball.com. **Website:** www.senators-baseball.com.
Affiliation (first year): Washington Nationals (2005). **Years in League:** 1924-35, 1987-

OWNERSHIP, MANAGEMENT
Operated By: Senators Partners, LLC.
Chairman: Michael Reinsdorf. **CEO:** Bill Davidson. **President:** Kevin Kulp. **General Manager:** Randy Whitaker.
Assistant GM, Game Operations: Aaron Margolis. **Accounting Manager:** Donna Demczak. **Accounting, Assistant:** Gina Wirful. **Senior Corporate Sales Executive:** Todd Matthew. **Senior Sales Executive, Corporate Development:** Nate DeFazio. **Director, Ticket Sales:** Jonathan Boles. **Senior Account Executives:** Jessica Kauffman, Andrew Madden. **Account Executive:** Chuck Heisley, Brian Becka, Josh Mohn. **Box Office Manager:** Matt McGrady. **Box Office Intern:**

Joe Simowski. **Director, Merchandise:** Ann Marie Naumes. **Merchandise Intern:** Madison Bentley. **Director, Stadium Operations:** Tim Foreman. **Head Groundskeeper:** Brandon Forsburg. **Director, Broadcasting/Media Relations:** Terry Byrom. **Broadcaster/Media Relations Intern:** Perry Mattern. **Community Relations Coordinator:** Blair Jewell. **Community Relations Intern:** Nikki Reist. **Director, Digital/New Media:** Ashley Grotte. **Game Entertainment Coordinator:** Sean Purcell. **Ticket Sales Interns:** Samantha Jarvis, Morgan Bagg, Danny Keich, Ryan Binas. **Graphics Intern:** Allasyn Lieneck.

FIELD STAFF
Manager: Brian Daubach. **Coach:** Mark Harris. **Pitching Coach:** Chris Michalak. **Trainer:** Eric Montague. **Strength Coach:** Tony Rogowski.

GAME INFORMATION
Radio Announcers: Terry Byrom, Perry Mattern. **No. of Games Broadcast:** 142. **Flagship Station:** 1460-AM.
PA Announcer: Chris Andre. **Official Scorers:** Terry Walters, Bruce Bashore, Jeff McGaw.
Stadium Name: Metro Bank Park. **Location:** I-83, exit 23 (Second Street) to Market Street, bridge to City Island. **Ticket Price Range:** $5-13.50.
Visiting Club Hotel: Park Inn by Radisson, 5401 Carlisle Pike, Mechanicsburg, PA 17050. **Telephone:** (800) 772-7829.
Visiting Team Workout Facility: Gold's Gym, 3401 Hartzdale Dr, Camp Hill, PA 17011. **Telephone:** (717) 303-2070.

NEW BRITAIN ROCK CATS

Office Address: 230 John Karbonic Way, New Britain, CT 06051. **Mailing Address:** PO Box 1718, New Britain, CT 06050.
Telephone: (860) 224-8383. **Fax:** (860) 225-6267.
E-Mail Address: rockcats@rockcats.com. **Website:** www.rockcats.com.
Affiliation (first year): Colorado Rockies (2015). **Years in League:** 1983-

OWNERSHIP/MANAGEMENT
Operated By: New Britain Double Play LLC. **Directors:** Josh Solomon, Jim Solomon, Jennifer Goorno.
General Manager: Tim Restall. **Vice President, Corporate Partnerships/Marketing:** Mike Ambramson. **Director, Broadcasting/Media Relations:** Jeff Dooley. **Director, Corporate Tickets:** Steve Given. **Director, Group Sales:** Josh Montinieri. **Director, Creative Services:** Ted Seavey.
Senior Manager, Hospitality: Andres Levy. **Ticket Operations Manager:** Dylan Conway. **Merchandise Manager:** Kristin Zemke. **Group Sales Managers:** Steve Mekkelsen, Matt DiBona. **Manager, Media/Group Sales:** Pat O'Sullivan. **Community Relations/Marketing Manager:** Brianna Bruneau. **Corporate Sales Managers:** Andrew Vallejo, Shawn Perry. **Client Services Manager:** Amanda Goldsmith. **Marketing Coordinator:** Lori Soltis. **Controller:** Jim Bonfiglio.

FIELD STAFF
Manager: Darin Everson. **Coach:** Ron Gideon. **Pitching Coach:** Dave Burba. **Hitting Coach:** Jeff Salazar. **Trainer:** Billy Whitehead.

GAME INFORMATION
Radio Announcer: Jeff Dooley. **No. of Games Broadcast:** 142. **Flagship Station:** Fox Sports Radio 1410, WMRD 1150-AM.
PA Announcer: John Sheatsley. **Official Scorer:** Ed Smith.
Stadium Name: New Britain Stadium. **Location:** From I-84, take Route 72 East (exit 35 of Route 9 South (exit 39A), left at Ellis St. (exit 25), left at South Main St., stadium one mile on right. From Route 91 or Route 5, take Route 9 North to Route 71 (exit 24), first exit. **Ticket Price Range:** $6-20.
Visiting Club Hotel: Holiday Inn Express, 120 Laning St, Southington, CT 06489. **Telephone:** (860) 276-0736.

NEW HAMPSHIRE
FISHER CATS

Address: 1 Line Dr, Manchester, NH 03101.
Telephone: (603) 641-2005. **Fax:** (603) 641-2055.
E-Mail Address: info@nhfishercats.com. **Website:** www.nhfishercats.com.
Affiliation (first year): Toronto Blue Jays (2004). **Years in League:** 2004-

OWNERSHIP/MANAGEMENT
Operated By: DSF Sports. **Owner:** Art Solomon. **President/General Manager:** Rick Brenner.
Senior VP, Sales: Mike Ramshaw. **Senior VP/Assistant GM:** Jenna Raizes. **General Counsel/VP, Business Operations:** Steve Pratt. **Corporate Controller:** Debbie Morin. **Executive Director, Sales:** Erik Lesniak. **Executive Director, Box Office Operations:** Tim Hough. **Executive Director, Broadcast/Media Relations:** Tom Gauthier. **Executive Director, Stadium Operations:** DJ White. **Director, Ticket Sales:** Ben Carr. **Director, Hospitality/Special Events:** Stephanie Fournier. **Sports Turf Manager:** Dan Boyle. **Director, Production/Graphic Design:** Sean Hladick. **Stadium Operations**

Manager: Eric Costin. **Production/Social Media Assistant Manager:** David Rodriguez. **Corporate Sales Manager:** Jon Mersereau. **Merchandise Manager:** Brianne Hemmila. **Ticket Sales Account Executives:** Lindsey House, Chris Biskup, Kevin Caputo. **Ticket Office Assistant:** Jeff McMahon. **Radio/Media Relations Assistant:** Ben Gellman-Chomsky. **General Manager, Advantage Food/Beverage:** Al Foley.

FIELD STAFF
Manager: Bobby Meacham. **Hitting Coach:** Stubby Clapp. **Pitching Coach:** Bob Stanley. **Athletic Trainer:** Bob Tarpey. **Strength/Conditioning:** Brian Pike.

GAME INFORMATION
Radio Announcers: Tom Gauthier, Bob Lipman, Ben Gellman-Chomsky. **No. of Games Broadcast:** 142. **Flagship Station:** WGIR 610-AM.
PA Announcer: Unavailable. **Official Scorers:** Chick Smith, Lenny Parker, Greg Royce, Pete Dupuis.
Stadium Name: Northeast Delta Dental Stadium. **Location:** From I-93 North, take I-293 North to exit 5 (Granite Street), right on Granite Street, right on South Commercial Street, right on Line Drive. **Ticket Price Range:** $6-12.
Visiting Club Hotel: Country Inn & Suites, 250 South River Rd., Bedford, N.H. 03110. **Telephone:** (603) 666-4600.

PORTLAND SEA DOGS

Office Address: 271 Park Ave, Portland, ME 04102. **Mailing Address:** PO Box 636, Portland, ME 04104.
Telephone: (207) 874-9300. **Fax:** (207) 780-0317.
E-Mail address: seadogs@seadogs.com. **Website:** www.seadogs.com.
Affiliation (first year): Boston Red Sox (2003). **Years in League:** 1994-

OWNERSHIP/MANAGEMENT
Operated By: Portland, Maine Baseball, Inc. **Chairman:** Bill Burke.
Treasurer: Sally McNamara. **President:** Charles Eshbach. **Executive Vice President/General Manager:** Geoff Iacuessa. **Senior VP:** John Kameisha. **VP, Financial Affairs/Game Operations:** Jim Heffley. **Assistant GM, Media Relations:** Chris Cameron. **Executive Director, Sales:** Dennis Meehan. **Ticket Office Manager:** Dennis Carter. **Account Executive, Sales/Promotions:** Courtney Rague. **Account Executives, Sales:** Ashley Montgomery, Lindsay Oliver. **Director, Broadcasting:** Mike Antonellis. **Director, Food Services:** Mike Scorza. **Assistant Director, Food Services:** Greg Moyes. **Office Manager:** Lyndsey Berry. **Clubhouse Managers:** Craig Candage Sr, Nick Fox. **Head Groundskeeper:** Rick Anderson.

FIELD STAFF
Manager: Billy McMillon. **Coach:** Dave Joppie. **Pitching Coach:** Kevin Walker. **Trainer:** Brandon Henry.

GAME INFORMATION
Radio Announcer: Mike Antonellis. **No. of Games Broadcast:** 142. **Flagship Station:** WPEI 95.9 FM.
PA Announcer: Paul Coughlin. **Official Scorer:** Thom Hinton.
Stadium Name: Hadlock Field. **Location:** From South, I-295 to exit 5, merge onto Congress Street, left at St John Street, merge right onto Park Ave; From North, I-295 to exit 6A, right onto Park Ave. **Ticket Price Range:** $5-10.
Visiting Club Hotel: Fireside Inn & Suites, 81 Riverside St., Portland, ME 04103. **Telephone:** (207) 774-5601.

READING FIGHTIN PHILS

Office Address: Route 61 South/1900 Centre Ave, Reading, PA 19605. **Mailing Address:** PO Box 15050, Reading, PA 19612.
Telephone: (610) 370-2255. **Fax:** (610) 373-5868.
E-Mail Address: info@fightins.com. **Website:** www.fightins.com.
Affiliation (first year): Philadelphia Phillies (1967). **Years in League:** 1933-35, 1952-61, 1963-65, 1967-

OWNERSHIP/MANAGEMENT
Operated By: E&J Baseball Club, Inc. **Principal Owner:** Reading Baseball LP. **Managing Partner:** Craig Stein.
General Manager: Scott Hunsicker. **Assistant GM:** Ashley Peterson. **Executive Director, Sales:** Joe Bialek. **Controller:** Kristyne Haver. **Head Groundskeeper:** Dan "Dirt" Douglas. **Executive Director, Baseball Operations/Merchandise:** Kevin Sklenarik. **Executive Director, Graphic Arts/Game Entertainment:** Matt Jackson. **Executive Director, Tickets:** Mike Becker. **Executive Director, Community Relations/Fan Development:** Mike Robinson.
Director, Food/Beverage: Eric Freeman. **Director, Business Development:** Anthony Pignetti. **Director, Groups:** Jim Taipalus. **Video Director:** Andy Kauffman. **Office Manager:** Deneen Giesen. **Director, Marketing:** Tonya Petrunak. **Director, Educational Programs/Music/Game Presentation:** Todd Hunsicker. **Director, Public Relations/Media Relations:** Eric Scarcella. **Manager, Fundraising/Sales Rep:** Andrew Nelson. **Assistant Director, Groups:** Jon Nally. **Manager, Concessions/Sales Representative:** Travis Hart. **Manager, Operations/Sales Representative:** Brian Hoeper. **Manager, Tickets/New Media:** Jenn Pirri. **Manager, Groups/Extra Events/Game Presentation:** Stephen Thomas. **Managers, Groups:** Bill Richards, Derek Lupia.

FIELD STAFF
Manager: Dusty Wathan. **Coach:** Frank Cacciatore. **Pitching Coach:** Dave Lundquist.

GAME INFORMATION

Radio Announcer: Mike Ventola. **No. of Games Broadcast:** 142. **Flagship Station:** WRAW 1340-AM.
PA Announcer: Justin Choate. **Official Scorers:** Paul Jones, Brian Kopetsky, Josh Leiboff, Dick Shute.
Stadium Name: FirstEnergy Stadium. **Location:** From east, take Pennsylvania Turnpike West to Morgantown exit, to 176 North, to 422 West, to Route 12 East, to Route 61 South exit; From west, take 422 East to Route 12 East, to Route 61 South exit; From north, take 222 South to Route 12 exit, to Route 61 South exit; From south, take 222 North to 422 West, to Route 12 East exit at Route 61 South. **Standard Game Times:** 7:05 pm, 6:35 (April-May), Sun 1:35. **Ticket Price Range:** $5-11.
Visiting Club Hotel: Crowne Plaza Reading Hotel 1741 Papermill Road, Wyomissing, PA 19610. **Telephone:** (610) 376-3811.

RICHMOND FLYING SQUIRRELS

Address: 3001 N Boulevard, Richmond, VA 23230.
Telephone: (804) 359-3866. **Fax:** (804) 359-1373.
E-Mail Address: info@squirrelsbaseball.com. **Website:** www.squirrelsbaseball.com.
Affiliation: San Francisco Giants (2009). **Years in League:** 2009-

OWNERSHIP/MANAGEMENT

Operated By: Navigators Baseball LP. **President/Managing Partner:** Lou DiBella.
CEO: Chuck Domino. **Vice President/COO:** Todd "Parney" Parnell.
General Manager: Bill Papierniak. **Controller:** Faith Casey. **Director, Corporate Sales:** Mike Murphy. **Corporate Sales Executives:** Will Bell. **Assistant GM, Sales:** Brendon Porter. **Director, Tickets:** Patrick Flower. **Box Office Manager:** Andy Webb. **Director, Suite Sales/Client Relations:** Jerrine Lee. **Director, Business Development:** Marty Steele. **Lead Broadcaster:** Jon Laaser. **Communications, Marketing/Broadcast Manager:** Jay Burnham. **Director, Promotions/In-Game Entertainment/Creative Services Manager:** Kellye Semonich. **Community Relations Manager:** Megan Angstadt. **Group Sales Executives:** Camp Peery, Chris Walker, Garrett Erwin, Deidre Geron. **Executive Director, Food/Beverage/Merchandise:** Ben Rothrock. **Assistant Directors, Food/Beverage:** Mike Caddell. **Director, Tasty Goodness/Chef/Catering:** Josh Barban. **Director, Field Operations:** Steve Ruckman. **Assistant Director, Field Operations:** Tyler Lenz. **Director, Stadium Operations:** Steve Pump.

FIELD STAFF

Manager: Jose Alguacil. **Hitting Coach:** Ken Joyce. **Pitching Coach:** Steve Kline. **Athletic Trainer:** David Getsoff. **Strength/Conditioning Coach:** Adam Vish.

GAME INFORMATION

Radio Announcers: Jon Laaser, Jay Burnham. **No. of Games Broadcast:** 142. **Flagship Station:** Sports Radio 910 WRNL-AM.
PA Announcer: Jimmy Barrett. **Official Scorer:** Scott Day.
Stadium Name: The Diamond. **Location:** Right off I-64 at the Boulevard exit. **Standard Game Times:** 7:05 pm, Sat 6:35, Sun 5:05. **Ticket Price Range:** $7-12.
Visiting Club Hotel: Comfort Suites at Virginia Center Commons, 10601 Telegraph Road, Glen Allen, VA. **Telephone:** (804) 262-2000.

TRENTON THUNDER

Address: One Thunder Road, Trenton, NJ 08611.
Telephone: (609) 394-3300. **Fax:** (609) 394-9666.
E-Mail address: fun@trentonthunder.com. **Website:** www.trentonthunder.com.
Affiliation (first year): New York Yankees (2003). **Years in League:** 1994-

OWNERSHIP/MANAGEMENT

Operated By: Garden State Baseball, LLP. **General Manager/COO:** Will Smith.

Senior VP, Corporate Sales/Partnerships: Eric Lipsman. **Director, Merchandising:** Joe Pappalardo. **Director, Finance/Baseball Operations:** Jeff Hurley. **Director, Ticket Operations:** Matt Pentima. **Director, Creative/Audiovisual Services:** Greg Lavin. **Director, Marketing/Partnerships:** Lydia Rios. **Director, Community Relations/Database Management:** TJ Jahn. **Director, Food/Beverage:** Chris Champion. **Director, Ticket Sales:** Nate Schneider. **Director, Stadium Operations:** Steve Brokowsky.

Office Manager: Susanna McGrogan. **Production Manager:** Chris Foster. **Group Sales Account Executive:** Lindsey Ravior. **Ticket Sales Account Executive:** Janelle Alfano. **Ticket Sales Account Representative:** Sean O'Brien, Sol Presnky. **Group Sales Account Representative:** Matt Mango, Dean Fritz, Jack Rymal, Jon Bodnar, Nick Luongo, Chuck Keller. **Group Sales Coordinator:** Mike Heyer. **Assistant, Administrative/Community Relations:** Amanda Rossetti. **Assistant, Broadcast/Media Relations:** Adam Giardino. **Assistant, Tickets:** Steven Carpenter. **Assistant, Promotions:** Rob Faulstick, Christina Jennings. **Head Groundskeeper:** Mike Kerns. **Assistant Groundskeeper:** Danny Bradley. **Superintendent:** Scott Ribsam. **Chef:** Corey Anderson.

FIELD STAFF

Manager: Al Pedrique. **Hitting Coach:** P.J. Pilittere. **Pitching Coach:** Jose Rosado. **Coach:** Michel Hernandez. **Trainer:** Lee Meyer. **Strength/Conditioning Coach:** Orlando Crance.

GAME INFORMATION

Radio Announcers: Adam Giardino, Jon Mozes. **No. of Games Broadcast:** 142. **Flagship Station:** WTSR 91.3 FM. **PA Announcer:** Unavailable. **Official Scorers:** Jay Dunn, Greg Zak.

Stadium Name: Arm & Hammer Park. **Location:** From I-95, take Route 1 North to Route 29 South, stadium entrance just before tunnel; From NJ Turnpike, take Exit 7A and follow I-195 West, Road will become Rte 29, Follow through tunnel and ballpark is on left. **Standard Game Times:** 7 pm, Sun 1/5. **Ticket Price Range:** $11-13.

Visiting Club Hotel: Wyndham Garden Trenton. **Telephone:** (609) 421-4000.

SOUTHERN LEAGUE

Mailing Address: 2551 Roswell Rd, Suite 330, Marietta, GA 30062.
Telephone: (770) 321-0400. **Fax:** (770) 321-0037.
E-Mail Address: loriwebb@southernleague.com. **Website:** www.southernleague.com.
Years League Active: 1964-

President: Lori Webb.
Vice President: Steve DeSalvo. **Directors:** Buck Rogers (Biloxi), Jonathan Nelson (Birmingham), Rich Mozingo (Chattanooga), Reese Smith (Jackson), Peter Bragan, Jr. (Jacksonville), Steve DeSalvo (Mississippi), Mike Savit (Mobile), Sherrie Myers(Montgomery), Bruce Baldwin (Pensacola), Doug Kirchhofer (Tennessee).
Director, Operations: John Harris.
Division Structure: North—Birmingham, Chattanooga, Jackson, Montgomery, Tennessee. South—Biloxi, Jacksonville, Mississippi, Mobile, Pensacola.
Regular Season: 140 games (split schedule). **2015 Opening Date:** April 9. **Closing Date:** Sept. 7.
All-Star Game: June 23 at Montgomery.
Playoff Format: First-half division winners meet second-half division winners in best-of-five series. Winners meet in best of five series for league championship.
Roster Limit: 25. **Player Eligibility Rule:** No restrictions.
Brand of Baseball: Rawlings.
Umpires: Unavailable.

Lori Webb

STADIUM INFORMATION

Club	Stadium	Opened	Dimensions LF	CF	RF	Capacity	2014 Att.
*Biloxi	MGM Stadium	2015	N/A	N/A	N/A	6,000	94,929
Birmingham	Regions Field	2013	320	400	325	8,500	437,612
Chattanooga	AT&T Field	2000	325	400	330	6,362	242,627
Jackson	Ballpark at Jackson	1998	310	395	320	6,000	135,248
Jacksonville	Baseball Grounds of Jacksonville	2003	321	420	317	11,000	300,538
Mississippi	Trustmark Park	2005	335	402	332	7,416	211,200
Mobile	Hank Aaron Stadium	1997	325	400	310	6,000	106,297
Montgomery	Riverwalk Stadium	2004	314	380	332	7,000	244,534
Pensacola	Bayfront Stadium	2012	325	400	335	6,000	311,687
Tennessee	Smokies Park	2000	330	400	330	6,000	283,038

* Team played in Huntsville in 2014.

BILOXI SHUCKERS

Address: 714 Howard Ave, Biloxi, MS 39530
Telephone: (228) 233-3465.
E-Mail Address: info@biloxishuckers.com. **Website:**www.biloxishuckers.com.
Affiliation (first year): Milwaukee Brewers (1999). **Years in League:** 1985-

OWNERSHIP/MANAGEMENT
Operated By: Biloxi Baseball LLC. **President:** Ken Young. **General Manager:** Buck Rogers.
Director, Media/Broadcaster: Chris Harris. **Manager, Publications/Social Media:** Cristina Coca. **Director, Sales:** Chris Birch. **Retail Manager:** Babs Rogers. **Ticket Sales Executives:** Allan Lusk, Kevin Trembley. **Director, Stadium Operations:** Trevor Matifes. **Head Groundkeeper:** Jamie Hill. **Office Manager:** Lisa Turner.

FIELD STAFF
Manager: Carlos Subero. **Coach:** Sandy Guerrero. **Pitching Coach:** Chris Hook. **Athletic Trainer:** Steve Patera. **Strength/Conditioning Coach:** Nate Dine.

GAME INFORMATION
PA Announcer: Unavailable. **Official Scorer:** Unavailable.
Stadium Name: MGM Park. **Location:** I-10 to I-110 South toward beach, take Ocean Springs exit onto US 90 (Beach Blvd), travel east one block, turn left on Caillavet Street, stadium is on left. **Ticket Price Range:** $10-$27.
Visiting Club Hotel: Four Points Sheraton Biloxi.

BIRMINGHAM BARONS

Office Address: 1401 1st Ave South, Birmingham, AL, 35233. **Mailing Address:** PO Box 877, Birmingham, AL, 35201.
Telephone: (205) 988-3200. **Fax:** (205) 988-9698.
E-Mail Address: barons@barons.com. **Website:** www.barons.com.
Affiliation (first year): Chicago White Sox (1986). **Years in League:** 1964-65, 1967-75, 1981-

OWNERSHIP/MANAGEMENT

Principal Owners: Don Logan, Jeff Logan, Stan Logan.
General Manager: Jonathan Nelson. **Chief Financial Officer:** Randy Prince. **Director, Broadcasting:** Curt Bloom. **Director, Customer Service:** George Chavous. **Director, Media Relations:** Tyler Brown. **Director, Production:** Mike Ferko. **Director, Retail Sales:** Becky York. **Director, Sales:** John Cook. **Director, Stadium Operations:** Nick Lampasona. **Director, Tickets:** David Madison. **Director, Group Sales:** Charlie Santiago. **Group Sales Managers:** Jessica O'Rear, Brett Oates. **Corporate Event Planners:** Sydney Wilbanks, Emily Stuenkel. **Special Events Coordinators:** Fabian Truss, Claire Griffith. **Head Groundskeeper:** Daniel Ruggiero. **Assistant Groundskeeper:** Eric Taylor. **Office Manager:** Shaunte Bailey. **Corporate Sales Manager:** Don Leo. **Season Ticket Manager:** Danny Franklyn. **Inventory Control Accountant:** Ruth Allison.
General Manager, Parkview Catering: Eric Crook. **Concessions Manager:** Brian Diciaccio. **Executive Chef:** Matt Jett. **Catering Managers:** Ginny Bryant, Matt Mullinax.

FIELD STAFF

Manager: Julio Vinas. **Hitting Coach:** Jaime Dismuke. **Pitching Coach:** Britt Burns.

GAME INFORMATION

Radio Announcer: Curt Bloom. **No of Games Broadcast:** 140. **Flagship Station:** News Radio 105.5 WERC-FM.
PA Announcers: Derek Scudder. **Official Scorers:** AA Moore, Grant Martin.
Stadium Name: Regions Field. **Location:** I-65 (exit 259B) in Birmingham. **Standard Game Times:** 7:05 pm, Sat 6:30, Sun 2:05. **Ticket Price Range:** $7-14.
Visiting Club Hotel: Sheraton Birmingham Hotel, 2101 Richard Arrington Junior Boulevard North, Birmingham, AL 35203. **Telephone:** (205) 324-5000.

CHATTANOOGA LOOKOUTS

Office Address: 201 Power Alley, Chattanooga, TN 37402. **Mailing Address:** PO Box 11002, Chattanooga, TN 37401.
Telephone: (423) 267-2208. **Fax:** (423) 267-4258.
E-Mail Address: lookouts@lookouts.com. **Website:** www.lookouts.com.
Affiliation (first year): Minnesota Twins (2015). **Years in League:** 1964-65, 1976-

OWNERSHIP/MANAGEMENT

Operated By: Scenic City Baseball LLC.
Principal Owner: Frank Burke. **President/General Manager:** Rich Mozingo.
Assistant GM: Harold Craw. **Director, Group Sales:** Andrew Zito. **Group Sales Mangers:** Morgan Billups, Jennifer Crum. **Director, Ticketing:** Rebecca Ramos. **Media Relations Manager:** Dan Kopf. **Marketing/Promotions Manager:** Alex Tainsh. **Director, Concessions:** Steve Sullivan. **Director, Broadcasting:** Larry Ward. **Director, Business Administration/Accounting:** Anastasia McCowan. **Retail Manager:** Emily Dillard. **Head Groundskeeper:** Brandon Moore.

FIELD STAFF

Manager: Doug Mientkiewicz. **Hitting Coach:** Chad Allen. **Pitching Coach:** Stu Cliburn.

GAME INFORMATION

Radio Announcers: Larry Ward, Jim Reynolds. **No. of Games Broadcast:** 140. **Flagship Station:** 105.1 WALV-FM.
PA Announcer: Ron Hall. **Official Scorers:** Wirt Gammon, Andy Paul, David Jenkins.
Stadium Name: AT&T Field. **Location:** From I-24, take US 27 North to exit 1C (4th Street), first left onto Chestnut Street, left onto Third Street. **Ticket Price Range:** $5-9.
Visiting Club Hotel: Holiday Inn, 2232 Center Street, Chattanooga, TN 37421. **Telephone:** (423) 485-1185.

JACKSON GENERALS

Address: 4 Fun Place, Jackson, TN 38305.
Telephone: (731) 988-5299. **Fax:** (731) 988-5246.
E-Mail Address: sarge@jacksongeneralsbaseball.com. **Website:** www.jacksongeneralsbaseball.com.
Affiliation (first year): Seattle Mariners (2007). **Years in League:** 1998-

OWNERSHIP/MANAGEMENT

Operated by: Jackson Baseball Club LP.

Chairman: David Freeman. **President:** Reese Smith. **General Manager:** Jason Compton.

Vice President, Sales/Marketing: Mike Peasley. **VP, Finance:** Charles Ferrell. **Turf Manager:** Marty Wallace. **Manager, Media Relations/Broadcasting:** Brandon Liebhaber. **Manager, Ticket Operations:** Blake Leonard. **Manager, Stadium Operations:** Lewis Crider. **Manager, Catering/Concessions:** Eric Kormanik. **Manager, Promotions/Merchandise:** Nick Hall. **Manager, Corporate Sales:** Mark Kaufman. **Manager, Group Ticket Sales:** Chris Freeman. **Manager, Publications/ Design:** Stephanie Godlewski. **Manager, Community Relations:** Tabitha Causey. **Manager, Stadium Security:** Robert Jones. **Manager, Home Clubhouse Operations:** CJ Fedewa.

FIELD STAFF

Manager: Jim Horner. **Coach:** Roy Howell. **Pitching Coach:** Lance Painter. **Trainer:** B.J. Downie.

GAME INFORMATION

Radio Announcer: Brandon Liebhaber. **No. of Games Broadcast:** 140. **Flagship Station:** 94.1/94.3 FM and 1390 AM. **PA Announcer:** Dan Reeves. **Official Scorer:** Mike Henson.

Stadium Name: The Ballpark in Jackson. **Location:** From I-40, take exit 85 South on FE Wright Drive, left onto Ridgecrest Road. **Standard Game Times:** 7:05 pm, Sat 6:05, Sun 2:05 or 6:05. **Ticket Price Range:** $6-10.

Visiting Club Hotel: Doubletree Hotel, 1770 Hwy 45 Bypass, Jackson, TN 38305. **Telephone:** (731) 664-6900.

JACKSONVILLE SUNS

Office Address: 301 A Philip Randolph Blvd, Jacksonville, FL 32202. **Mailing Address:** PO Box 4756, Jacksonville, FL 32201.

Telephone: (904) 358-2846. **Fax:** (904) 358-2845.

E-Mail Address: info@jaxsuns.com. **Website:** www.jaxsuns.com.

Affiliation (first year): Miami Marlins (2009). **Years In League:** 1970-

OWNERSHIP/MANAGEMENT

Operated by: Baseball Jax Inc.

Senior Madame Chairman: Mary Frances Bragan.

President: Peter Bragan Jr. **General Manager:** Chris Peters. **Director, Field Operations:** Christian Galen. **Director, Merchandise:** Trevor Johnson. **Assistant GM:** Casey Nichols. **Senior Director, Business Administration:** Barbara O'Berry. **Director, Video Services:** Brian Delettre. **Director, Group Sales:** January Putt. **Director, Ticket Operations:** Rachel Piersall. **Director, Stadium Operations:** Corey Kernan. **Director, Community Relations:** Theresa Viets. **Director, Broadcasting:** Roger Hoover. **Stadium Operations Manager:** Steven Unser. **General Manager, Ballpark Foods:** Jamie Davis. **Assistant GM, Ballpark Foods/Finance:** Mitch Buska. **Manager Account Executives:** Sam Shiner, Chris Peach, Dan Zbikowski.

FIELD STAFF

Manager: Andy Barkett. **Hitting Coach:** Kevin Randel. **Pitching Coach:** John Duffy.

GAME INFORMATION

Radio Announcer: Roger Hoover. **No. of Games Broadcast:** 140. **Flagship Station:** 94.1 FM-WSOS. **PA Announcer:** Unavailable. **Official Scorer:** Jason Eliopulos.

Stadium Name: Bragan Field at The Baseball Grounds of Jacksonville. **Location:** I-95 South to Martin Luther King Parkway exit, follow Gator Bowl Blvd around Everbank Field; I-95 North to Exit 347 (Emerson Street), go right to Hart Bridge Expressway, take Sports Complex exit, left at light to stop sign, take left and follow around Everbank Field; From Mathews Bridge, take A Philip Randolph exit, right on A Philip Randolph, straight to stadium. **Standard Game Times:** 7:05 pm, Sun 3:05/6:05. **Ticket Price Range:** $7.50-$22.50.

Visiting Club Hotel: Hyatt Regency Jacksonville Riverfront, 225 Coastline Drive, Jacksonville, FL 32202. **Telephone:** (904) 633-9095.

MISSISSIPPI BRAVES

Office Address: Trustmark Park, 1 Braves Way, Pearl, MS 39208. **Mailing Address:** PO Box 97389, Pearl, MS 39288.

Telephone: (601) 932-8788. **Fax:** (601) 936-3567.

E-Mail Address: mississippibraves@braves.com. **Website:** www.mississippibraves.com.

Affiliation: Atlanta Braves (2005). **Years in League:** 2005-

OWNERSHIP/MANAGEMENT

Operated By: Atlanta National League Baseball Club Inc.

General Manager: Steve DeSalvo. **Assistant GM:** Jim Bishop. **Ticket Manager:** Nick Anderson. **Merchandise Manager:** Sarah Banta. **Media Relations Manager:** Miranda Black. **Director, Sales:** Dave Burke. **Sales Associates:** Joe Crocker, Sean Guillotte, Destin Smith, Gerrod Speer, Marrieo Stovall. **Head Chef:** Tina Funches. **Suites/Catering Manager:** Debbie Herrington. **Stadium Operations Manager:** Matt McCoy. **Promotions/Entertainment Manager:** Brian Prochilo. **Concessions Manager:** Felicia Thompson. **Office Manager:** Christy Shaw. **Restaurant Manager:** Gene Slaughter. **Director, Field/Facility Operations:** Matt Taylor. **Receptionist:** Katie Patterson.

FIELD STAFF

Manager: Aaron Holbert. **Coach:** Jamie Dismuke. **Pitching Coach:** Dennis Lewallyn. **Trainer:** Ricky Alcantara.

GAME INFORMATION

Radio Announcer: Kyle Tate. **No. of Games Broadcast:** 140. **Flagship Station:** WYAB 103.9 FM.
PA Announcer: Derrel Palmer. **Official Scorer:** Mark Beason.
Stadium Name: Trustmark Park. **Location:** I-20 to exit 48/Pearl (Pearson Road). **Ticket Price Range:** $6-$20.
Visiting Club Hotel: Holiday Inn Trustmark Park, 110 Bass Pro Drive, Pearl, MS 39208. **Telephone:** (601) 939-5238.

MOBILE BAYBEARS

Address: Hank Aaron Stadium, 755 Bolling Brothers Blvd., Mobile, AL 36606.
Telephone: (251) 479-2327. **Fax:** (251) 476-1147.
E-Mail Address: Info@mobilebaybears.com. **Website:** www.MobileBayBears.com.
Affiliation (first year): Arizona Diamondbacks (2007). **Years in League:** 1966, 1970, 1997- current

OWNERSHIP/MANAGEMENT

Operated by: HWS Baseball Group. **Principal Owner:** Mike Savit. **Executive Vice President:** Mike Gorrasi.
General Manager: Chris Morgan. **Assistant GM, Sales:** Bradley Reynolds. **Assistant GM, Operations:** Ari Rosenbaum. **Director, Business Operations/Finance:** Betty Adams. **Director, Sales:** Kyne Sheehy. **Director, Stadium Operations:** Nathan Breiner. **Director, Broadcasting/ Media Relations:** Justin Baker. **Director, Concessions:** Justin Gunsaulus. **Account Executive:** Matt Baranofsky. **PR/Promotions/Broadcasting Assistant:** Melanie Newman. **PR/Promotions Assistant:** Jordan Dravis. **Stadium Operations Assistants:** Chris Ganoe, David Neubauer. **Groundskeeper:** Gulf Coast Sports Fields.

FIELD STAFF

Manager: Robby Hammock. **Hitting Coach:** Jason Camilli. **Pitching Coach:** Wellington Cepeda. **Athletic Trainer:** Masa Abe. **Strength Coach:** Matt Tenney. **Home Clubhouse Manager:** Dustin Hann.

GAME INFORMATION

Radio Announcer: Justin Baker. **No. of Games Broadcast:** 140. **Website:** www.BayBearsRadio.com.
PA Announcer: Unavailable. **Official Scorer:** Unavailable.
Stadium Name: Hank Aaron Stadium. **Location:** I-65 to exit 1 (Government Blvd East), right at Satchel Paige Drive, right at Bolling Bros Blvd. **Standard Game Times:** 6:35pm (April-May), 7:05 (Fri-Sat) 7:05 (Sun), 2:05 (April-May), Sunday: 5:05 pm (June-Sept). **Ticket Price Range:** $6-16.
Visiting Club Hotel: Riverview Plaza, 64 S Water St, Mobile, AL 36602. **Telephone:** (251) 438-4000.

MONTGOMERY BISCUITS

Address: 200 Coosa St., Montgomery, AL 36104.
Telephone: (334) 323-2255. **Fax:** (334) 323-2225.
E-Mail address: info@biscuitsbaseball.com. **Website:** www.biscuitsbaseball.com.
Affiliation (first year): Tampa Bay Rays (2004). **Years in League:** 1965-1980, 2004-

OWNERSHIP/MANAGEMENT

Operated By: Montgomery Professional Baseball LLC. **Principal Owners:** Sherrie Myers, Tom Dickson.
President: Greg Rauch. **General Manager:** Scott Trible. **Director, Marketing:** Staci Wilkenson. **Director, Client Services/Media Partnerships:** Jonathan Vega. **Sponsorship Service Representative:** Jordan Thomas. **Corporate Account Executive:** Cory Eirich. **Group Sales Representatives:** Greg Liebbe, Dru Knizacky. **Sales Assistant:** Julie Gauthier. **Events Coordinator:** Brittney Sheffield. **Communications Services Coordinator:** Sarah Stephan. **Multimedia Specialist:** Richie Wilson. **Broadcaster, Media Relations:** Aaron Vargas. **Director, Retail Operations:** Steve Keller. **Director, Stadium Operations:** Steve Blackwell. **Box Office Manager:** Anna Del Castillo. **Head Groundskeeper:** Alex English. **Director, Food/Beverage:** Dave Parker. **Executive Chef:** Dwayne Gulley. **Executive Director, Business Operations:** Linda Fast. **Business Manager:** Tracy Mims. **Administrative Assistant:** Bill Sisk. **Season Ticket Concierge:** Bob Rabon.

FIELD STAFF

Manager: Brady Williams. **Hitting Coach:** Ozzie Timmons. **Pitching Coach:** RC Lichtenstein.

GAME INFORMATION

Radio Announcer: Aaron Vargas. **No of Games Broadcast:** 140. **Flagship Station:** WLWI 1440-AM.
PA Announcer: Rick Hendrick. **Official Scorer:** Brian Wilson.
Stadium Name: Montgomery Riverwalk Stadium. **Location:** I-65 to exit 172, east on Herron Street, left on Coosa Street. **Ticket Price Range:** $9-13.
Visiting Club Hotel: Candlewood Suites, 9151 Boyd-Cooper Pkwy, Montgomery, AL 36117. **Telephone:** (334) 277-0677.

PENSACOLA BLUE WAHOOS

Address: 351 West Cedar St., Pensacola, FL 32502.
Telephone: (850) 934-8444. **Fax:** (850) 791-6256.
E-Mail Address: info@bluewahoos.com. **Website:** www.bluewahoos.com.
Affiliation (third year): Cincinnati Reds (2012). **Years in League:** 2012-

OWNERSHIP/MANAGEMENT

Operated by: Northwest Florida Professional Baseball LLC. **Principal Owners:** Quint Studer, Rishy Studer. **Minority Owner:** Bubba Watson.

President: Bruce Baldwin. **Executive Vice President:** Jonathan Griffith. **Receptionist:** Pam Handlin. **Operations Coordinator:** Mike Crenshaw. **Creative Services Manager:** Adam Waldron. **Director, Sports Turf Management:** Ray Sayre. **Sales Manager:** Chuck Arnold. **Sales Executive:** Brian Larkin. **Director, Human Relations:** Dick Baker. **Media Relations Manager:** Maryjane Gardner. **Broadcaster:** Tommy Thrall. **Director, Guest Relations/Community Relations:** Donna Kirby. **Director, Merchandise:** Denise Richardson. **Box Office Manager:** Eric Kroll. **Director, Food/Beverage:** Mark Micallef. **Finance Director:** Amber McClure. **Groups Sales Executives:** Joey DiChiara, Michael Taylor.

FIELD STAFF

Manager: Pat Kelly. **Hitting Coach:** Alex Pelaez. **Pitching Coach:** Jeff Fassero. **Trainer:** Charles Leddon.

GAME INFORMATION

Radio Announcers: Tommy Thrall. **No. of Games Broadcast:** 140. **Flagship Station:** Unavailable.
PA Announcer: Josh Gay. **Official Scorer:** Brenton Goebel.
Stadium Name: Pensacola Bayfront Stadium. **Standard Game Times:** 6:30 pm, Sat 6:30, Sun 4 pm. **Ticket Price Range:** $6-$18.
Visiting Club Hotels: Hilton Garden Inn, Hampton Inn, Homewood Suites.

TENNESSEE SMOKIES

Address: 3540 Line Drive, Kodak, TN 37764.
Telephone: (865) 286-2300. **Fax:** (865) 523-9913.
E-Mail Address: info@smokiesbaseball.com. **Website:** www.smokiesbaseball.com.
Affiliation (ninth year): Chicago Cubs (2007-). **Years in League:** 1964-67, 1972-

OWNERSHIP/MANAGEMENT

Owner: Randy Boyd. **President:** Doug Kirchhofer. **Vice President:** Chris Allen. **General Manager:** Brian Cox.

GM, Smokies Hospitality: Jeff Shoaf. **Director, Corporate Sales:** Jeremy Boler. **Senior Director, Corporate Marketing:** Craig Jenkins. **Director, Ticket/Group Sales:** Tim Volk. **Director, Community Relations:** Lauren Chesney. **Director, Field Maintenance:** Anthony DeFeo. **Director, Food/Beverage:** Brandon Roberts. **Director, In-Game Entertainment:** Kristi Servais. **Director, Media Relations:** Andrew Green. **Director, Merchandise:** Matt Strutner. **Director, Stadium Operations:** Bryan Webster. **Box Office Manager:** Michael McMullen. **Sponsorship Service Manager:** Baylor Love. **Senior Account Executive, Groups:** Jason Moody. **Business Manager:** Suzanne French. **Account Executives:** Tyler Castro, Adam Grigsby, Eric Harrell,Whitley Patterson. **Corporate Sales Executive:** Thomas Kappel. **Receptionist:** Tolena Trout

FIELD STAFF

Manager: Buddy Bailey. **Hitting Coach:** Desi Wilson. **Pitching Coach:** Storm Davis. **Trainer:** Shane Nelson.

GAME INFORMATION

Radio Announcer: Mick Gillispie. **No. of Games Broadcast:** 140. **Flagship Station:** WNML 99.1-FM/990-AM.
PA Announcer: Unavailable. **Official Scorers:** Jared Smith, Bernie Reimer.
Stadium Name: Smokies Stadium. **Location:** I-40 to exit 407, Highway 66 North. **Standard Game Times:** 7:05 pm, Sat 7:05 pm, Sun 2/5. **Ticket Price Range:** $6-11.
Visiting Club Hotel: Hampton Inn & Suites Sevierville, 105 Stadium Drive, Kodak, TN 37764. **Telephone:** (865) 465-0590.

TEXAS LEAGUE

TEXAS LEAGUE OF PROFESSIONAL BASEBALL CLUBS

Mailing Address: 2442 Facet Oak, San Antonio, TX 78232.
Telephone: (210) 545-5297. **Fax:** (210) 545-5298.
E-Mail Address: texasleague@sbcglobal.net. **Website:** www.texas-league.com.

Years League Active: 1888-1890, 1892, 1895-1899, 1902-1942, 1946-

President/Treasurer: Tom Kayser. **Vice Presidents:** Matt Gifford, Bill Valentine.

Corporate Secretary: Ken Schrom. **Assistant to the President:** Casey Greene.

Directors: Jon Dandes (Northwest Arkansas), Ken Schrom (Corpus Christi), William DeWitt III (Springfield), Dale Hubbard (Tulsa), Chuck Greenberg (Frisco), E. Miles Prentice (Midland), Russ Meeks (Arkansas), Burl Yarbrough (San Antonio).

Tom Kayser

Division Structure: North—Arkansas, Northwest Arkansas, Springfield, Tulsa. South—Corpus Christi, Frisco, Midland, San Antonio.

Regular Season: 140 games (split schedule). **2015 Opening Date:** April 9. **Closing Date:** Sept 7.

All-Star Game: June 30 at Corpus Christi.

Playoff Format: First-half division winners play second-half division winners in best of five series. Winners meet in best of five series for league championship.

Roster Limit: 25. **Player Eligibility Rule:** No restrictions.

Brand of Baseball: Rawlings.

Umpires: Mike Cascioppo (Escondido, CA), Nestor Ceja (Arleta, CA), Matt Czajak (Flower Mound, TX), Derek Eaton (Tracy, CA), Bryan Fields (Dallas, TX), Clayton Hamm (Spicewood, TX), Ramon Hernandez (Columbia, MD), Lee Meyers (Madera, CA), Clayton Park (Georgetown, TX), Ronnie Teague (Cypress, TX), Brett Terry (Beaverton OR), Jake Wilburn (Fort Worth, TX

STADIUM INFORMATION

				Dimensions			
Club	Stadium	Opened	LF	CF	RF	Capacity	2014 Att.
Arkansas	Dickey-Stephens Park	2007	332	413	330	5,842	326,179
Corpus Christi	Whataburger Field	2005	325	400	315	5,362	393,769
Frisco	Dr Pepper Ballpark	2003	335	409	335	10,216	449,773
Midland	Citibank Ballpark	2002	330	410	322	4,669	299,586
NW Arkansas	Arvest Ballpark	2008	325	400	325	6,500	319,109
San Antonio	Nelson Wolff Municipal Stadium	1994	310	402	340	6,200	294,539
Springfield	John Q. Hammons Field	2003	315	400	330	6,750	354,227
Tulsa	ONEOK Field	2010	330	400	307	7,833	403,732

ARKANSAS TRAVELERS

Office Address: Dickey-Stephens Park, 400 West Broadway, North Little Rock, AR 72114.
Mailing Address: PO Box 3177, Little Rock, AR 72203.
Telephone: (501) 664-1555. **Fax:** (501) 664-1834.
E-Mail address: travs@travs.com. **Website:** www.travs.com.
Affiliation (first year): Los Angeles Angels (2001). **Years in League:** 1966-

OWNERSHIP/MANAGEMENT

Ownership: Arkansas Travelers Baseball Club, Inc. **President:** Russ Meeks.

General Manager: Paul Allen. **Director, Broadcasting/Media Relations:** Robbie Aaron. **Director, Finance:** Patti Clark. **Director, In-Game Entertainment:** Tommy Adam. **Assistant GM, Merchandise:** Rusty Meeks. **Park Superintendent:** Greg Johnston. **Assistant Park Superintendent:** Reggie Temple. **Director, Luxury Suites/Account Executive:** Jared Schein. **Assistant GM, Tickets:** Drew Williams. **Director, Marketing:** Lance Restum. **Director, Stadium Operations/ Account Executive:** Jeff Goldsmith. **Corporate Event Planners:** Mandy Valentine, Eric Schrader, Justin Phillips

FIELD STAFF

Manager: Bill Richardson. **Coach:** Tom Tornincasa. **Pitching Coach:** Pat Rice. **Trainer:** Greg Spence. **Strength/ Conditioning Coach:** Andrew Chappell.

GAME INFORMATION

Radio Announcers: Robbie Aaron. **No. of Games Broadcast:** 140. **Flagship Station:** KARN 920 AM.

PA Announcer: Russ McKinney. **Official Scorer:** Tim Cooper.

Stadium Name: Dickey-Stephens Park. **Location:** I-30 to Broadway exit, proceed west to ballpark, located at Broadway Avenue and the Broadway Bridge. **Standard Game Time:** 7:10 pm. **Ticket Price Range:** $3-12.

Visiting Club Hotel: Wyndham Riverfront, 2 Riverfront Place, N. Little Rock, AR 72114. **Telephone:** (501) 371-9000.

CORPUS CHRISTI HOOKS

Address: 734 East Port Ave, Corpus Christi, TX 78401.
Telephone: (361) 561-4665. **Fax:** (361) 561-4666.
E-Mail Address: info@cchooks.com. **Website:** www.cchooks.com.
Affiliation (first year): Houston Astros (2005). **Years in League:** 1958-59, 2005-

OWNERSHIP/MANAGEMENT

Owned/Operated By: Houston Astros.
President: Ken Schrom. **Vice President/General Manager:** Michael Wood.
Director, Sales/Marketing: Andy Steavens. **Senior Director, Sponsor Services:** Elisa Macias. **Senior Director, Communications:** Matt Rogers. **Director, Finance:** Kim Harris. **Director, Stadium Operations:** Jeremy Sturgeon. **Director, Ballpark Entertainment:** JD Davis. **Director, Season Ticket Services:** Jeff Mackor. **Director, Group Sales:** Amanda Pruett. **Media Relations Manager:** Michael Coffin. **Ticket Operations Manager:** Danielle Norris-O'Toole. **Game Day Staff Manager:** Brad Crabtree. **Senior Service Desk Technician, Jack Ruiz. Media Relations Coordinator:** Chris Blake. **Community Outreach Coordinator:** Courtney Merritt. **Social Media Coordinator:** Gil Perez. **Video Production Coordinator:** Amy Johnson. **Accounting Analyst:** Jessica Fearn. **Account Executive:** Zach Kaddatz. **Retail Manager:** Daniel Sanchez. **Maintenance Manager:** Daniel Castillo. **Stadium Operations:** Mike Shedd. **Clubhouse Manager:** Brad Starr. **Field Superintendent:** Nick Rozdilski.

FIELD STAFF

Manager: Rodney Linares. **Hitting Coach:** Dan Radison. **Pitching Coach:** Doug Brocail. **Infield Instructor:** Tom Lawless. **Athletic Trainer:** Grant Hufford. **Strength Coach:** Mark Spadavecchia.

GAME INFORMATION

Radio Announcers: Michael Coffin, Chris Blake, Gene Kasprzyk. **No. of Games Broadcast:** 140. **Flagship Station:** KKTX-AM 1360.
PA Announcer: Layne Berman.
Stadium Name: Whataburger Field. **Location:** I-37 to end of interstate, left at Chaparral, left at Hirsh Ave. **Ticket Price Range:** $6-17.
Visiting Club Hotel: Holiday Inn Corpus Christi Downtown Marina, 707 North Shoreline Blvd, Corpus Christi, Texas, 78401. **Telephone:** (361) 882-1700.

FRISCO ROUGHRIDERS

Address: 7300 RoughRiders Trail, Frisco, TX 75034.
Telephone: (972) 731-9200. **Fax:** (972) 731-5355.
E-Mail Address: info@ridersbaseball.com. **Website:** www.ridersbaseball.com.
Affiliation (first year): Texas Rangers (2003). **Years in League:** 2003-

OWNERSHIP/MANAGEMENT

Operated by: Frisco RoughRiders LP. **Chairman/CEO/Managing Partner:** Chuck Greenberg.
President: Scott Sonju. **Executive Vice President/General Manager:** Jason Dambach. **Chief Operating Officer:** Scott Burchett. **VP, Accounting/Finance:** Dustin Alban.
Senior Director, Corporate Partnerships: Steven Nelson. **Director, Operations:** Scott Arnold. **Director, Partner Services:** Matt Ratliff. **Director, Partner/Event Services:** Kristin Russell. **Director, Ticket Sales:** Andrew Sidney. **Director, Ticket Operations:** Kyle Gehring. **Director, Game Entertainment:** Regina Pierce. **Director, Community Development:** LaShawn Moore. **Head Groundskeeper:** David Bicknell. **Director, Maintenance:** Alfonso Bailon. **Assistant Director, Maintenance:** Gustavo Bailon.
Operations Coordinator: Tyler Waddles. **Manager, Broadcasting/Media Development:** Alex Vispoli. **Ticket Operations Manager:** Kyle Kahn. **Partner Services Manager:** David Kosydar. **Merchandise Manager:** Jennifer Adamczyk. **Partner/Event Services Coordinator:** Scott Fults. **Partner/Event Services Coordinator:** Kathryne Buckley. **Graphic Design/Social Media Coordinator:** Byron Towles. **Senior Manager, Group Sales:** Reese Haymes. **Senior Manager, Outside Sales:** Ross Lanford. **Corporate Marketing Managers:** Roman Crescimanno, David Dwyer, Lisa Gonzalez, Bryan Henderson, Kayla Lara, Matt Martin, Garret Randle. **Group Sales Executives:** Tom Baker, Logan Brown, Sander Bryan, Tyler Ellis, Jessica English, Jon Fletcher, Monica Man, Ben Berenson, Mike Cordisco.

FIELD STAFF

Manager: Joe Mikulik. **Hitting Coach:** Jason Hart. **Pitching Coach:** Jeff Andrews. **Trainer:** Carlos Olivas. **Strength/Conditioning:** Eric McMahon.

GAME INFORMATION

Broadcaster: Alex Vispoli. **No. of Games Broadcast:** 140. **Flagship Station:** www.RidersBaseball.com.
PA Announcer: John Clemens. **Official Scorer:** Lary Bump.
Stadium Name: Dr Pepper Ballpark. **Location:** Intersection of Dallas North Tollway & State Highway 121. **Standard Game Times:** 7:05 pm, Sunday 4:05 (April-May) 6:05 (June-Sept).
Visiting Club Hotel: Comfort Suites at Frisco Square, 9700 Dallas Parkway, Frisco, TX 75033. **Phone:** (972) 668-9700. **Fax:** (972) 668-9701.

MIDLAND ROCKHOUNDS

Address: Security Bank Ballpark, 5514 Champions Drive, Midland, TX 79706.
Telephone: (432) 520-2255. **Fax:** (432) 520-8326.
Website: www.midlandrockhounds.org.
Affiliation (first year): Oakland Athletics (1999). **Years in League:** 1972-

OWNERSHIP/MANAGEMENT

Operated By: Midland Sports, Inc. **Principal Owners:** Miles Prentice, Bob Richmond.
President: Miles Prentice. **Executive Vice President:** Bob Richmond. **General Manager:** Monty Hoppel.
Assistant GM: Jeff VonHolle. **Assistant GM, Marketing/Tickets:** Jamie Richardson. **Assistant GM, Merchandise/ Facilities:** Ray Fieldhouse. **Assistant GM, Media Relations:** Greg Bergman. **Director, Broadcasting/Publications:** Bob Hards. **Director, Business Operations:** Eloisa Galvan. **Head Groundskeeper:** Eric Campbell. **Office Manager:** Frances Warner. **Director, Public Relations:** Brian Smith. **Director, Group Sales:** Morgan Halpert. **Director, Client Services:** Shelley Haenggi. **Director, Ticket Operations:** Andrew Brown. **Sales/Marketing Executive:** John English. **Coordinator, Community Relations:** Courtnie Golden. **Complex Coordinator:** Sarah Jones. **Coordinator, Game Entertainment:** Russ Pinkerton. **Home Clubhouse Manager:** Derek Smith. **Visiting Clubhouse Manager:** TJ Leonard. **Complex Operations Manager:** CJ Bahr. **Assistant Groundskeeper:** Levi Driesen. **Director, Business Operations:** Eloisa Galvan. **Executive Director, Communications:** Brian Smith. **Office/ Box Office Manager:** Frances Warner. **Director, Group Sales:** Morgan Halpert.
Director, Ticket Operations: Andrew Brown. **Director, Client Services:** Shelly Haenggi. **Director, Stadium Operations:** C.J. Bahr. **Assistant Director, Stadium Operations:** Joe Peters. **Head Groundskeeper:** Monty Sowell. **Assistant Groundskeeper:** Levi Driesen. **Director, Broadcasting, Publications:** Bob Hards. **Game Entertainment/ Video Board Coordinator:** Russ Pinkerton. **Website/Creative Design Coordinator:** Frank Longobardo. **Community Relations Coordinator:** Courtnie Golden. **Assistant Concessions Manager:** Preston Madill. **Sales Executive:** Blake Fosse. **Administrative Assistant, Communications:** Alec Martinez. **Group Sales Assistant:** Andrew Petersen. **Assistant Office/Box Office Manager:** Calie Bloom. **Home Clubhouse Manager:** Derek Smith. **Visiting Clubhouse Manager:** Ari Vieira.

FIELD STAFF

Manager: Ryan Christenson. **Hitting Coach:** Eric Martins. **Pitching Coach:** John Wasdin. **Trainer:** Justin Whitehouse. **Strength/Conditioning:** AJ Seeliger.

GAME INFORMATION

Radio Announcer: Bob Hards. **No. of Games Broadcast:** 140. **Flagship Station:** KCRS 550 AM.
PA Announcer: Wes Coles. **Official Scorer:** Steve Marcom.
Stadium Name: Security Bank Ballpark. **Location:** From I-20, exit Loop 250 North to Highway 191 intersection. **Standard Game Times:** 7 pm. **Ticket Price Range:** $7-16.
Visiting Club Hotel: Sleep Inn and Suites, 5612 Deauville Blvd, Midland, TX 79706. **Telephone:** (432) 694-4200.

NORTHWEST ARKANSAS NATURALS

Address: 3000 S 56th Street, Springdale, AR 72762.
Telephone: (479) 927-4900. **Fax:** (479) 756-8088.
E-Mail Address: tickets@nwanaturals.com. **Website:** www.nwanaturals.com.
Affiliation (first year): Kansas City Royals (1995). **Years in League:** 1987-

OWNERSHIP/MANAGEMENT

Principal Owner: Rich Products Corp. **Chairman:** Robert Rich Jr. **President, Rich Entertainment:** Melinda Rich. **President, Rich Baseball:** Jon Dandes.
General Manager: Justin Cole. **Sales Manager:** Mark Zaiger. **Business Manager:** Morgan Helmer. **Marketing/PR Manager:** Dustin Dethlefs. **Ballpark Operations Director:** Jeff Windle. **Head Groundskeeper:** Brock White. **Ticket Office Coordinator:** Sam Ahern. **Broadcaster/Baseball Operations Coordinator:** Benjamin Kelly. **Promotions Coordinator:** Julie Fitzpatrick. **Production Coordinator:** Patrick Wallace. **Account Executives:** Brad Ziegler, Matt Fanning, Jon Tucker, Trey Garner, Tim Uryasz. **Coordinator, Special Events:** Adam Wright. **Coordinator, Operations:** Marshall Schellhardt. **Merchandise Coordinator:** Paige Peugh. **Equipment Manager:** Danny Helmer.

FIELD STAFF

Manager: Vance Wilson. **Hitting Coach:** Brandon Moore. **Pitching Coach:** Jim Brower.

GAME INFORMATION

Radio Announcers: Benjamin Kelly. **No. of Games Broadcast:** 140. **Flagship:** KQSM 92.1-FM.
PA Announcer: Bill Rogers. **Official Scorer:** Chris Ledeker.
Stadium Name: Arvest Ballpark. **Location:** I-540 to US 412 West (Sunset Ave); Left on 56th St. **Ticket Price Range:** $7-13. **Standard Game Times:** 7:05 pm, Sun 2:05 pm (April-May), 6:05 pm (June-August).
Visiting Club Hotel: Holiday Inn Springdale, 1500 S 48th St, Springdale, AR 72762. **Telephone:** (479) 751-8300.

SAN ANTONIO MISSIONS

Address: 5757 Highway 90 West, San Antonio, TX 78227.
Telephone: (210) 675-7275. **Fax:** (210) 670-0001.
E-Mail Address: sainfo@samissions.com. **Website:** www.samissions.com.
Affiliation (first year): San Diego Padres (2007). **Years in League:** 1888, 1892, 1895-99, 1907-42, 1946-64, 1968-

OWNERSHIP/MANAGEMENT
Operated by: Elmore Sports Group. **Principal Owner:** David Elmore.
President: Burl Yarbrough. **General Manager:** Dave Gasaway. **Assistant GMs:** Mickey Holt, Jeff Long, Bill Gerlt. **GM, Diamond Concessions:** Mike Lindal. **Controller:** Eric Olivarez. **Director, Broadcasting:** Mike Saeger. **Office Manager:** Delia Rodriguez. **Box Office Manager:** Rob Gusick. **Director, Operations:** John Hernandez. **Director, Group Sales:** George Levandoski. **Director, Public Relations:** Rich Weimert. **Field Superintendent:** Rob Gladwell.

FIELD STAFF
Manager: Jamie Quirk Hitting Coach: Morgan Burkhart. **Pitching Coach:** Jimmy Jones. **Trainer:** Daniel Turner.

GAME INFORMATION
Radio Announcer: Mike Saeger. **No. of Games Broadcast:** 140. **Flagship Station:** 860-AM.
PA Announcer: Roland Ruiz. **Official Scorer:** David Humphrey.
Stadium Name: Nelson Wolff Stadium. **Location:** From I-10, I-35 or I-37, take US Hwy 90 West to Callaghan Road exit. **Standard Game Times:** 7:05 pm, Sun 2:05/6:05.
Visiting Club Hotel: Holiday Inn Northwest/Sea World. **Telephone:** (210) 520-2508.

SPRINGFIELD CARDINALS

Address: 955 East Trafficway, Springfield, MO 65802.
Telephone: (417) 863-0395. **Fax:** (417) 832-3004.
E-Mail Address: springfield@cardinals.com. **Website:** springfieldcardinals.com.
Affiliation (first year): St. Louis Cardinals (2005). **Years in League:** 2005-

OWNERSHIP/MANAGEMENT
Operated By: St. Louis Cardinals.
Vice President/General Manager: Matt Gifford. **VP, Baseball/Business Operations:** Scott Smulczenski. **VP, Facility Operations:** Bill Fischer. **Director, Ticket Operations:** Angela Deke. **VP, Sales/Marketing:** Dan Reiter. **Manager, Promotions/Productions:** Kent Shelton. **Manager, Market Development:** Scott Bailes. **Manager, Stadium/Game Day Operations:** Aaron Lowrey. **Manager, Public Relations/Broadcaster:** Andrew Buchbinder. **Manager, Sales/Marketing:** Zack Pemberton. **Manager, Inside Sales:** Chris Kaempfe. **Manager, Fan Interaction:** Faith Lorhan. **Box Office Supervisor/Office Assistant:** Ayrica Batson. **Head Groundskeeper:** Brock Phipps. **Assistant Head Groundskeeper:** Derek Edwards.

FIELD STAFF
Manager: Dann Bilardello. **Hitting Coach:** Erik Pappas. **Pitching Coach:** Jason Simontacchi. **Trainer:** Scott Ensell.

GAME INFORMATION
Radio Announcer: Andrew Buchbinder. **No. of Games Broadcast:** 140. **Flagship Station:** JOCK 98.7 FM.
PA Announcer: Unavailable. **Official Scorers:** Mark Stillwell, Tim Tourville.
Stadium Name: Hammons Field. **Location:** Highway 65 to Chestnut Expressway exit, west to National, south on National, west on Trafficway. **Standard Game Time:** 7:10 pm. **Ticket Price Range:** $6-28.
Visiting Club Hotel: University Plaza Hotel, 333 John Q Hammons Parkway, Springfield, MO 65806. **Telephone:** (417) 864-7333.

TULSA DRILLERS

Address: 201 N. Elgin, Tulsa, OK 74120.
Telephone: (918) 744-5998. **Fax:** (918) 747-3267.
E-Mail Address: mail@tulsadrillers.com. **Website:** www.tulsadrillers.com.
Affiliation (first year): Los Angeles Dodgers (2015). **Years in League:** 1933-42, 1946-65, 1977-

OWNERSHIP/MANAGEMENT
Operated By: Tulsa Baseball Inc. **Co-Chairmen:** Dale Hubbard, Jeff Hubbard.
President/GM: Mike Melega. **Executive VP/Assistant GM:** Jason George. **Bookkeeper:** Cheryll Couey. **Executive Assistant:** Kara Biden. **VP, Stadium Operations:** Mark Hilliard. **VP, Media/Public Relations:** Brian Carroll. **VP, Marketing/Business Development:** Rob Gardenhire. **Director, Merchandise:** Tom Jones. **Senior Account Executive:** Geoff Beaty. **Director, Promotions/Game Entertainment:** Justin Gorski. **Director, Video Production:** Alan Ramseyer. **Head**

Groundskeeper: Gary Shepherd. **Director, Group Sales:** Matt Larson. **Director, Business Development:** Kevin Butcher. **Assistant Bookkeeper:** Jenna Savill. **Manager, Ticket Sales:** Joanna Hubbard. **Mascot Coordinator:** Vincent Pace. **Facilities Manager:** Stevelan Hamilton. **Manager, Graphic Design/Social Media:** Jordan Suskind. **Manager, Video Production:** Jase Chilcoat.

Receptionist: Lynda Davis. **Ticket Office Intern:** Mallory Overton. **Group Sales Intern:** Courtni Daily. **Stadium Operations Intern:** Brady May. **Merchandise Intern:** Chad Denton. **Media Intern:** Wes Leander. **Promotions Intern:** Justin Johnston. **Video Intern:** Graham Jenkins. **Director, Food Services:** Cody Malone. **Director, Concessions:** Wayne Campbell. **Concessions Manager:** Sara Bush. **Catering Manager:** Brandon Gilliam. **Clubhouse Manager:** Sam Salabura.

FIELD STAFF

Manager: Razor Shines. **Hitting Coach:** Shawn Wooten. **Pitching Coach:** Matt Herges. **Coach:** Leo Garcia. **Trainer:** Aaron Schumacher. **Strength Coach:** Paul Sterrett.

GAME INFORMATION

Radio Announcer: Dennis Higgins. **No. of Games Broadcast:** 140. **Flagship Station:** KTBZ 1430-AM.

PA Announcer: Kirk McAnany. **Official Scorers:** Bruce Howard, Duane DaPron, Larry Lewis, Barry Lewis.

Stadium Name: ONEOK Field. **Location:** I-244 to Cincinnati/Detroit Exit (6A); north on Detroit Ave, right onto John Hope Franklin Blvd, right on Elgin Ave. **Standard Game Times:** 7:05 pm, Sun 2:05 (April-June), 7:05 (July-Aug).

Visiting Club Hotel: Hyatt Regency, 100 E 2nd St, Tulsa, OK 74103. **Telephone:** (918) 582-9000.

CALIFORNIA LEAGUE

Address: 3600 South Harbor Blvd, Suite 122, Oxnard, CA 93035.
Telephone: (805) 985-8585. **Fax:** (805) 985-8580.
Website: www.californialeague.com. **E-Mail:** info@californialeague.com.
Years League Active: 1941-1942, 1946-
President: Charlie Blaney. **Vice President:** Tom Volpe.

Directors: Bobby Brett (Rancho Cucamonga), Jake Kerr (Lancaster), Dave Elmore (Inland Empire), D.G. Elmore (Bakersfield), Dave Heller (High Desert), Gary Jacobs (Lake Elsinore), Mike Savit (Modesto), Tom Seidler (Visalia), Tom Volpe (Stockton), Dan Orum (San Jose).

Director, Operations/Marketing: Matt Blaney. **Historian:** Chris Lampe. **Legal Counsel:** Jonathan Light. **CPA:** Jeff Hass.

Division Structure: North—Bakersfield, Modesto, San Jose, Stockton, Visalia. South—High Desert, Inland Empire, Lake Elsinore, Lancaster, Rancho Cucamonga.

Regular Season: 140 games (split schedule). **2015 Opening Date:** April 9. **Closing Date:** Sept 7.

Playoff Format: Six teams make the playoffs. First-half winners in each division earn first-round bye; second-half winners meet wild cards with next best overall records in best of three quarterfinals. Winners meet first-half champions in best of five semifinals. Winners meet in best of five series for league championship.

Charlie Blaney

All-Star Game: Cal League-Carolina League, June 23 at Rancho Cucamonga.

Roster Limit: 25 active (35 under control). **Player Eligibility:** No more than two players and one player/coach on active list may have more than six years experience.

Brand of Baseball: Rawlings.

Umpires: Sean Allen, Jonathan Felczak, Reid Gibbs, Adrian Gonzalez, Jeff Gorman, Kyle McCrady, Malachi Moore, Jason Starkovich, Clint Vondrak, Lewis Williams III.

			Dimensions				
Club	Stadium	Opened	LF	CF	RF	Capacity	2014 Att.
Bakersfield	Sam Lynn Ballpark	1941	328	354	328	2,700	57,057
High Desert	Mavericks Stadium	1991	340	401	340	3,808	147,231
Inland Empire	San Manuel Stadium	1996	330	410	330	5,000	195,841
Lake Elsinore	The Diamond	1994	330	400	310	7,866	220,069
Lancaster	Clear Channel Stadium	1996	350	410	350	4,500	170,532
Modesto	John Thurman Field	1952	312	400	319	4,000	172,902
Rancho Cucamonga	LoanMart Field	1993	335	400	335	6,615	166,993
San Jose	Municipal Stadium	1942	320	390	320	5,208	200,124
Stockton	Banner Island Ballpark	2005	300	399	326	5,200	195,500
Visalia	Rawhide Ballpark	1946	320	405	320	2,468	120,003

BAKERSFIELD BLAZE

Office Address: 4009 Chester Ave, Bakersfield, CA 93301. **Mailing Address:** PO Box 10031, Bakersfield, CA 93389.

Telephone: (661) 716-4487. **Fax:** (661) 322-6199.

E-Mail Address: blaze@bakersfieldblaze.com. **Website:** www.bakersfieldblaze.com.

Affiliation: Seattle Mariners (2015). **Years In League:** 1941-42, 1946-75, 1978-79, 1982-

OWNERSHIP/MANAGEMENT

Principal Owner: Elmore Sports Group/D.G. Elmore.

General Manager: Elizabeth Martin. **Assistant GM, Media/Marketing:** Dan Besbris. **Assistant GM, Ticketing/Groups:** Mike Candela. **Director, Concessions Marketing:** Chris Henstra. **Director, Stadium Operations:** Jeff MacDonald. **Director, Group/Ticket Sales:** Billy Brosemer. **Head Groundskeeper:** Unavailable.

FIELD STAFF

Manager: Eddie Menchaca. **Hitting Coach:** Max Venable. **Pitching Coach:** Andrew Lorraine.

GAME INFORMATION

Radio: Dan Besbris. **Flagship Station:** 1230-AM.

PA Announcer: Mike Cushine. **Official Scorer:** Tim Wheeler.

Stadium Name: Sam Lynn Ballpark. **Location:** Highway 99 to California Avenue, east two miles to Chester Avenue, north two miles to stadium. **Standard Game Time:** Variable due to setting sun. 7:30 pm. **Ticket Price Range:** $7-13.

Visiting Club Hotel: Marriott at the Convention Center, 801 Truxtun Ave, Bakersfield, CA 93301. **Telephone:** (661) 323-1900.

HIGH DESERT MAVERICKS

Address: 12000 Stadium Way, Adelanto, CA 92301.
Telephone: (760) 246-6287.
E-Mail Address: info@hdmavs.com. **Website:** www.hdmavs.com.
Affiliation: Texas Rangers (2015). **Years in League:** 1991-

OWNERSHIP/MANAGEMENT
   Operated By: Main Street California. **Managing Partner:** Dave Heller. **President:** Jim Coufos. **General Manager:** Ryan Cook. **Assistant GM:** Tony Wardell. **Head Groundskeeper:** Ryan CowanController: Jane Korn. **Marketing Director:** Unavailable. **Ticket Sales:** Unavailable.

FIELD STAFF
   Manager: Spike Owen. **Hitting Coach:** Bobby Rose. **Pitching Coach:** Steve Mintz.

GAME INFORMATION
   Radio Announcer: Unavailable.
   PA Announcer: Unavailable. **Official Scorer:** Unavailable.
   Stadium Name: Heritage Field. **Location:** I-15 North to Highway 395 to Adelanto Road. **Standard Game Times:** 6:05 pm, Sun 3:05 (1st half), 5:05 (2nd half). **Ticket Price Range:** $6-$15.
   Visiting Club Hotel: Unavailable.

INLAND EMPIRE 66ERS

Address: 280 South E St., San Bernardino, CA 92401.
Telephone: (909) 888-9922. **Fax:** (909) 888-5251.
Website: www.66ers.com.
Affiliation (first year): Los Angeles Angels (2011). **Years in League:** 1941, 1987-

OWNERSHIP/MANAGEMENT
   Operated by: Inland Empire 66ers Baseball Club of San Bernardino. **Principal Owners:** David Elmore, Donna Tuttle. **President:** David Elmore. **Chairman:** Donna Tuttle.
   General Manager: Joe Hudson. **Assistant GM:** Ryan English. **Director, Broadcasting:** Steve Wendt. **Director, Group Sales:** Steve Pelle. **Director, Marketing:** Matt Kowallis. **Director, Promotions:** Adam Franey. **Director, Ticket Operations and Sales:** Seam Peterson Manager, Operations: John Jensen. **Manager:** Social Media, Jennifer Colgate. **Manager, Creative Services:** Mark Altenbach. **Group Account Executive** Jarrett Stark. **Group Account Executive:** Stephanie O' Quinn. **Coordinator, Marketing:** Julie Brady. **Coordinator, Promotions:** Peter Ercey. **Administrative Assistant:** Angie Geibel. **Head Groundskeeper:** Dominick Guerrero. **CFO:** John Fonseca.

FIELD STAFF
   Manager: Denny Hocking. **Hitting Coach:** Brent Del Chiaro. **Pitching Coach:** Matt Wise. **Trainer:** Omar Uribe.

GAME INFORMATION
   Radio Announcer: Steve Wendt. **Flagship Station:** 66ers Radio on TuneIn.
   PA Announcer: J.J. Gould. **Official Scorer:** Bill Maury-Holmes.
   Stadium Name: 66ers Stadium. **Location:** From south, I-215 to 2nd Street exit, east on 2nd, right on G Street; from north, I-215 to 3rd Street exit, left on Rialto, right on G Street. **Standard Game Times:** 7:05 pm; Sun 2:05 (April-June), 5:05 (July-Aug). **Ticket Price Range:** $5.50-15.
   Visiting Club Hotel: Hampton Inn Highland: 27959 Highland Avenue, Highland, California, 92346. **Telephone:** (909) 862-8000.

LAKE ELSINORE STORM

Address: 500 Diamond Drive, Lake Elsinore, CA 92530
Telephone: (951) 245-4487. **Fax:** (951) 245-0305.
E-Mail Address: info@stormbaseball.com. **Website:** www.stormbaseball.com.
Affiliation (first year): San Diego Padres (2001). **Years in League:** 1994-.

OWNERSHIP/MANAGEMENT
   Owners: Gary Jacobs, Len Simon.
   President/General Manager: Dave Oster. **General Manager:** Raj Narayanan.
   Assistant GM/Senior Graphics, Animation Designer: Mark Beskid. **Director of Finance/Business Administration:** Rick Riegler. **Assistant Director, Finance:** Andres Pagan. **Director, Broadcasting:** Sean McCall. **Director, First Impressions:** Peggy Mitchell. **Director, Marketing:** Tagg Bozied. **Assistant Director, Marketing:** Tyler Zickel. **Director, Community Relations/Group Sales:** Courtney Kessler. **Director, Player-Community Relations/Clubhouse Manager:** Terrance Tucker. **Sales Executives:** Kasey Rawitzer, Cutter Chanley. **Communications Director:** Eric Theiss. **Director, Ticketing:** Eric Colunga. **Assistant Director, Ticketing:** Tanner Grabianowski. **Director, Mascot Operations:**

Stephen Webster. **Director, Merchandise:** Donna Grunow. **Assistant Director, Merchandise:** Tommy Pompo. **Head Groundskeeper:** Joe Jimenez. **Assistant Groundskeeper:** Jordan Schrader. **Director, Storm Events:** Josh Ferguson. **Director, Stadium Operations:** Patrick Kennedy. **Assistant Director, Stadium Operations:** Casey Scott. Maintenance **Supervisor:** Jassiel Reza. **Director, Food/ Beverage:** Andrew Nelson. **Director, Concessions:** Chris Kidder. **Director, Diamond Club Events:** Christina Constancio.

FIELD STAFF

Manager: Michael Collins. **Coach:** Rod Barajas. **Pitching Coach:** Glendon Rusch.

GAME INFORMATION

Radio Announcer: Sean McCall. **No. of Games Broadcast:** 140. **Flagship Station:** Radio 94.5.
PA Announcer: Joe Martinez. **Official Scorer:** Lloyd Nixon.
Stadium Name: The Diamond. **Location:** From I-15, exit at Diamond Drive, west one mile to stadium. **Standard Game Times:** 6:05 pm, Thurs/Fri 7:05 pm, Sun 2:05 (first half), 5:05 (second half). **Ticket Price Range:** $10-14.
Visiting Club Hotel: Lake Elsinore Hotel and Casino, 20930 Malaga St, Lake Elsinore, CA 92530. **Telephone:** (951) 674-3101.

LANCASTER JETHAWKS

Address: 45116 Valley Central Way, Lancaster, CA 93536.
Telephone: (661) 726-5400. **Fax:** (661) 726-5406.
Email Address: info@jethawks.com. **Website:** www.jethawks.com.
Affiliation (first year): Houston Astros (2009). **Years in League:** 1996-

OWNERSHIP/MANAGEMENT

Operated By: Hawks Nest LLC. **Principal Owner/Managing General Partner:** Jake Kerr. **Partner:** Jeff Mooney. **President:** Andy Dunn. **Executive Vice President:** Tom Backemeyer. **General Manager:** William Thornhill. **Assistant GM, Tickets/Merchandise:** Will Murphy. **Director, Facility/Baseball Operations:** John Laferney. **Group Sales Manager:** Dylan Baker. **Community Relations / Promotions Manager:** Mike Hirsch. **Finance Director:** Brenda Baczkowski. **Sales/ Marketing Coordinator:** Alyssa Harrington.

FIELD STAFF

Manager: Omar Lopez. **Coach:** Darryl Robinson. **Pitching Coach:** Don Alexander.

GAME INFORMATION

Radio Announcer: Jason Schwartz. **No. of Games Broadcast:** 140. **Flagship Station:** www.jethawks.com.
PA Announcer: John Tyler. **Official Scorer:** David Guenther.
Stadium Name: The Hangar. **Location:** Highway 14 in Lancaster to Avenue I exit, west one block to stadium. **Standard Game Times:** 6:30 pm, Sun 2 (April-June), 5 (July-Sept). **Ticket Price Range:** $6-12.
Visiting Club Hotel: Comfort Inn, 1825 W Avenue J-12, Lancaster CA 93534. **Telephone:** (661) 723-2001.

MODESTO NUTS

Office Address: 601 Neece Dr, Modesto, CA 95351. **Mailing Address:** PO Box 883, Modesto, CA 95353.
Telephone: (209) 572-4487. **Fax:** (209) 572-4490.
E-Mail Address: fun@modestonuts.com. **Website:** www.modestonuts.com.
Affiliation (first year): Colorado Rockies (2005). **Years in League:** 1946-64, 1966-

OWNERSHIP/MANAGEMENT

Operated by: HWS Group IV. **Principal Owner:** Mike Savit.
Executive Vice President: Michael Gorrasi. **General Manager:** Tyler Richardson. **Vice President, HWS Beverage:** Ed Mack. **Director, Brand Management:** Robert Moullette. **Director, Ticket Sales :** Austin Weltner. **Director, In-Game Entertainment:** Joe Tichy. **Manager, Brand Representatives:** Nicola Norris.

FIELD STAFF

Manager: Fred Ocasio. **Coach:** Drew Saylor. **Pitching Coach:** Dave Burba

GAME INFORMATION

Radio Announcer: Unavailable.
PA Announcer: Unavailable. **Official Scorer:** Unavailable.
Stadium Name: John Thurman Field. **Location:** Highway 99 in southwest Modesto to Tuolomne Boulevard exit, west on Tuolomne for one block to Neece Drive, left for 1/4 mile to stadium. **Standard Game Times:** 7:05 pm, Sun 1:05pm/6:05 pm. **Ticket Price Range:** $7 -13.
Visiting Club Hotel: Unavailable.

RANCHO CUCAMONGA
QUAKES

Office Address: 8408 Rochester Ave., Rancho Cucamonga, CA 91730. **Mailing Address:** P.O. Box 4139, Rancho Cucamonga, CA 91729.
Telephone: (909) 481-5000. **Fax:** (909) 481-5005.
E-Mail Address: info@rcquakes.com. **Website:** www.rcquakes.com.
Affiliation (first year): Los Angeles Dodgers (2011). **Years in League:** 1993-

OWNERSHIP/MANAGEMENT

Operated By: Brett Sports & Entertainment. **Principal Owner:** Bobby Brett.
President: Brent Miles. **Vice President/General Manager:** Grant Riddle. **Vice President/Tickets:** Monica Ortega. **Assistant General Manager, Group Sales:** Linda Rathfon. **Assistant General Manager, Sponsorships:** Chris Pope. **Sponsorship Account Executive:** Kevin Cabori, Dori Eisenthal. **Promotions Coordinator:** Bobbi Salcido. **Director, Group Sales:** Kyle Burleson. **Group Sales Operations Coordinator:** Eric Jensen. **Director, Season Tickets:** Melinda Balandra. **Account Executive:** Derek Jimenez, Carly Nicola. **Director, Accounting:** Amara McClellan. **Director, Public Relations/Voice of the Quakes:** Mike Lindskog. **Office Manager:** Shelley Scebbi. **Director, Food/Beverage:** Jose Reyna.

FIELD STAFF

Manager: P.J. Forbes. **Hitting Coach:** Mike Eylward. **Pitching Coach:** Bill Simas.

GAME INFORMATION

Radio Announcer: Mike Lindskog.
PA Announcer: Chris Albaugh. **Official Scorer:** Ryan Wilson.
Stadium Name: LoanMart Field. **Location:** I-10 to I-15 North, exit at Foothill Boulevard, left on Foothill, left on Rochester to Stadium. **Standard Game Times:** 7:05 pm; Sun 2:05 (April-June), 5:05 (July-Sept.). **Ticket Price Range:** $8-12.
Visiting Club Hotel: Best Western Heritage Inn, 8179 Spruce Ave, Rancho Cucamonga, CA 91730. **Telephone:** (909) 466-1111.

SAN JOSE GIANTS

Office Address: 588 E Alma Ave, San Jose, CA 95112. **Mailing Address:** PO Box 21727, San Jose, CA 95151.
Telephone: (408) 297-1435. **Fax:** (408) 297-1453.
E-Mail Address: info@sjgiants.com. **Website:** www.sjgiants.com.
Affiliation (first year): San Francisco Giants (1988). **Years in League:** 1942, 1947-58, 1962-76, 1979-

OWNERSHIP/MANAGEMENT

Operated by: Progress Sports Management. **Principal Owners:** San Francisco Giants, Heidi Stamas, Richard Beahrs.
President/CEO: Daniel Orum. **Chief Operating Officer/General Manager:** Mark Wilson. **Chief Marketing Officer:** Juliana Paoli. **VP, Ballpark Operations:** Lance Motch. **VP, Finance/Human Resources:** Tyler Adair. **VP, Ticketing:** Kellen Minteer. **Director, Player Personnel:** Linda Pereira. **Director, Broadcasting:** Joe Ritzo. **Director, Food/Beverage/Human Resources:** Elizabeth Espinoza. **Director, Marketing/Media Relations:** Ben Taylor. **Manager, Partnerships and Youth Development Program:** John Rally. **Coordinator, Marketing:** Matt Alongi. **Assistant, Marketing/Retail:** Sarah Acosta. **Account Executive:** Jeff Di Giorgio. **Ticket Services Coordinator:** Andrew Molyneux. **Junior Account Executive:** Liana Louie.

FIELD STAFF

Manager: Russ Morman. **Hitting Coach:** Lipso Nava. **Pitching Coach:** Mike Couchee. **Trainer:** Garrett Havig. **Strength/Conditioning Coach:** Mike Lidge.

GAME INFORMATION

Radio Announcers: Joe Ritzo, Justin Allegri. **No. of Games Broadcast:** 140. **Flagship:** www.sjgiants.com. **Television Announcers:** Joe Ritzo, Joe Castellano. **No. of Games Broadcast:** 20 home games on Comcast Hometown Network, 70 on MiLB.TV.
PA Announcer: Russ Call. **Official Scorer:** Mike Hohler.
Stadium Name: Municipal Stadium. **Location:** South on I-280, Take 10th/11th Street Exit, Turn right on 10th Street, Turn left on Alma Ave; North on I-280: Take the 10th/11th Street Exit, Turn left on 10th Street, Turn Left on Alma Ave. **Standard Game Times:** 7 pm, 6:30 PM, Sat 5 PM, Sun 1 PM (5 PM after June 30). **Ticket Price Range:** $7-16.
Visiting Club Hotel: DoubleTree by Hilton Hotel San Jose, 2050 Gateway Place, San Jose, CA 95110. **Telephone:** (408) 453-4000.

STOCKTON PORTS

Address: 404 W Fremont St, Stockton, CA 95203.
Telephone: (209) 644-1900. **Fax:** (209) 644-1931.
E-Mail Address: info@stocktonports.com. **Website:** www.stocktonports.com.
Affiliation (first year): Oakland Athletics (2005). **Years in League:** 1941, 1946-72, 1978-

OWNERSHIP/MANAGEMENT

Operated By: 7th Inning Stretch LLC.
President: Pat Filippone. **Assistant General Manager:** Bryan Meadows. **Director, Tickets:** Tim Pollack. **Director, Marketing:** Taylor McCarthy. **Director, Corporate Sales:** Aaron Morales. **Community Relations Manager:** Kellie Ryan. **Stadium Operations Manager:** Max Bochman. **Ticket Operations Manager:** Dustin Coder. **Manager, Graphics/Website:** Mark Fanta. **Account Executive:** Scott Gillies. **Group Sales Account Executive:** Justice Hoyt. **Sponsorship/Ticket Sales Executive:** Greg Bell. **Bookkeeper:** Vang Hang. **Front Office Manager:** Deborah Pelletier. **Ovations General Manager:** Mike Bristow.

FIELD STAFF

Manager: Rick Magnante. **Hitting Coach:** Brian McArn. **Pitching Coach:** Rick Rodriguez. **Trainer:** Travis Tims.

GAME INFORMATION

Radio Announcer: Zack Bayrouty. **No of Games Broadcast:** 140. **Flagship Station:** KWSX 1280 AM. **TV:** Comcast Hometown Network, Channel 104, Regional Telecast.
PA Announcer: Mike Conway. **Official Scorer:** Paul Muyskens.
Stadium Name: Banner Island Ballpark. **Location:** From I-5/99, take Crosstown Freeway (Highway 4) exit El Dorado Street, north on El Dorado to Fremont Street, left on Fremont. **Standard Game Times:** 7:05 pm. **Ticket Price Range:** $6-$15.
Visiting Club Hotel: Hampton Inn Stockton, 5045 South State Route 99 East, Stockton, CA 95215. **Telephone:** (209) 946-1234.

VISALIA RAWHIDE

Address: 300 N Giddings St, Visalia, CA 93291.
Telephone: (559) 732-4433. **Fax:** (559) 739-7732.
E-Mail Address: info@rawhidebaseball.com. **Website:** www.rawhidebaseball.com.
Affiliation (first year): Arizona Diamondbacks (2007). **Years in League:** 1946-62, 1968-75, 1977-

OWNERSHIP/MANAGEMENT

President: Tom Seidler. **General Manager:** Jennifer Pendergraft. **Executive Assistant:** Jill Webb. **Office Assistant:** Julian Rifkind. **Assistant GM, Ticketing/Groups/Events:** Charlie Saponara. **Ticketing Coordinator:** Heather Dominguez. **Event Manager:** Lauren Lopes. **Director, Broadcasting/Media Relations:** Donny Baarns. **Community Relations/Groups:** Jon Bueno. **Assistant GM, Ballpark Operations:** Cody Gray. **Head Groundskeeper:** James Templeton. **Operations Assistant, Food/Beverage:** Erik Clark. **Ballpark Operations Assistant:** Les Kissick.

FIELD STAFF

Manager: Robby Hammock. **Hitting Coach:** Bobby Smith. **Pitching Coach:** Gil Heredia. **Trainer:** Takashi Onuki.

GAME INFORMATION

Radio Announcers: Donny Baarns. **No. of Games Broadcast:** 140. **Flagship Station:** KJUG 1270-AM.
PA Announcer: Brian Anthony. **Official Scorer:** Harry Kargenian.
Stadium Name: Rawhide Ballpark. **Location:** From Highway 99, take 198 East to Mooney Boulevard exit, left at second signal on Giddings; four blocks to ballpark. **Standard Game Times:** 7 pm, Sun 1 (first half), 6 (second half). **Ticket Price Range:** $5-20.
Visiting Club Hotel: Comfort Inn & Suites, 9300 W. Airport Dr, Visalia, CA 93277. **Telephone:** (559) 651-3700.

CAROLINA LEAGUE

Address: 1806 Pembroke Rd., Suite 2-B, Greensboro, NC 27408.
Telephone: (336) 691-9030. **Fax:** (336) 464-2737.
E-Mail Address: office@carolinaleague.com. **Website:** www.carolinaleague.com.
Years League Active: 1945-.
President/Treasurer: John Hopkins.

Vice President: Art Silber (Potomac). **Executive VP:** Steve Bryant (Carolina). **Corporate Secretary:** Ken Young (Frederick). **Directors:** Tim Zue (Salem), Paul Sunwall (Lynchburg), Chuck Greenberg (Myrtle Beach), Dave Ziedelis (Frederick), Steve Bryant (Carolina), Clark Minker (Wilmington), Billy Prim (Winston-Salem), Art Silber (Potomac). **Administrative Assistant:** Marnee Larkins.

Division Structure: North—Frederick, Lynchburg, Potomac, Wilmington. South—Carolina, Myrtle Beach, Salem, Winston-Salem.

Regular Season: 140 games (split schedule). **2015 Opening Date:** April 9. **Closing Date:** Sept 7.

All-Star Game: Carolina League vs California League, June 22 at Rancho Cucamonga.

Playoff Format: First-half division winners play second-half division winners in best of three series; if a team wins both halves, it plays division opponent with next-best second-half record. Division series winners meet in best of five series for Mills Cup.

John Hopkins

Roster Limit: 25 active. **Player Eligibility Rule:** No age limit. No more than two players and one player/coach on active list may have six or more years of prior minor league service.

Brand of Baseball: Rawlings.

Umpires: Erich Bacchus (Germantown, MD), Adam Beck (Winter Springs, FL), Chase Eade (Meridianville, AL), Travis Godec (Roanoke, VA), Richard Grassa (Lindenhurst, NY), Cody Oakes (Delhi, IA), Michael Provine (Newtown, PA), Skyler Shown (Owensboro, KY).

STADIUM INFORMATION

Club	Stadium	Opened	LF	CF	RF	Capacity	2014 Att.
Carolina	Five County Stadium	1991	330	400	309	6,500	215,149
Frederick	Harry Grove Stadium	1990	325	400	325	5,400	324,446
Lynchburg	City Stadium	1939	325	390	325	4,281	158,750
Myrtle Beach	TicketReturn.com Field	1999	308	405	328	5,200	241,026
Potomac	Pfitzner Stadium	1984	315	400	315	6,000	243,559
Salem	Salem Memorial Stadium	1995	325	401	325	5,502	220,782
Wilmington	Frawley Stadium	1993	325	400	325	6,532	278,316
Winston-Salem	BB&T Ballpark	2010	315	399	323	5,500	299,645

Dimensions

CAROLINA MUDCATS

Office Address: 1501 NC Hwy 39, Zebulon, NC 27597. **Mailing Address:** PO Drawer 1218, Zebulon, NC 27597.
Telephone: (919) 269-2287. **Fax:** (919) 269-4910.
E-Mail Address: muddy@carolinamudcats.com. **Website:** www.carolinamudcats.com.
Affiliation (first year): Atlanta Braves (2015). **Years in League:** 2012-

OWNERSHIP/MANAGEMENT

Operated by: Mudcats Baseball, LLC. **Majority Owner/President:** Steve Bryant.

Vice President/General Manager: Joe Kremer. **General Manager, Operations:** Eric Gardner. **Executive Sales Assistant/Office Manager:** Jackie DiPrimo. **Director, Stadium Operations:** Patrick Ennis. **Director, Food/Beverage:** Dwayne Lucas. **Director, Merchandise/Box Office Manager:** Janell Bullock. **Director, Creative Services/Marketing:** Aaron Bayles. **Director, Fan Experience:** Beckie Reid. **Director, Video Production:** Dave Maynard. **Director, Ticketing:** Brian Cassidy. **Ticket/Corporate Sales Executive:** Yogi Brewington, Samantha Colein, Aaron Freeman, Mike Link, Duke Sanders. **Director, Field Operations:** John Packer. **Director, Broadcasting/Media Relations:** Unavailable.

FIELD STAFF

Manager: Luis Salazar. **Hitting Coach:** Carlos Mendez. **Pitching Coach:** Derrick Lewis. **Trainer:** Joe Toenjes.

GAME INFORMATION

Radio Announcer: Unavailable. **No. of Games Broadcast:** 140. **Flagship Station:** Unavailable.
PA Announcer: Unavailable. **Official Scorer:** John Hobgood.
Stadium Name: Five County Stadium. **Location:** From Raleigh, US 64 East to 264 East, exit at Highway 39 in Zebulon.
Standard Game Times: 7 pm, Sat 6, Sun 2. **Ticket Price Range:** $10-11.
Visiting Club Hotel: Unavailable.

FREDERICK KEYS

Address: 21 Stadium Dr., Frederick, MD 21703.
Telephone: (301) 662-0013. **Fax:** (301) 662-0018.
E-Mail Address: info@frederickkeys.com. **Website:** www.frederickkeys.com.
Affiliation (first year): Baltimore Orioles (1989). **Years in League:** 1989-

OWNERSHIP/MANAGEMENT

Ownership: Maryland Baseball Holding LLC.
President: Ken Young. **General Manager:** Dave Ziedelis. **Director, Ticket Operations:** Ben Sealy. **Director, Marketing:** Bridget McCabe. **Promotions Manager:** Christine Roy. **Manager, Broadcasting/Public Relations:** Geoff Arnold. **Marketing Assistant:** Catie Graf. **Director, Group Sales:** Matt Miller. **Account Managers:** Amanda Kostolansky, Chris Colletti, Casey O'Brien. **Director, Sponsorship/Broadcaster:** Doug Raftery. **Account Managers:** Taylor Fisher, Elizabeth Wenger. **Box Office Assistants:** Chris Williams, Matthew Baker. **Director, Stadium Operations:** Kari Collins. **Head Groundskeeper:** Mike Soper. **Clubhouse Manager:** Adam Barron. **Office Manager:** Katy Bobbitt. **Finance Manager:** Tami Hetrick. **General Manager-Ovations:** Alan Cranfill.

FIELD STAFF

Manager: Orlando Gomez. **Hitting Coach:** Unavailable. **Pitching Coach:** Kennie Steenstra. **Athletic Trainer:** Pat Wesley.

GAME INFORMATION

Radio Announcers: Geoff Arnold, Doug Raftery.
PA Announcer: Andy Redmond. **Official Scorers:** Bob Roberson, Dennis Hetrick, Luke Stillson.
Stadium Name: Harry Grove Stadium. **Location:** From I-70, take exit 54 (Market Street), left at light; From I-270, take exit 32 (I-70Baltimore/Hagerstown) toward Baltimore (I-70), to exit 54 at Market Street. **Ticket Price Range:** $9-12.
Visiting Club Hotel: Comfort Inn Frederick, 7300 Executive Way, Frederick, MD 21704. **Telephone:** (301) 668-7272.

LYNCHBURG HILLCATS

Office Address: Lynchburg City Stadium, 3180 Fort Ave, Lynchburg, VA 24501. **Mailing Address:** PO Box 10213, Lynchburg, VA 24506.
Telephone: (434) 528-1144. **Fax:** (434) 846-0768.
E-Mail Address: info@lynchburg-hillcats.com. **Website:** www.Lynchburg-hillcats.com.
Affiliation (first year): Cleveland Indians (2015). **Years in League:** 1966-

OWNERSHIP/MANAGEMENT

Operated By: Lynchburg Baseball Corp.
President/CFO: Paul Sunwall. **General Manager:** Ronnie Roberts. **Head Groundskeeper/Sales:** Darren Johnson. **Director, Broadcasting:** Kyle West. **Director, Food/Beverage:** Zach Willis. **Director, Promotions:** Ashley Stephenson. **Director, Group Sales:** Brad Goodale. **Ticket Manager:** John Hutt. **Office Manager:** Diane Arrington.

FIELD STAFF

Manager: Mark Budzinski. **Hitting Coach:** Unavailable. **Pitching Coach:** Tony Arnold. **Trainer:** Bobby Ruiz.

GAME INFORMATION

Radio Announcer: Kyle West. **No. of Games Broadcast:** 140. **Flagship Station:** WVGM-93.3 FM.
PA Announcer: Chuck Young. **Official Scorers:** Malcolm Haley, Chuck Young.
Stadium Name: Calvin Falwell Field at Lynchburg City Stadium. **Location:** US 29 Business South to Lynchburg City Stadium (exit 6); US 29 Business North to Lynchburg City Stadium (exit 4). **Ticket Price Range:** $7-10.
Visiting Club Hotel: Microtel Inn & Suites by Wyndham, 5704 Seminole Ave., Lynchburg, VA 24502. **Telephone:** (434) 239-2300.

MYRTLE BEACH PELICANS

Mailing Address: 1251 21st Avenue N. Myrtle Beach, SC 29577.
Telephone: (843) 918-6000. **Fax:** (843) 918-6001.
E-Mail Address: info@myrtlebeachpelicans.com. **Website:** www.myrtlebeachpelicans.com.
Affiliation (first year): Chicago Cubs (2015). **Years in League:** 1999-

OWNERSHIP/MANAGEMENT

Operated By: Myrtle Beach Pelicans LP. **President/Managing Partner:** Chuck Greenberg.
VP/General Manager: Andy Milovich. **Merchandise Manager:** Dan Bailey. **Senior Director, Business Development:** Guy Schuman. **Media Relations/Broadcaster:** Nathan Barnett. **Sports Turf Manager:** Corey Russell. **Turf Assistant:** Kevin Schmidt. **Senior Director, Finance:** Anne Frost. **Senior Director, Community Development:** Jen Borowski. **Senior Director, Marketing:** Kristin Call. **Administrative Assistant:** Beth Freitas. **Facility Operations Manager:** Mike

Snow. **Director, Food/Beverage:** Brad Leininger. **Director, Video Production:** Kyle Guertin. **Assistant GM/Sales:** Zach Brockman. **Box Office Manager:** Shannon Samanka. **Group Sales Manager:** Glenn Goodwin, Justin Bennett. **Account Executives:** Gandy Henry, Todd Chapman. **Corporate Sales Manager:** Katelyn Guild. **Official Scorer:** Steve Walsh.

FIELD STAFF
Manager: Mark Johnson. **Pitching Coach:** David Rosario. **Hitting Coach:** Mariano Duncan. **Assistant Coach:** Chris Gutierrez. **Athletic Trainer:** Peter Fagan.

GAME INFORMATION
PA Announcer: Unavailable. **Official Scorer:** Steve Walsh.
Stadium Name: Ticketreturn.com Field at Pelicans Ballpark. **Location:** US Highway 17 Bypass to 21st Ave. North, half mile to stadium. **Standard Game Times:** Unavailable. **Ticket Price Range:** $9-$15.
Visiting Club Hotel: Hampton Inn-Broadway at the Beach, 1140 Celebrity Circle, Myrtle Beach, SC 29577. **Telephone:** (843) 916-0600.

POTOMAC NATIONALS

Office Address: 7 County Complex Ct, Woodbridge, VA 22192. **Mailing Address:** PO Box 2148, Woodbridge, VA 22195.
Telephone: (703) 590-2311. **Fax:** (703) 590-5716.
E-Mail Address: info@potomacnationals.com. **Website:**www.potomacnationals. com.
Affiliation (first year): Washington Nationals (2005). **Years in League:** 1978-

OWNERSHIP/MANAGEMENT
Operated By: Potomac Baseball LLC.
Principal Owner: Art Silber. **President:** Lani Silber Weiss.
Senior Vice President/General Manager: Josh Olerud. **Assistant GM, Director, Sales:** Zach Prehn. **Ticket Director:** Brett Adams. **Director, Media Relations/Broadcasting:** Bryan Holland. **Director, Food Services/Merchandise Director:** Aaron Johnson. **Director, Stadium Operations:** Arthur Bouvier. **Senior Group Sales Director:** Andrew Stinson. **Group Sales Executives:** Julie Goldberg, Jacob Martinez. **Director, Community Relations:** Ricky Goykin. **Director, Creative Design:** Alexis Deegan. **Manager, Business Operations:** Shawna Hooke.

FIELD STAFF
Manager: Tripp Keister. **Hitting Coach:** Brian Rupp. **Pitching Coach:** Franklin Bravo. **Trainer:** TD Swinford

GAME INFORMATION
Radio Announcer: Bryan Holland. **No. of Games Broadcast:** 140. **Flagship:** www.potomacnationals.com.
PA Announcer: Unavailable. **Official Scorer:** David Vincent, Ben Trittipoe.
Stadium Name: Richard Pfitzner Stadium. **Location:** From I-95, take exit, 158B and continue on Prince William Parkway for five miles, right into County Complex Court. **Standard Game Times:** 7:05 pm, Sat 6:35, Sun 1:05 (first half), Sun 6:05 (second half). **Ticket Price Range:** $8-15.
Visiting Club Hotel: Country Inn and Suites, Prince William Parkway, Woodbridge, VA 22192. **Telephone:** (703) 492-6868.

SALEM RED SOX

Office Address: 1004 Texas St., Salem, VA 24153. **Mailing Address:** PO Box 842, Salem, VA 24153.
Telephone: (540) 389-3333. **Fax:** (540) 389-9710.
E-Mail Address: info@salemsox.com. **Website:** www.salemsox.com.
Affiliation (first year): Boston Red Sox (2009). **Years in League:** 1968-

OWNERSHIP/MANAGEMENT
Operated By: Carolina Baseball LLC/Fenway Sports Group.
President: Sam Kennedy. **General Manager:** Ryan Shelton. **VP/Senior Assistant GM:** Allen Lawrence. **Director, Corporate Sponsorships:** Steven Elovich. **Marketing/Promotions Manager:** Samantha Barney. **VP, Operations:** Tim Anderson. **Facilities Manager:** Matt Bird. **Group Sales Account Executive:** Casey Eliff. **Ticket Operations/Retention Manager:** Dustin Davis. **Food/Beverage Manager:** Patrick Pelletier. **Head Groundskeeper:** Ross Groenevelt. **Clubhouse Manager:** Chipper Cripps.

FIELD STAFF
Manager: Carlos Febles. **Hitting Coach:** Jon Nunnally. **Pitching Coach:** Paul Abbott. **Trainer:** David Herrera.

GAME INFORMATION
Radio Announcer: Evan Lepler. **No. of Games Broadcast:** 140. **Flagship Station:** ESPN 1240-AM.
PA Announcer: Unavailable. **Official Scorer:** Billy Wells.
Stadium Name: Salem Memorial Ballpark. **Location:** I-81 to exit 141 (Route 419), follow signs to Salem Civic Center Complex. **Standard Game Times:** 7:05 pm, Sat/Sun 6:05/4:05. **Ticket Price Range:** $7-13.
Visiting Club Hotel: Comfort Suites Ridgewood Farms, 2898 Keagy Rd., Salem, VA 24153. **Telephone:** (540) 375-4800.

WILMINGTON BLUE ROCKS

Address: 801 Shipyard Drive, Wilmington, DE 19801.
Telephone: (302) 888-2015. **Fax:** (302) 888-2032.
E-Mail Address: info@bluerocks.com. **Website:** www.bluerocks.com.
Affiliation (first year): Kansas City Royals (2007). **Years in League:** 1993-

OWNERSHIP/MANAGEMENT

Operated by: Wilmington Blue Rocks LP. **Honorary President:** Matt Minker.
Owners: Main Street Baseball, Clark Minker. **General Manager:** Chris Kemple.
Assistant GM: Andrew Layman. **Director, Broadcasting/Media Relations:** Matt Janus. **Broadcasting/Media Relations Assistants:** Jonathan Kohut, Jackson Baird. **Director, Advertising Sales:** Brian Radle. **Director, Merchandise:** Jim Beck. **Director, Marketing:** Joe Valenti. **Director, Community Affairs:** Kevin Linton. **Director, Tickets:** Stefani Rash. **Manager, Game Entertainment:** Mike Diodati. **Box Office Manager:** Mark Cunningham. **Group Sales Executives:** Eric Little, Brent Kepner. **Director, Field Operations:** Steve Gold. **Office Manager:** Erin Del Negro.

FIELD STAFF

Manager: Brian Buchanan. **Hitting Coach:** Abraham Nunez. **Pitching Coach:** Steve Luebber. **Athletic Trainer:** James Stone.

GAME INFORMATION

Radio Announcers: Matt Janus, Jonathan Kohut, Jackson Baird. **No. of Games Broadcast:** 140. **Flagship Station:** 89.7 WGLS-FM.
PA Announcer: Kevin Linton. **Official Scorer:** Dick Shute.
Stadium Name: Judy Johnson Field at Daniel Frawley Stadium. **Location:** I-95 North to Maryland Ave (exit 6), right on Maryland Ave, and through traffic light onto Martin Luther King Blvd, right at traffic light on Justison St, follow to Shipyard Dr; I-95 South to Maryland Ave (exit 6), left at fourth light on Martin Luther King Blvd, right at fourth light on Justison St, follow to Shipyard Dr. **Standard Game Times:** 6:35 pm, 7:05 (Fri/Sat), Sun 1:35 p.m. **Ticket Price Range:** $4-14.
Visiting Club Hotel: Clarion Belle, 1612 N DuPont Hwy, New Castle, DE 19720. **Telephone:** (302) 299-1408.

WINSTON-SALEM DASH

Office Address: 926 Brookstown Ave, Winston-Salem, NC 27101.
Stadium Address: 951 Ballpark Way, Winston-Salem, NC 27101.
Telephone: (336) 714-2287. **Fax:** (336) 714-2288.
Website: www.wsdash.com. **E-Mail Address:** info@wsdash.com.
Affiliation (first year): Chicago White Sox (1997). **Years in League:** 1945-

OWNERSHIP/MANAGEMENT:

Operated by: Sports Menagerie LLC. **Principal Owner:** Billy Prim.
President: Geoff Lassiter. **Vice President/Chief Financial Officer:** Kurt Gehsmann. **VP, Baseball Operations:** Ryan Manuel. **VP, Ticket Sales:** C.J. Johnson. **VP, Corporate Partnerships:** Corey Bugno. **Director, Corporate Partnerships:** Darren Hill. **Director, Group Sales:** Russell Parmele. **Director, Entertainment/Community Relations:** Annie Stoltenberg. **Director, Facility Management:** Jeff Brown. **Director, Media Relations/Broadcasting:** Brian Boesch. **Staff Accountant:** Amanda Elbert.
Creative Services Manager: Kristin DiSanti. **Sponsor Services Account Managers:** Mimi Driscoll, Nick Jones. **Business Development Representatives:** Taylor Boyle, Bryan Ferrer, Paul Stephens. **Group Sales Representative:** Tommy Grant. **Ticket Sales/Service Representatives:** Sean Aquadro, Ira Dogruyol, Whitley Shannon. **Box Office Manager:** Kenny Lathan. **Box Office Supervisor:** Paul Williams. **Head Groundskeeper:** Paul Johnson.

FIELD STAFF

Manager: Tim Esmay. **Hitting Coach:** Charlie Poe. **Pitching Coach:** J.R. Perdew.

GAME INFORMATION

Radio Announcer: Brian Boesch. **No. of Games Broadcast:** 140. **Flagship Station:** 600 AM-WSJS (Thursdays) or wsdash.com (all games).
PA Announcer: Unavailable. **Official Scorer:** Bill Grainger.
Stadium Name: BB&T Ballpark. **Location:** I-40 Business to Peters Creek Parkway exit (exit 5A). **Standard Game Times:** 7 pm, Sat 6:30, Sun 2/5.
Visiting Club Hotel: Unavailable.

FLORIDA STATE LEAGUE

Office Address: 104 E Orange Ave Daytona Beach, FL 32114. **Mailing Address:** PO Box 349, Daytona Beach, FL 32115.
Telephone: (386) 252-7479. **Fax:** (386) 252-7495.
E-Mail Address: fslbaseball@cfl.rr.com. **Website:** www.floridastateleague.com.
Years League Active: 1919-1927, 1936-1941, 1946- .

President/Treasurer: Chuck Murphy.
Executive Vice President: Ken Carson. **VPs:** North—Ken Carson. South—Paul Taglieri.
Corporate Secretary: Horace Smith Jr. **Special Adviser:** Ben Hayes.
Directors: Mike Bauer (Jupiter/Palm Beach), Ken Carson (Dunedin), Jared Forma (Charlotte), Trevor Gooby (Bradenton), Jason Hochberg (Fort Myers), Josh Lawther (Daytona), Ron Myers (Lakeland), Kyle Smith (Brevard County), Vance Smith (Tampa), Paul Taglieri (St. Lucie), John Timberlake (Clearwater).
Office Manager: Laura LeCras.
Division Structure: North—Brevard County, Clearwater, Daytona, Dunedin, Lakeland, Tampa. South—Bradenton, Charlotte, Fort Myers, Jupiter, Palm Beach, St. Lucie.
Regular Season: 140 games (split schedule). **2015 Opening Date:** April 9. **Closing Date:** September 6.
All-Star Game: June 20 at St. Lucie.
Playoff Format: First-half division winners meet second-half winners in best of three series. Winners meet in best of five series for league championship.
Roster Limit: 25. **Player Eligibility Rule:** No age limit. No more than two players and one player-coach on active list may have six or more years of prior minor league service.
Brand of Baseball: Rawlings.
Umpires: Jordan Albarado (Scott, LA), Ryan Benson (Danbury, CT), Scott Costello (Barrie, Ontario), Ryan Doherty (Littleton, CO), Joe George (Springfield, IL), Ben Levin (Cincinnati, OH), Alexander MacKay (Evergreen, CO), Brennan Miller (Fairfax Station, VA), Kirk Struble (Kirkland, WA), Nate Tomlinson (Ogdenburg, WI), Matt Winter (Hubbard, IA), Michael Wiseman (White Lake, MI).

Chuck Murphy

STADIUM INFORMATION

| Club | Stadium | Opened | Dimensions | | | Capacity | 2014 Att. |
			LF	CF	RF		
Bradenton	McKechnie Field	1923	335	400	335	8,654	104,584
Brevard County	Space Coast Stadium	1994	340	404	340	7,500	78,465
Charlotte	Charlotte Sports Park	2009	343	413	343	5,028	118,430
Clearwater	Bright House Field	2004	330	400	330	8,500	195,063
Daytona	Jackie Robinson Ballpark	1930	317	400	325	4,200	143,273
Dunedin	Florida Auto Exchange Stadium	1977	335	400	327	5,509	60,044
Fort Myers	Hammond Stadium	1991	330	405	330	7,900	119,102
Jupiter	Roger Dean Stadium	1998	330	400	325	6,871	71,713
Lakeland	Joker Marchant Stadium	1966	340	420	340	7,828	64,396
Palm Beach	Roger Dean Stadium	1998	330	400	325	6,871	74,887
St. Lucie	Mets Stadium	1988	338	410	338	7,000	94,650
Tampa	Steinbrenner Field	1996	318	408	314	11,026	111,521

BRADENTON MARAUDERS

Address: 1701 27th Street East, Bradenton, FL 34208.
Telephone: (941) 747-3031. **Fax:** (941) 747-9442.
E-Mail Address: MaraudersInfo@pirates.com. **Website:** www.BradentonMarauders.com.
Affiliation (first year): Pittsburgh Pirates (2010). **Years in League:** 1919-20, 1923-24, 1926, 2010-.

OWNERSHIP/MANAGEMENT
Operated By: Pittsburgh Associates.
Senior Director, Florida Operations: Trevor Gooby. **Manager, McKechnie Operations:** A.J. Grant. **Manager, Florida Operations:** Unavailable. **Manager, Sales/Marketing:** Rachelle Madrigal. **Coordinator, Florida Operations, Ray Morris Coordinator, Concessions:** Phil Green. **Coordinator, Sales:** Anne Putnam. **Coordinator, Sales/Marketing:** Mike Warren. **Coordinator, Ticket Operations:** Justin Kristich. **Coordinator, Marketing/Community Relations:** Carley Paganelli. **Coordinator, Florida Operations:** Unavailable. **Coordinator, Communication/Broadcasting:** Nate March. **Head Groundskeeper:** Victor Madrigal.

FIELD STAFF

Manager: Michael Ryan. **Coach:** Ryan Long. **Pitching Coach:** Scott Elarton. **Athletic Trainer:** Justin Ahrens.

GAME INFORMATION

PA Announcer: Art Ross. **Official Scorer:** Dave Taylor.
Stadium Name: McKechnie Field. **Location:** I-75 to exit 220 (220B from I-75N) to SR 64 West/Manatee Ave, Left onto 9th St West, McKechnie Field on the left. **Standard Game Times:** 6:30 pm, Sun 1 (1st half), 5 (second half). **Ticket Price Range:** $6-10, $1 Sundays.
Visiting Club Hotel: Courtyard by Marriott Bradenton Sarasota Waterfront, 100 Riverfront Drive West, Bradenton, FL 34205. **Telephone:** (941) 747-3727.

BREVARD COUNTY MANATEES

Address: 5800 Stadium Pkwy, Suite 101, Viera, FL 32940.
Telephone: (321) 633-9200. **Fax:** (321) 633-4418.
E-Mail Address: info@spacecoaststadium.com. **Website:** www.manateesbaseball.com.
Affiliation (first year): Milwaukee Brewers (2005). **Years in League:** 1994-

OWNERSHIP/MANAGEMENT

Operated By: Central Florida Baseball Group LLC.
Chairman: Tom Winters. **Vice Chairman:** Dwight Titus. **President:** Charlie Baumann. **General Manager:** Kyle Smith. **Assistant GM:** Chad Lovitt. **Director, Business Operations/Finance:** Kelley Wheeler. **Director, Broadcasting:** Dave Walkovic. **Director, Community Relations/Promotions:** Jennifer Garcia. **Outside Sales Manager:** Tom Snyder. **Group Sales Manager:** Evija Vilde. **Inside Sales/Box Office Manager:** Chad Stevens. **Accounting Manager:** Max Caron. **Clubhouse Manager:** Ryan McDonald. **Head Groundskeeper:** Doug Lopas.

FIELD STAFF

Manager: Joe Ayrault. **Coaches:** Ned Yost IV, Reggie Williams. **Pitching Coach:** Dave Chavarria. **Trainer:** Tommy Craig. **Strength/Conditioning Coordinator:** Jonah Mergen.

GAME INFORMATION

PA Announcer: J.C. Meyerholz. **Official Scorer:** Unavailable.
Stadium Name: Space Coast Stadium. **Location:** I-95 North to Wickham Rd (exit 191), left onto Wickham, right at traffic circle onto Lake Andrew Drive for 1 1/2 miles through the Brevard County government office complex to the four-way stop, right on Stadium Parkway, Space Coast Stadium 1/2 mile on the left; I-95 South to Rockledge exit (exit 195), left onto Stadium Parkway, Space Coast Stadium is 3 miles on right. **Standard Game Times:** 6:35 pm, Sun 5:05. **Tickets:** $6 - $10.
Visiting Club Hotel: Holiday Inn Melbourne-Viera Hotel and Conference Center. **Telephone:** (321) 255-0077.

CHARLOTTE STONE CRABS

Address: 2300 El Jobean Road, Building A, Port Charlotte, FL 33948.
Telephone: (941) 206-4487. **Fax:** (941) 206-3599.
E-Mail Address: info@stonecrabsbaseball.com. **Website:** www.stonecrabsbaseball.com.
Affiliation (first year): Tampa Bay Rays (2009). **Years in League:** 2009-

OWNERSHIP/MANAGEMENT

Operated By: Ripken Baseball.
General Manager: Jared Forma. **Assistant GM:** Holly Jones. **Marketing Manager:** Mary Hegley. **Community Relations Manager:** Sammy DiTonno. **Accountant:** Lori Engleman. **Accounting Clerk:** Sue Denny. **Corporate Sponsorship Sales:** Bill Cox. **Box Office Manager:** Cooper Fazio. **Director, Food/Beverage:** Matt Vanderhoff. **Manager, Food/Beverage:** Marshall Clapper. **Manager, Corporate Sponsorship Sales:** Bill Holohan. **Account Representatives:** Marcus Sheehan, Hallie Rubins, Patrick Wondrak.

FIELD STAFF

Manager: Michael Johns. **Coach:** Joe Szekely. **Pitching Coach:** Steve Watson. **Trainer:** Scott Thurston.

GAME INFORMATION

PA Announcer: Josh Grant. **Official Scorer:** Rich Spedaliere.
Stadium Name: Charlotte Sports Park. **Location:** I-75 to Exit 179, turn left onto Toldeo Blade Blvd then right on El Jobean Rd. **Ticket Price Range:** $7-12.
Visiting Club Hotel: Days Inn, 1941 Tamiami Trail, Port Charlotte, FL 33948. **Telephone:** 941-627-8900.

CLEARWATER THRESHERS

Address: 601 N Old Coachman Road, Clearwater, FL 33765.
Telephone: (727) 712-4300. **Fax:** (727) 712-4498.
Website: www.threshersbaseball.com.
Affiliation (first year): Philadelphia Phillies (1985). **Years in League:** 1985-

OWNERSHIP/MANAGEMENT

Operated by: Philadelphia Phillies.
Chairman: Bill Giles. **President:** David Montgomery. **Director, Florida Operations/General Manager:** John Timberlake. **Business Manager:** Dianne Gonzalez. **Assistant GM/Director, Sales:** Dan McDonough. **Assistant GM, Ticketing:** Jason Adams. **Office Administration:** DeDe Angelillis. **Manager, Group Sales:** Dan Madden. **Senior Sales Associate:** Bobby Mitchell. **Manager, Ballpark Operations:** Jerry Warren. **Operations Assistant:** Sean McCarthy. **Coordinator, Facility Maintenance:** Cory Sipe. **Manager, Special Events:** Doug Kemp. **Manager, Community Relations/Promotions:** Amanda Koch. **Clubhouse Manager:** Mark Meschede. **Manager, Food/Beverage:** Brad Dudash. **Assistant, Food/Beverage:** Brittany Jones. **Suites Manager:** Wendy Armstrong. **Ticket Office Managers:** Pat Privelege, Kyle Webb. **Group Sales Assistant:** Aaron Frey. Audio/Video: Nic Repper. **Buyer/Manager, Merchandise:** Robin Warner. **PR Assistant:** Rob Stretch.

FIELD STAFF

Manager: Greg Legg. **Coach:** Rob Ducey. **Pitching Coach:** Steve Schrenk.

GAME INFORMATION

PA Announcer: Don Guckian. **Official Scorer:** Larry Wiederecht.
Stadium Name: Bright House Field. **Location:** US 19 North and Drew Street in Clearwater. **Standard Game Times:** 7 pm, Fri/Sat 6:30. **Ticket Price Range:** $5-10.
Visiting Club Hotel: La Quinta Inn, 21338 US Highway 19 N, Clearwater, FL 33765. **Telephone:** (727) 799-1565.

DAYTONA TORTUGAS

Address: 110 E Orange Ave, Daytona Beach, FL 32114.
Telephone: (386) 257-3172. **Fax:** (386) 523-9490.
E-Mail Address: info@daytonatortugas.com. **Website:** www.daytonatortugas.com.
Affiliation (first year): Cincinnati Reds (2015). **Years in League:** 1920-24,1928, 1936-41, 1946-73, 1977-87, 1993-

OWNERSHIP/MANAGEMENT

Operated By: Big Game Florida LLC. **Principal Owner/President:** Andrew Rayburn.
General Manager: Josh Lawther. **Assistant GMs:** Clint Cure & Jim Jaworski. **Director, Broadcasting/Media Relations:** Robbie Aaron. **Assistant GM, Stadium Operations:** JR Laub. **Director, Ticket Operations:** Paul Krenzer. **Manager, Food/Beverage:** Kevin Dwyer. **Director, Merchandise:** Wade Becker. **Office Manager:** Tammy Devine. **Head Groundskeeper:** Blake Chapman.

FIELD STAFF

Manager: Eli Marrero. **Hitting Coach:** Kevin Mahar. **Pitching Coach:** Tony Fossas. **Trainer:** Kyle Utne.

GAME INFORMATION

Radio Announcer: Robbie Aaron. **No. of Games Broadcast:** 140. **Flagship Station:** AM-1230 WSBB.
PA Announcer: Tim Lecras. **Official Scorer:** Don Roberts.
Stadium Name: Jackie Robinson Ballpark. **Location:** I-95 to International Speedway Blvd Exit (Route 92), east to Beach Street, south to Magnolia Ave east to ballpark; A1A North/South to Orange Ave west to ballpark. **Standard Game Time:** 7:05 p.m. **Ticket Price Range:** $6-12.
Visiting Club Hotel: Holiday Inn Resort Daytona Beach Oceanfront, 1615 S. Atlantic Ave Daytona Beach, FL 32118. **Telephone:** (386) 255-0921.

DUNEDIN BLUE JAYS

Address: 373 Douglas Ave Dunedin, FL 34698.
Telephone: (727) 733-9302. **Fax:** (727) 734-7661.
E-Mail Address: dunedin@bluejays.com. **Website:** dunedinbluejays.com.
Affiliation (first year): Toronto Blue Jays (1987). **Years in League:** 1978-79, 1987-

OWNERSHIP/MANAGEMENT

Director/General Manager, Florida Operations: Shelby Nelson. **Assistant GM:** Mike Liberatore.
Accounting Manager: Gayle Gentry. **Manager, Group Sales/Retail/Community Relations:** Kathi Beckman. **Community Relations Coordinator:** Tim Vieira. **Ticket Operations Coordinator:** Hunter Haas. **Administrative Assistant/**

Receptionist: Michelle Smith. **Stadium Operations Supervisor:** Leon Harrell. **Stadium Operations Supervisor:** Zac Phelps. **Senior Advisor:** Ken Carson. **Head Superintendent:** Patrick Skunda. **Assistant Superintendent:** Matt Johnson.

FIELD STAFF

Manager: Omar Malavé. **Hitting Coach:** John Tamargo Jr. **Pitching Coach:** Vince Horsman. **Trainer:** Shawn McDermott.

GAME INFORMATION

PA Announcer: Bill Christie. **Official Scorer:** Unavailable.

Stadium Name: Florida Auto Exchange Stadium. **Location:** From I-275, north on Highway 19, left on Sunset Point Rd for 4.5 miles, right on Douglas Ave; stadium is on right. **Standard Game Times:** 6:30 pm, Sun 5. **Ticket Price Range:** $7.

Visiting Club Hotel: La Quinta, 21338 US Highway 19 North, Clearwater, FL. **Telephone:** (727) 799-1565.

FORT MYERS MIRACLE

Address: 14400 Six Mile Cypress Pkwy, Fort Myers, FL 33912.

Telephone: (239) 768-4210. **Fax:** (239) 768-4211.

E-Mail Address: miracle@miraclebaseball.com. **Website:** www.miraclebaseball.com.

Affiliation (first year): Minnesota Twins (1993). **Years in League:** 1926, 1978-87, 1991-

OWNERSHIP/MANAGEMENT

Operated By: SJS Beacon Baseball. **Owner:** Jason Hochberg. **Chief Operating Officer:** Steve Gliner.

General Manager: Andrew Seymour. **Senior Director, Business Operations:** Suzanne Reaves. **Senior Director, Business Development:** John Kuhn. **Director, Broadcasting/Media Relations:** Brice Zimmerman. **Director, Food/Beverage:** Kevin Bush. **Director, Ticket Operations/Sales Advisor:** Bill Levy. **Sales Advisor:** Delroy Gay. **Manager, Community Relations/Merchandise:** Ashley Adams. **Merchandise Operations:** John Acquavella. **Assistant, Food/Beverage:** Danny Barbosa. **Administrative Assistant:** Karleen Halfmann. **Head Groundskeeper:** Keith Blasingim. **Clubhouse Manager:** Brock Rasmussen.

FIELD STAFF

Manager: Jeff Smith. **Coach:** Jim Dwyer. **Pitching Coach:** Ivan Arteaga. **Trainer:** Alan Rail.

GAME INFORMATION

Radio Announcer: Brice Zimmerman. **No. of Games Broadcast:** 140. **Internet Broadcast:** www.miraclebaseball.com. **PA Announcer:** Bill Banfield. **Official Scorer:** Scott Pedersen.

Stadium Name: William H. Hammond Stadium at the CenturyLink Sports Complex. **Location:** Exit 131 off I-75, west on Daniels Parkway, left on Six Mile Cypress Parkway. **Standard Game Times:** 7:05 pm, Sat 6:05; Sun 4:05. **Ticket Price Range:** $5-11.

Visiting Club Hotel: Unavailable.

JUPITER HAMMERHEADS

Address: 4751 Main Street, Jupiter, FL 33458.

Telephone: (561) 775-1818. **Fax:** (561) 691-6886.

E-Mail Address: f.desk@rogerdeanstadium.com. **Website:** www.jupiterhammerheads.com.

Affiliation (first year): Miami Marlins (2002). **Years in League:** 1998-

OWNERSHIP/MANAGEMENT

Owned By: Miami Marlins, Jupiter Stadium, LTD.

General Manager, Jupiter Stadium, LTD: Mike Bauer. **Executive Assistant:** Kacey Wilcoxson. **Assistant GM, Jupiter Stadium LTD/GM Jupiter Hammerheads:** Unavailable. **Assistant GM, Jupiter Stadium:** Alex Inman. **Director, Accounting:** John McCahan. **Corporate Partnerships Manager:** Katherine Deal. **Director, Ticketing:** Haile Urquhart. **Marketing/Media Relations Manager:** Jeffrey Draluck. **Manager, Event Services:** Alex Inman. **Director, Grounds:** Jordan Treadway. **Assistant Directors, Grounds:** Micah Bennett, Drew Wolcott. **Stadium Building Manager:** Walter Herrera. **Merchandise Manager:** Linda Hanson. **Ticket Manager:** Aimee Erbacher. **Press Box:** Houston Stutz. **Office Manager:** Dianne Detling.

FIELD STAFF

Manager: Brian Schneider. **Coach:** Corey Hart. **Pitching Coach:** Joe Coleman.

GAME INFORMATION

PA Announcers: Dick Sanford, John Frost, Lou Palmer. **Official Scorer:** Brennan McDonald.

Stadium Name: Roger Dean Stadium. **Location:** I-95 to exit 83, east on Donald Ross Road for 1/4 mile. **Standard Game Times:** 6:35 pm, Sat 5:35pm, Sun 1:05 or 5:05 p.m. **Ticket Price Range:** $7.00-$10.00.

Visiting Club Hotel: Fairfield Inn by Marriott, 6748 Indiantown Road, Jupiter, FL 33458. **Telephone:** (561) 748-5252.

LAKELAND FLYING TIGERS

Address: 2125 N Lake Ave, Lakeland, FL 33805.
Telephone: (863) 686-8075. **Fax:** (863) 688-9589.
Website: www.lakelandflyingtigers.com.
Affiliation (first year): Detroit Tigers (1967). **Years in League:** 1919-26, 1953-55, 1960, 1962-64, 1967-.

OWNERSHIP/MANAGEMENT

Owned By: Detroit Tigers, Inc. **Principal Owner:** Mike Ilitch. **President:** David Dombrowski.
Director, Florida Operations: Ron Myers. **General Manager:** Zach Burek. **Manager, Administration/Operations:** Shannon Follett. **Ticket Manager:** Ryan Eason. **Group Sales Manager:** Dan Lauer. **Receptionist:** Maria Walls.

FIELD STAFF

Manager: Dave Huppert. **Coach:** Nelson Santovenia. **Pitching Coach:** Jorge Cordova. **Trainer:** Jason Schwartzman . **Clubhouse Manager:** Bo Bianco

GAME INFORMATION

PA Announcer: Unavailable . **Official Scorer:** Ed Luteran.
Stadium Name: Joker Marchant Stadium. **Location:** Exit 33 on I-4 to 33 South, 1.5 miles on left. **Standard Game Times:** 6:30, Sat 6, Sun 1. **Ticket Price Range:** $4-7.
Visiting Club Hotel: Imperial Swan Hotel & Suites, 4141 South Florida Ave. Lakeland, FL 33813. **Telephone:** (863) 647-3000.

PALM BEACH CARDINALS

Address: 4751 Main Street, Jupiter, FL 33458.
Telephone: (561) 775-1818. **Fax:** (561) 691-6886.
E-Mail Address: f.desk@rogerdeanstadium.com. **Website:**www.palmbeachcardinals.com. **Affiliation (first year):** St. Louis Cardinals (2003). **Years in League:** 2003-

OWNERSHIP/MANAGEMENT

Owned By: St. Louis Cardinals. **Operated By:** Jupiter Stadium LTD.
General Manager, Jupiter Stadium, LTD: Mike Bauer. **Executive Assistant:** Kacey Wilcoxson. **Assistant GM, Jupiter Stadium LTD/GM Palm Beach Cardinals:** Alex Inman. **Assistant GM, Jupiter Stadium:** Unavailable. **Director, Accounting:** John McCahan. **Corporate Partnerships Manager:** Katherine Deal. **Director, Ticketing:** Haile Urquhart. **Manager, Marketing/Media Relations:** Jeffrey Draluck. **Manager, Event Services:** Alex Inman. **Director, Grounds:** Jordan Treadway. **Assistant Directors, Grounds:** Micah Bennett, Drew Wolcott. **Stadium Building Manager:** Walter Herrera. **Merchandise Manager:** Linda Hanson. **Ticket Manager:** Aimee Erbacher. **Press Box:** Natalie Bohonsky. **Office Manager:** Dianne Detling.

FIELD STAFF

Manager: Oliver Marmol. **Hitting Coach:** Ramon Ortiz. **Pitching Coach:** Randy Niemann. **Athletic Trainer:** Keith Joynt.

GAME INFORMATION

PA Announcers: John Frost, Dick Sanford, Lou Palmer. **Official Scorer:** Lou Villano.
Stadium Name: Roger Dean Stadium. **Location:** I-95 to exit 83, east on Donald Ross Road for 1/4 mile. **Standard Game Times:** 6:35 pm, Sat 5:35pm, Sun 1:05/5:05 p.m. **Ticket Price Range:** $7- $10.
Visiting Club Hotel: Fairfield Inn by Marriott, 6748 Indiantown Road, Jupiter, FL 33458. **Telephone:** (561) 748-5252.

ST. LUCIE METS

Address: 525 NW Peacock Blvd., Port St Lucie, FL 34986.
Telephone: (772) 871-2100. **Fax:** (772) 878-9802.
Website: www.stluciemets.com.
Affiliation (first year): New York Mets (1988). **Years in League:** 1988-

OWNERSHIP/MANAGEMENT

Operated by: Sterling Mets LP. **Chairman/CEO:** Fred Wilpon. **President:** Saul Katz. **COO:** Jeff Wilpon. **Executive Director, Minor League Facilities:** Paul Taglieri. **General Manager:** Traer Van Allen.
Executive Assistant: Cynthia Malaspino. **Staff Accountant:** Shannon Murray. **Director, Food/Beverage Operations:** Eric Page. **Director, Ticketing/Merchandise:** Stephen Fox. **Manager, Sales/Corporate Partnerships:** Lauren Mahoney. **Manager, Ticketing/Merchandise:** Kyle Gleockler. **Manager, Food/Beverage Operations:** John Gallagher. **Manager, Media/Broadcast Relations:** Adam MacDonald. **Manager, Group Sales/Community Relations:** Kasey Blair.

FIELD STAFF

Manager: Luis Rojas. **Hitting Coach:** Joel Fuentes. **Pitching Coach:** Phil Regan. **Trainer:** Matt Hunter. **Strength Coach:**

Dane Inderrieden.

GAME INFORMATION
PA Announcer: Evan Nine. **Official Scorer:** Unavailable.
Stadium Name: Tradition Field. **Location:** Exit 121 (St Lucie West Blvd) off I-95, east 1/2 mile, left on NW Peacock Blvd.
Standard Game Times: 6:30 pm, Sun 1. **Ticket Price Range:** $5.50-$8.50.
Visiting Club Hotel: SpringHill Suites, 2000 NW Courtyard Circle, Port St Lucie, FL 34986. **Telephone:** (772) 871-2929.

TAMPA YANKEES

Address: One Steinbrenner Drive, Tampa, FL 33614.
Telephone: (813) 875-7753. **Fax:** (813) 673-3174.
E-Mail Address: vsmith@yankees.com. **Website:** tybaseball.com.
Affiliation (first year): New York Yankees (1994). **Years in League:** 1919-27, 1957-1988, 1994-

OWNERSHIP/MANAGEMENT
Operated by: New York Yankees LP. **Principal Owner:** Harold Z Steinbrenner.
General Manager: Vance Smith. **Assistant GM, Sales/Marketing:** Matt Gess. **Community Relations Coordinator:** AmySue Manzione. **Ticket Operations:** Jennifer Magliocchetti. **Digital/Social Media Coordinator:** Jessica Lack. **Operations Coordinator:** Jeremy Ventura. **Head Groundskeeper:** Ritchie Anderson.

FIELD STAFF
Manager: Dave Bialas. **Hitting Coach:** Tom Slater. **Pitching Coach:** Tommy Phelps. **Coach:** JD Closser. **Trainer:** Michael Becker. **Strength/Conditioning:** Joe Siara.

GAME INFORMATION
Radio: www.tybaseball.com.
PA Announcer: Unavailable. **Official Scorer:** Unavailable.
Stadium Name: George M Steinbrenner Field. **Location:** I-275 to Dale Mabry Hwy, North on Dale Mabry Hwy (Facility is at corner of West Martin Luther King Blvd/Dale Mabry Hwy). **Standard Game Times:** 7 pm, Sat 6, Sun 1. **Ticket Price Range:** $4-6.
Visiting Club Hotel: Unavailable.

MIDWEST LEAGUE

Address: 210 South Michigan Street, 5th Floor-Plaza Building, South Bend, Indiana 46601.

Telephone: (574) 532-1221. **Fax:** (574) 234-4220.

E-Mail Address: mwl@midwestleague.com, dickn@sni-law.com. **Website:** www.midwestleague.com.

Years League Active: 1947-.

President/Legal Counsel/Secretary: Richard A. Nussbaum, II.

President Emeritus: George H. Spelius.

Directors: Andrew Berlin (South Bend), Stuart Katzoff (Bowling Green), Chuck Brockett (Burlington), Lew Chamberlin (West Michigan), Dennis Conerton (Beloit), Paul Davis (Clinton), Tom Dickson (Lansing), Jason Freier (Fort Wayne), David Heller (Quad Cities), Greg Seyfer (Cedar Rapids), Nicholas Sakellariadis (Dayton), Brad Seymour (Lake County), Paul Barbeau (Great Lakes), Rocky Vonachen (Peoria), Bob Froehlich (Kane County), Rob Zerjav (Wisconsin).

League Administrator: Holly Voss.

Division Structure: East—Bowling Green, Dayton, Fort Wayne, Lake County, Lansing, South Bend, Great Lakes, West Michigan. West—Beloit, Burlington, Cedar Rapids, Clinton, Kane County, Peoria, Quad Cities, Wisconsin.

Regular Season: 140 games (split schedule). **2015 Opening Date:** April 9. **Closing Date:** Sept 7.

All-Star Game: June 23 at Peoria.

Playoff Format: Eight teams qualify. First-half and second-half division winners and wild-card teams meet in best of three quarterfinal series. Winners meet in best of three series for division championships. Division champions meet in best of five series for league championship.

Roster Limit: 25 active. **Player Eligibility Rule:** No age limit. No more than two players and one player-coach on active list may have more than five years experience.

Brand of Baseball: Rawlings ROM-MID.

Umpires: Unavailable.

Richard Nussbaum

STADIUM INFORMATION

Club	Stadium	Opened	Dimensions LF	CF	RF	Capacity	2014 Att.
Beloit	Pohlman Field	1982	325	380	325	3,500	63,505
Bowling Green	Bowling Green Ballpark	2009	312	401	325	4,559	180,350
Burlington	Community Field	1947	338	403	318	3,200	70,649
Cedar Rapids	Veterans Memorial Stadium	2000	315	400	325	5,300	171,011
Clinton	Ashford University Field	1937	335	390	325	4,000	111,329
Dayton	Fifth Third Field	2000	338	402	338	7,230	573,309
Fort Wayne	Parkview Field	2009	336	400	318	8,100	406,715
Great Lakes	Dow Diamond	2007	332	400	325	5,200	230,019
Kane County	Fifth Third Bank Ballpark	1991	335	400	335	7,400	415,571
Lake County	Classic Park	2003	320	400	320	7,273	226,454
Lansing	Cooley Law School Stadium	1996	305	412	305	11,000	338,249
Peoria	Peoria Chiefs Stadium	2002	310	400	310	7,500	217,632
Quad Cities	Modern Woodmen Park	1931	343	400	318	4,024	237,005
South Bend	Coveleski Regional Stadium	1987	336	405	336	5,000	258,836
West Michigan	Fifth Third Ballpark	1994	317	402	327	10,051	391,653
Wisconsin	Fox Cities Stadium	1995	325	400	325	5,500	250,131

BELOIT SNAPPERS

Office Address: 2301 Skyline Drive, Beloit, WI 53511. **Mailing Address:** PO Box 855, Beloit, WI 53512.

Telephone: (608) 362-2272. **Fax:** (608) 362-0418.

E-Mail Address: snappy@snappersbaseball.com. **Website:** www.snappersbaseball.com.

Affiliation (first year): Oakland Athletics (2013). **Years in League:** 1982-

OWNERSHIP/MANAGEMENT

Operated by: Beloit Professional Baseball Association Inc.

Chairman: Dennis Conerton. **President:** Dennis Conerton. **Corporate Sales/Promotions:** Bill Czaja. **Director, Media Relations/Marketing:** Robert Coon. **Director, Tickets:** Kelvin Long. **Director, Community Relations/Merchandise:** Crystal Bowen. **Head Groundskeeper:** Dalton Deckert.

FIELD STAFF

Manager: Fran Riordan. **Hitting Coach:** Steve Connelly. **Pitching Coach:** Craig Lefferts. **Trainer:** Brian Thorson.

GAME INFORMATION
Radio Announcer: Dave Krapf. **No. of Games Broadcast:** Home–40. **Flagship Station:** Jacksonville Community Radio 103.5 FM.

PA Announcer: Robert Coon. **Official Scorer:** Unavailable.

Stadium Name: Pohlman Field. **Location:** I-90 to exit 185-A, right at Cranston Road for 1 1/2 miles; I-43 to Wisconsin 81 to Cranston Road, right at Cranston for 1 1/2 miles. **Standard Game Times:** 7 pm, 6:30 (April-May), Sun 2. **Ticket Price Range:** $6.50-10.

Visiting Club Hotel: Rodeway Inn, 2956 Milwaukee Rd, Beloit, WI 53511. **Telephone:** (608) 364-4000.

BOWLING GREEN HOT RODS

Address: Bowling Green Ballpark, 300 8th Avenue, Bowling Green, KY 42101.
Telephone: (270) 901-2121. **Fax:** (270) 901-2165.
E-Mail Address: fun@bghotrods.com. **Website:** www.bghotrods.com.
Affiliation (first year): Tampa Bay Rays (2009). **Years in League:** 2010-

OWNERSHIP/MANAGEMENT
Operated By: Manhattan Sports Capital Acquisition. **President/Managing Partner:** Stuart Katzoff. **Partner:** Jerry Katzoff. **General Manager/COO:** Adam Nuse. **Assistant General Manager:** Eric Leach. **Director, Finance:** Stephanie Morton. **Director, Marketing/Community Relations:** Jennifer Johnson. **Broadcast/Media Relations Manager:** Andrew Kappes. **Sports Turf Manager:** John Gides. **Director, Operations:** Jeremy Mosby. **Director, Sales:** Matt Ingram. **Director, Ballpark Entertainment:** Billy Sims-Roush. **Digital Media Manager:** Stephanie Umek. **Account Executives:** Daniel Langdon, Devin Stovall, Kyle Wolz.

FIELD STAFF
Manager: Reinaldo Ruiz. **Hitting Coach:** Dan Dement. **Pitching Coach:** Bill Moloney. **Trainer:** Nick Flynn.

GAME INFORMATION
Radio Announcer: Andrew Kappes. **No. of Games Broadcast:** 140. **Flagship Station:** WBGN 1340-AM.
PA Announcer: Unavailable. **Official Scorer:** Unavailable.
Stadium Name: Bowling Green Ballpark. **Location:** From I-65, take Exit 26 (KY-234/Cemetery Road) into Bowling Green for 3 miles, left onto College Street for .2 miles, right onto 8th Avenue. **Standard Game Times:** 7:05 pm, Sun 2:05. **Ticket Price Range:** $7-15.
Visiting Club Hotel: Jameson Inn & Suites. **Telephone:** (270) 282-7130.

BURLINGTON BEES

Office Address: 2712 Mount Pleasant St, Burlington, IA 52601. **Mailing Address:** PO Box 824, Burlington, IA 52601.
Telephone: (319) 754-5705. **Fax:** (319) 754-5882.
E-Mail Address: staff@gobees.com. **Website:** www.gobees.com.
Affiliation (first year): Los Angeles Angels (2013). **Years in League:** 1962-

OWNERSHIP/MANAGEMENT
Operated By: Burlington Baseball Association Inc.
President: Dave Walker. **General Manager:** Chuck Brockett. **Assistant GM/Director, Group Outings:** Kim Brockett. **Director, Tickets/Merchandising:** Jill Mason. **Media/Community Relations:** Michael Broskowski. **Groundskeeper:** TJ Brewer.

FIELD STAFF
Manager: Chad Tracy. **Hitting Coach:** Ryan Barba. **Pitching Coach:** Ethan Katz. **Trainer:** Chris Wells. **Strength/Conditioning:** Adam Auer.

GAME INFORMATION
Radio Announcer: Michael Broskowski. **No. of Games Broadcast:** 140. **Flagship Station:** KBUR 1490-AM.
PA Announcer: Sean Cockrell . **Official Scorer:** Ted Gutman.
Stadium Name: Community Field. **Location:** From US 34, take US 61 North to Mt. Pleasant Street, east 1/8 mile. **Standard Game Times:** 6:30 pm, Sun 2. **Ticket Price Range:** $4-8.
Visiting Club Hotel: Pzazz Best Western FunCity, 3001 Winegard Dr., Burlington, IA 52601. **Telephone:** (319) 753-2223.

CEDAR RAPIDS KERNELS

Office Address: 950 Rockford Road SW, Cedar Rapids, IA 52404. **Mailing Address:** PO Box 2001, Cedar Rapids, IA 52406.
Telephone: (319) 363-3887. **Fax:** (319) 363-5631.
E-Mail Address: kernels@kernels.com. **Website:** www.kernels.com.
Affiliation (first year): Minnesota Twins (2013). **Years in League:** 1962-

OWNERSHIP/MANAGEMENT

President: Greg Seyfer. **Chief Executive Officer:** Doug Nelson. **General Manager:** Scott Wilson. **Manager, IT/Communications:** Andrew Pantini. **Sports Turf Manager:** Jesse Roeder. **Director, Ticket/Group Sales:** Andrea Brommelkamp. **Director, Finance:** Charlie Patrick. **Sales Associate:** Morgan Hawk. **Manager, Entertainment/Community Relations:** Ryne George. **Director, Corporate Sales/Marketing:** Jessica Fergesen. **Coordinator, History:** Marcia Moran. **Manager, Ticket Office:** Sammy Brzostowski. **Manager, Stadium Operations:** Joe Krumm.

FIELD STAFF

Manager: Jake Mauer. **Hitting Coach:** Tommy Watkins. **Pitching Coach:** Henry Bonilla. **Trainer:** Curtis Simondet.

GAME INFORMATION

Radio Announcer: Morgan Hawk. **No. of Games Broadcast:** 140. **Flagship Station:** KMRY 1450-AM/93.1-FM. **PA Announcers:** Bob Hoyt, Josh Paulson. **Official Scorers:** Steve Meyer, Josh Schroeder, Shane Severson. **Stadium Name:** Perfect Game Field at Veterans Memorial Stadium. **Location:** From I-380 North, take the Wilson Ave exit, turn left on Wilson Ave, after the railroad tracks, turn right on Rockford Road, proceed .8 miles, stadium is on left; From I-380 South, exit at First Avenue, proceed to Eighth Avenue (first stop sign) and turn left, stadium entrance is on right (before tennis courts). **Standard Game Times:** 6:35 pm, Sun 2:05. **Ticket Price Range:** $7-11 in advance, $8-12 day of game. **Visiting Club Hotel:** Best Western Cooper's Mill, 100 F Ave NW, Cedar Rapids, IA 52405. **Telephone:** (319) 366-5323.

CLINTON LUMBERKINGS

Office Address: Ashford University Field, 537 Ball Park Drive, Clinton, IA 52732.
Mailing Address: PO Box 1295, Clinton, IA 52733.
Telephone: (563) 242-0727. Fax: (563) 242-1433.
E-Mail Address: lumberkings@lumberkings.com. Website: www.lumberkings.com.
Affiliation (first year): Seattle Mariners (2009). Years in League: 1956-

OWNERSHIP/MANAGEMENT

Operated By: Clinton Baseball Club Inc.
President: Paul Davis. **General Manager:** Ted Tornow. **Director, Broadcasting/Media Relations:** Mike Weisman. **Director, Operations:** Tyler Oehmen. **Director, Concessions:** Kathy Ward. **Manager, Stadium/Sportsturf:** Shaun Thomas. **Accountant:** Ryan Marcum. **Assistant Director, Operations:** Morty Kriner. **Director, Facility Compliance:** Tom Whaley. **Office Procurement Manager:** Les Moore. **Clubhouse Manager:** Jon Weinberg.

FIELD STAFF

Manager: Chris Prieto. **Coach:** Mike Kinkade. **Pitching Coach:** Cibney Bello. **Trainer:** Geoff Swanson. **Strength/Conditioning:** Taylor Nakamura.

GAME INFORMATION

Radio Announcer: Mike Weisman. **No. of Games Broadcast:** 140. **Flagship Station:** WCCI 100.3 FM. **PA Announcer:** Brad Seward. **Official Scorer:** Unavailable. **Stadium Name:** Ashford University Field. **Location:** Highway 67 North to Sixth Ave. North, right on Sixth, cross railroad tracks, stadium on right. **Standard Game Times:** 6:30 pm, Sun 2. **Ticket Price Range:** $5-8. **Visiting Club Hotel:** Oak Tree Inn, 2300 Valley W Ct., **Clinton, IA 52732. Telephone:** (563) 243-1000.

DAYTON DRAGONS

Office Address: Fifth Third Field, 220 N Patterson Blvd, Dayton, OH 45402. Mailing Address: PO Box 2107, Dayton, OH 45401.
Telephone: (937) 228-2287. Fax: (937) 228-2284.
E-Mail Address: dragons@daytondragons.com. Website: www.daytondragons.com.
Affiliation (first year): Cincinnati Reds (2000). Years in League: 2000-

OWNERSHIP/MANAGEMENT

Operated By: Palisades Arcadia Baseball LLC. **President:** Robert Murphy.
Executive Vice President: Eric Deutsch. **Executive VP/General Manager:** Gary Mayse. **VP, Accounting/Finance:** Mark Schlein. **VP, Corporate Partnerships:** Jeff Webb, Brad Eaton. **VP, Sponsor Services:** Brandy Guinaugh.
Director, Media Relations: Tom Nichols. **Director, Group Sales:** Mike Vujea. **Senior Director, Entertainment:** Kaitlin Rohrer. **Director, Entertainment:** Chelsie Cooper. **Senior Marketing Manager:** Lindsey Huerter. **Marketing Managers:** Jacob Coy, Greg Lees, Jason McKendry, Colleen Santella. **Box Office Manager:** Stefanie Mitchell. **Assistant Box Office Manager:** Katelyn Hoover. **Senior Corporate Marketing Managers:** Trafton Eutsler, Viterio Jones. **Corporate Marketing Managers:** Lance Camden, Evan Elkins, Travis Green, Andrew Hayes, Matt Heithaus, Carl Hertzberg, Sam Schneider, Jacob Swartz. **Senior Operations Director:** Joe Eaglowski. **Facilities Operations Manager:** Joe Elking. **Baseball Operations Manager:** John Wallace. **Entertainment Assistant:** Chelsie Cooper. **Manager, Retail Operations:** Zack Spencer. **Customer Service Representative:** Amber Mingus. **Office Manager/Executive Assistant to the President:** Leslie Stuck. **Staff Accountant:** Dorothy Day. **Administrative Secretary:** Barbara Van Schaik. **Sports Turf Manager:** Britt Barry. **Event Operations Manager:** Cody Oakes.

FIELD STAFF

Manager: Jose Nieves. **Hitting Coach:** Luis Bolivar. **Pitching Coach:** Tom Browning. **Coach:** Corky Miller. **Trainer:** Andrew Cleves.

GAME INFORMATION

Radio Announcers: Tom Nichols, Keith Raad. **No. of Games Broadcast:** 140. **Flagship Station:** WONE 980 AM. **Television Announcer:** Tom Nichols. **No. of Games Broadcast:** Home-25. **Flagship Station:** WHIO 7.2.

PA Announcer: Ben Oburn. **Official Scorers:** Matt Lindsay, Mike Lucas, Matt Zircher.

Stadium Name: Fifth Third Field. **Location:** I-75 South to downtown Dayton, left at First Street; I-75 North, right at First Street exit. **Ticket Price Range:** $7-$15.

Visiting Club Hotel: Courtyard by Marriott, 100 Prestige Place, Miamisburg, OH 45342. **Phone:** 937-433-3131. **Fax:** 937-433-0285.

FORT WAYNE TINCAPS

Address: 1301 Ewing St Fort Wayne, IN 46802.
Telephone: (260) 482-6400. **Fax:** (260) 471-4678.
E-Mail Address: info@tincaps.com. **Website:** www.tincaps.com.
Affiliation (first year): San Diego Padres (1999). **Years in League:** 1993-

OWNERSHIP/MANAGEMENT

Operated By: Hardball Capital. **Owner:** Jason Freier. **President:** Mike Nutter.

Vice President, Corporate Partnerships: David Lorenz. **VP, Sales/Finance:** Brian Schackow. **VP, Marketing:** Michael Limmer. **VP, Ticket Sales:** Brad Shank. **Creative Director:** Tony DesPlaines. **Video Production Manager:** Melissa Darby. **Assistant Video Production Manager:** Jared Law. **Manager, Community Engagement/Promotions:** Tara Cahill. **Manager, Broadcasting/Media Relations:** John Nolan. **Assistant Director, Group Sales:** Jared Parcell. **Senior Ticket Account Manager:** Justin Shurley. **Senior Ticket Account Manager:** Brent Harring. **Ticket Account Manager:** Austin Allen, Dalton McGill. **Corporate Partnerships Managers:** Evan Ashton, Tyler Baker. **Special Events Coordinator:** Holly Raney. **Director of Food/Beverage:** Bill Lehn. **Executive Chef/Culinary Director:** Scott Kammerer. **Catering Director:** Brandon Tinkle. **Food/Beverage Operations Manager:** Dan Krleski. **Head Groundskeeper:** Keith Winter. **Assistant Groundskeeper:** Andrew Burnette. **Director, Facilities:** Tim Burkhart. **Assistant Director, Maintenance:** Donald Miller. **Accounting Manager/Facilities Manager:** Erik Lose. **Merchandise Manager:** Jen Wall. **Human Resources Administrator/Office Manager:** Cathy Tinney.

FIELD STAFF

Manager: Francisco Morales. **Hitting Coach:** Unavailable. **Pitching Coach:** Burt Hooton.

GAME INFORMATION

Radio Announcers: John Nolan, Kevin Fitzgerald, Mike Maahs. **No. of Games Broadcast:** 140. **Flagship Station:** WKJG 1380-AM. **TV Announcers:** John Nolan, Dave Doster, Javi DeJesus. **No. of Games Broadcast:** Home−70. **Flagship Station:** XFINITY Channel 81.

PA Announcer: Jared Parcell. **Official Scorers:** Rich Tavierne, Bill Salyer, Bill Scott, Dave Coulter.

Stadium Name: Parkview Field. **Location:** 1301 Ewing St, Fort Wayne, IN, 46802 (Downtown Fort Wayne). **Ticket Price Range:** $5-$12.50.

Visiting Club Hotel: Quality Inn, 1734 West Washington Center Rd, Fort Wayne, IN, 46818 (260-489-5554).

GREAT LAKES LOONS

Address: 825 East Main St, Midland, MI 48640.
Telephone: (989) 837-2255. **Fax:** (989) 837-8780.
E-Mail Address: info@loons.com. **Website:** www.loons.com.
Affiliation (first year): Los Angeles Dodgers (2007). **Years in League:** 2007-

OWNERSHIP/MANAGEMENT

Operated By: Michigan Baseball Operations. **Stadium Ownership:** Michigan Baseball Foundation. **Founder/Foundation President:** William Stavropoulos.

President: Paul Barbeau. **Vice President/General Manager:** Scott Litle. **VP, Facilities/Operations:** Dan Straley. **VP, Finance:** Jana Chotivkova. **VP Marketing/Entertainment:** Chris Mundhenk. **General Manager, Dow Diamond Events:** Dave Gomola. **Assistant GM, Corporate Partnerships/Director, Development (MBF):** Eric Ramseyer. **VP, Talent Management/Guest Services:** Ann Craig. **Production Coordinator:** Trent Elliott. **Assistant GM, Ticket Sales:** Tiffany Wardynski. **Director, Accounting:** Jamie Start. **Director, Group Sales:** James Cahilellis, Nick Knieling. **Programming:** Matt DeVries. **Director, Ticket Sales:** Thom Pepe. **Assistant to MBF President:** Marge Parker. **Accounting Manager:** Hope Wright. **Communications Director:** Bruce Gunther. **Business Development Manager:** Tim Jacques. **Manager, Concessions:** James Reed. **Manager, Corporate Partnerships:** Eric Ramseyer. **Group Sales Coordinator:** Tyler Kring. **Retail Manager:** Jenean Clarkson. **Promotions Manager:** Amber Ferris. **Stadium Operations Manager:** Dan Straley. **GM, Food/Beverage:** Jenny Smart. **Director, Food/Beverage:** Andrea Noonan. **Head Groundskeeper:** Nick Wolcott. **Administrative Assistant:** Melissa Kehoe. **Director, Sales, 100.9-FM:** Jay Arons. **Business Manager, 100.9-FM:** Robin Gover. **General Manager, 100.9-FM:** Jerry O'Donnell.

FIELD STAFF

Manager: Bill Haselman. **Hitting Coach:** Johnny Washington. **Pitching Coach:** Bill Simas.

GAME INFORMATION

Play-by-Play Broadcaster: Brad Golder. **No. of Games Broadcast:** 140. **Flagship Station:** WLUN 100.9-FM. **PA Announcer:** Jerry O'Donnell. **Official Scorers:** Terry Wilczek, Terry Lynch. **Stadium Name:** Dow Diamond. **Location:** I-75 to US-10 W, Take the M-20/US-10 Business exit on the left toward downtown Midland, Merge onto US-10 W/MI-20 W (also known as Indian Street), Turn left onto State Street, The entrance to the stadium is at the intersection of Ellsworth and State Streets. **Standard Game Times:** 6:05 pm (April), 7:05 (May-Sept), Sun 2:05. **Ticket Price Range:** $6-9. **Visiting Club Hotel:** Holiday Inn, 810 Cinema Drive, Midland, MI 48642. **Telephone:** (989) 794-8500.

KANE COUNTY COUGARS

Address: 34W002 Cherry Lane, Geneva, IL 60134
Telephone: (630) 232-8811. **Fax:** (630) 232-8815
E-Mail Address: info@kanecountycougars.com. **Website:** www.kccougars.com
Affiliation (first year): Arizona Diamondbacks (2015). **Years in League:** 1991-

OWNERSHIP/MANAGEMENT

Operated By: Cougars Baseball Partnership/American Sports Enterprises, Inc. **Chairman/Chief Executive Officer/President:** Bob Froehlich. **Owners:** Bob Froehlich, Cheryl Froehlich. **Board of Directors:** Bob Froehlich, Cheryl Froehlich, Stephanie Froehlich, Chris Neidhart, Marianne Neidhart.
Vice President/General Manager: Curtis Haug. **Senior Director, Finance/Administration:** Douglas Czurylo. **Finance/Accounting Manager:** Lance Buhmann. **Accounting:** Sally Sullivan. **Senior Director, Ticketing:** R. Michael Patterson. **Senior Ticket Sales Representative:** Alex Miller. **Sales Representatives:** Joe Golota, Derek Weber, Sean Freed. **Sales Representative/Promotions Assistant:** Derek Harrigan. **Director, Ticket Services/Community Relations:** Amy Mason. **Senior Ticket Operations Representative:** Paul Quillia. **Ticket Operations Representative:** Jack Luse. **Director, Security:** Dan Klinkhamer. **Promotions Director:** Justin Cohen. **Director, Public Relations:** Shawn Touney. **Design/Graphics:** Emmet Broderick. **Media Placement Coordinator:** Bill Baker.
Webmaster: Kevin Sullivan. **Video Manager:** Mike Forrest. **Director, Food/Beverage:** Jon Williams. **Catering Manager:** Alexa McNeice. **Business Manager:** Robin Hull. **Concessions Manager:** Dan McIntosh. **Executive Chef:** Ron Kludac. **Senior Director, Stadium Operations:** Mike Klafehn. **Director, Maintenance:** Jeff Snyder. **Head Groundskeeper:** Dave Wasielewski.

FIELD STAFF

Manager: Mark Grudzielanek. **Hitting Coach:** Vince Harrison. **Pitching Coach:** Doug Bochtler. **Trainer:** Rafael Freitas. **Strength/Conditioning Coach:** Sean Light. **Clubhouse Manager:** Scott Anderson.

GAME INFORMATION

Radio Announcers: Wayne Randazzo, Joe Brand. **No. of Games Broadcast:** 140. **Flagship Station:** WBIG 1280-AM. **PA Announcer:** Kevin Sullivan. **Official Scorer:** Wayne Randazzo. **Stadium Name:** Fifth Third Bank Ballpark. **Location:** From east or west, I-88 Ronald Reagan Memorial Tollway) to Farnsworth Ave. North exit, north five miles to Cherry Lane, left into stadium; from northwest, I-90 (Jane Addams Memorial Tollway) to Randall Rd. South exit, south to Fabyan Parkway, east to Kirk Rd., north to Cherry Lane, left into stadium complex. **Standard Game Times:** 6:30 pm, Sun 1. **Ticket Price Range:** $9-15. **Visiting Club Hotel:** Pheasant Run Resort, 4051 E Main St, St. Charles, IL 60174. **Telephone:** (630) 584-6300.

LAKE COUNTY CAPTAINS

Address: Classic Park, 35300 Vine St., Eastlake, OH 44095-3142.
Telephone: (440) 975-8085. **Fax:** (440) 975-8958.
E-Mail Address: bseymour@captainsbaseball.com. **Website:** www.captainsbaseball.com.
Affiliation (first year): Cleveland Indians (2003). **Years in League:** 2010-

OWNERSHIP/MANAGEMENT

Operated By: Cascia LLC. **Owners:** Peter and Rita Carfagna, Ray and Katie Murphy.
Chairman/Secretary/Treasurer: Peter Carfagna. **Vice Chairman:** Rita Carfagna. **Vice President:** Ray Murphy. **VP, General Manager:** Brad Seymour. **Assistant GM, Sales:** Neil Stein.
Director, Media Relations: Craig Deas. **Manager, Promotions:** Drew LaFollette. **Director, Captains Concessions:** John Klein. **Director, Stadium Operations:** Josh Porter. **Director, Turf Operations:** Dan Stricko. **Director, Finance:** Rob Demko. **Director, Ticket Operations/Merchandise:** Jen Yorko. **Director, Ticket Sales:** Amy Gladieux. **Ticket Sales Account Executives:** Christy Buchar, Nick Dobrinich, Brian Fisher. **Office Assistant:** Jim Carfagna.

FIELD STAFF

Manager: Shaun Larkin. **Coach:** Unavailable. **Pitching Coach:** Steve Karsay.

Radio Announcer: Craig Deas. **No. of Games Broadcast:** 140. **Flagship Station:** WINT 1330-AM.
PA Announcer: George Phillips. **Official Scorers:** Glen Blabolil, Mike Mohner.
Stadium Name: Classic Park. **Location:** From Ohio State Route 2 East, exit at Ohio 91, go left and the stadium is 1/4 mile north on your right; From Ohio State Route 90 East, exit at Ohio 91, go right and the stadium in approximately five miles north on your right. **Standard Game Times:** 6:30 pm (April-May), 7 (May-Sept), Sun 1:30.
Visiting Club Hotel: Red Roof Inn 4166 State Route 306, Willoughby, Ohio 44094. **Telephone:** (440)-946-9872.

LANSING LUGNUTS

Address: 505 E Michigan Ave, Lansing, MI 48912.
Telephone: (517) 485-4500. **Fax:** (517) 485-4518.
E-Mail Address: info@lansinglugnuts.com. **Website:** www.lansinglugnuts.com.
Affiliation (first year): Toronto Blue Jays (2005). **Years in League:** 1996-

OWNERSHIP/MANAGEMENT
Operated By: Take Me Out to the Ballgame LLC. **Principal Owners:** Tom Dickson, Sherrie Myers.
General Manager: Nick Grueser. **Assistant, GM Sales:** Nick Brzezinski. **Community Relations Manager:** Angela Sees. **Director, Business Operations:** Heather Viele. **Business Coordinator:** Brianna Pfeil. **Corporate Sales Manager:** Kohl Tyrrell. **Corporate Account Executive:** Bill Adler. **Senior Group Sales Representative:** Faith Brooks. **Group Sales Representative:** Eric Pionk. **Box Office/Team Relations Manager:** Josh Calver. **Season Ticket Specialist:** Greg Kruger. **Assistant Retail Director:** Matt Hicks. **Stadium Operations Manager:** Dennis Busse. **Head Groundskeeper:** Lenny Yoder. **Senior Food/Beverage Director:** Brett Telder. **Assistant Food/Beverage Director:** Andrew Creswell. **Director, Marketing:** Linda Frederickson. **Special Events Manager:** Katie Niles. **Digital Media/Marketing Manager:** Ben Owen. **Creative Services/Production Assistant:** Ken Foldenauer. **Corporate Partnerships Manager:** Michaela Vryhof. **Corporate Partnerships Representative:** Ashley Loudan.

FIELD STAFF
Manager: Ken Huckaby. **Hitting Coach:** Kenny Graham. **Pitching Coach:** Jeff Ware. **Athletic Trainer:** Drew Macdonald.

GAME INFORMATION
Radio Announcer: Jesse Goldberg-Strassler. **No of Games Broadcast:** 140. **Flagship Station:** WQTX 92.1-FM.
PA Announcer: Unavailable. **Official Scorer:** Unavailable.
Stadium Name: Cooley Law School Stadium. **Location:** I-96 East/West to US 496, exit at Larch Street, north of Larch, stadium on left. **Ticket Price Range:** $8-$23.50.
Visiting Club Hotel: Unavailable.

PEORIA CHIEFS

Address: 730 SW Jefferson, Peoria, IL 61605.
Telephone: (309) 680-4000. **Fax:** (309) 680-4080.
E-Mail Address: feedback@chiefsnet.com. **Website:** www.peoriachiefs.com.
Affiliation (first year): St. Louis Cardinals (2013). **Years in League:** 1983-

OWNERSHIP/MANAGEMENT
Operated By: Peoria Chiefs Community Baseball Club LLC. **President:** Rocky Vonachen.
General Manager: Brendan Kelly. **Manager, Box Office:** Ryan Sivori. **Director, Media/Baseball Operations:** Nathan Baliva. **Marketing Manager:** Hannah Wolfe. **Vice President, Ticket Sales:** Jason Mott. **Manager, Entertainment/Community Relations:** Katie Nichols. **Account Executives:** Sam Connell, Matt Szczupakowski, Kate Voss. **Head Groundskeeper:** Mike Reno. **Director, Food/Beverage:** Austin Punzel.

FIELD STAFF
Manager: Joe Kruzel. **Hitting Coach:** Jobel Jimenez. **Pitching Coach:** Jason Simontacchi. **Trainer:** Michael Petrarca.

GAME INFORMATION
Radio Announcer: Nathan Baliva. **No. of Games Broadcast:** 140. **Flagship Station:** www.peoriachiefs.com, Peoria Chiefs App in iTunes.
PA Announcer: Unavailable. **Official Scorers:** Bryan Moore, Nathan Baliva.
Stadium Name: Dozer Park. **Location:** From South/East, I-74 to exit 93 (Jefferson St), continue one mile, stadium is one block on left; From North/West, I-74 to Glen Oak Exit, turn right on Glendale, which turns into Kumpf Blvd, turn right on Jefferson, stadium on left. **Standard Game Times:** 7 pm, 6:30 (April-May, after Aug 18), Sat 6:30, Sun 2. **Ticket Price Range:** $7-11.
Visiting Club Hotel: Quality Inn & Suites, 4112 Brandywine Dr, Peoria, IL, 61614. **Telephone:** (309) 685-2556.

QUAD CITIES RIVER BANDITS

Address: 209 S Gaines St, Davenport, IA 52802.
Telephone: (563) 324-3000. **Fax:** (563) 324-3109.
E-Mail Address: bandit@riverbandits.com. **Website:** www.riverbandits.com.
Affiliation (first year): Houston Astros (2013). **Years in League:** 1960-

OWNERSHIP/MANAGEMENT
Operated by: Main Street Iowa LLC, David Heller, Bob Herrfeldt.
General Manager: Andrew Chesser. **VP, Sales:** Shawn Brown. **Assistant GM, Baseball Operations:** Travis Painter. **Assistant GM, Special Events:** Taylor Satterly. **Assistant GM, Amusements:** Mike Clark. **Finance Manager:** Dustin Miller. **Director, Community Relations:** Denise Clark. **Director, Marketing/Promotions:** Alexandria Sheffler. **Director, Media Relations:** Marco LaNave. **Director, Sales/Ticketing:** Joe Kubly. **Manager, Production:** Stacy Issen. **Manager, Sales:** Paul Kleinhans-Schulz. **Manager, Special Events:** Alli Costello. **Head Groundskeeper:** Scott Blanchette. **Account Executive:** Arsal Shareef. **Director, Food/Beverage:** Patrick Delaney. **Manager, Concessions:** Michael Riffle. **Executive Chef:** Tom Whalen.

FIELD STAFF
Manager: Josh Bonifay. **Hitting Coach:** Joel Chimelis. **Pitching Coach:** Dave Borkowski. **Outfield/Baserunning Development Specialist:** Tim Garland. **Athletic Trainer:** Corey O'Brien. **Strength/Conditioning Coach:** Dwayne Peterson.

GAME INFORMATION
Radio Announcer: Marco LaNave. **No. of Games Broadcast:** 140. **Flagship Station:** 1170-AM KBOB.
PA Announcer: Scott Werling. **Official Scorer:** Unavailable.
Stadium Name: Modern Woodmen Park. **Location:** From I-74, take Grant Street exit left, west onto River Drive, left on South Gaines Street; from I-80, take Brady Street exit south, right on River Drive, left on South Gaines Street. **Standard Game Times:** 7 pm; Sat 6, Sun 1:15 (April-June/Aug 9), Sun 5:15 pm (July-Aug 2). **Ticket Price Range:** $5-13.
Visiting Club Hotel: Clarion Hotel, 5202 Brady St, Davenport, IA 52806. **Telephone:** (563) 391-1230.

SOUTH BEND CUBS

Office Address: 501 W South St, South Bend, IN 46601. **Mailing Address:** PO Box 4218, South Bend, IN 46634.
Telephone: (574) 235-9988. **Fax:** (574) 235-9950.
E-Mail Address: cubs@southbendcubs.com. **Website:** www.southbendcubs.com.
Affiliation (first year): Chicago Cubs (2015). **Years in League:** 1988-

OWNERSHIP/MANAGEMENT
Owner: Andrew Berlin.
President: Joe Hart. **Vice President/Business Development:** Nick Brown. **Assistant General Manager, Tickets:** Andy Beuster. **Assistant GM, Operations:** Peter Argueta. **Director, Finance/Human Resources:** Cheryl Carlson. **Box Office Manager:** Devon Hastings. **Director, Creative Services/Promotions:** Chris Hagstrom. **Production Manager:** Nick Ruthrauff. **Merchandise Manager:** Brandy Beehler. **Account Executives:** Mike Frissore, Mitch McKamey, Ben Wiley, Alex Withorn. **Head Groundskeeper:** Robert Sedlak. **Groundskeeper:** T.J. Wohlever. **Director, Food/ Beverage:** Nick Barkley. **Catering/Business Manager:** Katy Balcerzak.

FIELD STAFF
Manager: Jimmy Gonzalez. **Hitting Coach:** Jesus Feliciano. **Pitching Coach:** Brian Lawrence. **Assistant Coach:** Osmin Melendez. **Trainer:** Jonathan Fierro. **Strength Coach:** Unavailable.

GAME INFORMATION
Radio Announcer: Darin Pritchett. **Flagship Station:** 96.1 FM WSBT.
PA Announcer: Unavailable. **Official Scorer:** Peter Yarbro.
Stadium Name: Four Winds Field. **Location:** I-80/90 toll road to exit 77, take US 31/33 south to South Bend to downtown (Main Street), to Western Ave right on Western, left on Taylor. **Standard Game Times:** 7:05 pm, Fri 7:35, Sun 2:05. **Ticket Price Range:** Advance $9-11, Day of Game $10-12.
Visiting Club Hotel: DoubleTree by Hilton Hotel South Bend. **Telephone:**(574) 234-2000.

WEST MICHIGAN WHITECAPS

Office Address: 4500 West River Dr, Comstock Park, MI 49321. **Mailing Address:** PO Box 428, Comstock Park, MI 49321.
Telephone: (616) 784-4131. **Fax:** (616) 784-4911.
E-Mail Address: playball@whitecapsbaseball.com. **Website:** www.whitecapsbase-

ball.com.
Affiliation (first year): Detroit Tigers (1997). **Years in League:** 1994-

OWNERSHIP/MANAGEMENT
Operated By: Whitecaps Professional Baseball Corp. **Principal Owners:** Denny Baxter, Lew Chamberlin.
President: Scott Lane. **Vice President:** Jim Jarecki. **Vice President, Sales:** Steve McCarthy.
Facility Events Manager: Mike Klint. **Operations Manager:** Tyler Edema. **Director, Food/Beverage:** Matt Timon.
Community Relations Coordinator: Jessica Muzevuca. **Director, Marketing/Media:** Mickey Graham. **Promotions Manager:** Keith Roelfsema. **Multimedia Manager:** Elaine Cunningham. **Box Office Manager:** Shaun Pynnonen.
Groundskeeper: Michael Huie. **Facility Maintenance Manager:** John Passarelli. **Director, Ticket Sales:** Chad Sayen.

FIELD STAFF
Manager: Andrew Graham. **Coach:** Nelson Santovenia. **Pitching Coach:** Mike Henneman. **Trainer:** T.J. Obergefell.

GAME INFORMATION
Radio Announcers: Ben Chiswick, Dan Elve. **No. of Games Broadcast:** 140. **Flagship Station:** WBBL 107.3-FM.
PA Announcers: Mike Newell, Bob Wells. **Official Scorers:** Mike Dean, Don Thomas.
Stadium Name: Fifth Third Ballpark. **Location:** US 131 North from Grand Rapids to exit 91 (West River Drive). **Ticket Price Range:** $6-14.
Visiting Club Hotel: Holiday Inn Express-GR North, 358 River Ridge Dr NW, Walker, MI 49544. **Telephone:** (616) 647-4100.

WISCONSIN TIMBER RATTLERS

Office Address: 2400 N Casaloma Dr, Appleton, WI 54913. **Mailing Address:** PO Box 7464, Appleton, WI 54912.
Telephone: (920) 733-4152. **Fax:** (920) 733-8032.
E-Mail Address: info@timberrattlers.com. **Website:** www.timberrattlers.com.
Affiliation (first year): Milwaukee Brewers (2009). **Years in League:** 1962-

OWNERSHIP/MANAGEMENT
Operated By: Appleton Baseball Club, Inc. **Chairman:** Doug Westemeier.
President/General Manager: Rob Zerjav. **Vice President/Assistant GM:** Aaron Hahn. **Controller:** Cathy Spanbauer.
Director, Food/Beverage: Ryan Grossman. **Director, Stadium Operations/Security:** Ron Kaiser. **Director, Community Relations:** Dayna Baitinger. **Director, Media Relations:** Chris Mehring. **Corporate Partnerships:** Ryan Cunniff, Jerrad Radocay. **Director, Merchandise:** Jay Gruszynski. **Director, Tickets:** Ryan Moede. **Banquet Sales/Events Manager:** Hillary Basten. **Assistant Manager, Banquets/Events:** Kim Chonos. **Executive Chef:** Tim Hansen. **Assistant, Food/Beverage Director:** Chumley Hodgson. **Assistant Stadium Operations Manager:** Aaron Johnson. **Director, Group Sales:** Seth Merrill. **Group Sales:** Brittany Ezze, Kaitlynn Sablich. **Creative Director:** Ann Mollica. **Graphic Designer:** Jake Hansel. **Marketing Coordinator:** Hilary Bauer. **Entertainment Coordinator:** Jacob Jirschele. **Staff Accountant:** Sara Mortimer. **Production Manager:** Jarred Drake. **Clubhouse Manager:** Travis Voss. **Office Manager:** Mary Robinson.
Groundskeeper: Jake Hannes.

FIELD STAFF
Manager: Matt Erickson. **Coach:** Liu Rodriguez. **Coach:** Chuckie Caufield. **Pitching Coach:** Gary Lucas. **Trainer:** Jeff Paxson.

GAME INFORMATION
Radio Announcer: Chris Mehring. **No. of Games Broadcast:** 140. **Flagship Station:** WNAM 1280-AM. **Television Announcers:** Bob Brainerd, Dean Leisgang, Ted Stefaniak, Brad Woodall. **No. of Games Broadcast:** 43. **Television Affiliates:** Time Warner Cable SportsChannel, WACY-TV.
PA Announcer: Joey D. **Official Scorer:** Jay Gruszynski.
Stadium Name: Neuroscience Group Field at Fox Cities Stadium. **Location:** Highway 41 to Highway 15 (00) exit, west to Casaloma Drive, left to stadium. **Standard Game Times:** 7:05 pm, 6:35 (April-May), Sat 6:35, Sun 1:05. **Ticket Price Range:** $6-25.
Visiting Club Hotel: Microtel Inn & Suites, 321 Metro Dr, Appleton, WI 54913. **Telephone:** (920) 997-3121.

SOUTH ATLANTIC LEAGUE

SOUTH ATLANTIC LEAGUE
"THE LEAGUE OF CHOICE" EST. 1903

Address: 13575 58th Street North, Suite 141, Clearwater, FL 33760-3721.
Telephone: (727) 538-4270. **Fax:** (727) 499-6853.
E-Mail Address: office@saloffice.com. **Website:** www.southatlanticleague.com.
Years League Active: 1904-1964, 1979-
President/Secretary/Treasurer: Eric Krupa.
First Vice President: Chip Moore (Rome). **Second VP:** Craig Brown (Greenville).
Directors: Don Beaver (Hickory), Cooper Brantley (Greensboro), Craig Brown (Greenville), Brian DeWine (Asheville), Joseph Finley (Lakewood), Jason Freier (Savannah), Marvin Goldklang (Charleston), Chip Moore (Rome), Bruce Quinn (Hagerstown), Brad Smith (Kannapolis), Andy Shea (Lexington), Jeff Eiseman (Augusta), Tom Volpe (Delmarva), Tim Wilcox (West Virginia).
Division Structure: North—Delmarva, Greensboro, Hagerstown, Hickory, Kannapolis, Lakewood, West Virginia. South—Asheville, Augusta, Charleston, Greenville, Lexington, Rome, Savannah.
Regular Season: 140 games (split schedule). **2015 Opening Date:** April 9. **Closing Date:** Sept 7.
All-Star Game: June 23 at Asheville.
Playoff Format: First-half and second-half division winners meet in best of three series. Winners meet in best of five series for league championship.
Roster Limit: 25 active. **Player Eligibility Rule:** No age limit. No more than two players and one player-coach on active list may have more than five years of experience.
Brand of Baseball: Rawlings.
Umpires: Tucker Beneville (Efland, NC), Grant Conrad (Lafayette, LA), Tyler Ferguson (Stayton, OR), Derek Gonzales (Orem, UT), Christopher Lloyd (Long Beach, CA), Takahito Matsuda (Seiyo, Ehime, Japan), Edwin Moscoso (Palo Nego, Aragua, Venezuela), Justin Robinson (St. Louis, MO), Randy Rosenberg (Arlington, VA), Patrick Sharshel (Highlands Ranch, CO), Alexis Trujillo (Stockton, CA), Kyle Wallace (San Antonio, TX), Ronald Whiting (Fairmont, WV).

Eric Krupa

STADIUM INFORMATION

| Club | Stadium | Opened | Dimensions | | | Capacity | 2014 Att. |
			LF	CF	RF		
Asheville	McCormick Field	1992	326	373	297	4,000	174,893
Augusta	Lake Olmstead Stadium	1995	330	400	330	4,322	169,194
Charleston	Joseph P. Riley Jr. Ballpark	1997	306	386	336	5,800	280,075
Delmarva	Arthur W. Perdue Stadium	1996	309	402	309	5,200	210,130
Greensboro	NewBridge Bank Park	2005	322	400	320	7,599	369,170
Greenville	Fluor Field	2006	310	400	302	5,000	346,187
Hagerstown	Municipal Stadium	1931	335	400	330	4,600	61,683
Hickory	L.P. Frans Stadium	1993	330	401	330	5,062	148,414
Kannapolis	CMC-NorthEast Stadium	1995	330	400	310	4,700	119,377
Lakewood	FirstEnergy Park	2001	325	400	325	6,588	380,573
Lexington	Whitaker Bank Ballpark	2001	320	401	318	6,033	282,158
Rome	State Mutual Stadium	2003	335	400	330	5,100	177,531
Savannah	Historic Grayson Stadium	1941	290	410	310	8,000	124,013
West Virginia	Appalachian Power Park	2005	330	400	320	4,300	140,484

ASHEVILLE TOURISTS

Address: McCormick Field, 30 Buchanan Place, Asheville, NC 28801.
Telephone: (828) 258-0428. **Fax:** (828) 258-0320.
E-Mail Address: info@theashevilletourists.com. **Website:** www.theashevilletourists.com.
Affiliation (first year): Colorado Rockies (1994). **Years in League:** 1976-

OWNERSHIP/MANAGEMENT
Operated By: DeWine Seeds Silver Dollar Baseball, LLC. **President:** Brian DeWine.
General Manager: Larry Hawkins. **Assistant General Manager:** Jon Clemmons. **Senior Sales Executive:** Chris Smith. **Box Office Manager:** Megan Lachey. **Business Manager:** Ryan Straney. **Community Relations Manager:** Michelle Buss. **Manager, Media Relations/Broadcasting:** Doug Maurer. **Group Sales Associates:** Dave McKurth, Samantha Fischer, Eliot Williams, Ryan Smith. **Outside Sales Associate:** Bob Jones. **Stadium Operations Director:** Patrick Spence. **Senior Director of Food & Beverage:** Nick Wardell (Pro Sports Catering). **Head Groundskeeper:** Matt Dierdorff. **Publications/Website:** Bill Ballew.

FIELD STAFF
Manager: Warren Schaeffer. **Hitting Coach:** Mike Devereaux. **Pitching Coach:** Mark Brewer. **Development Supervisor:** Marv Foley:

GAME INFORMATION

Radio Announcer: Doug Maurer. **No. of Games Broadcast:** 140. **Flagship Station:** WRES 100.7-FM.
PA Announcer: Rick Rice. **Official Scorer:** Jim Baker, Steven Grandy.
Stadium Name: McCormick Field. **Location:** I-240 to Charlotte Street South exit, south one mile on Charlotte, left on McCormick Place. **Ticket Price Range:** $6-11.50.
Visiting Club Hotel: Quality Inn, 1 Skyline Drive, Arden, NC 28704. **Telephone:** (828) 684-6688.

AUGUSTA GREENJACKETS

Office Address: 78 Milledge Rd, Augusta, GA 30904. **Mailing Address:** PO Box 3746 Hill Station, Augusta, GA 30914.
Telephone: (706) 922-WINS(9467). **Fax:** (706) 736-1122.
E-Mail Address: info@greenjacketsbaseball.com. **Website:** www.greenjacketsbaseball.com.
Affiliation (first year): San Francisco Giants (2005). **Years in League:** 1988-

OWNERSHIP/MANAGEMENT

Ownership Group: AGON Sports & Entertainment. **Owner:** Chris Schoen. **President:** Jeff Eiseman.
General Manager: Tom Denlinger. **Assistant GM:** Brandon Greene. **Director, Ticket Sales:** Mike Van Hise. **Accounting:** Debbie Brown. **Corporate Sales Manager:** Dan Szatkowski. **Stadium Operations Manager:** David Ryther. **Promotions/Marketing Coordinator:** Caitlyn Smith. **Assistant Ticket Sales Manager:** Keaton Kovacs. **Account Executive:** Jon Fonvielle. **Group Sales Executive:** Derek Herron. **Groundskeeper:** Zach Severns.

FIELD STAFF

Manager: Nestor Rojas. **Hitting Coach:** Todd Linden. **Pitching Coach:** Jerry Cram. **Coach:** Hector Borg.

GAME INFORMATION

PA Announcer: Unavailable.
Stadium Name: Lake Olmstead Stadium. **Location:** I-20 to Washington Road exit, east to Broad Street exit, left on Milledge Road. **Standard Game Times:** 7 pm; Sun 2. **Ticket Price Range:** $7-15.
Visiting Club Hotel: Quality Inn, 1455 Walton Way, Augusta, GA 30901. **Telephone:** (706) 722-2224.

CHARLESTON RIVERDOGS

Office Address: 360 Fishburne St, Charleston, SC 29403. **Mailing Address:** PO Box 20849, Charleston, SC 29413.
Telephone: (843) 723-7241. **Fax:** (843) 723-2641.
E-Mail Address: admin@riverdogs.com. **Website:** www.riverdogs.com.
Affiliation (first year): New York Yankees (2005). **Years in League:** 1973-78, 1980-

OWNERSHIP/MANAGEMENT

Operated by: The Goldklang Group/South Carolina Baseball Club LP.
Chairman: Marv Goldklang. **President:** Mike Veeck. **Director, Fun:** Bill Murray. **Co-Owners:** Peter Freund, Gene Budig, Al Phillips.
Executive Vice President/General Manager: Dave Echols. **VP, Corporate Sales:** Andy Lange. **VP, Special Events:** Melissa Azevedo. **Assistant GM:** Ben Abzug. **Director, Marketing:** Noel Blaha. **Director, Promotions:** Joey Cain. **Director, Broadcasting/Media Relations:** Dan Acheson. **Director, Food/Beverage:** Josh Shea. **Director, Merchandise:** Mike DeAntonio. **Director, Community Relations:** Haley Kirchner. **Director, Ticket Sales:** Jake Terrell. **Business Manager:** Dale Stickney. **Box Office Manager:** Erin Killian. **Special Events Manager:** Kristen Wolfe. **Food/Beverage Manager:** Jay Weekley. **Sales Representative:** Ryan Gill, Will Senn. **Operations Assistant:** Harris Seletsky. **Head Groundskeeper:** Mike Williams. **Clubhouse Manager:** Kenneth Bassett.

FIELD STAFF

Manager: Luis Dorante. **Hitting Coach:** Greg Colbrunn. **Pitching Coach:** Tim Norton. **Coach:** Travis Chapman. **Trainer:** Jimmy Downam. **Strength/Conditioning Coach:** Anthony Velazquez.

GAME INFORMATION

Radio Announcer: Dan Acheson. **No. of Games Broadcast:** 140. **Flagship Station:** WTMA 1250-AM.
PA Announcer: Unavailable. **Official Scorer:** Mike Hoffman.
Stadium Name: Joseph Riley Jr. Ballpark. **Location:** 360 Fishburne St, Charleston, SC 29403, From US 17, take Lockwood Dr. North, right on Fishburne St. **Standard Game Times:** 7:05pm, Sat 6:05pm, Sun 5:05. **Ticket Price Range:** $5-18.
Visiting Club Hotel: Unavailable.

DELMARVA SHOREBIRDS

Office Address: 6400 Hobbs Rd, Salisbury, MD 21804. **Mailing Address:** PO Box 1557, Salisbury, MD 21802.
 Telephone: (410) 219-3112. **Fax:** (410) 219-9164.
 E-Mail Address: info@theshorebirds.com. **Website:** www.theshorebirds.com.
 Affiliation (first year): Baltimore Orioles (1997). **Years in League:** 1996-

OWNERSHIP/MANAGEMENT

 Operated By: 7th Inning Stretch, LP. **Directors:** Tom Volpe, Pat Filippone.
 General Manager: Chris Bitters. **Assistant GM:** Jimmy Sweet. **Director, Community Relations/Marketing:** Shawn Schoolcraft. **Business Development Executive:** Alyssa Dooyema. **Director, Tickets:** Brandon Harms. **Group Sales Manager:** Andrew Bryda. **Box Office Manager:** Benjamin Posner. **Ticket Sales Account Executives:** Zac Penman, Eric Sichau, Skip Krantz. **Director, Stadium Operations:** Matt Bernhardt. **Head Groundskeeper:** Tim Young. **Director, Broadcasting:** Doug Newton. **Communications Services Coordinator:** Steve Uhlmann. **Accounting Manager:** Gail Potts. **Office Manager:** Audrey Vane.

FIELD STAFF

 Manager: Ryan Minor. **Hitting Coach:** Howie Clark. **Pitching Coach:** Blaine Beatty. **Athletic Trainer:** Trek Schuler.

GAME INFORMATION

 Radio Announcer: Doug Newton. **No. of Games Broadcast:** 140. **Flagship Station:** 960 WTGM.
 PA Announcer: Unavailable. **Official Scorer:** Gary Hicks.
 Stadium Name: Arthur Perdue Stadium. **Location:** From US 50 East, right on Hobbs Rd; From US 50 West, left on Hobbs Road. **Standard Game Time:** 7:05 pm. **Ticket Price Range:** $8-13.
 Visiting Club Hotel: Sleep Inn, 406 Punkin Court, Salisbury, MD 21804. **Telephone:** (410) 572-5516.

GREENSBORO GRASSHOPPERS

Address: 408 Bellemeade St, Greensboro, NC 27401.
 Telephone: (336) 268-2255. **Fax:** (336) 273-7350.
 E-Mail Address: info@gsohoppers.com. **Website:** www.gsohoppers.com.
 Affiliation (first year): Miami Marlins (2003). **Years in League:** 1979-

OWNERSHIP/MANAGEMENT

 Operated By: Greensboro Baseball LLC. **Principal Owners:** Cooper Brantley, Wes Elingburg, Len White.
 President/General Manager: Donald Moore. **Vice President, Baseball Operations:** Katie Dannemiller. **CFO:** Benjamin Martin. **Assistant GM/Head Groundskeeper:** Jake Holloway. **Assistant GM, Sales/Marketing:** Tim Vangel. **Director, Ticket Sales:** Erich Dietz. **Director, Promotions/Community Relations:** Courtney Campbell. **Director, Production/Entertainment:** Shawn Russell. **Director, Creative Services:** Amanda Williams. **Office Administrator:** Hillary Overmyer. **Senior Sales Associate:** Todd Olson. **Sales Associate:** Daniel Midkiff. **Sales Associate:** Stephen Johnson. **Director, Stadium Operations:** Tim Hardin. **Assistant Groundskeeper:** Kaid Musgrave.

FIELD STAFF

 Manager: Kevin Randel. **Coach:** Unavailable. **Pitching Coach:** Jeremy Powell. **Trainer:** Ben Cates.

GAME INFORMATION

 Radio Announcer: Andy Durham. **No. of Games Broadcast:** 140. **Flagship Station:** WPET 950-AM.
 PA Announcer: Jim Scott. **Official Scorer:** Wayne Butler.
 Stadium Name: NewBridge Bank Park. **Location:** From I-85, take Highway 220 South (exit 36) to Coliseum Blvd, continue on Edgeworth Street,ballpark at corner of Edgeworth and Bellemeade Streets. **Standard Game Times:** 7 pm, Sun 4. **Ticket Price Range:** $7-11.00.
 Visiting Club Hotel: Days Inn 6102 Landmark Center Boulevard, Greensboro, NC 27407. **Telephone:** (336) 553-2763.

GREENVILLE DRIVE

Address: 945 South Main St, Greenville, SC 29601
Telephone: (864) 240-4500. **Fax:** (864) 240-4501.
E-Mail Address: info@greenvilledrive.com. **Website:** www.greenvilledrive.com.
Affiliation (first year): Boston Red Sox (2005) Years in League: 2005-

OWNERSHIP/MANAGEMENT
Operated By: Greenville Drive, LLC. **Co-Owner/President:** Craig Brown.
General Manager: Eric Jarinko. **Executive Vice President:** Nate Lipscomb. **VP, Finance:** Eric Blagg. **VP, Sales:** Kevin Jenko. **Senior Director, Business Development:** Emily Dymski. **Director, Game Entertainment:** Sam LoBosco. **Director, Events/Community Relations:** Jennifer Brown. **Media Relations Manager:** Cameron White. **Marketing Manager:** Alex Fiedler. **Creative Services Manager:** Clint Boyleston. **Creative Services Manager:** James Fowler. **Account Executives:** Thomas Berryhill, Daniel Medvedev. **Inside Sales Representative:** Matthew Tezza. **Box Office/Merchandise Manager:** Steve Seman. **Merchandise Operations Manager:** Corey Brothers. **Box Office Operations Manager:** Joseph Talbert. **Director, Food/Beverage:** Matt Weeks. **Director, Operations:** Eric Anastasi. **Head Groundskeeper:** Greg Burgess. **Assistant Groundskeeper:** Chris Rinebold. **General Accountant:** Joe Persia. **Office Manager:** Laura Wade.

FIELD STAFF
Manager: Darren Fenster. **Hitting Coach:** Nelson Paulino. **Pitching Coach:** Walter Miranda. **Head Athletic Trainer:** Satoshi Kajiyama.

GAME INFORMATION
Radio Announcer: Ed Jenson. **No. of Games Broadcast:** Home-70, Away-16. **Flagship Station:** www.greenvilledrive.com.
PA Announcer: Doug Mayer. **Official Scorer:** Jordan Caskey. **Stadium Name:** Fluor Field at the West End. **Location:** From south, I-85N to exit 42 toward downtown Greenville, turn left onto Augusta Road, stadium is two miles on the left; From north, I-85S to I-385 toward Greenville, turn left onto Church Street, turn right onto University Ridge. **Standard Game Times:** 7:05 PM, Sun 4:05 PM. **Ticket Price Range:** $6-9.
Visiting Club Hotel: Baymont Inn and Suites, 246 Congaree Road, Greenville, SC 29607. **Telephone:** (864) 288-1200.

HAGERSTOWN SUNS

Address: 274 E Memorial Blvd, Hagerstown, MD 21740.
Telephone: (301) 791-6266. **Fax:** (301) 791-6066.
E-Mail Address: info@hagerstownsuns.com. **Website:** www.hagerstownsuns.com.
Affiliation (first year): Washington Nationals (2007). **Years in League:**1993-

OWNERSHIP/MANAGEMENT
Principal Owner/Operated by: Hagerstown Baseball LLC. **President:** Bruce Quinn.
General Manager: Chris Easom. **Assistant GM:** Bob Bruchey. **Director, Media Relations:** Eli Pearlstein. **Director, F&B/Stadium Operations:** Andrew Houston. **Manager, Promotions/Game Day Production:** Ashley Bowling. **Manager, Box Office/Ticket Operations:** Brice Ballentine. **Group Sales Assistant:** Shane Ganley.

FIELD STAFF
Manager: Patrick Anderson. **Hitting Coach:** Luis Ordaz. **Pitching Coach:** Sam Narron. **Trainer:** Don Neidig.

GAME INFORMATION
Radio Announcer: Eli Pearlstein. **No. of Games Broadcast:** Home-70. **Flagship Station:** WJEJ-1240 AM.
PA Announcer: Rick Reeder. **Official Scorer:** Will Kauffman.
Stadium Name: Municipal Stadium. **Location:** Exit 32B (US 40 West) on I-70 West, left at Eastern Boulevard; Exit 6A (US 40 East) on I-81, right at Eastern Boulevard. **Standard Game Times:** 7:05 pm, Sun 3:05. **Ticket Price Range:** $9-12.
Visiting Club Hotel: Unavailable.

HICKORY CRAWDADS

Office Address: 2500 Clement Blvd. NW, Hickory, NC 28601. **Mailing Address:** PO Box 1268, Hickory, NC 28603.
   Telephone: (828) 322-3000. **Fax:** (828) 322-6137.
   E-Mail Address: crawdad@hickorycrawdads.com. **Website:** www.hickorycrawdads.com.
   Affiliation (first year): Texas Rangers (2009). **Years in League:** 1952, 1960, 1993-

OWNERSHIP/MANAGEMENT

   Operated by: Hickory Baseball Inc. **Principal Owners:** Don Beaver, Luther Beaver, Charles Young.
   President: Don Beaver. **General Manager:** Mark Seaman. **Assistant GM:** Charlie Downs. **Director, Promotions:** Pete Subsara. **Director, Broadcasting/Media Relations:** Aaron Cox. **Business Manager:** Donna White. **Director, Community Relations/Events:** Megan Meade. **Clubhouse Manager:** Mitch Brasher. **Director, Ticket Operations:** Gian D'Amico. **Director, Creative Services:** Crystal Lin. **Director, Group Sales:** Travis Gortman. **Executive Director, Sales/Merchandise:** Douglas Locascio. **Head Groundskeeper:** Zach Van Voorhees. **Director, Food/Beverage:** Teddy Ingraham. **Group Sales Executives:** Zach Miller, Kyle May.

FIELD STAFF

   Manager: Corey Ragsdale. **Hitting Coach:** Josue Perez. **Pitching Coach:** Oscar Marin. **Trainer:** Sean Fields. **Strength/Conditioning:** Wade Lamont.

GAME INFORMATION

   Radio Announcer: Aaron Cox. **No. of Games Broadcast:** 140. **Flagship Station:** hickorycrawdads.com.
   PA Announcers: Ralph Mangum, Jason Savage, Steve Jones. **Official Scorers:** Mark Parker, Paul Fogelman.
   Stadium Name: LP Frans Stadium. **Location:** I-40 to exit 123 (Lenoir North), 321 North to Clement Blvd, left for 1/2 mile. **Standard Game Times:** 7 pm, Sun 5.
   Visiting Club Hotel: Crowne Plaza, 1385 Lenior-Rhyne Boulevard SE, Hickory, NC 28602. **Telephone:** (828) 323-1000.

KANNAPOLIS INTIMIDATORS

Office Address: 2888 Moose Road, Kannapolis, NC 28083. **Mailing Address:** PO Box 64, Kannapolis, NC 28082.
   Telephone: (704) 932-3267. **Fax:** (704) 938-7040.
   E-Mail Address: info@intimidatorsbaseball.com. **Website:** www.intimidatorsbaseball.com. **Affiliation (first year):** Chicago White Sox (2001). **Years in League:** 1995-

OWNERSHIP/MANAGEMENT

   Operated by: Smith Family Baseball Inc. **President:** Brad Smith.
   General Manager: Randy Long. **Head Groundskeeper:** Billy Ball. **Director, Stadium Operations:** Darren Cozart. **Director, Communications:** Josh Feldman. **Assistant Groundskeeper:** Mitchell Hooten.

FIELD STAFF

   Manager: Tommy Thompson. **Hitting Coach:** Robert Sasser. **Pitching Coach:** Jose Bautista. **Trainer:** James Kruk. **Strength/Conditioning Coach:** George Timke.

GAME INFORMATION

   Radio Announcer: Josh Feldman. **No. of Games Broadcast:** All 140 games. **Flagship Station:** www.intimidators-baseball.com.
   PA Announcer: Sean Fox. **Official Scorer:** Brent Stastny.
   Stadium Name: CMC-NorthEast Stadium. **Location:** Exit 63 on I-85, west on Lane Street to Stadium Drive. **Standard Game Times:** 7:05 pm, Sun 5:05. **Ticket Price Range:** $5-$10.
   Visiting Club Hotel: Spring Hill Suites. **Address:** 7811 Gateway Lane NW, Concord, NC 28027. **Telephone:** (704) 979-2500.

LAKEWOOD BLUECLAWS

Address: 2 Stadium Way, Lakewood, NJ 08701.
Telephone: (732) 901-7000. **Fax:** (732) 901-3967.
E-Mail Address: info@blueclaws.com. **Website:** www.blueclaws.com
Affiliation (first year): Philadelphia Phillies (2001). **Years in League:** 2001-

OWNERSHIP/MANAGEMENT

Operated by: American Baseball Company LLC. **President:** Joseph Finley.
Chief Revenue/Operating Officer: Adam Lorber. **Senior Vice President, Business Operations:** Chris Tafrow. **VP, Ticket Sales/Service:** Jim McNamara. **VP, Sponsorship:** Zack Rosenberg. **VP, Operations/Special Events:** Steve Farago. **Chief Financial Officer:** Bernadette Miller. **Front Office Manager:** JoAnne Bell. **Director, Community Relations:** Jim DeAngelis. **Director, Media Relations:** Greg Giombarrese. **Director, Outside Sales:** Mike Ryan. **Director, Ticket Sales:** Rob Vota. **Director, Group Sales:** Kevin Fenstermacher. **Director, Food/Beverage:** Kyle Lindquist. **Director, Grounds:** Mike Morvay.
Sponsorship Sales Managers: Dave Ricci, Wade Johnson, David Houck. **Manager, Marketing/Sponsorship Services:** Zack Nicol. **Ticket Sales Managers:** Sean Mihalik, Vicki Pumpple, Greg Heroy. **Ticket Operations Manager:** Libby Rowe. **Ticket Service Coordinator:** Paige Selle. **Ticket Service Coordinator:** Garrett Herr. **Group Sales Managers:** Joe Pilon, Rob McGillick, Andrew Gilberti, Matt Freeman, Kyle Volp, Frank Skrajewski, Brittany Sullivan, Mike Kasel. **Marketing Manager:** Jamie Stone. **Events/Operations Manager:** Kevin Moodhe. **Merchandise Manager:** Lisa Szymendera.

FIELD STAFF

Manager: Shawn Williams. **Hitting Coach:** Nelson Prada. **Pitching Coach:** Aaron Fultz.

GAME INFORMATION

Radio Announcers: Greg Giombarrese. **No. of Games Broadcast:** 140. **Flagship Station:** WOBM 1160-AM.
PA Announcers: Kevin Clark. **Official Scorers:** Joe Bellina.
Stadium Name: FirstEnergy Park. **Location:** Route 70 to New Hampshire Avenue, North on New Hampshire for 2.5 miles to ballpark. **Standard Game Times:** 7:05 pm, 6:35 pm (April-May); Sun 1:05, 5:05 (July-Aug). **Ticket Price Range:** $7-12.
Visiting Team Hotel: Clarion Hotel Toms River, 815 Route 37 West, Toms River, NJ 08755. **Telephone:** (732) 341-3400.

LEXINGTON LEGENDS

Address: 207 Legends Lane, Lexington, KY 40505.
Telephone: (859) 252-4487. **Fax:** (859) 252-0747.
E-Mail Address: webmaster@lexingtonlegends.com. **Website:** www.lexingtonle-gends.com.
Affiliation (first year): Kansas City Royals (2013). **Years in League:** 2001-

OWNERSHIP/MANAGEMENT

Operated By: STANDS LLC. **Principal Owner:** Susan Martinelli Shea. **CEO:** Andy Shea.
Executive Vice President/General Manager: Gary Durbin. **Director, Stadium Operations/Manager, Human Resources:** Shannon Kidd. **Business Manager:** Tina Wright. **Senior Corporate Accounts Manager:** Jeremy Dixon. **Director, Ticket Operations:** David Barry. **Creative Marketing Director:** Ty Cobb. **Director, Broadcasting/Media Relations:** Keith Elkins. **Senior Account Executive:** Ron Borkowski. **Director, Community Relations/Special Events:** Sarah Bosso. **Audio Visual Production Manager:** Nick Juhasz. **Head Groundskeeper:** Jason Boston. **Facility Specialist:** Steve Moore.

FIELD STAFF

Manager: Omar Ramirez. **Hitting Coach:** Damon Hollins. **Pitching Coach:** Carlos Reyes. **Bench Coach:** Glenn Hubbard. **Athletic Trainer:** Mark Keiser.

GAME INFORMATION

Radio Announcer: Keith Elkins. **No. of Games Broadcast:** 140. **Flagship Station:** WLXG 1300-AM.
PA Announcer: Ty Cobb. **Official Scorer:** Unavailable.
Stadium Name: Whitaker Bank Ballpark. **Location:** From I-64/75, take exit 113, right onto North Broadway toward downtown Lexington for 1.2 miles, past New Circle Road (Highway 4), right into stadium, located adjacent to Northland Shopping Center. **Standard Game Times:** 7:05 pm, Sun 2:05 (through May 31), 6:05 (June-Aug). **Ticket Price Range:** $4-$24.
Visiting Club Hotel: Ramada Inn and Conference Center, 2143 N Broadway, Lexington, KY 40505. **Telephone:** (859) 299-1261.

ROME BRAVES

Office Address: State Mutual Stadium, 755 Braves Blvd, Rome, GA 30161. **Mailing Address:** PO Box 1915, Rome, GA 30162-1915.
Telephone: (706) 378-5100. **Fax:** (706) 368-6525.
E-Mail Address: rome.braves@braves.com. **Website:** www.romebraves.com.
Affiliation (first year): Atlanta Braves (2003). **Years in League:** 2003-

OWNERSHIP MANAGEMENT

Operated By: Atlanta National League Baseball Club Inc.
General Manager: Michael Dunn. **Assistant GM:** Jim Jones.
Director, Stadium Operations: Eric Allman. **Director, Ticket Manager:** Jeff Fletcher. **Director, Culinary Director:** Owen Reppert. **Director, Food/Beverage:** Brad Smith. **Special Projects Manager:** Erin White. **Administrative Manager:** Christina Shaw. **Account Representatives:** Dale Billodeaux, Katie Aspin. **Head Groundskeeper:** Phil Grefrath. **Retail Manager:** Starla Roden. **Warehouse Operations Manager:** Morgan McPherson. **Neighborhood Outreach Coordinator:** Laura Harrison.

FIELD STAFF

Manager: Randy Ingle. **Coach:** Bobby Moore. **Pitching Coach:** Gabe Luckert. **Trainer:** Kyle Damschroder.

GAME INFORMATION

Radio Announcer: Kevin Karel. **No. of Games Broadcast:** 140. **Flagship Station:** 99.5 FM The Jock, RomeBraves.com (home games).
PA Announcer: Tony McIntosh. **Official Scorers:** Jim O'Hara, Lyndon Huckaby.
Stadium Name: State Mutual Stadium. **Location:** I-75 North to exit 190 (Rome/Canton), left off exit and follow Highway 411/Highway 20 to Rome, right at intersection on Highway 411 and Highway 1 (Veterans Memorial Highway), stadium is at intersection of Veterans Memorial Highway and Riverside Parkway. **Ticket Price Range:** $4-10.
Visiting Club Hotel: Days Inn, 840 Turner McCall Blvd, Rome, GA 30161. **Telephone:** (706) 295-0400.

SAVANNAH SAND GNATS

Office Address: 1401 E Victory Dr, Savannah, GA 31404. **Mailing Address:** PO Box 3783, Savannah, GA 31414.
Telephone: (912) 351-9150. **Fax:** (912) 352-9722.
E-Mail Address: info@sandgnats.com. **Website:** www.sandgnats.com.
Affiliation (first year): New York Mets (2007). **Years in League:** 1904-1915, 1936-1960, 1962, 1984-

OWNERSHIP/MANAGEMENT

Operated By: Savannah Professional Baseball, LLC. **President:** John Katz. **Vice President:** Scott Burton.
Director, Business Development: Brittany Petersen. **Director, Marketing/Promotions:** Jonathan Mercier. **Director, Ticketing Operations:** Joe Shepard. **Head Groundskeeper:** Cameron Richardson. **Communications/Graphics Manager:** Jeff Berger. **Groups/Hospitality Manager:** Scotty Rhodes. **Food/Beverage Manager:** Josh Andrews. **Account Executives:** Jeremy Keen, Matthew Strader, Robert Willis and Dalton Workman.

FIELD STAFF

Manager: Jose Leger. **Hitting Coach:** Valentino Pascucci. **Pitching Coach:** Marc Valdes. **Trainer:** Eric Velazquez.

GAME INFORMATION

Radio Announcer: Toby Hyde. **No. of Games Broadcast:** 140. **Flagship Station:** WBMQ 960-AM.
PA Announcer: Sean Brown. **Official Scorer:** Steven Linsday.
Stadium Name: Historic Grayson Stadium. **Location:** From I-16 E to 37th St. exit, left on 37th, right on Abercorn St., left on Victory Drive; From I-95 to exit 16, east on 204, right on Victory Drive, Stadium is on right in Daffin Park. **Standard Game Times:** 7:05 pm, Sat 6:05, Sun 2:05. **Ticket Price Range:** $7-10.
Visiting Club Hotel: Unavailable.

WEST VIRGINIA POWER

Address: 601 Morris St, Suite 201, Charleston, WV 25301.
Telephone: (304) 344-2287. **Fax:** (304) 344-0083.
E-Mail Address: info@wvpower.com. **Website:** www.wvpower.com
Affiliation (first year): Pittsburgh Pirates (2009) **Years in League:** 1987-

OWNERSHIP/MANAGEMENT

Operated By: West Virginia Baseball, LLC. **Managing Partner:** Tim Wilcox. **Executive Vice President:** Ken Fogel. **General Manager:** Tim Mueller. **Assistant GM, Operations:** Jeremy Taylor. **Merchandise Manager:** Nick Crawford. **Accountant:** Darren Holstein. **Director, Marketing/Media:** Adam Marco. **Head Groundskeeper:** Chris Mason. **Director, Food/Beverage:** Nate Michel. **Box Office Manager:** Nikki Mirth. **Group Sales Manager:** Gary Olson. **Client Services/Entertainment Manager:** Jordan Pence. **Account Executive:** John Schraer. **Production Manager:** Jay Silverman.

FIELD STAFF

Manager: Brian Esposito. **Coach:** Keoni Di Renne. **Pitching Coach:** Mark DiFelice.

GAME INFORMATION

Radio Announcer: Adam Marco. **No. of Games Broadcast:** 140. **Flagship Stations:** ESPN 104.5 FM, WSWW 1490-AM. **PA Announcer:** Unavailable. **Official Scorer:** Unavailable.
Stadium Name: Appalachian Power Park. **Location:** I-77 South to Capitol Street exit, left on Lee Street, left on Brooks Street. **Standard Game Times:** 7:05 pm, Sun 2:05. **Ticket Price Range:** $7-11.
Visiting Club Hotel: Charleston Capitol Hotel,1000 Washington Street East, Charleston, WV 25301. **Telephone:** (304) 343-4661.

NEW YORK-PENN LEAGUE

Address: 204 37th Ave. North, #366, St. Petersburg, Florida 33704.
Telephone: (727) 289-7112. **Fax:** (727) 683-9691.
Website: www.newyork-pennleague.com.
Years League Active: 1939-

President: Ben Hayes.
President Emeritus: Robert Julian. **Treasurer:** Jon Dandes (West Virginia). **Secretary:** Doug Estes (Williamsport).
Directors: Tim Bawmann (Lowell), Steve Cohen (Brooklyn), Jon Dandes (West Virginia), Tim Lewis (Aberdeen), Doug Selby (Auburn), Bill Gladstone (Tri-City), Marvin Goldklang (Hudson Valley), Chuck Greenberg (State College), Kyle Bostick (Vermont), Michael Savit (Mahoning Valley), Miles Prentice (Connecticut), Naomi Silver (Batavia), Glenn Reicin (Staten Island), Peter Freund (Williamsport).
Office Manager: Laurie Hayes. **League Historian:** Charles Wride. **Media Associate:** Makenzie Burrows.
Division Structure: McNamara—Aberdeen, Brooklyn, Hudson Valley, Staten Island. Pinckney—Auburn, Batavia, Mahoning Valley, State College, West Virginia, Williamsport. Stedler—Lowell, Connecticut, Tri-City, Vermont.
Regular Season: 76 games. **2015 Opening Date:** June 19. **Closing Date:** Sept 7.
All-Star Game: Aug. 18 at Aberdeen.
Playoff Format: Division winners and wild-card team meet in best of three series. Winners meet in best of three series for league championship.
Roster Limit: 35 active and eligible to play in any given game. **Player Eligibility Rule:** No more than four players 23 or older; no more than three players on active list may have four or more years of prior service.
Brand of Baseball: Rawlings.
Umpires: Unavailable.

Ben Hayes

STADIUM INFORMATION

Club	Stadium	Opened	LF	CF	RF	Capacity	2014Att.
Aberdeen	Ripken Stadium	2002	310	400	310	6,000	150,300
Auburn	Falcon Park	1995	330	400	330	2,800	44,640
Batavia	Dwyer Stadium	1996	325	400	325	2,600	33,376
Brooklyn	KeySpan Park	2001	315	412	325	7,500	231,628
Connecticut	Dodd Stadium	1995	309	401	309	6,270	78,118
Hudson Valley	Dutchess Stadium	1994	325	400	325	4,494	159,084
Lowell	Edward LeLacheur Park	1998	337	400	301	4,842	165,129
Mahoning Valley	Eastwood Field	1999	335	405	335	6,000	109,545
State College	Medlar Field at Lubrano Park	2006	325	399	320	5,412	134,927
Staten Island	Richmond County Bank Ballpark	2001	325	400	325	6,500	122,442
Tri-City	Joseph L. Bruno Stadium	2002	325	400	325	5,000	161,171
Vermont	Centennial Field	1922	323	405	330	4,000	84,091
*West Virginia	WVU Baseball Park	2015	325	400	325	Unavailable	24,246*
Williamsport	Bowman Field	1923	345	405	350	4,200	61,249

*Team played at Jamestown in 2014

ABERDEEN IRONBIRDS

Address: 873 Long Drive, Aberdeen, MD 21001
Telephone: (410)297-9292 Fax: (210)297-6653
E-Mail address: Info@ironbirdsbaseball.com. **Website:** www.ironbirdsbaseball.com
Affiliation (first year): Baltimore Orioles (2002). **Years in league:** 2002-

OWNERSHIP/MANAGEMENT
Operated By: Ripken Professional Baseball LLC.
Principal Owner: Cal Ripken Jr. **Co-Owner/Executive Vice President:** Bill Ripken.
General Manager: Joe Harrington. **Assistant GM:** Brad Cox. **Director, Ticket Operations:** Ian Clark. **Training/Sales Coach:** Lee Greely. **Director, Retail Merchandising:** Don Eney. **Video Production Coordinator:** Mike Zapalowicz. **Lead Facilities Coordinator:** Larry Gluch. **Head Groundskeeper:** Patrick Coakley

FIELD STAFF
Manager: Luis Pujols. **Pitching Coach:** Justin Lord. **Coach:** Scott Thomas. **Trainer:** Brian Guzman.

GAME INFORMATION
Radio Announcer: Unavailable. **No. of Games Broadcast:** 76. **Flagship Station:** MiLB.com.
PA Announcer: Danny Mays. **Official Scorer:** Joe Stetka.
Stadium Name: Ripken Stadium. **Location:** I-95 to exit 85 (route 22), west on 22, right onto long drive. **Ticket Price range:** $9-27.50.
Visiting Club Hotel: Unavailable.

AUBURN DOUBLEDAYS

Address: 130 N Division St, Auburn, NY 13021.
Telephone: (315) 255-2489. **Fax:** (315) 255-2675.
E-Mail Address: info@auburndoubledays.com. **Website:** www.auburndoubledays.com.
Affiliation (first year): Washington Nationals (2011). **Years in League:** 1958-80, 1982-

OWNERSHIP/MANAGEMENT
Owned by: City of Auburn. **Operated by:** Auburn Community Non-Profit Baseball Association Inc.
President: Doug Selby. **General Manager:** Michael Voutsinas.

FIELD STAFF
Manager: Gary Cathcart. **Coach:** Amaury Garcia. **Pitching Coach:** Tim Redding.

GAME INFORMATION
Radio Announcer: David Lauterbach. **No of Games Broadcast:** Unavailable. **Flagship Station:** Unavailable.
PA Announcer: Unavailable. **Official Scorer:** Unavailable.
Stadium Name: Falcon Park. **Location:** I-90 to exit 40, right on Route 34 South for 8 miles to York Street, right on York, left on North Division Street. **Standard Game Times:** 7:05 pm (M-Sa), 5:05 pm (Su). **Ticket Price Range:** $5-9.
Visiting Club Hotel: Unavailable.

BATAVIA MUCKDOGS

Address: Dwyer Stadium, 299 Bank St, Batavia, NY 14020.
Telephone: (585) 343-5454. **Fax:** (585) 343-5620.
E-Mail Address: tsick@muckdogs.com. **Website:** www.muckdogs.com.
Affiliation (first year): Miami Marlins (2013). **Years in League:** 1939-53, 1957-59, 1961-

OWNERSHIP/MANAGEMENT
Operated By: Red Wings Management, LLC.
General Manager: Travis Sick. **Assistant GM:** Mike Ewing. **Director, Stadium Operations:** Don Rock. **Director, Merchandise:** Kathy Bills. **Clubhouse Manager:** John Versage.

FIELD STAFF
Manager: Angel Espada. **Hitting Coach:** Rigoberto Silverio. **Pitching Coach:** Brendan Sagara. **Trainer:** Michael Bibbo.

GAME INFORMATION
Radio Announcer: Matthew Coller. **No. of Games Broadcast:** Home-38 Away-20. **Flagship Station:** WBTA 1490-AM.
PA Announcer: Wayne Fuller. **Official Scorer:** Paul Bisig. **Stadium Name:** Dwyer Stadium. **Location:** I-90 to exit 48, left on Route 98 South, left on Richmond Avenue, left on Bank Street. **Standard Game Times:** 7:05 pm, Sun 1:05/5:05. **Ticket Price Range:** $6.00-8.00. **Visiting Club Hotel:** Days Inn of Batavia, 200 Oak St, Batavia, NY 14020. **Telephone:** (585) 344-6000.

BROOKLYN CYCLONES

Address: 1904 Surf Ave, Brooklyn, NY 11224.
Telephone: (718) 372-5596. **Fax:** (718) 449-6368.
E-Mail Address: info@brooklyncyclones.com. **Website:** www.brooklyncyclones.com.
Affiliation (first year): New York Mets (2001). **Years in League:** 2001-

OWNERSHIP/MANAGEMENT
Chairman, CEO: Fred Wilpon. **President:** Saul Katz. **COO:** Jeff Wilpon.
Vice President: Steve Cohen. **General Manager:** Kevin Mahoney. **Assistant GM:** Gary Perone. **Director, Communications:** Billy Harner. **Manager, Ticket Operations:** Greg Conway. **Graphics Manager:** Kevin Jimenez. **Operations Manager:** Vladimir Lipsman. **Community Relations Manager:** JoshMevorach. **Head Groundskeeper:** Mike Meola. **Community Outreach/Promotions:** King Henry. **Account Executives:** Jared Silverman, Tommy Cardona, Nicole Kneessy, Sal LaMonica, Craig Coughlin, Josh Hernandez, Angelina Tennis, Ricky Viola. **Staff Accountant:** Tatiana Isdith. **Administrative Assistant, Community Relations:** Sharon Lundy-Ross.

FIELD STAFF

Manager: Tom Gamboa. **Coach:** Unavailable. **Pitching Coach:** Tom Signore.

GAME INFORMATION

Radio Announcer: Stu Johnson. **No. of Games Broadcast:** 76. **Flagship Station:** WKRB 90.3-FM.
PA Announcer: Mark Frotto. **Official Scorer:** Mike Damon.
Stadium Name: MCU Park. **Location:** Belt Parkway to Cropsey Ave South, continue on Cropsey until it becomes West 17th St, continue to Surf Ave, stadium on south side of Surf Ave; By subway, west/south to Stillwell Ave./Coney Island station. **Ticket Price Range:** $8-17.
Visiting Club Hotel: Unavailable.

CONNECTICUT TIGERS

Address: 14 Stott Avenue, Norwich, CT 06360.
Telephone: (860) 887-7962. **Fax:** (860) 886-5996.
E-Mail Address: info@cttigers.com. **Website:** www.cttigers.com.
Affiliation (first year): Detroit Tigers (1999). **Years in League:** 2010-

OWNERSHIP/MANAGEMENT

Operated By: Oneonta Athletic Corp. **President:** Miles Prentice.
Senior Vice President: CJ Knudsen. **VP/General Manager:** Eric Knighton. **Assistant GM:** Dave Schermerhorn. **Director, Concessions/Merchandise:** Heather Bartlett. **Director, Sales:** Brent Southworth. **Box Office Manager:** Josh Postler. **Director, Group Sales/Operations:** Jack Kasten. **Director, Business Development:** Brad Favreau. **Head Groundskeeper:** Ryan Lefler

FIELD STAFF

Manager: Mike Rabelo. **Hitting Coach:** Scott Dwyer. **Pitching Coach:** Carlos Chantres. **Trainer:** Chris Vick.

GAME INFORMATION

PA Announcer: Ed Weyant. **Official Scorer:** Chris Cote.
Stadium Name: Dodd Stadium. **Location:** Exit 82 off I-395. **Standard Game Times:** 7:05 pm, Sun 4:05. **Ticket Price Range:** $8-20.
Visiting Club Hotel: Unavailable.

HUDSON VALLEY RENEGADES

Office Address: Dutchess Stadium, 1500 Route 9D, Wappingers Falls, NY 12590. **Mailing Address:** PO Box 661, Fishkill, NY 12524.
Telephone: (845) 838-0094. **Fax:** (845) 838-0014.
E-Mail Address: info@hvrenegades.com. **Website:** www.hvrenegades.com.
Affiliation (first year): Tampa Bay Rays (1996). **Years in League:** 1994-

OWNERSHIP/MANAGEMENT

Operated by: Keystone Professional Baseball Club Inc.
Principal Owner: Marv Goldklang. **President:** Jeff Goldklang
Senior Vice President/General Manager: Eben Yager.
Vice President: Rick Zolzer. **Assistant GM:** Kristen Huss. **Director, Stadium Operations:** Tom Hubmaster. **Director, Baseball Communications:** Joe Ausanio. **Director, Business Operations:** Vicky DeFreese. **Director, Sales:** Sean Kammerer. **Director, Promotions/Merchandise:** Breven Zimmerman. **Director, Marketing/Communications:** Corinne Adams. **Manager, New Business Development:** Dave Neff. **Manager, Director, Food/Beverage:** Teri Bettencourt. **Head Groundskeeper:** Tim Merante. **Community Relations Specialist:** Bob Outer. **Ticket Sales Associates:** Chris Winslow, Dan Horne, Casey Vecchio.

FIELD STAFF

Manager: Tim Parenton. **Hitting Coach:** Manny Castillo. **Pitching Coach:** Brian Reith.

GAME INFORMATION

Radio Announcer: Unavailable. **No. of Games Broadcast:** Home–38. **Flagship Stations:** WKIP 1450-AM.
PA Announcer: Rick Zolzer. **Official Scorers:** Unavailable.
Stadium Name: Dutchess Stadium. **Location:** I-84 to exit 11 (Route 9D North), north one mile to stadium. **Standard Game Times:** 7:05 pm, Sun 5:05. **Visiting Club Hotel:** Days Inn, 20 Schuyler Blvd and Route 9, Fishkill, NY 12524. **Telephone:** (845) 896-4995.
Visiting Club Hotel: Unavailable.

LOWELL SPINNERS

Address: 450 Aiken St, Lowell, MA 01854.
Telephone: (978) 459-2255. **Fax:** (978) 459-1674.
E-Mail Address: info@lowellspinners.com. **Website:** www.lowellspinners.com.
Affiliation (first year): Boston Red Sox (1996). **Years in League:** 1996-

OWNERSHIP/MANAGEMENT
Operated By: Diamond Action Inc. **Owner/CEO:** Drew Weber.
President/General Manager: Tim Bawmann. **Executive Vice President, Sales:** Brian Lindsay. **VP/Controller:** Patricia Harbour. **Executive VP, Communications:** Jon Goode. **VP, Stadium Operations:** Dan Beaulieu. **Director, Facility Management:** Gareth Markey. **Assistant GM, Media Relations:** Jon Boswell. **Director, Merchandising:** Jeff Cohen. **VP, Group Ticketing:** Jon Healy. **Director, Ticket Operations:** Justin Williams. **Director, Game Day Entertainment:** Matt Steinberg. **Head Groundskeeper:** Jeff Paolino. **Clubhouse Manager:** Del Christman.

FIELD STAFF
Manager: Joe Oliver. **Hitting Coach:** Iggy Suarez. **Pitching Coach:** Lance Carter. **Athletic Trainer:** Nick Faciana.

GAME INFORMATION
Radio Announcer: John Leahy. **No. of Games Broadcast:** 76. **Flagship Station:** WCAP 980-AM.
PA Announcer: Mike Riley. **Official Scorer:** David Rourke.
Stadium Name: Edward A LeLacheur Park. **Location:** From Route 495 and 3, take exit 35C (Lowell Connector), follow connector to exit 5B (Thorndike Street) onto Dutton Street, left onto Father Morrissette Boulevard, right on Aiken Street. **Standard Game Times:** 7:05 pm. **Ticket Price Range:** $7-10 (advance); $9-12 (day of game).
Visiting Club Hotel: Radisson of Chelmsford, 10 Independence Dr, Chelmsford, MA 01879. **Telephone:** (978) 356-0800.

MAHONING VALLEY
SCRAPPERS

Address: 111 Eastwood Mall Blvd, Niles, OH 44446.
Telephone: (330) 505-0000. **Fax:** (303) 505-9696.
E-Mail Address: info@mvscrappers.com. **Website:** www.mvscrappers.com.
Affiliation (first year): Cleveland Indians (1999). **Years in League:** 1999-

OWNERSHIP/MANAGEMENT
Operated By: HWS Baseball Group. **Managing General Partner:** Michael Savit. **Vice President, HWS Baseball/General Manager:** Jordan Taylor. **Assistant GM, Marketing:** Heather Sahli. **Assistant GM, Sales:** Matt Thompson. **Manager, Box Office:** Roxanne Herrington. **Assistant GM, Operations:** Brad Hooser. **Group Sales Manager:** Chris Sumner. **Head Groundskeeper:** Ryan Olszewski. **Manager, Accounting:** Courtney Perrino. **Manager, Community Relations & Merchandise:** Kate Walsh.

FIELD STAFF
Manager: Travis Fryman. **Coach:** Larry Day. **Pitching Coach:** Greg Hibbard.

GAME INFORMATION
Radio Announcer: Unavailable. **No. of Games Broadcast:** 76. **Flagship Station:** SportsRadio 1240 AM.
PA Announcer: Unavailable. **Official Scorer:** Craig Antush.
Stadium Name: Eastwood Field. **Location:** I-80 to 11 North to 82 West to 46 South; stadium located behind Eastwood Mall. **Ticket Price Range:** $8-12.
Visiting Club Hotel: Days Inn & Suites, 1615 Liberty St, Girard, OH 44429. **Telephone:** (330) 759-9820.

STATE COLLEGE SPIKES

Address: 112 Medlar Field, Lubrano Park, University Park, PA 16802.
Telephone: (814) 272-1711. **Fax:** (814) 272-1718.
Website: www.statecollegespikes.com.
Affiliation (first year): St. Louis Cardinals (2013). **Years in League:** 2006-.

OWNERSHIP/MANAGEMENT
Operated By: Spikes Baseball LP. **Chairman/Managing Partner:** Chuck Greenberg.
President: Jason Dambach. **General Manager:** Scott Walker. **Assistant GM, Operations:** Dan Petrazzolo. **Assistant GM, Marketing:** Matt Hoover. **Accounting Manager:** Karen Mahon. **Business/Box Office Manager:** Steve Christ. **Manager, Ticket Sales:** Brian DeAngelis. **Manager, Entertainment/Promotions:** Ben Love. **Ticket Account Executives:** Erik Hoffman. **Manager, Corporate Partnerships:** Don DiBastiani. **Sports Turf Manager:** Matt Neri.

FIELD STAFF

Manager: Johnny Rodriguez. **Hitting Coach:** Roger LaFrancois. **Pitching Coach:** Darwin Marrero. **Trainer:** Dan Martin.

GAME INFORMATION

PA Announcer: Unavailable. **Official Scorer:** Unavailable.
Stadium Name: Medlar Field at Lubrano Park. **Location:** From west, US 322 to Mount Nittany Expressway, I-80 to exit 158 (old exit 23/Milesburg), follow Route 150 South to Route 26 South; From east, I-80 to exit 161 (old exit 24/Bellefonte) to Route 26 South or US 220/I-99 South. **Standard Game Times:** 7:05 pm, Sun 6:05. **Ticket Price Range:**$6-14.
Visiting Club Hotel: Ramada Conference Center State College, 1450 Atherton St, State College, PA 16801. **Telephone:** (814) 238-3001.

STATEN ISLAND YANKEES

Stadium Address: 75 Richmond Terrace, Staten Island, NY 10301.
Telephone: (718) 720-9265. **Fax:** (718) 273-5763.
Website: www.siyanks.com.
Affiliation (first year): New York Yankees (1999). **Years in League:** 1999-

OWNERSHIP/MANAGEMENT

Principal Owners: Nostalgic Partners. **CEO:** Steven Violetta. **President/General Manager:** Jane Rogers.
Director, Corporate Partnerships: Jill Wright. **Director, Manager, Corporate Partnerships:** Stephen Mortley. **Entertainment:** John D'Agostino. **Senior Director of Finance:** Anthony Di Flaurio. **Vice President, Sales:** Neal Desormeaux. **Ticket Operations Manager:** Dana Rommel. **Senior Sales Executive:** David Percarpio. **Sales Executives:** Steven Liss, Andrew Lupo, Joseph Mola, Bill Glass. **Senior Director, Marketing:** Michael Holley. **Marketing Manager:** Ian Fontenot. **Manager, Stadium Operations:** Mike Rogers. **Stadium Operations:** Bobby Brown.

FIELD STAFF

Manager: Patrick Osborn. **Hitting Coach:** Ty Hawkins. **Pitching Coach:** Butch Henry. **Defensive Coach:** Eric Duncan.

GAME INFORMATION

Radio Announcer: Unavailable. **No. of Games Broadcast:** 76. **Flagship Station:** Unavailable.
PA Announcer: Unavailable. **Official Scorer:** Unavailable.
Stadium Name: Richmond County Bank Ballpark at St George. **Location:** From I-95, take exit 13E (1-278 and Staten Island), cross Goethals Bridge, stay on I-278 East and take last exit before Verrazano Narrows Bridge, north on Father Capodanno Boulevard, which turns into Bay Street, which goes to ferry terminal; ballpark next to Staten Island Ferry Terminal. **Standard Game Times:** 7 pm, Sun 4.
Visiting Club Hotel: Unavailable.

TRI-CITY VALLEYCATS

Office Address: Joseph L Bruno Stadium, 80 Vandenburg Ave, Troy, NY 12180. **Mailing Address:** PO Box 694, Troy, NY 12181.
Telephone: (518) 629-2287. **Fax:** (518) 629-2299.
E-Mail Address: info@tcvalleycats.com. **Website:** www.tcvalleycats.com.
Affiliation (first year): Houston Astros (2002). **Years in League:** 2002-

OWNERSHIP/MANAGEMENT

Operated By: Tri-City ValleyCats Inc. **Principal Owners:** Martin Barr, John Burton, William Gladstone, Rick Murphy, Alfred Roberts, Stephen Siegel.
President: William Gladstone. **Vice President/General Manager:** Rick Murphy. **Assistant GM:** Matt Callahan. **Fan Development/Community Relations Manager:** Michelle Skinner. **Business Development Manager:** Jason Lecuyer. **Stadium Operations Manager:** Keith Sweeney. **Media Relations Manager:** Chris Chenes. **Account Executives:** Chris Dawson, Ben Whitehead. **Box Office Manager:** Jessica Kaszeta.

FIELD STAFF

Manager: Ed Romero. **Hitting Coach:** Russ Steinhorn. **Pitching Coach:** Chris Holt. **Trainer:** John Gregorich.

GAME INFORMATION

Radio Announcer: Sam Sigal. **No. of Games Broadcast:** 76. **Flagship Station:** MiLB.com.
PA Announcer: Anthony Pettograsso. **Official Scorer:** Dave Bestle
Stadium Name: Joseph Bruno Stadium. **Location:** From north, I-87 to exit 7 (Route 7), go east 1 1/2 miles to I-787 South, to Route 378 East, go over bridge to Route 4, right to Route 4South, one mile to Hudson Valley Community College campus on left; From south, I-87 to exit 23 (I-787), I-787 north six miles to exit for Route 378 east, over bridge to Route 4, right to Route 4 South, one mile to campus on left; From east, Massachusetts Turnpike to exit B-1 (I-90), nine miles to Exit 8 (Defreestville), left off ramp to Route 4 North, five miles to campus on right; From west, I-90 to exit 24 (I-90 East), I-90 East for six miles to I-787 North (Troy), 2.2 miles to exit for Route 378 East, over bridge to Route 4, right to Route 4 south for one mile to campus on left. **Standard Game Times:** 7 pm, Sun 5. **Ticket Price Range:** $5.50-$10.50.
Visiting Club Hotel: Travelodge, 831 New Loudon Road, Latham, NY 12110. **Telephone:** (518) 785-6626.

VERMONT LAKE MONSTERS

Address: 1 King Street Ferry Dock, Burlington, VT 05401.
Telephone: (802) 655-4200. **Fax:** (802) 655-5660.
E-Mail Address: info@vermontlakemonsters.com. **Website:** www.vermontlakemonsters.com.
Affiliation (first year): Oakland Athletics (2011). **Years in League:** 1994-

OWNERSHIP/MANAGEMENT
Operated by: Vermont Expos Inc. **Principal Owner/President:** Ray Pecor Jr. **Vice President:** Kyle Bostwick. **General Manager:** Joe Doud. **Executive Director, Sales & Marketing:** Nate Cloutier. **Accounts Manager/Merchandise Director:** Kate Echo. **Director, Manager, Box Office:** Unavailable. **Director, Promotions/Community Relations:** Noelle Richard. **Director, Media Relations:** Paul Stanfield. **Clubhouse Operations:** Phil Schelzo.

FIELD STAFF
Manager: Aaron Nieckula. **Hitting Coach:** Tommy Everidge. **Pitching Coach:** Carlos Chavez.

GAME INFORMATION
Radio Announcers: George Commo. **No. of Games Broadcast:** Home-38, Away-12. **Flagship Station:** 960 The Zone.
PA Announcer: Unavailable. **Official Scorer:** Unavailable.
Stadium Name: Centennial Field. **Location:** I-89 to exit 14W, right on East Avenue for one mile, right at Colchester Avenue. **Standard Game Times:** 7:05 pm, Sat 6:05, Sun 5:05. **Ticket Price Range:** $5-8.
Visiting Club Hotel: Sheraton Hotel & Conference Center. **Telephone:** (802) 865-6600.

WEST VIRGINIA BLACK BEARS

Office Address: 2040 Jedd Gyorko Drive, Morgantown, WV 26504. **Mailing Address:** PO Box 4680 Morgantown, WV 26504.
Telephone: (304)293-7910. **Website:** www.westvirginiablackbears.com.
Affiliation (first year): Pittsburgh Pirates (2015). **Years in League:** 2015-

OWNERSHIP/MANAGEMENT
Operated By: Rich Baseball Operations. **President:** Robert Rich Jr. **Chief Operating Officer:** Jonathan Dandes.
General Manager: Matthew Drayer. **Assistant GM, Sales:** John Pogorzelski. **Assistant GM, Operations:** Ernie Galusky.

FIELD STAFF
Manager: Wyatt Toregas. **Hitting Coach:** Jonathan Prieto. **Pitching Coach:** Tom Filer.

GAME INFORMATION
PA Announcer: Unavailable. **Official Scorer:** Unavailable.
Stadium Name: WVU Baseball Park. **Game Times:** 7:05 pm, Sun 4:05.
Visiting Club Hotel: Unavailable.

WILLIAMSPORT CROSSCUTTERS

Office Address: Bowman Field, 1700 W Fourth St, Williamsport, PA 17701. **Mailing Address:** PO Box 3173, Williamsport, PA 17701.
Telephone: (570) 326-3389. **Fax:** (570) 326-3494.
E-Mail Address: mail@crosscutters.com. **Website:** www.crosscutters.com.
Affiliation (first year): Philadelphia Phillies (2007). **Years in League:** 1968-72, 1994-

OWNERSHIP/MANAGEMENT
Operated By: Cutting Edge Baseball, LLC. **Principal Owner:** Peter Freund. **Vice President/General Manager:** Doug Estes. **VP, Marketing/Public Relations:** Gabe Sinicropi. **Director, Concessions:** Bill Gehron. **Director, Ticket Operations/Community Relations:** Sarah Budd. **Director, Partner Services:** Jennifer Lorson.

FIELD STAFF
Manager: Nelson Prada. **Coach:** Shawn Williams. **Pitching Coach:** Aaron Fultz. **Trainer:** Michael Hefta.

GAME INFORMATION
Radio Announcers: Todd Bartley, Ian Catherine. **No. of Games Broadcast:** 76. **Flagship Station:** WLYC 1050-AM,

NORTHWEST LEAGUE

Address: 140 N Higgins Ave., No. 211, Missoula, MT, 59802.
Telephone: (406) 541-9301. **Fax:** (406) 543-9463.
E-Mail Address: mellisnwl@aol.com. **Website:** www.northwestleague.com
Years League Active: 1954-
President/Treasurer: Mike Ellis.
Vice President: Mike McMurray (Hillsboro). **Corporate Secretary:** Jerry Walker (Salem-Keizer).
Directors: Dave Elmore (Eugene), Bobby Brett (Spokane), Tom Volpe (Everett), Jake Kerr (Vancouver), Mike McMurray (Hillsboro), Brent Miles (Tri-City), Jerry Walker (Salem-Keizer), Jeff Eiseman (Boise).
Administrative Assistant: Judy Ellis.
Division Structure: South—Boise, Hillsboro, Eugene, Salem-Keizer. North—Everett, Spokane, Tri-City, Vancouver.
Regular Season: 76 games (split schedule). **2015 Opening Date:** June 18. **Closing Date:** Sept. 6.
All-Star Game: Aug. 4, in Spokane.
Playoff Format: First-half division winners meet second-half division winners in best of three series. Winners meet in best of three series for league championship.
Roster Limit: 35 active, 35 under control. **Player Eligibility Rule:** No more than three players on active list may have four or more years of prior service.
Brand of Baseball: Rawlings.
Umpires: Unavailable.

Mike Ellis

STADIUM INFORMATION

Club	Stadium	Opened	Dimensions LF	CF	RF	Capacity	2014 Att.
Boise	Memorial Stadium	1989	335	400	335	3,426	87,519
Eugene	PK Park	2010	335	400	325	4,000	108,067
Everett	Everett Memorial Stadium	1984	324	380	330	3,682	92,642
Hillsboro	Hillsboro Ballpark	2013	325	400	325	4,500	138,732
Salem-Keizer	Volcanoes Stadium	1997	325	400	325	4,100	95,083
Spokane	Avista Stadium	1958	335	398	335	7,162	193,865
Tri-City	Dust Devils Stadium	1995	335	400	335	3,700	85,679
Vancouver	Nat Bailey Stadium	1951	335	395	335	6,500	180,187

BOISE HAWKS

Address: 5600 N. Glenwood St. Boise, ID 83714.
Telephone: (208) 322-5000. **Fax:** (208) 322-6846.
Website: www.boisehawks.com.
Affiliation (first year): Colorado Rockies (2015). **Years in League:** 1975-76, 1978, 1987-

OWNERSHIP/MANAGEMENT
Operated by: Boise Professional Baseball LLC. **Managing Partner:** Jeff Eiseman.
President: Todd Rahr. **General Manager:** Bob Flannery. **Dir., Stadium Ops/Food & Beverage:** Jake Lusk. **Corporate/Group Sales Manager:** Britt Talbert. **Ticket Sales Manager:** Sam Annabel. **Manager, Marketing:** Joe Kelly. **Manager, Stadium Ops:** Jeff Israel. **Manager, Accounting/Office:** Angela Phillips. **Account Executives:** Stephen Gall, Patrick Leipold. **Asst., Media Relations:** Nathan Kroehn.

FIELD STAFF
Development Supervisor: Fred Nelson. **Manager:** Frank Gonzales. **Hitting Coach:** Andy Gonzalez. **Pitching Coach:** Doug Jones. **Trainer:** Mickey Clarizio.

GAME INFORMATION
Radio Announcer: Unavailable. **No. of Games Broadcast:** Unavailable. **Flagship Station:** Unavailable.
PA Announcer: Unavailable. **Official Scorer:** Curtis Haines.
Stadium Name: Memorial Stadium. **Location:** I-84 to Cole Rd., north to Western Idaho Fairgrounds at 5600 North Glenwood St. **Standard Game Time:** 7:15 pm. **Ticket Price Range:** $7-16.
Visiting Club Hotel: Unavailable.

EUGENE EMERALDS

Office Address: 2760 Martin Luther King Jr. Blvd, Eugene, OR 97401. **Mailing Address:** PO Box 10911, Eugene, OR 97440.
Telephone: (541) 342-5367. **Fax:** (541) 342-6089.
E-Mail Address: info@emeraldsbaseball.com. **Website:** www.emeraldsbaseball.com.
Affiliation (first year): Chicago Cubs (2015). **Years in League:** 1955-68, 1974-

OWNERSHIP/MANAGEMENT
Operated By: Elmore Sports Group Ltd. **Principal Owner:** David Elmore.
General Manager: Allan Benavides. **Assistant GM:** Sarah Heth. **Assistant GM:** Matt Dompe. **Director, Food/Beverage:** Nikki Ochs. **Director, Tickets:** Peter Billups. **Assistant Dir. Of Tickets:** Chris Bowers. **Account Executive:** Patrick Zajac. **Graphic Designer:** Danny Crowley. **Director, Community Affairs:** Anne Culhaine.

FIELD STAFF
Manager: Gary Van Tol. **Hitting Coach:** Ricardo Medina. **Pitching Coach:** Anderson Tavares. **Assistant Coach:** Termel Sledge

GAME INFORMATION
Radio Announcer: Matt Dompe. **No. of Games Broadcast:** 76. **Flagship Station:** 95.3-FM The Score.
PA Announcer: Ted Welker. **Official Scorer:** George McPherson.
Stadium Name: PK Park. **Standard Game Time:** 7:05 pm, Sun 5:01. **Ticket Price Range:** $7-$13.
Visiting Club Hotel: Unavailable.

EVERETT AQUASOX

Mailing Address: 3802 Broadway, Everett, WA 98201.
Telephone: (425) 258-3673. **Fax:** (425) 258-3675.
E-Mail Address: info@aquasox.com. **Website:** www.aquasox.com.
Affiliation (first year): Seattle Mariners (1995). **Years in League:** 1984-

OWNERSHIP/MANAGEMENT
Operated by: 7th Inning Stretch, LLC. **Directors:** Tom Volpe, Pat Filippone.
Executive Vice President/General Manager: Tom Backemeyer. **Assistant GM:** Katie Crawford Woods. **VP, Corporate Sponsorships:** Brian Sloan. **Director, Corporate Partnerships/Broadcasting:** Pat Dillon. **Group Sales/Merchandise Manager:** Erica Fensterbush. **Director, Food/Beverage:** Nick Reuter. **Director, Tickets:** Not Available. **Account Executives:** Duncan Jensen, Andrew Garrison, Greg Bell. **Finance Manager:** Tony Ackerman. **Head Groundskeeper:** Not Available.

FIELD STAFF
Manager: Rob Mummau. **Hitting Coach:** Mike Davis. **Pitching Coach:** Jason Blanton. **Trainer:** Shane Zdebiak.

GAME INFORMATION
Radio Announcer: Pat Dillon. **No. of Games Broadcast:** 76. **Flagship Station:** KRKO 1380-AM.
PA Announcer: Tom Lafferty. **Official Scorer:** Pat Castro.
Stadium Name: Everett Memorial Stadium. **Location:** I-5, exit 192. **Standard Game Times:** 7:05 pm, Sun 4:05. **Ticket Price Range:** $7-17.
Visiting Club Hotel: Holiday Inn, Downtown Everett, 3105 Pine St, Everett, WA 98201. **Telephone:** (425) 339-2000.

HILLSBORO HOPS

Address: 4460 NW 229th Ave., Hillsboro, OR, 97124.
Telephone: (503) 640-0887. **E-Mail Address:** info@hillsborohops.com. **Website:** www.hillsborohops.com.
Affiliation (first year): Arizona Diamondbacks (2001). **Years in League:** 2013-

OWNERSHIP/MANAGEMENT
Operated by: Short Season LLC. **Managing Partners:** Mike McMurray, Mark Mays, Josh Weinman, Myron Levin. **President:** Mike McMurray.
General Manager: K.L. Wombacher. **Chief Financial Officer:** Laura McMurray. **Director, Ballpark Operations:** Juan Huitron. **Director, Tickets:** Jason Gavigan. **Director, Merchandise:** Lauren Wombacher. **Director, Media Relations/Broadcasting:** Rich Burk.

FIELD STAFF
Manager: Shelley Duncan. **Hitting Coach:** Javier Colina. **Pitching Coach:** Doug Drabek.

GAME INFORMATION

PA Announcer: Brian Rogers. **Official Scorer:** Unavailable.
Stadium Name: Ron Tonkin Field. **Location:** 4460 NW 229th, Hillsboro, OR, 97124. **Standard Game Times:** 7:05 pm, Sun 4:05. **Ticket Price Range:** $7-$16.
Visiting Club Hotel: Comfort Inn, Hillsboro. **Telephone:** (503) 648-3500.

SALEM-KEIZER VOLCANOES

Office Address: 6700 Field of Dreams Way, Keizer, OR 97303. **Mailing Address:** PO Box 20936, Keizer, OR 97307.
Telephone: (503) 390-2225. **Fax:** (503) 390-2227.
E-Mail Address: Volcanoes@volcanoesbaseball.com. **Website:** www.volcanoesbaseball.com.
Affiliation (first year): San Francisco Giants (1997). **Years in League:** 1997-

OWNERSHIP/MANAGEMENT

Operated By: Sports Enterprises Inc. **Principal Owners:** Jerry Walker, Bill Tucker.
President/General Manager: Jerry Walker. **President, Stadium Operations:** Rick Nelson. **President, Business Operations:** Tom Leip. **Senior Account Executive/Game Day Operations:** Jerry Howard. **Director, Broadcasting/Media Relations:** Rob Schreier. **Director, Ticket Office Operations:** Bea Howard. **Director, Business Development:** Justin Lacche.

FIELD STAFF

Manager: Gary Davenport. **Coach:** Ricky Ward. **Pitching Coach:** Jerry Cram.

GAME INFORMATION

Radio Announcer: Rob Schreier. **No. of Games Broadcast:** 76. **Flagship Station:** KBZY AM-1490.
PA Announcer: Unavailable. **Official Scorer:** Scott Sepich.
Stadium Name: Volcanoes Stadium. **Location:** I-5 to exit 260 (Chemawa Road), west one block to Stadium Way NE, north six blocks to stadium. **Standard Game Times:** 6:35 pm, Sun 5:05. **Ticket Price Range:** $7-30.
Visiting Club Hotel: Comfort Suites, 630 Hawthorne Ave SE, Salem, OR 97301. **Telephone:** (503) 585-9705.

SPOKANE INDIANS

Office Address: Avista Stadium, 602 N Havana, Spokane, WA 99202. **Mailing Address:** PO Box 4758, Spokane, WA 99220.
Telephone: (509) 535-2922. **Fax:** (509) 534-5368.
E-Mail Address: mail@spokaneindiansbaseball.com. **Website:** www.spokaneindiansbaseball.com.
Affiliation (first year): Texas Rangers (2003). **Years in League:** 1972, 1983-

OWNERSHIP/MANAGEMENT

Operated By: Longball Inc. **Principal Owner:** Bobby Brett. **Co-Owner/Senior Adviser:** Andrew Billig.
Vice President/General Manager: Chris Duff. **Senior Vice President:** Otto Klein. **VP, Tickets:** Josh Roys. **Director, Business Operations:** Lesley DeHart. **Assistant GM, Sponsorships:** Kyle Day. **Assistant GM, Tickets:** Nick Gaebe. **Director, Concessions/Operations:** Justin Stottlemyre. **Director, Public Relations:** Dustin Toms. **Sponsorships and Community Relations:** Yvette Yzaguirre, Elise Rooney. **Senior Account Executive:** Chris Combo. **Account Executives:** Thane Jackson, Karly Searl. **Group Sales Coordinators:** Olivia Johnson, Darby Moore. **CFO:** Greg Sloan. **Director, Accounting:** Dawnelle Shaw. **Head Groundskeeper:** David Yearout. **Assistant Director, Stadium Operations:** Larry Blummer.

FIELD STAFF

Manager: Tim Hulett. **Hitting Coach:** Unavailable. **Pitching Coach:** Jose Jaimes. **Strength/Conditioning Coach:** Ed Yong. **Trainer:** Zach Jones.

GAME INFORMATION

Radio Announcer: Mike Boyle. **No. of Games Broadcast:** 76. **Flagship Station:** 1510 KGA.
PA Announcer: Scott Lewis. **Official Scorer:** Todd Gilkey.
Stadium Name: Avista Stadium at the Spokane Fair and Expo Center. **Location:** From west, I-90 to exit 283B (Thor/Freya), east on Third Avenue, left onto Havana; From east, I-90 to Broadway exit, right onto Broadway, left onto Havana. **Standard Game Time:** 6:30 pm, Sun 3:30 pm. **Ticket Price Range:** $5-13.
Visiting Club Hotel: Mirabeau Park Hotel & Convention Center, N 1100 Sullivan Rd, Spokane, WA 99037. **Telephone:** (509) 924-9000.

TRI-CITY DUST DEVILS

Address: 6200 Burden Blvd, Pasco, WA 99301.
Telephone: (509) 544-8789. **Fax:** (509) 547-9570.
E-Mail Address: info@dustdevilsbaseball.com. **Website:** www.dustdevilsbaseball.
com.
Affiliation (first year): San Diego Padres (2015). **Years in League:** 1955-1974,
1983-1986, 2001-

OWNERSHIP/MANAGEMENT
Operated by: Northwest Baseball Ventures. **Principal Owners:** George Brett, Hoshino Dreams Corp, Brent Miles.
President: Brent Miles.
Vice President/General Manager: Derrel Ebert. **VP, Business Operations:** Tim Gittel. **Assistant GM:** Dan O'Neill.
Director of Season Ticket Sales: Andy Wood. **Promotions Manager:** Ann Shaffer. **Sponsorships Manager:** Brennan
McIntire. **Group Sales Coordinator:** Joey Edminster. **Account Executive:** Jason Bravo. **Account Executive:** Trevor
Shively. **Head Groundskeeper:** Michael Angel.

FIELD STAFF
Manager: Unavailable. **Hitting Coach:** Unavailable. **Pitching Coach:** Nelson Cruz.

GAME INFORMATION
Radio Announcer: Chris King. **No. of Games Broadcast:** 76. **Flagship Station:** 870-AM KFLD.
PA Announcer: Patrick Harvey. **Official Scorers:** Tony Wise, Scott Tylinski.
Stadium Name: Gesa Stadium. **Location:** I-182 to exit 9 (Road 68), north to Burden Blvd, right to stadium. **Standard
Game Time:** 7:15 pm. **Ticket Price Range:** $7-10.
Visiting Club Hotel: Red Lion Hotel-Columbia Center, 1101 N Columbia Center Blvd, Kennewick, WA 99336.
Telephone: (509) 783-0611.

VANCOUVER CANADIANS

Address: Scotiabank Field at Nat Bailey Stadium, 4601 Ontario St, Vancouver, British
Columbia V5V 3H4.
Telephone: (604) 872-5232. **Fax:** (604) 872-1714.
E-Mail Address: staff@canadiansbaseball.com. **Website:** www.canadiansbaseball.com.
Affiliation (fifth year): Toronto Blue Jays (2011). **Years in League:** 2000-

OWNERSHIP/MANAGEMENT
Operated by: Vancouver Canadians Professional Baseball LLP. **Managing General Partner:** Jake Kerr. **Partner:** Jeff
Mooney. **President:** Andy Dunn.
General Manager: JC Fraser. **Assistant General Manager:** Allan Bailey. **Financial Controller:** Andrew Remedios.
VP, Sales/Marketing: Graham Wall. **Director, Communications/Broadcast:** Rob Fai. **Director, Community Relations/
Social Media:** Jeff Holloway. **Manager, Sales/Marketing Services:** Jennifer Wilcock. **Manager, Group Sales:** Andrew
Forsyth. **Manager, Sales/Promotions:** Michael Richardson. **Manager, Ballpark Operations:** Cale Reining. **Coordinator,
Sales:** Lindsay Scharf. **Head Groundskeeper:** Matt Horan.

FIELD STAFF
Manager: John Schneider. **Hitting Coach:** Dave Pano. **Pitching Coach:** Jim Czajkowski. **Trainer:** Reggie Mungrue.

GAME INFORMATION
Radio Announcer: Rob Fai. **No. of Games Broadcast:** 76. **Flagship Station:** TSN 1040-AM.
PA Announcer: Don Andrews/John Ashbridge. **Official Scorer:** Mike Hanafin. **Stadium Name:** Scotiabank Field at Nat
Bailey Stadium. **Location:** From downtown, take Cambie Street Bridge, left on East 25th Ave./King Edward Ave, right on
Main Street, right on 33rd Ave, right on Ontario St to stadium; From south, take Highway 99 to Oak Street, right on 41st
Ave, left on Main Street to 33rd Ave, right on Ontario St to stadium. **Standard Game Times:** 7:05 pm, Sun 1:05. **Ticket
Price Range:** $9-20.
Visiting Club Hotel: Accent Inns, 10551 Edwards Dr, Richmond, BC V6X 3L8. **Telephone:** (604) 273-3311.

APPALACHIAN LEAGUE

APPALACHIAN LEAGUE
of professional baseball clubs

ROOKIE ADVANCED

Mailing Address: 759 182nd Ave. E., Redington Shores, FL 33708.
Telephone: 704-252-2656.
E-Mail Address: office@appyleague.net. **Website:** www.appyleague.com.
Years League Active: 1921-25, 1937-55, 1957-
President/Treasurer: Lee Landers. **Corporate Secretary:** David Lane (Greeneville).
Directors: Charlie Wilson (Bluefield), Larry Broadway (Bristol), Ronnie Richardson (Burlington), Jonathan Schuerholz (Danville), Brad Steil (Elizabethton), Quinton McCracken (Greeneville), Gary LaRocque (Johnson City), Ian Levin (Kingsport), Mitch Lukevics (Princeton), Eric Schmitt (Pulaski).
Executive Committee: Mike Mains (Elizabethton), David Lane (Greeneville), Dan Moushon (Burlington), Gary La Rocque (St. Louis), Charlie Wilson (Toronto), Larry Broadway (Pittsburgh).
Board of Trustees Representative: Mitch Lukevics (Tampa Bay).
League Administrator: Bobbi Landers.
Division Structure: East—Bluefield, Burlington, Danville, Princeton, Pulaski. West—Bristol, Elizabethton, Greeneville, Johnson City, Kingsport.
Regular Season: 68 games. **2015 Opening Date:** June 23. **Closing Date:** September 1.
All-Star Game: None.
Playoff Format: First- and second-place teams in each division play each other in best of three series. Winners meet in best of three series for league championship.
Roster Limit: 35 active, 35 under control. **Player Eligibility Rule:** No more than three players on the active roster may have three or more years of prior minor league service.
Brand of Baseball: Rawlings.
Umpires: Unavailable

Lee Landers

STADIUM INFORMATION

| Club | Stadium | Opened | Dimensions | | | Capacity | 2014 Att. |
			LF	CF	RF		
Bluefield	Bowen Field	1939	335	400	335	2,250	26,646
Bristol	DeVault Memorial Stadium	1969	325	400	310	2,000	25,743
Burlington	Burlington Athletic Stadium	1960	335	410	335	3,000	40,497
Danville	Dan Daniel Memorial Park	1993	330	400	330	2,588	30,385
Elizabethton	Joe O'Brien Field	1974	335	414	326	1,500	26,590
Greeneville	Pioneer Park	2004	331	400	331	2,400	48,619
Johnson City	Howard Johnson Field	1956	320	410	320	2,500	40,351
Kingsport	Hunter Wright Stadium	1995	330	410	330	2,500	30,464
Princeton	Hunnicutt Field	1988	330	396	330	1,950	24,848
Pulaski	Calfee Park	1935	335	405	310	2,500	26,160

BLUEFIELD BLUE JAYS

Office Address: Stadium Drive, Bluefield, WV 24701. **Mailing Address:** PO Box 356, Bluefield, WV 24701.
Telephone: (304) 324-1326. **Fax:** (304) 324-1318.
E-Mail Address: babybirds1@comcast.net. **Website:** www.bluefieldjays.com.
Affiliation (first year): Toronto Blue Jays (2011). **Years in League:** 1946-55, 1957-

OWNERSHIP/MANAGEMENT

Director: Charlie Wilson (Toronto Blue Jays). **Vice President:** Bill Looney. **Counsel:** David Kersey.
President: George McGonagle. **General Manager:** Jeff Gray. **Director, Field Operations/Grounds:** Mike White.

FIELD STAFF

Manager: Dennis Holmberg. **Coach:** Ken Huckaby. **Pitching Coach:** Antonio Caceres.

GAME INFORMATION

PA Announcer: Unavailable. **Official Scorer:** Unavailable.
Stadium Name: Bowen Field. **Location:** I-77 to Bluefield exit 1, Route 290 to Route 460 West, fourth light right onto Leatherwood Lane, left at first light, past Chevron station and turn right, stadium quarter-mile on left. **Ticket Price Range:** $5.
Visiting Club Hotel: Quality Inn Bluefield, 3350 Big Laurel Highway/460 West, Bluefield, WV 24701. **Telephone:** (304) 325-6170.

BRISTOL PIRATES

Ballpark Location: 1501 Euclid Ave, Bristol, VA 24201. **Mailing Address:** PO Box 1434, Bristol, VA 24203.
Telephone: (276) 206-9946. **Fax:** (276) 669-7686.
E-Mail Address: gm@bristolbaseball.com. **Website:** www.bristolpiratesbaseball.com
Affiliation (first year): Pittsburgh Pirates (2014). **Years in League:** 1921-25, 1940-55, 1969-

OWNERSHIP/MANAGEMENT
Owned by: Pittsburgh Pirates. **Operated by:** Bristol Baseball Inc. **Director:** Larry Broadway (Pittsburgh Pirates).
President/General Manager: Mahlon Luttrell. **Vice Presidents:** Lucas Hobbs, Tim Johnston, Mark Young. **Treasurer:** Jean Luttrell. **Secretary:** Perry Hustad.

FIELD STAFF
Manager: Edgar Varela. **Hitting Coach:** Terry Alexander. **Pitching Coach:** Miguel Bonilla. **Trainer:** Lee Slagle.

GAME INFORMATION
Radio: milb.com.
PA Announcer: Josh Buckles. **Official Scorer:** Tim Johnston.
Stadium Name: DeVault Memorial Stadium. **Location:** I-81 to exit 3 onto Commonwealth Ave, right on Euclid Ave for half-mile. **Standard Game Time:** 7 pm, 6 pm Sunday. **Ticket Price Range:** $3-6.
Visiting Club Hotel: Holiday Inn, 3005 Linden Drive Bristol, VA 24202. **Telephone:** (276) 466-4100.

BURLINGTON ROYALS

Office Address: 1450 Graham St, Burlington, NC 27217. **Mailing Address:** PO Box 1143, Burlington, NC 27216.
Telephone: (336) 222-0223. **Fax:** (336) 226-2498.
E-Mail Address: info@burlingtonroyals.com. **Website:** www.burlingtonroyals.com
Affiliation (first year): Kansas City Royals (2007). **Years in League:** 1986-

OWNERSHIP/MANAGEMENT
Operated by: Burlington Baseball Club Inc. **Director:** Ronnie Richardson (Kansas City). **President:** Miles Wolff. **Vice President:** Dan Moushon.
General Manager: Ryan Keur. **Assistant GM:** Jared Orton. **Director, Stadium Operations:** Mike Thompson.

FIELD STAFF
Manager: Scott Thorman. **Hitting Coach:** Jesus Azuaje. **Pitching Coach:** Carlos Martinez.

GAME INFORMATION
Radio Announcer: Matt Krause. **No. of Games Broadcast:** Home-34, Away-10. **Flagship:** www.burlingtonroyals.com.
PA Announcer: Tyler Williams. **Official Scorer:** Dale Hunt.
Stadium Name: Burlington Athletic Stadium. **Location:** I-40/85 to exit 145, north on Route 100 (Maple Avenue) for 1.5 miles, right on Mebane Street for 1.5 miles, right on Beaumont, left on Graham. **Standard Game Time:** 7 p.m. **Ticket Price Range:** $5-9.
Visiting Club Hotel: Unavailable.

DANVILLE BRAVES

Office Address: Dan Daniel Memorial Park, 302 River Park Dr, Danville, VA 24540. **Mailing Address:** PO Box 378, Danville, VA 24543.
Telephone: (434) 797-3792. **Fax:** (434) 797-3799.
E-Mail Address: info@dbraves.com. **Website:** www.dbraves.com.
Affiliation (first year): Atlanta Braves (1993). **Years in League:** 1993-

OWNERSHIP/MANAGEMENT
Operated by: Atlanta National League Baseball Club Inc. **Director:** Ronnie Richardson (Atlanta Braves).
General Manager: David Cross. **Assistant GM:** Bob Kitzmiller. **Operations Manager:** Tyler Bishop. **Head Groundskeeper:** Mark Washburn.

FIELD STAFF
Manager: Rocket Wheeler. **Coach:** Ivan Cruz. **Pitching Coach:** Dan Meyer. **Athletic Trainer:** Joe Luat.

GAME INFORMATION
Radio Announcer: Nick Pierce. **No. of Games Broadcast:** Home-34. **Flagship Station:** www.dbraves.com.
PA Announcer: Jay Stephens. **Official Scorer:** Mark Bowman.
Stadium Name: American Legion Field Post 325 Field at Dan Daniel Memorial Park. **Location:** US 29 Bypass to River Park Drive/Dan Daniel Memorial Park exit; follow signs to park. **Standard Game Times:** 7 pm, Sun 4. **Ticket Price Range:**

$5-8.
Visiting Club Hotel: Comfort Inn & Suites, 100 Tower Drive, Danville, VA 24540.

ELIZABETHTON TWINS

Office Address: 300 West Mill St., Elizabethton, TN 37643. **Stadium Address:** 208 N Holly Lane, Elizabethton, TN 37643. **Mailing Address:** 136 S Sycamore St., Elizabethton, TN 37643. **Telephone:** (423) 547-6441. **Fax:** (423) 547-6442.
E-Mail Address: etwins@cityofelizabethton.org. **Website:** www.elizabethtontwins.com.
Affiliation (first year): Minnesota Twins (1974). **Years in League:** 1937-42, 1945-51, 1974-

OWNERSHIP/MANAGEMENT
Operator: City of Elizabethton. **Director:** Brad Steil. **President:** Harold Mains.
General Manager: Mike Mains. **Clubhouse Operations/Head Groundskeeper:** David McQueen.

FIELD STAFF
Manager: Ray Smith. **Coach:** Unavailable. **Pitching Coach:** Jeff Reed. **Trainer:** Steven Taylor.

GAME INFORMATION
Radio Announcer: Nick Hyder. **No. of Games Broadcast:** 34–Home, 6–Away. **Flagship Station:** WBEJ 1240-AM.
PA Announcer: Tom Banks. **Official Scorer:** Unavailable.
Stadium Name: Joe O'Brien Field. **Location:** I-81 to Highway I-26, exit at Highway 321/67, left on Holly Lane. **Standard Game Time:** 7 pm. **Ticket Price Range:** $3-6.
Visiting Club Hotel: Holiday Inn, 101 W Springbrook Dr, Johnson City, TN 37601. **Telephone:** (423) 282-4611.

GREENEVILLE ASTROS

Office Address: 135 Shiloh Road, Greeneville, TN 37743. **Mailing Address:** PO Box 5192, Greeneville, TN 37743.
Telephone: (423) 638-0411. **Fax:** (423) 638-9450.
E-Mail Address: greeneville@astros.com. **Website:** www.greenevilleastros.com.
Affiliation (first year): Houston Astros (2004). **Years in League:** 2004-

OWNERSHIP/MANAGEMENT
Operated by: Houston Astros Baseball Club. **Director:** Quinton McCracken (Houston Astros).
General Manager: David Lane. **Assistant GM:** Hunter Reed. **Account Executive:** Ben Spillner, Kelsey Thompson.
Head Groundskeeper: Kelly Rensel. **Clubhouse Operations:** Unavailable.

FIELD STAFF
Manager: Lamarr Rodgers. **Hitting Coach:** Cesar Cedeno. **Pitching Coach:** Josh Miller.

GAME INFORMATION
Radio Announcer: Steve Wilhoit. **Flagship Station:** greenevilleastros.com.
PA Announcer: Bobby Rader. **Official Scorer:** Johnny Painter.
Stadium Name: Pioneer Park. **Location:** On the campus of Tusculum College, 135 Shiloh Rd Greeneville, TN 37743. **Standard Game Time:** 7 pm, Sat/Sun 6 pm. **Ticket Price Range:** $6-9.
Visiting Club Hotel: Quality Inn, 3160 E Andrew Johnson Hwy, Greeneville, TN 37745. **Telephone:** (423) 638-7511.

JOHNSON CITY CARDINALS

Office Address: 111 Legion St., Johnson City, TN 37601. **Mailing Address:** PO Box 179, Johnson City, TN 37605.
Telephone: (423) 461-4866. **Fax:** (423) 461-4864.
E-Mail Address: contact@jccardinals.com. **Website:** www.jccardinals.com.
Affiliation (first year): St. Louis Cardinals (1975). **Years in League:** 1911-13, 1921-24, 1937-55, 1957-61, 1964-

OWNERSHIP/MANAGEMENT
Owned by: St. Louis Cardinals. **Operated by:** Johnson City Sports Foundation Inc. **President:** Lee Sowers. **Director:** John Vuch.
General Manager: Tyler Parsons. **Assistant GM:** Zac Clark.

FIELD STAFF
Manager: Chris Swauger. **Hitting Coach:** George Greer. **Pitching Coach:** Darwin Marrero.

GAME INFORMATION
PA Announcer: Unavailable. **Official Scorer:** Unavailable.

Stadium Name: Howard Johnson Field at Cardinal Park. **Location:** I-26 to exit 23, left on East Main, through light onto Legion Street. **Standard Game Time:** 7 pm. **Ticket Price Range:** $5-$7.
Visiting Club Hotel: Holiday Inn, 101 W Springbrook Dr, Johnson City, TN 37601. **Telephone:** (423) 282-4611.

KINGSPORT METS

Address: 800 Granby Rd, Kingsport, TN 37660.
Telephone: (423) 224-2626. **Fax:** (423) 224-2625.
E-Mail Address: info@kmets.com. **Website:** www.kmets.com
Affiliation (first year): New York Mets (1980). **Years in League:** 1921-25, 1938-52, 1957, 1960-63, 1969-82, 1984-

OWNERSHIP/MANAGEMENT
Operated By: New York Mets. **Director:** Ian Levin.
General Manager: Brian Paupeck.

FIELD STAFF
Manager: Luis Rivera. **Coach:** Yunir Garcia. **Pitching Coach:** Jonathan Hurst.

GAME INFORMATION
PA Announcer: Brad Jones. **Official Scorer:** Jon Moorehouse.
Stadium Name: Hunter Wright Stadium. **Location:** I-26, Exit 1 (Stone Drive), left on West Stone Drive (US 11W), right on Granby Road. **Game Times:** Mon-Sat: 7 pm, Sun 4, doubleheaders 5. **Ticket Price Range:** $4-7.
Visiting Club Hotel: Quality Inn, 3004 Bays Mountain Plaza, Kingsport, TN 37664. **Telephone:** (423) 230-0534.

PRINCETON RAYS

Office Address: 345 Old Bluefield Rd, Princeton, WV 24739. **Mailing Address:** PO Box 5646, Princeton, WV 24740.
Telephone: (304) 487-2000. **Fax:** (304) 487-8762.
E-Mail Address: princetonrays@frontier.com . **Website:** www.princetonrays.net.
Affiliation (first year): Tampa Bay Rays (1997). **Years in League:** 1988-

OWNERSHIP/MANAGEMENT
Operated By: Princeton Baseball Association Inc. **Director:** Mitch Lukevics. **President:** Mori Williams.
General Manager: Jim Holland. **Director, Stadium Operations:** Mick Bayle. **Clubhouse Manager:** Anthony Dunagan. **Administrative Assistant:** Tommy Thomason. **Chaplain:** Craig Stout.

FIELD STAFF
Manager: Danny Sheaffer. **Coach:** Craig Albernaz. **Pitching Coach:** Jose Gonzalez. **Athletic Trainer:** James Ramsdell.

GAME INFORMATION
Radio Announcer: Kyle Cooper. **No. of Games Broadcast:** 34–Away. **Flagship Station:** WAEY-103.3FM.
PA Announcer: Unavailable. **Official Scorer:** Unavailable.
Stadium Name: Hunnicutt Field. **Location:** Exit 9 off I-77, US 460 West to downtown exit, left on Stafford Drive; stadium located behind Mercer County Technical Education Center. **Standard Game Times:** 7 pm, Sun 5:30. **Ticket Price Range:** $4-6.
Visiting Club Hotel: Days Inn, I-77 and Ambrose Lane, Princeton, WV 24740. **Telephone:** (304) 425-8100.

PULASKI YANKEES

Office Address: 700 South Washington Ave., Pulaski VA 24301. **Mailing Address:** PO 1499, Christiansburg, VA 24301.
Telephone: (540) 980-1070.
E-Mail Address: info@pulaskiyankees.net
Affiliation (first year): New York Yankees (2015). **Years in League:** 1946-50, 1952-55, 1957-58, 1969-77, 1982-92, 1997-2006, 2008-

OWNERSHIP/MANAGEMENT
Operated By: Calfee Park Baseball Inc. **Park Owners:** David Hagan, Larry Shelor.
General Manager: Mike Fintel. **Director, Public Relations/Marketing:** Blair Hoke.

FIELD STAFF
Manager: Tony Franklin. **Hitting Coach:** Edwar Gonzalez. **Pitching Coach:** Justin Pope. **Defensive Coach:** Hector Rabago. **Trainer:** Josh DiLoreto. **Strength Coach:** James Gonzalez.

GAME INFORMATION

PA Announcer: Unavailable. **Official Scorer:** Unavailable.

Stadium Name: Calfee Park. **Location:** Interstate 81 to Exit 89-B (Route 11), north to Pulaski, right on Pierce Avenue. **Ticket Price Range:** $4-6.

Visiting Club Hotel: Unavailable.

PIONEER LEAGUE

Office Address: 180 S Howard Street, Spokane, WA 99201. **Mailing Address:** PO Box 2564, Spokane, WA 99220.
Telephone: (509) 456-7615. **Fax:** (509) 456-0136.
E-Mail Address: fanmail@pioneerleague.com. **Website:** www.pioneerleague.com.
Years League Active: 1939-42, 1946-

President: Jim McCurdy.

Directors: Dave Baggott (Ogden), Matt Ellis (Missoula), DG Elmore (Helena), Kevin Greene (Idaho Falls), Michael Baker (Grand Junction), Jeff Katofsky (Orem), Vinny Purpura (Great Falls), Bob Herrfeldt (Billings).

League Administrator: Teryl MacDonald. **Executive Director:** Mary Ann McCurdy.

Division Structure: North—Billings, Great Falls, Helena, Missoula.South—Grand Junction, Idaho Falls, Ogden, Orem.

Regular Season: 76 games (split schedule). **2015 Opening Date:** June 16. **Closing Date:** Sept. 4.

All-Star Game: Pioneer League vs. Northwest League, Aug. 4, Spokane.

Playoff Format: First-half division winners meet second-half division winners in best of three series. Winners meet in best of three series for league championship.

Roster Limit: 35 active, 35 dressed for each game. **Player Eligibility Rule:** No player on active list may have three or more years of prior minor league service.

Brand of Baseball: Rawlings.

Umpires: Unavailable.

Jim McCurdy

STADIUM INFORMATION

Club	Stadium	Opened	Dimensions LF	CF	RF	Capacity	2014 Att.
Billings	Dehler Park	2008	329	410	350	3,071	105,538
Grand Junction	Sam Suplizio Field	1949	302	400	333	7,014	81,382
Great Falls	Centene Stadium at Legion Park	1956	335	414	335	3,800	49,520
Helena	Kindrick Field	1939	335	400	325	1,700	30,764
Idaho Falls	Melaleuca Field	1976	340	400	350	3,400	79,895
Missoula	Ogren Park at Allegiance Field	2004	309	398	287	3,500	84,429
Ogden	Lindquist Field	1997	335	396	334	5,000	108,504
Orem	Home of the Owlz	2005	305	408	312	4,500	83,1799

BILLINGS MUSTANGS

Office Address: Dehler Park, 2611 9th Avenue North, Billings, MT 59101. **Mailing Address:** PO Box 1553, Billings, MT 59103-1553.
Telephone: (406) 252-1241. **Fax:** (406) 252-2968.
E-Mail Address: mustangs@billingsmustangs.com. **Website:** billingsmustangs.com.
Affiliation (first year): Cincinnati Reds (1974). **Years in League:** 1948-63, 1969-

OWNERSHIP/MANAGEMENT

Operated By: Billings Pioneer Baseball Club.
President: Woody Hahn.
General Manager: Gary Roller. **Senior Director, Corporate Sales/Partnerships:** Chris Marshall. **Senior Director, Stadium Operations:** Matt Schoonover. **Senior Director, Broadcasting/Media Relations:** Ryan Schuiling. **Senior Director, Food Services:** Curt Prchal. **Senior Director, Field Maintenance/Facilities:** John Barta.

FIELD STAFF

Manager: Dick Schofield. **Hitting Coach:** Jolbert Cabrera. **Pitching Coach:** Derrin Ebert.

GAME INFORMATION

Radio Broadcaster: Kyle Riley. **No. of Games Broadcast:** 76. **Flagship Station:** 910-AM KBLG.
PA Announcer: Rob Kovatch. **Official Scorer:** George Kimmet.
Stadium Name: Dehler Park. **Location:** I-90 to Exit 450, north on 27th Street North to 9th Avenue North. **Standard Game Times:** 7:05 pm, Sat 6:05, Sun 1:05. **Ticket Price Range:** $4 - $10.
Visiting Club Hotel: Unavailable.

GRAND JUNCTION ROCKIES

Address: 1315 North Ave, Grand Junction, CO 81501.
Telephone: (970) 255-7625. **Fax:** (970) 241-2374.
E-Mail Address: timray@gjrockies.com. **Website:** www.gjrockies.com.
Affiliation (first year): Colorado Rockies (2001). **Years in League:** 2001-

OWNERSHIP/MANAGEMENT
Principal Owners/Operated by: GJR LLC.
General Manager: Tim Ray. **Assistant GM:** BJ Miller. **Director, Food and Beverage:** Mick Ritter.

FIELD STAFF
Developmental Supervisor: Tony Diaz. **Manager:** Anthony Sanders. **Hitting Coach:** Lee Stevens. **Pitching Coach:** Ryan Kibler. **Trainer:** John Duff.

GAME INFORMATION
Radio Announcer: Adam Spolane. **No. of Games Broadcast:** 76. **Flagship Station:** The Vault 100.7 FM.
PA Announcer: Unavailable. **Official Scorers:** Chris Hanks, Dan Kenyon.
Stadium Name: Suplizio Field. **Location:** 1315 North Ave, Grand Junction, CO 81501. **Standard Game Times:** 7:05 pm, Sun 4:05. **Ticket Price Range:** $7-9.
Visiting Club Hotel: Unavailable.

GREAT FALLS VOYAGERS

Address: 1015 25th St N, Great Falls, MT 59401.
Telephone: (406) 452-5311. **Fax:** (406) 454-0811.
E-Mail Address: voyagers@gfvoyagers.com. **Website:** www.gfvoyagers.com.
Affiliation (first year): Chicago White Sox (2003). **Years in League:** 1948-1963, 1969-

OWNERSHIP/MANAGEMENT
Operated By: Great Falls Baseball Club, Inc. **President:** Vinney Purpura.
General Manager: Scott Reasoner. **Assistant GM:** Matt Coakley. **Sales Manager:** Scott Lettre.

FIELD STAFF
Manager: Cole Armstrong. **Coach:** Greg Briley. **Pitching Coach:** Brian Drahman.

GAME INFORMATION
Radio Announcer: Rob Low. **No. of Games Broadcast:** 76. **Flagship Station:** KXGF-1400 AM.
PA Announcer: Chris Evans. **Official Scorer:** Mike Lewis.
Stadium Name: Centene Stadium. **Location:** From I-15 to exit 281 (10th Ave S), left on 26th, left on Eighth Ave North, right on 25th, ballpark on right, past railroad tracks. **Ticket Price Range:** $5-10.
Visiting Club Hotel: Townhouse Inn of Great Falls, 1411 10th Ave S, Great Falls, MT 59405. **Telephone:** (406) 761-4600.

HELENA BREWERS

Office Address: 1300 N. Ewing, Helena, MT 59601. **Mailing Address:** PO Box 6756, Helena, MT 59604.
Telephone: (406) 495-0500. **Fax:** (406) 495-0900.
E-Mail Address: info@helenabrewers.net. **Website:** www.helenabrewers.net.
Affiliation (first year): Milwaukee Brewers (2003). **Years in League:** 1978-2000, 2003-

OWNERSHIP/MANAGEMENT
Operated by: Helena Baseball Club LLC. **Principal Owner:** David Elmore.
General Manager: Paul Fetz. **Director, Operations/Ticketing:** Travis Hawks. **Director, Group Sales/Marketing:** Dylan LaPlante. **Radio Announcer/Director, Broadcasting/Media Relations:** Dustin Daniel. **Community Relations/Entertainment:** Helen Scholar.

FIELD STAFF
Manager: Tony Diggs. **Hitting Coach:** Jason Dubois. **Pitching Coach:** Rolando Valles.

GAME INFORMATION
Radio Announcer: Dustin Daniel. **No. of Games Broadcast:** 76. **Flagship Station:** Unavailable.
PA Announcer: Kevin Smith. **Official Scorers:** Kevin Higgens, Craig Struble, Jim Shope, Andrew Gideon.

Stadium Name: Kindrick Field. **Location:** Cedar Street exit off I-15, west to Last Chance Gulch, left at Memorial Park.
Standard Game Time: 7:05 pm, Sun 1:05. **Ticket Price Range:** $6-10.
Visiting Club Hotel: Red Lion Colonial. **Telephone:** (406) 443-2100.

IDAHO FALLS CHUKARS

Office Address: 900 Jim Garchow Way, Idaho Falls, ID 83402. **Mailing Address:** PO 2183, Idaho, ID 83403.
Telephone: (208) 522-8363. **Fax:** (208) 522-9858.
E-Mail Address: chukars@ifchukars.com. **Website:** www.ifchukars.com.
Affiliation (first year): Kansas City Royals (2004). **Years in League:** 1940-42, 1946-

OWNERSHIP/MANAGEMENT

Operated By: The Elmore Sports Group. **Principal Owner:** David Elmore.
President/General Manager: Kevin Greene. **Assistant GM:** Paul Henderson. **Director, Operations:** Alex Groh.
Clubhouse Manager: Patrick Greene. **Head Groundskeeper:** Ryan Coleman.

FIELD STAFF

Manager: Justin Gemoll. **Hitting Coach:** Andre David. **Pitching Coach:** Jeff Suppan.

GAME INFORMATION

Radio Announcer: John Balginy. **No. of Games Broadcast:** 76. **Flagship Station:** KUPI/ESPN 980-AM.
PA Announcer: Unavailable. **Official Scorer:** John Balginy.
Stadium Name: Melaleuca Field. **Location:** I-15 to West Broadway exit, left onto Memorial Drive, right on Mound Avenue, 1/4 mile to stadium. **Standard Game Times:** 7:15 pm, Sun 4:00. **Ticket Price Range:** $8-12.
Visiting Club Hotel: Guesthouse Inn & Suites, 850 Lindsay Blvd, Idaho Falls, ID 83402. **Telephone:** (208) 522-6260.

MISSOULA OSPREY

Address: 140 N Higgins, Suite 201, Missoula, MT 59802.
Telephone: (406) 543-3300. **Fax:** (406) 543-9463.
E-Mail Address: info@missoulaosprey.com. **Website:** www.missoulaosprey.com.
Affiliation (first year): Arizona Diamondbacks (1999). **Years in League:** 1956-60, 1999-

OWNERSHIP/MANAGEMENT

Operated By: Mountain Baseball LLC. **President:** Mike Ellis. **Executive Vice Presidents:** Judy Ellis, Matt Ellis.
Vice President/General Manager: Jeff Griffin. **Retail Manager:** Kim Klages Johns. **Office Manager/Bookkeeper:** Nola Hunter. **Ticket Sales Executive:** Taylor Rush. **Ticket Sales Executive:** A.J. Russell.

FIELD STAFF

Manager: Joe Mather. **Hitting Coach:** Tack Wilson. **Pitching Coach:** Jeff Bajenaru. **Strength/Conditioning:** Steven Candelaria. **Trainer:** Chris Schepel.

GAME INFORMATION

Radio Announcer: Tyler Geivett. **No. of Games Broadcast:** 76. **Flagship Station:** ESPN 102.9 FM.
PA Announcer: Tom Schultz. **Official Scorer:** Dan Hunter.
Stadium Name: Ogren Park Allegiance Field. **Location:** Take Orange Street to Cregg Lane, west on Cregg Lane, stadium west of McCormick Park. **Standard Game Times:** 7:05 pm, Sun 5:05. **Ticket Price Range:** $6-13.
Visiting Club Hotel: Comfort Inn-University, 1021 E. Broadway, Missoula, MT 59802. **Telephone:** (406) 549-7600.

OGDEN RAPTORS

Address: 2330 Lincoln Ave, Ogden, UT 84401.
Telephone: (801) 393-2400. **Fax:** (801) 393-2473.
E-Mail Address: homerun@ogden-raptors.com. **Website:** www.ogden-raptors.com.
Affiliation (first year): Los Angeles Dodgers (2003). **Years in League:** 1939-42, 1946-55, 1966-74, 1994-

OWNERSHIP/MANAGEMENT

Operated By: Ogden Professional Baseball, Inc. **Principal Owners:** Dave Baggott, John Lindquist.
President/General Manager: Dave Baggott. **Director Media Relations/Broadcaster:** Brandon Hart. **Director, Food Services:** Geri Kopinski. **Director, Food Service Personnel:** Louise Hillard. **Director, Security:** Scott McGregor. **Director, Ticket Operations:** Kylie Johnson. **Director, Information Technology:** Chris Greene. **Public Relations:** Pete Diamond. **Groundskeeper:** Kenny Kopinski. **Assistant Groundskeeper:** Bob Richardson.

FIELD STAFF

Manager: John Shoemaker. **Hitting Coach:** Darryl Brinkley. **Pitching Coach:** Bobby Cuellar.

GAME INFORMATION

   Radio Announcer: Brandon Hart. **No. of Games Broadcast:** 76. **Flagship Station:** 97.5 FM.
   PA Announcer: Pete Diamond. **Official Scorer:** Dennis Kunimura.
   Stadium Name: Lindquist Field. **Location:** I-15 North to 21th Street exit, east to Lincoln Avenue, south three blocks to park. **Standard Game Times:** 7 pm, Sun 4. **Ticket Price Range:** $4-10.
   Visiting Club Hotel: Unavailable.

OREM OWLZ

   Address: 970 W. University Parkway, Orem, UT 84058.
   Telephone: (801) 377-2255. **Fax:** (801) 377-2345.
   E-Mail Address: fan@oremowlz.com. **Website:** www.oremowlz.com.
   Affiliation: Los Angeles Angels (2001). **Years in League:** 2001-

OWNERSHIP/MANAGEMENT

   Operated By: Bery Bery Gud To Me LLC. **Principal Owner:** Jeff Katofsky.
   General Manager: Justo Vazquez. **Assistant GM:** Jillian Dingee. **IT Manager:** Julie Hatch. **Director, Sales/Marketing:** Abby Lyman.

FIELD STAFF

   Manager: Dave Stapleton. **Coach:** Buck Coats. **Pitching Coach:** John Slusarz.

GAME INFORMATION

   Radio Announcer: Trevor Amicone. **No. of Games Broadcast:** 76. **Flagship Station:** Unavailable.
   PA Announcer: Unavailable. **Official Scorer:** Rachel Hartgrove.
   Stadium Name: Home of the Owlz. **Location:** Exit 269 (University Parkway) off I-15 at Utah Valley University campus. **Ticket Price Range:** $4-12.
   Visiting Club Hotel: Holiday Inn & Suites, 1290 W. University Parkway, Orem, UT 8405.

ARIZONA LEAGUE

Office Address: 620 W Franklin St., Boise, ID 83702. **Mailing Address:** PO Box 1645, Boise, ID 83701.
Telephone: (208) 429-1511. **Fax:** (208) 429-1525.
E-Mail Address: bobrichmond@qwestoffice.net
Years League Active: 1988-
President/Treasurer: Bob Richmond.
Vice President: Alan Lee (Giants). **Corporate Secretary:** Ted Polakowski (Athletics).
Administrative Assistant: Rob Richmond.
Divisional Alignment: East—Angels, Athletics, Cubs, Diamondbacks, Giants. Central—Brewers, Dodgers, Indians, Reds, White Sox. West—Mariners, Padres, Rangers, Royals.
Regular Season: 56 games (split schedule). **2015 Opening Date:** June 20. **Closing Date:** Aug 29.
Playoff Format: Division champions from the first and second half qualify (six teams). Two teams with best overall records receive first-round bye. Remaining four teams meet in one-game playoffs. Winners advance to one-game championship.
All-Star Game: None.
Roster Limit: 35 active. **Player Eligibility Rule:** No player may have three or more years of prior minor league service.

Clubs	Playing Site	Manager	Coach	Pitching Coach
Angels	Angels Complex, Tempe	Elio Sarmiento	B. Betancourth/P. McAnulty	J. Cuevas/R. O'Malley
Athletics	Papago Park Baseball Complex, Phoenix	Ruben Escalera	Juan Dilone	Unavailable
Brewers	Maryvale Baseball Complex, Phoenix	Nestor Corredor	Al LeBoeuf	Steve Cline
Cubs	Fitch Park, Mesa	Carmelo Martinez	Oscar Bernard	Ron Villone
D-backs	Salt River Fields at Talking Stick	Mike Benjamin	Jacob Cruz	Larry Pardo
Dodgers	Camelback Ranch, Glendale	Jack McDowell	Aaron Bates	Greg Sabat
Giants	Giants complex, Scottsdale	Nestor Rojas	Billy Horton	L. McCall/M. Rodriguez
Indians	Goodyear Ballpark	Anthony Medrano	J. Betances/D. Malave	Rigo Beltran
Mariners	Peoria Sports Complex	Darrin Garner	A. Bottin/J. Lofton	Rich Dorman
Padres	Peoria Sports Complex	Rod Barajas	Carlos Sosa	Dave Rajsich
Rangers	Surprise Recreation Campus	Kenny Holmberg	K. Hook/S. Manriquez	J. Seaver/B. Shouse
Reds	Goodyear Ballpark	Ray Martinez	Travis Dawkins	Elmer Dessens/Tom Brown
Royals	Goodyear Ballpark	Darryl Kennedy	N. Liriano/W. Aikens	M. Davis/R. Colon
White Sox	Camelback Ranch, Glendale	Mike Gellinger	Gary Ward	Felipe Lira

GULF COAST LEAGUE

Operated By: Minor League Baseball.
Address: 9550 16th St. North, St. Petersburg, FL 33716.
Telephone: (727) 456-1734. **Fax:** (727) 821-5819.
Website: www.milb.com. **E-Mail Address:** gcl@milb.com.
Vice President, Baseball/Business Operations: Tim Brunswick. **Manager, Baseball/Business Operations:** Andy Shultz.
Regular Season: 60 games. **2015 Opening Date:** June 22. **Closing Date:** Aug 29.
Divisional Alignment: East—Cardinals, Marlins, Mets, Nationals. Northeast—Astros, Braves, Tigers, Yankees 2. Northwest—Blue Jays, Phillies, Pirates, Yankees 1. South—Orioles, Rays, Red Sox, Twins.
Playoff Format: Division winners play one-game semifinals. Winners meet in best of three series for league championship.
All-Star Game: None.
Roster Limit: 35 active, 30 in uniform and eligible to play in any given game. At least 10 must be pitchers as of July 1.
Player Eligibility Rule: No player may have three or more years of prior minor league service.
Brand of Baseball: Rawlings.

Clubs	Playing Site	Manager	Coach(es)	Pitching Coach
Astros	Astros Complex, Kissimmee	Marty Malloy	Vinnie Lopez	Hector Mercado
Blue Jays	Mattick Training Center, Dunedin	Cesar Martin	Paul Elliott	Willie Collazo
Braves	ESPN Wide World of Sports, Orlando	Robinson Cancel	Rick Albert	Willie Martinez
Cardinals	Cardinals Complex, Jupiter	Steve Turco	Roberto Espinoza	Cale Johnson
Marlins	Roger Dean Stadium Complex, Jupiter	Julio Garcia	Danny Santin	Manny Olivera
Mets	Mets Complex, Port St Lucie	Jose Carreno	Ender Chavez	Royce Ring
Nationals	Nationals Complex, Viera	Michael Barrett	J. Mejia/J. Head	Michael Tejera
Orioles	Ed Smith Stadium Complex, Sarasota	Matt Merullo	M. May/R. Sambo	Wilson Alvarez
Phillies	Carpenter Complex, Clearwater	Roly de Armas	Rafael DeLima	Steve Schrenk
Pirates	Pirate City, Bradenton	Milver Reyes	Kory DeHaan	Elvin Nina
Rays	Charlotte Sports Park, Port Charlotte	Jim Morrison	W. Rincones/H. Torres	Marty DeMerritt
Red Sox	Jet Blue Park, Fort Myers	Tom Kotchman	J. Zamora/D. Tomlin	Dick Such
Tigers	Tigertown, Lakeland	Basilio Cabrera	Edgar Alfonzo	Jaime Garcia
Twins	Lee County Sports Complex, Fort Myers	Ramon Borrego	Ingram/Valentin/Dinkelman	Martinez/Vasquez
Yankees 1	Himes Complex, Tampa	Julio Mosquera	Caonabo Cosme	Elvys Quezada
Yankees 2	Himes Complex, Tampa	Marc Bombard	Jason Brown	Unavailable

INDEPENDENT LEAGUES

AMERICAN ASSOCIATION

Office Address: 1415 Hwy 54 West, Suite 210, Durham, NC 27707.
Telephone: (919) 401-8150. **Fax:** (919) 401-8152. **Website:** www.americanassociationbaseball.com.
Year Founded: 2006.
Commissioner: Miles Wolff. **President:** Dan Moushon.
Director, Umpires: Kevin Winn.
Division Structure—North Division: Fargo-Moorhead RedHawks, St. Paul Saints, Sioux Falls Canaries, Winnipeg Goldeyes.
Central Division: Gary SouthShore RailCats, Kansas City T-Bones, Lincoln Saltdogs, Sioux City Explorers.
South Division: Amarillo Thunderheads, Grand Prairie AirHogs, Joplin Blasters, Laredo Lemurs, Wichita Wingnuts.
Regular Season: 100 games.
2015 Opening Date: May 21. **Closing Date:** Sept. 7.
Playoff Format: Three division winners and one wild card play in best-of-five series. Winners play for best-of-five American Association championship.
Roster Limit: 22.
Eligibility Rule: Minimum of four first-year players; maximum of five veterans (at least six or more years of professional service).
Brand of Baseball: Rawlings.
Statistician: Pointstreak.com, 602-1595 16th Avenue, Richmond Hill, ON Canada L4B 3N9.

STADIUM INFORMATION

Club	Stadium	Opened	Dimensions LF	CF	RF	Capacity	2014 Att.
Amarillo	Amarillo National Bank Stadium	1949	355	429	355	7,500	81,834
Fargo-Moorhead	Newman Outdoor Field	1996	318	408	314	4,513	186,306
Gary SouthShore	U.S. Steel Yard	2002	320	400	335	6,139	164,286
Grand Prairie	QuikTrip Park at Grand Prairie	2008	330	400	330	5,445	60,747
Joplin	Joe Becker Stadium	1913	330	400	330	4,200	N/A
Kansas City	CommunityAmerica Ballpark	2003	300	396	328	6,537	248,989
Laredo	Uni-Trade Stadium	2012	335	405	335	6,000	132,562
Lincoln	Haymarket Park	2001	335	395	325	4,500	166,503
St. Paul	CHS Field	2015	330	396	320	7,140	248,106
Sioux City	Lewis and Clark Park	1993	330	400	330	3,630	50,746
Sioux Falls	Sioux Falls Stadium	1964	312	410	312	4,656	139,784
Wichita	Lawrence-Dumont Stadium	1934	344	401	312	6,055	147,706
Winnipeg	Shaw Park	1999	325	400	325	7,481	258,429

AMARILLO THUNDERHEADS

Office Address: 801 S Polk St, Amarillo, TX 79101.
Telephone: (806) 242-4653. **Fax:** (806) 322-1839.
Email Address: stephanie@806prosports.com. **Website:** www.gothunderheads.com.
General Manager: Stephanie Tucker.
Field Manager: Bobby Brown.

GAME INFORMATION
Stadium Name: Amarillo National Bank Stadium. **Location:** Take Grand Street exit and proceed north on Grand Street; turn left onto SE 3rd Ave.
Standard Game Times: 7:05, Saturday 6:05, Sunday 2:05.

FARGO-MOORHEAD
REDHAWKS

Office Address: 1515 15th Ave N, Fargo, ND 58102.
Telephone: (701) 235-6161. **Fax:** (701) 297-9247.
Email Address: redhawks@fmredhawks.com. **Website:** www.fmredhawks.com.
Operated by: Fargo Baseball LLC.
President: Bruce Thom. **Chief Executive Officer:** Brad Thom.
General Manager: Josh Buchholz. **Director, Accounting:** Rick Larson. **Director, Ticket Operations:** Michael Larson. **Director, Promotions/Merchandise:** Karl Hoium. **Director, Group Sales:** Corey Eidem. **Head Groundskeeper:** Tim Jallen. **Director, Stadium Operations:** Michael Stark. **Director, Food/Beverage:** Sean Kiernan.

Manager/Director, Player Procurement: Doug Simunic. **Player Procurement Consultant:** Jeff Bittiger. **Pitching Coach:** Michael Schlact. **Coaches:** Bucky Burgau, Kole Zimmerman, Robbie Lopez. **Trainer:** Unavailable. **Clubhouse Manager:** Chris Krick.

GAME INFORMATION
Radio Announcer: Scott Miller. **No. of Games Broadcast:** 100. **Flagship Station:** 740-AM The FAN.
Stadium Name: Newman Outdoor Field. **Location:** I-29 North to exit 67, east on 19th Ave North, right on Albrecht Boulevard. **Standard Game Times:** 7:02 pm, Sat 6, Sun 1.

GARY SOUTHSHORE RAILCATS

Office Address: One Stadium Plaza, Gary, IN 46402.
Telephone: (219) 882-2255. **Fax:** (219) 882-2259.
Email Address: info@railcatsbaseball.com. **Website:** www.railcatsbaseball.com.
Operated by: PLS Holdings.
Owner/CEO: Pat Salvi. **Owner:** Lindy Salvi.
President, Salvi Sports Enterprises: Pete Laven. **General Manager:** Bryan Lyter. **Assistant GM/Director, Tickets:** David Kay. **Senior Executive, Corporate Partnerships:** Percy Thornbor. **Account Executive:** David Kerr. **Manager, Community Relations/Merchandise:** Crystal Torres. **Account Executive/Marketing Assistant:** Briana Schafer. **Marketing Consultant:** Renee Connelly.
Manager: Greg Tagert. **Pitching Coach:** Chad Rhoades. **Coaches:** Mick Curran, Joe Beck, Juan Alonso. **Clubhouse Manager:** James Johnson.

GAME INFORMATION
Broadcaster: Dan Vaughan. **No. of Games Broadcast:** 100. **Flagship Station:** WLPR 89.1-FM.
Stadium Name: US Steel Yard. **Location:** I-80/94 to Broadway Exit (Exit 10), north on Broadway to Fifth Avenue, east one block to stadium. **Standard Game Times:** 7:10 pm, Sat 6:10, Sun 2:10.

GRAND PRAIRIE AIRHOGS

Office Address: 1600 Lone Star Parkway, Grand Prairie, TX 75050.
Telephone: (972) 504-9383. **Fax:** (972) 504-2288.
Websites: www.airhogsbaseball.com.
Operated By: Southern Independent Baseball, LLC.
Owner: Gary Elliston. **Vice President/General Manager:** John Bilbow. **Assistant GM:** Katy White. **Sales:** Karen Lucchesi.
Manager: Eric Champion.

GAME INFORMATION
No of Games Broadcast: 100. **Webcast:** www.airhogsbaseball.com.
Stadium Name: QuikTrip Park at Grand Prairie. **Location:** From I-30, take Beltline Road exit going north, take Lone Star Park entrance towards the stadium.
Standard Game Times: 7:05 pm, Sun 2:05.

JOPLIN BLASTERS

Office Address: 407 South Pennsylvania Avenue, Joplin, MO 64801.
Telephone: (417) 437-6105.
E-mail address: info@joplinblasters.com.
Website: www.joplinblasters.com.
CEO: Gabriel Suarez. **Executive VP/GM:** Shawn Suarez. **Executive VP, Business Operations:** Matt LaBranche.
Manager: Carlos Lezcano.
Stadium Name: Joe Becker Stadium. **Standard Game Times:** 6:35 p.m., **Sunday 5:**05 p.m.

KANSAS CITY T-BONES

Office Address: 1800 Village West Parkway, Kansas City, KS 66111.
Telephone: (913) 328-5618. **Fax:** (913) 328-5674.
Email Address: tickets@tbonesbaseball.com.
Website: www.tbonesbaseball.com.
Operated By: T-Bones Baseball Club, LLC; Ehlert Development.
Owner: John Ehlert. **President:** Adam Ehlert.

VP/General Manager: Chris Browne. **Senior Director, Corporate Sales:** Jeff Husted. **Senior Director, Broadcasting/Media Relations:** Matt Fulks. **Assistant Director, Group Sales:** Stephen Hardwick. **Director, Ticket Sales:** Crystal Collins. **Manager, Promotions:** Joe Goll. **Account Executive:** Connor Terry. **Group Sales Associates:** Scott Hull and Nick Restivo. **Director, Operations; Rylan Brody. Head Groundskeeper:** Gary Hinton. **Bookkeeper:** Karen Slaughter. **Director, Merchandise:** Kacy Muller.

Manager: John Massarelli. **Coaches:** Frank White, Bill Sobbe, Dave Schaub.

GAME INFORMATION

Radio Announcer: Nathan Moore. **No. of Games Broadcast:** 100. **Flagship Station:** KMBZ 1660-AM.

Stadium Name: CommunityAmerica Ballpark. **Location:** State Avenue West off I-435 and State Avenue. **Standard Game Times:** 7:05 pm, 5:05 pm (Sun).

LAREDO LEMURS

Office Address: 6320 Sinatra Drive, Laredo, TX 78045.

Telephone: (956) 753-6877. **Fax:** (956) 791-0672.

Website: www.laredolemurs.com.

Managing Partner: Mark Schuster.

Corporate Sales: Susan Gusman, Juan Salinas. **Office Manager/Receptionist:** Victoria Cardenas. **Promotions Coordinator:** Tanyn Walters. **Clubhouse Manager:** Gibby Vela-Cuellar.

Manager: Pete Incaviglia.

GAME INFORMATION

Announcer: Unavailable. **No. of Games Broadcast:** 100. **Webcast:** www.laredolemurs.com.

Stadium Name: Uni-Trade Stadium. **Location:** From North: I-35 to Exit 9 turn left onto Loop 20/Bob Bullock Blvd, south on Loop 20 for 3 miles, make right onto Sinatra Blvd, stadium on left; From South: I-35 to Exit 2 turn right onto Hwy 59 for 4 miles, turn left onto Loop 20 North for 2 miles, turn left onto Sinatra Drive, stadium on left.

Standard Game Times: 7:30 pm.

LINCOLN SALTDOGS

Office Address: 403 Line Drive Circle, Suite A, Lincoln, NE 68508.

Telephone: (402) 474-2255. **Fax:** (402) 474-2254.

Email Address: info@saltdogs.com. **Website:** www.saltdogs.com.

Owner: Jim Abel. **President/GM:** Charlie Meyer.

Director, Marketing: Bret Beer. **Director, Broadcasting/Communications:** Drew Bontadelli. **Director, Stadium Operations:** Dave Aschwege. **Director, Sales:** Steve Zoucha. **Director, Merchandise/Promotions:** Anne Duchek. **Director, Video Production:** Bill Homan. **Assistant Director, Stadium Operations:** Dan Busch. **Manager, Ticket Sales:** Colter Clarke. **Athletic Turf Manager:** Josh Klute. **Assistant Athletic Turf Managers:** Jeremy Johnson, Jen Roeber. **Office Manager:** Shelby Meier.

Manager: Ken Oberkfell. **Trainers:** Corey Courtney, Kyle Younkin.

GAME INFORMATION

Radio Announcer: Drew Bontadelli. **No. of Games Broadcast:** 100. **Flagship Station:** KFOR 1240-AM. **Webcast Address:** www.kfor1240.com.

Stadium Name: Haymarket Park. **Location:** I-80 to Cornhusker Highway West, left on First Street, right on Sun Valley Boulevard, left on Line Drive.

Standard Game Times: 6:35, Friday 7:05, Saturday 6:05, Sunday 5:05.

ST. PAUL SAINTS

Office Address: 360 Broadway Street, St. Paul, MN 55101.

Telephone: (651) 644-3517. **Fax:** (651) 644-1627.

Email Address: funisgood@saintsbaseball.com.

Website: www.saintsbaseball.com.

Principal Owners: Marv Goldklang, Bill Murray, Mike Veeck. **Chairman:** Marv Goldklang. **President:** Mike Veeck. **Vice-President/Owner:** Jeff Goldklang.

Executive Vice President/General Manager: Derek Sharrer. **Executive VP:** Tom Whaley. **Assistant GMs:** Scott Bush, Chris Schwab. **VP, Customer Service/Community Partnerships:** Annie Huidekoper. **Director, Broadcast/Media Relations:** Sean Aronson. **Box Office Manager:** Alex Harkaway. **Manager, Promotions:** Sierra Bailey. **Manager, Corporate Activation:** Tyson Jeffers. **Manager, Marketing Services:** Kelly Hagenson. **Manager, Fan Services & Community Relations:** Emily Vickers. **Events Manager:** Jillian Beard.

Account Executives: Mark Jeffrey, Casey Odell, Allison Wenker. **Marketing Associate:** Jordan Lynn. **Director, Operations:** Curtis Nachtsheim. **Office Manager:** Gina Kray. **Director,Food/Beverage:** Justin Grandstaff. **Director, Catering:** Effie Minitsios. **Head Groundskeeper:** Nick Baker.

Manager: George Tsamis. **Coaches:** Kerry Ligtenberg, Ole Sheldon. **Clubhouse Manager:** Ed Luka.

GAME INFORMATION
Radio Announcer: Sean Aronson. **No. of Games Broadcast:** 100. **Flagship Station:** Club 1220 AM. **Webcast Address:** www.saintsbaseball.com.
Stadium Name: CHS Field. **Location:** From the west take I-94 to the 7th St. Exit and head south to 5th & Broadway. From the east take I-94 to the Mounds Blvd/US-61N exit. Turn left on Kellogg and a right on Broadway until you reach 5th St.
Standard Game Times: 7:05 pm, Sun 5:05.

SIOUX CITY EXPLORERS

Office Address: 3400 Line Drive, Sioux City, IA 51106.
Telephone: (712) 277-9467. **Fax:** (712) 277-9406.
Email Address: promotions@xsbaseball.com. **Website:** www.xsbaseball.com.
President: Matt Adamski.
VP/General Manager: Shane M Tritz. **Director, Ticketing:** Stephanie Warnke.
Media Relations Assistant: Shawn Tiemann. **Office Manager:** Julie Stinger.
Field Manager: Steve Montgomery. **Pitching Coach:** Bobby Post. **Hitting Coach:** Kyle Nichols. **Clubhouse Manager:** Mike Ward.

GAME INFORMATION
Radio Announcer: Dave Nitz. **No. of Games Broadcast:** 100. **Flagship Station:** KSCJ 1360-AM. **Webcast Address:** www.xsbaseball.com.
Stadium Name: Lewis and Clark Park. **Location:** I-29 to Singing Hills Blvd, North, right on Line Drive.
Standard Game Times: 7:05 pm, Sun 6:05.

SIOUX FALLS CANARIES

Office Address: 1001 N West Ave, Sioux Falls, SD 57104.
Telephone: (605) 333-0179. **Fax:** (605) 333-0139.
Email Address: info@sfcanaries.com. **Website:** www.sfcanaries.com.
Operated by: Sioux Falls Sports, LLC.
CEO/President/Managing Partner: Tom Garrity.
Executive VP, Business Operations: Jim Olander. **GM/VP, Ticket Sales:** Matt Ferguson. **Director, Sales:** Rico Velazquez. **Assistant GM, Baseball Operations:** Duell Higbe. **Assistant GM, Business Operations:** Brita Bragnalo. **Sales Executives:** Denny Majeske, Korey McDonald, Brian Olthoff. **Director, Game Operations & Merchandise:** Anthony Hegstrom. **Stadium Operations:** Larry McKenny, Duell Higbe.
Manager: Chris Paterson. **Trainer:** Derek West.

GAME INFORMATION
Radio Announcer: JJ Hartigan. **No. of Games Broadcast:** 100. **Flagship Station:** KWSN 1230-AM. **Webcast Address:** www.kwsn.com.
Stadium Name: Sioux Falls Stadium. **Location:** I-29 to Russell Street, east one mile, south on West Avenue.
Standard Game Times: 7:05 pm, Sat 6:05 pm, Sun 4:05.

WICHITA WINGNUTS

Office Address: 300 South Sycamore, Wichita, KS 67213.
Telephone: (316) 264-6887. **Fax:** (316) 264-2129.
Website: www.wichitawingnuts.com.
Owners: Steve Ruud, Dan Waller, Gary Austerman, Nate Robertson.
President/General Manager: Josh Robertson. **Assistant GM/Director, Corporate Sales:** Brian Turner. **Manager, Finance:** Jared Johnson. **Director, Stadium Operations:** Jeff Kline. **Director, Group Sales:** Toby Antonson. **Manager, Communications:** Jason Kempf. **Manager, Ticket Sales/Community Relations:** Robert Slaughter. **Manager, Merchandise/Game Day Staff:** Meryl Loop. **Director, Food and Beverage:** Greg Read.
Manager: Kevin Hooper. **Coaches:** Jose Amado, Luke Robertson, Jim Foltz.

GAME INFORMATION
Broadcaster: Jason Kempf. **No. of Games Broadcast:** 100. **Flagship Station:** KWME 92.7-FM.
Webcast Address: www.wichitawingnuts.com.
Stadium Name: Lawrence-Dumont Stadium. **Location:** 135 North to Kellogg (54) West, Take Seneca Street exit North to Maple, Go East on Maple to Sycamore, Stadium is located on corner of Maple and Sycamore.
Standard Game Times: 7:05 pm, Sun 1:05.

WINNIPEG GOLDEYES

Office Address: One Portage Ave E, Winnipeg, Manitoba R3B 3N3.
Telephone: (204) 982-2273. **Fax:** (204) 982-2274.
Email Address: goldeyes@goldeyes.com. **Website:** www.goldeyes.com.
Operated by: Winnipeg Goldeyes Baseball Club, Inc.
Principal Owner/President: Sam Katz.
General Manager: Andrew Collier. **Assistant GM:** Regan Katz. **CFO:** Jason McRae-King. **Director, Sales/Marketing:** Dan Chase. **Manager, Box Office:** Kevin Arnst. **Manager, Promotions:** Allison Pattison. **Manager, Media Relations:** Scott Unger. **Manager, Retail:** Sean Seywright. **Manager, Food/Beverage:** Marty Adey. **Coordinator, Food/Beverage:** Melissa Schlichting. **Account Executives:** Nikki O'Donnell, Steve Schuster. **Consultant, Media Relations:** Scott Taylor. **Administrator, Sales/Marketing:** Angela Sanche. **IT:** Wayne Jackson. **Controller:** Judy Jones. Director, Security: Murray Allan. **Facility Manager:** Don Ferguson. **Executive Assistant:** Sherri Rheubottom. **Administrative Assistant:** Bonnie Benson.

Manager/Director, Player Procurement: Rick Forney. **Coaches:** Jamie Vermilyea, Tom Vaeth. **Trainer:** Stephen Wady. **Clubhouse Manager:** Jamie Samson. **Assistant Clubhouse Manager:** Jake Zelenewich.

GAME INFORMATION

Radio Announcer: Steve Schuster. **No. of Games Broadcast:** 100. **Flagship Station:** The Jewel 100.5 FM. **Television Announcers:** Scott Taylor. **No. of Games Telecast:** Home-10, Away-0. **Station:** Shaw TV/Shaw Direct.
Stadium Name: Shaw Park. **Location:** North on Pembina Highway to Broadway, East on Broadway to Main Street, North on Main Street to Water Avenue, East on Water Avenue to Westbrook Street, North on Westbrook Street to Lombard Avenue, East on Lombard Avenue to Mill Street, South on Mill Street to ballpark.
Standard Game Times: 7 pm, Sat 6, Sun 1:30.

ATLANTIC LEAGUE

Mailing Address: Clipper Magazine Stadium, 650 N. Prince St., Lancaster, Pa., 17603.
Telephone: (717) 509-4487. **Fax:** (717) 509-8476.
Email Address: info@atlanticleague.com. **Website:** www.atlanticleague.com.
Year Founded: 1998.

Senior Vice President/Founder: Frank Boulton. **Sr. Vice President:** Jon Danos. **Senior Vice President:** Josh Kalafer. **Senior Vice President:** Peter Kirk. **Senior Vice President:** Seth Waugh.

President: Rick White. **Executive Director, Baseball Operations:** Joe Klein. **Controller:** Emily Merrill. **League Operations Manager:** Jasson Read.

Division Structure: Liberty Division—Bridgeport, Camden, Long Island, Somerset. Freedom Division—Lancaster, Somerset, Southern Maryland, Sugar Land, York.

Regular Season: 140 games (split-schedule).
2015 Opening Date: April 24. **Closing Date:** Sept 20.
All-Star Game: July 8 in Bridgeport.

Playoff Format: First-half division winners meet second-half winners in best of five series. Winners meet in best-of-five final for league championship.

Roster Limit: 25. Teams may keep 27 players from start of season until May 31.
Eligibility Rule: No restrictions.
Brand of Baseball: Rawlings.
Statistician: Statistician: Pointstreak.com, 602 - 1595 16th Avenue, Richmond Hill, ON, Canada L4B 3N9.

STADIUM INFORMATION

			Dimensions				
Club	**Stadium**	**Opened**	**LF**	**CF**	**RF**	**Capacity**	**2014 Att.**
Bridgeport	The Ballpark at Harbor Yard	1998	325	405	325	5,300	150,284
Camden	Campbell's Field	2001	325	405	325	6,425	214,891
Lancaster	Clipper Magazine Stadium	2005	372	400	300	6,000	301,935
Long Island	Citibank Park	2000	325	400	325	6,002	344,543
Somerset	Commerce Bank Ballpark	1999	317	402	315	6,100	348,512
So. Maryland	Regency Stadium	2008	305	400	320	6,000	221,694
Sugar Land	Constellation Field	2012	348	405	325	7,500	383,465
York	Sovereign Bank Stadium	2007	300	400	325	5,000	267,695

BRIDGEPORT BLUEFISH

Office Address: 500 Main St, Bridgeport, CT 06604. **Telephone:** (203) 345-4800. **Fax:** (203) 345-4830. **Website:** www.bridgeportbluefish.com.

Operated by: Past Time Partners, LLC.

Principal Owner/CEO, Past Time Partners: Frank Boulton. **Senior VP, Past Time Partners:** Mike Pfaff. **Partners, Past Time Partners:** Tony Rosenthal, Fred Heyman, Jeffrey Serkes.

General Manager: Jamie Toole. **Director, Public Relations/Baseball Operations:** Paul Herrmann. **Director, Ticket Operations:** Drew LaBov. **Director, Stadium Operations:** Dan Gregory. **Director, Community Relations/Promotions:** Marisa Marvin. **Director, Business Operations/Merchandise:** Gregory Hodges. **Director of Finance:** Virdene Compton. **Assistant Director, Stadium Operations:** Anthony Polito. **Corporate Partnership Coordinator:** Jeff Gabriel.

Manager: Ricky VanAsselberg. **Trainer:** Ericka Ventura.

GAME INFORMATION

Radio Announcer: Michael Mohr. **No. of Games Broadcast:** 70 (webcast). **Flagship Station:** 1490 WGCH. **PA Announcer:** Bill Jensen. **Official Scorer:** Chuck Sadowski.

Stadium Name: The Ballpark at Harbor Yard. **Location:** I-95 to exit 27, Route 8/25 to exit 1. **Standard Game Times:** 7:05 pm, Sat 6:05, Sun 1:35.

Visiting Club Hotel: Holiday Inn Bridgeport, 1070 Main St, Bridgeport, CT 06604. **Telephone:** (203) 334-1234.

CAMDEN RIVERSHARKS

Office Address: 401 N Delaware Ave, Camden, NJ 08102.
Telephone: (856) 963-2600. **Fax:** (856) 963-8534.
Email Address: riversharks@riversharks.com. **Website:** www.riversharks.com.
Operated by: Camden Baseball, LLC. **Principal Owners:** Frank Boulton, Peter Kirk.

Controller: Tony Conte. **Assistant General Manager:** Lindsay Rosenberg. **Director, Ticketing:** Mark Schieber. **Director, Corporate Partnerships:** Drew Nelson. **Director, Youth Baseball Operations:** Scott DuPont Director, Group Sales: David Koehler Marketing Manager: Mike Barone. **Group Sales Manager:** Joe Bartlett. **Box Office Manager:** Chris Zabady. **Corporate Partnerships Coordinator:** Shaughn Marion. **Community Relations**

Coordinator: Rebecca Anderson. **Marketing Assistant:** Caitlin Graham. **Group Sales Coordinator:** Jason Tremblay. **Creative Services Coordinator:** Nick Deterding. Creative Services Coordinator: Deanna Lugo. **Broadcasting/Media Relations Manager:** Tom Willms. Stadium Operations Manager: Frank Slavinski.
Manager: Chris Widger.

GAME INFORMATION

Radio: www.riversharks.com. **Broadcaster:** Tom Willms. **PA Announcer:** Kevin Casey. **Official Scorer:** Dick Shute.
Stadium Name: Campbell's Field. **Location:** From Philadelphia, right on Sixth Street, right after Ben Franklin Bridge toll booth, right on Cooper Street until it ends at Delaware Ave; From Camden, I-676 to exit 5B, follow signs to field. **Standard Game Times:** 7:05 pm, Sat 5:35, Sun 1:35. Gates open one hour prior to game time.
Visiting Club Hotel: Holiday Inn, Route 70 and Sayer Avenue, Cherry Hill, NJ 08002. **Telephone:** (856) 663-5300.

LANCASTER BARNSTORMERS

Office Address: 650 North Prince St, Lancaster, PA 17603.
Telephone: (717) 509-4487. **Fax:** (717) 509-4486.
Email Address: info@lancasterbarnstormers.com.
Website: www.lancasterbarnstormers.com.
Operated by: Lancaster Barnstormers Baseball Club, LLC.
Principal Owners: Dakota Baseball
Partner: Robert Liss. **General Manager:** Kristen Simon. **Vice President, Fan Experience:** Anthony DeMarco. **VP, Business Development:** Vince Bulik. **VP, Sales/Marketing:** Ann Marie Hall. **Director, Stadium Operations:** Don Pryer. **Director, Sky Boxes/Ticket Services:** Maureen Wheeler. **Director, Business Development:** Bob Ford. **Accounting Manager:** Leanne Beaghan. **Stadium Operations Manager:** Andrew Wurst.
Box Office Manager: Holly Shelton, Creative Services Coordinator: John Brennan. **Business Development Representatives:** Terry Christopher, Philip Benigno, Quinton Collins, Zachary Cunningham, Melissa Tucker. **Partnership Marketing Representative:** Holly Love Client Services Representatives: Liz Welch, Amber Guinther. **Experience Sales Representative:** Alex Einhorn. **Head Groundskeeper:** Patrick Hilton
Manager: Butch Hobson. **Clubhouse Manager:** John Thomas.

GAME INFORMATION

Radio Announcer: Dave Collins. **No. of Games Broadcast:** Home-70, Away-70. **Flagship Stations:** WLAN 1390 AM PA Announcer: John Witwer. **Official Scorer:** Joel Schreiner.
Stadium Name: Clipper Magazine Stadium. **Location:** From Route 30, take Fruitville Pike or Harrisburg Pike toward downtown Lancaster, stadium on North Prince between Clay Street and Frederick Street. **Standard Game Times:** 7 p.m., Sun 1 p.m.

LONG ISLAND DUCKS

Mailing Address: 3 Court House Dr, Central Islip, NY 11722
Telephone: (631) 940-3825. **Fax:** (631) 940-3800.
Email Address: info@liducks.com. **Website:** www.liducks.com
Operated by: Long Island Ducks Professional Baseball, LLC. **Founder/CEO:** Frank Boulton. **Owner/Chairman:** Seth Waugh. **Owner/Senior VP, Baseball Operations:** Bud Harrelson.
President/General Manager: Michael Pfaff. **Assistant GM/Senior VP, Sales:** Doug Cohen. **Director, Administration:** Gerry Anderson. **Director, Group Sales:** John Wolff. **Director, Season Sales:** Brad Kallman. **Manager, Box Office:** Ben Harper. **Director, Merchandise & Client Relations:** Jason Randall. **Director, Media Relations/Broadcasting:** Michael Polak. **Director, Marketing & Promotions:** Jordan Schiff. **Manager, Corporate Sales:** Chris Burns. **Staff Accountant:** Annmarie DeMasi. **Account Executives:** Anthony Rubino, Ashley Bush. **Coordinator, Facilities Maintenance:** Ryan Reeves. **Coordinator, Administration:** Michelle Jensen. **Assistant, Group Sales:** Sean Smith.
Manager: Kevin Baez. **Coaches:** Bud Harrelson, Lew Ford. **Trainers:** Tony Amin, Dorothy Pitchford, Adam Lewis

GAME INFORMATION

Radio Announcers: Michael Polak, Chris King, David Weiss. **No. of Games Broadcast:** 140 on www.liducks.com. **Flagship Station:** 103.9-FM LI News Radio. **PA Announcer:** Bob Ottone. **Official Scorer:** Michael Polak.

SOMERSET PATRIOTS

Office Address: One Patriots Park, Bridgewater, NJ 08807.
Telephone: (908) 252-0700. **Fax:** (908) 252-0776.
Website: www.somersetpatriots.com.
Operated by: Somerset Baseball Partners, LLC.
Principal Owners: Steve Kalafer, Josh Kalafer, Jonathan Kalafer.
Chairman: Steve Kalafer.
President/General Manager: Patrick McVerry. **Senior Vice President, Marketing:** Dave Marek. **VP, Public Relations:** Marc Russinoff. **VP, Operations:** Bryan Iwicki. **VP, Ticket Operations:** Matt Kopas. **Senior Director, Tickets:** Brian Cahill. **Director, Merchandise:** Rob Crossman. **Director of Sales/Marketing:** Kevin Fleming. **Director of Operations:** Tom McCartney. **Director of Promotions:** Deanna Liotard. **Media Relations Manager:** Marc Schwartz. **Account Executive:** Nick Cherrillo. **Group Sales Managers:** Laura Sigle, Chris Kornmann. **Executive Assistant to GM:** Michele DaCosta. **Senior Vice President/ Treasurer:** Ron Schulz. **Accountant:** Stephanie DePass. **Receptionist:** Lorraine Ott. **GM, Centerplate:** Mike McDermott. **Head Groundskeeper:** Dan Purner.
Manager: Brett Jodie. **Hitting/3B Coach:** Shane Spencer. **Pitching Coach:** Cory Domel. **Director of Player Personnel:** Jon Hunton. **Trainer:** H.R. **Gorski. Manager Emeritus:** Sparky Lyle.

GAME INFORMATION

Radio Announcer: Justin Antweil. **No. of Games Broadcast:** Home-70, Away-70. **Flagship Station:** WCTC 1450-AM. **Live Video Streams:** Home-20 (SPN.tv). **PA Announcer:** Paul Spychala.
Official Scorer: John Nolan.
Ballpark Name: TD Bank Ballpark. **Location:** Route 287 North to exit 13B/Route 287 South to exit 13 (Somerville Route 28 West); follow signs to ballpark. **Standard Game Times:** 7:05 pm, Sun 1:35/5:05.
Visiting Club Hotel: Hotel Somerset-Bridgewater.

SOUTHERN MARYLAND
BLUE CRABS

Office Address: 11765 St Linus Dr, Waldorf, MD 20602.
Telephone: 301-638-9788. **Fax:** 301-638-9788.
Email address: info@somdbluecrabs.com. **Website:** www.somdbluecrabs.com.
Principal Owners: Opening Day Partners LLC, Brooks Robinson.
General Manager: Patrick Day. **Assistant GM:** Courtney Knichel. **Finance Manager:** Theresa Coffey. **Sales Account Executives:** Parris Armstrong, Patrick Pruitt, Del Baxter. **Director, Corporate Sales:** Candace Gick. **Creative Services:** Garret Young. **Corporate Partnerships Coordinator:** Kyle Lockrow. **Community Relations:** Greg Jensen. **Stadium Operations:** Derek Kauffman. **GM, Centerplate Concessions/Merchandise:** Anthony Hilla.
Manager: Lance Burkhart. **Hitting Coach:** Jeremy Owens. **Pitching Coach:** Joe Gannon

GAME INFORMATION

Radio: All home games, www.somdbluecrabs.com.
Stadium: Regency Furniture Stadium. **Standard Game Times:** 7:05 pm, Sat 6:35, Sun 2:05.

SUGAR LAND SKEETERS

Office Address: 1 Stadium Drive, Sugar Land Texas 77498.
Telephone: (281) 240-4487.
General Manager: Chris Jones. **Assistant GM:** JT Onyett. **Special Assistant:** Deacon Jones. **Accounting Manager:** Tina Gately. **Director, Human Resources:** Kimberly Ciszewski. **Senior Director, Community Development:** Kyle Dawson. **Director, Operations:** Donnie Moore. **Sponsorship Services Director:** Jacqueline Holm. **Sponsorship Sales Manager:** Ryan Derr. **Group Services Manager:** Chris Parsons. **Senior Sales Manager and Broadcaster:** Ira Liebman. **Senior Sales Manager:** Tyler Stamm. **Senior Sales Manager:** Teneisha Hall. **Senior Sales Manager,** Sunny Okpon. **Senior Sales Manager,** Grant Wilson. **Ticket Sales Director:** Colt Riley. **Box Office Manager:** Jennifer Schwarz. **Ticket Sales Assistant,** Lauren Hundley. **Customer Service Manager:** Adam Mettler. **Marketing/Communications Manager:** Molly Hughes. **Graphic Designer and Game Producer:** Nick Guenther. **Head Groundskeeper:** Brad Detmore. **Assistant Groundskeeper:** Richard Mendez. **Special Events Sales Director:** Matt Thompson. **Special Events Sales Manager:** Jessica Anderson. **Legends Hospitality General Manager:** Matt Coonrad. **Legends Merchandise Manager:** Jackie Beers. **Legends Warehouse Manager:** George Wasai, Jr.
Manager: Gary Gaetti. **Pitching Coach:** Jeff Scott.

GAME INFORMATION

Radio Announcer: Ira Liebman. **No. of Games Broadcast:** 140. **Flagship Station:** KBRZ Sports Radio. **Standard Game Times:** 7:05 pm, Sat/Sun 6:05/2:05. **Directions to Ballpark:** Southbound HWY 59—Take the exit toward Corporate Dr/US-90/Stafford/Sugar Land. **Turn right onto HWY 6. Travel northbound to Imperial Blvd. Turn right onto Imperial Blvd from HWY 6.**

Visiting Club Hotel: Sugar Land Marriott Town Square.

YORK REVOLUTION

Office Address: 5 Brooks Robinson Way, York, PA 17401.
Telephone: (717) 801-4487. **Fax:** (717) 801-4499.
Email Address: info@yorkrevolution.com.
Website: www.yorkrevolution.com.
Operated by: York Professional Baseball Club, LLC.
Principal Owners: York Professional Baseball Club, LLC.
President: Eric Menzer. **General Manager/Vice President of Operations:** John Gibson. **Vice President, Business Development:** Nate Tile. **Vice President, Finance:** Lori Brunson. **Director, Ticketing:** Cindy Brown. **Box Office Manager:** Bob Gibson. **Director, Marketing/Communications:** Paul Braverman. **Marketing Manager:** Aysa Alwood. **Director, Group Sales:** Kaylee Swanson. **Senior Account Executive:** Mike Coleman. **Account Executives:** Brandon Tesluk, Brittany Percich, Sarah Campbell, Kelsie Lehigh, Whitney Goulish, Cameron Lipnicky. **Director, Client Services:** Reed Gunderson. **Special Events Coordinator:** Adam Nugent.

Stadium Operations Manager: Lewis LaBar. **Baseball Operations Manager:** Nate Sterner. **Head Groundskeeper:** Mike Urich. **Creative Director:** Corey Shaud. **Legends Hospitality GM, Concessions/Merchandise/Catering:** Brett Herman. **Legends Hospitality Catering Manager:** Adam Baumbach. **Legends Hospitality Chef:** Tiffany Eger.

Manager: Mark Mason. **Pitching Coach:** Paul Fletcher. **Bench/Third-Base Coach:** Enohel Polanco.

GAME INFORMATION

Radio Announcer: Darrell Henry. **No. of Games Broadcast:** 140. **Flagship Station:** WOYK 1350 AM. **PA Announcer:** Ray Jensen. **Official Scorer:** Brian Wisler.

Stadium Name: Santander Stadium. **Location:** Take Route 30 West to North George Street. **Directions:** Turn left onto North George Street; follow that straight for four lights, Santander Stadium is on left. **Standard Game Times:** 6:30 pm, Sun 5 pm, 2 pm (April/Sept).

Visiting Club Hotel: The Yorktowne Hotel, 48 E Market Street, York, PA 17401. **Telephone:** (717) 848-1111.

CAN-AM LEAGUE

Office Address: 1415 Hwy 54 West, Suite 210, Durham, NC 27707.
Telephone: (919) 401-8150. **Fax:** (919) 401-8152. **Website:** www.canamleague.com.
Year Founded: 2005.
Commissioner: Miles Wolff. **President:** Dan Moushon. **Director, Umpires:** Kevin Winn.
Regular Season: 97 games. **2015 Opening Date:** May 21. **Closing Date:** Sept 7.
Playoff Format: Top four teams meet in best-of-five semifinals; winners meet in best-of-five finals.
Roster Limit: 22. **Eligibility Rule:** Minimum of five and maximum of eight first-year players; minimum of five players must be an LS-4 or higher; a maximum of four may be veterans.
Brand of Baseball: Rawlings. **Statistician:** Pointstreak.com.

STADIUM INFORMATION

| Club | Stadium | Opened | Dimensions | | | Capacity | 2014 Att. |
			LF	CF	RF		
New Jersey	Yogi Berra Stadium	1998	308	398	308	3,784	76,423
Ottawa	Ottawa Baseball Stadium	1993	325	404	325	10,332	N/A
Quebec	Stade Municipal	1938	315	385	315	4,500	121,305
Rockland	Provident Bank Park	2011	323	403	313	4,750	146,383
Sussex County	Skylands Stadium	1994	330	392	330	4,200	N/A
Trois-Rivieres	Stade Fernand-Bedard	1938	342	372	342	4,500	72,543

NEW JERSEY JACKALS

Office Address: One Hall Dr, Little Falls, NJ 07424.
Telephone: (973) 746-7434. **Fax:** (973) 655-8006.
Email Address: info@jackals.com. **Website:** www.jackals.com.
Operated by: Floyd Hall Enterprises, LLC. **Chairman:** Floyd Hall.
President: Greg Lockard. **Executive Vice President:** Larry Hall. **Vice President, Finance/Operations:** Jennifer Fertig.
Director, Group Sales & Operations: Michael Berhang. **Manager, Client Services:** Joe Hale. **Coordinator, Group Sales & Community Relations:** Stephanie DiBrita. **Coordinator, Group Sales/Operations:** Matt Julian. **Facilities Manager:** Aldo Licitra. **Concessions Manager:** Eric McConnell. **Clubhouse Manager:** Wally Brackett.
Manager: Joe Calfapietra. **Coaches:** Ed Ott, Ani Ramos, Chuck Stewart. **Trainer:** Jonathan Salazar.

GAME INFORMATION

Webcast Announcer: Michael Cohen. **No. of Games Broadcast:** 97. **Webcast Address:** www.jackals.com.
Stadium Name: Yogi Berra Stadium. **Location:** On the campus of Montclair State University; Route 80 or Garden State Parkway to Route 46, take Valley Road exit to Montclair State University. **Standard Game Times:** 7:05 pm, Sat 6:35, Sun 2:05.

OTTAWA CHAMPIONS

Office Address: 300 Coventry Road, Ottawa, ON K1K 4P5.
Telephone: (613) 745-2255. **Fax:** (613) 745-3289.
Email address: info@ottawachampions.com. **Website:** www.ottawachampions.com.
Owner: Miles Wolff. **President:** David Gourlay. **General Manager:** Ben Hodge.
Director, Sales: Davyd Balloch. **Director, Media Relations:** Andrew Denny.
Manager: Hal Lanier. **Coach:** Sebastien Boucher.

GAME INFORMATION

Webcast address: www.ottawachampions.com
Stadium Name: Ottawa Baseball Stadium. **Location:** From Hwy #417 "Queensway," take Vanier Parkway (Exit #117). Turn right on to Coventry Road. Ottawa Stadium is at your immediate right. **Standard Game Times:** Mon-Sat 7:05 p.m., Sun 1:35.

QUEBEC CAPITALES

Office Address: 100 Rue du Cardinal Maurice-Roy, Quebec City, QC G1K 8Z1.
Telephone: (418) 521-2255. **Fax:** (418) 521-2266.
Email Address: info@capitalesdequebec.com. **Website:** www.capitalesdequebec.com.
Owner: Jean Tremblay.
President/GM: Michel Laplante. **Assistant GM:** Julie Lefrançois. **Director, Media Relations:** Maxime Aubry. **Group Sales Representative:** Jean Marois. **Corporate Sales Representative:** Bobby Baril. **Director, Ticketing and Community Relations:** Anne-Marie Nappert.

Manager: Patrick Scalabrini. Coaches: TJ Stanton, Goefrey Tomlinson. Trainer: Jean-François Brochu.

GAME INFORMATION
Broadcaster: François Paquet. Games Broadcast: 97. Flagship Station: CHEQ 101.5-FM. Webcast Address: www.fm1015.ca.
Stadium Name: Stade Municipal de Québec. Location: Highway 40 to Highway 173 (Centre-Ville) exit 2 to Parc Victoria. Standard Game Times: 7:05 pm, Sat 6:05 pm, Sun 1:05.

ROCKLAND BOULDERS

Office Address: 1 Provident Bank Park Drive, Pomona, NY 10970.
Telephone: (845) 364-0009. Fax: (845) 364-0001.
E-Mail Address: info@rocklandboulders.com. Website: www.rocklandboulders.com.
President: Ken Lehner. Executive Vice President/General Manager: Shawn Reilly.
Assistant General Manager: Seth Cantor. CFO: Maria Wainwright. Manager, Suites/Catering: Kaylee del Rosario. Manager, Promotions and Public Relations: Christian Heimall. Manager, Ticket Operations: Brett Kaufman. Manager, Box Office: Rachael Kutash. Manager, Retail Store: Deidra Verona. Account Executives: Karen McCombs, Kevin Mendi, Patrick Rutkowski, Tom Triglia. Promotions/Operations Assistant: Steph Stierle. Manager, Concessions: George McElroy. Coordinator, Facility Operations: Nick Barbalato. Director, Security: Jeff Rinaldi. Audio/Visual Specialist: Jim Houston. Bookkeeper: Michele Almash.
Manager: Jamie Keefe. Coaches: Bobby Jones, Chad Duesler. Trainer: Lori Rahim. Clubhouse Manager: Louie Jimenez.

GAME INFORMATION
Broadcaster: Seth Cantor. No. of Games Broadcast: 60. Flagship Station: WBNR 1260-AM. Webcast Address: www.rocklandboulders.com. Stadium Name: Provident Bank Park. Location: Take Exit 12 towards Route 45, make left at stop sign on Conklin Road, make left on Route 45, turn right on Pomona Road, take 1st right on Fireman's Memorial Drive.
Standard Game Times: 7 pm, Saturday 6:35, Sun 2:05/5:05.

SUSSEX COUNTY MINERS

Office Address: 94 Championship Place, Suite 11, August, NJ 07822.
Telephone: (973) 383-7644. Fax : (973) 383-7522.
Email Address : contact@skylandsstadium.com.
Website: www.sussexcountyminers.com
President: Al Dorso. General Manager: Dave Chase.
Manager: Steve Shirley.

GAME INFORMATION
Stadium Name: Skylands Stadium. Location: In New Jersey, I-80 to exit 34B (Route 15 North) to Route 565 North; From Pennsylvania, I-84 to Route 6 (Matamoras) to Route 206 North to Route 565 North. Standard Game Times: 7:05, Sunday 2:05.

TROIS-RIVIÈRES AIGLES

Office Address: 1760 Avenue Gilles-Villeneuve, Trois-Rivières, QC G9A 5K8.
Telephone: (819) 379-0404. Fax: (819) 379-5087.
Email Address: info@lesaiglestr.com. Website: www.lesaiglestr.com
President: Marc-André Bergeron. General Manager: René Martin. Director, Communications/Marketing: Simon Laliberté. Assistant, Communications/Marketing: Hugues Marcil. Director, Stadium Operations: Real Lajoie.
Manager: Pete LaForest. Coaches: Maxime Poulin, Matt Rusch.

GAME INFORMATION
Broadcaster: Simon Laliberté. No. of Games Broadcast: TBA. Webcast address: www.lesaiglestr.com.
Stadium Name: Stade Fernand-Bedard. Location: Take Hwy 40 West, exit Boul. des forges/Centre-ville, keep right, turn right at light, turn right at stop sign.
Standard Game Times: 7:05 pm, Sun 1:35.

FRONTIER LEAGUE

Office Address: 2041 Goose Lake Rd Suite 2A, Sauget, IL 62206.
Telephone: (618) 215-4134. **Fax:** (618) 332-2115.
Email Address: office@frontierleague.com. **Website:** www.frontierleague.com.
Year Founded: 1993.
Commissioner: Bill Lee.
Deputy Commissioner: Steve Tahsler.
President: Rich Sauget (Gateway). **Executive Committee:** Clint Brown (Florence), Steve Malliet (Normal/River City), Nick Semaca (Joliet), Leslye Wuerfel (Traverse City).
Board of Directors: Tim Arseneau (Southern Illinois), Bill Bussing (Evansville), Steven Edelson (Lake Erie), Chris Hanners (Rockford), Al Oremus (Windy City), Pat Salvi (Schaumburg), Stu Williams (Washington).
Division Structure: East—Evansville, Florence, Frontier Greys, Lake Erie, Southern Illinois, Traverse City, Washington. West—Gateway, Joliet, Normal, River City, Rockford, Schaumburg, Windy City.
Regular Season: 96 games. **2015 Opening Date:** May 14. **Closing Date:** Sept 6.
All-Star Game: July 15 at Schaumburg.
Playoff Format: Top 4 non-division winners have a single-game series, with winners advancing to a best-of-3 Divisional Round. Championship Series is best-of-5.
Roster Limit: 24. **Eligibility Rule:** Minimum of eleven Rookie 1/Rookie 2 players. No player may be 27 prior to Jan. 1 of current season with the exception of one player that may not be 30 years of age prior to Jan. 1 of the current season.
Brand of Baseball: Rawlings.
Statistician: Pointstreak, 602-1595 16th Avenue, Richmond Hill, ONT L4B 3N9.

STADIUM INFORMATION

| Club | Stadium | Opened | Dimensions | | | Capacity | 2014 Att. |
			LF	CF	RF		
Evansville	Bosse Field	1915	315	415	315	5,110	111,709
Florence	UC Health Stadium	2004	325	395	325	4,200	105,539
Gateway	GCS Ballpark	2002	318	395	325	5,500	156,840
Joliet	Silver Cross Field	2002	330	400	327	6,229	92,992
Lake Erie	All-Pro Freight	2009	325	400	325	5,000	106,009
Normal	The Corn Crib	2010	356	400	344	7,000	109,952
River City	T.R. Hughes Ballpark	1999	320	382	299	4,989	81,662
Rockford	Aviators Stadium	2006	315	393	312	3,279	72,340
Schaumburg	Schaumburg Stadium	1999	355	400	353	8,107	157,393
So. Illinois	Rent One Park	2007	325	400	330	4,500	147,287
Traverse City	Wuerfel Park	2006	320	400	320	4,600	143,585
Washington	CONSOL Energy Park	2002	325	400	325	3,200	84,533
Windy City	Standard Bank Stadium	1999	335	390	335	2,598	74,481

EVANSVILLE OTTERS

Mailing Address: 23 Don Mattingly Way, Evansville, IN 47711.
Telephone: (812) 435-8686.
Operated by: Evansville Baseball, LLC.
President: Bill Bussing. **Senior Vice President:** Bix Branson. **General Manager:** Joel Padfield. **Director, Operations:** Jake Riffert. **Account Executive/Director, Media Relations/Broadcasting:** Mike Radomski. **Controller:** Casie Williams. **Sports Turf Manager:** Lance Adler.
Manager: Andy McCauley.

GAME INFORMATION

Radio Announcer: Mike Radomski. **No. of Games Broadcast:** Home-51, Away-45. **Flagship Station:** WUEV 91.5-FM.
PA Announcer: Zane Clodfelter.
Stadium Name: Bosse Field. **Location:** US 41 to Lloyd Expressway West (IN-62), Main St Exit, Right on Main St, ahead 1 mile to Bosse Field. **Standard Game Times:** 6:35 pm, Sun 5:05; Doubleheaders 5:35 p.m.
Visiting Club Hotel: Comfort Inn & Suites, 3901 Hwy 41 N, Evansville, IN 47711.

FLORENCE FREEDOM

Office Address: 7950 Freedom Way, Florence, KY, 41042.
Telephone: (859) 594-4487. **Fax:** (859) 594-3194.
Email Address: info@florencefreedom.com.
Operated by: Canterbury Baseball, LLC.
President: Clint Brown. **General Manager:** Josh Anderson. **Assistant GM,**
Operations: Kim Brown. **Assistant GM, Marketing/Promotions:** Sarah Eichenberger. **Director, Ticket Sales:** Zach

Ziler. **Groups Sales Manager:** Amanda Sipple. **Director, Food/Beverage:** Joel Bogart. **Director, Broadcasting/Media Relations:** Aaron Morse. **Business Manager:** Shelli Bitter. **Director, Amateur Baseball:** Tyler Brake. **Box Office Manager:** Chanel Lessing. **Stadium Maintenance Director:** Mike Conrad.

Manager: Dennis Pelfrey. **Pitching Coach:** Chad Rhoades. **Hitting Coach:** AJ Cicconi.

GAME INFORMATION

Official Scorer: Joe Gall.
Stadium: UC Health Stadium. **Location:** I71/75 South to exit 180, left onto US 42, right on Freedom Way; I-71/75 North to exit 180. **Standard Game Times:** 6:35 pm, Fri 7:05, Sat-Sun 6:05.
Visiting Club Hotel: Howard Johnson.

FRONTIER GREYS

Mailing Address: 2041 Goose Lake Road, Suite 2A, Sauget, IL 62206.
Telephone: (618) 215-4134.
Website: www.frontiergreys.com. **E-Mail:** frontiergreys@yahoo.com
Operated by: Frontier League Baseball Travel Team, LLC.
President: Steve Tahsler. **Secretary:** Bill Lee.
Director, Operations: Spencer Holtzinger
Field manager: Vinny Ganz. **Bench Coach:** Jeremiah Knackstedt.
Spring Training Facility: Glik Park, 12525 Sportsman Road, Highland, IL 62249

GATEWAY GRIZZLIES

Telephone: (618) 337-3000. **Fax:** (618) 332-3625.
Email Address: info@gatewaygrizzlies.com. **Website:** www.gatewaygrizzlies.com
Operated by: Gateway Baseball, LLC.
Managing Officer: Richard Sauget.
General Manager: Steven Gomric. **Assistant General Manager:** Alex Wilson. **Director Stadium Operations/Finance:** Zach Buettner. **Director, Events:** Kurt Ringkamp. **Director, Community Relations:** Christina Cathcart. **Radio Broadcaster/Media Relations Director:** Sam Levitt. **Director, Group Sales:** Jim Fox. **Director of Merchandise:** Monica Rodriguez. **Director, Ticket Sales:** James Caldwell. **Groups/Corporate Sales Coordinator:** Chris Kellerman.

Manager: Phil Warren. **Pitching Coach:** Randy Martz. **Bench Coach:** Mike Breyman. **Hitting Coach:** Zach Borowiak. **Trainer:** Geof Manzo.

GAME INFORMATION

Radio Announcer: Sam Levitt. **No of Games Broadcast:** Home-54, Away-44. **PA Announcer:** Tom Calhoun.
Stadium Name: GCS Ballpark. **Location:** I-255 at exit 15 (Mousette Lane). **Standard Game Times:** 7:05 pm, Sun 6:05/3:05.

JOLIET SLAMMERS

Office Address: 1 Mayor Art Schultz Dr, Joliet, IL 60432
Telephone: (815) 722-2287. **Fax:** (815) 726-4304.
E-Mail Address: info@jolietslammers.com. **Website:** www.jolietslammers.com
Operated by: Joliet Community Baseball & Entertainment, LLC.
Owner: Joliet Community Baseball & Entertainment, LLC
General Manager/Operations: Chris Franklin, Box Office Manager: Heather Mills. **Director of Food/Beverage:** Tom Fremarek. **Director, Community Relations:** Ken Miller. **Account Executive, Ticket Sales:** Porscha Johnson. **Account Executive, Ticket Sales:** Shawn Hardy, **Account Executive, Ticket Sales:** Megan Becker **Team Doctor:** Dr. Pzinger. **Physical Therapy Athletic Trainer:** Andrew Gates. **Photographer:** Carmen Arrigo.
Manager: Jess Isom. **Coach:** Matt Kennedy. **Pitching Coach:** Pascual Santiago.

GAME INFORMATION:

No. of Games Broadcast: 96. **Flagship Station:** 1340 AM WJOL. **Official Scorer:** Dave Laketa. **Stadium Name:** Silver Cross Field. **Location:** 1 Mayor Art Schultz Drive, Joliet, IL 60432. **Standard Game Times:** 7:05pm; Sat 6:05pm; Sun 5:05pm. **Visiting Club Hotel:** Joliet Fairfield Inn & Suites

LAKE ERIE CRUSHERS

Mailing Address: 2009 Baseball Blvd, Avon, OH, 44011.
Telephone: (440) 934-3636. **Fax:** (440) 934-2458.
Email Address: info@lakeeriecrushers.com. **Website:** www.lakeeriecrushers.com.
Operated by: Avon Pro Baseball LLC.
Managing Officer: Steven Edelson.
Assistant GM, Operations: Paul Siegwarth. **Accountant:** Kathleen Hudson. **Box Office Manager:** Unavailable. **Director, Concessions/Catering:** Unavailable. **Director, Promotions:** Beckie Reid. **Account Executives:** Matt Kendeigh, Mark Yates. **Director, Broadcasting:** Andy Barch.
Manager: Chris Mongiardo.

GAME INFORMATION

Stadium Name: All Pro Freight Stadium. **Location:** Intersection of I-90 and Colorado Ave in Avon, OH. **Standard Game Times:** 7:05 pm, Sun 2:05.

NORMAL CORNBELTERS

Mailing Address: 1000 West Raab Road, Normal, IL 61761.
Telephone: 309-454-2255 (BALL). **Fax:** 309- 454-2287 (BATS).
Ownership: Normal Baseball Group.
President/General Manager: Steve Malliet. **Director, Ticket Operations:** Justin Cartor. **Communications/Baseball Operations Manager:** Mike Rains. **Director, Stadium Operations/Game Operations:** Jeff Holtke. **Director, Sales:** Mike Petrini. **Group Sales Manager:** Brendan O'Neill. **Group Sales Manager:** Tony Giardina. **Business Manager:** Deana Roberts
Field Manager: Brooks Carey

GAME INFORMATION

Radio Announcer: Greg Halbleib. **Flagship Station:** Online only at www.Normalbaseball.com No. **of Games Broadcast:** All 51 games streaming online at www.normalbaseball.com
Stadium Name: The Corn Crib. **Location:** From I-55 North, go south on I-55 and take the 165 exit, turn left at light, turn right on Raab Road to ballpark on right; From I-55 South, go north on I-55 and take the 165 exit, merge onto Route 51 (Main Street), turn right on Raab Road to ballpark on right. **Standard Game Times:** 6:35 pm, Sun 3:05.

RIVER CITY RASCALS

Office Address: 900 TR Hughes Blvd, O'Fallon, MO 63366.
Telephone: (636) 240-2287. **Fax:** (636) 240-7313.
Email Address: info@rivercityrascals.com. **Website:** www.rivercityrascals.com.
Operated by: PS and J Professional Baseball Club LLC.
Owners: Tim Hoeksema, Jan Hoeksema, Fred Stratton, Anne Stratton, Pam Malliet, Steve Malliet, Michael Veeck, Greg Wendt.
President/General Manager: Dan Dial. **Assistant GM:** Lisa Fegley. **Senior Director, Ticket Operations:** Courtney Oakley. **Director, Stadium Operations:** Tom Bauer. **Director, Food/Beverage:** Maureen Stranz. **Business Manager:** Carrie Green. **Account Executive:** Tim McConkey.
Manager: Steve Brook. **Assistant Coach:** Eric Williams.

GAME INFORMATION

No. of Games Broadcast: Home-51, Away-45.
PA Announcer: Randy Moehlman.
Stadium Name: TR Hughes Ballpark. **Location:** I-70 to exit 219, north on TR Hughes Road, follow signs to ballpark. **Standard Game Times:** 6:35 pm, Sun 4:05.
Visiting Club Hotel: America's Best Value Inn 1310 Bass Pro Drive St Charles, MO. **Telephone:** (636) 947-5900.

ROCKFORD AVIATORS

Office Address: 4503 Interstate Blvd Loves Park, IL 61111.
Telephone: (815) 885-2255. **Fax:** (815) 885-2204.
Website: www.rockfordaviators.com
Owned by: Rock River Valley Baseball. **CEO:** W Chris Hanners.
General Manager: Brad Sholes. **Director, Media/Community Relations:** Jared Revlett.
Field Manager: James Frisbie. **Hitting Coach:** Jeff Brooks. **Pitching Coach:** John Foster

GAME INFORMATION

Radio Announcer: Jared Revlett. **No. of Games Broadcast:** 96. **Flagship Station:** Meridix Network (Online Streaming). **PA Announcer:** Brett Myhres.

Stadium Name: Aviators Stadium. **Location:** I-90 (Jane Addams Tollway) to Riverside Blvd exit (automatic toll booth), east to Interstate Dr, north on Interstate Drive to dead end. **Standard Game Times:** Varies.

Visiting Club Hotel: Clock Tower Resort, 7801 East State Street Rockford, Ill, 61108. **Telephone:** (800) 358-7666.

SCHAUMBURG BOOMERS

Office Address: 1999 Springinsguth Road, Schaumburg, IL 60193
Email Address: info@boomersbaseball.com Website: www.boomersbaseball.com
Owned by: Pat and Lindy Salvi
President/General Manager: Andy Viano. **VP, Corporate Sales:** Jeff Ney. **Director, Marketing/Media:** Ed McCaskey. **Business Manager:** Todd Fulk. **Director, Facilities:** Mike Tlusty. **Director, Sales:** Mike Kline. **Director, Food/Beverage:** Rich Essegian. **Broadcaster:** Tim Calderwood. **Manager, Ticket Operations:** Adam Dolezal. **Account Executive:** Ryan Kukla.
Manager: Jamie Bennett. **Hitting Coach:** CJ Thieleke. **Pitching Coach:** TJ Nall. **First-Base Coach:** Bill Frato.

GAME INFORMATION

Broadcaster: Tim Calderwood. **No. of Games Broadcast:** Home-54, Away-42. **Flagship Station:** WRMN 1410 AM Elgin. **Official Scorer:** Ken Trendel.

Stadium: Schaumburg Boomers Stadium. **Location:** I-290 to Thorndale Ave Exit, head West on Elgin-O'Hare Expressway until Springinsguth Road Exit, second left at Springinsguth Road (shared parking lot with Schaumburg Metra Station). **Visiting Club Hotel:** AmericInn Hotel & Suites, 1300 East Higgins Road, Schaumburg IL 60173.

SOUTHERN ILLINOIS MINERS

Office Address: Rent One Park, 1000 Miners Drive, Marion, IL 62959.
Telephone: (618) 998-8499. **Fax:** (618) 969-8550.
Email Address: info@southernillinoisminers.com. **Website:** www.southernillinoisminers.com.
Operated by: Southern Illinois Baseball Group. **Owner:** Jayne Simmons.
Vice President: Tim Arseneau. **Director, Extra Events/Stadium Operations:** Casey Petermeyer. **Director, Ticket Operations:** Billy Leitner. **Director, Sponsorships/Promotions:** Jon Brownfield. **Director, Video Production/Creative Services:** Heath Hooker. **Director, Radio Broadcasting/Media Relations:** Jason Guerette Director, Finance: Cathy Perry. **Senior Account Executive:** Jon Basil. **Account Executive:** Phoenix Strawn Client Service Manager, McKenna Moffett
Manager: Mike Pinto. **Hitting Coach:** Pat O'Sullivan. **Pitching Coach:** Preston Vancil. **Bench Coach:** Ralph Santana. **Coach/Advance Scout:** John Lakin. **Advance Scout:** Chris Colwell. **Strength/Conditioning Coordinator:** Chris Stone.

GAME INFORMATION

No. of Games Broadcast: 96. **Flagship Station:** 97.7 WHET-FM.
Stadium Name: Rent One Park. **Location:** US 57 to Route 13 East, right at Halfway Road to Fairmont Drive. **Standard Game Times:** 7:05 pm, Sat 6:05, Sun 5:05.
Visiting Club Hotel: America's Best Value Inn 1802 Bittle Place, Marion, IL 62959.

TRAVERSE CITY BEACH BUMS

Office Address: 333 Stadium Dr, Traverse City, MI 49685.
Telephone: (231) 943-0100. **Fax:** (231) 943-0900.
Email Address: info@tcbeachbums.com. **Website:** www.tcbeachbums.com.
Operated by: Traverse City Beach Bums, LLC.
Managing Member/President/COO: John Wuerfel. **Member/GM:** Leslye Wuerfel.
Vice President/Director, Baseball Operations: Jason Wuerfel. **Director, Ticketing:** Ben Holcomb. **Director, Food/Beverage:** Tom Goethel. **Director, Media/Broadcasting:** Scott Montesano. **Director, Promotion/Community Events:** Brandon Rexin. **Maintenance Supervisor:** Ken Allen. **Bookkeeping:** Gretchen Bensinger.
Field Manager: Dan Rohn. **Hitting Coach:** Dominick Gaudioso. **Pitching Coach:** Greg Cadaret

GAME INFORMATION

No. of Games Broadcast: 96. **Flagship Stations:** Classic Rock The Bear 95.5 FM & 107.5 FM. **PA Announcer:** Bill Froelich. **Stadium Name:** Wuerfel Park. **Location:** Three miles south of the Grand Traverse Mall just off US-31 and M-37 in Chums Village. Stadium is visible from the highway. **Standard Game Times:** 7:05 pm, Sun 5:05 p.m.

WASHINGTON WILD THINGS

Office Address: One Washington Federal Way, Washington, PA 15301.
Telephone: (724) 250-9555. **Fax:** (724) 250-2333.
Email Address: info@washingtonwildthings.com.
Website: www.washingtonwildthings.com.
Owned by: Sports Facility, LLC. **Operated by:** Washington Frontier League Baseball, LLC.
President/Chief Executive Officer: Stuart Williams. **General Manager:** Francine Williams. **Director, Marketing/Communications/Corporate Relations:** Christine Blaine. **Assistant GM:** Steven Zavacky. **Corporate Partnership Account Executives:** Zack Kaminski, Jason Havelka. **Ticket Manager:** Brian King. **Account Executive:** Austin Snodgrass. **Special Events/Operations:** Wayne Herrod.
PR/Social Media Manager: Deb Hilton. **Controller:** JJ Heider. **Assistant Controller:** Jordan Millorino. **Creative Services:** Bryan Leones.
Manager: Bob Bozutto.

GAME INFORMATION

Stadium Name: CONSOL Energy Park. **Location:** I-70 to exit 15 (Chestnut Street), right on Chestnut Street to Washington Crown Center Mall, right at mall entrance, right on to Mall Drive to stadium. **Standard Game Times:** 7:05 Sunday 2:35 p.m.
Visiting Club Hotel: Red Roof Inn.

WINDY CITY THUNDERBOLTS

Office Address: 14011 South Kenton Avenue, Crestwood, IL 60445-2252.
Telephone: (708) 489-2255. **Fax:** (708) 489-2999.
Email Address: info@wcthunderbolts.com. **Website:** www.wcthunderbolts.com.
Owned by: Crestwood Professional Baseball, LLC.
General Manager: Mike Lucas. **Assistant GM:** Mike VerSchave. **Director, Community Relations:** Marissa Miller. **Senior Sales Executive:** Bill Waliewski. **Group Sales Coordinator:** Ryan Syring.
Field Manager: Ron Biga. **Pitching Coach:** Brian Smith. **Hitting Coach:** Pete Pirman.

GAME INFORMATION

Radio Announcer: Terry Bonadonna. **No. of Games Broadcast:** 96. **Flagship Station:** WXAV, 88.3 FM. **Official Scorer:** Chris Gbur
Stadium Name: Standard Bank Stadium. **Location:** I-294 to South Cicero Ave, exit (Route 50), south for 1 1/2 miles, left at Midlothian Turnpike, right on Kenton Ave; I-57 to 147th Street, west on 147th to Cicero, north on Cicero, right on Midlothian Turnpike, right on Kenton. **Standard Game Times:** 7:05 pm, Sat 6:05, Sun 2:05/5:05.
Visiting Club Hotel: Georgioís Comfort Inn, 8800 W 159th St, Orland Park, IL 60462. **Telephone:** (708) 403-1100.

ADDITIONAL LEAGUES

PACIFIC ASSOCIATION OF PROFESIONAL BASEBALL CLUBS

Mailing address: 1201 B Street, San Rafael, CA, 94901
Telephone: (415) 485-1563 Email: info@pacificsbaseball.com
mailto: info@pacificsbaseball.com   Website: www.pacproclubs.com
Ownership Group: Redwood Sports & Entertainment Group, Sonoma Sports & Entertainment Inc.,
Teams: San Rafael Pacifics, Sonoma Stompers, Vallejo Admirals, Pittsburg Mettle
Roster Limit: 22. **Eligibility Rules:** None.
Brand of Baseball: Rawlings.

PECOS LEAGUE

Address: PO Box 271489, Houston, Texas 77277. **Telephone:** 575-680-2212.
Website: www.PecosLeague.com. **E-mail:** info@pecosleague.com
Year Founded: 2010.
Divisions: Northern Division-Las Vegas Train Robbers (Las Vegas New Mexico); Santa Fe Fuego (Santa Fe Fuego); Garden City Wind(Garden City, Kansas); Trinidad Triggers (Trinidad Triggers). **South Division-**Alpine Cowboys (Alpine Texas);Las Cruces Vaqueros(Las Cruces New Mexico); Roswell Invaders (Roswell New Mexico); White Sands Pupfish (Alamogordo New Mexico).
Regular Season: 70 games. **2015 Opening Date:** May 19.
Playoff Format: Division champs play best-of-3 series.
Roster Limit: 22.
Eligibility Rules: Players must be age 25 and under. **Brand of Baseball:** National League.

INTERNATIONAL

AMERICAS

MEXICO
MEXICAN LEAGUE

Member, National Association
NOTE: The Mexican League is a member of the National Association of Professional Baseball Leagues and has a Triple-A classification. However, its member clubs operate largely independent of the 30 major league teams, and for that reason the league is listed in the international section.

Address: Av Insurgentes Sur #797 3er. piso. Col. Napoles. C.P. 03810, Benito Juarez, Mexico, D.F. **Telephone:** 52-55-5557-1007. **Fax:** 52-55-5395-2454. **E-Mail Address:** oficina@lmb.com.mx. **Website:** www.lmb.com.mx.

Years League Active: 1955-.

President: Plinio Escalante Bolio. **Operations Manager:** Nestor Alba Brito.

Division Structure: North—Aguascalientes, Laguna, Mexico City, Monclova, Monterrey, Reynosa, Saltillo, Tijuana. South—Campeche, Ciudad del Carmen, Oaxaca, Puebla, Quintana Roo, Tabasco, Veracruz, Yucatan.

Regular Season: 110 games (split-schedule). **2015 Opening Date:** April 3. **Closing Date:** Aug 14.

All-Star Game: May 29-31, Merida, Yucatan.

Playoff Format: Eight teams qualify, including first- and second-half division winners plus wild-card teams with best overall records; Quarterfinals, semifinals and finals are all best-of-seven series.

Roster Limit: 28. **Roster Limit, Imports:** 6.

AGUASCALIENTES RAILROADMEN
Office Address: López Mateos # 101 Torre "A" Int 214 y 215, Plaza Cristal, Colonia San Luis, CP 20250. **Telephone:** (52) 449-915-1596. **Fax:** (52) 614-459-0336. **E-Mail Address:** Not available. **Website:** www.rielerosags.com.

President: Mario Rodriguez. **General Manager:** Iram Campos Lara.

Manager: Mario Mendoza.

CAMPECHE PIRATES
Office Address: Calle Filiberto Qui Farfan No. 2, Col. Camino Real, CP 24020, Campeche, Campeche. **Telephone:** (52) 981-827-4759. **Fax:** (52) 981-827-4767. **E-Mail Address:** piratas@prodigy.net.mx. **Website:** www.piratasdecampeche.mx.

President: Gabriel Escalante Castillo. **General Manager:** Gabriel Lozano Berron.

Manager: Dan Firova.

CIUDAD DEL CARMEN DOLPHINS
Telephone: (52) 938-286-1627. **E-Mail Address:** contacto@delfinesbeisbol.com.mx. **Website:** http://www.delfinesbeisbol.com.mx

President: Carlos Mejía Berrio.

Manager: Felix Fermin.

LAGUNA COWBOYS
Office Address: Juan Gutenberg s/n, Col Centro, CP 27000, Torreon, Coahuila. **Telephone:** (52) 871-718-5515. **Fax:** (52) 871-717-4335. **E-Mail Address:** Not available. **Website:** www.clubvaqueroslaguna.com/.

President: Ricardo Martin Bringas. **General Manager:** Victor Andres Favela Lopez.

Manager: Lino Rivera.

MEXICO CITY RED DEVILS
Office Address: Av Cuauhtemoc #451-101, Col Narvarte, CP 03020, Mexico DF. **Telephone:** (52) 555-639-8722. **Fax:** (52) 555-639-9722. **E-Mail Address:** diablos@sportsya.com. **Website:** www.diablos.com.mx.

President: Roberto Mansur Galán. **General Manager:** Roberto Castellon.

Manager: Miguel Ojeda.

MONCLOVA STEELERS
Office Address: Cuauhtemoc #299, Col Ciudad Deportiva, CP 25750, Monclova, Coahuila. **Telephone:** (52) 866-636-2650. **Fax:** (52) 866-636-2688. **E-Mail Address:** acererosdelnorte@prodigy.net.mx. **Website:** www.acereros.com.mx.

President: Donaciano Garza Gutierrez. **General Manager:** Oscar Romero Tirado

Manager: Homar Rojas.

MONTERREY SULTANS
Office Address: Av Manuel Barragan s/n, Estadio Monterrey, Apartado Postal 870, Monterrey, Nuevo Leon, CP 66460. **Telephone:** (52) 81-8351-0209. **Fax:** (52) 81-8351-8022. **E-Mail Address:** sultanes@sultanes.com.mx. **Website:** www.sultanes.com.mx.

President: José Maiz Mier. **General Manager:** Leobardo Figueroa.

Manager: Miguel Flores.

OAXACA WARRIORS
Office Address: M Bravo 417 Col Centro 68000, Oaxaca, Oaxaca. **Telephone:** (52) 951-515-5522. **Fax:** (52) 951-515-4966. **E-Mail Address:** oaxacaguerreros@gmail.com. **Website:** http://www.guerreros.mx.

President: Lorenzo Peón Escalante. **General Manager:** Guillermo Spindola Morales.

Manager: Hector Alvarez.

PUEBLA PARROTS
Office Address: Calz Zaragoza S/N, Unidad Deportiva 5 de Mayo, Col Maravillas, CP 72220, Puebla, Puebla. **Telephone:** (52) 222-222-2116. **Fax:** (52) 222-222-2117. **E-Mail Address:** oficina@pericosdepuebla.com.mx. **Website:** www.pericosdepuebla.com.mx.

President: Juan Villareal. **General Manager:** Jose Raul Melendez Habib.

Manager: Joe Alvarez.

QUINTANA ROO TIGERS
Office Address: Av Mayapan Mz 4 Lt 1 Super Mz 21, CP 77500, Cancun, Quintana Roo. **Telephone:** (52) 998-887-3108. **Fax:** (52) 998-887-1313. **E-Mail Address:** tigres@tigrescapitalinos.com.mx. **Website:** www.tigresqr.mx.

President: Cuauhtémoc Rodriguez. **General Manager:** Francisco Minjarez Garcia.

Manager: Jerry Royster.

REYNOSA BRONCOS
Office Address: Paris 511, Esq c/ Tiburcio Garza Zamora Altos, Locales 6 y 7, Col Beatty, Reynosa, Tamps. **Telephone:** (52) 922-3462. **Fax:** (52) 925-7118. **E-Mail Address:** broncosdereynosa@gmail.com. **Website:** www.broncosdereynosa.com.mx.

President: Eliud Villarreal Garza. **General Manager:** Leonardo Clayton Rodríguez.

Manager: Roberto Mendez.

SALTILLO SARAPE MAKERS
Office Address: Blvd Nazario Ortiz Esquina con Blvd Jesus Sanchez, CP 25280, Saltillo, Coahuila. **Telephone:** (52) 844-416-9455. **Fax:** (52) 844-439-1330. **E-Mail Address:** aley@grupoley.com. **Website:** www.saraperos.com.mx.

President: Alvaro Ley Lopez. **General Manager:**

Eduardo Valenzuela Guajardo.
Manager: Juan Rodriguez.

TABASCO OLMECS
Office Address: Av Circuito Deportiva S/N, Col Atasta, Villahermosa, Tabasco, CP 86100. **Telephone:** (52) 993-352-2787. **Fax:** (52) 993-352-2788. **E-Mail Address:** club@olmecastabasco.com. **Website:** www.olmecastabasco.com/.
President: Raul Gonzalez Rodriguez. **General Manager:** Luis Guzman Ramos.
Manager: Alonso Tellez.

TIJUANA BULLS
Office Address: Blvd Agua Caliente #11720, Col Hipodromo 22020, Tijuana, BC. **Telephone:** (52) 664-633-3195. **E-Mail Address:** Not available. **Website:** www.torosdetijuana.com.
General Manager: Carlos Orozco.
Manager: Jesus Someras.

VERACRUZ RED EAGLES
Office Address: Av Jacarandas S/N, Esquina España, Fraccionamiento Virginia, CP 94294, Boca del Rio, Veracruz. **Telephone:** (52) 229-935-5004. **Fax:** (229) 935-5008. **E-Mail Address:** rojosdelaguila@terra.com.mx. **Website:** www.aguiladeveracruz.com.
President: Jose Antonio Mansur Beltran. **General Manager:** Grimaldo Martinez Gonzalez.
Manager: Alfonso Jimenez.

YUCATAN LIONS
Office Address: Calle 50 #406-B, Entre 35 y 37, Col Jesus Carranza, CP 97109, Merida, Yucatán. **Telephone:** (52) 999-926-3022. **Fax:** (52) 999-926-3631. **E-Mail Addresses:** mserrano@leones.mx. **Website:** www.leones.mx.
President: Erick Ernesto Arellano Hernández. **General Manager:** José Rivero Ancona.
Manager: Orlando Sanchez Marquez.

MEXICAN ACADEMY

Rookie Classification
Mailing Address: Angel Pola No 16, Col Periodista, CP 11220, Mexico, DF Telephone: (52) 555-557-1007. **Fax:** (52) 555-395-2454. **E-Mail Address:** mbl@prodigy.net.mx. **Website:** www.lmbacademia.com.mx.
President: C.P. Plinio Escalante Bolio. **Director General:** Raul Martinez.
Regular Season: 50 games. **Opening Date:** Not available. **Closing Date:** Not available.

DOMINICAN REPUBLIC
DOMINICAN SUMMER LEAGUE

Member, National Association
Rookie Classification
Mailing Address: Calle Segunda No 64, Reparto Antilla, Santo Domingo, Dominican Republic. **Telephone/Fax:** (809) 532-3619. **Website:** www.dominicansummerleague.com. **E-Mail Address:** ligadeverano@codetel.net.do.
Years League Active: 1985-.
President: Orlando Diaz.
Member Clubs/Division Structure: Boca Chica North—Angels, Astros Orange, Cubs, Marlins, Mets 2, Phillies, Pirates, Rangers 1, Rangers 2, Yankees 2. **Boca Chica South**—Cardinals, Giants, Mariners, Mets 1, Nationals, Orioles 2, Red Sox, Reds/Diamobacks, Rockies, Yankees 1. **Boca Chica Northwest**—Astros Blue, Athletics, Dodgers, Indians, Rays, Royals. **Boca Chica Baseball City**—Diamondbacks, Orioles 1, Padres, Reds, Twins, White Sox. **San Pedro de Macoris**—Blue Jays, Braves, Brewers, Tigers.
Regular Season: 72 games. **Opening Date:** Unavailable. **Closing Date:** Unavailable.
Playoff Format: Six teams qualify for playoffs, including four division winners and two wild-card teams. Teams with two best records receive a bye to the semifinals; four other playoff teams play best-of-three series. Winners advance to best-of-three semifinals. Winners advance to best-of-five championship series.
Roster Limit: 35 active. **Player Eligibility Rule:** No player may have four or more years of prior minor league service. No draft-eligible player from the U.S. or Canada (not including players from Puerto Rico) may participate in the DSL. No age limits apply.

VENEZUELA
VENEZUELAN SUMMER LEAGUE

Member, National Association
Rookie Classification
Mailing Address: Torre Movilnet, Oficina 10, Piso 9, Valencia, Carabobo, Venezuela. **Telephone:** (58) 241-823-8101. **Fax:** (58) 241-824-3340.
Years League Active: 1997-.
Administrator: Franklin Moreno, Ramon Feriera Jr. **Coordinator:** Ramon Feriera.
Participating Organizations: Cubs, Mariners, Phillies, Rays, Tigers.
Regular Season: 70 games.
Playoffs: Best-of-three series between top two teams in regular season.
Roster Limit: 35 active. **Player Eligibility Rule:** No player may have four or more years of prior minor league service. No draft-eligible player from the U.S. or Canada (not including players from Puerto Rico) may participate in the VSL. No age limits apply.

CHINA
CHINA BASEBALL LEAGUE

Mailing Address: 5, Tiyuguan Road, Beijing 100763, China. **Telephone:** (86) 10-6716-9082. **Fax:** (86) 10-6716-2993. **Website:** baseball.sport.org.cn.
Years League Active: 2002-

Chairman: Hu Jian Guo. **Vice Chairmen:** Tom McCarthy, Shen Wei. **Executive Director:** Yang Jie. **General Manager, Marketing/Promotion:** Lin Xiao Wu.
Member Clubs: Beijing Tigers, Guangdong Leopards, Henan Elephants, Jiangsu Pegasus, Shanghai Golden Eagles, Sichuan Dragons, Tianjin Lions.
Regular Season: 28 games.
Playoff Format: Top two teams meet in one-game championship.

JAPAN
NIPPON PROFESSIONAL BASEBALL

Mailing Address: Mita Bellju Building, 11th Floor, 5-36-7 Shiba, Minato-ku, Tokyo 108-0014. **Telephone:** 03-6400-1189. **Fax:** 03-6400-1190.
Website: www.npb.or.jp, www.npb.or.jp/eng
Commissioner: Katsuhiko Kumazaki.
Executive Secretary: Atsushi Ihara. **Director, Baseball Operations:** Nobby Ito. **Director, Public Relations:** Katsuhisa Matsuzaki.
Director, Central League Operations: Kazuhide Kinefuchi. **Director, Pacific League Operations:** Kazuo Nakano.
Nippon Series: Best-of-seven series between Central and Pacific League representatives, begins Oct 24.
All-Star Series: July 17 at Tokyo Dome; July 18 at Mazda Stadium, Hiroshima.
Roster Limit: 70 per organization (one major league club, one minor league club). Major league club is permitted to register 28 players at a time, though just 25 may be available for each game.
Roster Limit, Imports: Four in majors (no more than three position players or pitchers); unlimited in minors.

CENTRAL LEAGUE
Regular Season: 143 games.
2015 Opening Date: March 27. **Closing Date:** Sept 27.
Playoff Format: Second-place team meets third-place team in best-of-three series. Winner meets first-place team in best-of-seven series to determine representative in Japan Series (first-place team has one-game advantage to begin series).

CHUNICHI DRAGONS
Mailing Address: Chunichi Bldg 6F, 4-1-1 Sakae, Naka-ku, Nagoya 460-0008. **Telephone:** 052-261-8811. **Fax:** 052-263-7696.
Chairman: Bungo Shirai. **President:** Takao Sasaki. **General Manager:** Hiromitsu Ochiai. **Field Manager:** Motonobu Tanishige.
2015 Foreign Players: Anderson Hernandez, Hector Luna, Ricardo Nanita, Amaury Rivas, Raul Valdes.

HANSHIN TIGERS
Mailing Address: 2-33 Koshien-cho, Nishinomiya-shi, Hyogo-ken 663-8152. **Telephone:** 0798-46-1515. **Fax:** 0798-46-3555.
Chairman: Shinya Sakai. **President:** Nobuo Minami. **General Manager:** Katsuhiro Nakamura. **Field Manager:** Yutaka Wada.
2015 Foreign Players: Mauro Gomez, Randy Messenger, Matt Murton, Seung-Hwan Oh, Tom O'Malley (Coach).

HIROSHIMA TOYO CARP
Mailing Address: 2-3-1 Minami Kaniya, Minami-ku, Hiroshima 732-8501. **Telephone:** 082-554-1000. **Fax:** 082-568-1190.
President: Hajime Matsuda. **General Manager:** Kiyoaki Suzuki. **Field Manager:** Koichi Ogata.
2015 Foreign Players: Brad Eldred, Jesus Guzman, Deunte Heath, Kris Johnson, Rainel Rosario, Mike Zagurski.

TOKYO YAKULT SWALLOWS
Mailing Address: Seizan Bldg, 4F, 2-12-28 Kita Aoyama, Minato-ku, Tokyo 107-0061. **Telephone:** 03-3405-8960. **Fax:** 03-3405-8961.
Chairman: Sumiya Hori. **President:** Tsuyoshi KInugasa. **Senior Director:** Junji Ogawa. **Field Manager:** Mitsuru Manaka.

2015 Foreign Players: Wladimir Balentien, Tony Barnette, Lastings Milledge, Logan Ondrusek, Orlando Roman.

YOKOHAMA DeNA BAYSTARS
Mailing Address: Kannai Arai Bldg, 7F, 1-8 Onoe-cho, Naka-ku, Yokohama 231-0015. **Telephone:** 045-681-0811. **Fax:** 045-661-2500.
Owner: Tomoko Namba. **President:** Jun Ikeda. **General Manager:** Shigeru Takada. **Field Manager:** Kiyoshi Nakahata.
2015 Foreign Players: Aarom Baldiris, Yulieski Gourriel, Yoslan Herrera, Jose Lopez, Guillermo Moscoso,

YOMIURI GIANTS
Mailing Address: Yomiuri Shimbun Bldg, 26F, 1-7-1 Otemachi, Chiyoda-ku, Tokyo 100-8151. **Telephone:** 03-3246-7733. **Fax:** 03-3246-2726.
Chairman: Kojiro Shiraishi. **President:** Tsunekazu Momoi. **General Manager:** Atsushi Harasawa. **Field Manager:** Tatsunori Hara.
2015 Foreign Players: Leslie Anderson, Frederich Cepeda, Scott Mathieson, Hector Mendoza, Miles Mikolas, Aaron Poreda.

PACIFIC LEAGUE
Regular Season: 143 games.
2015 Opening Date: March 27. **Closing Date:** Oct. 1.
Playoff Format: Second-place team meets third-place team in best-of-three series. **Winner meets first-place team in best-of-seven series to determine league's representative in Japan Series (first-place team has one-game advantage to begin series).**

CHIBA LOTTE MARINES
Mailing Address: 1 Mihama, Mihama-ku, Chiba-shi, Chiba-ken 261-8587. **Telephone:** 03-5682-6341.
Chairman: Takeo Shigemitsu. **President:** Shinya Yamamuro. **Field Manager:** Tsutomu Ito.
2015 Foreign Players: Kuan-Yu Chen, Luis Cruz, Alfredo Despaigne, Chad Huffman, Dae-Eun Rhee, Carlos Rosa.

FUKUOKA SOFTBANK HAWKS
Mailing Address: Fukuoka Yahoo! **Japan Dome, Hawks Town, Chuo-ku, Fukuoka 810-0065. Telephone:** 092-847-1006. **Fax:** 092-844-4600.
Owner: Masayoshi Son. **Chairman:** Sadaharu Oh. **President:** Yoshimitsu Goto. **Field Manager:** Kimiyasu Kudo.
2015 Foreign Players: Barbaro Canizares, Dae Ho Lee, Dennis Sarfate, Jason Standridge, Rick VandenHurk, Brian Wolfe.

HOKKAIDO NIPPON HAM FIGHTERS
Mailing Address: 1 Hitsujigaoka, Toyohira-ku, Sapporo 062-8655. **Telephone:** 011-857-3939. **Fax:** 011-857-3900.
Chairman: Hiroji Okoso. **President:** Junichi Fujii. **General Manager:** Hiroshi Yoshimura. **Field Manager:** Hideki Kuriyama.
2015 Foreign Players: Mike Crotta, Victor Garate, Jeremy Hermida, Brandon Laird, Luis Mendoza.

ORIX BUFFALOES
Mailing Address: 3-Kita-2-30 Chiyozaki, Nishi-ku, Osaka 550-0023. **Telephone:** 06-6586-0221. **Fax:** 06-6586-0240.
Chairman: Yoshihiko Miyauchi. **President:** Hiroaki Nishina. **General Manager:** Ryuzo Setoyama. **Field Manager:** Hiroshi Moriwaki.
2015 Foreign Players: Tony Blanco, Bryan Bullington, Brandon Dickson, Esteban German, Alex Maestri.

SAITAMA SEIBU LIONS

Mailing Address: 2135 Kami-Yamaguchi, Tokorozawa-shi, Saitama-ken 359-1189. **Telephone:** 04-2924-1155. **Fax:** 04-2928-1919.

President: Hajime Iqo. **Field Manager:** Norio Tanabe.

2015 Foreign Players: Shun-rin Kaku, Wade LeBlanc, Ernesto Mejia, Miguel Mejia, Anthony Seratelli, Esmerling Vasquez.

TOHOKU RAKUTEN GOLDEN EAGLES

Mailing Address: 2-11-6 Miyagino, Miyagino-ku, Sendai-shi, Miyagi-ken 983-0045. **Telephone:** 022-298-5300. **Fax:** 022-298-5360.

Chairman: Hiroshi Mikitani. **President:** Yozo Tachibana. **Field Manager:** Hiromoto "Dave" Okubo.

2015 Foreign Players: Rhiner Cruz, Jim Heuser, Kam Mickolio, Kenny Ray, Gaby Sanchez, Zealous Wheeler.

KOREA

KOREA BASEBALL ORGANIZATION

Mailing Address: 946-16 Dokokdong, Kangnam-gu, Seoul, Korea. **Telephone:** (02) 3460-4600. **Fax:** (02) 3460-4639.

Years League Active: 1982-.

Website: www.koreabaseball.com.

Commissioner: Koo Bon-Neung. **Secretary General:** Yang Hae-Young.

Member Clubs: Doosan Bears, Hanwha Eagles, Kia Tigers, KT Wiz, LG Twins, Lotte Giants, NC Dinos, Nexen Heroes, Samsung Lions, SK Wyverns.

Regular Season: 128 games. **2015 Opening Date:** March 28.

Playoffs: Third- and fourth-place teams meet in best-of-three series; winner advances to meet second-place team in best-of-five series; winner meets first-place team in best-of-seven Korean Series for league championship.

Roster Limit: 26 active through Sept 1, when rosters expand to 31. **Imports:** Two active.

TAIWAN

CHINESE PROFESSIONAL BASEBALL LEAGUE

Mailing Address: 2F, No 32, Pateh Road, Sec 3, Taipei, Taiwan 10559. **Telephone:** 886-2-2577-6992. **Fax:** 886-2-2577-2606. **Website:** www.cpbl.com.tw.

Years League Active: 1990-.

Commissioner: Jenn-Tai Hwang. **Deputy Secretary General:** Hueimin Wang. **E-Mail Address:** richard.wang@cpbl.com.tw.

Member Clubs: Brother Elephants, EDA Rhinos, Lamigo Monkeys, Uni Lions.

Regular Season: 120 games. **2015 Opening Date:** Not available. **Playoffs:** Half-season winners are eligible for the postseason. If a non-half-season winner team possesses a higher overall winning percentage than any other half-season winner, then this team gains a wild-card and will play a best-of-five series against the half-season winner with lower winner percentage.

The winner of the playoff series advances to Taiwan Series (best-of-seven).

EUROPE

NETHERLANDS

DUTCH MAJOR LEAGUE

Mailing Address: Koninklijke Nederlandse Baseball en Softball Bond (Royal Dutch Baseball and Softball Association), Postbus 2650, 3430 GB Nieuwegein, Holland. **Telephone:** 31-30-751-3650. **Fax:** 31-30-751-3651. **Website:** www.knbsb.nl.

Member Clubs: ADO, Amsterdam Pirates, Dordrecht, HCAW, Kinheim, Neptunus, Mampaey Hawks, UVV, Vaessen Pioniers.

President: Bob Bergkamp.

ITALY

ITALIAN BASEBALL LEAGUE

Mailing Address: Federazione Italiana Baseball Softball, Viale Tiziano 74, 00196 Roma, Italy. **Telephone:** 39-06-32297201. **Fax:** 39-06-36858201. **Website:** www.fibs.it.

Member Clubs: Bologna, Godo, Grosseto, Nettuno, Novara, Parma, Rimini, San Marino.

President: Riccardo Fraccari.

WINTER BASEBALL

CARIBBEAN BASEBALL CONFEDERATION

Mailing Address: Frank Feliz Miranda No 1 Naco, Santo Domingo, Dominican Republic. **Telephone:** (809) 381-2643. **Fax:** (809) 565-4654.

Commissioner: Juan Francisco Puello. **Secretary:** Benny Agosto.

Member Countries: Colombia, Dominican Republic, Mexico, Nicaragua, Puerto Rico, Venezuela (Colombia and Nicaragua do not play in the Caribbean Series).

2016 Caribbean Series: Dominican Republic, February.

DOMINICAN LEAGUE

Office Address: Estadio Quisqueya, 2da Planta, Ens La Fe, Santo Domingo, Dominican Republic. **Telephone:**

(809) 567-6371. **Fax:** (809) 567-5720. **E-Mail Address:** ligadom@hotmail.com. **Website:** www.lidom.com.

Years League Active: 1951-.

President: Leonardo Matos Berrido. **Executive Director:** Jorge Torres Ocumarez.

Member Clubs: Aguilas Cibaenas, Estrellas de Oriente, Gigantes del Cibao, Leones del Escogido, Tigres del Licey, Toros del Este.

Regular Season: 50 games. **2015 Opening Date:** Unavailable.

Playoff Format: Top four teams meet in 18-game round-robin. Top two teams advance to best-of-nine series for league championship. Winner advances to Caribbean Series.

Roster Limit: 30. **Imports:** 7.

MEXICAN PACIFIC LEAGUE

Mailing Address: Blvd Solidaridad No 335, Plaza las Palmas, Edificio A, Nivel 1, Local 4, Hermosillo, Sonora, Mexico CP 83246. **Telephone:** (52) 662-310-9714. **Fax:** (52) 662-310-9715. **E-Mail Address:** ligadelpacifico@liga-delpacifico.com.mx. **Website:** www.ligadelpacifico.com.mx.

Years League Active: 1958-.
President: Omar Canizales Soto. **Administration:** Remigio Valencia. **General Manager:** Christian O. Valencia Veliz. **Media Manager:** Pedro A. Gutierrez.
Member Clubs: Culiacan Tomateros, Hermosillo Naranjeros, Jalisco Charros, Los Mochis Caneros, Mazatlan Venados, Mexicali Aguilas, Navojoa Mayos, Obregon Yaquis.
Regular Season: 68 games. **2015 Opening Date:** Unavailable.
Playoff Format: Six teams advance to best-of-seven quarterfinals. Three winners and losing team with best record advance to best-of-seven semifinals. Winners meet in best-of-seven series for league championship. Winner advances to Caribbean Series.
Roster Limit: 30. **Imports:** 5.

PUERTO RICAN LEAGUE

Office Address: Avenida Munoz Rivera 1056, Edificio First Federal, Suite 501, Rio Piedras, PR 00925. **Mailing Address:** PO Box 191852, San Juan, PR 00019. **Telephone:** (787) 765-6285, 765-7285. **Fax:** (787) 767-3028. **Website:** www.ligapr.com.
Years League Active: 1938-2007; 2008-
President: Hector Rivera.
Member Clubs: Caguas Criollos, Carolina Gigantes, Mayaguez Indios, San Juan Senadores, Santurce Canjrejeros.
Regular Season: 40 games. **2015 Opening Date:** Unavailable.
Playoff Format: Top four teams meet in best-of-seven semifinal series. Winners meet in best-of-nine series for league championship. Winner advances to Caribbean Series.
Roster Limit: 30. **Imports:** 5.

VENEZUELAN LEAGUE

Mailing Address: Avenida Casanova, Centro Comercial "El Recreo,"Torre Sur, Piso 3, Oficinas 6 y 7, Sabana Grande, Caracas, Venezuela. **Telephone:** (58) 212-761-6408. **Fax:** (58) 212-761-7661. **Website:** www.lvbp.com.
Years League Active: 1946-.
President: Oscar Prieto Párraga. **Vice Presidents:** Humberto Angrisano, Domingo Santander. **General Manager:** Domingo Alvarez.
Member Clubs: Anzoategui Caribes, Aragua Tigres, Caracas Leones, La Guaira Tiburones, Lara Cardenales, Magallanes Navegantes, Margarita Bravos, Zulia Aguilas.
Regular Season: 64 games. **2015 Opening Date:** Unavailable.
Playoff Format: Top two teams in each division, plus a wild-card team, meet in 16-game round-robin series. Top two finishers meet in best-of-seven series for league championship. Winner advances to Caribbean Series.
Roster Limit: 26. **Imports:** 7.

COLOMBIAN LEAGUE

Office/Mailing Address: Cra54 No 47-01 Estadio Tomas Arrieta, Baranquilla, Colombia. **Telephone:** 370-5083. **E-mail Address:** ligadebeisbolprocol@hotmail.com. **Website:** www.lcbp.com.co.
President: Edinson Renteria. **Vice Presidents:** Edgar Perez, George Baladi, Orlando Covo.
Member Clubs: Barranquilla Caimanes, Cartegena Tigres, Monteria Leones, Sincelejo Toros.
Regular season: 65 games. **2015 Opening Date:** Unavailable.
Playoff Format: Top two teams meet in best-of-seven finals for league championship.

AUSTRALIA

AUSTRALIAN BASEBALL LEAGUE

Mailing Address: Suite 203/46 Market St, Sydney NSW 2000, Australia. **Telephone:** (61) 2-8226-0225. **Fax:** (61)-2-8226-0293. **E-Mail Address:** admin@theABL.com.au. **Website:** www.theabl.com.
CEO: Peter Wermuth. **General Manager:** Ben Foster.
Teams: Adelaide Bite, Brisbane Bandits, Canberra Cavalry, Melbourne Aces, Perth Heat, Sydney Blue Sox.
Playoff Format: First-place team plays second-place team in major semifinal; third-place team plays fourth-place team in minor semifinal, both best of three series. Loser of major semifinal plays winner of minor semifinal in best of three series. Winner of that series plays winner of major semifinal in best of three series for league championship.

DOMESTIC LEAGUE

ARIZONA FALL LEAGUE

Mailing Address: 2415 E Camelback Road, Suite 850, Phoenix, AZ 85016. **Telephone:** (602) 281-7250. **Fax:** (602) 281-7313. **E-Mail Address:** afl@mlb.com. **Website:** www.mlb.com.
Years League Active: 1992-.
Operated by: Major League Baseball.
Executive Director: Steve Cobb. **Administrator:** Darlene Emert. **Communications:** Paul Jensen.
Teams: Glendale Desert Dogs, Mesa Solar Sox, Peoria Javelinas, Salt River Rafters, Scottsdale Scorpions, Surprise Saguaros.
2015 Opening Date: Unavailable. Play usually opens in mid-October. **Playoff Format:** Division champions meet in one-game championship.
Roster Limit: 30. Players with less than one year of major league service are eligible, with one foreign player and one player below the Double-A level allowed per team.

MINOR LEAGUE SCHEDULES

TRIPLE-A

INTERNATIONAL LEAGUE

BUFFALO BISONS

APRIL
9-10 . . . . Rochester
11-12 . . . . . at Rochester
13-15 . . . . . .Pawtucket
16-19 . . . . . Lehigh Valley
20-22 . . . . at Pawtucket
23-26 . . . at Lehigh Valley
27-30 . . . . .Norfolk

MAY
1-3 . . . . Louisville
5-7 . . . . .at Durham
8-10 . . . . at Norfolk
11-13 . . . . Durham
14-17 . . . . Toledo
18-20 . . . . . at Columbus
21-24 . . . . . . .at Toledo
25-27 . . . . . .Indianapolis
29-31 . . . . Rochester

JUNE
1-3 . . . . . . at Indianapolis
4-7 . . . . at Louisville
8-10 . . . . . . Scranton/WB
11 . . . . Charlotte
13-14 . . . . Charlotte
15-18 . . . . at Lehigh Valley
19-21 . . . . . . at Syracuse
23-25 . . . . . Lehigh Valley
26-28 . . . . at Scranton/WB

29-30 . . . . Gwinnett

JULY
1 . . . . Gwinnett
2-3 . . . . Syracuse
4-6 . . . . . at Scranton/WB
7-9 . . . . . . at Rochester
10-12 . . . . . Scranton/WB
16-19 . . . . Columbus
20-23 . . . . Syracuse
24-26 . . . . . at Pawtucket
27-30 . . . . . at Syracuse
31 . . . . .Pawtucket

AUGUST
1-2 . . . . .Pawtucket
4-6 . . . . .at Charlotte
7-9 . . . . at Gwinnett
10-13 . . . . Rochester
14-16 . . . . . at Syracuse
17-19 . . . . at Rochester
21-23 . . . . Syracuse
24-26 . . . at Lehigh Valley
27-28 . . . . . . .Pawtucket
29-31 . . . . . Scranton/WB

SEPTEMBER
1-2 . . . . Syracuse
3-4 . . . . . at Scranton/WB
5-7 . . . . . . at Pawtucket

CHARLOTTE KNIGHTS

APRIL
9-12 . . . . .Norfolk
13-14 . . . . Durham
15-16 . . . . . .at Gwinnett
17-19 . . . . . . Gwinnett
20-23 . . . . . .at Durham
24-26 . . . . at Norfolk
27-29 . . . . Toledo
30 . . . . Scranton/WB

MAY
1-3 . . . . Scranton/WB
5-7 . . . . at Columbus
8-10 . . . . .at Toledo
11-14 . . . . Louisville
15-17 . . . . .Syracuse
18-20 . . . at Scranton/WB
21-24 . . at Lehigh Valley
25-28 . . . . Columbus
29-31 . . . . . Lehigh Valley

JUNE
2-4 . . . . .at Durham
5-7 . . . . .Norfolk
8-10 . . . . . . at Pawtucket
11 . . . . at Buffalo
13-14 . . . . at Buffalo
16-18 . . . . . . .Pawtucket
19-21 . . . . . .Indianapolis
22-25 . . . . . . at Syracuse

26-28 . . . . . at Rochester
29-30 . . . . at Norfolk

JULY
1 . . . . at Norfolk
2-3 . . . . Gwinnett
4-6 . . . . .at Gwinnett
7-9 . . . . Durham
10-12 . . . . . . at Norfolk
16-19 . . . . .Norfolk
20-23 . . . . Durham
24-26 . . . . . .at Gwinnett
27-30 . . . . . .at Louisville
31 . . . . . . at Indianapolis

AUGUST
1-2 . . . . . . at Indianapolis
4-6 . . . . Buffalo
7-9 . . . . Rochester
10-13 . . . . Gwinnett
14-16 . . . . .at Toledo
17-18 . . . . . at Columbus
20-23 . . . . . .Indianapolis
24-26 . . . . Gwinnett
27-30 . . . . . . .at Durham
31 . . . . at Norfolk

SEPTEMBER
1 . . . . at Norfolk
2-4 . . . . Durham
5-7 . . . . .at Gwinnett

COLUMBUS CLIPPERS

APRIL
9-12 . . . . . at Indianapolis
13-14 . . . . .at Louisville

16-17 . . . . .at Toledo
18-19 . . . . Toledo
20-22 . . . . . .Indianapolis

23-26 . . . . Louisville
27-30 . . . . at Rochester

MAY
1-3 . . . . at Syracuse
5-7 . . . . Charlotte
8-10 . . . . . . .Pawtucket
11-13 . . . at Lehigh Valley
14-17 . . . . at Pawtucket
18-20 . . . . Buffalo
21-24 . . . . Gwinnett
25-28 . . . . at Charlotte
29-31 . . . . . .at Gwinnett

JUNE
1-3 . . . . Toledo
5-7 . . . . .at Toledo
8-10 . . . . Louisville
11-14 . . . . Syracuse
15-17 . . . . at Norfolk
18-21 . . . . .at Durham
22-24 . . . . . . .Norfolk
26-28 . . . . . . Durham
29-30 . . . . at Indianapolis

JULY
1 . . . . at Indianapolis
2-3 . . . . . .at Louisville
4-6 . . . . Toledo

7-9 . . . . .at Toledo
10-12 . . . . . .Indianapolis
16-19 . . . . . at Buffalo
20-21 . . . . . Louisville
22-23 . . . . . .at Louisville
24-26 . . . . . . Rochester
27-30 . . . . . .Indianapolis
31 . . . . . at Scranton/WB

AUGUST
1-2 . . . . . at Scranton/WB
4-6 . . . . . . Scranton/WB
7-9 . . . . . . Lehigh Valley
11-13 . . . . .at Louisville
14-16 . . . . . Gwinnett
17-18 . . . . . Charlotte
19-21 . . . . . at Norfolk
22-23 . . . . . .at Durham
24-26 . . . . . .at Toledo
27-28 . . . . . . Toledo
29-30 . . . . . Louisville
31 . . . . . . .Indianapolis

SEPTEMBER
1 . . . . .Indianapolis
2-3 . . . . . . at Indianapolis
4-5 . . . . . . at Louisville
6-7 . . . . Toledo

DURHAM BULLS

APRIL
9-12 . . . . . . .at Gwinnett
13-14 . . . . . .at Charlotte
15-17 . . . . . . .Norfolk
18-19 . . . . . at Norfolk
20-23 . . . . . . Charlotte
24-26 . . . . . Gwinnett
27-30 . . . at Lehigh Valley

MAY
1-3 . . . . at Pawtucket
5-7 . . . . Buffalo
8-10 . . . . . . at Syracuse
11-13 . . . . . . at Buffalo
14-17 . . . Scranton/WB
18-20 . . . . at Rochester
21-24 . . at Scranton/WB
25-27 . . . . . . Rochester
29-31 . . . . . . Syracuse

JUNE
2-4 . . . . Charlotte
5-7 . . . . .at Gwinnett
8-10 . . . . . Lehigh Valley
11-14 . . . . at Louisville
15-17 . . . .at Indianapolis
18-21 . . . . . . Columbus
23-25 . . . . Toledo
25-28 . . . . at Columbus
29-30 . . . . . . .at Toledo

JULY
1 . . . . .at Toledo
2-3 . . . . at Norfolk
4-6 . . . . .Norfolk
7-9 . . . . .at Charlotte
10-12 . . . . . . Gwinnett
16-19 . . . . . . .Pawtucket
20-23 . . . . . .at Charlotte
24-26 . . . . . . at Norfolk
27-29 . . . . . .at Gwinnett
31 . . . . Gwinnett

AUGUST
1-2 . . . . Gwinnett
3-6 . . . . .Indianapolis
7-9 . . . . Louisville
10-11 . . . . . at Norfolk
12-13 . . . . .Norfolk
14-16 . . . at Indianapolis
17-18 . . . . at Louisville
19-21 . . . . Toledo
22-23 . . . . Columbus
25-26 . . . . . at Norfolk
27-30 . . . . . . Charlotte
31 . . . . Gwinnett

SEPTEMBER
1 . . . . Gwinnett
2-4 . . . . .at Charlotte
5-7 . . . . .Norfolk

GWINNETT BRAVES

APRIL
9-12 . . . . Durham
13-14 . . . . .Norfolk
15-16 . . . . Charlotte
17-19 . . . . . .at Charlotte
20-23 . . . . . . at Norfolk
24-26 . . . . . .at Durham
27-29 . . . . . Scranton/WB
30 . . . . Toledo

MAY
1-3 . . . . Toledo
5-7 . . . . at Scranton/WB
8-10 . . . . . at Lehigh Valley
11-14 . . . . Syracuse
15-17 . . . . . . Louisville
18-20 . . . . .at Toledo
21-24 . . . . at Columbus
25-28 . . . . . Lehigh Valley
29-31 . . . . Columbus

JUNE	
2-4 . . . . at Norfolk	24-26 . . . . Charlotte
5-7 . . . . Durham	27-29 . . . . Durham
8-10 . . . . .Norfolk	31 . . . . .at Durham
11-14 . . . . at Indianapolis	**AUGUST**
15-17 . . . . . . at Louisville	1-2 . . . . .at Durham
19-21 . . . . .Pawtucket	3-6 . . . . Rochester
22-25 . . . . . .Indianapolis	7-9 . . . . Buffalo
26-28 . . . . . at Pawtucket	10-13 . . . . . .at Charlotte
29-30 . . . . at Buffalo	14-16 . . . . . at Columbus
JULY	17-18 . . . . .at Toledo
1 . . . . at Buffalo	20-23 . . . . Louisville
2-3 . . . . .at Charlotte	24-26 . . . . . .at Charlotte
4-6 . . . . Charlotte	27-30 . . . . .Norfolk
7-9 . . . . .Norfolk	31 . . . . .at Durham
10-12 . . . . . .at Durham	**SEPTEMBER**
16-19 . . . . . . at Syracuse	1 . . . . .at Durham
20-23 . . . . . at Rochester	2-4 . . . . at Norfolk
	5-7 . . . . Charlotte

INDIANAPOLIS INDIANS

APRIL		JULY	
9-12 . . . . .Columbus		1 . . . . .Columbus	
13-14 . . . . Toledo		2-3 . . . . .at Toledo	
15-17 . . . . Louisville		4-6 . . . . Louisville	
18-19 . . . . . . at Louisville		7-9 . . . . at Louisville	
20-22 . . . . at Columbus		10-12 . . . . at Columbus	
23-26 . . . . . . .at Toledo		16-19 . . . . . .at Toledo	
27-28 . . . . . at Louisville		20-23 . . . . . Scranton/WB	
29-30 . . . . . . Louisville		24-26 . . . . . . Louisville	
MAY		27-30 . . . . at Columbus	
1-3 . . . . Lehigh Valley		31 . . . . Charlotte	
5-7 . . . . Rochester		**AUGUST**	
8-10 . . . . at Scranton/WB		1-2 . . . . Charlotte	
11-13 . . . . . at Pawtucket		3-6 . . . . .at Durham	
14-17 . . . . .Norfolk		7-9 . . . . at Norfolk	
18-20 . . . . . . .Pawtucket		11-13 . . . . Toledo	
22-24 . . . . . . at Syracuse		14-16 . . . . Durham	
25-27 . . . . . . at Buffalo		17-18 . . . . .Norfolk	
28-31 . . . . Toledo		20-23 . . . . . .at Charlotte	
JUNE		24-26 . . . . . . Louisville	
1-3 . . . . Buffalo		27-28 . . . . . at Louisville	
4-7 . . . . . at Lehigh Valley		29-30 . . . . .at Toledo	
8-10 . . . . . at Rochester		31 . . . . at Columbus	
11-14 . . . . Gwinnett		**SEPTEMBER**	
15-17 . . . . Durham		1 . . . . at Columbus	
19-21 . . . . .at Charlotte		2-3 . . . . Columbus	
22-25 . . . . at Gwinnett		4-5 . . . . Toledo	
26-28 . . . . Syracuse		6-7 . . . . . at Louisville	
29-30 . . . . . . Columbus			

LEHIGH VALLEY IRONPIGS

APRIL		
9-12 . . . . .Pawtucket	11-14 . . . . at Norfolk	
13-15 . . . . Syracuse	15-18 . . . . Buffalo	
16-19 . . . . at Buffalo	19-21 . . . . Scranton/WB	
20-22 . . . at Scranton/WB	23-25 . . . . . at Buffalo	
23-26 . . . . Buffalo	26-28 . . . . . . Louisville	
27-30 . . . . Durham	29-30 . . . . Scranton/WB	
MAY	**JULY**	
1-3 . . . . . . at Indianapolis	1 . . . . Scranton/WB	
4-6 . . . . at Louisville	2-3 . . . . Rochester	
8-10 . . . . Gwinnett	4-6 . . . . at Rochester	
11-13 . . . . Columbus	7-9 . . . . .Pawtucket	
14-17 . . . . at Rochester	10-12 . . . . at Pawtucket	
18-20 . . . . at Syracuse	16-19 . . . . at Rochester	
21-24 . . . . Charlotte	20-23 . . . . Toledo	
25-28 . . . . at Gwinnett	24-26 . . . . . . Syracuse	
29-31 . . . . . .at Charlotte	27-28 . . . at Scranton/WB	
JUNE	29-30 . . . . Scranton/WB	
2-3 . . . . Rochester	31 . . . . .Norfolk	
4-7 . . . . .Indianapolis	**AUGUST**	
8-10 . . . . . . .at Durham	1-2 . . . . .Norfolk	
	3-6 . . . . .at Toledo	

	JULY	
7-9 . . . . at Columbus	27-28 . . . . at Scranton/WB	
11-13 . . . . . at Syracuse	29-31 . . . . . . at Syracuse	
14-16 . . . . .Pawtucket	**SEPTEMBER**	
18-20 . . . . at Scranton/WB	1-2 . . . . at Pawtucket	
21-23 . . . . at Pawtucket	3-4 . . . . Syracuse	
24-26 . . . . Buffalo	5-7 . . . . Rochester	

LOUISVILLE BATS

APRIL		JULY	
9-12 . . . . Toledo		1 . . . . Syracuse	
13-14 . . . . Columbus		2-3 . . . . Columbus	
15-17 . . . . at Indianapolis		4-6 . . . . . . at Indianapolis	
18-19 . . . . .Indianapolis		7-9 . . . . .Indianapolis	
21-22 . . . . .at Toledo		10-12 . . . . . . .at Toledo	
23-26 . . . . at Columbus		16-19 . . . . Scranton/WB	
27-28 . . . . .Indianapolis		20-21 . . . . at Columbus	
29-30 . . . . Indianapolis		22-23 . . . . . . Columbus	
MAY		24-26 . . . . at Indianapolis	
1-3 . . . . at Buffalo		27-30 . . . . Charlotte	
4-6 . . . . . . Lehigh Valley		31 . . . . Toledo	
8-10 . . . . Rochester		**AUGUST**	
11-14 . . . . . .at Charlotte		1-2 . . . . Toledo	
15-17 . . . . at Gwinnett		3-6 . . . . at Norfolk	
18-20 . . . . .Norfolk		7-9 . . . . .at Durham	
21-24 . . . . . .Pawtucket		11-13 . . . . . . Columbus	
25-27 . . . . Toledo		14-16 . . . . . . .Norfolk	
29-31 . . . . at Pawtucket		17-18 . . . . Durham	
JUNE		20-23 . . . . . .at Gwinnett	
1-3 . . . . at Syracuse		24-26 . . . . at Indianapolis	
4-7 . . . . Buffalo		27-28 . . . . .Indianapolis	
8-10 . . . . at Columbus		29-30 . . . . at Columbus	
11-14 . . . . Durham		31 . . . . .at Toledo	
15-17 . . . . Gwinnett		**SEPTEMBER**	
19-21 . . . . at Rochester		1-3 . . . . .at Toledo	
22-25 . . . . Scranton/WB		4-5 . . . . Columbus	
26-28 . . . at Lehigh Valley		6-7 . . . . . . .Indianapolis	
29-30 . . . . Syracuse			

NORFOLK TIDES

APRIL		JULY	
9-12 . . . . at Charlotte		1 . . . . Charlotte	
13-14 . . . . . . at Gwinnett		2-3 . . . . Durham	
15-17 . . . . .at Durham		4-6 . . . . .at Durham	
18-19 . . . . Durham		7-9 . . . . .at Gwinnett	
20-23 . . . . Gwinnett		10-12 . . . . . . Charlotte	
24-26 . . . . Charlotte		16-19 . . . . . .at Charlotte	
27-30 . . . . . . at Buffalo		20-23 . . . . . . .Pawtucket	
MAY		24-26 . . . . Durham	
1-3 . . . . at Rochester		28-30 . . . . . at Pawtucket	
4-6 . . . . at Syracuse		31 . . . . . at Lehigh Valley	
8-10 . . . . Buffalo		**AUGUST**	
11-13 . . . . . Scranton/WB		1-2 . . . . . at Lehigh Valley	
14-17 . . . . at Indianapolis		3-6 . . . . Louisville	
18-20 . . . .at Louisville		7-9 . . . . . . .Indianapolis	
21-24 . . . . . . Rochester		10-11 . . . . Durham	
25-28 . . . . . . Syracuse		12-13 . . . . . .at Durham	
29-31 . . . at Scranton/WB		14-16 . . . . at Louisville	
JUNE		17-18 . . . . at Indianapolis	
2-4 . . . . Gwinnett		19-21 . . . . Columbus	
5-7 . . . . .at Charlotte		22-23 . . . . Toledo	
8-10 . . . . . . .at Charlotte		25-26 . . . . . . Durham	
11-14 . . . . . Lehigh Valley		27-30 . . . . . .at Gwinnett	
15-17 . . . . . . Columbus		31 . . . . Charlotte	
18-21 . . . . .at Toledo		**SEPTEMBER**	
22-24 . . . . at Columbus		1 . . . . Charlotte	
26-28 . . . . . Toledo		2-4 . . . . Gwinnett	
29-30 . . . . Charlotte		5-7 . . . . . . .at Durham	

PAWTUCKET RED SOX

APRIL
9-12 . . . . at Lehigh Valley
13-15 . . . . at Buffalo
16-19 . . . . Rochester
20-22 . . . . Buffalo
23-26 . . . . at Scranton/WB
27-30 . . . . Syracuse

MAY
1-3 . . . . Durham
5-7 . . . . .at Toledo
8-10 . . . . . . at Columbus
11-13 . . . . . . .Indianapolis
14-17 . . . . Columbus
18-20 . . . . at Indianapolis
21-24 . . . . . at Louisville
25-27 . . . . . Scranton/WB
29-31 . . . . Louisville

JUNE
1-3 . . . . . at Scranton/WB
4-5 . . . . at Rochester
6-7 . . . . at Syracuse
8-10 . . . . Charlotte
11-14 . . . . Toledo
16-18 . . . . . . .at Charlotte
19-21 . . . . at Gwinnett
22-25 . . . . Rochester
26-28 . . . . Gwinnett
29-30 . . . . . at Rochester

JULY
1 . . . . at Rochester
2-3 . . . . Scranton/WB
4-6 . . . . at Syracuse
7-9 . . . . at Lehigh Valley
10-12 . . . . Lehigh Valley
16-19 . . . . . . .at Durham
20-23 . . . . . . at Norfolk
24-26 . . . . Buffalo
28-30 . . . . Norfolk
31 . . . . at Buffalo

AUGUST
1-2 . . . . at Buffalo
3-5 . . . . at Syracuse
6-9 . . . . Syracuse
10-13 . . . at Scranton/WB
14-16 . . . . at Lehigh Valley
17-19 . . . . Syracuse
21-23 . . . . Lehigh Valley
24-26 . . . . . Scranton/WB
27-28 . . . . . . at Buffalo
29-31 . . . . . at Rochester

SEPTEMBER
1-2 . . . . Lehigh Valley
3-4 . . . . Rochester
5-7 . . . . Buffalo

ROCHESTER RED WINGS

APRIL
9-10 . . . . at Buffalo
11-12 . . . . Buffalo
13-15 . . . at Scranton/WB
16-19 . . . . . at Pawtucket
20-23 . . . . at Syracuse
24-26 . . . . . . Syracuse
27-30 . . . . Columbus

MAY
1-3 . . . . .Norfolk
5-7 . . . . . .at Indianapolis
8-10 . . . . at Louisville
11-13 . . . . Toledo
14-17 . . . . . . Lehigh Valley
18-20 . . . . Durham
21-24 . . . . . at Norfolk
25-27 . . . . . .at Durham
29-31 . . . . at Buffalo

JUNE
2-3 . . . . . at Lehigh Valley
4-5 . . . . .Pawtucket
6-7 . . . . Scranton/WB
8-10 . . . . . . .Indianapolis
11-14 . . . at Scranton/WB
16-18 . . . . . . Scranton/WB
19-21 . . . . . . Louisville
22-25 . . . . at Pawtucket
26-28 . . . . Charlotte
29-30 . . . . . . .Pawtucket

JULY
1 . . . . .Pawtucket
2-3 . . . . . at Lehigh Valley
4-6 . . . . . . Lehigh Valley
7-9 . . . . Buffalo
10-12 . . . . . . at Syracuse
16-19 . . . . . . Lehigh Valley
20-23 . . . . Gwinnett
24-26 . . . . at Columbus
27-29 . . . . . . .at Toledo
31 . . . . Syracuse

AUGUST
1-2 . . . . Syracuse
3-6 . . . . .at Gwinnett
7-9 . . . . .at Charlotte
10-13 . . . . at Buffalo
14-16 . . . . . Scranton/WB
17-19 . . . . Buffalo
21-23 . . . at Scranton/WB
24-26 . . . . . . at Syracuse
27-28 . . . . Syracuse
29-31 . . . . . . .Pawtucket

SEPTEMBER
1-2 . . . . Scranton/WB
3-4 . . . . . . at Pawtucket
5-7 . . . . . at Lehigh Valley

SCRANTON/WILKES-BARRE RAILRIDERS

APRIL
9-12 . . . . Syracuse
13-15 . . . . Rochester
16-19 . . . . at Syracuse
20-22 . . . . Lehigh Valley
23-26 . . . . . .Pawtucket
27-29 . . . . . at Gwinnett
30 . . . . .at Charlotte

MAY
1-3 . . . . .at Charlotte

5-7 . . . . Gwinnett
8-10 . . . . . .Indianapolis
11-13 . . . . . at Norfolk
14-17 . . . . .at Durham
18-20 . . . . Charlotte
21-24 . . . . Durham
25-27 . . . at Pawtucket
29-31 . . . . .Norfolk

JUNE
1-3 . . . . .Pawtucket

SYRACUSE CHIEFS

APRIL
9-12 . . . . at Scranton/WB
13-15 . . . at Lehigh Valley
16-19 . . . Scranton/WB
20-23 . . . . . . Rochester
24-26 . . . . at Rochester
27-30 . . . . at Pawtucket

MAY
1-3 . . . . Columbus
4-6 . . . . .Norfolk
8-10 . . . . Durham
11-14 . . . . . at Gwinnett
15-17 . . . . . .at Charlotte
18-20 . . . . . Lehigh Valley
22-24 . . . . .Indianapolis
25-28 . . . at Norfolk
29-31 . . . . . . .at Durham

JUNE
1-3 . . . . Louisville
4-5 . . . . . . Scranton/WB
6-7 . . . . .Pawtucket
8-10 . . . . .at Toledo
11-14 . . . . at Columbus
15-17 . . . . Toledo
19-21 . . . . Buffalo
22-25 . . . . Charlotte
26-28 . . . . at Indianapolis
29-30 . . . . . .at Louisville

JULY
1 . . . . .at Louisville
2-3 . . . . at Buffalo
4-6 . . . . .Pawtucket
7-9 . . . . . at Scranton/WB
10-12 . . . . . . Rochester
16-19 . . . . Gwinnett
20-23 . . . . . . at Buffalo
24-26 . . . at Lehigh Valley
27-30 . . . . Buffalo
31 . . . . at Rochester

AUGUST
1-2 . . . . at Rochester
3-5 . . . . .Pawtucket
6-9 . . . . at Pawtucket
11-13 . . . . . Lehigh Valley
14-16 . . . . Buffalo
17-19 . . . . . at Pawtucket
21-23 . . . . . . at Buffalo
24-26 . . . . Rochester
27-28 . . . . . at Rochester
29-31 . . . Lehigh Valley

SEPTEMBER
1-2 . . . . at Buffalo
3-4 . . . . . at Lehigh Valley
5-7 . . . . Scranton/WB

TOLEDO MUD HENS

APRIL
9-12 . . . . . . .at Louisville
13-14 . . . . at Indianapolis
16-17 . . . . Columbus
18-19 . . . . . at Columbus
21-22 . . . . . . Louisville
23-26 . . . . . .Indianapolis
27-29 . . . . . .at Charlotte
30 . . . . at Gwinnett

MAY
1-3 . . . . .at Gwinnett
5-7 . . . . .Pawtucket
8-10 . . . . Charlotte
11-13 . . . . . at Rochester
14-17 . . . . . . at Buffalo
18-20 . . . . . . Gwinnett
21-24 . . . . Buffalo
25-27 . . . . . .at Louisville
28-31 . . . at Indianapolis

JUNE
1-3 . . . . . . at Columbus
5-7 . . . . Columbus

8-10 . . . . Syracuse
11-14 . . . . at Pawtucket
15-17 . . . . . at Syracuse
18-21 . . . . .Norfolk
23-25 . . . . . . .at Durham
26-28 . . . . at Norfolk
29-30 . . . . Durham

JULY
1 . . . . Durham
2-3 . . . . .Indianapolis
4-6 . . . . at Columbus
7-9 . . . . Columbus
10-12 . . . . . . Louisville
16-19 . . . . . .Indianapolis
20-23 . . . at Lehigh Valley
24-26 . . . at Scranton/WB
27-29 . . . . Rochester
31 . . . . .at Louisville

AUGUST
1-2 . . . . at Louisville
3-6 . . . . Lehigh Valley
7-9 . . . . Scranton/WB

11-13 . . . . . at Indianapolis
14-16 . . . . Charlotte
17-18 . . . . Gwinnett
19-21 . . . . . . .at Durham
22-23 . . . . at Norfolk
24-26 . . . . Columbus
27-28 . . . . . at Columbus

29-30 . . . . . .Indianapolis
31 . . . . Louisville

SEPTEMBER
1-3 . . . . Louisville
4-5 . . . . . at Indianapolis
6-7 . . . . . . at Columbus

PACIFIC COAST LEAGUE

ALBUQUERQUE ISOTOPES

APRIL
9-12 . . . . Reno
13-16 . . . . .Tacoma
17-20 . . . . .at Reno
21-24 . . . . at Tacoma
25-28 . . . . . .at Las Vegas
30 . . . . Salt Lake

MAY
1-3 . . . . .Salt Lake
4-7 . . . . Las Vegas
8-11 . . . . . at Sacramento
12-15 . . . . Fresno
16-19 . . . . . . Sacramento
21-24 . . . . at Round Rock
25-28 . . .at New Orleans
29-31 . . . . .Omaha

JUNE
1 . . . . .Omaha
2-5 . . . . Iowa
6-9 . . . . at Salt Lake
11-14 . . . . at Tacoma
15-17 . . . . El Paso
18-21 . . . . .Tacoma

23-25 . . . . at El Paso
26-29 . . . . . . at Salt Lake
30 . . . . Reno

JULY
1-3 . . . . Reno
4-7 . . . . . . .at Las Vegas
8-11 . . . . at El Paso
16-19 . . . . Las Vegas
20-23 . . . . .at Reno
24-27 . . . . . .Sacramento
28-31 . . . . . . .Salt Lake

AUGUST
1-4 . . . . .at Fresno
5-9 . . . . El Paso
11-14 . . . . Fresno
15-18 . . . . . at Memphis
19-22 . . . . . at Nashville
23-26 . . .Oklahoma City
27-30 . . . Colorado Springs
31 . . . . .at Fresno

SEPTEMBER
1-3 . . . . .at Fresno
4-7 . . . . . . at Sacramento

COLORADO SPRINGS SKY SOX

APRIL
9-12 . . . . .Nashville
13-16 . . . . .Round Rock
17-20 . . . . at Nashville
21-24 . . . . at Round Rock
25-28 . . . . Iowa
30 . . . . .Omaha

MAY
1-3 . . . . .Omaha
4-7 . . . . .at Memphis
8-12 . . . . .at Iowa
12-15 . . . . Memphis
16-19 . . . . . .Round Rock
21-24 . . . . at Salt Lake
25-28 . . . . . .at Las Vegas
29-31 . . . . . .Sacramento

JUNE
1 . . . . .Sacramento
2-5 . . . . Fresno
6-9 . . . . at Omaha
11-14 . . . . .at Iowa
15-17 . . . . .Oklahoma City
18-21 . . . . . New Orleans

23-25 . . . at Oklahoma City
26-29 . . . . . . .at Memphis
30 . . . . at Nashville

JULY
1-3 . . . . at Nashville
4-7 . . . . Memphis
8-12 . . . . . . Oklahoma City
16-19 . . . .at New Orleans
20-23 . . . . .Nashville
24-27 . . . . . . at Omaha
28-31 . . . .at New Orleans

AUGUST
1-4 . . . . Iowa
5-9 . . . . at Oklahoma City
11-14 . . . at Round Rock
15-18 . . . . Reno
19-22 . . . . .Tacoma
23-26 . . . . . at El Paso
27-30 . . . at Albuquerque
31 . . . . .Omaha

SEPTEMBER
1-3 . . . . .Omaha
4-7 . . . . New Orleans

EL PASO CHIHUAHUAS

APRIL
9-12 . . . . .Tacoma
13-16 . . . . Reno
17-20 . . . . at Tacoma
21-24 . . . . . .Sacramento
25-28 . . . . .Salt Lake
30 . . . . . at Sacramento

MAY
1-3 . . . . . . at Sacramento
4-7 . . . . .at Fresno
8-11 . . . . Las Vegas
12-15 . . . . .at Reno
16-19 . . . . Fresno
21-24 . . . .at New Orleans
25-28 . . . . . at Round Rock

29-31 . . . . Iowa

JUNE
1 . . . . Iowa
2-5 . . . . .Omaha
6-9 . . . . .at Las Vegas
11-14 . . . . .Sacramento
15-17 . . . at Albuquerque
18-21 . . . . . . .Salt Lake
23-25 . . . . . Albuquerque
26-29 . . . . . . at Tacoma
30 . . . . Fresno

JULY
1-3 . . . . Fresno
4-7 . . . . at Salt Lake
8-12 . . . . Albuquerque
16-19 . . . . .at Fresno

FRESNO GRIZZLIES

APRIL
9-12 . . . . Las Vegas
13-16 . . . . Salt Lake
17-20 . . . .at Las Vegas
21-24 . . . . at Salt Lake
25-28 . . . . Reno
30 . . . . .at Tacoma

MAY
1-3 . . . . at Tacoma
4-7 . . . . El Paso
8-11 . . . . .Tacoma
12-15 . . . . . Albuquerque
16-19 . . . . . . at El Paso
21-24 . . . . .Nashville
25-28 . . . . Memphis
29-31 . . . at Oklahoma City

JUNE
1 . . . . . at Oklahoma City
2-5 . . . .at Colorado Springs
6-9 . . . . Reno
11-14 . . . . . . at Salt Lake
15-17 . . . at Sacramento
18-21 . . . . . . Las Vegas

23-25 . . . . . .Sacramento
26-29 . . . . . .at Reno
30 . . . . at El Paso

JULY
1-3 . . . . at El Paso
4-7 . . . . .Tacoma
8-12 . . . . . at Sacramento
16-19 . . . . El Paso
20-23 . . . .at Las Vegas
24-27 . . . . . . at Tacoma
29-31 . . . . .at Reno

AUGUST
1-4 . . . . Albuquerque
5-9 . . . . .Sacremento
11-14 . . . at Albuquerque
15-18 . . . . . New Orleans
19-22 . . . . . .Round Rock
24-26 . . . . . . .at Iowa
27-30 . . . . . . at Omaha
31 . . . . Albuquerque

SEPTEMBER
1-3 . . . . Albuquerque
4-7 . . . . .Salt Lake

IOWA CUBS

APRIL
9-12 . . . . at Memphis
13-16 . . . .at New Orleans
17-20 . . . . .Oklahoma City
21-24 . . . . . New Orleans
25-28 . .at Colorado Springs
30 . . . . . . .Oklahoma City

MAY
1-3 . . . . . .Oklahoma City
4-7 . . . . at Nashville
8-11 . . . . Colorado Springs
12-15 . . . . .Nashville
16-19 . . . at Oklahoma City
21-24 . . . . .Tacoma
25-28 . . . . Reno
29-31 . . . . . at El Paso

JUNE
1 . . . . at El Paso
2-5 . . . . . at Albuquerque
6-9 . . . . Memphis
11-14 . . . Colorado Springs
15-17 . . . . . . at Omaha
18-21 . . . . . at Round Rock

23-25 . . . . .Omaha
26-29 . . . . . New Orleans
30 . . . . .Round Rock

JULY
1-3 . . . . .Round Rock
4-7 . . . . . .at New Orleans
8-11 . . . . at Omaha
16-19 . . . . Memphis
20-23 . . . . . . .Round Rock
24-27 . . . . . at Memphis
28-31 . . . . . at Nashville

AUGUST
1-4 . . . .at Colorado Springs
5-9 . . . . .Omaha
11-14 . . . . .Nashville
15-18 . . . . . .at Las Vegas
19-22 . . . . at Salt Lake
24-26 . . . . Fresno
27-30 . . . . . . .Sacramento
31 . . . . . at Oklahoma City

SEPTEMBER
1-3 . . . . . at Oklahoma City
4-7 . . . . . . at Round Rock

20-23 . . . . . at Sacramento
24-27 . . . . . . at Salt Lake
28-31 . . . . .Tacoma

AUGUST
1-4 . . . . Reno
5-9 . . . . . at Albuquerque
11-14 . . . . Las Vegas
15-18 . . . . . at Nashville
19-22 . . . . . at Memphis
23-26 . . . Colorado Springs
27-30 . . . .Oklahoma City
31 . . . . .at Las Vegas

SEPTEMBER
1-3 . . . . .at Las Vegas
4-7 . . . . .at Reno

LAS VEGAS 51S

APRIL
9-12	at Fresno
13-16	at Sacramento
17-20	Fresno
21-24	at Reno
25-28	Albuquerque
30	Reno

MAY
1-3	Reno
4-7	at Albuquerque
8-11	at El Paso
12-15	Sacramento
16-19	at Tacoma
21-24	Oklahoma City
25-28	Colorado Springs
29-31	at Nashville

JUNE
1	at Nashville
2-5	at Memphis
6-9	El Paso
11-14	Reno
15-17	Salt Lake
18-21	at Fresno
23-25	at Salt Lake
25-29	Sacramento
30	at Tacoma

JULY
1-3	at Tacoma
4-7	Albuquerque
8-11	Salt Lake
16-19	at Albuquerque
20-23	Fresno
24-27	at Reno
28-31	at Sacramento

AUGUST
1-4	Tacoma
5-9	at Salt Lake
11-14	at El Paso
15-18	Iowa
19-22	Omaha
23-26	at New Orleans
27-30	at Round Rock
31	El Paso

SEPTEMBER
1-3	El Paso
4-7	Tacoma

MEMPHIS REDBIRDS

APRIL
9-12	Iowa
13-16	Omaha
17-20	at Round Rock
21-24	at Omaha
25-28	Round Rock
30	at New Orleans

MAY
1-3	at New Orleans
4-7	Colorado Springs
8-11	New Orleans
12-15	at Colorado Springs
16-19	Omaha
21-24	at Sacramento
25-28	at Fresno
29-31	Salt Lake

JUNE
1	Salt Lake
2-5	Las Vegas
6-9	at Iowa
11-14	Round Rock
15-17	at Nashville
18-21	at Oklahoma City
23-25	Nashville
26-29	Colorado Springs
30	Oklahoma City

JULY
1-3	Oklahoma City
4-7	at Colorado Springs
8-12	Nashville
16-19	at Iowa
20-23	at New Orleans
24-27	Iowa
28-31	Oklahoma City

AUGUST
1-4	at Round Rock
5-9	at Nashville
11-14	at Omaha
15-18	Albuquerque
19-22	El Paso
23-26	at Tacoma
27-30	at Reno
31	New Orleans

SEPTEMBER
1-3	New Orleans
4-7	at Oklahoma City

NASHVILLE SOUNDS

APRIL
9-12	at Colorado Springs
13-16	at Oklahoma City
17-20	Colorado Springs
21-24	Oklahoma City
25-28	at New Orleans
30	at Round Rock

MAY
1-3	at Round Rock
4-7	Iowa
8-11	Round Rock
12-15	at Iowa
16-19	New Orleans
21-24	at Fresno
25-28	at Sacramento
29-31	Las Vegas

JUNE
1	Las Vegas
2-5	Salt Lake
6-9	at New Orleans
11-14	at Oklahoma City
15-17	Memphis
18-21	Omaha
23-25	at Memphis
26-29	Oklahoma City
30	Colorado Springs

JULY
1-3	Colorado Springs
4-7	at Round Rock
8-12	at Memphis
16-19	Omaha
20-23	at Colorado Springs
24-27	New Orleans
28-31	Iowa

AUGUST
1-4	at Omaha

NEW ORLEANS ZEPHYRS

APRIL
9-12	Omaha
13-16	Iowa
17-20	at Omaha
21-24	at Iowa
25-28	Nashville
30	Memphis

MAY
1-3	Memphis
4-7	at Oklahoma City
8-11	at Memphis
12-15	Oklahoma City
16-19	at Nashville
21-24	El Paso
25-28	Albuquerque
29-31	at Reno

JUNE
1	at Reno
2-5	at Tacoma
6-9	Nashville
11-14	Omaha
15-17	at Round Rock
18-21	at Colorado Springs
23-25	Round Rock
26-29	at Iowa
30	at Omaha

JULY
1-3	at Omaha
4-7	Iowa
8-12	at Round Rock
16-19	Colorado Springs
20-23	Memphis
24-27	at Nashville
28-31	Colorado Springs

AUGUST
1-4	at Oklahoma City
5-9	Round Rock
11-14	Oklahoma City
15-18	at Fresno
19-22	at Sacramento
23-26	Las Vegas
27-30	Salt Lake
31	at Memphis

SEPTEMBER
1-3	at Memphis
4-7	at Colorado Springs

OKLAHOMA CITY DODGERS

APRIL
9-12	Round Rock
13-16	Nashville
17-20	at Iowa
21-24	at Nashville
25-28	Omaha
30	at Iowa

MAY
1-3	at Iowa
4-7	New Orleans
8-11	at Omaha
12-15	at New Orleans
16-19	Iowa
21-24	at Las Vegas
25-28	at Salt Lake
29-31	Fresno

JUNE
1	Fresno
2-5	Sacramento
6-9	at Round Rock
11-14	Nashville
15-17	at Colorado Springs
18-21	Memphis

JULY
1-3	at Memphis
4-7	Omaha
8-12	at Colorado Springs
16-19	Round Rock
20-23	at Omaha
24-27	at Round Rock
28-31	at Memphis

AUGUST
1-4	New Orleans
5-9	Colorado Springs
11-14	at New Orleans
15-18	Tacoma
19-22	Reno
23-26	at Albuquerque
27-30	at El Paso
31	Iowa

SEPTEMBER
1-3	Iowa
4-7	Memphis

OMAHA STORM CHASERS

APRIL
9-12	at New Orleans
13-16	at Memphis
17-20	New Orleans
21-24	Memphis
25-28	at Oklahoma City
30	at Colorado Springs

MAY
1-3	at Colorado Springs
4-7	Round Rock
8-11	Oklahoma City
12-15	at Round Rock
16-19	at Memphis
21-24	Reno
25-28	Tacoma
29-31	at Albuquerque

JUNE
1	at Albuquerque
2-5	at El Paso
6-9	Colorado Springs
11-14	at New Orleans
15-17	Iowa
18-21	at Nashville
23-25	at Iowa

25-29 . . . . . . Round Rock
30 . . . . New Orleans
JULY
1-3. . . . . . New Orleans
4-7. . . . at Oklahoma City
8-11 . . . . Iowa
16-19 . . . . at Nashville
20-23 . . .Oklahoma City
24-27 . . . Colorado Springs
28-31 . . . . at Round Rock

RENO ACES

APRIL
9-12 . . . . at Albuquerque
13-16 . . . . at El Paso
17-20 . . . . . Albuquerque
21-24 . . . . Las Vegas
25-28 . . . . at Fresno
30 . . . . . . .at Las Vegas
MAY
1-3. . . . . . .at Las Vegas
4-7. . . . . . . .Sacramento
8-11 . . . . . at Salt Lake
12-15 . . . . El Paso
16-19 . . . . . . .Salt Lake
21-24 . . . . at Omaha
25-28 . . . . at Iowa
29-31 . . . . . New Orleans
JUNE
1. . . . . New Orleans
2-5. . . . . . . .Round Rock
6-9. . . . . . . .at Fresno
11-14 . . . . at Las Vegas
15-17 . . . . . . .Tacoma
18-21 . . . . at Sacramento

ROUND ROCK EXPRESS

APRIL
9-12 . . . . at Oklahoma City
13-16 . .at Colorado Springs
17-20 . . . . . . Memphis
21-24 . . . Colorado Springs
25-28 . . . .at Memphis
30 . . . . .Nashville
MAY
1-3. . . . . .Nashville
4-7. . . . . at Omaha
8-11 . . . . . at Nashville
12-15 . . . . .Omaha
16-19 . .at Colorado Springs
21-24 . . . . Albuquerque
25-28 . . . . El Paso
29-31 . . . . . . at Tacoma
JUNE
1. . . . . at Tacoma
2-5. . . . . .at Reno
6-9. . . .Oklahoma City
11-14 . . . .at Memphis
15-17 . . . . . New Orleans
18-21 . . . . Iowa

SACRAMENTO RIVER CATS

APRIL
9-12 . . . . Salt Lake
13-16 . . . . Las Vegas
17-20 . . . . at Salt Lake
21-24 . . . . . . at El Paso

AUGUST
1-4. . . . . .Nashville
5-9. . . . . at Iowa
11-14 . . . . . . Memphis
15-18 . . . at Salt Lake
19-22 . . .at Las Vegas
23-26 . . . .Sacramento
27-30 . . . . Fresno
31 . . .at Colorado Springs
SEPTEMBER
1-3. . .at Colorado Springs
4-7. . . . . .Nashville

23-25 . . . . at Tacoma
26-29 . . . . Fresno
30 . . . . . at Albuquerque
JULY
1-3. . . . . . at Albuquerque
4-7. . . . . . . .Sacramento
8-11 . . . . .Tacoma
16-19 . . . at Salt Lake
20-23 . . . . Albuquerque
24-27 . . . . . Las Vegas
29-31 . . . . Fresno
AUGUST
1-4. . . . . at El Paso
5-9. . . . . . . at Tacoma
11-14 . . . . . . .Salt Lake
15-18 . .at Colorado Springs
19-22 . . . at Oklahoma City
23-26 . . . . . . .Nashville
27-30 . . . . . . Memphis
31 . . . . . at Sacramento
SEPTEMBER
1-3. . . . . . at Sacramento
4-7. . . . . El Paso

23-25 . . . .at New Orleans
25-29 . . . . at Omaha
30 . . . . .at Iowa
JULY
1-3. . . . . .at Iowa
4-7. . . . . .Nashville
8-12 . . . . . . New Orleans
16-19 . . . at Oklahoma City
20-23 . . . . . . .at Iowa
24-27 . . . .Oklahoma City
28-31 . . . . .Omaha
AUGUST
1-4. . . . . Memphis
5-9. . . . . .at New Orleans
11-14 . . . . Colorado Springs
15-18 . . . . at Sacramento
19-22 . . . . . . .at Fresno
23-26 . . . . . . .Salt Lake
27-30 . . . . . . Las Vegas
31 . . . . at Nashville
SEPTEMBER
1-3. . . . . at Nashville
4-7. . . . . Iowa

25-28 . . . . .Tacoma
30 . . . . El Paso
MAY
1-3. . . . . El Paso
4-7. . . . . .at Reno

8-11 . . . . Albuquerque
12-15 . . . . .at Las Vegas
16-19 . . . . . Albuquerque
21-24 . . . . . . Memphis
25-28 . . . . . . .Nashville
29-31 . .at Colorado Springs
JUNE
1 . . . .at Colorado Springs
2-5. . . . at Oklahoma City
6-9. . . . . .Tacoma
11-14 . . . . . . at El Paso
15-17 . . . . Fresno
18-21 . . . . Reno
23-25 . . . . . . .at Fresno
26-29 . . . . . .at Las Vegas
30 . . . . Salt Lake
JULY
1-3. . . . . .Salt Lake

SALT LAKE BEES

APRIL
9-12 . . . . . at Sacramento
13-16 . . . . .at Fresno
17-20 . . . . . Sacramento
21-24 . . . . Fresno
25-28 . . . . . at El Paso
30 . . . . . at Albuquerque
MAY
1-3. . . . . at Albuquerque
4-7. . . . . .Tacoma
8-11 . . . . Reno
12-15 . . . . . at Tacoma
16-19 . . . . . . .at Reno
21-24 . . . Colorado Springs
25-28 . . Oklahoma City
29-31 . . . . . at Memphis
JUNE
1. . . . . at Memphis
2-5. . . . . . at Nashville
6-9. . . . . . Albuquerque
11-14 . . . . Fresno
15-17 . . . .at Las Vegas
18-21 . . . . at El Paso

TACOMA RAINIERS

APRIL
9-12 . . . . at El Paso
13-16 . . . . at Albuquerque
17-20 . . . . El Paso
21-24 . . . . . Albuquerque
25-28 . . . . at Sacramento
30 . . . . Fresno
MAY
1-3. . . . . Fresno
4-7. . . . . . . at Salt Lake
8-11 . . . . . . .at Fresno
12-15 . . . . . . .Salt Lake
16-19 . . . . . Las Vegas
21-24 . . . . at Iowa
25-28 . . . . . at Omaha
29-31 . . . . . .Round Rock
JUNE
1. . . . . .Round Rock
2-5. . . . . . . New Orleans
6-9. . . . . . at Sacramento
11-14 . . . . . Albuquerque
15-17 . . . . . . .at Reno
18-21 . . . . at Albuquerque

4-7. . . . . .at Reno
8-12 . . . . Fresno
16-19 . . . . . . at Tacoma
20-23 . . . . El Paso
24-27 . . . . at Albuquerque
28-31 . . . . . . Las Vegas
AUGUST
1-4. . . . . . . at Salt Lake
5-9. . . . . .at Fresno
10-14 . . . . . . at Tacoma
15-18 . . . . . .Round Rock
19-22 . . . . . New Orleans
23-26 . . . . . at Omaha
27-30 . . . . . . .at Iowa
31 . . . . Reno
SEPTEMBER
1-3. . . . . Reno
4-7. . . . . . . Albuquerque

23-25 . . . . Las Vegas
26-29 . . . . . . Albuquerque
30 . . . . . . at Sacramento
JULY
1-3. . . . . at Sacramento
4-7. . . . . El Paso
8-11 . . . . . .at Las Vegas
16-19 . . . . Reno
20-23 . . . . . . at Tacoma
24-27 . . . . El Paso
28-31 . . . at Albuquerque
AUGUST
1-4. . . . . .Sacramento
5-8. . . . . . . Las Vegas
11-14 . . . . . . .at Reno
15-18 . . . . . . .Omaha
19-22 . . . . Iowa
23-26 . . . . at Round Rock
27-30 . . . .at New Orleans
31 . . . . .Tacoma
SEPTEMBER
1-3. . . . . .Tacoma
4-7. . . . . .at Fresno

23-25 . . . . Reno
26-29 . . . . El Paso
30 . . . . Las Vegas
JULY
1-3. . . . . Las Vegas
4-7. . . . . .at Fresno
8-12 . . . . .at Reno
16-19 . . . . . .Sacramento
20-23 . . . . . . .Salt Lake
24-27 . . . . Fresno
28-31 . . . . . . at El Paso
AUGUST
1-4. . . . . . . .at Las Vegas
5-9. . . . . Reno
11-14 . . . . . . .Sacramento
15-18 . . at Oklahoma City
19-22 . .at Colorado Springs
23-26 . . . . Memphis
27-30 . . . . . . .Nashville
31 . . . . at Salt Lake
SEPTEMBER
1-3. . . . . . . at Salt Lake
4-7. . . . . . . .at Las Vegas

DOUBLE-A

EASTERN LEAGUE

AKRON RUBBERDUCKS

APRIL
9-12	Binghamton
13-15	Trenton
16-19	at Altoona
20-22	at Reading
23-26	Bowie
27-29	Altoona

MAY
1-3	at Trenton
4-7	at Bowie
8-10	Binghamton
11-13	at Erie
14-17	at Altoona
19-21	New Britain
22-25	at Binghamton
26-28	Trenton
29-31	Erie

JUNE
2-4	at Harrisburg
5-7	at New Britain
9-11	New Hampshire
12-14	at Reading
16-18	Altoona
19-22	Erie
23-26	at Reading
27-29	Binghamton

30	Bowie

JULY
1-3	Bowie
4-6	at Richmond
7-9	at Bowie
10-12	Reading
16-19	at Erie
20-22	at Richmond
23-26	Altoona
27-29	Bowie
30-31	at Altoona

AUGUST
1-2	at Altoona
4-6	at Harrisburg
7-9	Portland
11-13	at New Hampshire
14-16	at Portland
18-20	Harrisburg
21-23	Erie
24-26	at Trenton
27-30	Richmond
31	Erie

SEPTEMBER
1-3	Erie
4-7	at Harrisburg

ALTOONA CURVE

APRIL
9-12	at Harrisburg
13-15	at Richmond
16-19	Akron
20-22	Harrisburg
24-26	at Erie
27-29	at Akron

MAY
1-3	Erie
4-7	Richmond
8-10	at Harrisburg
11-13	Bowie
14-17	Akron
19-21	at Portland
22-25	at New Hampshire
26-28	at New Britain
29-31	Binghamton

JUNE
2-4	New Britain
5-8	at Erie
9-11	at Reading
12-14	New Hampshire
16-18	at Akron
19-22	Harrisburg
23-26	Erie
27-29	at Harrisburg

30	at Trenton

JULY
1-3	at Trenton
4-6	Harrisburg
7-9	at Erie
10-13	Bowie
16-19	at Richmond
20-22	Erie
23-26	at Akron
27-29	Richmond
30-31	Akron

AUGUST
1-2	Akron
4-6	at New Britain
7-9	Richmond
11-13	Binghamton
14-16	at Richmond
18-20	Portland
21-23	at Bowie
24-26	Reading
27-30	Trenton
31	at Bowie

SEPTEMBER
1-3	at Bowie
4-7	at Binghamton

BINGHAMTON METS

APRIL
9-12	at Akron
13-16	at Erie
16-19	Harrisburg
20-22	Erie
23-26	at New Hampshire
27-29	at Portland

MAY
1-3	New Hampshire
4-7	Portland
8-10	at Akron
11-13	at Richmond
14-17	New Hampshire
19-21	at Harrisburg
22-25	Akron

26-28	Portland
29-31	at Altoona

JUNE
2-4	Trenton
5-7	Reading
9-11	at Bowie
12-14	New Britain
16-18	at Portland
19-21	at New Hampshire
23-26	Harrisburg
27-29	at Akron
30	at Erie

JULY
1-3	at Erie
4-6	Portland
7-9	New Britain
10-13	at Portland
16-19	Trenton

BOWIE BAYSOX

APRIL
9-12	at Richmond
13-15	at Harrisburg
16-19	Erie
20-21	Richmond
23-26	at Akron
27-29	at Erie

MAY
1-3	Harrisburg
4-7	Akron
8-10	at Richmond
11-13	at Altoona
14-17	Richmond
19-21	at Trenton
22-25	at Richmond
26-28	Erie
29-31	Harrisburg

JUNE
2-4	at New Hampshire
5-7	at Portland
9-11	Binghamton
12-14	Portland
16-18	at New Britain
19-22	Trenton
23-26	New Britain
27-29	at Erie

ERIE SEAWOLVES

APRIL
9-12	Trenton
13-15	Binghamton
16-19	at Bowie
20-22	at Binghamton
24-26	Altoona
27-29	Bowie

MAY
1-3	at Altoona
4-7	at Trenton
8-10	Reading
11-13	Akron
14-17	at Reading
18-20	Richmond
22-25	Trenton
26-28	Bowie
29-31	at Akron

JUNE
2-4	Reading
5-8	Altoona

20-22	at New Britain
23-26	at Trenton
27-29	New Britain
30-31	at Richmond

AUGUST
1-2	at Richmond
4-6	Bowie
7-9	Trenton
11-13	at Altoona
14-16	at New Britain
18-20	Richmond
21-23	at New Hampshire
24-26	Erie
27-30	New Hampshire
31	at Reading

SEPTEMBER
1-3	at Reading
4-7	Altoona

30	at Akron

JULY
1-3	at Akron
4-6	Erie
7-9	Akron
10-13	at Altoona
16-19	Harrisburg
20-22	Reading
23-26	at Harrisburg
27-29	at Akron
30-31	Trenton

AUGUST
1-2	Trenton
4-6	at Binghamton
7-9	New Hampshire
10-13	Richmond
14-16	at Harrisburg
18-20	Trenton
21-23	Altoona
24-26	at New Britain
27-30	at Reading
31	Altoona

SEPTEMBER
1-3	Altoona
4-7	at Erie

9-11	at Trenton
12-14	at Richmond
15-17	New Hampshire
19-22	at Akron
23-26	at Altoona
27-29	Bowie
30	Binghamton

JULY
1-3	Binghamton
4-6	at Bowie
7-9	Altoona
10-13	at Harrisburg
16-19	Akron
20-22	at Altoona
23-26	Richmond
27-29	at Reading
30-31	at New Britain

AUGUST
1-2	at New Britain
4-6	Portland

7-9 . . . . .Harrisburg
11-13 . . . . . . at Portland
14-16 . . at New Hampshire
18-20 . . . . . New Britain
21-23 . . . . .at Akron
24-26 . . . . at Binghamton

27-30 . . . . . .Harrisburg
31 . . . . at Akron

SEPTEMBER
1-3 . . . . at Akron
4-7 . . . . .Bowie

HARRISBURG SENATORS

APRIL
9-12 . . . . Altoona
13-15 . . . . .Bowie
16-19 . . . .at Binghamton
20-22 . . . . . .at Altoona
23-26 . . . . Reading
27-29 . . . . New Britain

MAY
1-3 . . . . .at Bowie
4-6 . . . . . at New Britain
8-10 . . . . Altoona
11-13 . . . . Reading
14-17 . . . . . . at Trenton
19-21 . . . . . Binghamton
22-25 . . . . . New Britain
26-28 . . . . . at Richmond
29-31 . . . . . . at Bowie

JUNE
2-4 . . . . .Akron
5-7 . . . . . . at Trenton
8-11 . . . . . at New Britain
12-14 . . . . . . Trenton
16-18 . . . . . Richmond
19-22 . . . . . . .at Altoona
23-26 . . .at Binghamton
27-29 . . . . Altoona

30 . . . . .Richmond

JULY
1-3 . . . . Richmond
4-6 . . . . .at Altoona
7-9 . . . . . at Richmond
10-13 . . . . Erie
16-19 . . . . at Bowie
20-22 . . . New Hampshire
23-26 . . . . .Bowie
27-29 . . at New Hampshire
30-31 . . . . . . at Portland

AUGUST
1-2 . . . . at Portland
4-6 . . . . .Akron
7-9 . . . . at Erie
11-13 . . . . . . .at Reading
14-16 . . . . .Bowie
18-20 . . . . . . at Akron
21-23 . . . . Portland
24-26 . . . . at Richmond
27-30 . . . . . . at Erie
31 . . . . .Richmond

SEPTEMBER
1-3 . . . . Richmond
4-7 . . . . .Akron

NEW BRITAIN ROCK CATS

APRIL
9-12 . . at New Hampshire
13-15 . . . . . at Portland
16-19 . . . New Hampshire
20-22 . . . . Portland
23-26 . . . . at Richmond
27-29 . . . . at Harrisburg

MAY
1-3 . . . . Richmond
4-6 . . . . .Harrisburg
8-10 . . . . . . at Portland
11-13 . at New Hampshire
14-17 . . . . . . Portland
19-21 . . . . . . at Akron
22-25 . . . . at Harrisburg
26-28 . . . . . . Altoona
29-31 . . . New Hampshire

JUNE
2-4 . . . . .at Altoona
5-7 . . . . .Akron
8-11 . . . . . . .Harrisburg
12-14 . . .at Binghamton
16-18 . . . . . . .Bowie
19-22 . . . . . at Richmond
23-26 . . . . . . at Bowie
27-29 . . . . Richmond

30 . . . . Reading

JULY
1-3 . . . . Reading
4-6 . . . at New Hampshire
7-9 . . . . .at Binghamton
10-13 . . . New Hampshire
16-19 . . . . . .at Reading
20-22 . . . . Binghamton
23-26 . . . . Reading
27-29 . . . .at Binghamton
30-31 . . . . Erie

AUGUST
1-2 . . . . Erie
4-6 . . . . Altoona
7-9 . . . . .at Reading
11-13 . . . . Trenton
14-16 . . . . . Binghamton
18-20 . . . . . . at Erie
21-23 . . . . . .at Reading
24-26 . . . . .Bowie
27-30 . . . . . Portland
31 . . . . at Trenton

SEPTEMBER
1-3 . . . . at Trenton
4-7 . . . . . . at Portland

NEW HAMPSHIRE FISHER CATS

APRIL
9-12 . . . . . . New Britain
13-15 . . . . Reading
16-19 . . . . at New Britain
20-22 . . . . . . at Trenton
23-26 . . . . . Binghamton
27-29 . . . . Trenton

MAY
1-3 . . . . . .at Binghamton
4-6 . . . . .at Reading
8-10 . . . . Trenton
11-13 . . . . . New Britain
14-17 . . . .at Binghamton
18-20 . . . . . .at Reading

22-25 . . . . Altoona
26-28 . . . . Reading
29-31 . . . . at New Britain

JUNE
2-4 . . . . .Bowie
5-7 . . . . Richmond
9-11 . . . . at Akron
12-14 . . . .at Altoona
15-17 . . . . . . at Erie
19-22 . . . . . Binghamton
23-26 . . . . Portland
27-29 . . . . at Trenton
30 . . . . at Portland

JULY
1-3 . . . . at Portland
4-6 . . . . . New Britain
7-9 . . . . Trenton
10-13 . . at New Britain
16-19 . . . . Portland

AUGUST
1-2 . . . . Reading
4-6 . . . . . . at Richmond
7-9 . . . . at Bowie
11-13 . . . . .Akron
14-16 . . . . Erie
17-20 . . . . . .at Reading
21-23 . . . . . Binghamton
24-26 . . . . at Portland
27-30 . . . .at Binghamton
31 . . . . Portland

SEPTEMBER
1-3 . . . . Portland
4-7 . . . . .at Trenton

PORTLAND SEA DOGS

APRIL
9-12 . . . . Reading
13-15 . . . . . New Britain
16-19 . . . . at Trenton
20-22 . . . at New Britain
23-26 . . . . . Trenton
27-29 . . . . . Binghamton

MAY
1-3 . . . . .at Reading
4-7 . . . . . .at Binghamton
8-10 . . . . . . New Britain
11-13 . . . . Trenton
14-17 . . . at New Britain
19-21 . . . . Altoona
22-25 . . . . Reading
26-28 . . .at Binghamton
29-31 . . . . at Trenton

JUNE
2-4 . . . . Richmond
5-7 . . . . .Bowie
9-11 . . . . . . at Richmond
12-14 . . . . . . at Bowie
16-18 . . . . . Binghamton
19-22 . . . . . .at Reading
23-26 . . at New Hampshire
27-29 . . . . Reading

30 . . . . . New Hampshire

JULY
1-3 . . . . . New Hampshire
4-6 . . . . . .at Binghamton
7-9 . . . . .at Reading
10-13 . . . . . Binghamton
16-19 . . at New Hampshire
20-22 . . . . Trenton
23-26 . . . . . New Hampshire
27-29 . . . . . at Trenton
30-31 . . . . . .Harrisburg

AUGUST
1-2 . . . . .Harrisburg
4-6 . . . . at Erie
7-9 . . . . at Akron
11-13 . . . . Erie
14-16 . . . . .Akron
18-20 . . . .at Altoona
21-23 . . . . at Harrisburg
24-26 . . . New Hampshire
27-30 . . . . at New Britain
31 . . . . at New Hampshire

SEPTEMBER
1-3 . . . at New Hampshire
4-7 . . . . New Britain

READING FIGHTIN PHILS

APRIL
9-12 . . . . . . at Portland
13-15 . . at New Hampshire
17-19 . . . . . . Richmond
20-22 . . . . .Akron
23-26 . . . . at Harrisburg
27-29 . . . . at Richmond

MAY
1-3 . . . . Portland
4-6 . . . . . New Hampshire
8-10 . . . . . . at Erie
11-13 . . . at Harrisburg
14-16 . . . . Erie
17-19 . . . . . New Hampshire
22-25 . . . . . at Portland
26-28 . . at New Hampshire
29-31 . . . . Richmond

JUNE
1 . . . . Richmond
2-4 . . . . at Erie
5-7 . . . . . .at Binghamton
9-11 . . . . Altoona
12-14 . . . . .Akron

15-17 . . . . . . .at Trenton
19-22 . . . . Portland
23-26 . . . . .Akron
27-29 . . . . at Portland
30 . . . . . at New Britain

JULY
1-3 . . . . . at New Britain
4-6 . . . . Trenton
7-9 . . . . Portland
10-12 . . . . .at Akron
16-19 . . . . . New Britain
20-22 . . . . . . .at Bowie
23-26 . . . . at New Britain
27-29 . . . . Erie
30-31 . . at New Hampshire

AUGUST
1-2 . . . at New Hampshire
4-6 . . . . . . .at Trenton
7-9 . . . . New Britain
11-13 . . . . . .Harrisburg
14-16 . . . . . at Trenton
17-20 . . . New Hampshire
21-23 . . . . . . New Britain

24-26 . . . . .at Altoona
27-30 . . . . .Bowie
31 . . . . Binghamton

SEPTEMBER
1-3 . . . . Binghamton
4-7 . . . . at Richmond

RICHMOND FLYING SQUIRRELS

APRIL
9-12 . . . . .Bowie
13-15 . . . . Altoona
17-19 . . . . .at Reading
20-21 . . . . at Bowie
23-26 . . . . . . New Britain
27-29 . . . . Reading

MAY
1-3 . . . . . . at New Britain
4-7 . . . . . .at Altoona
8-10 . . . . .Bowie
11-13 . . . . . Binghamton
14-17 . . . . at Bowie
18-20 . . . . at Erie
22-25 . . . . . . .Bowie
26-28 . . . . . .Harrisburg
29-31 . . .at Reading

JUNE
1 . . . . .at Reading
2-4 . . . . . . at Portland
5-7 . . at New Hampshire
9-11 . . . . . . Portland
12-14 . . . . . . Erie
16-18 . . . . . at Harrisburg
19-22 . . . . . New Britain
23-26 . . . . Trenton

27-29 . . . . at New Britain
30 . . . . at Harrisburg

JULY
1-3 . . . . . . at Harrisburg
4-6 . . . . .Akron
7-9 . . . . . . .Harrisburg
10-13 . . . . . . .at Trenton
16-19 . . . . Altoona
20-22 . . . . . . .Akron
23-26 . . . . . . at Erie
27-29 . . . . .at Altoona
30-31 . . . . . Binghamton

AUGUST
1-2 . . . . . . Binghamton
4-6 . . . . New Hampshire
7-9 . . . . . . .at Altoona
10-13 . . . . at Bowie
14-16 . . . . Altoona
18-20 . . .at Binghamton
21-23 . . . . . at Trenton
24-26 . . . .Harrisburg
27-30 . . . . . at Akron
31 . . . . at Harrisburg

SEPTEMBER
1-3 . . . . . . .at Harrisburg
4-7 . . . . Reading

TRENTON THUNDER

APRIL
9-12 . . . . at Erie
13-15 . . . . . . at Akron
16-19 . . . . . . Portland
20-22 . . . . New Hampshire
23-26 . . . . at Portland
27-29 . . at New Hampshire

MAY
1-3 . . . . .Akron
4-7 . . . . Erie
8-10 . . at New Hampshire
11-13 . . . . at Portland
14-17 . . . . . .Harrisburg
19-21 . . . . . .Bowie
22-25 . . . . . at Erie
26-28 . . . . at Akron
29-31 . . . . . Portland

JUNE
2-4 . . . . . .at Binghamton
5-7 . . . . . .Harrisburg
9-11 . . . . Erie
12-14 . . . . at Harrisburg
16-18 . . . . . Reading
19-22 . . . . . at Bowie
23-26 . . . . . at Richmond
27-29 . . . . New Hampshire

30 . . . . Altoona

JULY
1-3 . . . . Altoona
4-6 . . . . . . .at Reading
7-9 . . at New Hampshire
10-13 . . . . Richmond
16-19 . . .at Binghamton
20-22 . . . . at Portland
23-26 . . . . . Binghamton
27-29 . . . . . . Portland
30-31 . . . . . .at Bowie

AUGUST
1-2 . . . . at Bowie
4-6 . . . . Reading
7-9 . . . .at Binghamton
11-13 . . . . at New Britain
14-16 . . . . Reading
18-20 . . . . at Bowie
21-23 . . . . Richmond
24-26 . . . . .Akron
27-30 . . . .at Altoona
31 . . . . New Britain

SEPTEMBER
1-3 . . . . New Britain
4-7 . . . . . New Hampshire

SOUTHERN LEAGUE

BILOXI SHUCKERS

APRIL
9-13 . . . . . . at Pensacola
15-19 . . . . . . at Mobile
20-24 . . . . . .Jacksonville
25-29 . . . . at Pensacola
30 . . . . Mobile

MAY
1-4 . . . . Mobile
6-10 . . . . .Mississippi
11-15 . . . . . . .at Jackson
16-10 . . . . .Jacksonville
21-25 . . . . . Birmingham

27-31 . . . at Chattanooga

JUNE
1-5 . . . . . .at Birmingham
6-10 . . . . Mobile
11-15 . . . . at Mississippi
17-21 . . . . . Montgomery
25-29 . . . . at Jacksonville

JULY
1-3 . . . . .Mississippi
4-8 . . . . . at Montgomery
9-13 . . . . at Tennessee
15-19 . . . Chattanooga
20-21 . . . . . . Mobile

BIRMINGHAM BARONS

APRIL
9-13 . . . . Mobile
15-19 . . . at Chattanooga
20-24 . . . . . . Pensacola
25-29 . . at Jacksonville
30 . . . . .Tennessee

MAY
1-4 . . . . .Tennessee
6-10 . . . . at Montgomery
11-15 . . . . Chattanooga
16-20 . . . . . at Mobile
21-25 . . . . at Biloxi
27-31 . . . . .Jacksonville

JUNE
1-5 . . . . Biloxi
6-10 . . . . at Tennessee
11-15 . . . Chattanooga
17-21 . . . . .at Jackson
25-29 . . . . Jackson

JULY
1-3 . . . . . at Chattanooga
4-8 . . . . .Tennessee
9-13 . . . . . . .at Jackson
15-19 . . . . . Pensacola
20-21 . . . . . at Tennessee
23-27 . . at Jacksonville
28-31 . . . . .Mississippi

AUGUST
1 . . . . .Mississippi
2-6 . . . . . at Tennessee
7-11 . . . . at Pensacola
13-17 . . . . Montgomery
18-22 . . at Mississippi
23-27 . . . .Jacksonville
28-31 . . . . . Chattanooga

SEPTEMBER
1 . . . . .Chattanooga
3-7 . . . . . at Montgomery

CHATTANOOGA LOOKOUTS

APRIL
9-13 . . . . . at Montgomery
15-19 . . . . Birmingham
20-24 . . at Mississippi
25-29 . . . at Tennessee
30 . . . . .Jacksonville

MAY
1-4 . . . . .Jacksonville
6-10 . . . . Jackson
11-15 . . .at Birmingham
16-20 . . . . Montgomery
21-25 . . . . . at Mobile
27-31 . . . . Biloxi

JUNE
1-3 . . . . .Tennessee
4-5 . . . . at Tennessee
6-10 . . . . . .at Jackson
11-15 . . .at Birmingham
17-21 . . . .Jacksonville
25-29 . . . at Montgomery

JULY
1-3 . . . . Birmingham
4-8 . . . . . at Jacksonville
9-13 . . . . . .Mississippi
15-19 . . . . . at Biloxi
20-21 . . . . . Montgomery
22-23 . . . . . .Tennessee
24-26 . . . . at Tennessee
28-31 . . . . . Pensacola

AUGUST
1 . . . . Pensacola
2-6 . . . . . . .at Jackson
7-11 . . . . Mobile
12-16 . . . . . .Tennessee
18-22 . . . . at Pensacola
23-27 . . . . . .Tennessee
28-31 . . . at Birmingham

SEPTEMBER
1 . . . . .at Birmingham
3-7 . . . . Jackson

JACKSON GENERALS

APRIL
9-13 . . . . . at Jacksonville
15-19 . . . . .Mississippi
20-24 . . . . . . .Tennessee
25-29 . . at Montgomery
30 . . . . Pensacola

MAY
1-4 . . . . Pensacola
6-10 . . . . at Chattanooga
11-15 . . . . Biloxi
16-20 . . . at Tennessee

21-25 . . . . . . at Pensacola
26-30 . . . . . Montgomery

JUNE
1-5 . . . . . . at Mississippi
6-10 . . . . . . Chattanooga
11-15 . . . . . . at Mobile
17-21 . . . . . Birmingham
25-29 . . at Birmingham

JULY
1-3 . . . . Mobile
4-8 . . . . . . .at Mississippi

9-13 . . . . . . Birmingham	7-11 . . . . . at Tennessee
15-19 . . . . at Mobile	12-16 . . . . . Jacksonville
20-21 . . . . . .Mississippi	18-22 . . . . Biloxi
22-26 . . . . . Montgomery	23-27 . . . at Montgomery
28-31 . . . . at Biloxi	28-31 . . . . Pensacola

AUGUST	SEPTEMBER
1 . . . . at Biloxi	1 . . . . Pensacola
2-6 . . . . Chattanooga	3-7 . . . . . at Chattanooga

JACKSONVILLE SUNS

APRIL	JULY
9-13 . . . . Jackson	1-3 . . . . at Pensacola
15-19 . . . . . Montgomery	4-8 . . . . Chattanooga
20-24 . . . . Mobile	9-13 . . . . Mobile
25-29 . . . . . Birmingham	15-19 . . . . at Mississippi
30 . . . . . at Chattanooga	20-21 . . . . . at Pensacola
MAY	23-27 . . . . . . Birmingham
1-4 . . . . . at Chattanooga	28-31 . . . . . . at Mobile
5-9 . . . . at Mobile	AUGUST
11-15 . . . . . . Pensacola	1 . . . . at Mobile
16-20 . . . . . . at Biloxi	2-6 . . . . Pensacola
21-25 . . . . . .Mississippi	7-11 . . . . at Montgomery
27-31 . . . at Birmingham	12-16 . . . . . at Jackson
JUNE	18-22 . . . . Mobile
1-5 . . . . Montgomery	23-27 . . . at Birmingham
6-10 . . . . . at Pensacola	28-31 . . . at Tennessee
11-15 . . . . . . .Tennessee	SEPTEMBER
17-21 . . . at Chattanooga	1 . . . . at Tennessee
25-29 . . . . Biloxi	3-7 . . . . .Mississippi

MISSISSIPPI BRAVES

APRIL	JULY
9-13 . . . . .Tennessee	1-3 . . . . Biloxi
15-19 . . . . . . .at Jackson	4-8 . . . . Jackson
20-24 . . . . . Chattanooga	9-13 . . . at Chattanooga
25-29 . . . . . at Mobile	15-19 . . . . . Jacksonville
30 . . . . Montgomery	20-21 . . . . . .at Jackson
MAY	22-26 . . . . Mobile
1-4 . . . . . . Montgomery	28-31 . . . at Birmingham
6-10 . . . . at Biloxi	AUGUST
11-15 . . . . Mobile	1 . . . . . . .at Birmingham
16-20 . . . . at Jacksonville	2-6 . . . . . . Montgomery
21-25 . . . at Jacksonville	7-11 . . . . at Biloxi
27-31 . . . . . Pensacola	12-16 . . . . . at Mobile
JUNE	18-22 . . . . . Birmingham
1-5 . . . . Jackson	23-27 . . . . . at Pensacola
6-10 . . . . at Montgomery	28-31 . . . . Biloxi
11-15 . . . . Biloxi	SEPTEMBER
17-21 . . . . at Tennessee	1 . . . . Biloxi
25-29 . . . . . . Pensacola	3-7 . . . . . at Jacksonville

MOBILE BAYBEARS

APRIL	17-21 . . . . . at Pensacola
9-13 . . . .at Birmingham	25-29 . . . . . . .Tennessee
15-19 . . . . Biloxi	JULY
20-24 . . . at Montgomery	1-3 . . . . .at Jackson
25-29 . . . . . .Mississippi	4-8 . . . . Pensacola
30 . . . . at Biloxi	9-13 . . . . . at Jacksonville
MAY	15-19 . . . . . . Jackson
1-4 . . . . at Biloxi	20-21 . . . . . . at Biloxi
5-9 . . . . . . Jacksonville	22-26 . . . . at Mississippi
11-15 . . . at Mississippi	28-31 . . . . . Jacksonville
16-20 . . . . . Birmingham	AUGUST
21-25 . . . . Chattanooga	1 . . . . Jacksonville
27-31 . . . at Tennessee	2-6 . . . . Biloxi
JUNE	7-11 . . . . at Chattanooga
1-5 . . . . Pensacola	12-16 . . . . . .Mississippi
6-10 . . . . at Biloxi	18-22 . . . . at Jacksonville
11-15 . . . . . . Jackson	23-27 . . . . at Biloxi

28-31 . . . . . Montgomery

MONTGOMERY BISCUITS

APRIL	JULY
9-13 . . . . . . Chattanooga	1-3 . . . . at Tennessee
15-19 . . . . . at Jacksonville	4-8 . . . . Biloxi
20-24 . . . . Mobile	9-13 . . . . at Pensacola
25-29 . . . . Jackson	15-19 . . . . .Tennessee
30 . . . . . . at Mississippi	20-21 . . . . at Chattanooga
MAY	22-26 . . . . . . at Jackson
1-4 . . . . . . at Mississippi	28-31 . . . . . . .Tennessee
6-10 . . . . . Birmingham	AUGUST
11-15 . . . . at Tennessee	1 . . . . .Tennessee
16-20 . . . . at Chattanooga	2-6 . . . . . .at Mississippi
21-25 . . . . . .Tennessee	7-11 . . . . . Jacksonville
26-30 . . . . . at Jackson	13-17 . . . at Birmingham
JUNE	18-22 . . . at Tennessee
1-5 . . . . . at Jacksonville	23-27 . . . . Jackson
6-10 . . . . . . .Mississippi	28-31 . . . . . . at Mobile
11-15 . . . . . . Pensacola	SEPTEMBER
17-21 . . . . . . at Biloxi	1 . . . . at Mobile
25-29 . . . . Chattanooga	3-7 . . . . . . Birmingham

PENSACOLA BLUE WAHOOS

APRIL	JULY
9-13 . . . . Biloxi	1-3 . . . . Jacksonville
15-19 . . . . at Tennessee	4-8 . . . . at Mobile
20-24 . . . . .at Birmingham	9-13 . . . . . Montgomery
25-29 . . . . Biloxi	15-19 . . . at Birmingham
30 . . . . .at Jackson	20-21 . . . . . Jacksonville
MAY	22-26 . . . . Biloxi
1-4 . . . . . . .at Jackson	28-31 . . . at Chattanooga
5-9 . . . . .Tennessee	AUGUST
11-15 . . . at Jacksonville	1 . . . . . . at Chattanooga
16-20 . . . . .Mississippi	2-6 . . . . . at Jacksonville
21-25 . . . . . . Jackson	7-11 . . . . . . Birmingham
27-31 . . . . at Mississippi	12-16 . . . . . . at Biloxi
JUNE	18-22 . . . . . Chattanooga
1-5 . . . . . . at Mobile	23-27 . . . . .Mississippi
6-10 . . . . . .Jacksonville	28-31 . . . . . .at Jackson
11-15 . . . at Montgomery	SEPTEMBER
17-21 . . . . . . Mobile	1 . . . . .at Jackson
25-29 . . . . at Mississippi	3-7 . . . . Mobile

TENNESSEE SMOKIES

APRIL	JULY
9-13 . . . . . . at Mississippi	1-3 . . . . Montgomery
15-19 . . . . Pensacola	4-8 . . . . .at Birmingham
20-24 . . . . . .at Jackson	9-13 . . . . Biloxi
25-29 . . . . . Chattanooga	15-19 . . . . at Montgomery
30 . . . . . .at Birmingham	20-21 . . . . . Birmingham
MAY	22-23 . . . at Chattanooga
1-4 . . . . . at Birmingham	24-26 . . . . . Chattanooga
5-9 . . . . at Pensacola	28-31 . . . at Montgomery
11-15 . . . . . Montgomery	AUGUST
16-20 . . . . . . Jackson	1 . . . . at Montgomery
21-25 . . . at Montgomery	2-6 . . . . . . Birmingham
27-31 . . . . Mobile	7-11 . . . . Jackson
JUNE	12-16 . . . . at Chattanooga
1-3 . . . . . at Chattanooga	18-22 . . . . . Montgomery
4-5 . . . . . . Chattanooga	23-27 . . . at Chattanooga
6-10 . . . . . . Birmingham	28-31 . . . . . Jacksonville
11-15 . . . at Jacksonville	SEPTEMBER
17-21 . . . . . . .Mississippi	1 . . . . Jacksonville
25-29 . . . . . . at Mobile	3-7 . . . . at Biloxi

TEXAS LEAGUE

ARKANSAS TRAVELERS

APRIL		JULY	
9-11 . . . . at Frisco		2-4 . . . . at Midland	
12-14 . . . . at Midland		5-7 . . . . at Frisco	
16-18 . . . . .Frisco		8-10 . . . . Midland	
19-21 . . . . Midland		11-13 . . . . .Frisco	
23-26 . . . . . .at Springfield		15-18 . . . . .at Tulsa	
27-30 . . . . Tulsa		19-22 . . . . . Springfield	
MAY		23-26 . . . . .at Tulsa	
1-4 . . . . Springfield		27-29 . . . . . NW Arkansas	
5-8 . . . . .at Tulsa		30-31 . . . . Tulsa	
9-12 . . . . . NW Arkansas		AUGUST	
14-17 . . . . Tulsa		1-2 . . . . Tulsa	
18-21 . . . . at NW Arkansas		3-5 . . . . . at NW Arkansas	
22-25 . . . . .at Springfield		6-9 . . . . . . .at Springfield	
26-28 . . . . San Antonio		11-13 . . . . . Corpus Christi	
29-31 . . . . . Corpus Christi		14-16 . . . . . San Antonio	
JUNE		18-20 . . .at Corpus Christi	
2-4 . . . . . .at San Antonio		21-23 . . . . at San Antonio	
5-7 . . . . . .at Corpus Christi		25-28 . . . . Tulsa	
9-12 . . . . . . Springfield		29-31 . . . . at NW Arkansas	
13-16 . . . . at NW Arkansas		SEPTEMBER	
17-20 . . . . .at Tulsa		1-4 . . . . .at NW Arkansas	
21-24 . . . . . NW Arkansas		5-7 . . . . NW Arkansas	
25-28 . . . . . Springfield			

CORPUS CHRISTI HOOKS

APRIL		JULY	
9-11 . . . . . . .at Springfield		2-4 . . . . .at Tulsa	
12-14 . . . . .at Tulsa		5-7 . . . . . .at Springfield	
16-18 . . . . . . Springfield		8-10 . . . . Tulsa	
19-21 . . . . Tulsa		11-13 . . . . . . Springfield	
23-26 . . . . at Frisco		15-18 . . . . . . at Frisco	
27-30 . . . . . . at Midland		19-22 . . . . . . Midland	
MAY		23-26 . . . . at Frisco	
1-4 . . . . .Frisco		27-29 . . . . . San Antonio	
5-8 . . . . Midland		30-31 . . . . . . at Midland	
9-12 . . . . .at San Antonio		AUGUST	
14-17 . . . . . . at Frisco		1-2 . . . . at Midland	
18-21 . . . . . San Antonio		3-5 . . . . . at San Antonio	
22-25 . . . . . Midland		6-9 . . . . Midland	
26-28 . . . . . NW Arkansas		11-13 . . . . . . at Arkansas	
29-31 . . . . . . at Arkansas		14-16 . . . at NW Arkansas	
JUNE		18-20 . . . . . . .Arkansas	
2-4 . . . . NW Arkansas		21-23 . . . . . NW Arkansas	
5-7 . . . . .Arkansas		25-28 . . . . . . at Midland	
9-12 . . . . at Midland		29-31 . . . . . San Antonio	
13-16 . . . .at San Antonio		SEPTEMBER	
17-20 . . . . .Frisco		1-4 . . . . .Frisco	
21-24 . . . . . San Antonio		5-7 . . . . . .at San Antonio	
25-28 . . . . .Frisco			

FRISCO ROUGHRIDERS

APRIL			
9-11 . . . . .Arkansas		29-31 . . . . Tulsa	
12-14 . . . . . NW Arkansas		JUNE	
16-18 . . . . . at Arkansas		2-4 . . . . .at Springfield	
19-21 . . . . at NW Arkansas		5-7 . . . . .at Tulsa	
23-26 . . . . . Corpus Christi		9-12 . . . . . . San Antonio	
27-30 . . . . .at San Antonio		13-16 . . . . . . at Midland	
MAY		17-20 . . . .at Corpus Christi	
1-4 . . . . . .at Corpus Christi		21-24 . . . . Midland	
5-8 . . . . San Antonio		25-28 . . . . .at Corpus Christi	
9-12 . . . . at Midland		JULY	
14-17 . . . . Corpus Christi		2-4 . . . . NW Arkansas	
18-21 . . . . Midland		5-7 . . . . .Arkansas	
22-25 . . . . .at San Antonio		8-10 . . . . at NW Arkansas	
26-28 . . . . Springfield		11-13 . . . . . . at Arkansas	

MIDLAND ROCKHOUNDS

APRIL		JULY	
9-11 . . . . . . NW Arkansas		2-4 . . . . .Arkansas	
12-14 . . . . .Arkansas		5-7 . . . . NW Arkansas	
16-18 . . . at NW Arkansas		8-10 . . . . at Arkansas	
19-21 . . . . .Arkansas		11-13 . . . . at NW Arkansas	
23-26 . . . . . San Antonio		15-18 . . . . . San Antonio	
27-30 . . . . Corpus Christi		19-22 . . .at Corpus Christi	
MAY		23-26 . . . . . San Antonio	
1-4 . . . . . .at San Antonio		27-29 . . . . at Frisco	
5-8 . . .at Corpus Christi		30-31 . . . . Corpus Christi	
9-12 . . . . .Frisco		AUGUST	
14-17 . . . . . San Antonio		1-2 . . . . Corpus Christi	
18-21 . . . . at Frisco		3-5 . . . . .Frisco	
22-25 . . .at Corpus Christi		6-9 . . . . . .at Corpus Christi	
26-28 . . . . Tulsa		11-13 . . . . . . Springfield	
29-31 . . . . . . Springfield		14-16 . . . . Tulsa	
JUNE		18-20 . . . . . .at Springfield	
2-4 . . . . .at Tulsa		21-23 . . . . .at Tulsa	
5-7 . . . . . . .at Springfield		25-28 . . . . . Corpus Christi	
9-12 . . . . . Corpus Christi		29-31 . . . . .Frisco	
13-16 . . . . .Frisco		SEPTEMBER	
17-20 . . . .at San Antonio		1-4 . . . . . . .at San Antonio	
21-24 . . . . at Frisco		5-7 . . . . at Frisco	
25-28 . . .at San Antonio			

NORTHWEST ARKANSAS NATURALS

APRIL			
9-11 . . . . at Midland		21-24 . . . . at Arkansas	
12-14 . . . . at Frisco		25-28 . . . . Tulsa	
16-18 . . . . Midland		JULY	
19-21 . . . . .Frisco		2-4 . . . . at Frisco	
23-26 . . . . .at Tulsa		5-7 . . . . at Midland	
27-30 . . . . . . Springfield		8-10 . . . . .Frisco	
MAY		11-13 . . . . Midland	
1 . . . . Tulsa		15-18 . . . .at Springfield	
2 . . . . .at Tulsa		19-22 . . . . Tulsa	
3-4 . . . . Tulsa		23-25 . . . .at Springfield	
5-8 . . . . . .at Springfield		27-29 . . . . at Arkansas	
9-12 . . . . . . at Arkansas		30-31 . . . . . . Springfield	
14-17 . . . . . Springfield		AUGUST	
18-21 . . . . . .Arkansas		1-2 . . . . Springfield	
22-24 . . . . Tulsa		3-5 . . . . .Arkansas	
25 . . . . .at Tulsa		6-9 . . . . .at Tulsa	
26-28 . . . . Corpus Christi		11-13 . . . . . San Antonio	
29-31 . . . . . San Antonio		14-16 . . . . Corpus Christi	
JUNE		18-20 . . . at San Antonio	
2-4 . . . . .at Corpus Christi		21-23 . . . .at Corpus Christi	
5-7 . . . . . at San Antonio		25-28 . . . . . Springfield	
9-10 . . . . Tulsa		29-31 . . . . .Arkansas	
11-12 . . . . .at Tulsa		SEPTEMBER	
13-16 . . . . .Arkansas		1-4 . . . . .at Tulsa	
17-20 . . . . .at Springfield		5-7 . . . . at Arkansas	

MIDLAND ROCKHOUNDS (top of page continued)

15-18 . . . . . Corpus Christi		11-13 . . . . Tulsa	
19-22 . . . . .at San Antonio		14-16 . . . . . . Springfield	
23-26 . . . . Corpus Christi		18-20 . . . . .at Tulsa	
27-29 . . . . Midland		21-23 . . . . . .at Springfield	
30-31 . . . . .at San Antonio		25-28 . . . . . San Antonio	
AUGUST		29-31 . . . . . . at Midland	
1-2 . . . . .at San Antonio		SEPTEMBER	
3-5 . . . . at Midland		1-4 . . . . . .at Corpus Christi	
6-9 . . . . San Antonio		5-7 . . . . Midland	

SAN ANTONIO MISSIONS

APRIL
9-11 . . . . .at Tulsa
12-14 . . . . .at Springfield
16-18 . . . . Tulsa
19-21 . . . . . Springfield
23-26 . . . . at Midland
27-30 . . . . .Frisco

MAY
1-4 . . . . Midland
5-8 . . . . at Frisco
9-12 . . . . . Corpus Christi
14-17 . . . . at Midland
18-21 . . .at Corpus Christi
22-25 . . . . .Frisco
26-28 . . . . . . at Arkansas
29-31 . . . . at NW Arkansas

JUNE
2-4 . . . . .Arkansas
5-7 . . . . at NW Arkansas
9-12 . . . . at Frisco
13-16 . . . . Corpus Christi
17-20 . . . . . . Midland
21-24 . . .at Corpus Christi
25-28 . . . . Midland

JULY
2-4 . . . . .at Springfield
5-7 . . . . .at Tulsa
8-10 . . . . Springfield
11-13 . . . . Tulsa
15-18 . . . . at Midland
19-22 . . . . .Frisco
23-26 . . . . . . at Midland
27-29 . . . .at Corpus Christi
30-31 . . . . .Frisco

AUGUST
1-2 . . . . .Frisco
3-5 . . . . . Corpus Christi
6-9 . . . . at Frisco
11-13 . . . at NW Arkansas
14-16 . . . . . at Arkansas
18-20 . . . . . NW Arkansas
21-23 . . . . .Arkansas
25-28 . . . . . . at Frisco
29-31 . . . .at Corpus Christi

SEPTEMBER
1-4 . . . . Midland
5-7 . . . . . Corpus Christi

SPRINGFIELD CARDINALS

APRIL
9-11 . . . . . Corpus Christi
12-14 . . . . . San Antonio
16-18 . . .at Corpus Christi
19-21 . . . at San Antonio
23-26 . . . . . . Arkansas
27-30 . . . . at NW Arkansas

MAY
1-4 . . . . at Arkansas
5-8 . . . . . . NW Arkansas
9-12 . . . . .at Tulsa
14-17 . . . . at NW Arkansas
18-21 . . . . Tulsa
22-25 . . . . .Arkansas
26-28 . . . . at Frisco
29-31 . . . . . . at Midland

JUNE
2-4 . . . . .Frisco
5-7 . . . . Midland
9-12 . . . . at Arkansas
13-16 . . . . .at Tulsa
17-20 . . . . NW Arkansas
21-24 . . . . Tulsa
25-28 . . . . at Arkansas

JULY
1-3 . . . . at Modesto
4-6 . . . . .Stockton
7-10 . . . . at San Jose
11-13 . . . . .at Visalia
15-17 . . . . . . .Modesto
18-21 . . . . at Stockton
23-26 . . . . San Jose
27-29 . . . . . .High Desert
30-31 . . . .at Inland Empire

TULSA DRILLERS

APRIL
9-11 . . . . . . San Antonio
12-14 . . . . . Corpus Christi
16-18 . . . .at San Antonio
19-21 . . .at Corpus Christi
23-26 . . . . NW Arkansas
27-30 . . . . . . at Arkansas

MAY
1 . . . . . . at NW Arkansas
2 . . . . NW Arkansas
3-4 . . . . at NW Arkansas
5-8 . . . . .Arkansas
9-12 . . . . Springfield
14-17 . . . . . at Arkansas
18-21 . . .at Springfield
22-24 . . . . at NW Arkansas
25 . . . . . . NW Arkansas
26-28 . . . . . at Midland
29-31 . . . . at Frisco

JUNE
2-4 . . . . Midland
5-7 . . . . .Frisco
9-10 . . . . at NW Arkansas
11-12 . . . . NW Arkansas
13-16 . . . . . Springfield
17-20 . . . . . . .Arkansas

21-24 . . . .at Springfield
25-28 . . . . at NW Arkansas

JULY
2-4 . . . . . . Corpus Christi
5-7 . . . . . . San Antonio
8-10 . . . .at Corpus Christi
11-13 . . . . .at San Antonio
15-18 . . . . .Arkansas
19-22 . . . at NW Arkansas
23-26 . . . . . . .Arkansas
27-29 . . . . . Springfield
30-31 . . . . at Arkansas

AUGUST
1-2 . . . . at Arkansas
3-5 . . . . . . .at Springfield
6-9 . . . . . . NW Arkansas
11-13 . . . . at Frisco
14-16 . . . . at Midland
18-20 . . . . .Frisco
21-23 . . . . . Midland
25-28 . . . . at Arkansas
29-31 . . . . . Springfield

SEPTEMBER
1-4 . . . . NW Arkansas
5-7 . . . . . .at Springfield

3-5 . . . . Tulsa
6-9 . . . . .Arkansas
11-13 . . . . . at Midland
14-16 . . . . at Frisco
18-20 . . . . . Midland
21-23 . . . . .Frisco
25-28 . . . at NW Arkansas
29-31 . . . . .at Tulsa

SEPTEMBER
1-4 . . . . .Arkansas
5-7 . . . . Tulsa

HIGH CLASS A

CALIFORNIA LEAGUE

BAKERSFIELD BLAZE

APRIL
9-12 . . Rancho Cucamonga
13-15 . . . . . . .Modesto
16-19 . . . . . . at San Jose
20-22 . . . . . at Stockton
23-26 . . . . . . San Jose
27-29 . . . . .Stockton

MAY
1-3 . . . . .at Visalia
4-7 . . . . at Modesto
8-9 . . . . Visalia
11 . . . . Visalia
12-14at Rancho Cucamonga
15-18 . . . . . at High Desert
19-21 . . . . .Stockton
22-25 . . . . . .High Desert
27-29 . . . . at Visalia
30-31at Rancho Cucamonga

JUNE
1-2 . .at Rancho Cucamonga
4-7 . . . . Visalia
8-10 . . . . at San Jose

11-14 . . . . .Modesto
15-17 . . . . Inland Empire
18-21 . . . . . at Stockton
25-28 . . . . Lancaster
30 . . . . at Modesto

JULY
1-3 . . . . at Modesto
4-6 . . . . .Stockton
7-10 . . . . at San Jose
11-13 . . . . .at Visalia
15-17 . . . . . . .Modesto
18-21 . . . . at Stockton
23-26 . . . . San Jose
27-29 . . . . . .High Desert
30-31 . . . .at Inland Empire

AUGUST
1-2 . . . . .at Inland Empire
3-5 . . . . .at Lancaster
6-8 . . . . .Modesto
11-13 . . . . at Lake Elsinore
14-16 . . . . . . at Modesto
17-19 . . . . . Lake Elsinore
20-23 . . . . . . at San Jose

24-27 . . . . Visalia
28-30 . . . . . at High Desert

HIGH DESERT MAVERICKS

APRIL
9-12 . . . . .at Visalia
13-15 . . . . at Lake Elsinore
16-19 . . . . Lancaster
20-22 . . . . . Lake Elsinore
23-26 . . . .at Inland Empire
27-29 . . . . .Modesto

MAY
1-3 . . . . . at Lake Elsinore
4-7 . . . . . Inland Empire
8-10 . . Rancho Cucamonga
12-14 . . . . . . at Stockton
15-18 . . . . . . Bakersfield
19-21 . . . . . .at Lancaster
22-25 . . . . at Bakersfield
27-29 . . . . San Jose
30-31 . . . . Lancaster

JUNE
1-2 . . . . Lancaster
4-7 . . . . at San Jose
8-10 . . . . . . Lake Elsinore
11-14 . . . . San Jose

SEPTEMBER
1-3 . . . . Lancaster
4-7 . . . . San Jose

15-17at Rancho Cucamonga
18-21 . . . . . . at Modesto
25-28 . . . . Visalia
30 . .at Rancho Cucamonga

JULY
1-3 . .at Rancho Cucamonga
4-6 . . . . .Modesto
7-10 . . . . . . Lake Elsinore
11-13 . . . . . . .at Lancaster
15-17 . Rancho Cucamonga
18-21 . . . . Inland Empire
23-26 . . . at Lake Elsinore
27-29 . . . .at Bakersfield
30-31 . . . . Lancaster

AUGUST
1-2 . . . . Lancaster
3-5 . .at Rancho Cucamonga
6-9 . . . . .at Lancaster
11-13 . Rancho Cucamonga
14-16 . . . . Inland Empire
17-19at Rancho Cucamonga
20-23 . . . .at Inland Empire

24-27 . . . . .Stockton
28-30 . . . . . . Bakersfield

INLAND EMPIRE 66ERS

APRIL
9-12 . . . . .Stockton
13-15 . Rancho Cucamonga
15-19 . . . . . at Modesto
20-22 . . . . . at San Jose
23-26 . . . . . .High Desert
28-30 . . . . Lake Elsinore

MAY
1-3 . .at Rancho Cucamonga
4-7 . . . . . . at High Desert
8-10 . . . . .Modesto
12-14 . . . . at Lake Elsinore
15-18 . . . . Lancaster
19-21 . Rancho Cucamonga
22-25 . . . . . .at Lancaster
27-29 . . . . Lake Elsinore
30-31 . . . . . . San Jose

JUNE
1-2 . . . . San Jose
4-7 . . . . at Lake Elsinore
8-10 . . . . . at Stockton
11-14 . . . . Visalia
15-17 . . . .at Bakersfield
18-21 . . . . at San Jose
25-28 . . . . . . .Stockton

30 . . . . .at Lancaster

JULY
1-3 . . . . .at Lancaster
4-6 . . . Rancho Cucamonga
7-10 . . . . . . at Modesto
11-13at Rancho Cucamonga
15-17 . . . . Lancaster
18-21 . . . . at High Desert
23-26 . Rancho Cucamonga
27-29 . . . at Lake Elsinore
30-31 . . . . . . Bakersfield

AUGUST
1-2 . . . . Bakersfield
3-5 . . . . . . Lake Elsinore
6-9 . . . . at Visalia
11-13 . . . . Lancaster
14-16 . . at High Desert
17-19 . . . . . .at Lancaster
20-23 . . . . . .High Desert
24-27 . . . . San Jose
28-30 . . . . at Stockton

SEPTEMBER
1-3 . . . . .High Desert
4-7 . .at Rancho Cucamonga

LAKE ELSINORE STORM

APRIL
9-12 . . . . .Modesto
13-15 . . . . . .High Desert
16-19at Rancho Cucamonga
20-22 . . . at High Desert
23-26 . Rancho Cucamonga
28-30 . . .at Inland Empire

MAY
1-3 . . . . .High Desert
4-7 . . . . at San Jose
8-10 . . . . .at Lancaster
12-14 . . . . Inland Empire
15-18at Rancho Cucamonga
19-21 . . . . Visalia
22-25 . . . . . . .Stockton
27-29 . . .at Inland Empire
30-31 . . . . at Stockton

JUNE
1-2 . . . . at Stockton
4-7 . . . . . Inland Empire
8-10 . . . . at High Desert
11-14 . . . . Lancaster
15-17 . . . . . . .Stockton
18-21 . . . . .at Lancaster
25-28 . Rancho Cucamonga

30 . . . . .at Visalia

JULY
1-3 . . . . .at Visalia
4-6 . . . . Lancaster
7-10 . . . . at High Desert
11-13 . . . . . . at Stockton
15-17 . . . . Visalia
18-21 . . . . . at Modesto
23-26 . . . . . .High Desert
27-29 . . . . Inland Empire
30-31at Rancho Cucamonga

AUGUST
1-2 . .at Rancho Cucamonga
3-5 . . . . .at Inland Empire
6-9 . . . . San Jose
11-13 . . . . . . Bakersfield
14-16at Rancho Cucamonga
17-19 . . . .at Bakersfield
20-23 . . . . Lancaster
24-27 . . . . .Modesto
28-30 . . . . . .at Lancaster

SEPTEMBER
1-3 . . Rancho Cucamonga
4-7 . . . . at Visalia

LANCASTER JETHAWKS

APRIL
9-12 . . . . San Jose
13-15 . . . . . . .Stockton
16-19 . . . at High Desert
20-22at Rancho Cucamonga
23-26 . . . . . . .Modesto
28-30 . Rancho Cucamonga

MAY
1-3 . . . . at Modesto
4-7 . . . . at Stockton
8-10 . . . . . . Lake Elsinore

12-14 . . . . . . at Visalia
15-18 . . .at Inland Empire
19-21 . . . . . .High Desert
22-25 . . . Inland Empire
27-29 . . . . at Stockton
30-31 . . . . at High Desert

JUNE
1-2 . . . . . at High Desert
4-7 . . Rancho Cucamonga
8-10 . . . . .at Visalia
11-14 . . . at Lake Elsinore

15-17 . . . . Visalia
18-21 . . . . Lake Elsinore
25-28 . . . . at Bakersfield
30 . . . . Inland Empire

JULY
1-3 . . . . . . Inland Empire
4-6 . . . at Lake Elsinore
7-10 .at Rancho Cucamonga
11-13 . . . . . .High Desert
15-17 . . .at Inland Empire
18-21 . . . . at San Jose
23-26 . . . . .Stockton
27-29 . Rancho Cucamonga
30-31 . . . . at High Desert

AUGUST
1-2 . . . . Bakersfield
3-5 . . . . . . Lake Elsinore
6-9 . . . . at Visalia
11-13 . . . . Lancaster
14-16 . . at High Desert
17-19 . . . . . .at Lancaster
20-23 . . . . . .High Desert
24-27 . . . . San Jose
28-30 . . . . at Stockton

SEPTEMBER
1-3 . . . . .High Desert
4-7 . .at Rancho Cucamonga

15-17 . . . . Visalia
18-21 . . . . . Lake Elsinore
25-28 . . . . at Bakersfield
30 . . . . Inland Empire

JULY
1-3 . . . . . . Inland Empire
4-6 . . . . at Lake Elsinore
7-10 .at Rancho Cucamonga
11-13 . . . . . .High Desert
15-17 . . .at Inland Empire
18-21 . . . . at San Jose
23-26 . . . . .Stockton
27-29 . Rancho Cucamonga
30-31 . . . . at High Desert

MODESTO NUTS

APRIL
9-12 . . . . at Lake Elsinore
13-15 . . . .at Bakersfield
16-19 . . . . Inland Empire
20-22 . . . . Visalia
23-26 . . . .at Lancaster
27-29 . . . . at High Desert

MAY
1-3 . . . . Lancaster
4-7 . . . . Bakersfield
8-10 . . . .at Inland Empire
12-14 . . . . . at San Jose
15-18 . . . . at Stockton
19-21 . . . . at San Jose
22-24 . . . . Visalia
27-29at Rancho Cucamonga
30-31 . . . . . . at Visalia

JUNE
1-2 . . . . at Visalia
4-7 . . . . .Stockton
8-10 . . Rancho Cucamonga
11-14 . . . .at Bakersfield
15-17 . . . . . at San Jose
18-21 . . . . . .High Desert
25-28 . . . . at San Jose

30 . . . . Bakersfield

JULY
1-3 . . . . Bakersfield
4-6 . . . . . . at High Desert
7-10 . . . . . Inland Empire
11-13 . . . . San Jose
15-17 . . . . . . .at Bakersfield
18-21 . . . . Lake Elsinore
23-26 . . . . . . .at Visalia
27-29 . . . . at Stockton
30-31 . . . . Visalia

AUGUST
1-2 . . . . Visalia
3-5 . . . . San Jose
6-9 . . . . . .at Bakersfield
11-13 . . . . .Stockton
14-16 . . . . . . Bakersfield
17-19 . . . . . . at Visalia
20-23 . . . . . . .Stockton
24-27 . . . at Lake Elsinore
28-30 . . . . Visalia

SEPTEMBER
1-3 . . . . at San Jose
4-7 . . . . at Stockton

RANCHO CUCAMONGA QUAKES

APRIL
9-12 . . . . . .at Bakersfield
13-15 . . . .at Inland Empire
16-19 . . . . . Lake Elsinore
20-22 . . . . . Lancaster
23-26 . . . at Lake Elsinore
28-30 . . . . . .at Lancaster

MAY
1-3 . . . . . . Inland Empire
4-7 . . . . Visalia
8-10 . . . . . at High Desert
12-14 . . . . . . Bakersfield
15-18 . . . . Lake Elsinore
19-21 . . . .at Inland Empire
22-25 . . . . . at San Jose
27-29 . . . . . . .Modesto
30-31 . . . . . . Bakersfield

JUNE
1-2 . . . . Bakersfield
4-7 . . . . . . .at Lancaster
8-10 . . . . . at Modesto
11-14 . . . . . . .Stockton
15-17 . . . . . .High Desert
18-21 . . . . . . at Visalia
25-28 . . . . at Lake Elsinore

30 . . . . .High Desert

JULY
1-3 . . . . .High Desert
4-6 . . . . .at Inland Empire
7-10 . . . . Lancaster
11-13 . . . . Inland Empire
15-17 . . . . at High Desert
18-21 . . . . Visalia
23-26 . . .at Inland Empire
27-29 . . . . . .at Lancaster
30-31 . . . . . Lake Elsinore

AUGUST
1-2 . . . . Lake Elsinore
3-5 . . . . .High Desert
6-9 . . . . at Stockton
11-13 . . . . at High Desert
14-16 . . . . . Lake Elsinore
17-19 . . . . . .High Desert
21-23 . . . . .at Visalia
24-27 . . . . .at Lancaster
28-30 . . . . San Jose

SEPTEMBER
1-3 . . . . . at Lake Elsinore
4-7 . . . . . . Inland Empire

SAN JOSE GIANTS

APRIL
9-12 . . . . at Lancaster
13-15 . . . . at Visalia
16-19 . . . . . . Bakersfield
20-22 . . . . . Inland Empire
23-26 . . . .at Bakersfield
28-30 . . . . Visalia

MAY
1-3 . . . . at Stockton
4-7 . . . . Lake Elsinore
8-10 . . . . Stockton
12-14 . . . . at Modesto
15-18 . . . . at Visalia
19-21 . . . . Modesto
22-25 . Rancho Cucamonga
27-29 . . . at High Desert
30-31 . . . .at Inland Empire

JUNE
1-2 . . . . .at Inland Empire
4-7 . . . . .High Desert
8-10 . . . . . . Bakersfield
11-14 . . . . at High Desert
15-17 . . . . . . at Modesto
18-21 . . . . . Inland Empire
25-28 . . . . Modesto

STOCKTON PORTS

APRIL
9-12 . . . . .at Inland Empire
13-15 . . . . . .at Lancaster
16-19 . . . . Visalia
20-22 . . . . Bakersfield
23-26 . . . . . . at Visalia
27-29 . . . . .at Bakersfield

MAY
1-3 . . . . San Jose
4-7 . . . . Lancaster
8-10 . . . . at San Jose
12-14 . . . . . .High Desert
15-18 . . . . Modesto
19-21 . . . .at Bakersfield
22-25 . . at Lake Elsinore
27-29 . . . . Lancaster
30-31 . . . . . Lake Elsinore

JUNE
1-2 . . . . Lake Elsinore
4-7 . . . . at Modesto
8-10 . . . . Inland Empire
11-14at Rancho Cucamonga
15-17 . . . . at Lake Elsinore
18-21 . . . . . Bakersfield
25-28 . . . .at Inland Empire

VISALIA RAWHIDE

APRIL
9-12 . . . . . . .High Desert
13-15 . . . . San Jose
16-19 . . . . . at Stockton
20-22 . . . . at Modesto
23-26 . . . . . Stockton
28-30 . . . . at San Jose

MAY
1-3 . . . . Bakersfield
4-7 . .at Rancho Cucamonga
8-9 . . . . . . .at Bakersfield
11 . . . . . .at Bakersfield
12-14 . . . . Lancaster
15-18 . . . . San Jose
19-21 . . . . at Lake Elsinore

30 . . . . at Stockton

JULY
1-3 . . . . at Stockton
4-6 . . . . Visalia
7-10 . . . . Bakersfield
11-13 . . . . . . at Modesto
15-17 . . . . .Stockton
18-21 . . . . Lancaster
23-26 . . . .at Bakersfield
27-29 . . . . . . at Visalia
30-31 . . . . Stockton

AUGUST
1-2 . . . . .Stockton
3-5 . . . . at Modesto
6-9 . . . . . at Lake Elsinore
11-13 . . . . Visalia
14-16 . . . . Lancaster
17-19 . . . . . at Stockton
20-23 . . . . . . Bakersfield
24-27 . . . .at Inland Empire
28-30at Rancho Cucamonga

SEPTEMBER
1-3 . . . . .Modesto
4-7 . . . . . . .at Bakersfield

30 . . . . San Jose

JULY
1-3 . . . . San Jose
4-6 . . . . . . .at Bakersfield
7-10 . . . . Visalia
11-13 . . . . Lake Elsinore
15-17 . . . . . at San Jose
18-21 . . . . . . Bakersfield
23-26 . . . .at Lancaster
27-29 . . . . Modesto
30-31 . . . . at San Jose

AUGUST
1-2 . . . . . . at San Jose
3-5 . . . . at Visalia
6-9 . . . Rancho Cucamonga
11-13 . . . . at Modesto
14-16 . . . . Visalia
17-19 . . . . . San Jose
20-23 . . . . at Modesto
24-27 . . . . at High Desert
28-30 . . . . Inland Empire

SEPTEMBER
1-3 . . . . .at Visalia
4-7 . . . . .Modesto

22-25 . . . . . at Modesto
27-29 . . . . . Bakersfield
30-31 . . . . . . Modesto

JUNE
1-2 . . . . Modesto
4-7 . . . . . .at Bakersfield
8-10 . . . . Lancaster
11-14 . . . .at Inland Empire
15-17 . . . .at Lancaster
18-21 . Rancho Cucamonga
25-28 . . . . at High Desert
30 . . . . . Lake Elsinore

JULY
1-3 . . . . Lake Elsinore
4-6 . . . . at San Jose

7-10 . . . . at Stockton
11-13 . . . . . . Bakersfield
15-17 . . at Lake Elsinore
18-21at Rancho Cucamonga
23-26 . . . . .Modesto
27-29 . . . . . . San Jose
30-31 . . . . at Modesto

AUGUST
1-2 . . . . . . at Modesto
3-5 . . . . .Stockton

6-9 . . . . . . Inland Empire
11-13 . . . . . . at San Jose
14-16 . . . . . at Stockton
17-19 . . . . .Modesto
20-23 . Rancho Cucamonga
24-27 . . . .at Bakersfield
28-30 . . . . at Modesto

SEPTEMBER
1-3 . . . . .Stockton
4-7 . . . . . . Lake Elsinore

CAROLINA LEAGUE

CAROLINA MUDCATS

APRIL
9-12 . . . . .Salem
13-15 . . . . . Wilmington
16-19 . . . . . . at Salem
20-22 . . . at Winston-Salem
23-26 . . . . .Salem
28-30 . . . at Lynchburg

MAY
1-4 . . . . .Frederick
5-7 . . . . .Lynchburg
8-11 . . . . at Salem
12-14 . . . at Myrtle Beach
15-17 . . . Myrtle Beach
18-21 . . . . at Potomac
22-25 . . . . . at Wilmington
27-29 . . . . Myrtle Beach
30-31 . . . . . Wilmington

JUNE
1-2 . . . . Wilmington
4-7 . . . . at Myrtle Beach
8-11 . . . . . . .Potomac
12-14 . . . .Winston-Salem
15-17 . . . . at Frederick
18-21 . . . . at Potomac
25-27 . . . . . Myrtle Beach

FREDERICK KEYS

APRIL
9-12 . . . . .Winston-Salem
13-15 . . . . . . .Lynchburg
16-19 . . . . at Wilmington
20-22 . . . at Lynchburg
23-26 . . . . . Wilmington
28-30 . . . . at Salem

MAY
1-4 . . . . .at Carolina
5-7 . . . . .Winston-Salem
8-11 . . . . . at Potomac
12-14 . . . . .at Lynchburg
15-17 . . . . . . .Potomac
19-21 . . . . at Myrtle Beach
22-25 . . . . at Lynchburg
27-29 . . . . .Salem
30-31 . . . . .Lynchburg

JUNE
1-2 . . . . .Lynchburg
4-7 . . . . . . at Wilmington
8-11 . . . . Myrtle Beach
12-14 . . . . at Potomac
15-17 . . . . . . Carolina
18-21 . . . . Wilmington
25-27 . . . . . at Salem

28-30 . . . . . . at Potomac

JULY
1-3 . . . . .Winston-Salem
4-6 . . . . . . Myrtle Beach
7-9 . . . . at Salem
10-13 . . . at Myrtle Beach
15-18 . . . .Winston-Salem
19-21 . . . . . . .Wilmington
22-24 . . . at Winston-Salem
25-27 . . . at Myrtle Beach
28-30 . . . . . . .Frederick
31 . . . . . . at Wilmington

AUGUST
1-2 . . . . . . at Wilmington
4-6 . . . . .Winston-Salem
7-9 . . . . .Potomac
11-13 . . . . at Wilmington
14-16 . . . . at Frederick
18-20 . . . . .Salem
21-23 . . at Winston-Salem
24-26 . . . . . Wilmington
27-30 . . . . . . .Lynchburg

SEPTEMBER
1-3 . . . . .at Frederick
4-7 . . . . . . .at Lynchburg

28-30 . . . . Wilmington

JULY
1-3 . . . . .Potomac
4-6 . . . at Winston-Salem
7-9 . . . . . at Wilmington
10-13 . . . . .Salem
15-18 . . . . at Wilmington
19-21 . . . . .Potomac
22-24 . . . . at Potomac
25-27 . . . .Winston-Salem
28-30 . . . . . .at Carolina
31 . . . . Myrtle Beach

AUGUST
1-2 . . . . . Myrtle Beach
4-6 . . . . at Salem
7-9 . . . . at Myrtle Beach
11-13 . . . . . . .Lynchburg
14-16 . . . . Carolina
18-20 . . . . at Lynchburg
21-23 . . . Myrtle Beach
24-26 . . . . at Potomac
27-30 . . at Winston-Salem

SEPTEMBER
1-3 . . . . Carolina
4-7 . . . . . .Winston-Salem

LYNCHBURG HILLCATS

APRIL
9-12 . . . . at Potomac
13-15 . . . . . . at Frederick
16-19 . . . . . . .Potomac
20-22 . . . . . . .Frederick
24-27 . . . . . at Potomac
28-30 . . . . . Carolina

MAY
1-4 . . . . Myrtle Beach
5-7 . . . . .at Carolina
8-11 . . . . at Wilmington
12-14 . . . . . . .Frederick
15-17 . . . . . . .Wilmington
19-21 . . . . . . at Salem
22-25 . . . . . .Frederick
27-29 . . at Winston-Salem
30-31 . . . . . at Frederick

JUNE
1-2 . . . . at Frederick
4-7 . . . . . .Winston-Salem
8-9 . . . . .Salem
10-11 . . . . at Salem
12-14 . . . . at Myrtle Beach
15-17 . . . . . . .Potomac
18-21 . . . . at Myrtle Beach
25-27 . . . . .Winston-Salem

28-30 . . . . at Salem

JULY
1-3 . . . . . at Wilmington
4-6 . . . . .Salem
7-9 . . . . at Potomac
10-13 . . . . . .Wilmington
15-16 . . . . .Salem
17-18 . . . . at Salem
19-21 . . . at Winston-Salem
22-24 . . . . . Myrtle Beach
25-27 . . . . at Wilmington
28-30 . . . . .Salem
31 . . . . . at Winston-Salem

AUGUST
1-2 . . . . . at Winston-Salem
4-6 . . . . .Potomac
7-9 . . . . .Wilmington
11-13 . . . . . . at Frederick
14-16 . . . at Myrtle Beach
18-20 . . . . .Frederick
21-23 . . . . .Potomac
24-26 . . . . . . at Salem
27-30 . . . . .at Carolina

SEPTEMBER
1-3 . . . . .Salem
4-7 . . . . Carolina

MYRTLE BEACH PELICANS

APRIL
9-12 . . . . Wilmington
13-15 . . . . .Salem
16-19 . . . at Winston-Salem
20-22 . . . . at Salem
23-26 . . . .Winston-Salem
28-30 . . . . at Wilmington

MAY
1-4 . . . . at Lynchburg
5-7 . . . . .Salem
8-11 . . . at Winston-Salem
12-14 . . . . Carolina
15-17 . . . . .at Carolina
19-21 . . . . . . .Frederick
22-25 . . . . . . .Potomac
27-29 . . . . .at Carolina
30-31 . . . at Potomac

JUNE
1-2 . . . . at Potomac
4-7 . . . . Carolina
8-11 . . . . . . at Frederick
12-14 . . . . . . .Lynchburg
15-17 . . . at Winston-Salem
18-21 . . . . . . .Lynchburg
25-27 . . . . . . .at Carolina

28-30 . . . at Winston-Salem

JULY
1-3 . . . . .Salem
4-6 . . . . .at Carolina
7-9 . . . . . . .Winston-Salem
10-13 . . . . Carolina
15-18 . . . . . . at Potomac
19-21 . . . . .Salem
22-24 . . . . . at Lynchburg
25-27 . . . . . . Carolina
28-30 . . . . . . .Potomac
31 . . . . at Frederick

AUGUST
1-2 . . . . at Frederick
4-6 . . . . Wilmington
7-9 . . . . .Frederick
11-13 . . . . . . at Salem
14-16 . . . . . . .Lynchburg
18-20 . . at Winston-Salem
21-23 . . . . . . at Frederick
24-26 . . . .Winston-Salem
27-30 . . . . . . Wilmington

SEPTEMBER
1-3 . . . . at Potomac
4-7 . . . . . . at Wilmington

POTOMAC NATIONALS

APRIL
9-12 . . . . .Lynchburg
13-15 . . . . .Winston-Salem
16-19 . . . . at Lynchburg
20-22 . . . . . at Wilmington
24-27 . . . . . . .Lynchburg
28-30 . . . at Winston-Salem

MAY
1-4 . . . . .at Salem
5-7 . . . . Wilmington
8-11 . . . . .Frederick
12-14 . . . . at Wilmington
15-17 . . . . . at Frederick
19-21 . . . . Carolina

22-25 . . . . at Myrtle Beach
27-29 . . . . . . Wilmington
30-31 . . . . . Myrtle Beach

JUNE
1-2 . . . . . . Myrtle Beach
4-7 . . . . at Salem
8-11 . . . . .at Carolina
12-14 . . . . . . .Frederick
15-17 . . . .at Lynchburg
18-21 . . . . Carolina
25-27 . . . . at Wilmington
28-30 . . . . Carolina

SALEM RED SOX

APRIL
9-12 . . . . .at Carolina
13-15 . . . at Myrtle Beach
16-19 . . . . Carolina
20-22 . . . Myrtle Beach
23-26 . . . . . .at Carolina
28-30 . . . . . . .Frederick

MAY
1-4 . . . . .Potomac
5-7 . . . . . at Myrtle Beach
8-11 . . . . Carolina
12-14 . . . .Winston-Salem
15-17 . . . at Winston-Salem
19-21 . . . . . . .Lynchburg
22-25 . . . .Winston-Salem
27-29 . . . . at Frederick
30-31 . . . at Winston-Salem

JUNE
1-2 . . . . at Winston-Salem
4-7 . . . . .Potomac
8-9 . . . . . at Lynchburg
10-11 . . . . . . .Lynchburg
12-14 . . . . . Wilmington
15-17 . . . at Wilmington
18-21 . . . at Winston-Salem
25-27 . . . . .Frederick

28-30 . . . . . . .Lynchburg

JUNE
1-3 . . . . . at Myrtle Beach
4-6 . . . . . at Lynchburg
7-9 . . . . Carolina
10-13 . . . . at Frederick
15-16 . . . . at Lynchburg
17-18 . . . . . . .Lynchburg
19-21 . . at Myrtle Beach
22-24 . . . . . .Wilmington
25-27 . . . . . . .Potomac
28-30 . . at Lynchburg
31 . . . . . . at Potomac

AUGUST
1-2 . . . . at Potomac
4-6 . . . . .Frederick
7-9 . . . . at Winston-Salem
11-13 . . . . Myrtle Beach
14-16 . . . .Winston-Salem
18-20 . . . . . . .at Carolina
21-23 . . . at Wilmington
24-26 . . . . . . .Lynchburg
27-30 . . . . . . .Potomac

SEPTEMBER
1-3 . . . . at Lynchburg
4-7 . . . . at Potomac

WILMINGTON BLUE ROCKS

APRIL
9-12 . . . . at Myrtle Beach
13-15 . . . . .at Carolina
16-19 . . . . . . .Frederick
20-22 . . . . .Potomac
23-26 . . . . at Frederick
28-30 . . . . . Myrtle Beach

MAY
1-4 . . . . . .Winston-Salem
5-7 . . . . at Potomac
8-11 . . . . .Lynchburg
12-14 . . . . .Potomac
15-17 . . . . at Lynchburg
19-21 . . . . .Winston-Salem
22-25 . . . . Carolina
27-29 . . . . . . at Potomac
30-31 . . . . . . .at Carolina

JUNE
1-2 . . . . .at Carolina
4-7 . . . . .Frederick
8-11 . . . at Winston-Salem
12-14 . . . . at Salem
15-17 . . . . .Salem
18-21 . . . . at Frederick
25-27 . . . . .Potomac

28-30 . . . . . . at Frederick

JULY
1-3 . . . . .Lynchburg
4-6 . . . . at Potomac
7-9 . . . . .Frederick
10-13 . . . . at Lynchburg
15-18 . . . . . . .Frederick
19-21 . . . . . . .at Carolina
22-24 . . . . . . at Salem
25-27 . . . . . .Lynchburg
28-30 . . at Winston-Salem
31 . . . . Carolina

AUGUST
1-2 . . . . Carolina
4-6 . . . . . at Myrtle Beach
7-9 . . . . . . at Lynchburg
11-13 . . . . Carolina
14-16 . . . . . at Potomac
18-20 . . . . .Potomac
21-23 . . . . .Salem
24-26 . . . . . .at Carolina
27-30 . . . . at Myrtle Beach

SEPTEMBER
1-3 . . . . . .Winston-Salem
4-7 . . . . Myrtle Beach

WINSTON-SALEM DASH

APRIL	
9-12	at Frederick
13-15	at Potomac
16-19	Myrtle Beach
20-22	Carolina
23-26	at Myrtle Beach
28-30	Potomac

MAY	
1-4	at Wilmington
5-7	at Frederick
8-11	Myrtle Beach
12-14	at Salem
15-17	Salem
19-21	at Wilmington
22-25	at Salem
27-29	Lynchburg
30-31	Salem

JUNE	
1-2	Salem
4-7	at Lynchburg
8-11	Wilmington
12-14	at Carolina
15-17	Myrtle Beach
19-21	Salem
25-27	at Lynchburg

28-30	Myrtle Beach

JULY	
1-3	at Carolina
4-6	Frederick
7-9	at Myrtle Beach
10-13	Potomac
15-18	at Carolina
19-21	Lynchburg
22-24	Carolina
25-27	at Frederick
28-30	Wilmington
31	Lynchburg

AUGUST	
1-2	Lynchburg
4-6	at Carolina
7-9	Salem
11-13	at Potomac
14-16	at Salem
18-20	Myrtle Beach
21-23	Carolina
24-26	at Myrtle Beach
27-30	Frederick

SEPTEMBER	
1-3	at Wilmington
4-7	at Frederick

FLORIDA STATE LEAGUE

BRADENTON MARAUDERS

APRIL	
9-10	at St. Lucie
11-12	St. Lucie
13-16	at Dunedin
17-19	Jupiter
20-22	Charlotte
23-25	at Jupiter
26-28	at Charlotte
30	St. Lucie

MAY	
1	St. Lucie
2-3	at St. Lucie
4	Fort Myers
5-6	Fort Myers
7-9	at Palm Beach
11-14	at Brevard County
15-17	Palm Beach
18	Fort Myers
19-20	at Fort Myers
21-24	at Lakeland
26-29	Daytona
30-31	Jupiter

JUNE	
1	Jupiter
2-3	St. Lucie
4	at Fort Myers
5	Fort Myers
6	at Fort Myers
8-9	at Clearwater
10-11	Clearwater
12	Fort Myers
13	at Fort Myers

14	Fort Myers
15-18	Tampa
22-24	at Charlotte
25-26	at St. Lucie
27-30	Brevard County

JULY	
1-3	Charlotte
4-6	at Jupiter
7-9	Palm Beach
10-13	at Daytona
15-18	Lakeland
19-21	at Palm Beach
22-25	Dunedin
26-27	at Clearwater
28-29	Clearwater
30-31	at Tampa

AUGUST	
1-2	at Tampa
4-6	Jupiter
7-9	at Charlotte
10-12	at Jupiter
13-15	Charlotte
16-17	St. Lucie
18-19	at St. Lucie
20-22	Fort Myers
23-25	at Palm Beach
27-29	at Fort Myers
30-31	Palm Beach

SEPTEMBER	
1	Palm Beach
2-3	St. Lucie
5-6	at St. Lucie

BREVARD COUNTY MANATEES

APRIL	
9	at Daytona
10	Daytona
11	at Daytona
12	Daytona
13-14	St. Lucie
15-16	at St. Lucie
17-19	Dunedin
20-22	Lakeland
23-25	at Dunedin
26-28	at Lakeland
30	Daytona

MAY	
1	at Daytona
2	Daytona
3	at Daytona
4-6	at Clearwater
7-9	Tampa
11-14	Bradenton
15-17	at Tampa
18-20	Clearwater
21-24	at Fort Myers
25-29	Charlotte
30-31	Lakeland

JUNE	
1	Lakeland
2	at Daytona
3	Daytona
4-6	Dunedin
8-11	at Palm Beach
12-14	at Clearwater
15-18	Jupiter
22-24	at Lakeland
25	at Daytona

26	Daytona
27-30	at Bradenton

JULY	
1-3	at Dunedin
4-6	Clearwater
7-9	at Tampa
10-13	at Charlotte
15-18	Fort Myers
19-21	Tampa
22-23	at St. Lucie
24-25	St. Lucie
26-29	Palm Beach
30-31	at Jupiter

AUGUST	
1-2	at Jupiter
4-6	Tampa
7-9	at Dunedin
10-12	at Tampa
13-15	Dunedin
16	Daytona
17	at Daytona
18	Daytona
19	at Daytona
20-22	at Clearwater
23-25	at Lakeland
27-29	Clearwater
30-31	Lakeland

SEPTEMBER	
1	Lakeland
3	Daytona
4	at Daytona
5	Daytona
6	at Daytona

CHARLOTTE STONE CRABS

APRIL	
9	Fort Myers
10-11	at Fort Myers
12	Fort Myers
13-14	Daytona
15-16	at Daytona
17-19	at Palm Beach
20-22	at Bradenton
23-25	Palm Beach
26-28	Bradenton
30	at Fort Myers

MAY	
1-2	Fort Myers
3	at Fort Myers
4-6	at Jupiter
7-9	St. Lucie
11-14	at Clearwater
15-17	at St. Lucie
18-20	Jupiter
21-24	Tampa
26-29	at Brevard County
30-31	at Palm Beach

JUNE	
1	at Palm Beach
2	at Fort Myers
3	Fort Myers
4-6	Jupiter
8-11	at Dunedin
12-14	at Jupiter
15-18	Lakeland
22-24	Bradenton
25	Fort Myers

26	at Fort Myers
27-30	Clearwater

JULY	
1-3	at Bradenton
4-6	Palm Beach
7-9	at St. Lucie
10-13	Brevard County
15-18	at Tampa
19-21	St. Lucie
22-23	at Daytona
24-25	Daytona
26-29	Dunedin
30-31	at Lakeland

AUGUST	
1-2	at Lakeland
4-6	at Palm Beach
7-9	Bradenton
10-12	Palm Beach
13-15	at Bradenton
16	Fort Myers
17-18	at Fort Myers
19	Fort Myers
20-22	Jupiter
23-25	St. Lucie
27-29	at Jupiter
30-31	at St. Lucie

SEPTEMBER	
1	at St. Lucie
3	Fort Myers
4	at Fort Myers
5	Fort Myers
6	at Fort Myers

CLEARWATER THRESHERS

APRIL
9 . . . . .Dunedin
10 . . . . at Dunedin
11 . . . . .Dunedin
12 . . . . at Dunedin
13-16 . . . . at Jupiter
17-19 . . . . . .Lakeland
20-21 . . . . Tampa
22 . . . . .at Tampa
23-25 . . . . . at Lakeland
26-27 . . . . . . .at Tampa
28 . . . . Tampa
30 . . . . at Dunedin

MAY
1 . . . . at Dunedin
2-3 . . . . .Dunedin
4-6 . . . . Brevard County
7-9 . . . . . . at Daytona
11-14 . . . . . Charlotte
15-17 . . . . . . Daytona
18-20 . .at Brevard County
21-24 . . . . at Palm Beach
25-29 . . . . . . .Fort Myers
30-31 . . . . at Daytona

JUNE
1 . . . . at Daytona
2 . . . . .Dunedin
3 . . . . at Dunedin
4-6 . . . . .at Tampa
8-9 . . . . .Bradenton
10-11 . . . . . at Bradenton
12-14 . . . . Brevard County

15-18 . . . . St. Lucie
22-24 . . . . Daytona
25 . . . . at Dunedin
26 . . . . .Dunedin
27-30 . . . . . .at Charlotte

JULY
1-3 . . . . Tampa
4-6 . . . .at Brevard County
7-9 . . . . .Lakeland
10-13 . . . at Fort Myers
15-18 . . . Palm Beach
19-21 . . . . . . at Lakeland
22-25 . . . . Jupiter
26-27 . . . . . . .Bradenton
27-28 . . . . at Bradenton
30-31 . . . . at St. Lucie

AUGUST
1-2 . . . . at St. Lucie
4-6 . . . . .Lakeland
7-9 . . . . .at Tampa
10-12 . . . . at Lakeland
13-15 . . . . Tampa
16 . . . . Dunedin
17-19 . . . . at Dunedin
20-22 . . Brevard County
23-25 . . . . . . Daytona
27-29 . .at Brevard County
30-31 . . . . at Daytona

SEPTEMBER
1 . . . . at Daytona
3 . . . . at Dunedin
4-6 . . . . Dunedin

DAYTONA TORTUGAS

APRIL
9 . . . . . . Brevard County
10 . . . .at Brevard County
11 . . . . . Brevard County
12 . . .at Brevard County
13-14 . . . . . .at Charlotte
15-16 . . . . . . Charlotte
17-19 . . . . . . Tampa
20-22 . . . . Dunedin
23-25 . . . . .at Tampa
26-28 . . . . at Dunedin
30 . . . . .at Brevard County

MAY
1 . . . . . . Brevard County
2 . . . .at Brevard County
3 . . . . . . Brevard County
4-6 . . . . . . at Lakeland
7-9 . . . . . . Clearwater
11-14 . . . . . . Palm Beach
15-17 . . . . .at Clearwater
18-20 . . . . . .Lakeland
21-24 . . . . Jupiter
26-29 . . . . at Bradenton
30-31 . . . . . Clearwater

JUNE
1 . . . . Clearwater
2 . . . . . . Brevard County
3 . . . . .at Brevard County
4-6 . . . . at Lakeland
8-11 . . . . St. Lucie
12-14 . . . . . . Tampa
15-18 . . . . . at Fort Myers
22-24 . . . . . at Clearwater
25 . . . . . . Brevard County

26 . . . . .at Brevard County
27-30 . . . . . at Palm Beach

JULY
1-3 . . . . .Lakeland
4-6 . . . . .at Tampa
7-9 . . . . .Dunedin
10-13 . . . . .Bradenton
15-18 . . . . at Jupiter
19-21 . . . . . . at Dunedin
22-23 . . . . . . Charlotte
24-25 . . . . .at Charlotte
26-29 . . . . . . at St. Lucie
30-31 . . . . . . .Fort Myers

AUGUST
1-2 . . . . .Fort Myers
4-6 . . . . .Dunedin
7-9 . . . . . . at Lakeland
10-12 . . . . at Dunedin
13-15 . . . . .Lakeland
16 . . . .at Brevard County
17 . . . . . Brevard County
18 . . . .at Brevard County
19 . . . . Brevard County
20-22 . . . . .at Tampa
23-25 . . . . . Clearwater
27-29 . . . . Tampa
30-31 . . . . . Clearwater

SEPTEMBER
1 . . . . Clearwater
3 . . . . .at Brevard County
4 . . . . . Brevard County
5 . . . . .at Brevard County
6 . . . . . . Brevard County

DUNEDIN BLUE JAYS

APRIL
9 . . . . . . .at Clearwater
10 . . . . . Clearwater
11 . . . . . .at Clearwater
12 . . . . . . Clearwater
13-16 . . . . . . .Bradenton
17-19 . . .at Brevard County
20-22 . . . . at Daytona
23-25 . . . . Brevard County
26-28 . . . . Daytona
30 . . . . Clearwater

MAY
1 . . . . Clearwater
2-3 . . . . . .at Clearwater
4-6 . . . . .at Tampa
7-9 . . . . .Lakeland
11-14 . . . . at Fort Myers
15-17 . . . . . . at Lakeland
18-20 . . . . Tampa
21-24 . . . . . . St. Lucie
26-29 . . . . at Jupiter
30-31 . . . . Tampa

JUNE
1 . . . . Tampa
2 . . . . . .at Clearwater
3 . . . . Clearwater
4-6 . . . .at Brevard County
8-11 . . . . Charlotte
12-14 . . . . . .Lakeland
15-18 . . . . at Palm Beach

FORT MYERS MIRACLE

APRIL
9 . . . . .at Charlotte
10-11 . . . . Charlotte
12 . . . . . .at Charlotte
13-14 . . . . . .at Tampa
15-16 . . . . Tampa
17-19 . . . . . . St. Lucie
20-22 . . . at Palm Beach
23-25 . . . . . . at St. Lucie
26-28 . . . . . Palm Beach
30 . . . . Charlotte

MAY
1-2 . . . . . . .at Charlotte
3 . . . . Charlotte
4 . . . . .Bradenton
5-6 . . . . at Bradenton
7-9 . . . . Jupiter
11-14 . . . . Dunedin
15-17 . . . . at Jupiter
18 . . . . at Bradenton
19-20 . . . . . . .Bradenton
21-24 . . . . Brevard County
26-29 . . . .at Clearwater
30-31 . . . . . at St. Lucie

JUNE
1 . . . . at St. Lucie
2 . . . . Charlotte
3 . . . . . .at Charlotte
4 . . . . .Bradenton
5 . . . . at Bradenton
6 . . . . .Bradenton
8-11 . . . . . at Lakeland
12 . . . . . . at Bradenton
13 . . . . .Bradenton
14 . . . . at Bradenton

22-24 . . . . .at Tampa
25 . . . . Clearwater
26 . . . . . . .at Clearwater
27-30 . . . . . . .Fort Myers

JULY
1-3 . . . . . Brevard County
4-6 . . . . at Lakeland
7-9 . . . . at Daytona
10-13 . . . . Jupiter
15-18 . . . . at St. Lucie
19-21 . . . . Daytona
22-25 . . . . . at Bradenton
26-29 . . . . at Charlotte
30-31 . . . . Palm Beach

AUGUST
1-2 . . . . Palm Beach
4-6 . . . . at Daytona
7-9 . . . . . Brevard County
10-12 . . . . Daytona
13-15 . . .at Brevard County
16 . . . . . . .at Clearwater
17-19 . . . . . . Clearwater
20-22 . . . . at Lakeland
23-25 . . . . . . .at Tampa
27-29 . . . . . .Lakeland
30-31 . . . . . Tampa

SEPTEMBER
1 . . . . Tampa
3 . . . . Clearwater
4-6 . . . . . . .at Clearwater

15-18 . . . . Daytona
22-24 . . . . . Palm Beach
25 . . . . . . .at Charlotte
26 . . . . Charlotte
27-30 . . . . . at Dunedin

JULY
1-3 . . . . . at Palm Beach
4-6 . . . . St. Lucie
7-9 . . . . at Jupiter
10-13 . . . . . Clearwater
15-18 . . .at Brevard County
19-21 . . . . Jupiter
22-23 . . . . . .at Tampa
24-25 . . . . . . Tampa
26-29 . . . . . .Lakeland
30-31 . . . . at Daytona

AUGUST
1-2 . . . . at Daytona
4-6 . . . . St. Lucie
7-9 . . . . at Palm Beach
10-12 . . . . at St. Lucie
13-15 . . . Palm Beach
16 . . . . . . .at Charlotte
17-18 . . . . . Charlotte
19 . . . . . .at Charlotte
20-22 . . . . at Bradenton
23-25 . . . . Jupiter
27-29 . . . . .Bradenton
30-31 . . . . . at Jupiter

SEPTEMBER
1 . . . . at Jupiter
3 . . . . . . .at Charlotte
4 . . . . Charlotte
5 . . . . .at Charlotte
6 . . . . Charlotte

JUPITER HAMMERHEADS

APRIL
9 . . . . Palm Beach
10 . . . . . . at Palm Beach
11 . . . . Palm Beach
12 . . . . at Palm Beach
12 . . . . at Palm Beach
13-16 . . . . . . Clearwater
17-19 . . . . . at Bradenton
20-22 . . . . . . at St. Lucie
23-25 . . . . . . .Bradenton
26-28 . . . . St. Lucie
30 . . . . . . at Palm Beach

MAY
1 . . . . . . at Palm Beach
2-3. . . . . Palm Beach
4-6. . . . . Charlotte
7-9. . . . . . at Fort Myers
11-14 . . . . . . .Lakeland
15-17 . . . . . .Fort Myers
18-20 . . . . . at Charlotte
21-24 . . . . . . at Daytona
26-29 . . . . . . .Dunedin
30-31 . . . at Bradenton

JUNE
1 . . . . at Bradenton
2 . . . . . . at Palm Beach
3 . . . . Palm Beach
4-6. . . . . . . at Charlotte
8-11. . . . . . . .at Tampa
12-14 . . . . . . Charlotte
15-18 . . .at Brevard County

22-24 . . . . St. Lucie
25-26 . . . . . . Palm Beach
27-30 . . . . . . at Lakeland

JULY
1-3. . . . . at St. Lucie
4-6. . . . . .Bradenton
7-9. . . . . .Fort Myers
10-13 . . . . . . at Dunedin
15-18 . . . . Daytona
19-21 . . . at Fort Myers
22-25 . . . at Clearwater
26-29 . . . . Tampa
30-31 . . . Brevard County

AUGUST
1-2. . . . . Brevard County
4-6. . . . . . . at Bradenton
7-9. . . . . . . at St. Lucie
10-12 . . . . . .Bradenton
13-15 . . . . St. Lucie
16-18 . . . at Palm Beach
19 . . . . . . Palm Beach
20-22 . . . .at Charlotte
23-25 . . . at Fort Myers
27-29 . . . . . . Charlotte
30-31 . . . . .Fort Myers

SEPTEMBER
1 . . . . .Fort Myers
3 . . . . . at Palm Beach
4-5. . . . . . Palm Beach
6 . . . . . . at Palm Beach

LAKELAND FLYING TIGERS

APRIL
9 . . . . Tampa
10 . . . . .at Tampa
11 . . . . Tampa
12 . . . . .at Tampa
13-16 . . . . . . Palm Beach
17-19 . . . . at Clearwater
20-22 . .at Brevard County
23-25 . . . . . . Clearwater
26-28 . . . Brevard County
30 . . . . Tampa

MAY
1-3. . . . . .at Tampa
4-6. . . . . Daytona
7-9. . . . . at Dunedin
11-14 . . . . at Jupiter
15-17 . . . . Dunedin
18-20 . . . . . at Daytona
21-24 . . . . . . .Bradenton
26-29 . . . . at St. Lucie
30-31 . .at Brevard County

JUNE
1 . . . . .at Brevard County
2-3. . . . . Tampa
4-6. . . . . Daytona
8-11. . . . . . . .Fort Myers
12-14 . . . . at Dunedin
15-18 . . . . . at Charlotte
22-24 . . . Brevard County

25 . . . . Tampa
26 . . . . .at Tampa
27-30 . . . . Jupiter

JULY
1-3. . . . . at Daytona
4-6. . . . . Dunedin
7-9. . . . . .at Clearwater
10-13 . . . . St. Lucie
15-18 . . . . . at Bradenton
19-21 . . . . Clearwater
22-25 . . at Palm Beach
25-29 . . . at Fort Myers
30-31 . . . . . Charlotte

AUGUST
1-2. . . . . Charlotte
4-6. . . . . . . .at Clearwater
7-9. . . . . . . Daytona
10-12 . . . . . Clearwater
13-15 . . . . . at Daytona
16-17 . . . . Tampa
18-19 . . . . . .at Tampa
20-22 . . . . . . Dunedin
23-25 . . . Brevard County
27-29 . . . . at Dunedin
30-31 . . .at Brevard County

SEPTEMBER
1 . . . . .at Brevard County
3-4. . . . . Tampa
5-6. . . . . .at Tampa

PALM BEACH CARDINALS

APRIL
9 . . . . at Jupiter
10 . . . . Jupiter
11 . . . . at Jupiter
12 . . . . Jupiter
13-16 . . . at Lakeland
17-19 . . . . Charlotte
20-22 . . . . . . .Fort Myers
23-25 . . . at Charlotte
26-28 . . . at Fort Myers
30 . . . . Jupiter

MAY
1 . . . . Jupiter
2-3. . . . . at Jupiter
4-6. . . . . at St. Lucie
7-9. . . . . .Bradenton
11-14 . . . . at Daytona
15-17 . . . . at Bradenton
18-20 . . . . . St. Lucie
21-24 . . . . Clearwater
26-29 . . . . . .at Tampa
30-31 . . . . . Charlotte

JUNE
1 . . . . Charlotte
2 . . . . Jupiter
3 . . . . at Jupiter
4-6. . . . . St. Lucie
8-11. . . . Brevard County
12-14 . . . . at St. Lucie
15-18 . . . . Dunedin

22-24 . . . at Fort Myers
25-26 . . . . . . at Jupiter
27-30 . . . . Daytona

JULY
1-3. . . . . .Fort Myers
4-6. . . . . at Charlotte
7-9. . . . . . at Bradenton
10-13 . . . . Tampa
15-18 . . . . . at Clearwater
19-21 . . . . . .Bradenton
22-25 . . . . . . .Lakeland
26-29 . . .at Brevard County
30-31 . . . . . . at Dunedin

AUGUST
1-2. . . . . . . at Dunedin
4-6. . . . . Charlotte
7-9. . . . . .Fort Myers
10-12 . . . . .at Charlotte
13-15 . . . . at Fort Myers
16-18 . . . . Jupiter
19 . . . . at Jupiter
20-22 . . . . St. Lucie
23-25 . . . . . . .Bradenton
27-29 . . . . at St. Lucie
30-31 . . . . . at Bradenton

SEPTEMBER
1 . . . . at Bradenton
3 . . . . Jupiter
4-5. . . . . at Jupiter
6 . . . . Jupiter

ST. LUCIE METS

APRIL
9-10 . . . . .Bradenton
11-12 . . . . . at Bradenton
13-15 . . .at Brevard County
16 . . . . . Brevard County
17-19 . . . . . at Fort Myers
20-22 . . . . Jupiter
23-25 . . . . . . .Fort Myers
26-28 . . . . . . at Jupiter
30 . . . . at Bradenton

MAY
1 . . . . at Bradenton
2-3. . . . . .Bradenton
4-6. . . . . Palm Beach
7-9. . . . . . .at Charlotte
11-14 . . . . Tampa
15-17 . . . . Charlotte
18-20 . . . at Palm Beach
21-24 . . . . at Dunedin
26-29 . . . . . .Lakeland
30-31 . . . . . .Fort Myers

JUNE
1 . . . . .Fort Myers
2-3. . . . . . . at Bradenton
4-6. . . . . at Palm Beach
8-11. . . . . . . at Daytona
12-14 . . . . Palm Beach
15-18 . . . . .at Clearwater
22-24 . . . . . . at Jupiter

25-26 . . . . . . .Bradenton
27-30 . . . . . . .at Tampa

JULY
1-3. . . . . Jupiter
4-6. . . . . . at Fort Myers
7-9. . . . . Charlotte
10-13 . . . . . at Lakeland
15-18 . . . . . . Dunedin
19-21 . . . .at Charlotte
22-23 . . . Brevard County
24-25 . . .at Brevard County
26-29 . . . . Daytona
30-31 . . . . . . Clearwater

AUGUST
1-2. . . . . Clearwater
4-6. . . . . . . at Fort Myers
7-9. . . . . Jupiter
10-12 . . . . . .Fort Myers
13-15 . . . . . . at Jupiter
16-17 . . . . . at Bradenton
18-19 . . . . . . .Bradenton
20-22 . . . at Palm Beach
23-25 . . . . . at Charlotte
27-29 . . . Palm Beach
30-31 . . . . . Charlotte

SEPTEMBER
1 . . . . Charlotte
3-4. . . . . . . at Bradenton
5-6. . . . . .Bradenton

TAMPA YANKEES

APRIL
9	at Lakeland
10	Lakeland
11	at Lakeland
12	Lakeland
13-14	Fort Myers
15-16	at Fort Myers
17-19	at Daytona
20-21	at Clearwater
22	Clearwater
23-25	Daytona
26-27	Clearwater
28	at Clearwater
30	at Lakeland

MAY
1-3	Lakeland
4-6	Dunedin
7-9	at Brevard County
11-14	at St. Lucie
15-17	Brevard County
18-20	at Dunedin
21-24	at Charlotte
26-29	Palm Beach
30-31	at Dunedin

JUNE
1	at Dunedin
2-3	at Lakeland
4-6	Clearwater
8-11	Jupiter
12-14	at Daytona
15-18	at Bradenton
22-24	Dunedin
25	at Lakeland
26	Lakeland
27-30	St. Lucie

JULY
1-3	at Clearwater
4-6	Daytona
7-9	Brevard County
10-13	at Palm Beach
15-18	Charlotte
19-21	at Brevard County
22-23	Fort Myers
24-25	at Fort Myers
26-29	at Jupiter
31	Bradenton

AUGUST
1-2	Bradenton
4-6	at Brevard County
7-9	Clearwater
10-12	Brevard County
13-15	at Clearwater
16-17	at Lakeland
18-19	Lakeland
20-22	Daytona
23-25	Dunedin
27-29	at Daytona
30-31	at Dunedin

SEPTEMBER
1	at Dunedin
3-4	at Lakeland
5-6	Lakeland

LOW CLASS A

MIDWEST LEAGUE

BELOIT SNAPPERS

APRIL
9-11	at Clinton
12-14	at Cedar Rapids
15-17	Quad Cities
18-20	at Clinton
21-23	Burlington
24-26	Clinton
28-30	at Peoria

MAY
1-3	at Kane County
4-6	Burlington
7-9	Cedar Rapids
11-14	at Quad Cities
15-17	at Peoria
18-21	Kane County
22-25	Cedar Rapids
26-28	at Burlington
29-31	at Wisconsin

JUNE
1	at Wisconsin
3-5	Fort Wayne
6-8	Lake County
10-12	at Bowling Green
13-15	at Dayton
16-18	Peoria
19-21	Wisconsin
25-28	at Burlington
29-30	at Quad Cities

JULY
1	at Quad Cities
2-3	Wisconsin
4-5	at Wisconsin
6-7	at Cedar Rapids
8-9	Cedar Rapids
10-13	Wisconsin
15-17	at Peoria
18-20	Clinton
21-23	Burlington
24-26	at Cedar Rapids
28-30	Quad Cities
31	Peoria

AUGUST
1-2	Peoria
4-6	at Great Lakes
7-9	at Lansing
11-13	South Bend
14-16	West Michigan
18-20	at Peoria
21-23	Burlington
24-26	Kane County
27-29	at Wisconsin
30-31	at Kane County

SEPTEMBER
1	at Kane County
2-4	at Clinton
5-7	Quad Cities

BOWLING GREEN HOT RODS

APRIL
9-11	at South Bend
12-14	at Lake County
15-17	at Dayton
18-20	Lake County
21-23	Dayton
24-26	Lansing
28-30	at Great Lakes

MAY
1-3	at Lansing
4-6	Lake County
7-9	South Bend
11-14	at West Michigan
15-17	Fort Wayne
18-21	West Michigan
22-25	at South Bend
26-28	Lansing
29-31	Great Lakes

JUNE
1	Great Lakes
3-5	at Kane County
6-8	at Clinton
10-12	Beloit
13-15	Wisconsin
16-18	at Lansing
19-21	at Fort Wayne
25-28	Dayton
29-30	at Fort Wayne

JULY
1	at Fort Wayne
2-3	at South Bend
4-5	South Bend
6-7	Dayton
8-9	at Dayton
10-13	at West Michigan
15-17	Great Lakes
18-20	at Lake County
21-23	at Lansing
24-26	Fort Wayne
28-30	West Michigan
31	Lansing

AUGUST
1-2	Lansing
4-6	at Quad Cities
7-9	at Cedar Rapids

BURLINGTON BEES

APRIL
9-11	Wisconsin
12-14	Kane County
15-17	at Wisconsin
18-20	Cedar Rapids
21-23	at Beloit
24-26	at Quad Cities
28-30	Kane County

MAY
1-3	at Peoria
4-6	at Beloit
7-9	Peoria
11-14	at Kane County
15-17	Clinton
18-21	Wisconsin
22-25	at Clinton
26-28	Beloit
29-31	Quad Cities

JUNE
1	Quad Cities
3-5	at Lansing
6-8	at Great Lakes
10-12	South Bend
13-15	West Michigan
16-18	at Cedar Rapids
19-21	at Quad Cities
25-28	Beloit
29-30	Kane County

JULY
1	Kane County
2-3	Cedar Rapids
4-5	at Cedar Rapids
6-7	at Peoria
8-9	Peoria
10-13	at Quad Cities
15-17	at Cedar Rapids
18-20	Peoria
21-23	at Beloit
24-26	Quad Cities
28-30	at Kane County
31	at Clinton

AUGUST
1-2	at Clinton
4-6	Fort Wayne
7-9	Lake County
11-13	at Bowling Green
14-16	at Dayton
18-20	Clinton
21-23	Beloit
24-26	at Wisconsin
27-29	Clinton
30-31	Quad Cities

SEPTEMBER
1	Quad Cities
2-4	at Peoria
5-7	Wisconsin

CEDAR RAPIDS KERNELS

APRIL
9-11	at Kane County
12-14	Beloit
15-17	Peoria
18-20	at Burlington
21-23	at Wisconsin
24-26	Kane County
28-30	at Quad Cities

MAY
1-3	Clinton
4-6	at Wisconsin
7-9	at Beloit
11-14	Peoria
15-17	Quad Cities
18-21	Peoria
22-25	at Beloit

The following partial columns from the middle of the page (Bowling Green continued):

JUNE (Bowling Green, continued)
10-13	at West Michigan
15-17	Great Lakes
18-20	at Lake County
21-23	at Lansing
24-26	Fort Wayne
28-30	West Michigan
31	Lansing

AUGUST (Bowling Green, continued)
1-2	Lansing
4-6	at Quad Cities
7-9	at Cedar Rapids
11-13	Burlington
14-16	Peoria
18-20	Fort Wayne
21-23	at Lansing
24-26	at Great Lakes
27-29	at Dayton
30-31	South Bend

SEPTEMBER (Bowling Green, continued)
1	South Bend
2-4	Lake County
5-7	at Fort Wayne

26-28 . . . . Wisconsin
29-31 . . . . .Clinton

JUNE
1 . . . . .Clinton
3-5 . . . . . at South Bend
6-8 . . . . at West Michigan
10-12 . . . . Great Lakes
13-15 . . . . Lansing
16-18 . . . . . . .Burlington
19-21 . . . . . at Clinton
25-28 . . . . Quad Cities
29-30 . . . . . at Wisconsin

JULY
1 . . . . at Wisconsin
2-3 . . . . . . at Burlington
4-5 . . . . .Burlington
6-7 . . . . .Beloit
8-9 . . . . at Beloit
10-13 . . . . at Kane County
15-17 . . . . . . .Burlington

CLINTON LUMBERKINGS

APRIL
9-11 . . . . .Beloit
12-14 . . . . at Quad Cities
15-17 . . . at Kane County
18-20 . . . . .Beloit
21-23 . . . at Kane County
24-26 . . . . . . at Beloit
28-30 . . . . . . Wisconsin

MAY
1-3 . . . . . at Cedar Rapids
4-6 . . . . Peoria
7-9 . . . . . . Kane County
11-14 . . . . . at Wisconsin
15-17 . . . at Burlington
18 21 . . . . . . Quad Cities
22-25 . . . . . .Burlington
26-28 . . . . at Peoria
29-31 . . . at Cedar Rapids

JUNE
1 . . . . . at Cedar Rapids
3-5 . . . . .Dayton
6-8 . . . . .Bowling Green
10-12 . . .at Lake County
13-15 . . .at Fort Wayne
16-18 . . . . . Quad Cities
19-21 . . . . Cedar Rapids
25-28 . . . . . at Wisconsin
29-30 . . . . Peoria

DAYTON DRAGONS

APRIL
9-11 . . . . at West Michigan
12-14 . . . . . . South Bend
15-17 . . . . Bowling Green
18-20 . . . . . . .at Lansing
21-23 . . at Bowling Green
24-26 . . . West Michigan
28-30 . . . . .at Fort Wayne

MAY
1-3 . . . . . . at Great Lakes
4-6 . . . . Fort Wayne
7-9 . . . . . . West Michigan
11-14 . . . . at Great Lakes
15-17 . . .at Lake County
18-21 . . . . . . Great Lakes
22-25 . . at West Michigan
26-28 . . . . . South Bend
29-31 . . . . Lansing

JUNE
1 . . . . Lansing

18-20 . . . . at Quad Cities
21-23 . . . . . . Wisconsin
24-26 . . . . .Beloit
28-30 . . . . at Clinton
31 . . . . . at Kane County

AUGUST
1-2 . . . . . at Kane County
4-6 . . . . .Dayton
7-9 . . . . . . .Bowling Green
11-13 . . .at Lake County
14-16 . . . .at Fort Wayne
18-20 . . . . Kane County
21-23 . . . . . at Clinton
24-26 . . . . Peoria
27-29 . . . . Kane County
30-31 . . . . .at Peoria

SEPTEMBER
1 . . . . .at Peoria
2-4 . . . . . at Wisconsin
5-7 . . . . .Clinton

JULY
1 . . . . Peoria
2-3 . . . . . at Kane County
4-5 . . . . . Kane County
6-7 . . . . at Quad Cities
8-9 . . . . . . Quad Cities
10-13 . . . . Peoria
15-17 . . . . . Kane County
18-20 . . . . at Beloit
21-23 . . . . at Peoria
24-26 . . . . . at Wisconsin
28-30 . . . . . Cedar Rapids
31 . . . . .Burlington

AUGUST
1-2 . . . . .Burlington
4-6 . . . . at West Michigan
7-9 . . . . . at South Bend
11-13 . . . . Lansing
14-16 . . . . . . Great Lakes
18-20 . . . at Burlington
21-23 . . . . . Cedar Rapids
24-26 . . . . at Quad Cities
27-29 . . . . at Burlington
30-31 . . . . Wisconsin

SEPTEMBER
1 . . . . Wisconsin
2-4 . . . . .Beloit
5-7 . . . . . at Cedar Rapids

3-5 . . . . at Clinton
6-8 . . . . . at Kane County
10-12 . . . . . Wisconsin
13-15 . . . . .Beloit
16-18 . . . . at South Bend
19-21 . . . . Lake County
25-28 . . at Bowling Green
29-30 . . . . . . Great Lakes

JULY
1 . . . . Great Lakes
2-3 . . . . . . Fort Wayne
4-5 . . . . . .at Fort Wayne
6-7 . . . . at Bowling Green
8-9 . . . . . .Bowling Green
10-13 . . . . Lansing
15-17 . . at West Michigan
18-20 . . . . . Fort Wayne
21-23 . . . . West Michigan
24-26 . . . . . . .at Lansing
28-30 . . . . .at Fort Wayne

31 . . . . South Bend

AUGUST
1-2 . . . . South Bend
4-6 . . . . at Cedar Rapids
7-9 . . . . at Quad Cities
11-13 . . . . Peoria
14-16 . . . . . .Burlington
18-20 . . . at South Bend

FORT WAYNE TINCAPS

APRIL
9-11 . . . . . . at Great Lakes
12-14 . . . . Lansing
15-17 . . . . South Bend
18-20 . . . at West Michigan
21-23 . . . . . .at Lansing
24-26 . . . . South Bend
28-30 . . . . .Dayton

MAY
1-3 . . . . . . at South Bend
4-6 . . . . at Dayton
7-9 . . . . Lansing
11-14 . . . . Lake County
15-17 . . . at Bowling Green
18-21 . . .at Lake County
22-25 . . . . . .at Lansing
26-28 . . . . . Great Lakes
29-31 . . . . West Michigan

JUNE
1 . . . . West Michigan
3-5 . . . . at Beloit
6-8 . . . . . at Wisconsin
10-12 . . . . Kane County
13-15 . . . . .Clinton
16-18 . . at West Michigan
19-21 . . . .Bowling Green
25-28 . . . at Great Lakes
29-30 . . . .Bowling Green

GREAT LAKES LOONS

APRIL
9-11 . . . . Fort Wayne
12-14 . . at West Michigan
15-17 . . . . Lansing
18-20 . . . at South Bend
21-23 . . . West Michigan
24-26 . . . .at Lake County
28-30 . . . .Bowling Green

MAY
1-3 . . . . .Dayton
4-6 . . . . . . at South Bend
7-9 . . . .at Lake County
11-14 . . . . .Dayton
15-17 . . . . . South Bend
18-21 . . . . . . at Dayton
22-25 . . . . Lake County
26-28 . . . .at Fort Wayne
29-31 . . at Bowling Green

JUNE
1 . . . . . at Bowling Green
3-5 . . . . Peoria
6-8 . . . . .Burlington
10-12 . . at Cedar Rapids
13-15 . . . . at Quad Cities
16-18 . . . . Lake County
19-21 . . . . . .at Lansing
25-28 . . . . . Fort Wayne
29-30 . . . . . at Dayton

JULY
1 . . . . at Dayton
2-3 . . . . . West Michigan
4-5 . . . . at West Michigan
6-7 . . . . .at Lansing
8-9 . . . . Lansing
10-13 . . . . .at Fort Wayne
15-17 . . . at Bowling Green
18-20 . . . . Lansing
21-23 . . . . . at South Bend
24-26 . . . . . . Lake County
28-30 . . . . . South Bend
31 . . . . . .at Lake County

AUGUST
1-2 . . . . .at Lake County
4-6 . . . . .Beloit
7-9 . . . . Wisconsin
11-13 . . . at Kane County
14-16 . . . . . at Clinton
18-20 . . . at West Michigan
21-23 . . . . .Dayton
24-26 . . . . . .Bowling Green
27-29 . . . . at South Bend
30-31 . . . West Michigan

SEPTEMBER
1 . . . . West Michigan
2-4 . . . . .at Lansing
5-7 . . . . . West Michigan

21-23 . . . . at Great Lakes
24-26 . . . .at Lake County
27-29 . . . .Bowling Green
30-31 . . . . Lake County

SEPTEMBER
1 . . . . Lake County
2-4 . . . . . . at South Bend
5-7 . . . . Lansing

KANE COUNTY COUGARS

APRIL
9-11 . . . . . . Cedar Rapids
12-14 . . . . . . at Burlington
15-17 . . . . Clinton
18-20 . . . . . . Quad Cities
21-23 . . . . Clinton
24-26 . . . . Cedar Rapids
28-30 . . . . . at Burlington

MAY
1-3 . . . . Beloit
4-6 . . . . Quad Cities
7-9 . . . . at Clinton
11-14 . . . . . . .Burlington
15-17 . . . . . . at Wisconsin
18-21 . . . . . . at Beloit
22-25 . . . Wisconsin
26-28 . . . . at Quad Cities
29-31 . . . . . . at Peoria

JUNE
1 . . . . at Peoria
3-5 . . . . Bowling Green
6-8 . . . . .Dayton
10-12 . . . . .at Fort Wayne
13-15 . . . .at Lake County
16-18 . . . . . Wisconsin
19-21 . . . . . . Peoria
25-28 . . . . at Peoria
29-30 . . . at Burlington

JULY
1 . . . . at Burlington
2-3 . . . . Clinton
4-5 . . . . at Clinton
6-7 . . . . at Wisconsin
8-9 . . . . Wisconsin
10-13 . . . . . Cedar Rapids
15-17 . . . . . . at Clinton
18-20 . . . . Wisconsin
21-23 . . . . . . Quad Cities
24-26 . . . . at Peoria
28-30 . . . . . . .Burlington
31 . . . . Cedar Rapids

AUGUST
1-2 . . . . . . Cedar Rapids
4-6 . . . . . at South Bend
7-9 . . . . at West Michigan
11-13 . . . . Great Lakes
14-16 . . . . Lansing
18-20 . . . at Cedar Rapids
21-23 . . . . Quad Cities
24-26 . . . . . . at Beloit
27-29 . . . at Cedar Rapids
30-31 . . . . Beloit

SEPTEMBER
1 . . . . Beloit
2-4 . . . . . . at Quad Cities
5-7 . . . . Peoria

LAKE COUNTY CAPTAINS

APRIL
10-11 . . . . . . at Lansing
12-14 . . . . Bowling Green
15-17 . . . . West Michigan
18-20 . . at Bowling Green
21-23 . . . . at South Bend
24-26 . . . . . . Great Lakes
28-30 . . . . . . Lansing

MAY
1-3 . . . . at West Michigan
4-6 . . . . at Bowling Green
7-9 . . . . Great Lakes
11-14 . . . . .at Fort Wayne
15-17 . . . . Dayton
18-21 . . . . . . Fort Wayne
22-25 . . . . at Great Lakes
26-28 . . . . West Michigan
29-31 . . . . South Bend

JUNE
1 . . . . South Bend
3-5 . . . . . . at Wisconsin
6-8 . . . . at Beloit
10-12 . . . . Clinton
13-15 . . . . . Kane County
16-18 . . at Great Lakes
19-21 . . . . at Dayton
25-28 . . . . South Bend
29-30 . . . at West Michigan

JULY
1 . . . . . at West Michigan
2-3 . . . . Lansing
4-5 . . . . .at Lansing
6-7 . . . . at West Michigan
8-9 . . . . . . West Michigan
10-13 . . . . at South Bend
15-17 . . . . .at Fort Wayne
18-20 . . . . Bowling Green
21-23 . . . . . . Fort Wayne
24-26 . . . . at Great Lakes
28-30 . . . . Lansing
31 . . . . Great Lakes

AUGUST
1-2 . . . . Great Lakes
4-6 . . . . at Peoria
7-9 . . . . . . at Burlington
11-13 . . . . . Cedar Rapids
14-16 . . . . . . Quad Cities
18-20 . . . . at Lansing
21-23 . . . . West Michigan
24-26 . . . . .Dayton
27-29 . . . .at Fort Wayne
30-31 . . . . at Dayton

SEPTEMBER
1 . . . . at Dayton
2-4 . . . . at Bowling Green
5-7 . . . . South Bend

LANSING LUGNUTS

APRIL
10-11 . . . . . Lake County
12-14 . . . . .at Fort Wayne
15-17 . . . . at Great Lakes
18-20 . . . . Dayton
21-23 . . . . Fort Wayne
24-26 . . at Bowling Green
28-30 . . . . at Lake County

MAY
1-3 . . . . . . .Bowling Green
4-6 . . . . . . West Michigan
7-9 . . . . . .at Fort Wayne
11-14 . . . . at South Bend
15-17 . . . at West Michigan
18-21 . . . . . . South Bend
22-25 . . . . . . Fort Wayne
26-28 . . . at Bowling Green
29-31 . . . . at Dayton

PEORIA CHIEFS

APRIL
9-11 . . . . . . Quad Cities
12-14 . . . . . at Wisconsin
15-17 . . . at Cedar Rapids
18-20 . . . . . Wisconsin
21-23 . . . . . Quad Cities
24-26 . . . at Wisconsin
28-30 . . . . .Beloit

MAY
1-3 . . . . .Burlington
4-6 . . . . Clinton
7-9 . . . . at Burlington
11-14 . . . at Cedar Rapids
15-17 . . . . .Beloit
18-21 . . . . Cedar Rapids
22-25 . . . at Quad Cities
26-28 . . . . Clinton
29-31 . . . . Kane County

JUNE
1 . . . . Kane County
3-5 . . . . . at Great Lakes
6-8 . . . . .at Lansing
10-12 . . . . West Michigan
13-15 . . . . South Bend
16-18 . . . . at Beloit
19-21 . . . at Kane County
25-28 . . . . Kane County
29-30 . . . . . at Clinton

JULY
1 . . . . at Clinton
2-3 . . . . . . at Quad Cities
4-5 . . . . Quad Cities
6-7 . . . . .Burlington
8-9 . . . . . . at Burlington
10-13 . . . . . . at Clinton
15-17 . . . . .Beloit
18-20 . . . . at Burlington
21-23 . . . . Clinton
24-26 . . . . . Kane County
28-30 . . . . at Wisconsin
31 . . . . at Beloit

AUGUST
1-2 . . . . at Beloit
4-6 . . . . Lake County
7-9 . . . . Fort Wayne
11-13 . . . . at Dayton
14-16 . . . at Bowling Green
18-20 . . . . .Beloit
21-23 . . . . Wisconsin
24-26 . . . . at Cedar Rapids
27-29 . . . . at Quad Cities
30-31 . . . . Cedar Rapids

SEPTEMBER
1 . . . . Cedar Rapids
2-4 . . . . .Burlington
5-7 . . . . . at Kane County

QUAD CITIES RIVER BANDITS

APRIL
9-11 . . . . at Peoria
12-14 . . . . Clinton
15-17 . . . . at Beloit
18-20 . . . . Kane County
21-23 . . . . at Peoria
24-26 . . . . .Burlington
28-30 . . . . . Cedar Rapids

MAY
1-3 . . . . at Wisconsin
4-6 . . . . . at Kane County
7-9 . . . . Wisconsin
11-14 . . . . .Beloit
16-18 . . . at Cedar Rapids
19-21 . . . . . . at Clinton
22-25 . . . . Peoria
26-28 . . . . Kane County
29-31 . . . at Burlington

JUNE
1 . . . . at Burlington
3-5 . . . . . at West Michigan

JUNE
1 . . . . at Dayton
3-5 . . . . .Burlington
6-8 . . . . Peoria
10-12 . . . at Quad Cities
13-15 . . . at Cedar Rapids
16-18 . . . . Bowling Green
19-21 . . . . Great Lakes
25-28 . . . West Michigan
29-30 . . . . at South Bend

JULY
1 . . . . at South Bend
2-3 . . . . . .at Lake County
4-5 . . . . . Lake County
6-7 . . . . Great Lakes
8-9 . . . . at Great Lakes
10-13 . . . . at Dayton
15-17 . . . . . South Bend
18-20 . . . . at Great Lakes

JUNE
6-8 . . . . . . at South Bend
10-12 . . . . Lansing
13-15 . . . . . Great Lakes
16-18 . . . . . at Clinton
19-21 . . . . .Burlington
25-28 . . . at Cedar Rapids
29-30 . . . . Beloit

JULY
1 . . . . .Beloit
2-3 . . . . Peoria
4-5 . . . . .at Peoria
6-7 . . . . Clinton
8-9 . . . . at Clinton
10-13 . . . . .Burlington
15-17 . . . . . at Wisconsin
18-20 . . . . . Cedar Rapids
21-23 . . . . at Kane County
24-26 . . . . at Burlington
28-30 . . . . at Beloit
31 . . . . Wisconsin

JULY (Peoria continued right)
21-23 . . . . . Bowling Green
24-26 . . . . Dayton
28-30 . . . . .at Lake County
31 . . . . . at Bowling Green

AUGUST
1-2 . . . . . at Bowling Green
4-6 . . . . Wisconsin
7-9 . . . . .Beloit
11-13 . . . . at Clinton
14-16 . . . at Kane County
18-20 . . . . . Lake County
21-23 . . . . . Bowling Green
24-26 . . . . . at Fort Wayne
27-29 . . . at West Michigan
30-31 . . . Fort Wayne

SEPTEMBER
1 . . . . Fort Wayne
2-4 . . . . Great Lakes
5-7 . . . . at Dayton

MINOR LEAGUES

AUGUST
1-2 . . . . Wisconsin
4-6 . . . . . . Bowling Green
7-9 . . . . Dayton
11-13 . . . . . at Fort Wayne
14-16 . . . . at Lake County
18-20 . . . . . . Wisconsin
21-23 . . . . at Kane County
24-26 . . . . Clinton
27-29 . . . . Peoria
30-31 . . . . at Burlington

SEPTEMBER
1 . . . . at Burlington
2-4 . . . . . . Kane County
5-7 . . . . at Beloit

SOUTH BEND CUBS

APRIL
9-11 . . . . . Bowling Green
12-14 . . . . . . at Dayton
15-17 . . . . .at Fort Wayne
18-20 . . . . . Great Lakes
21-23 . . . . Lake County
24-26 . . . . at Fort Wayne
28-30 . . . at West Michigan

MAY
1-3 . . . . Fort Wayne
4-6 . . . . Great Lakes
7-9 . . . . . at Bowling Green
11-14 . . . . Lansing
15-17 . . . . at Great Lakes
18-21 . . . . . .at Lansing
22-25 . . . . Bowling Green
26-28 . . . . . at Dayton
29-31 . . . .at Lake County

JUNE
1 . . . . . . .at Lake County
3-5 . . . . . . Cedar Rapids
6-8 . . . . Quad Cities
10-12 . . . . . at Burlington
13-15 . . . . at Peoria
16-18 . . . . Dayton
19-21 . . . . West Michigan
25-28 . . . .at Lake County
29-30 . . . . . . Lansing

WEST MICHIGAN WHITECAPS

APRIL
9-11 . . . . .Dayton
12-14 . . . . . . Great Lakes
15-17 . . . .at Lake County
18-20 . . . . . Fort Wayne
21-23 . . . . at Great Lakes
24-26 . . . . . at Dayton
28-30 . . . . . . South Bend

MAY
1-3 . . . . Lake County
4-6 . . . . .at Lansing
7-9 . . . . at Dayton
11-14 . . . . Bowling Green
15-17 . . . . Lansing
18-21 . . . at Bowling Green
22-25 . . . . . . .Dayton
26-28 . . . . Lake County
29-31 . . . . .at Fort Wayne

JUNE
1 . . . . .at Fort Wayne
3-5 . . . . Quad Cities
6-8 . . . . Cedar Rapids
10-12 . . . . at Peoria
13-15 . . . . . at Burlington
16-18 . . . . . Fort Wayne
19-21 . . . . at South Bend
25-28 . . . . . . .al Lansing
29-30 . . . . . Lake County

JULY
1 . . . . Lake County
2-3 . . . . . at Great Lakes
4-5 . . . . . Great Lakes
6-7 . . . . . . Lake County
8-9 . . . . . .at Lake County
10-13 . . . . Bowling Green
15-17 . . . . Dayton
18-20 . . . . at South Bend
21-23 . . . . . . at Dayton
24-26 . . . . . South Bend
28-30 . . at Bowling Green
31 . . . . . . at Fort Wayne

AUGUST
1-2 . . . . . .at Fort Wayne
4-6 . . . . Clinton
7-9 . . . . . . Kane County
11-13 . . . . . at Wisconsin
14-16 . . . . at Beloit
18-20 . . . . . Great Lakes
21-23 . . . .at Lake County
24-26 . . . . . South Bend
27-29 . . . . . . Lansing
30-31 . . . . at Great Lakes

SEPTEMBER
1 . . . . at Great Lakes
2-4 . . . . Fort Wayne
5-7 . . . . . . at Great Lakes

WISCONSIN TIMBER RATTLERS

APRIL
9-11 . . . . . . at Burlington
12-14 . . . . Peoria
15-17 . . . . . . .Burlington
18-20 . . . . Peoria
21-23 . . . . Cedar Rapids
24-26 . . . . Peoria
28-30 . . . . . . at Clinton

MAY
1-3 . . . . Quad Cities
4-6 . . . . . . Cedar Rapids
7-9 . . . . . at Quad Cities
11-14 . . . . .Clinton
15-17 . . . . Kane County
18-21 . . . . at Burlington
22-25 . . . at Kane County
26-28 . . at Cedar Rapids
29-31 . . . . Beloit

JUNE
1 . . . . Beloit
3-5 . . . . . . Lake County
6-8 . . . . Fort Wayne
10-12 . . . . . . at Dayton
13-15 . . at Bowling Green
16-18 . . at Kane County
19-21 . . . . . . at Beloit
25-28 . . . . . . .Clinton
29-30 . . . . Cedar Rapids

JULY
1 . . . . Cedar Rapids
2-3 . . . . at Beloit
4-5 . . . . .Beloit
6-7 . . . . . . Kane County
8-9 . . . . . at Kane County
10-13 . . . . . . at Beloit
15-17 . . . . . Quad Cities
18-20 . . . at Kane County
21-23 . . . at Cedar Rapids
24-26 . . . . .Clinton
28-30 . . . . Peoria
31 . . . . . at Quad Cities

AUGUST
1-2 . . . . . . at Quad Cities
4-6 . . . . .at Lansing
7-9 . . . . . at Great Lakes
11-13 . . . . . West Michigan
14-16 . . . . . South Bend
18-20 . . at Quad Cities
21-23 . . . . . . ı at Peoria
24-26 . . . . . .Burlington
27-29 . . . . .Beloit
30-31 . . . . . at Clinton

SEPTEMBER
1 . . . . at Clinton
2-4 . . . . . . Cedar Rapids
5-7 . . . . . . at Burlington

SOUTH ATLANTIC LEAGUE

ASHEVILLE TOURISTS

APRIL
9-12 . . . . at Rome
13-15 . . . . . . at Hickory
16-19 . . . . . Greenville
20-22 . . . . . .Hickory
23-26 . . . . . at Greenville
28-30 . . . . Charleston

MAY
1-4 . . . . Lexington
6-8 . . . . .at Delmarva
9-12 . . . at Lakewood
14-17 . . . . .Rome
18-20 . . . . Kannapolis
21-24 . . . at Augusta
25-27 . . . .at Savannah
28-31 . . . . . . Augusta

JUNE
1-3 . . . . Savannah
4-7 . . . . . . .at Charleston
9-11 . . . . .Rome
12-15 . . . . Charleston
16-18 . . . .at Savannah
19-21 . . . .at Charleston
25-29 . . . . .at Kannapolis

JULY
30 . . . . Charleston
1-3 . . . . Charleston
4-7 . . . . at Lexington
8-12 . . . . Greenville
14-16 . . . . . .at Savannah
17-20 . . . . at Greenville
22-24 . . . . . . .Hickory
25-28 . . . . .Rome
30-31 . . . . . . .at Savannah

AUGUST
1-2 . . . . . .at Savannah
3-5 . . . . . .at Kannapolis
6-9 . . . . . . West Virginia
11-13 . . . at Greenville
14-16 . . . . Augusta
17-19 . . . . Kannapolis
20-23 . . . . at Rome
25-28 . . . . . Savannah
29-31 . . . . .at Charleston

SEPTEMBER
1-2 . . . . . .at Charleston
3-7 . . . . .Greensboro

AUGUSTA GREENJACKETS

APRIL
9-12 . . . . . . at Greenville
13-15 . . . .at Charleston
16-19 . . . . .Rome
20-22 . . . . . Charleston
23-26 . . . . at Rome
28-30 . . . . . .Lakewood

MAY
1-4 . . . . Delmarva
6-8 . . . . . . .at Lakewood
9-12 . . . . . . .at Delmarva
14-17 . . . . . . .Hickory
18-20 . . . . .at Savannah
21-24 . . . . .Asheville
25-27 . . . . . Greenville
28-31 . . . . at Asheville

JUNE
1-3 . . . . . . .at Charleston
4-7 . . . . Lexington
9-11 . . . . . . at Greenville
12-15 . . . . at West Virginia
16-18 . . . . Lexington

BaseballAmerica.com

Baseball America 2015 Directory · **223**

19-21 . . . . Savannah
25-29 . . . . at Rome
30 . . . . .at Savannah

JULY
1-3. . . . . .at Savannah
4-7. . . . . Kannapolis
8-12. . . . . .Rome
14-16 . . . . . at Greenville
17-20 . . . . . . at Hickory
22-24 . . . . . . Greenville
25-28 . . . . Delmarva
30-31 . . . . at Rome

CHARLESTON RIVERDOGS

APRIL
9-12. . . . . . . Lexington
13-15 . . . . Augusta
16-19 . . . . . .at Savannah
20-22 . . . . . at Augusta
23-26 . . . . . . Savannah
28-30 . . . . . at Asheville

MAY
1-4. . . . . .Hickory
6-8. . . . . . . at Lexington
9-12 . . . at West Virginia
14-17 . . . . . . Greenville
18-20 . . . . at Rome
21-24 . . . . . at Greenville
25-27 . . . . .Rome
28-31 . . . . . . Savannah

JUNE
1-3. . . . . Augusta
4-7. . . . . .Asheville
9-11. . . . . . . at Hickory
12-15 . . . . at Asheville
16-18 . . . . . West Virginia
19-21 . . . . .Asheville
25-29 . . . . at Greenville

DELMARVA SHOREBIRDS

APRIL
9-12 . . . . . . .Greensboro
13-15 . . . . . . Kannapolis
16-19 . . . . at Greensboro
20-22 . . . . at Hagerstown
23-26 . . . . . .Greensboro
28-30 . . . . . .at Savannah

MAY
1-4. . . . . . . at Augusta
6-8. . . . . .Asheville
9-12. . . . . Augusta
14-17 . . . . at Greensboro
18-20 . . . . . . Lakewood
21-24 . . . at West Virginia
25-27 . . . . at Hickory
28-31 . . . . . West Virginia

JUNE
1-3. . . . . Lakewood
4-7. . . . . . .at Kannapolis
9-11. . . . . .Hagerstown
12-15 . . . . . Kannapolis
16-18 . . . . at Lakewood
19-21 . . . . at Hagerstown
25-29 . . . . . .Hagerstown

30 . . . . at Asheville

JULY
1-3. . . . . at Asheville
4-7. . . . . .Rome
8-12 . . . . Kannapolis
14-16 . . . . . . at Rome
17-20 . . . . . .at Savannah
22-24 . . . . Delmarva
25-28 . . . . . . Greenville
30-31 . . . . . . .at Delmarva

AUGUST
1-2. . . . . .at Delmarva
3-5. . . . . at Hagerstown
6-9. . . . . Savannah
11-13 . . . . Lexington
14-16 . . . . at Greenville
17-19 . . . . .Rome
20-23 . . . . Augusta
25-28 . . . . . . at Hickory
29-31 . . . . .Asheville

SEPTEMBER
1-2. . . . . .Asheville
3-7. . . . . at Augusta

30 . . . . .Lakewood

JULY
1-3. . . . . Lakewood
4-7. . . . . at West Virginia
8-12 . . . at Hagerstown
14-16 . . . . . . Lexington
17-20 . . . . . . Greensboro
22-24 . . . .at Charleston
25-28 . . . . . at Augusta
30-31 . . . . . . Charleston

AUGUST
1-2. . . . . Charleston
3-5. . . . . .Hickory
6-9. . . . . . at Hagerstown
10-12 . . . at West Virginia
14-16 . . . . . .Lakewood
17-19 . . . . . at Lakewood
20-23 . . . . . . Greenville
25-28 . . . .at Kannapolis
29-31 . . . . .Hickory

SEPTEMBER
1-2. . . . . .Hickory
3-7. . . . . . . at Lakewood

GREENSBORO GRASSHOPPERS

APRIL
9-12 . . . . . . .at Delmarva
13-15 . . . . at Lakewood
16-19 . . . . . . Delmarva
20-22 . . . . Lakewood
23-26 . . . . .at Delmarva
28-30 . . . . . . .Hickory

MAY
1-4. . . . . . . West Virginia
6-8. . . . . . . at Hickory
9-12 . . . . . . at Rome
14-17 . . . . . . Delmarva
18-20 . . . . at Hagerstown
21-24 . . . . at Lakewood
25-27 . . . .Hagerstown
28-31 . . . . . . Lakewood

JUNE
1-3. . . . . at West Virginia
4-7. . . . . . .Hagerstown
9-11. . . .at Kannapolis
12-15 . . . . at Lexington
16-18 . . . . . Greenville
19-21 . . . . . . Kannapolis
25-29 . . . . at West Virginia

30 . . . . . . at Hagerstown

JULY
1-3. . . . . . at Hagerstown
4-7. . . . . .Hickory
8-12 . . . . West Virginia
14-16 . . . . . . at Hickory
17-20 . . . . .at Delmarva
22-24 . . . . . Kannapolis
25-28 . . . . . . Savannah
30-31 . . . . at Kannapolis

AUGUST
1-2. . . . . . . .at Kannapolis
3-5. . . . . .Lakewood
6-9. . . . . Kannapolis
10-12 . . . . at Lakewood
14-16 . . . .at Savannah
17-19 . . . . . . Greenville
20-23 . . . . .Hickory
25-28 . . . . at Greenville
29-31 . . . . .Lakewood

SEPTEMBER
1-2. . . . . .Lakewood
3-7. . . . . at Asheville

GREENVILLE DRIVE

APRIL
9-12 . . . . Augusta
13-15 . . . . Lexington
16-19 . . . at Asheville
20-22 . . . at Lexington
23-26 . . . . . .Asheville
28-30 . . . .at Kannapolis

MAY
1-4. . . . . at Hagerstown
6-8. . . . . Savannah
9-12 . . . . .Hagerstown
14-17 . . . .at Charleston
18-20 . . . . . Lexington
21-24 . . . . . Charleston
25-27 . . . . . at Augusta
28-31 . . . . at Lexington

JUNE
1-3. . . . . Kannapolis
4-7. . . . . . . .at Savannah
9-11. . . . . . . Augusta
12-15 . . . . .Rome
16-18 . . . . . . Greensboro
19-21 . . . . at Lakewood
25-29 . . . . Charleston

30 . . . . at Hickory

JULY
1-3. . . . . at Hickory
4-7. . . . . Savannah
8-12 . . . . . at Asheville
14-16 . . . . . . Augusta
17-20 . . . . . .Asheville
22-24 . . . . . at Augusta
25-28 . . . .at Charleston
30-31 . . . . . . Lexington

AUGUST
1-2. . . . . Lexington
3-5. . . . . at West Virginia
6-9. . . . . at Lexington
11-13 . . . . . .Asheville
14-16 . . . . . Charleston
17-19 . . . . at Greensboro
20-23 . . . .at Delmarva
25-28 . . . .Greensboro
29-31 . . . . . . at Rome

SEPTEMBER
1-2. . . . . at Rome
3-7. . . . . Savannah

HAGERSTOWN SUNS

APRIL
9-12 . . . . . . at Hickory
13-15 . . . at West Virginia
16-19 . . . . . Lakewood
20-22 . . . . . Delmarva
23-26 . . . at Lakewood
28-30 . . . West Virginia

MAY
1-4. . . . . Greenville
6-8. . . . . at Rome
9-12 . . . . at Greenville
14-17 . . . . . West Virginia
18-20 . . . .Greensboro
21-24 . . . . at Lexington
25-27 . . . . at Greensboro
28-31 . . . . . . Kannapolis

JUNE
1-3. . . . . .Hickory
4-7. . . . . . at Greensboro
9-11. . . . . .at Delmarva
12-15 . . . . . Lakewood
15-17 . . . .at Kannapolis
19-21 . . . . . Delmarva
25-29 . . . . .at Delmarva
30 . . . . . . .Greensboro

JULY
1-3. . . . . . . .Greensboro
4-7. . . . . . at Lakewood
8-12 . . . . . . Delmarva
14-16 . . . at West Virginia
17-20 . . . . .at Kannapolis
22-24 . . . . Savannah
25-28 . . . . West Virginia

30-31 at Hickory

AUGUST

1-2 at Hickory
3-5 Charleston
7-9 Delmarva
11-13 at Augusta
14-16 at Kannapolis
17-19 Hickory
20-23 Lexington
25-28 at Lakewood
29-31 Kannapolis

SEPTEMBER

1-2 Kannapolis
3-7 at Lexington

HICKORY CRAWDADS

APRIL

9-12 Hagerstown
13-15 Asheville
16-19 at Kannapolis
20-22 at Asheville
23-26 Kannapolis
28-30 at Greensboro

MAY

1-4 at Charleston
6-8 Greensboro
9-12 Savannah
14-17 at Augusta
18-20 West Virginia
21-24 at Kannapolis
25-27 Delmarva
28-31 Rome

JUNE

1-3 at Hagerstown
4-7 at Lakewood
9-11 Charleston
12-15 Savannah
16-18 at Rome
19-21 at West Virginia
25-29 Lakewood
30 Greenville

JULY

1-3 Greenville
4-7 at Greensboro
8-12 at Lakewood
14-16 Greensboro
17-20 Augusta
22-24 at Asheville
25-28 at Lexington
30-31 Hagerstown

AUGUST

1-2 Hagerstown
3-5 at Delmarva
6-9 at Lakewood
11-13 Kannapolis
14-16 West Virginia
17-19 at Hagerstown
20-23 at Greensboro
25-28 Charleston
29-31 at Delmarva

SEPTEMBER

1-2 at Delmarva
3-7 Rome

KANNAPOLIS INTIMIDATORS

APRIL

9-12 at Lakewood
13-15 at Delmarva
16-19 Hickory
20-22 West Virginia
23-26 at Hickory
28-30 Greenville

MAY

1-4 Rome
6-8 at West Virginia
9-12 at Lexington
14-17 Lakewood
18-20 at Asheville
21-24 Hickory
25-27 Lexington
28-31 at Hagerstown

JUNE

1-3 at Greenville
4-7 Delmarva
9-11 Greensboro
12-15 at Delmarva
16-18 Hagerstown
19-21 at Greensboro
25-29 Asheville
30 West Virginia

JULY

1-3 West Virginia
4-7 at Augusta
8-12 at Charleston
14-16 Lakewood
17-20 Hagerstown
22-24 at Greensboro
25-28 at Lakewood
30-31 Greensboro

AUGUST

1-2 Greensboro
3-5 Asheville
6-9 at Greensboro
11-13 at Hickory
14-16 Hagerstown
17-19 at Asheville
20-23 at Savannah
25-28 Delmarva
29-31 at Hagerstown

SEPTEMBER

1-2 at Hagerstown
3-7 West Virginia

LAKEWOOD BLUECLAWS

APRIL

9-12 Kannapolis
13-15 Greensboro
16-19 at Hagerstown
20-22 at Greensboro
23-26 Hagerstown
28-30 at Augusta

MAY

1-4 at Savannah
6-8 Augusta
9-12 Asheville
14-17 at Kannapolis
18-20 at Delmarva
21-24 Greensboro
25-27 West Virginia
28-31 at Greensboro

JUNE

1-3 at Delmarva
4-7 Hickory
9-11 at Lexington
12-15 at Hagerstown
16-18 Delmarva
19-21 Greenville
25-29 at Hickory
30 at Delmarva

JULY

1-3 at Delmarva
4-7 Hagerstown
8-12 Hickory
14-16 at Kannapolis
17-20 at Rome
22-24 West Virginia
25-28 Kannapolis
30-31 at West Virginia

AUGUST

1-2 at West Virginia
3-5 at Greensboro
6-9 Hickory
10-12 Greensboro
14-16 at Delmarva
17-19 Delmarva
20-23 at West Virginia
25-28 Hagerstown
29-31 at Greensboro

SEPTEMBER

1-2 at Greensboro
3-7 Delmarva

LEXINGTON LEGENDS

APRIL

9-12 at Charleston
13-15 at Greenville
16-19 West Virginia
20-22 Greenville
23-26 at West Virginia
28-30 Rome

MAY

1-4 at Asheville
6-8 Charleston
9-12 Kannapolis
14-17 at Savannah
18-20 at Greenville
21-24 Hagerstown
25-27 at Kannapolis
28-31 Greenville

JUNE

1-3 at Rome
4-7 at Augusta
9-11 Lakewood
12-15 Greensboro
16-18 at Augusta
19-21 Rome
25-29 at Savannah
30 at Rome

JULY

1-3 at Rome
4-7 Asheville
8-12 Savannah
14-16 at Delmarva
17-20 at West Virginia
22-24 Rome
25-28 Hickory
30-31 at Greenville

AUGUST

1-2 at Greenville
3-5 Augusta
6-9 Greenville
11-13 at Charleston
14-16 at Rome
17-19 West Virginia
20-23 at Hagerstown
25-28 Rome
29-31 at West Virginia

SEPTEMBER

1-2 at West Virginia
3-7 Hagerstown

ROME BRAVES

APRIL

9-12 Asheville
13-15 Savannah
16-19 at Augusta
20-22 at Savannah
23-26 Augusta
28-30 at Lexington

MAY

1-4 at Kannapolis
6-8 Hagerstown
9-12 Greensboro
14-17 at Asheville
18-20 Charleston
21-24 Savannah
25-27 at Charleston
28-31 at Hickory

JUNE

1-3 Lexington
4-7 West Virginia
9-11 at Asheville
12-15 at Greenville
16-18 Hickory
19-21 at Lexington
25-29 Augusta
30 Lexington

JULY

1-3 Lexington
4-7 at Charleston
8-12 at Augusta
14-16 Charleston
17-20 Lakewood
22-24 at Lexington
25-28 at Asheville
30-31 Augusta

AUGUST

1-2 Augusta
3-5 Savannah
6-9 at Augusta
11-13 at Savannah
14-16 Lexington
17-19 at Charleston
20-23 Asheville
25-28 at Lexington
29-31 Greenville

SEPTEMBER

1-2 Greenville
3-7 at Hickory

SAVANNAH SAND GNATS

APRIL
9-12 . . . . . at West Virginia
13-15 . . . . at Rome
16-19 . . . . Charleston
20-22 . . . . Rome
23-26 . . . . . at Charleston
28-30 . . . . . . Delmarva

MAY
1-4 . . . . Lakewood
6-8 . . . . at Greenville
9-12 . . . . at Hickory
14-17 . . . . Lexington
18-20 . . . . Augusta
21-24 . . . . . . at Rome
25-27 . . . . Asheville
28-31 . . . . . . Charleston

JUNE
1-3 . . . . at Asheville
4-7 . . . . Greenville
9-11 . . . . at West Virginia
12-15 . . . . . at Hickory
16-18 . . . . Asheville
19-21 . . . . . at Augusta
25-29 . . . . . Lexington

30 . . . . Augusta

JULY
1-3 . . . . Augusta
4-7 . . . . at Greenville
8-12 . . . . . . at Lexington
14-16 . . . . Asheville
17-20 . . . . . . Charleston
22-24 . . . . . at Hagerstown
25-28 . . . . at Greensboro
30-31 . . . . Asheville

AUGUST
1-2 . . . . Asheville
3-5 . . . . at Rome
6-9 . . . . . at Charleston
11-13 . . . . Rome
14-16 . . . . . Greensboro
17-19 . . . . . at Augusta
20-23 . . . . . Kannapolis
25-28 . . . . at Asheville
29-31 . . . . . . Augusta

SEPTEMBER
1-2 . . . . Augusta
3-7 . . . . . at Greenville

WEST VIRGINIA POWER

APRIL
9-12 . . . . Savannah
13-15 . . . . . . .Hagerstown
16-19 . . . . . at Lexington
20-22 . . . . .at Kannapolis
23-26 . . . . . Lexington
28-30 . . . at Hagerstown

MAY
1-4 . . . . . . at Greensboro
6-8 . . . . Kannapolis
9-12 . . . . Charleston
14-17 . . . . at Hagerstown
18-20 . . . . . . at Hickory
21-24 . . . . . Delmarva
25-27 . . . . at Lakewood
28-31 . . . . . at Delmarva

JUNE
1-3 . . . . . . .Greensboro
4-7 . . . . at Rome
9-11 . . . . Savannah
12-15 . . . . Augusta
16-18 . . . . .at Charleston
19-21 . . . . .Hickory
25-29 . . . . . .Greensboro

30 . . . . . . .at Kannapolis

JULY
1-3 . . . . .at Kannapolis
4-7 . . . . Delmarva
8-12 . . . . . . at Greensboro
14-16 . . . . . .Hagerstown
17-20 . . . . . Lexington
22-24 . . . . . at Lakewood
25-28 . . . .at Hagerstown
30-31 . . . . . Lakewood

AUGUST
1-2 . . . . .Lakewood
3-5 . . . . Greenville
6-9 . . . . at Asheville
10-12 . . . . . Delmarva
14-16 . . . . . at Hickory
17-19 . . . . at Lexington
20-23 . . . . Lakewood
25-28 . . . . at Augusta
29-31 . . . . . Lexington

SEPTEMBER
1-2 . . . . Lexington
3-7 . . . . . .at Kannapolis

SHORT SEASON

NEW YORK-PENN LEAGUE

ABERDEEN IRONBIRDS

JUNE
19-21 . . . . Hudson Valley
22-24 . . . . . at Vermont
25-27 . . . . . . .at Lowell
28-30 . . . . .Batavia

JULY
1-3 . . . . Staten Island
4-6 . . . at Mahoning Valley
8-10 . . . . . Staten Island
11-13 . . . . . at Brooklyn
15-17 . . . . Hudson Valley
18-20 . . . . . . Tri-City
21-23 . . . . . State College
24-26 . . . . . Williamsport
28-30 . . . . at Auburn
31 . . . . . at Staten Island

AUGUST
1-2 . . . . . at Staten Island
3-5 . . . . .Connecticut
6-8 . . . . Tri-City
9-11 . . . .at Hudson Valley
12-14 . . . . at West Virginia
15-16 . . . . at Connecticut
19-20 . . . . Staten Island
21-23 . . . . .Brooklyn
24-26 . . . . at Staten Island
27-29 . . . . . at Brooklyn
30-31 . . . . Vermont

SEPTEMBER
1 . . . . Vermont
2-4 . . . . Lowell
5-7 . . . . .at Hudson Valley

AUBURN DOUBLEDAYS

JUNE
19-21 . . . . at Batavia
22-24 . . . . at State College
25-27 . . . . . West Virginia
28-30 . . . . . .Brooklyn

JULY
1-3 . . . . . .at Williamsport
4-6 . . . . State College
8 . . . . at Batavia
9 . . . . Batavia
10 . . . . at Batavia
11-13 . . . . . Staten Island
15-17 . . at Mahoning Valley
18-20 . . . . West Virginia
21-23 . . . . . . at Vermont
24-26 . . . . .at Lowell
28-30 . . . . . . Aberdeen
31 . . . . . . Hudson Valley

AUGUST
1-2 . . . . . . Hudson Valley
3-5 . . . . . at West Virginia
6-8 . . . . Williamsport
9-11 . . . .at Connecticut
12-14 . . . . at Tri-City
15-16 . . . . Batavia
19-20 . . . . at West Virginia
21 . . . . . .at Williamsport
22-23 . . . . . Williamsport
24-26 . .Mahoning Valley
27-29 . . at State College
30 . . . . Williamsport
31 . . . . . .at Williamsport

SEPTEMBER
1 . . . . . . .at Williamsport
2-4 . . . . .Mahoning Valley
5 . . . . at Batavia
6-7 . . . . Batavia

BATAVIA MUCKDOGS

JUNE
19-21 . . . . .Auburn
22-24 . . . .Mahoning Valley
25-27 . . . .at Williamsport
28-30 . . . . . at Aberdeen

JULY
1-3 . . . . .Mahoning Valley
4-6 . . . . . at West Virginia
8 . . . . .Auburn
9 . . . . at Auburn
10 . . . . .Auburn
11-13 . . . .at Hudson Valley
15-16 . . . . . Williamsport
17 . . . . . .at Williamsport
18-20 . . . . at State College
21-23 . . . . . . .Connecticut
24-26 . . . . Tri-City
28-30 . . . . at Staten Island

31 . . . . at Brooklyn

AUGUST
1-2 . . . . at Brooklyn
3-5 . . . . State College
6-8 . . . at Mahoning Valley
9-11 . . . . Vermont
12-14 . . . . Lowell
15-16 . . . . at Auburn
19-20 . at Mahoning Valley
21-23 . . . . State College
24-26 . . . at West Virginia
27-29 . . . . . Williamsport
30-31 . . . West Virginia

SEPTEMBER
1 . . . . West Virginia
2-4 . . . . . at State College
5 . . . . .Auburn
6-7 . . . . at Auburn

BROOKLYN CYCLONES

JUNE
19 . . . . . at Staten Island
20 . . . . Staten Island
21 . . . . . at Staten Island
22-24 . . . . Tri-City
25-27 . . . . .Connecticut
28-30 . . . . . . at Auburn

JULY
1 . . . .at Hudson Valley
2 . . . . . . Hudson Valley
3 . . . .at Hudson Valley
4-6 . . . . . . Williamsport
8 . . .at Hudson Valley
9 . . . . . Hudson Valley
10 . . . .at Hudson Valley
11-13 . . . . . . Aberdeen
15 . . . . at Staten Island
16 . . . . . Staten Island
17 . . . . at Staten Island
18-20 . . . . Vermont

21-23 . . . . at West Virginia
24-26 . . at Mahoning Valley
28 . . . . . .at Hudson Valley
29 . . . . . . Hudson Valley
30 . . . . . .at Hudson Valley
31 . . . . Batavia

AUGUST
1-2 . . . . Batavia
3-5 . . . . .at Lowell
6-8 . . . . at Vermont
9-10 . . . . at Staten Island
11 . . . . . . Staten Island
12-14 . . . . . State College
15 . . . .at Hudson Valley
16 . . . . . Hudson Valley
19-20 . . . . Lowell
21-23 . . . . . at Aberdeen
24 . . . . . . Hudson Valley
25 . . .at Hudson Valley
26 . . . . . Hudson Valley

27-29 . . . . Aberdeen
30-31 . . . . at Tri-City

SEPTEMBER
1 . . . . at Tri-City
2-4 . . . . . . at Connecticut
5-7 . . . . Staten Island

CONNECTICUT TIGERS

JUNE	
19-21 . . . . Tri-City	
22-24 . . . . . Staten Island	
25-27 . . . . . at Brooklyn	
28-30 . . . . Tri-City	

JULY	
1 . . . . Lowell	
2 . . . . at Lowell	
3 . . . . Lowell	
4-6 . . . . Vermont	
8-10 . . . . at State College	
11-13 . . . . at Williamsport	
15 . . . . at Lowell	
16 . . . . at Lowell	
17 . . . . at Lowell	
18-20 . . . . . Hudson Valley	
21-23 . . . . at Batavia	
24-26 . . . . . . at Vermont	

28-30 . . . . Mahoning Valley
31 . . . . West Virginia

AUGUST
1-2 . . . . West Virginia
3-5 . . . . at Aberdeen
6-8 . . . . at Lowell
9-11 . . . . Auburn
12-14 . . . . . at Vermont
15-16 . . . . . . Aberdeen
19-20 . . at Hudson Valley
21-23 . . . . Vermont
24-26 . . . . . . at Tri-City
27-29 . . . . Lowell
30-31 . . . at Staten Island

SEPTEMBER
1 . . . . at Staten Island
2-4 . . . . Brooklyn
5-7 . . . . at Tri-City

HUDSON VALLEY RENEGADES

JUNE	
19-21 . . . . . at Aberdeen	
22-24 . . . . Lowell	
25-27 . . . . Vermont	
28-30 . . . at West Virginia	

JULY	
1 . . . . Brooklyn	
2 . . . . at Brooklyn	
3 . . . . Brooklyn	
4-6 . . . . at Staten Island	
8 . . . . Brooklyn	
9 . . . . at Brooklyn	
10 . . . . Brooklyn	
11-13 . . . . Batavia	
15-17 . . . . . at Aberdeen	
18-20 . . . at Connecticut	
21-23 . . . . Williamsport	
24-26 . . . State College	
28 . . . . Brooklyn	
29 . . . . . . at Brooklyn	
30 . . . . Brooklyn	
31 . . . . at Auburn	

AUGUST
1-2 . . . . at Auburn
3-5 . . . . Tri-City
6 . . . . . . at Staten Island
7 . . . . Staten Island
8 . . . . . . at Staten Island
9-11 . . . . Aberdeen
12-14 . . at Mahoning Valley
15 . . . . Brooklyn
16 . . . . at Brooklyn
19-20 . . . . . Connecticut
21-22 . . . . . . at Tri-City
23 . . . . Tri-City
24 . . . . . at Brooklyn
25 . . . . Brooklyn
26 . . . . . . at Brooklyn
27 . . . . . . Staten Island
28 . . . . at Staten Island
29 . . . . . Staten Island
30-31 . . . . at Lowell

SEPTEMBER
1 . . . . at Lowell
2-4 . . . . at Vermont
5-7 . . . . Aberdeen

LOWELL SPINNERS

JUNE	
19-21 . . . . . . at Vermont	
22-24 . . . at Hudson Valley	
25-27 . . . . . Aberdeen	
28-30 . . . . . . at Vermont	

JULY	
1 . . . . . . at Connecticut	
2 . . . . Connecticut	
3 . . . . . . at Connecticut	
4-6 . . . . . . at Tri-City	
8-10 . . . . . West Virginia	
11-13 . . Mahoning Valley	
15 . . . . Connecticut	
16 . . . . . . Connecticut	
17 . . . . Connecticut	
18-20 . . at Staten Island	
21-23 . . . . . . Tri-City	
24-26 . . . . Auburn	

28-30 . . . . at Williamsport
31 . . . . . at State College

AUGUST
1-2 . . . . at State College
3-5 . . . . Brooklyn
6-8 . . . . . . Connecticut
9-11 . . . . . . at Tri-City
12-14 . . . . . . at Batavia
15-16 . . . . Tri-City
19-20 . . . . at Brooklyn
21-23 . . . . . Staten Island
24-26 . . . . Vermont
27-29 . . . at Connecticut
30-31 . . . . . Hudson Valley

SEPTEMBER
1 . . . . Hudson Valley
2-4 . . . . at Aberdeen
5-7 . . . . Vermont

MAHONING VALLEY SCRAPPERS

JUNE	AUGUST
19-21 . . . at West Virginia	1-2 . . . . at Tri-City
22-24 . . . . . . at Batavia	3-5 . . . . Williamsport
25-27 . . . . . State College	6-8 . . . . Batavia
28-30 . . . . . Williamsport	9-11 . . . . at State College
JULY	12-14 . . . . Hudson Valley
1-3 . . . . at Batavia	15-16 . . . . at Williamsport
4-6 . . . . Aberdeen	19-20 . . . . Batavia
8-10 . . . . . . at Vermont	21-23 . . . . West Virginia
11-13 . . . . at Lowell	24-26 . . . . . . at Auburn
15-17 . . . . Auburn	27-29 . . . at West Virginia
18-20 . . . at Williamsport	30-31 . . . . State College
21-23 . . . . Staten Island	**SEPTEMBER**
24-26 . . . . Brooklyn	1 . . . . State College
28-30 . . . at Connecticut	2-4 . . . . at Auburn
31 . . . . at Tri-City	5-7 . . . . . West Virginia

STATE COLLEGE SPIKES

JUNE	AUGUST
19 . . . . Williamsport	1-2 . . . . Lowell
20 . . . . . at Williamsport	3-5 . . . . at Batavia
21 . . . . . Williamsport	6-8 . . . . . at West Virginia
22-24 . . . . Auburn	9-11 . . . . Mahoning Valley
25-27 . . at Mahoning Valley	12-14 . . . . . at Brooklyn
28-30 . . . . at Staten Island	15-16 . . . . . West Virginia
JULY	19-20 . . . . . Williamsport
1-3 . . . . West Virginia	21-23 . . . . . . at Batavia
4-6 . . . . at Auburn	24-26 . . . . at Williamsport
8-10 . . . . Connecticut	27-29 . . . . Auburn
11-13 . . . . Tri-City	30-31 . . at Mahoning Valley
15-17 . . at West Virginia	**SEPTEMBER**
18-20 . . . . Batavia	1 . . . . at Mahoning Valley
21-23 . . . . at Aberdeen	2-4 . . . . Batavia
24-26 . . . at Hudson Valley	5-6 . . . . . . Williamsport
28-30 . . . . . Vermont	7 . . . . . . at Williamsport
31 . . . . Lowell	

STATEN ISLAND YANKEES

JUNE	AUGUST
19 . . . . Brooklyn	1-2 . . . . Aberdeen
20 . . . . . . at Brooklyn	3-5 . . . . at Vermont
21 . . . . Brooklyn	6 . . . . . . Hudson Valley
22-24 . . at Connecticut	7 . . . . at Hudson Valley
25-27 . . . . . at Tri-City	8 . . . . . at Hudson Valley
28-30 . . . . . State College	9-10 . . . . . . Brooklyn
JULY	11 . . . . . . at Brooklyn
1-3 . . . . . . at Aberdeen	12-14 . . . . . Williamsport
4-6 . . . . . Hudson Valley	15-16 . . . . . Vermont
8-10 . . . . . at Aberdeen	19-20 . . . at Aberdeen
11-13 . . . . . at Auburn	21-23 . . . . at Lowell
15 . . . . Brooklyn	24-26 . . . . . Aberdeen
16 . . . . . . at Brooklyn	27 . . . at Hudson Valley
17 . . . . Brooklyn	28 . . . . Hudson Valley
18-20 . . . . Lowell	29 . . . at Hudson Valley
21-23 . . at Mahoning Valley	30-31 . . . . . . Connecticut
24-26 . . . at West Virginia	**SEPTEMBER**
28-30 . . . . . . Batavia	1 . . . . Connecticut
31 . . . . Aberdeen	2-4 . . . . Tri-City
	5-7 . . . . at Brooklyn

TRI-CITY VALLEYCATS

JUNE	
19-21 . . . at Connecticut	4-6 . . . . Lowell
22-24 . . . . . at Brooklyn	8-10 . . . . at Williamsport
25-27 . . . . . Staten Island	11-13 . . . at State College
28-30 . . . at Connecticut	15-17 . . . . . Vermont
JULY	18-20 . . . . . Aberdeen
1-3 . . . . Vermont	21-23 . . . . . . at Lowell
	24-26 . . . . . . at Batavia

28-30 . . . . . . West Virginia	21-22 . . . . . Hudson Valley
31 . . . . . .Mahoning Valley	23 . . . . . .at Hudson Valley
AUGUST	24-26 . . . . . . .Connecticut
1-2. . . . .Mahoning Valley	27-29 . . . . at Vermont
3-5. . . . .at Hudson Valley	30-31 . . . . .Brooklyn
6-8. . . . . . . at Aberdeen	**SEPTEMBER**
9-11 . . . . Lowell	1 . . . . .Brooklyn
12-14 . . . . Auburn	2-4 . . . . . at Staten Island
15-16 . . . . .at Lowell	5-7 . . . . .Connecticut
19-20 . . . . . . at Vermont	

VERMONT LAKE MONSTERS

JUNE	**AUGUST**
19-21 . . . . Lowell	1-2. . . . . .at Williamsport
22-24 . . . . Aberdeen	3-5. . . . . Staten Island
25-27 . . .at Hudson Valley	6-8. . . . . .Brooklyn
28-30 . . . . . Lowell	9-11 . . . . at Batavia
JULY	12-14 . . . . . . .Connecticut
1-3. . . . . . . at Tri-City	15-16 . . . . at Staten Island
4-6. . . . . at Connecticut	19-20 . . . . Tri-City
8-10 . . .Mahoning Valley	21-23 . . .at Connecticut
11-13 . . . . . West Virginia	24-26 . . . . .at Lowell
15-17 . . . . . . at Tri-City	27-29 . . . . Tri-City
18-20 . . . . . at Brooklyn	30-31 . . . . . at Aberdeen
21-23 . . . . .Auburn	**SEPTEMBER**
24-26 . . . . . . .Connecticut	1 . . . . at Aberdeen
28-30 . . at State College	2-4 . . . . . Hudson Valley
31 . . . . . .at Williamsport	5-7 . . . . .at Lowell

WEST VIRGINIA BLACK BEARS

JUNE	**AUGUST**
19-21 . . .Mahoning Valley	1-2. . . . . .at Connecticut
22-24 . . . .at Williamsport	3-5. . . . . .Auburn
25-27 . . . . at Auburn	6-8. . . . . . . State College
28-30 . . . . . Hudson Valley	9-11 . . . .at Williamsport
JULY	12-14 . . . . Aberdeen
1-3. . . . . at State College	15-16 . . . at State College
4-6. . . . . Batavia	19-20 . . . . .Auburn
8-10 . . . . .at Lowell	21-23 . . at Mahoning Valley
11-13 . . . . . . at Vermont	24-26 . . . . Batavia
15-17 . . . . . State College	27-29 . . .Mahoning Valley
18-20 . . . . . at Auburn	30-31 . . . . . . at Batavia
21-23 . . . . .Brooklyn	**SEPTEMBER**
24-26 . . . . . Staten Island	1 . . . . at Batavia
28-30 . . . . at Tri-City	2-4 . . . . Williamsport
31 . . . . . . at Connecticut	5-7 . . . at Mahoning Valley

WILLIAMSPORT CROSSCUTTERS

JUNE	**AUGUST**
19 . . . . . at State College	1-2. . . . . Vermont
20 . . . . State College	3-5. . . at Mahoning Valley
21 . . . . . at State College	6-8. . . . . .at Auburn
22-24 . . . . . West Virginia	9-11 . . . . . West Virginia
25-27 . . . . Batavia	12-14 . . . . at Staten Island
28-30 . . at Mahoning Valley	15-16 . . .Mahoning Valley
JULY	19-20 . . . at State College
1-3. . . . . .Auburn	21 . . . . .Auburn
4-6. . . . . . . at Brooklyn	22-23 . . . . at Auburn
8-10 . . . . Tri-City	24-26 . . . . . State College
11-13 . . . . .Connecticut	27-29 . . . . at Batavia
15-16 . . . . at Batavia	30 . . . . .at Auburn
17 . . . . Batavia	31 . . . . .Auburn
18-20 . . .Mahoning Valley	**SEPTEMBER**
21-23 . . .at Hudson Valley	1 . . . . .Auburn
24-26 . . . . . at Aberdeen	2-4 . . . . . at West Virginia
28-30 . . . . . Lowell	5-6. . . . . at State College
31 . . . . Vermont	7 . . . . State College

NORTHWEST LEAGUE

BOISE HAWKS

JUNE	**AUGUST**
18-22 . . . . Tri-City	1-2. . . . . .Vancouver
23-25 . . . . at Eugene	6-8. . . . . at Hillsboro
26-30 . . . . . at Everett	9-11 . . . . .Eugene
JULY	12-16 . . . . at Tri-City
1-3. . . . . . . Salem-Keizer	17-19 . . . . .Eugene
4-8. . . . . at Spokane	20-22 . . . . . at Hillsboro
9-13 . . . . Everett	23-27 . . . . .at Vancouver
15-17 . . . at Salem-Keizer	28-30 . . . . at Salem-Keizer
18-22 . . . . Spokane	**SEPTEMBER**
23-25 . . . . .Hillsboro	1-3. . . . . .Hillsboro
26-28 . . . . . . at Eugene	4-6. . . . . . . Salem-Keizer
29-31 . . . . . .Vancouver	

EUGENE EMERALDS

JUNE	**AUGUST**
18-22 . . . . at Everett	1-2. . . . . at Spokane
23-25 . . . . Boise	6-8. . . . . . . Salem-Keizer
26-30 . . . . Tri-City	9-11 . . . . at Boise
JULY	12-16 . . . . Everett
1-3. . . . . at Hillsboro	17-19 . . . . at Boise
4-8. . . . . . . .Vancouver	20-22 . . . at Salem-Keizer
9-13 . . . . at Tri-City	23-27 . . . . Spokane
15-17 . . . . .Hillsboro	28-30 . . . . .Hillsboro
18-22 . . . . . at Vancouver	**SEPTEMBER**
23-25 . . . . . Salem-Keizer	1-3. . . . . at Salem-Keizer
26-28 . . . . Boise	4-6. . . . . at Hillsboro
29-31 . . . . . . at Spokane	

EVERETT AQUASOX

JUNE	**AUGUST**
18-22 . . . . .Eugene	1-2. . . . . at Salem-Keizer
23-25 . . . . . . at Spokane	6-8. . . . . Tri-City
26-30 . . . . Boise	9-11 . . . . at Vancouver
JULY	12-16 . . . . . . at Eugene
1-3. . . . . at Tri-City	17-19 . . . . Spokane
4-8. . . . . .Hillsboro	20-22 . . . . . . at Tri-City
9-13 . . . . at Boise	23-27 . . . . . Salem-Keizer
15-17 . . . . . . .Vancouver	28-30 . . . . Tri-City
18-22 . . . . . at Hillsboro	**SEPTEMBER**
23-25 . . . . Spokane	1-3. . . . . at Vancouver
26-28 . . . . . . .Vancouver	4-6. . . . . at Vancouver
29-31 . . . . at Salem-Keizer	

HILLSBORO HOPS

JUNE	**AUGUST**
18-22 . . . . . . at Spokane	1-2. . . . . at Tri-City
23-25 . . . . . Salem-Keizer	6-8. . . . . Boise
26-30 . . . . . at Vancouver	9-11 . . . . at Salem-Keizer
JULY	12-16 . . . . . . .Vancouver
1-3. . . . . .Eugene	17-19 . . . at Salem-Keizer
4-8. . . . . at Everett	20-22 . . . . Boise
9-13 . . . . Spokane	23-27 . . . . Tri-City
15-17 . . . . . . at Eugene	28-30 . . . . . . .at Eugene
18-22 . . . . Everett	**SEPTEMBER**
23-25 . . . . . . at Boise	1-3. . . . . at Boise
26-28 . . . . Salem-Keizer	4-6. . . . . .Eugene
29-31 . . . . at Tri-City	

SALEM-KEIZER VOLCANOES

JUNE	
18-22	Vancouver
23-25	at Hillsboro
26-30	Spokane

JULY	
1-3	at Boise
4-8	Tri-City
9-13	at Vancouver
15-17	Boise
18-22	at Tri-City
23-25	at Eugene
26-28	at Hillsboro
29-31	Everett

AUGUST	
1-2	Everett
6-8	at Eugene
9-11	Hillsboro
12-16	at Spokane
17-19	Hillsboro
20-22	Eugene
23-27	at Everett
28-30	Boise

SEPTEMBER	
1-3	Eugene
4-6	at Boise

SPOKANE INDIANS

JUNE	
18-22	Hillsboro
23-25	Everett
26-30	at Salem-Keizer

JULY	
1-3	at Vancouver
4-8	Boise
9-13	at Hillsboro
15-17	Tri-City
18-22	at Boise
23-25	at Everett
26-28	at Tri-City
29-31	Eugene

AUGUST	
1-2	Eugene
6-8	at Vancouver
9-11	Tri-City
12-16	Salem-Keizer
17-19	at Everett
20-22	Vancouver
23-27	at Eugene
28-30	Vancouver

SEPTEMBER	
1-3	Everett
4-6	at Tri-City

TRI-CITY DUST DEVILS

JUNE	
18-22	at Boise
23-25	Vancouver
26-30	at Eugene

JULY	
1-3	Everett
4-8	at Salem-Keizer
9-13	Eugene
15-17	at Spokane
18-22	Salem-Keizer
23-25	at Vancouver
26-28	Spokane
29-31	Hillsboro

AUGUST	
1-2	Hillsboro
6-8	at Everett
9-11	at Spokane
12-16	Boise
17-19	at Vancouver
20-22	Everett
23-27	at Hillsboro
28-30	at Everett

SEPTEMBER	
1-3	Vancouver
4-6	Spokane

VANCOUVER CANADIANS

JUNE	
18-22	at Salem-Keizer
23-25	at Tri-City
26-30	Hillsboro

JULY	
1-3	Spokane
4-8	at Eugene
9-13	Salem-Keizer
15-17	at Everett
18-22	Eugene
23-25	Tri-City
26-28	at Everett
29-31	at Boise

AUGUST	
1-2	at Boise
6-8	Spokane
9-11	Everett
12-16	at Hillsboro
17-19	Tri-City
20-22	at Spokane
23-27	Boise
28-30	at Spokane

SEPTEMBER	
1-3	at Tri-City
4-6	Everett

ROOKIE

APPALACHIAN LEAGUE

BLUEFIELD BLUE JAYS

JUNE	
23-25	Elizabethton
26-28	at Kingsport
29-30	at Burlington

JULY	
1	at Burlington
2-3	Pulaski
4	at Pulaski
5-7	Burlington
8-10	at Danville
11-13	Princeton
15-16	at Bristol
17	Bristol
18-20	Johnson City
21-23	at Greeneville
24-26	Danville
27	at Princeton
28-29	Princeton
30	at Princeton

31	at Johnson City

AUGUST	
1-2	at Johnson City
4-6	Greeneville
7-9	at Elizabethton
10	Pulaski
11-12	at Pulaski
13	Princeton
14-15	at Princeton
16-17	Bristol
18	at Bristol
20-22	Kingsport
23-25	at Pulaski
26	Princeton
27-29	at Danville
30-31	Burlington

SEPTEMBER	
1	Burlington

BRISTOL PIRATES

JUNE	
23-24	Greeneville
25	at Greeneville
26-28	Princeton
29-30	at Elizabethton

JULY	
1	at Elizabethton
2	Johnson City
3	at Johnson City
4	Johnson City

5-6	at Johnson City
7	Johnson City
8-10	Burlington
11	at Kingsport
12-13	Kingsport
15-16	Bluefield
17	at Bluefield
18-20	at Danville
21-23	at Burlington
24-27	at Pulaski
28-30	Greeneville

31	Danville

AUGUST	
1-2	Danville
4	at Kingsport
5	Kingsport
6	at Kingsport
7-8	at Greeneville
9	Greeneville
10-12	at Johnson City

SEPTEMBER	
1	at Elizabethton

BURLINGTON ROYALS

JUNE	
23-25	at Princeton
26-28	at Johnson City
29-30	Bluefield

JULY	
1	Bluefield
2-4	Kingsport
5-7	at Bluefield
8-10	at Bristol
11-13	Danville
15-17	at Pulaski
18-20	Elizabethton
21-23	Bristol
24-26	at Greeneville
27-28	at Danville
29-30	Danville

31	at Elizabethton

AUGUST	
1-2	at Elizabethton
4-6	Pulaski
7-9	Princeton
10-12	at Kingsport
13	Danville
14-15	at Danville
16-18	Pulaski
20-22	Johnson City
23-25	at Princeton
26	Danville
27-29	Greeneville
30-31	at Bluefield

SEPTEMBER	
1	at Bluefield

DANVILLE BRAVES

JUNE	
23-25	at Pulaski
26-28	at Greeneville
29-30	Kingsport

JULY	
1	Kingsport
2-3	Princeton
4	at Princeton
5-7	at Pulaski

8-10 . . . . .Bluefield	10 . . . . Princeton
11-13 . . . . . at Burlington	11-12 . . . . . .at Princeton
15-17 . . . . . Elizabethton	13 . . . . at Burlington
18-20 . . . . Bristol	14-15 . . . . . .Burlington
21-23 . . . . at Johnson City	16-18 . . . .at Elizabethton
24-26 . . . . . . at Bluefield	20-22 . . . . . . Greeneville
27-28 . . . . . .Burlington	23-25 . . . . . Johnson City
29-30 . . . . . at Burlington	26 . . . . at Burlington
31 . . . . .at Bristol	27-29 . . . . .Bluefield
AUGUST	30-31 . . . . . at Kingsport
1-2 . . . . .at Bristol	**SEPTEMBER**
4-6 . . . . Princeton	1 . . . . at Kingsport
7-9 . . . . Pulaski	

ELIZABETHTON TWINS

JUNE	**AUGUST**
23-25 . . . . at Bluefield	1-2 . . . . .Burlington
26-28 . . . . Pulaski	3-4 . . . . . at Johnson City
29-30 . . . . Bristol	6 . . . . . . at Johnson City
JULY	7-9 . . . . .Bluefield
1 . . . . Bristol	10 . . . . Greeneville
2 . . . . .at Greeneville	11 . . . . . . .at Greeneville
3 . . . . Greeneville	12 . . . . Greeneville
4 . . . . .at Greeneville	13-15 . . . . at Bristol
5-7 . . . . .at Princeton	16-18 . . . . Danville
8-10 . . . . . . at Kingsport	20-22 . . . . . . at Pulaski
11-13 . . . . .Johnston City	23-25 . . . .at Greeneville
15-17 . . . .at Danville	26 . . . . . at Johnson City
18-20 . . . . . at Burlington	27-29 . . . . Kingsport
21-23 . . . . Princeton	30-31 . . . . Bristol
24-26 . . . . . at Kingsport	**SEPTEMBER**
27-30 . . . . . Johnson City	1 . . . . Bristol
31 . . . . .Burlington	

GREENEVILLE ASTROS

JUNE	31 . . . . Kingsport
23-24 . . . . .at Bristol	**AUGUST**
25 . . . . Bristol	1 . . . . at Kingsport
26-28 . . . . Danville	2 . . . . Kingsport
29-30 . . . . . .at Princeton	4-6 . . . . . . at Bluefield
JULY	7-8 . . . . Bristol
1 . . . . .at Princeton	9 . . . . .at Bristol
2 . . . . Elizabethton	10 . . . .at Elizabethton
3 . . . .at Elizabethton	11 . . . . Elizabethton
4 . . . . Elizabethton	12 . . . . . .at Elizabethton
5-7 . . . . . . at Kingsport	13-15 . . . . at Pulaski
8-10 . . . . at Johnson City	16-18 . . . . . Johnson City
11-13 . . . . Pulaski	20-22 . . . . . .at Danville
15-17 . . . at Johnson City	23-25 . . . . . Elizabethton
18-20 . . . . . . Kingsport	26 . . . . Kingsport
21-23 . . . . .Bluefield	27-29 . . . . at Burlington
24-26 . . . . . .Burlington	30-31 . . . . Princeton
27 . . . . Kingsport	**SEPTEMBER**
28-30 . . . . .at Bristol	1 . . . . Princeton

JOHNSON CITY CARDINALS

JUNE	18-20 . . . . . . at Bluefield
23-24 . . . . . at Kingsport	21-23 . . . . Danville
25 . . . . Kingsport	24-26 . . . . . .at Princeton
26-28 . . . . . .Burlington	27-30 . . . .at Elizabethton
29-30 . . . . . . at Pulaski	31 . . . . .Bluefield
JULY	**AUGUST**
1-2 . . . . at Pulaski	1-2 . . . . .Bluefield
3 . . . . Bristol	3-4 . . . . Elizabethton
4 . . . . .at Bristol	6 . . . . Elizabethton
5-6 . . . . Bristol	7-9 . . . . at Kingsport
7 . . . . .at Bristol	10-12 . . . . Bristol
8-10 . . . . Greeneville	13 . . . . Kingsport
11-13 . . . .at Elizabethton	14 . . . . at Kingsport
15-17 . . . . . Greeneville	15 . . . . Kingsport

KINGSPORT METS

JUNE	**AUGUST**
23-24 . . . . . Johnson City	1 . . . . Greeneville
25 . . at Johnson City 26-28	2 . . . . .at Greeneville
Bluefield	4 . . . . Bristol
29-30 . . . . . . .at Danville	5 . . . . .at Bristol
JULY	6 . . . . Bristol
1 . . . . .at Danville	7-9 . . . . . . Johnson City
2-4 . . . . at Burlington	10-12 . . . . . . .Burlington
5-7 . . . . Greeneville	13 . . . . . at Johnson City
8-10 . . . . Elizabethton	14 . . . . Johnson City
11 . . . . Bristol	15 . . . . . at Johnson City
12-13 . . . . . . .at Bristol	16-18 . . . . Princeton
15-17 . . . .at Princeton	20-22 . . . . . at Bluefield
18-20 . . . .at Greeneville	23-25 . . . . .at Bristol
21-23 . . . . Pulaski	26-29 . . . .at Elizabethton
24-26 . . . . . Elizabethton	30-31 . . . . Danville
27 . . . . . . .at Greeneville	**SEPTEMBER**
28-30 . . . . . at Pulaski	1 . . . . Danville
31 . . . . at Greeneville	

PRINCETON RAYS

JUNE	30 . . . . .Bluefield
23-25 . . . . . .Burlington	31 . . . . Pulaski
26-28 . . . . .at Bristol	**AUGUST**
29-30 . . . . . Greeneville	1-2 . . . . at Pulaski
JULY	4-6 . . . . .at Danville
1 . . . . Greeneville	7-9 . . . . . . at Burlington
2-3 . . . . .at Danville	10 . . . . .at Danville
4 . . . . Danville	11-12 . . . . Danville
5-7 . . . . Elizabethton	13 . . . . at Bluefield
8-9 . . . . Pulaski	14-15 . . . . . . .Bluefield
10 . . . . at Pulaski	16-18 . . . . at Kingsport
11-13 . . . . . at Bluefield	20-22 . . . . Bristol
15-17 . . . . . Kingsport	23-25 . . . . .Burlington
18-20 . . . . Pulaski	26 . . . . at Bluefield
21-23 . . . .at Elizabethton	27-29 . . . . at Johnson City
24-26 . . . . . Johnson City	30-31 . . . . .at Greeneville
27 . . . . .Bluefield	**SEPTEMBER**
28-29 . . . . . at Bluefield	1 . . . . .at Greeneville

PULASKI YANKEES

JUNE	28-30 . . . . Kingsport
23-25 . . . . Danville	31 . . . . .at Princeton
25-28 . . . .at Elizabethton	**AUGUST**
29-30 . . . . . Johnson City	1-2 . . . . Princeton
JULY	4-6 . . . . at Burlington
1 . . . . Johnson City	7-9 . . . . .at Danville
2-3 . . . . at Bluefield	10 . . . . at Bluefield
4 . . . . .Bluefield	11-12 . . . . . . .Bluefield
5-7 . . . . Danville	13-15 . . . . . . Greeneville
8-9 . . . .at Princeton	16-18 . . . . at Burlington
10 . . . . Princeton	20-22 . . . . . Elizabethton
11-13 . . . .at Greeneville	23-25 . . . . .Bluefield
15-17 . . . . . .Burlington	26-29 . . . . . . .at Bristol
18-20 . . . . . .at Princeton	30-31 . . . . at Johnson City
21-23 . . . . . at Kingsport	**SEPTEMBER**
24-27 . . . . Bristol	1 . . . . at Johnson City

PIONEER LEAGUE

BILLINGS MUSTANGS

JUNE	
18-19	Great Falls
20-23	Missoula
24-25	at Great Falls
26-29	at Missoula
30	at Helena

JULY	
1	at Helena
2-5	Helena
7-10	at Orem
11-13	at Grand Junction
15-17	Orem
18-21	Grand Junction
22-23	at Great Falls
24-25	at Helena

26-29	Great Falls
30-31	at Missoula

AUGUST	
1-2	at Missoula
6-9	Ogden
10-12	Idaho Falls
14-16	at Ogden
17-20	at Idaho Falls
21-24	Missoula
25-28	at Great Falls
29-31	at Helena

SEPTEMBER	
1	at Helena
3-6	Helena
7-8	Great Falls

GRAND JUNCTION ROCKIES

JUNE	
18-21	at Idaho Falls
22-25	Orem
26-29	Idaho Falls
30	at Orem

JULY	
1-3	at Orem
4-6	at Ogden
7-10	Helena
11-13	Billings
15-17	at Helena
18-21	at Billings
23-26	Ogden
27-29	at Ogden

30-31	at Orem

AUGUST	
1-2	Orem
6-9	Missoula
10-12	Great Falls
14-16	at Missoula
17-20	at Great Falls
22-25	Idaho Falls
26-27	Orem
28-31	at Idaho Falls

SEPTEMBER	
1-2	at Orem
3-4	at Ogden
5-8	Ogden

GREAT FALLS VOYAGERS

JUNE	
18-19	at Billings
20	Helena
21-23	at Helena
24-25	Billings
26-28	Helena
29	at Helena
30	Missoula

JULY	
1	Missoula
2-3	at Missoula
4-5	Missoula
7-9	Idaho Falls
10-13	Ogden
15-17	at Ogden
18-21	at Idaho Falls
22-23	Billings

24-25	at Missoula
26-29	at Billings
30-31	Helena

AUGUST	
1-2	Helena
6-9	at Orem
10-12	at Grand Junction
14-16	Orem
17-20	Grand Junction
21-24	at Helena
25-28	Billings
29-30	Missoula

SEPTEMBER	
1-4	at Missoula
5-6	Missoula
7-8	at Billings

HELENA BREWERS

JUNE	
18-19	Missoula
20	at Great Falls
21-23	Great Falls
24-25	at Missoula
26-28	at Great Falls
29	Great Falls
30	Billings

JULY	
1	Billings
2-5	at Billings
7-10	at Grand Junction

11-13	at Orem
15-17	Grand Junction
18-21	Orem
22-23	at Missoula
24-25	Billings
26-27	Missoula
28-29	at Missoula
30-31	at Great Falls

AUGUST	
1-2	at Great Falls
6-9	Idaho Falls
10-12	Ogden
14-16	at Idaho Falls

17-20	at Ogden
21-24	Great Falls
25-26	at Missoula
27-28	Missoula
29-31	Billings

SEPTEMBER	
1	Billings
3-6	at Billings
7-8	Missoula

IDAHO FALLS CHUKARS

JUNE	
18-21	Grand Junction
22-25	at Ogden
26-29	at Grand Junction
30	Ogden

JULY	
1-3	Ogden
4-6	Orem
7-9	at Great Falls
10-13	at Missoula
15-17	Missoula
18-21	Great Falls
23-26	at Orem
27-29	Orem
30-31	Ogden

AUGUST	
1-2	at Ogden
6-9	at Helena
10-12	at Billings
14-16	Helena
17-20	Billings
22-25	at Grand Junction
26-27	at Ogden
28-31	Grand Junction

SEPTEMBER	
1-2	Ogden
3-4	at Orem
5-6	Orem
7-8	at Orem

MISSOULA OSPREY

JUNE	
18-19	at Helena
20-23	at Billings
24-25	Helena
26-29	Billings
30	at Great Falls

JULY	
1	at Great Falls
2-3	Great Falls
4-5	at Great Falls
7-9	Ogden
10-13	Idaho Falls
15-17	at Idaho Falls
18-21	at Ogden
22-23	Helena
24-25	Great Falls
26-27	at Helena

28-29	Helena
30-31	Billings

JULY	
1-2	Billings
6-9	at Grand Junction
10-12	at Orem
14-16	Grand Junction
17-20	Orem
21-24	at Billings
25-26	Helena
27-28	at Helena
29-30	at Great Falls

SEPTEMBER	
1-4	Great Falls
5-6	at Great Falls
7-8	at Helena

OGDEN RAPTORS

JUNE	
18-19	Orem
20-21	at Orem
22-25	Idaho Falls
26-27	Orem
28-29	at Orem
30	at Idaho Falls

JULY	
1-3	at Idaho Falls
4-6	Grand Junction
7-9	at Missoula
10-13	at Great Falls
15-17	Great Falls
18-21	Missoula
23-26	at Grand Junction

27-29	Grand Junction
30-31	at Idaho Falls

AUGUST	
1-2	Idaho Falls
6-9	at Billings
10-12	at Helena
14-16	Billings
17-20	Helena
22-25	at Orem
26-27	Idaho Falls
28-31	Orem

SEPTEMBER	
1-2	at Idaho Falls
3-4	Grand Junction
5-8	at Grand Junction

OREM OWLZ

JUNE	
18-19	at Ogden
20-21	Ogden
22-25	at Grand Junction
26-27	at Ogden
28-29	Ogden
30	Grand Junction

JULY	
1-3	Grand Junction
4-6	at Idaho Falls
7-10	Billings
11-13	Helena
15-17	at Billings
18-21	at Helena
23-26	Idaho Falls

17-20	at Ogden
21-24	Great Falls
25-26	at Missoula
27-28	Missoula
29-31	Billings

SEPTEMBER	
1	Billings
3-6	at Billings
7-8	Missoula

27-29 . . . . . at Idaho Falls	22-25 . . . . Ogden
30-31 . . . . Grand Junction	26-27 . . . at Grand Junction
AUGUST	28-31 . . . . at Ogden
1-2. . . . at Grand Junction	**SEPTEMBER**
6-9. . . . . Great Falls	1-2 . . . . . Grand Junction
10 12 . . . . Missoula	3-4 . . . . .Idaho Falls
14-16 . . . . at Great Falls	5-6 . . . . at Idaho Falls
17-20 . . . . . . at Missoula	7-8 . . . . .Idaho Falls

ARIZONA LEAGUE   * HOME GAMES ONLY

ANGELS

JUNE		
20 . . . . Athletics	26 . . . . Athletics
22 . . . . Brewers	27 . . . . Brewers
25 . . . . Cubs	31 . . . . Cubs
26 . . . . Royals	**AUGUST**
29 . . . . Padres	1 . . . . Indians
JULY	4 . . . . Rangers
2 . . . . White Sox	6 . . . . Royals
4 . . . . Athletics	9 . . . . Athletics
6 . . . . Giants	11 . . . . Giants
9 . . . . Mariners	15 . . . . .Diamondbacks
10 . . . . .Diamondbacks	17 . . . . Dodgers
16 . . . . Giants	20 . . . . Giants
17 . . . . Reds	22 . . . . Dodgers
21 . . . . .Diamondbacks	25 . . . . Cubs
22 . . . . Rangers	27 . . . . White Sox

ATHLETICS

JUNE		
22 . . . . Giants	24 . . . . Cubs
24 . . . . Mariners	28 . . . . Giants
27 . . . . .Diamondbacks	30 . . . . Royals
29 . . . . Brewers	**AUGUST**
JULY	2 . . . . . . .Diamondbacks
3 . . . . Cubs	5 . . . . Padres
5 . . . . Angels	8 . . . . Cubs
7 . . . . Dodgers	10 . . . . Angels
8 . . . . Cubs	12 . . . . Dodgers
12 . . . . .Diamondbacks	14 . . . . Angels
15 . . . . Rangers	17 . . . . Brewers
19 . . . . White Sox	18 . . . . Indians
21 . . . . Giants	23 . . . . Reds
23 . . . . Angels	25 . . . . .Diamondbacks
	27 . . . . Rangers
	28 . . . . Cubs

BREWERS

JUNE		
21 . . . . Angels	25 . . . . Cubs
24 . . . . Padres	28 . . . . Padres
26 . . . . Rangers	31 . . . . . .Diamondbacks
30 . . . . Athletics	**AUGUST**
JULY	2 . . . . Rangers
1 . . . . Dodgers	4 . . . . Reds
4 . . . . Reds	6 . . . . Dodgers
7 . . . . White Sox	9 . . . . Reds
10 . . . . Indians	12 . . . . White Sox
12 . . . . Mariners	15 . . . . Cleveland
15 . . . . Indians	16 . . . . Giants
16 . . . . White Sox	19 . . . . Royals
20 . . . . Royals	20 . . . . White Sox
21 . . . . Dodgers	25 . . . . Dodgers
	27 . . . . Mariners
	29 . . . . Indians

CUBS

JUNE		
20 . . . . Brewers	26 . . . . Brewers
23 . . . . .Diamondbacks	29 . . . . .Diamondbacks
24 . . . . Angels	30 . . . . Angels
28 . . . . Giants	**AUGUST**
30 . . . . Mariners	3 . . . . Giants
JULY	5 . . . . Dodgers
2 . . . . Athletics	7 . . . . White Sox
4 . . . . Indians	10 . . . . Padres
7 . . . . Padres	12 . . . . Rangers
10 . . . . Giants	13 . . . . Giants
13 . . . . Royals	18 . . . . Reds
16 . . . . .Diamondbacks	20 . . . . .Diamondbacks
18 . . . . Athletics	22 . . . . Athletics
20 . . . . Angels	24 . . . . Angels
23 . . . . White Sox	29 . . . . Athletics

DIAMONDBACKS

JUNE		
20 . . . . Giants	24 . . . . Mariners
22 . . . . Cubs	26 . . . . Giants
25 . . . . White Sox	28 . . . . Cubs
28 . . . . Athletics	**AUGUST**
30 . . . . Dodgers	1 . . . . Brewers
JULY	3 . . . . Athletics
1 . . . . Royals	5 . . . . Angels
5 . . . . Cubs	7 . . . . Athletics
6 . . . . Reds	11 . . . . Reds
11 . . . . Angels	13 . . . . Athletics
13 . . . . Rangers	16 . . . . Angels
18 . . . . Giants	18 . . . . Royals
19 . . . . Padres	22 . . . . Giants
22 . . . . Indians	23 . . . . Padres
	26 . . . . Angels
	27 . . . . Cubs

DODGERS

JUNE		
20 . . . . White Sox	24 . . . . Royals
22 . . . . Padres	26 . . . . White Sox
25 . . . . Reds	29 . . . . Rangers
27 . . . . Mariners	31 . . . . Reds
JULY	**AUGUST**
2 . . . . Brewers	2 . . . . Angels
3 . . . . .Diamondbacks	7 . . . . Brewers
5 . . . . White Sox	8 . . . . Giants
8 . . . . Indians	10 . . . . White Sox
10 . . . . Reds	13 . . . . Indians
12 . . . . Angels	15 . . . . Reds
16 . . . . Athletics	18 . . . . Rangers
19 . . . . Cubs	20 . . . . Athletics
22 . . . . Brewers	21 . . . . Indians
	26 . . . . Brewers
	27 . . . . Giants

GIANTS

JUNE		
21 . . . . . .Diamondbacks	23 . . . . Brewers
23 . . . . Athletics	24 . . . . Padres
26 . . . . Indians	27 . . . . . .Diamondbacks
27 . . . . Cubs	29 . . . . Athletics
30 . . . . Reds	**AUGUST**
JULY	1 . . . . Royals
2 . . . . .Diamondbacks	2 . . . . Cubs
7 . . . . Angels	5 . . . . Mariners
8 . . . . Rangers	7 . . . . Angels
12 . . . . Royals	10 . . . . Indians
13 . . . . Athletics	12 . . . . Angels
17 . . . . Dodgers	15 . . . . Cubs
19 . . . . Mariners	18 . . . . White Sox
	21 . . . . Angels

23 . . . . Cubs
25 . . . . Padres

INDIANS

JUNE
20 . . . . Reds
24 . . . . Rangers
25 . . . . Giants
29 . . . . Royals
JULY
1 . . . . White Sox
5 . . . . Padres
6 . . . . Dodgers
9 . . . . Brewers
11 . . . . Dodgers

9 . . . . Cubs
11 . . . . Dodgers
14 . . . . Brewers
16 . . . . Dodgers
19 . . . . Angels

MARINERS

JUNE
22 . . . . White Sox
25 . . . . Athletics
28 . . . . Dodgers
29 . . . . Cubs
JULY
2 . . . . Rangers
5 . . . . Giants
7 . . . . Royals
10 . . . . Padres
15 . . . . Angels
16 . . . . Indians
18 . . . . Brewers
21 . . . . Padres
23 . . . . . .Diamondbacks

PADRES

JUNE
20 . . . . Mariners
23 . . . . Dodgers
25 . . . . Brewers
27 . . . . White Sox
30 . . . . Angels
JULY
3 . . . . Royals
4 . . . . Rangers
8 . . . . . .Diamondbacks
9 . . . . Royals
13 . . . . Mariners
15 . . . . Reds
18 . . . . Rangers
20 . . . . Indians

RANGERS

JUNE
22 . . . . Royals
23 . . . . Indians
27 . . . . Brewers
29 . . . . Reds
JULY
1 . . . . Angels
3 . . . . Mariners

13 . . . . White Sox
17 . . . . . .Diamondbacks
19 . . . . Rangers
21 . . . . Cubs
24 . . . . Reds
26 . . . . Reds
30 . . . . Brewers
31 . . . . Athletics
AUGUST
4 . . . . Mariners
6 . . . . White Sox

20 . . . . Padres
24 . . . . Royals
25 . . . . Mariners
28 . . . . Reds

25 . . . . Royals
28 . . . . Dodgers
29 . . . . Reds
AUGUST
2 . . . . Padres
3 . . . . Indians
7 . . . . Rangers
10 . . . . . .Diamondbacks
12 . . . . Royals
15 . . . . Padres
17 . . . . Giants
20 . . . . Reds
22 . . . . . . White Sox
23 . . . . Rangers
28 . . . . Rangers
29 . . . . Royals

25 . . . . Athletics
26 . . . . Mariners
29 . . . . Indians
31 . . . . Giants
AUGUST
3 . . . . Reds
4 . . . . Cubs
8 . . . . Rangers
9 . . . . Rangers
12 . . . . . .Diamondbacks
14 . . . . Royals
18 . . . . Mariners
19 . . . . Cubs
22 . . . . Rangers
24 . . . . Brewers
28 . . . . . . White Sox

7 . . . . . .Diamondbacks
9 . . . . Cubs
11 . . . . Giants
12 . . . . Padres
17 . . . . Royals
20 . . . . . . Athletics
23 . . . . Dodgers
25 . . . . Indians

28 . . . . Royals
30 . . . . . . Mariners
AUGUST
1 . . . . . . White Sox
3 . . . . Dodgers
6 . . . . Giants
8 . . . . . . Mariners

REDS

JUNE
21 . . . . Indians
23 . . . . Royals
26 . . . . . . Dodgers
28 . . . . . . Rangers
JULY
1 . . . . Giants
3 . . . . Indians
5 . . . . Brewers
9 . . . . . . Athletics
11 . . . . . . White Sox
13 . . . . . . Dodgers
16 . . . . . . Padres
20 . . . . . Mariners
22 . . . . . White Sox
25 . . . . . . Angels

13 . . . . Padres
14 . . . . . . Mariners
17 . . . . . . Padres
19 . . . . . . Mariners
21 . . . . . . Royals
24 . . . . . Athletics
26 . . . . . . Royals
29 . . . . . . Padres

27 . . . . . . Indians
30 . . . . . . Padres
AUGUST
1 . . . . . . Dodgers
5 . . . . . . Brewers
6 . . . . . Diamondbacks
8 . . . . . . Indians
10 . . . . . Brewers
14 . . . . . . Cubs
16 . . . . . White Sox
19 . . . . . Athletics
21 . . . . Diamondbacks
24 . . . . . Mariners
26 . . . . . Giants
29 . . . . . Angels

ROYALS

JUNE
21 . . . . . Rangers
24 . . . . . Reds
27 . . . . . Angels
28 . . . . . Indians
JULY
2 . . . . . Padres
4 . . . . . Mariners
6 . . . . . Rangers
8 . . . . . Mariners
11 . . . . . Brewers
15 . . . . . Cubs
18 . . . . . Dodgers
19 . . . . . Reds
22 . . . . . Giants

23 . . . . . Padres
27 . . . . . Rangers
29 . . . . White Sox
AUGUST
3 . . . . . White Sox
4 . . . . Athletics
7 . . . . . Padres
9 . . . . . Mariners
11 . . . . . Rangers
13 . . . . . Mariners
16 . . . . . Rangers
17 . . . Diamondbacks
22 . . . . . Brewers
23 . . . . . Indians
27 . . . . . Padres
28 . . . Diamondbacks

WHITE SOX

JUNE
21 . . . . . Dodgers
23 . . . . . Mariners
26 . . . Diamondbacks
28 . . . . . Padres
30 . . . . . Indians
JULY
3 . . . . . Giants
6 . . . . . Brewers
8 . . . . . Reds
10 . . . . Athletics
12 . . . . . Cubs
17 . . . . . Brewers
18 . . . . . Angels
21 . . . . . Reds
24 . . . . . Rangers

27 . . . . . Dodgers
28 . . . . . Angels
31 . . . . . Mariners
AUGUST
2 . . . . . Royals
5 . . . . . Indians
8 . . . Diamondbacks
11 . . . . Brewers
13 . . . . . Reds
15 . . . Athletics
17 . . . . . Cubs
21 . . . . Brewers
23 . . . . Dodgers
25 . . . . . Reds
26 . . . . . Indians

GULF COAST LEAGUE
* HOME GAMES ONLY

ASTROS

JUNE
23 . . . . .Tigers
24 . . . . Yankees 2
26 . . . . Pirates
29 . . . . Phillies

JULY
1 . . . . Yankees 1
3 . . . . .Blue Jays
6 . . . . Braves
8 . . . . .Tigers
11 . . . . Yankees 2
14 . . . . Pirates
16 . . . . Phillies
18 . . . . Yankees 1
20 . . . . .Blue Jays
23 . . . . Braves

24 . . . . .Tigers
27 . . . . Yankees 2
29 . . . . Pirates
31 . . . . Phillies

AUGUST
3 . . . . Yankees 1
6 . . . . .Blue Jays
8 . . . . Braves
10 . . . . .Tigers
13 . . . . Yankees 2
15 . . . . Pirates
18 . . . . Phillies
20 . . . . Yankees 1
21 . . . . Braves
25 . . . . .Tigers
26 . . . . Yankees 2
29 . . . . Braves

BLUE JAYS

JUNE
22 . . . . Pirates
25 . . . . Yankees 1
26 . . . . Braves
29 . . . . .Tigers

JULY
2 . . . . Yankees 2
4 . . . . .Astros
6 . . . . Phillies
9 . . . . Pirates
10 . . . . Yankees 1
14 . . . . Braves
16 . . . . .Tigers
17 . . . . Yankees 2
21 . . . . .Astros
22 . . . . Phillies

24 . . . . Pirates
28 . . . . Yankees 1
29 . . . . Braves
31 . . . . .Tigers

AUGUST
4 . . . . Yankees 2
5 . . . . .Astros
8 . . . . Phillies
11 . . . . Pirates
12 . . . . Yankees 1
15 . . . . Braves
18 . . . . .Tigers
19 . . . . Yankees 2
22 . . . . Phillies
24 . . . . Pirates
27 . . . . Yankees 1
29 . . . . Phillies

BRAVES

JUNE
22 . . . . Yankees 2
25 . . . . .Tigers
27 . . . . .Blue Jays
30 . . . . Yankees 1

JULY
2 . . . . Phillies
4 . . . . Pirates
7 . . . . .Astros
9 . . . . Yankees 2
10 . . . . .Tigers
13 . . . . .Blue Jays
15 . . . . Yankees 1
18 . . . . Phillies
20 . . . . Pirates
22 . . . . .Astros
24 . . . . Yankees 2
28 . . . . .Tigers
30 . . . . .Blue Jays

AUGUST
1 . . . . Yankees 1
3 . . . . at Phillies
4 . . . . Phillies
6 . . . . Pirates
7 . . . . .Astros
11 . . . . Yankees 2
12 . . . . .Tigers
14 . . . . .Blue Jays
17 . . . . Yankees 1
19 . . . . Phillies

22 . . . . .Astros
24 . . . . Yankees 2
26 . . . . .Tigers
28 . . . . .Astros

GCL CARDINALS

JUNE
22 . . . . Nationals
24 . . . . Nationals
26 . . . . Marlins
29 . . . . Mets

JULY
1 . . . . Mets
2 . . . . Marlins
4 . . . . Marlins
7 . . . . Mets
10 . . . . Nationals
13 . . . . Mets
15 . . . . Mets
16 . . . . Nationals
18 . . . . Nationals
21 . . . . Marlins
24 . . . . Nationals
27 . . . . Marlins
29 . . . . Marlins
31 . . . . Mets

AUGUST
4 . . . . Marlins

7 . . . . Mets
10 . . . . Nationals
12 . . . . Nationals
13 . . . . Mets
15 . . . . Mets
18 . . . . Nationals

GCL MARLINS

JUNE
23 . . . . Mets
25 . . . . .Cardinals
27 . . . . .Cardinals
30 . . . . Nationals

JULY
3 . . . . .Cardinals
6 . . . . Nationals
8 . . . . Nationals
9 . . . . Mets
11 . . . . Mets
14 . . . . Nationals
17 . . . . Mets
20 . . . . .Cardinals
22 . . . . .Cardinals
23 . . . . Mets
25 . . . . Mets

28 . . . . .Cardinals
30 . . . . Nationals

AUGUST
1 . . . . Nationals
3 . . . . .Cardinals
5 . . . . .Cardinals
6 . . . . Nationals
8 . . . . Nationals
11 . . . . Mets
14 . . . . Nationals
17 . . . . Mets
19 . . . . Mets
21 . . . . .Cardinals
24 . . . . Nationals
27 . . . . Mets
29 . . . . .Cardinals

GCL METS

JUNE
22 . . . . Marlins
24 . . . . Marlins
26 . . . . Nationals
30 . . . . .Cardinals

JULY
2 . . . . Nationals
4 . . . . Nationals
6 . . . . .Cardinals
8 . . . . .Cardinals
10 . . . . Marlins
14 . . . . .Cardinals
16 . . . . Marlins
18 . . . . Marlins
21 . . . . Nationals
24 . . . . Marlins

27 . . . . Nationals
29 . . . . Nationals
30 . . . . .Cardinals

AUGUST
1 . . . . .Cardinals
4 . . . . Nationals
6 . . . . .Cardinals
8 . . . . .Cardinals
10 . . . . Marlins
12 . . . . Marlins
14 . . . . .Cardinals
18 . . . . Marlins
20 . . . . Nationals
22 . . . . Nationals
24 . . . . .Cardinals
26 . . . . Marlins
28 . . . . Nationals

GCL NATIONALS

JUNE
23 . . . . .Cardinals
25 . . . . Mets
27 . . . . Mets
29 . . . . Marlins

JULY
1 . . . . Marlins
3 . . . . Mets
7 . . . . Marlins
8 . . . . at Marlins
9 . . . . .Cardinals
11 . . . . .Cardinals
13 . . . . Marlins
15 . . . . Marlins
17 . . . . .Cardinals
20 . . . . Mets
22 . . . . Mets
23 . . . . .Cardinals
25 . . . . .Cardinals
28 . . . . Mets
31 . . . . Marlins

AUGUST
1 . . . . at Marlins
3 . . . . Mets
4 . . . . .at Mets

5 . . . . Mets
7 . . . . Marlins
11 . . . . .Cardinals
13 . . . . Marlins
15 . . . . Marlins
17 . . . . .Cardinals
19 . . . . .Cardinals
21 . . . . Mets
25 . . . . Marlins
27 . . . . .Cardinals
29 . . . . Mets

GCL ORIOLES

JUNE
23 . . . . Twins
25 . . . . Twins
26 . . . . .Rays
30 . . . . Red Sox

JULY
2 . . . . Red Sox
4 . . . . .Rays
6 . . . . Twins
8 . . . . Twins
10 . . . . .Rays

7 . . . . Mets
10 . . . . Nationals
12 . . . . Nationals
13 . . . . Mets
15 . . . . Mets
18 . . . . Nationals

20 . . . . Marlins
22 . . . . Marlins
25 . . . . Mets
26 . . . . Nationals
28 . . . . Marlins

13 . . . . Red Sox	10 . . . . Red Sox
15 . . . . Red Sox	11 . . . . .at Red Sox
18 . . . . .Rays	12 . . . . Red Sox
21 . . . . Twins	13 . . . . .at Red Sox
23 . . . . Twins	14 . . . . at Rays
24 . . . . .Rays	15 . . . . .Rays
28 . . . . Red Sox	17 . . . . at Twins
30 . . . . Red Sox	18 . . . . Twins

AUGUST

1 . . . . .Rays	19 . . . . at Twins
3 . . . . Twins	20 . . . . Twins
5 . . . . Twins	21 . . . . .Rays
7 . . . . .Rays	25 . . . . Red Sox
8 . . . . at Rays	27 . . . . Red Sox
	29 . . . . .Rays

GCL PHILLIES

JUNE

23 . . . . Yankees 1	3 . . . . Braves
24 . . . . Pirates	4 . . . . at Braves
27 . . . . .Tigers	5 . . . . . . .at Yankees 2
30 . . . . .Astros	6 . . . . Yankees 2

JULY

1 . . . . Braves	7 . . . . .Blue Jays
4 . . . . Yankees 2	8 . . . . at Blue Jays
7 . . . . .Blue Jays	10 . . . . Yankees 1
8 . . . . Yankees 1	11 . . . . . . .at Yankees 1
10 . . . . Pirates	12 . . . . .at Pirates
13 . . . . .Tigers	13 . . . . Pirates
15 . . . . .Astros	14 . . . . at Tigers
17 . . . . Braves	15 . . . . .Tigers
20 . . . . Yankees 2	17 . . . . .Astros
23 . . . . .Blue Jays	18 . . . . at Astros
25 . . . . Yankees 1	19 . . . . .at Braves
27 . . . . Pirates	20 . . . . Braves
28 . . . . .at Pirates	21 . . . . .Blue Jays
29 . . . . at Tigers	22 . . . . at Blue Jays
30 . . . . .Tigers	24 . . . . .at Yankees 1
31 . . . . at Astros	25 . . . . Yankees 1

AUGUST

1 . . . . .Astros	26 . . . . Pirates
	27 . . . . .at Pirates
	28 . . . . .Blue Jays
	29 . . . . at Blue Jays

GCL PIRATES

JUNE

22 . . . . at Blue Jays	25 . . . . .Blue Jays
23 . . . . .Blue Jays	27 . . . . at Phillies
24 . . . . at Phillies	28 . . . . Phillies
25 . . . . Phillies	29 . . . . .at Astros
26 . . . . at Astros	30 . . . . .Astros
27 . . . . .Astros	31 . . . . Yankees 2
29 . . . . Yankees 2	
30 . . . . .at Yankees 2	

AUGUST

	1 . . . . .at Yankees 2

JULY

1 . . . . .Tigers	3 . . . . at Tigers
2 . . . . at Tigers	4 . . . . .Tigers
3 . . . . Braves	5 . . . . Braves
4 . . . . .at Braves	6 . . . . .at Braves
6 . . . . Yankees 1	7 . . . . .at Yankees 1
7 . . . . .at Yankees 1	8 . . . . Yankees 1
8 . . . . .Blue Jays	10 . . . . .Blue Jays
9 . . . . at Blue Jays	11 . . . . at Blue Jays
10 . . . . at Phillies	12 . . . . Phillies
11 . . . . Phillies	13 . . . . at Phillies
13 . . . . .Astros	14 . . . . .Astros
14 . . . . at Astros	15 . . . . at Astros
15 . . . . .at Yankees 2	17 . . . . .at Yankees 2
16 . . . . Yankees 2	18 . . . . Yankees 2
17 . . . . .Tigers	19 . . . . at Tigers
18 . . . . at Tigers	20 . . . . .Tigers
20 . . . . .at Braves	21 . . . . Yankees 1
21 . . . . Braves	22 . . . . .at Yankees 1
22 . . . . .at Yankees 1	24 . . . . at Blue Jays
23 . . . . Yankees 1	25 . . . . .Blue Jays
24 . . . . at Blue Jays	26 . . . . at Phillies
	27 . . . . Phillies
	28 . . . . .at Yankees 1
	29 . . . . Yankees 1

GCL RAYS

JUNE

22 . . . . Red Sox	25 . . . . .Orioles
23 . . . . .at Red Sox	27 . . . . Twins
24 . . . . Red Sox	28 . . . . at Twins
25 . . . . .at Red Sox	29 . . . . Twins
26 . . . . at Orioles	30 . . . . at Twins
27 . . . . Orioles	31 . . . . Orioles
29 . . . . Twins	
30 . . . . at Twins	

AUGUST

	1 . . . . at Orioles

JULY

1 . . . . Twins	3 . . . . .at Red Sox
2 . . . . at Twins	4 . . . . Red Sox
3 . . . . Orioles	5 . . . . .at Red Sox
4 . . . . at Orioles	6 . . . . Red Sox
6 . . . . .at Red Sox	7 . . . . at Orioles
7 . . . . Red Sox	8 . . . . Orioles
8 . . . . .at Red Sox	10 . . . . at Twins
9 . . . . Red Sox	11 . . . . Twins
10 . . . . at Orioles	12 . . . . at Twins
11 . . . . Orioles	13 . . . . Twins
13 . . . . at Twins	14 . . . . Orioles
14 . . . . at Twins	15 . . . . at Orioles
15 . . . . at Twins	17 . . . . Red Sox
16 . . . . Twins	18 . . . . .at Red Sox
17 . . . . Orioles	19 . . . . Red Sox
18 . . . . at Orioles	20 . . . . .at Red Sox
20 . . . . Red Sox	21 . . . . at Orioles
21 . . . . .at Red Sox	22 . . . . Orioles
22 . . . . Red Sox	24 . . . . Twins
23 . . . . .at Red Sox	25 . . . . at Twins
24 . . . . at Orioles	26 . . . . Twins
	27 . . . . at Twins
	28 . . . . Orioles
	29 . . . . at Orioles

GCL RED SOX

JUNE

22 . . . . at Rays	27 . . . . Orioles
23 . . . . .Rays	28 . . . . at Orioles
24 . . . . at Rays	29 . . . . Orioles
25 . . . . .Rays	30 . . . . at Orioles
26 . . . . Twins	31 . . . . at Twins
27 . . . . at Twins	
29 . . . . Orioles	
30 . . . . at Orioles	

AUGUST

	1 . . . . Twins
	3 . . . . .Rays
	4 . . . . at Rays

JULY

1 . . . . Orioles	5 . . . . .Rays
2 . . . . at Orioles	6 . . . . at Rays
3 . . . . at Twins	7 . . . . Twins
4 . . . . Twins	8 . . . . at Twins
6 . . . . .Rays	10 . . . . at Orioles
7 . . . . at Rays	11 . . . . Orioles
8 . . . . .Rays	12 . . . . at Orioles
9 . . . . at Rays	13 . . . . Orioles
10 . . . . Twins	14 . . . . at Twins
11 . . . . at Twins	15 . . . . Twins
13 . . . . at Orioles	17 . . . . at Rays
14 . . . . Orioles	18 . . . . .Rays
15 . . . . at Orioles	19 . . . . at Rays
16 . . . . Orioles	20 . . . . .Rays
17 . . . . at Twins	21 . . . . Twins
18 . . . . Twins	22 . . . . at Twins
20 . . . . at Rays	24 . . . . Orioles
21 . . . . .Rays	25 . . . . at Orioles
22 . . . . at Rays	26 . . . . Orioles
23 . . . . .Rays	27 . . . . at Orioles
24 . . . . Twins	28 . . . . at Twins
25 . . . . at Twins	29 . . . . Twins

GCL TIGERS

JUNE

22	Astros
23	at Astros
24	Braves
25	at Braves
26	Phillies
27	at Phillies
29	at Blue Jays
30	Blue Jays

JULY

1	at Pirates
2	Pirates
3	Yankees 1
4	at Yankees 1
6	at Yankees 2
7	Yankees 2
8	at Astros
9	Astros
10	at Braves
11	Braves
13	at Phillies
14	Phillies
15	Blue Jays
16	at Blue Jays
17	at Pirates
18	Pirates
20	at Yankees 1
21	Yankees 1
22	Yankees 2
23	at Yankees 2
24	at Astros
25	Astros

27	Braves
28	at Braves
29	Phillies
30	at Phillies
31	at Blue Jays

AUGUST

1	Blue Jays
3	Pirates
4	at Pirates
5	Yankees 1
6	at Yankees 1
7	Yankees 2
8	at Yankees 2
10	at Astros
11	Astros
12	at Braves
13	Braves
14	Phillies
15	at Phillies
17	Blue Jays
18	at Blue Jays
19	Pirates
20	at Pirates
21	at Yankees 2
22	Yankees 2
24	Astros
25	at Astros
26	at Braves
27	Braves
28	Yankees 2
29	at Yankees 2

GCL TWINS

JUNE

22	Orioles
23	at Orioles
24	Orioles
25	at Orioles
26	at Red Sox
27	Red Sox
29	at Rays
30	Rays

JULY

1	at Rays
2	Rays
3	Red Sox
4	at Red Sox
6	at Orioles
7	Orioles
8	at Orioles
9	Orioles
10	at Red Sox
11	Red Sox
13	Rays
14	at Rays
15	Rays
16	at Rays
17	Red Sox
18	at Red Sox
20	Orioles
21	at Orioles
22	Orioles
23	at Orioles
24	at Red Sox
25	Red Sox

27	at Rays
28	Rays
29	at Rays
30	Rays
31	Red Sox

AUGUST

1	at Red Sox
3	at Orioles
4	Orioles
5	at Orioles
6	Orioles
7	at Red Sox
8	Red Sox
10	Rays
11	at Rays
12	Rays
13	at Rays
14	Red Sox
15	at Red Sox
17	Orioles
18	at Orioles
19	Orioles
20	at Orioles
21	at Red Sox
22	Red Sox
24	at Rays
25	Rays
26	at Rays
27	Rays
28	Red Sox
29	at Red Sox

GCL YANKEES 1

JUNE

22	Phillies
23	at Phillies
24	Blue Jays
25	at Blue Jays
26	at Yankees 2
27	Yankees 2
29	Braves
30	at Braves

JULY

1	at Astros
2	Astros
3	at Tigers
4	Tigers
6	at Pirates
7	Pirates
8	at Phillies
9	Phillies
10	at Blue Jays
11	Blue Jays
13	at Yankees 2
14	Yankees 2
15	at Braves
16	Braves
17	Astros
18	at Astros
20	Tigers
21	at Tigers
22	Pirates
23	at Pirates
24	Phillies
25	at Phillies

27	Blue Jays
28	at Blue Jays
29	Yankees 2
30	at Yankees 2
31	Braves

AUGUST

1	at Braves
3	at Astros
4	Astros
5	at Tigers
6	Tigers
7	Pirates
8	at Pirates
10	at Phillies
11	Phillies
12	at Blue Jays
13	Blue Jays
14	at Yankees 2
15	Yankees 2
17	at Braves
18	Braves
19	Astros
20	at Astros
21	at Pirates
22	Pirates
24	Phillies
25	at Phillies
26	Blue Jays
27	at Blue Jays
28	Pirates
29	at Pirates

GCL YANKEES 2

JUNE

22	at Braves
23	Braves
24	at Astros
25	Astros
26	Yankees 1
27	at Yankees 1
29	at Pirates
30	Pirates

JULY

1	Blue Jays
2	at Blue Jays
3	Phillies
4	at Phillies
6	Tigers
7	at Tigers
8	Braves
9	at Braves
10	Astros
11	at Astros
13	Yankees 1
14	at Yankees 1
15	Pirates
16	at Pirates
17	at Blue Jays
18	Blue Jays
20	at Phillies
21	Phillies
22	at Tigers
23	Tigers
24	at Braves

25	Braves
27	at Astros
28	Astros
29	at Yankees 1
30	Yankees 1
31	at Pirates

AUGUST

1	Pirates
3	Blue Jays
4	at Blue Jays
5	Phillies
6	at Phillies
7	at Tigers
8	Tigers
10	Braves
11	at Braves
12	Astros
13	at Astros
14	Yankees 1
15	at Yankees 1
17	Pirates
18	at Pirates
19	at Blue Jays
20	Blue Jays
21	Tigers
22	at Tigers
24	at Braves
25	Braves
26	at Astros
27	Astros
28	at Tigers
29	Tigers

INDEPENDENT

* Home games only

AMERICAN ASSOCIATION

AMARILLO THUNDERHEADS

MAY
26-28 . . . . St. Paul
29-31 . . . . Lincoln

JUNE
8-10 . . . . Sioux City
11-14 . . . . . . Trois-Rivieres
18-21 . . . . Laredo
22-24 . . . . . . Grand Prairie

JULY
3-5 . . . . Wichita
6-9 . . . . Joplin
20-22 . . . . . . Grand Prairie
23-26 . . . . Sioux Falls

AUGUST
5-7 . . . . Laredo
8-10 . . . . Trois-Rivieres
14-16 . . . . . . Grand Prairie
24-26 . . . . Kansas City
27-30 . . . . Laredo

FARGO-MOORHEAD REDHAWKS

MAY
25-27 . . . . Joplin

JUNE
2-4 . . . . Wichita
5-7 . . . . Laredo
15-18 . . . . Sioux Falls
19-21 . . . . Winnipeg
25-28 . . . . St. Paul

JULY
6-9 . . . . Winnipeg
10-12 . . . . . . Trois-Rivieres
29-31 . . . . . . Grand Prairie

AUGUST
1-3 . . . . St. Paul
11-13 . . . . Gary
17-20 . . . . Lincoln
21-23 . . . . Gary

SEPTEMBER
1-4 . . . . Trois-Rivieres
5-7 . . . . Amarillo

GARY SOUTHSHORE RAILCATS

MAY
21-24 . . . . Quebec
29-31 . . . . Kansas City

JUNE
12-14 . . . Fargo-Moorhead
16-18 . . . . Wichita
26-28 . . . . Lincoln
30 . . . . . Fargo-Moorhead

JULY
1-2 . . . . . Fargo-Moorhead
6-9 . . . . Sioux City
10-13 . . . . Sioux Falls
23-26 . . . . Sioux City
29-31 . . . . St. Paul

AUGUST
5-7 . . . . Winnipeg
8-10 . . . . Lincoln
18-20 . . . . Joplin
27-30 . . . . New Jersey

SEPTEMBER
5-7 . . . . Kansas City

GRAND PRAIRIE AIRHOGS

MAY
21-24 . . . . Winnipeg
26-28 . . . . Laredo

JUNE
1-3 . . . . St. Paul
5-7 . . . . Sioux City
15-17 . . . . Amarillo
18-20 . . . . . . Trois-Rivieres
29 . . . . Amarillo

JULY
1-2 . . . . Amarillo
3-5 . . . . Laredo
16-18 . . . . Wichita
23-26 . . . . Joplin

AUGUST
5-7 . . . . Sioux Falls
8-10 . . . . Laredo
17-19 . . . . Wichita
21-23 . . . . Amarillo

SEPTEMBER
1-4 . . . . Sioux City

JOPLIN BLASTERS

MAY
21-24 . . . . Wichita
29-31 . . . . Winnipeg

JUNE
2-3 . . . . Amarillo
11-14 . . . . . . Grand Prairie
15-18 . . . . Kansas City
22-24 . . . . Laredo

JULY
3-5 . . . . Lincoln
10-12 . . . . Sioux City
15-18 . . . . Amarillo
29-31 . . . . Laredo

AUGUST
1-4 . . . . . Gary SouthShore
11-13 . . . . Rockland
14-16 . . . . St. Paul
24-26 . . . . Lincoln
27-30 . . . . . . Grand Prairie

KANSAS CITY T-BONES

MAY
22-24 . . . . Lincoln
26-28 . . . . Sioux City

JUNE
4-6 . . . . Amarillo
8-10 . . . . . Fargo-Moorhead
19-21 . . . . Wichita

JULY
3-4 . . . . . Gary SouthShore
6-9 . . . . Grand Prairie
19-22 . . . Gary SouthShore
23-26 . . . . Winnipeg

AUGUST
5-7 . . . . Joplin
8-10 . . . . . Fargo-Moorhead
18-20 . . . . Amarillo
21-23 . . . . Joplin
27-30 . . . . St. Paul
31 . . . . Laredo

SEPTEMBER
1-3 . . . . Laredo

LAREDO LEMURS

MAY
21-24 . . . . Amarillo
29-31 . . . . St. Paul

JUNE
1-3 . . . . Lincoln
12-14 . . . . Kansas City
15-17 . . . . . . Trois-Rivieres
25-28 . . . . . . Grand Prairie
29-30 . . . . Joplin

JULY
1-2 . . . . Joplin
10-13 . . . . Amarillo
20-22 . . . . Joplin
23-26 . . . . Wichita

AUGUST
2-4 . . . . Sioux Falls
11-13 . . . . Amarillo
14-16 . . . . Wichita
24-26 . . . . . . Grand Prairie

SEPTEMBER
5-7 . . . . Sioux City

LINCOLN SALTDOGS

MAY
25-28 . . . Gary SouthShore

JUNE
5-7 . . . . Wichita
8-10 . . . . Winnipeg
19-21 . . . . Joplin
22-24 . . . Fargo-Moorhead
30 . . . . St. Paul

JULY
1-2 . . . . St. Paul
10-13 . . . . . . Grand Prairie
15-18 . . . . Kansas City
29-31 . . . . Sioux City

AUGUST
1-3 . . . . Amarillo
11-13 . . . . Kansas City
14-16 . . . . Rockland
21-23 . . . . Sioux City
27-30 . . . . Sioux Falls

SEPTEMBER
1-4 . . . . Joplin

SIOUX CITY EXPLORERS

MAY
21-23 . . . . Sioux Falls
29-31 . . . . Quebec

JUNE
1-3 . . . . Kansas City
11-13 . . . . Winnipeg
15-18 . . . . Lincoln
25-28 . . . . Amarillo

JULY
3-5 . . . . Sioux Falls
15-18 . . . . Laredo
20-22 . . . . Lincoln

AUGUST
1-3 . . . . Grand Prairie
5-7 . . . . . Fargo-Moorhead
11-13 . . . . St. Paul
14-17 . . . . Kansas City
24-26 . . . Gary SouthShore
27-30 . . . . Wichita

SIOUX FALLS CANARIES

MAY
24 . . . . Sioux City
26-28 . . . . Quebec
29-31 . . . Fargo-Moorhead

JUNE
1 . . . . Fargo-Moorhead
8-10 . . . . Grand Prairie
11-14 . . . . St. Paul

19-21 . . . . Sioux City	**AUGUST**
25-27 . . . . Winnipeg	8-10 . . . . Sioux City
29-30 . . . . .Wichita	14-16 . . . Gary SouthShore
JULY	18-20 . . . . Laredo
1 . . . . .Wichita	24-26 . . . .Fargo-Moorhead
6-9 . . . . .Lincoln	**SEPTEMBER**
16-18 . . . . St. Paul	5-7 . . . . .Joplin
29-31 . . . . . . Kansas City	

ST. PAUL SAINTS

MAY	19-22 . . . . Winnipeg
21-24 . . .Fargo-Moorhead	23-26 . . . . .Lincoln
JUNE	**AUGUST**
5-7 . . . . Sioux Falls	5-7 . . . . Lincoln
8-10 . . . . .Joplin	8-10 . . . . Winnipeg
19-21 . . Gary SouthShore	18-20 . . . . Sioux City
22-24 . . . . . Sioux City	21-23 . . . . . . .Sioux Falls
JULY	**SEPTEMBER**
3-5 . . . . . . .Fargo-Moorhead	1-4 . . . . . Gary SouthShore
6-9 . . . . .Ottawa	5-7 . . . . New Jersey

WICHITA WINGNUTS

MAY	14 . . . . .Joplin
26-28 . . . . Winnipeg	19-22 . . . . Sioux Falls
29-31 . . . . . Grand Prairie	**AUGUST**
JUNE	9-10 . . . . .Joplin
8-10 . . . . Laredo	11-13 . . . . . Grand Prairie
11-14 . . . . .Lincoln	21-23 . . . . Laredo
22-23 . . . . . Sioux Falls	24-26 . . . . St. Paul
25-28 . . . . .Joplin	**SEPTEMBER**
JULY	1-4 . . . . Amarillo
6-9 . . . . Laredo	5-7 . . . . Grand Prairie
10-13 . . . . . . Kansas City	

WINNIPEG GOLDEYES

JUNE	15-18 . . . . .Gary
2-4 . . . . Sioux Falls	29-31 . . . . Amarillo
5-7 . . . . .Joplin	**AUGUST**
15-17 . . . . St. Paul	1-3 . . . . Kansas City
22-24 . . Gary SouthShore	11-13 . . . . . . .Sioux Falls
29-30 . . . . Sioux City	14-16 . . .Fargo-Moorhead
JULY	28-31 . . .Fargo-Moorhead
1-2 . . . . Sioux City	**SEPTEMBER**
3-5 . . . . .Ottawa	1-4 . . . . .Sioux Falls
10-13 . . . . St. Paul	5-7 . . . . .Lincoln

FRONTIER LEAGUE

EVANSVILLE OTTERS

MAY	10-12 . . . . .Lake Erie
15-17 . . . . . Traverse City	17-19 . . . . .Joliet
22-24 . . . . Florence	24-26 . . . . . .Washington
JUNE	**AUGUST**
3-4 . . . . .Gateway	5-6 . . . . Frontier
10-11 . . . . Normal	7-9 . . . . .Southern Illinois
17-18 . . . . . Windy City	14-16 . . . . . Schaumburg
19-21 . . . . . Traverse City	19-20 . . . . Rockford
23-25 . . . . Frontier	26-27 . . . . Frontier
JULY	**SEPTEMBER**
1-2 . . . . Windy City	4-6 . . . . River City

FLORENCE FREEDOM

MAY	8-9 . . . . Evansville
14-16 . . . . .Joliet	22-23 . . . . .Rockford
19-21 . . . . Frontier	24-26 . . . .Southern Illinois
29-31 . . . . .Normal	**AUGUST**
JUNE	5-6 . . . . .Normal
3-4 . . . . Traverse City	14-16 . . . . Gateway
5-7 . . . . .Lake Erie	26-27 . . . . .Rockford
12-14 . . . . . Schaumburg	28-30 . . . . Frontier
19-21 . . .Southern Illinois	**SEPTEMBER**
24-25 . . . . . .Washington	1-3 . . . . Windy City
JULY	
3-5 . . . . River City	

FRONTIER GREYS

No home games

GATEWAY GRIZZLIES

MAY	3-4 . . . . Frontier
15-17 . . . . .Rockford	17-19 . . . . Frontier
25 . . . . Frontier	28-30 . . . . . . Evansville
26-28 . . . . Florence	31 . . . . Schaumburg
29-31 . . . . . .Washington	**AUGUST**
JUNE	1-2 . . . . Schaumburg
5-7 . . . . River City	7-9 . . . . . Traverse City
16-18 . . . . River City	11-13 . . . . Joliet
19-21 . . . . . Windy City	18-20 . . . . Frontier
26-28 . . . . .Rockford	25-27 . . . . .Normal
30 . . . . . .Southern Illinois	**SEPTEMBER**
JULY	1-3 . . . . .Southern Illinois
1-2 . . . . .Southern Illinois	4-6 . . . . .Lake Erie

JOLIET SLAMMERS

MAY	**JULY**
19-21 . . . . .Lake Erie	1-2 . . . . Traverse City
22-24 . . . . . . .Gateway	7-9 . . . . Frontier
JUNE	10-12 . . .Southern Illinois
2-4 . . . . Frontier	24-26 . . . . Windy City
5-7 . . . . Evansville	31 . . . . Frontier
9-11 . . . . . .Washington	**AUGUST**
16-18 . . . . Rockford	1-2 . . . . Frontier
19-21 . . . . River City	7-9 . . . . Florence
26-28 . . . . .Normal	18-20 . . . . Florence
30 . . . . Traverse City	25-27 . . . . . Schaumburg
	SEPTEMBER
	4-6 . . . . .Rockford

LAKE ERIE CRUSHERS

MAY	**JULY**
15-17 . . .Southern Illinois	3-5 . . . . Windy City
26-28 . . . . Evansville	17-19 . . . . . Schaumburg
29-31 . . . . Frontier	24-26 . . . . . Traverse City
JUNE	28-30 . . . . . . Florence
2-4 . . . . River City	**AUGUST**
12-14 . . . . . .Washington	4-6 . . . . .Rockford
16-18 . . . . Florence	7-9 . . . . Frontier
23-25 . . . . . . .Gateway	18-20 . . . . .Normal
26-28 . . . . . . Evansville	21-23 . . . . Joliet
	SEPTEMBER
	1-3 . . . . Joliet

NORMAL CORNBELTERS

MAY
19-21 . . . . Gateway
22-24 . . . . . . .Washington

JUNE
2-4 . . . . Windy City
5-7 . . . . . Southern Illinois
16-18 . . . . . Traverse City
19-21 . . . . Lake Erie
30 . . . . River City

JULY
1-2 . . . . River City
7-9 . . . . Schaumburg

10-12 . . . . Frontier
21-23 . . . . Joliet
24-26 . . . . Gateway

AUGUST
7-9 . . . . .Rockford
11-13 . . . . Florence
14-16 . . . . . . .Washington
21-23 . . . . Frontier

SEPTEMBER
1-3 . . . . Evansville
4-6 . . . . Schaumburg

RIVER CITY RASCALS

MAY
15-17 . . . . .Normal
22-24 . . . . Frontier
26-28 . . . . . .Washington

JUNE
9-11 . . . . Florence
12-14 . . . . .Normal
23-25 . . . . . . .Rockford
26-28 . . . . Frontier

JULY
7-9 . . . . .Lake Erie

10-12 . . . . Gateway
21-23 . . . . Schaumburg
24-26 . . . . Frontier

AUGUST
4-6 . . . . Joliet
7-9 . . . . Windy City
18-20 . . . Southern Illinois
21-23 . . . . . . Evansville
28-30 . . . . Lake Erie

SEPTEMBER
1-3 . . . . . . Traverse City

ROCKFORD AVIATORS

MAY
19-21 . . . . . Traverse City
26-28 . . . . Joliet
29-31 . . . . . Traverse City

JUNE
9-11 . . . . .Lake Erie
12-14 . . . . Frontier
19-21 . . . . Schaumburg
30 . . . . Florence

JULY
1-2 . . . . Florence
7-9 . . . . Grizzlies

10-12 . . . . . .Washington
17-19 . . . . River City
28-30 . . . . . Windy City
31 . . . . .Normal

AUGUST
1-2 . . . . .Normal
11-13 . . . . Evansville
14-16 . . . . River City
21-23 . . . Southern Illinois
28-30 . . . . .Normal

SEPTEMBER
1-3 . . . . Frontier

SCHAUMBURG BOOMERS

MAY
22-24 . . . . . . .Lake Erie
26-28 . . . . .Normal
29-31 . . . . River City

JUNE
5-7 . . . . Frontier
16-18 . . . . Frontier
23-25 . . . . Joliet
30 . . . . Frontier

JULY
1-2 . . . . Frontier
3-5 . . . . Evansville

10-12 . . . . Florence
24-26 . . . . .Rockford
28-30 . . . . Joliet

AUGUST
4-6 . . . . . Southern Illinois
7-9 . . . . .Washington
11-13 . . . . . Windy City
18-20 . . . . Traverse City
21-23 . . . . Florence
28-30 . . . . Gateway

SEPTEMBER
1-3 . . . . . . .Washington

SOUTHERN ILLINOIS MINERS

MAY
19-21 . . . . River City
22-24 . . . . .Rockford
28-31 . . . . Joliet

JUNE
2-4 . . . . Schaumburg
9-11 . . . . Frontier

12-14 . . . . . . Evansville
23-25 . . . . . Traverse City
26-28 . . . . . .Washington

JULY
3-5 . . . . .Normal
17-19 . . . . . Windy City
21-23 . . . . Gateway
28-30 . . . . Frontier

31 . . . . Evansville

AUGUST
1-2 . . . . Evansville
11-13 . . . . . . .Lake Erie
14-16 . . . . Frontier

TRAVERSE CITY BEACH BUMS

MAY
22-24 . . . . . . Windy City
26-28 . . . . . Frontier

JUNE
9-11 . . . . Gateway
12-14 . . . . Joliet
26-28 . . . . Schaumburg

JULY
3-5 . . . . .Rockford
7-9 . . . . . Southern Illinois
17-19 . . . . Florence
21-23 . . . . . Evansville

28-30 . . . . .Normal
31 . . . . .Lake Erie

AUGUST
1-2 . . . . .Lake Erie
4-6 . . . . . . .Washington
11-13 . . . . . River City
14-16 . . . . Joliet
21-23 . . . . Windy City
25-27 . . . . . .Washington

SEPTEMBER
4-6 . . . . Frontier

WASHINGTON WILD THINGS

MAY
15-17 . . . . Schaumburg
19-21 . . . . Evansville

JUNE
3-4 . . . . .Rockford
5-7 . . . . . . Traverse City
16-18 . . . . Southern Illinois
19-21 . . . . Frontier
30 . . . . .Lake Erie

JULY
1-2 . . . . .Lake Erie
3-5 . . . . Joliet

17-19 . . . . .Normal
21-23 . . . . . . .Lake Erie
29-30 . . . . River City
31 . . . . Florence

AUGUST
1-2 . . . . Florence
11-13 . . . . Frontier
18-20 . . . . Windy City
21-23 . . . . Gateway
28-30 . . . . . . Evansville

SEPTEMBER
4-6 . . . . Windy City

WINDY CITY THUNDERBOLTS

MAY
14 . . . . Schaumburg
15-16 . . . . Frontier
19-21 . . . . . Schaumburg
26-28 . . . . Southern Illinois
29-31 . . . . . Evansville

JUNE
5-7 . . . . .Rockford
10-11 . . . . Schaumburg
12-14 . . . . Gateway
23-25 . . . . .Normal
26-28 . . . . Florence

JULY
7-9 . . . . .Washington
10-12 . . . . Traverse City
20-23 . . . . Frontier
31 . . . . River City

AUGUST
1-2 . . . . River City
4-6 . . . . Gateway
14-16 . . . . . . .Lake Erie
25-27 . . . . River City
28-30 . . . . Joliet

ATLANTIC LEAGUE

BRIDGEPORT BLUEFISH

APRIL
24-26 . . . . Camden
28-30 . . . . Somerset

MAY
5-7 . . . . Long Island
15-17 . . . . Camden
22-25 . . . . . . Sugar Land
31 . . . . Somerset

JUNE
1-2 . . . . Somerset
11-14 . . . . . Long Island
23-25 . . . . Camden
29-30 . . Southern Maryland

JULY
1-2 . . . Southern Maryland
3-5 . . . . .York
13-16 . . Southern Maryland
17-19 . . . . . . Sugar Land
24-26 . . . . . Long Island

AUGUST
5-8 . . . . Lancaster
13-16 . . . . .York
24-26 . . . . . Long Island
27-30 . . . . . . Lancaster

SEPTEMBER
8-10 . . . . Sugar Land
15-16 . . . . Somerset
17-20 . . Southern Maryland

CAMDEN RIVERSHARKS

MAY
1-3 . . . . Bridgeport
8-11 . . . . Sugar Land
12-14 . . . . York
19-21 . . Southern Maryland
27-30 . . . . York

JUNE
4-6 . . . . Long Island
16-18 . . . . Lancaster
19-22 . . Southern Maryland
26-28 . . . . Lancaster
29-30 . . . . Somerset

JULY
1-2 . . . . Somerset

10-12 . . . . . . Bridgeport
20-23 . . . . Somerset
28-30 . . . . . Sugar Land
31 . . . . York

AUGUST
1-3 . . . . York
13-16 . . . . Somerset
17-20 . . . . Lancaster
24-26 . . Southern Maryland
27-30 . . . . . Sugar Land

SEPTEMBER
8-10 . . . . Long Island
11-13 . . . . . . Bridgeport

LANCASTER BARNSTORMERS

APRIL
30 . . . . York

MAY
1-3 . . . . Southern Maryland
5-7 . . . . York
15-18 . . . . . Long Island
19-21 . . . . . . Sugar Land
27-30 . . . . . . Bridgeport
31 . . . . Camden

JUNE
1-2 . . . . Camden
11-14 . . . . Somerset
19-22 . . . . York
23-25 . . . . Somerset

JULY
3-5 . . . . Camden
13-16 . . . . . . Long Island
17-19 . . . . York
28-30 . . . . . . Bridgeport
31 . . . . Somerset

AUGUST
1-3 . . . . Somerset
13-16 . . . . . Sugar Land
24-26 . . . . York

SEPTEMBER
1-3 . . . Southern Maryland
4-7 . . . . Camden
14-16 . . Southern Maryland
17-20 . . . . . . Long Island

LONG ISLAND DUCKS

MAY
1-3 . . . . Sugar Land
8-10 . . . . Lancaster
12-14 . . . . . . Bridgeport
22-24 . . . . Camden
31 . . . . York

JUNE
1-2 . . . . York
7-10 . . . Southern Maryland
16-18 . . . . . Sugar Land
19-22 . . . . . Bridgeport
29-30 . . . . Lancaster

JULY
1-2 . . . . Lancaster

3-5 . . . . Somerset
17-19 . . . . . . Somerset
20-23 . . . . York
28-30 . . . . . . Somerset
31 . . . . Bridgeport

AUGUST
1-3 . . . . Bridgeport
9-12 . . . . Camden
13-16 . Southern Maryland
21-23 . . . . Camden

SEPTEMBER
1-3 . . . . Bridgeport
4-7 . . . . Southern Maryland
11-13 . . . . . . Sugar Land

SOMERSET PATRIOTS

MAY
1-3 . . . . York
8-10 . . . . Bridgeport
12-14 . . . . Lancaster

19-21 . . . . . . Bridgeport
27-30 . . . . . Long Island

JUNE
3-6 . . . . Lancaster

7-10 . . . . Camden
16-18 . . . . . Bridgeport
19-22 . . . . Sugar Land
26-28 . . Southern Maryland

JULY
10-12 . . . . . Long Island
13-16 . . . . . . Camden
24-26 . . Southern Maryland

SOUTHERN MARYLAND BLUE CRABS

APRIL
24-26 . . . . Somerset
27-30 . . . . . . Long Island

MAY
5-7 . . . . Camden
12-14 . . . . . . Sugar Land
15-18 . . . . Somerset
22-25 . . . . Lancaster

JUNE
3-6 . . . . Bridgeport
11-14 . . . . Camden
23-25 . . . . York

JULY
3-5 . . . . Sugar Land

17-19 . . . . Camden
20-23 . . . . . Bridgeport
28-30 . . . . York
31 . . . . Sugar Land

AUGUST
1-3 . . . . Sugar Land
9-12 . . . . Bridgeport
17-20 . . . . York
21-23 . . . . Lancaster
27-30 . . . . . Long Island

SEPTEMBER
8-10 . . . . Lancaster
11-13 . . . . York

SUGAR LAND SKEETERS

APRIL
23-26 . . . . Lancaster
27-30 . . . . Camden

MAY
5-7 . . . . Somerset
15-18 . . . . York
27-31 . . Southern Maryland

JUNE
1-2 . . . Southern Maryland
7-10 . . . . . . Bridgeport
11-14 . . . . York

23-28 . . . . . . Long Island

JULY
10-12 . . Southern Maryland
22-26 . . . . Lancaster

AUGUST
5-8 . . . . Long Island
17-23 . . . . . . Bridgeport

SEPTEMBER
1-7 . . . . Somerset
14-20 . . . . Camden

YORK REVOLUTION

APRIL
24-26 . . . . . . Long Island
27-29 . . . . Lancaster

MAY
8-11 . . . Southern Maryland
19-21 . . . . . Long Island
22-25 . . . . Somerset

JUNE
3-6 . . . . Sugar Land
7-10 . . . . Lancaster
16-18 . . Southern Maryland
26-28 . . . . . . Bridgeport
29-30 . . . . . Sugar Land

JULY
1-2 . . . . Sugar Land
10-12 . . . . Lancaster
13-16 . . . . . Sugar Land
24-26 . . . . Camden

AUGUST
5-8 . . . . Southern Maryland
9-12 . . . . Lancaster
21-23 . . . . Somerset

SEPTEMBER
1-3 . . . . Camden
4-6 . . . . Bridgeport
14-16 . . . . . Long Island
17-20 . . . . Somerset

SPRING TRAINING SCHEDULES

ARIZONA CACTUS LEAGUE

ARIZONA DIAMONDBACKS

MARCH
4 . . . . at Colorado
5 . . . . .Colorado

6 . . . . Oakland
7 . . . . at Seattle
8 . . . . . . at San Francisco

8 . . . . .San Francisco
9 . . . . . . .at Chicago (AL)
10 . . . . at Oakland
11 . . . .Los Angeles (AL)
12 . . . . Cincinnati
13 . . . . at Cleveland
14 . . . . Seattle
14 . . . . . . .San Francisco

15 . . . . . . at San Francisco
16 . . . . Chicago (AL)
17 . . . . . at San Francisco
18 . . . . at Colorado
19 . . . . Chicago (NL)
20 . . . . . . .at Milwaukee
21 . . . . . . at San Diego
22 . . . . .Colorado

23 . . . . at Los Angeles (NL)
24 . . . . Milwaukee
26 . . . . San Diego
27 . . . at Los Angeles (AL)
27 . . . . Cleveland
28 . . . . Kansas City
29 . . . . at Colorado

CHICAGO (NL)

MARCH
5 . . . . Oakland
5 . . . at San Francisco
6 . . . . Cincinnati
7 . . . . at Colorado
8 . . . . Texas
9 . . . . San Diego
10 . . . . . . at Cleveland
11 . . . .Los Angeles (NL)
12 . . at Los Angeles (AL)
13 . . . . Cleveland
13 . . . . Oakland
14 . . . . Oakland
14 . . . . . at Milwaukee
15 . . . . . . Cincinnati
16 . . . . . at San Diego
17 . . . . . . Kansas City
18 . . at Los Angeles (NL)
19 . . . . at Arizona
20 . . . . .at Chicago (AL)
21 . . . . Seattle
22 . . . . San Diego
24 . . . . . . at Oakland
25 . . . . . . at Seattle
26 . . . .Los Angeles (AL)
27 . . . . . Chicago (AL)
28 . . . . . . .Colorado
28 . . . . . at Cincinnati
29 . . . . at Kansas City
30 . . .San Francisco
31 . . . . at Texas

APRIL
1 . . . . Milwaukee
3 . . . . at Arizona
4 . . . . at Arizona

CHICAGO WHITE SOX

MARCH
4 . . . at Los Angeles (NL)
5 . . . .Los Angeles (NL)
6 . . . . . at San Diego
7 . . . . Seattle
8 . . . . . . at Oakland
9 . . . . .Arizona
10 . . . . at Kansas City
11 . . . . Texas
12 . . . . at Texas
12 . . .San Francisco
13 . . . . . at Colorado
14 . . at Los Angeles (AL)
15 . . .Los Angeles (AL)
16 . . . . . . at Arizona
17 . . . . Seattle
18 . . . . . at Cincinnati
20 . . . . . . Chicago (NL)
21 . . . . . . Kansas City
22 . . . . . .at Milwaukee
23 . . . . . at San Diego
24 . . . . .Colorado
25 . . . . at Kansas City
26 . . . .Los Angeles (NL)
27 . . .at Chicago (NL)
28 . . . . Oakland
29 . . . . at Cleveland
30 . . . . . . Cleveland
31 . at Los Angeles (NL)

APRIL
1 . . . . at Seattle
1 . . . . San Diego
2 . . . . . . at Arizona

CINCINNATI REDS

MARCH
3 . . . . Cleveland
4 . . . . . . at Cleveland
5 . . . . Cleveland
6 . . . . . .at Chicago (NL)
7 . . . . . at Kansas City
8 . . . . Seattle
9 . . . .Los Angeles (NL)
9 . . . . . . at Colorado
10 . . . . .at Milwaukee
11 . . . . . Kansas City
12 . . . . . . at Arizona
13 . . at Los Angeles (NL)
14 . . . . . . .Colorado
15 . . . .at Chicago (NL)
16 . . .San Francisco
17 . . . . . at Cleveland
18 . . . . . Chicago (AL)
19 . . . . Texas
20 . . . at San Francisco
21 . . . . . at Oakland
22 . . . . Oakland
23 . . . . . . at Texas
25 . . . . Texas
26 . . . . . . Cleveland
27 . . . . . . Milwaukee
28 . . . . . Chicago (NL)
29 . . at Los Angeles (AL)
30 . . . . . . San Diego
31 . . . . .at Milwaukee

APRIL
1 . . . . .Arizona
2 . . . . Cleveland
3 . . . . .at Toronto
4 . . . . .at Toronto

CLEVELAND INDIANS

MARCH
3 . . . . at Cincinnati
4 . . . . Cincinnati
5 . . . . . . at Cincinnati
6 . . . . Kansas City
7 . . . . . .Los Angeles (NL)
8 . . . . at Texas
9 . . . . at Seattle
10 . . . . . Chicago (NL)
11 . . . . . . at Oakland
12 . . . . . . Kansas City

COLORADO ROCKIES

MARCH
4 . . . . .Arizona
5 . . . . at Arizona
6 . . at Los Angeles (AL)
7 . . . . . . Chicago (NL)
8 . . . . . at San Diego
9 . . . . . . Cincinnati
10 . . at Los Angeles (NL)
10 . . . . Seattle
11 . . . . . . at Seattle
12 . . . . at Milwaukee
13 . . . . Chicago (AL)
14 . . . . at Cincinnati
15 . . . . . Kansas City
17 . . . .Los Angeles (NL)
18 . . . . . . San Diego
18 . . . . .Arizona
19 . . . at Kansas City
20 . . . . Oakland
21 . . . . . at Cleveland
21 . . .Los Angeles (NL)
22 . . . . . at Arizona
23 . . . . . . Milwaukee
24 . . .at Chicago (AL)
25 . . .San Francisco
26 . . . . . . at Texas
27 . . . . at San Diego
28 . . .at Chicago (NL)
29 . . . . . . .Arizona
30 . . . . . at Oakland
31 . at San Francisco

APRIL
1 . . . . Texas
3 . . . . . . at Seattle
4 . . . . Seattle
4 . . . . . Kansas City

KANSAS CITY ROYALS

MARCH
4 . . . . at Texas
5 . . . . Texas
6 . . . . . at Cleveland
7 . . . . . . Cincinnati
8 . . at Los Angeles (AL)
9 . . . . at Milwaukee
10 . . . . Chicago (AL)
11 . . . at Cincinnati
11 . . . . . San Diego
12 . . . at Cleveland
13 . . . . . Oakland
14 . . .Los Angeles (AL)
15 . . . at Colorado
16 . . . . Cleveland
17 . .at Chicago (NL)
18 . . . . Milwaukee
19 . . . . .Colorado
20 . . . . at San Diego
21 . . . .at Chicago (AL)
22 . . .San Francisco
23 . . at San Francisco
25 . . . . Chicago (AL)
26 . . . . at Seattle
27 . . . . . Seattle
28 . . . . at Arizona
29 . . . Chicago (AL)
30 . . . . . at Texas
31 . . . at San Diego

APRIL
1 . . . . . .Los Angeles (NL)
3 . . . . . . at Houston
4 . . . . . . at Houston

LOS ANGELES ANGELS

MARCH
5 . . . . Milwaukee
6 . . . . .Colorado
7 . . . . at Oakland
8 . . . . Kansas City
9 . . . . . at Cincinnati
10 . . . . Texas
11 . . . . . at Arizona
12 . . . . . Chicago (NL)
13 . . . . . . San Diego
14 . . . at Kansas City
14 . . . . Chicago (AL)
15 . . .at Chicago (AL)
16 . . . . Texas
17 . . . . at Colorado
19 . . at Los Angeles (NL)
20 . . . . . at Cleveland
21 . . . . . .San Francisco
22 . . . at San Francisco
23 . . . . Seattle
24 . . . . . . at Texas
25 . . . . . . Cleveland
26 . . .at Chicago (NL)
27 . . . . . . .Arizona
28 . . .Los Angeles (NL)
29 . . . . . Cincinnati
30 . . . . . at Seattle
31 . . . . . . Oakland

APRIL
1 . . . . at Oakland
2 . . .Los Angeles (NL)
3 . . . .Los Angeles (NL)
4 . . . at Los Angeles (NL)

LOS ANGELES DODGERS

MARCH
4 . . . . Chicago (AL)
5 . . . . . .at Chicago (AL)
6 . . . . at Milwaukee
6 . . . . Seattle
7 . . . . at Cleveland
8 . . . . Milwaukee
9 . . . . . at San Francisco
10 . . . . .Colorado
11 . . . . . .at Chicago (NL)
12 . . . . . at San Diego
13 . . . . Cincinnati
14 . . . . Cleveland
15 . . . . . . at Seattle
16 . . . . Oakland
17 . . . . at Texas
18 . . . . . Chicago (NL)
19 . . . . .Los Angeles (AL)
20 . . . . . at Oakland
20 . . . . at Texas
21 . . . . at Texas
21 . . . . .at Colorado
22 . . . . Cleveland
23 . . . . Arizona
25 . . . . San Diego
26 . . . . . .at Chicago (AL)
27 . . . . . . .San Francisco
28 . . . at Los Angeles (AL)
29 . . . . at San Francisco
29 . . . . Texas
30 . . . . at Arizona
31 . . . . Chicago (AL)

APRIL
1 . . . . at Kansas City
2 . . at Los Angeles (AL)
3 . . . . at Los Angeles (AL)
4 . . . . . .Los Angeles (AL)

MILWAUKEE BREWERS

MARCH
5 . . . . . at Los Angeles (AL)
6 . . . . .Los Angeles (NL)
7 . . . . Texas
8 . . . at Los Angeles (NL)
9 . . . . Kansas City
10 . . . . Cincinnati
11 . . . . . at San Francisco
12 . . . . .Colorado
13 . . . . at Seattle
14 . . . . . . Chicago (NL)
15 . . . . at Texas
15 . . . . Oakland
17 . . . . . at San Diego
18 . . . . . . at Kansas City
19 . . . . . .San Francisco
20 . . . . .Arizona
21 . . . . at Texas
22 . . . . Chicago (AL)
23 . . . . . . .at Colorado
24 . . . . at Arizona
25 . . . . Oakland
26 . . . . Seattle
27 . . . . . . at Cincinnati
28 . . . . Cleveland
29 . . . . at Oakland
31 . . . . Cincinnati

APRIL
1 . . . . . . .at Chicago (NL)
2 . . . . . . at San Diego
3 . . . . . . at Cleveland
4 . . . . Cleveland

OAKLAND ATHLETICS

MARCH
3 . . . . .San Francisco
4 . . . . . at San Francisco
5 . . . . .at Chicago (NL)
6 . . . . at Arizona
7 . . . .Los Angeles (AL)
8 . . . . Chicago (AL)
9 . . . . at Texas
10 . . . . .Arizona
11 . . . . Cleveland
12 . . . . Seattle
13 . . . .at Chicago (NL)
13 . . . . at Kansas City
14 . . . . .at Chicago (NL)
14 . . . . . . .San Francisco
15 . . . . . . at Milwaukee
16 . . . at Los Angeles (NL)
17 . . . . San Diego
18 . . . . at Seattle
20 . . . . .Los Angeles (NL)
20 . . . . . . at Colorado
21 . . . . Cincinnati
22 . . . . . . at Cincinnati
23 . . . . at Cleveland
24 . . . . . . Chicago (NL)
25 . . . . at Milwaukee
26 . . . . at San Francisco
27 . . . . Texas
28 . . . . .at Chicago (AL)
29 . . . . Milwaukee
30 . . . . .Colorado
31 . . at Los Angeles (AL)

APRIL
1 . . . . . .Los Angeles (AL)
2 . . . . . at San Francisco
3 . . . . . . at San Francisco
4 . . . . . . .San Francisco

SAN DIEGO PADRES

MARCH
4 . . . . at Seattle
5 . . . . at Seattle
6 . . . . . . Chicago (AL)
7 . . . at San Francisco
8 . . . . .Colorado
9 . . . . .at Chicago (NL)
10 . . . . .San Francisco
11 . . . . . . at Kansas City
12 . . . .Los Angeles (NL)
13 . . . at Los Angeles (AL)
14 . . . . Texas
15 . . . . . . at Cleveland
16 . . . . . .at Chicago (NL)
17 . . . . Milwaukee
17 . . . . at Oakland
18 . . . . .at Colorado
20 . . . . Kansas City
21 . . . . .Arizona
22 . . . . .at Chicago (NL)
23 . . . . Chicago (AL)
24 . . . . Seattle
25 . . at Los Angeles (AL)
26 . . . . at Arizona
27 . . . . .Colorado
28 . . . . at Texas

SAN FRANCISCO GIANTS

29 . . . . Seattle
30 . . . . . . at Cincinnati
31 . . . . Kansas City

APRIL
1 . . . . . . .at Chicago (AL)
2 . . . . Milwaukee

MARCH
3 . . . . at Oakland
4 . . . . Oakland
5 . . . . Chicago (AL)
6 . . . . at Texas
7 . . . . San Diego
8 . . . . .Arizona
8 . . . . at Arizona
9 . . . . . .Los Angeles (NL)
10 . . . . . . at San Diego
11 . . . . Milwaukee
12 . . .at Chicago (AL)
13 . . . . Texas
14 . . . . at Oakland
14 . . . . .at Arizona
15 . . . . .Arizona
16 . . . . . . at Cincinnati
17 . . . . .Arizona
19 . . . . . .at Milwaukee
20 . . . . Cincinnati
21 . . . at Los Angeles (AL)
22 . . . .Los Angeles (AL)
22 . . . . . at Kansas City
23 . . . . Kansas City
24 . . . . at Cleveland
25 . . . . .at Colorado
26 . . . . Oakland
27 . . . at Los Angeles (NL)
28 . . . . at Seattle
29 . . . . .Los Angeles (NL)
30 . . . . .at Chicago (NL)
31 . . . . .Colorado

APRIL
1 . . . . Cleveland
2 . . . . Oakland
3 . . . . Oakland
4 . . . . at Oakland

SEATTLE MARINERS

MARCH
4 . . . . San Diego
5 . . . . San Diego
6 . . . at Los Angeles (NL)
7 . . . . .Arizona
7 . . . .at Chicago (AL)
8 . . . . . . at Cincinnati
9 . . . . Cleveland
10 . . . . at Colorado
11 . . . . .Colorado
12 . . . . at Oakland
13 . . . . Milwaukee
14 . . . . at Arizona
15 . . . . .Los Angeles (NL)
17 . . . . .at Chicago (AL)
18 . . . . Oakland
19 . . . . Cleveland
20 . . . . at Texas
21 . . . . . .at Chicago (NL)
22 . . . . Texas
23 . . . at Los Angeles (AL)
24 . . . . . . at San Diego
25 . . . . Chicago (NL)
26 . . . . Kansas City
26 . . . . . .at Milwaukee
27 . . . . Kansas City
28 . . . . . . .San Francisco
29 . . . . . at San Diego
30 . . . . .Los Angeles (AL)
31 . . . . . . at Cleveland

APRIL
1 . . . . Chicago (AL)
3 . . . . .Colorado
4 . . . . at Colorado

TEXAS RANGERS

MARCH
4 . . . . Kansas City
5 . . . . at Kansas City
6 . . . . . . .San Francisco
7 . . . . . .at Milwaukee
8 . . . .at Chicago (NL)
8 . . . . Cleveland
9 . . . . Oakland
10 . . . at Los Angeles (AL)
11 . . . .at Chicago (AL)
12 . . . . . . Chicago (AL)
13 . . . . at San Francisco
14 . . . . . at San Diego
15 . . . . Milwaukee
16 . . . at Los Angeles (AL)
17 . . . .Los Angeles (AL)
19 . . . . . . at Cincinnati
20 . . . . Seattle
20 . . . . .Los Angeles (NL)
21 . . . . .Los Angeles (NL)
21 . . . . Milwaukee
22 . . . . at Seattle
23 . . . . Cincinnati
24 . . . .Los Angeles (AL)
25 . . . . . at Cincinnati
26 . . . . . . .Colorado
27 . . . . . . at Oakland
28 . . . . San Diego
29 . . at Los Angeles (NL)
30 . . . . . Kansas City
31 . . . . . . Chicago (NL)
31 . . . . at Arizona

APRIL
1 . . . . .at Colorado
3 . . . . New York (NL)
4 . . . . New York (NL)

FLORIDA GRAPEFRUIT LEAGUE

ATLANTA BRAVES

MARCH
4 . . . . . . New York (NL)
5 . . . . at Detroit
6 . . . . .Washington
7 . . . . .Detroit
7 . . . . . .at New York (NL)
8 . . . . at Houston
9 . . . . at Washington
10 . . . . New York (NL)
11 . . . . St. Louis
12 . . . . . .at New York (AL)
13 . . . . Detroit

13 . . . . . .at New York (NL)
14 . . . . Houston
15 . . . . Toronto
16 . . . . at Houston
17 . . . . at Boston
18 . . . . . . New York (AL)
19 . . . . Miami
20 . . . . at Miami
21 . . . . St. Louis
21 . . . . .Washington
22 . . . . Detroit
23 . . . . at Houston

24 . . . . Philadelphia
26 . . . . . . at Pittsburgh
27 . . . . Boston
28 . . . . .at Toronto
29 . . . . .Pittsburgh
30 . . . . at Detroit
31 . . . . Houston
APRIL
1 . . . . . . .at Philadelphia
2 . . . . Baltimore
3 . . . . .at Baltimore
4 . . . . Baltimore

BALTIMORE ORIOLES

MARCH		
3 . . . . at Detroit	19 . . . . .Pittsburgh	
4 . . . . Detroit	20 . . . . at Boston	
5 . . . . at Tampa Bay	21 . . . . . . at Minnesota	
5 . . . . Toronto	22 . . . . St. Louis	
6 . . . . . . .at Toronto	24 . . . . . at Pittsburgh	
7 . . . . Boston	25 . . . . Toronto	
8 . . . . at Minnesota	26 . . . . . . at Detroit	
9 . . . . . Philadelphia	27 . . . . Tampa Bay	
10 . . . New York (AL)	28 . . . at New York (AL)	
11 . . . . Toronto	29 . . . . . . .Minnesota	
12 . . . . . at St. Louis	29 . . . . . . at Toronto	
13 . . . . . at Toronto	30 . . . at Tampa Bay	
14 . . . . . . Tampa Bay	31 . . . . . Tampa Bay	
15 . . . . . at Pittsburgh	**APRIL**	
16 . . . at Philadelphia	1 . . . . .Pittsburgh	
17 . . . . . .Minnesota	2 . . . . at Atlanta	
18 . . . . . at Minnesota	3 . . . . Atlanta	
	4 . . . . at Atlanta	

BOSTON RED SOX

MARCH		
5 . . . . . . at Minnesota	20 . . . . Baltimore	
6 . . . . Miami	21 . . . . . at Pittsburgh	
7 . . . . .at Baltimore	22 . . . . . . Philadelphia	
7 . . . . .Minnesota	23 . . . . St. Louis	
8 . . . . .at New York (NL)	24 . . . . .at Miami	
9 . . . . at St. Louis	26 . . . . . . .Minnesota	
10 . . . . . . Tampa Bay	27 . . . . at Atlanta	
11 . . . at New York (AL)	28 . . . . at Tampa Bay	
12 . . . . at Pittsburgh	29 . . . . . . Tampa Bay	
13 . . . . New York (AL)	30 . . . . . . .Minnesota	
14 . . . . . . .Pittsburgh	31 . . . . at Tampa Bay	
15 . . . at Philadelphia	**APRIL**	
16 . . . . New York (NL)	1 . . . . at Minnesota	
17 . . . . Atlanta	1 . . . . Toronto	
18 . . . . . . .Minnesota	2 . . . . . . at Minnesota	
19 . . . . at Toronto	3 . . . . .Minnesota	
	4 . . . . at Minnesota	

DETROIT TIGERS

MARCH		
3 . . . . Baltimore	19 . . . . . . at Washington	
4 . . . . .at Baltimore	20 . . . . . New York (AL)	
5 . . . . Atlanta	21 . . . . . New York (NL)	
6 . . . .at New York (NL)	22 . . . . at Atlanta	
7 . . . . at Atlanta	22 . . . . . . .Washington	
8 . . . . Houston	24 . . . . .at New York (AL)	
9 . . . . Toronto	25 . . . . Miami	
10 . . . . at Phillies	26 . . . . . . Baltimore	
11 . . . . . at Washington	27 . . . . . .at Toronto	
12 . . . . . at Houston	28 . . . . St. Louis	
12 . . . . . Philadelphia	29 . . . .at Philadelphia	
13 . . . . . . at Atlanta	30 . . . . Atlanta	
14 . . . at New York (AL)	31 . . . . .Pittsburgh	
14 . . . . . Philadelphia	**APRIL**	
15 . . . . . . at Miami	1 . . . . at Houston	
16 . . . . at St. Louis	2 . . . . . . New York (AL)	
17 . . . . . .Washington	3 . . . . Tampa Bay	
18 . . . . . at Pittsburgh	4 . . . . . . .at Tampa Bay	

HOUSTON ASTROS

MARCH		
5 . . . . . Philadelphia	19 . . . . .at New York (NL)	
6 . . . . at St. Louis	20 . . . . . . .Washington	
7 . . . . New York (AL)	21 . . . . at New York (AL)	
8 . . . . Atlanta	22 . . . . .Pittsburgh	
8 . . . . at Detroit	23 . . . . Atlanta	
9 . . . . . . .at Toronto	24 . . . .at New York (NL)	
10 . . . . . St. Louis	25 . . . .at Philadelphia	
12 . . . . Detroit	27 . . . . Miami	
13 . . . . . at Washington	28 . . . . . . at Miami	
14 . . . . . at Atlanta	29 . . . . New York (AL)	
15 . . . . . .Washington	30 . . . . Toronto	
16 . . . . . at Washington	31 . . . . . . at Atlanta	
16 . . . . Atlanta	**APRIL**	
17 . . . . at Pittsburgh	1 . . . . Detroit	
	3 . . . . Kansas City	

MIAMI MARLINS

MARCH		
5 . . . . St. Louis	20 . . . . Atlanta	
6 . . . . at Boston	21 . . . . . at Washington	
7 . . . . New York (NL)	22 . . . . . . .Minnesota	
8 . . . . at St. Louis	23 . . . . . New York (NL)	
9 . . . .at New York (NL)	24 . . . . Boston	
10 . . . .Washington	25 . . . . . . at Detroit	
11 . . . . New York (NL)	26 . . . . . . at St. Louis	
12 . . . . at Minnesota	27 . . . . . . at Houston	
13 . . . . . St. Louis	28 . . . . Houston	
14 . . . . at Washington	29 . . . . at Washington	
15 . . . . . . Detroit	30 . . . .at New York (NL)	
17 . . .at New York (NL)	31 . . . . . . at St. Louis	
17 . . . . St. Louis	**APRIL**	
18 . . . . . . .Washington	1 . . . . .Washington	
19 . . . . . . at Atlanta		

MINNESOTA TWINS

MARCH		
5 . . . . Boston	21 . . . . Baltimore	
6 . . . . at Tampa Bay	21 . . . . . at Tampa Bay	
7 . . . . . . at Boston	22 . . . . Miami	
8 . . . . . . Baltimore	23 . . . .at Philadelphia	
9 . . . . at Pittsburgh	24 . . . . Toronto	
10 . . . . at Toronto	25 . . . . . Tampa Bay	
11 . . . . Tampa Bay	26 . . . . . . at Boston	
12 . . . . Miami	27 . . . . . . .Pittsburgh	
13 . . . at Pittsburgh	28 . . . . . Philadelphia	
14 . . . . at St. Louis	29 . . . .at Baltimore	
15 . . . . . St. Louis	30 . . . . . . at Boston	
17 . . .at Baltimore	31 . . . . . New York (AL)	
18 . . . . Baltimore	**APRIL**	
18 . . . . . at Boston	1 . . . . Boston	
19 . . . . at Tampa Bay	2 . . . . Boston	
20 . . . . . .Pittsburgh	3 . . . . at Boston	
	4 . . . . Boston	

NEW YORK METS

MARCH		
4 . . . . at Atlanta	20 . . . . St. Louis	
5 . . . . . at Washington	21 . . . . . . at Detroit	
6 . . . . Detroit	22 . . . . New York (AL)	
7 . . . . . at Miami	23 . . . . . at Miami	
7 . . . . . . Atlanta	24 . . . . Houston	
8 . . . . . . Boston	25 . . .at New York (AL)	
9 . . . . . Miami	26 . . . . at Washington	
10 . . . . at Atlanta	27 . . . . at St. Louis	
11 . . . . at Miami	28 . . . .Washington	
12 . . . . .Washington	29 . . . . at St. Louis	
13 . . . . . Atlanta	30 . . . . . Miami	
14 . . . . .Washington	31 . . . at Washington	
15 . . . at Tampa Bay	**APRIL**	
16 . . . . at Boston	1 . . . . St. Louis	
17 . . . . . Miami	2 . . . . . . at Cardinals	
19 . . . . . at St. Louis	3 . . . . at Texas	
19 . . . . . Houston	4 . . . . at Texas	

NEW YORK YANKEES

MARCH	
3	at Philadelphia
4	Philadelphia
5	at Pittsburgh
6	at Philadelphia
6	Pittsburgh
7	at Houston
8	Washington
9	Tampa Bay
10	at Baltimore
11	Boston
12	Atlanta
13	at Boston
14	Detroit
14	at Toronto
15	Philadelphia
17	Toronto
18	at Atlanta
19	Philadelphia
20	at Detroit
21	Houston
22	at New York (NL)
23	at Washington
24	Detroit
25	New York (NL)
26	at Tampa Bay
27	at Philadelphia
28	Baltimore
29	at Houston
31	at Minnesota

APRIL	
1	Tampa Bay
2	at Detroit
2	Pittsburgh
3	Washington
4	at Washington

PHILADELPHIA PHILLIES

MARCH	
3	New York (AL)
4	at New York (AL)
5	at Houston
6	New York (AL)
7	Toronto
8	at Tampa Bay
9	at Baltimore
10	Detroit
11	Pittsburgh
12	at Detroit
13	Tampa Bay
14	at Detroit
15	Boston
15	at New York (AL)
16	Baltimore
17	Tampa Bay
19	at New York (AL)
20	at Pittsburgh
21	Toronto
22	at Boston
23	Minnesota
24	at Atlanta
25	Houston
26	at Toronto
27	New York (AL)
28	at Minnesota
29	Detroit
30	at Pittsburgh
31	at Toronto

APRIL	
1	Atlanta
2	Tampa Bay
3	Pittsburgh
4	Pittsburgh

PITTSBURGH PIRATES

MARCH	
3	at Toronto
4	Toronto
5	New York (AL)
6	at New York (AL)
7	Tampa Bay
8	at Toronto
9	Minnesota
10	at Tampa Bay
11	at Philadelphia
12	Boston
13	Minnesota
14	at Boston
15	Baltimore
17	Houston
18	Detroit
19	at Baltimore
20	Philadelphia
20	at Minnesota
21	Boston
22	at Houston
23	at Tampa Bay
24	Baltimore
26	Atlanta
27	at Minnesota
28	Toronto
29	at Atlanta
30	Philadelphia
31	at Detroit

APRIL	
1	at Baltimore
2	at New York (AL)
3	at Philadelphia
4	at Philadelphia

ST. LOUIS CARDINALS

MARCH	
5	at Miami
6	Houston
7	at Washington
8	Miami
9	Boston
10	at Houston
11	at Atlanta
12	Baltimore
13	at Miami
14	Minnesota
15	at Minnesota
16	Detroit
17	at Miami
19	New York (NL)
20	at New York (NL)
21	Atlanta
22	at Baltimore
23	at Boston
25	Washington
26	Miami
27	at Washington
27	New York (NL)
28	at Detroit
29	New York (NL)
30	Washington
31	Miami

APRIL	
1	at New York (NL)
2	New York (NL)

TAMPA BAY RAYS

MARCH	
5	Baltimore
6	Minnesota
7	at Pittsburgh
8	Philadelphia
9	at New York (AL)
10	Pittsburgh
10	at Boston
11	at Minnesota
12	Toronto
13	at Philadelphia
14	at Baltimore
15	New York (NL)
17	at Philadelphia
18	at Toronto
19	Minnesota
20	Toronto
21	Minnesota
22	at Toronto
23	Pittsburgh
25	at Minnesota
26	New York (AL)
27	at Baltimore
28	Boston
20	at Boston
30	Baltimore
31	Boston
31	at Baltimore

APRIL	
1	at New York (AL)
2	at Philadelphia
3	at Detroit
4	Detroit

TORONTO BLUE JAYS

MARCH	
3	Pittsburgh
4	at Pittsburgh
5	at Baltimore
6	Baltimore
7	at Philadelphia
8	Pittsburgh
9	at Detroit
9	Houston
10	Minnesota
11	at Baltimore
12	at Tampa Bay
13	Baltimore
14	New York (AL)
15	at Atlanta
17	at New York (AL)
18	Tampa Bay
19	Boston
20	at Tampa Bay
21	at Philadelphia
22	Tampa Bay
24	at Minnesota
25	at Baltimore
26	Philadelphia
27	Detroit
28	at Pittsburgh
28	Atlanta
29	Baltimore
30	at Houston
31	Philadelphia

APRIL	
1	at Boston
3	Cincinnati
4	Cincinnati

WASHINGTON NATIONALS

MARCH	
5	New York (NL)
6	at Atlanta
7	St. Louis
8	at New York (AL)
9	Atlanta
10	at Miami
11	Detroit
12	at New York (NL)
13	Houston
14	Miami
14	at New York (NL)
15	at Houston
16	Houston
17	at Detroit
18	at Miami
19	Detroit
20	at Houston
21	Miami
21	at Atlanta
22	at Detroit
23	New York (AL)
25	at St. Louis
26	New York (NL)
27	St. Louis
28	at New York (NL)
29	Miami
30	at St. Louis
31	New York (NL)

APRIL	
1	at Miami
3	at New York (AL)
4	New York (AL)

COLLEGES

COLLEGE ORGANIZATIONS

NATIONAL COLLEGIATE ATHLETIC ASSOCIATION

Mailing Address: PO Box 6222, Indianapolis, IN 46206. **Telephone:** (317) 917-6222. **Fax:** (317) 917-6826 (championships), 917-6710 (baseball).

E-Mail Addresses: Division I Championship: dleech@ncaa.org (Damani Leech), rlbuhr@ncaa.org (Randy Buhr), ctolliver@ncaa.org (Chad Tolliver), thalpin@ncaa.org (Ty Halpin), jhamilton@ncaa.org (JD Hamilton), kgiles@ncaa.org (Kim Giles). **Division II Championship:** ebreece@ncaa.org (Eric Breece). **Division III:** jpwilliams@ncaa.org (J.P. Williams).

Websites: www.ncaa.org, www.ncaa.com.

President: Dr. Mark Emmert. **Managing Director, Division I Championships/Alliances:** Damani Leech. **Director, Division I Championships/Alliances:** Randy Buhr. **Assistant Director, Championships/Alliances:** Chad Tolliver. **Division II Assistant Director, Championships/Alliances:** Eric Breece. **Division III Assistant Director, Championships/Alliances:** J.P. Williams. **Media Contact, Division I Championships, Alliances/College World Series:** J.D. Hamilton. **Playing Rules Contact:** Ty Halpin. **Statistics Contacts:** Jeff Williams (Division I and RPI); Mark Bedics (Division II); Sean Straziscar (Division III).

Chairman, Division I Baseball Committee: Dave Heeke (Director, Athletics, Central Michigan University). **Division I Baseball Committee:** Patrick Chun (Director of Athletics, Florida Atlantic); Joel Erdmann (Director, Athletics, South Alabama); Robert Goodman (Senior Associate Commissioner, Colonial Athletic Association); Dan Guerrero (Director of Athletics, UCLA; Dave Heeke (Director, Athletics, Central Michigan); Eric Hyman (Director, Athletics, Texas A&M); Ron Prettyman (Director, Athletics, Indiana St.); Ed Scott (Senior Associate Director, Athletics, Binghamton); Mike Buddie (Senior Associate Director, Athletics, Wake Forest University), Scott Sidwell (Director, Athletics, University of San Franscisco).

Chairman, Division II Baseball Committee: Doug Jones (Head Baseball Coach, Tusculum). **Chairman, Division III Baseball Committee:** Ben Shipp (Head Baseball Coach, Mary Hardin-Baylor).

2016 National Convention: Jan. 14-17 at Washington D.C.

2015 CHAMPIONSHIP TOURNAMENTS

NCAA DIVISION I
College World Series . . . . . Omaha, Neb., June 13-23/24
Super Regionals (8) . . . . Campus sites, June 5-8
Regionals (16). . . . . Campus sites, May 29-June 1

NCAA DIVISION II
World Series. . . USA Baseball National Training Complex
Cary, N.C., May 23-May 30
Regionals (8) Campus sites, May 14-17.

NCAA DIVISION III
39th annual World Series . . Neuroscience Group Field at
Fox Cities Stadium, Appleton, Wis., May 22-26
Regionals (8) . . . . Campus sites, May 13-17

NATIONAL JUNIOR COLLEGE ATHLETIC ASSOCIATION

Mailing Address: 1631 Mesa Ave., Suite B, Colorado Springs, CO 80906. **Telephone:** (719) 590-9788. **Fax:** (719) 590-7324. **E-Mail Address:** mkrug@njcaa.org. **Website:** www.njcaa.org.

Executive Director: Mary Ellen Leicht. **Director,**

Division I Baseball Tournament: Jamie Hamilton. **Director, Division II Baseball Tournament:** Billy Mayberry. **Director, Division III Baseball Tournament:** Bill Ellis. **Director Media Relations:** Mark Krug

2015 CHAMPIONSHIP TOURNAMENTS

DIVISION I
World Series. . . . . Grand Junction, CO, May 23-30
DIVISION II
World Series. . . . . Enid, OK, May 23-33
DIVISION III
World Series. . . . . Kinston, NC May 23-29

CALIFORNIA COMMUNITY COLLEGE ATHLETIC ASSOCIATION

Mailing Address: 2017 O St., Sacramento, CA 95811. **Telephone:** (916) 444-1600. **Fax:** (916) 444-2616. **E-Mail Addresses:** ccarter@cccaasports.org, jboggs@cccaasports.org. **Website:** www.cccaasports.org.

Executive Director: Carlyle Carter. **Director, Membership Services:** Unavailable. **Director, Championships:** George Mategakis. **Assistant Director, Sports Information/Communications:** Jason Boggs. **Director, Membership Services:** Jennifer Cardone, jcardone@cccaasports.org. **Business Operations Specialist:** Rina Kasim, rkasim@cccaasports.org. **Administrative Assistant:** Rima Trotter, rtrotter@cccaasports.org

2015 CHAMPIONSHIP TOURNAMENT

State Championship . . . . Fresno, CA, May 23-25

NORTHWEST ATHLETIC CONFERENCE

Mailing Address: Clark College TGB 121, 1933 Fort Vancouver Way, Vancouver, WA 98663. **Telephone:** (360) 992-2833. **Fax:** (360) 696-6210. **E-Mail Address:** nwaacc@clark.edu. **Website:** www.nwacsports.org.

Executive Director: Marco Azurdia. **Executive Assistant:** Carol Hardin. **Sports Information Director:** Tracy Swisher. **Director, External Operations:** Scott Archer. **Compliance Manager:** Jim Jackson.

2015 CHAMPIONSHIP TOURNAMENT

NWAC Championship. . . . . . Lower Columbia College
Longview, WA, May 21-25

AMERICAN BASEBALL COACHES ASSOCIATION

Office Address: 4101 Piedmont Parkway, Suite C, Greensboro, NC 27410. **Telephone:** (336) 821-3140. **Fax:** (336) 886-0000. **E-Mail Address:** abca@abca.org. **Website:** www.abca.org.

Executive Director: Craig Keilitz. **Associate Executive Director:** Nick Phillips. **Director, Exhibits/Branding:** Juahn Clark. **Communications/Business Manager:** Jon Litchfield. **Assistant Membership/Convention Coordinator:** Zach Haile.

Chairman: Mark Johnson. **President:** Ed Blankmeyer (St. John's).

2016 National Convention: Jan. 7-10, 2016, at Gaylord Opryland in Nashville, TN.

NCAA DIVISION I CONFERENCES

AMERICA EAST CONFERENCE

Mailing Address: 451 D Street, Suite 702, Boston, MA 02127. **Telephone:** (617) 695-6369. **Fax:** (617) 695-6380. **E-Mail Address:** hager@americaeast.com. **Website:** www.americaeast.com.

Baseball Members (First Year): Albany (2002), Binghamton (2002), Hartford (1990), Maine (1990), Maryland-Baltimore County (2004), Massachusetts-Lowell (2014), Stony Brook (2002).

Director, Strategic Media/Baseball Contact: Jared Hager.

2015 Tournament: Four teams, double-elimination, May 21-23 at LeLacheur Park, Lowell, Mass.

AMERICAN ATHLETIC CONFERENCE

Mailing Address: 15 Park Row West, Providence, RI 02903. **Telephone:** (401) 453-0660. **Fax:** (401) 751-8540. **E-Mail Address:** csullivan@theamerican.org. **Website:** www.theamerican.org.

Baseball Members (First Year): UCF (2014), Cincinnati (2014), Connecticut (2014), East Carolina (2015), Houston (2014), Memphis (2014), USF (2014), Tulane (2015).

Director, Communications: Chuck Sullivan.

2015 Tournament: Eight teams, double-elimination until the final, May 19-24 at Clearwater, Fla.

ATLANTIC COAST CONFERENCE

Mailing Address: 4512 Weybridge Ln., Greensboro, NC 27407. **Telephone:** (336) 851-6062. **Fax:** (336) 854-8797. **E-Mail Address:** sphillips@theacc.org. **Website:** www.theacc.com.

Baseball Members (First Year): Boston College (2006), Clemson (1954), Duke (1954), Florida State (1992), Georgia Tech (1980), Maryland (1954), Miami (2005), North Carolina (1954), North Carolina State (1954), Notre Dame (2014), Pittsburgh (2014), Virginia (1955), Virginia Tech (2005), Wake Forest (1954).

Associate Director, Communications: Steve Phillips.

2015 Tournament: Eight teams, group play. May 19-24, 2015 at Durham Bulls Athletic Park, Durham, NC.

ATLANTIC SUN CONFERENCE

Mailing Address: 3370 Vineville Ave., Suite 108-B, Macon, GA 31204. **Telephone:** (478) 474-3394. **Fax:** (478) 474-4272. **E-Mail Addresses:** pmccoy@atlanticsun.org. **Website:** www.atlanticsun.org.

Baseball Members (First Year): East Tennessee State (2006), Florida Gulf Coast (2008), Jacksonville (1999), Kennesaw State (2006), Lipscomb (2004), Mercer (1979), North Florida (2006), Northern Kentucky (2013), South Carolina-Upstate (2008), Stetson (1986).

Director, Sports Information: Patrick McCoy.

2015 Tournament: Eight teams, double-elimination. May 20-24 at Jacksonville, Fla.

ATLANTIC 10 CONFERENCE

Mailing Address: 11827 Canon Blvd., Suite 200, Newport News, VA 23606. **Telephone:** (757) 706-3059. **Fax:** (757) 706-3042. **E-Mail Address:** ckilcoyne@atlantic10.org. **Website:** www.atlantic10.com.

Baseball Members (First Year): Dayton (1996), Fordham (1996), George Mason (2014), George Washington (1977), La Salle (1996), Massachusetts (1977), Rhode Island (1981), Richmond (2002), St. Bonaventure (1980), Saint Joseph's (1983), Saint Louis (2006), Virginia

Commonwealth (2013).

Commissioner: Bernadette V. McGlade. **Director, Communications:** Drew Dickerson. **Assistant Director, Communications/Baseball Contact:** Chris Kilcoyne.

2015 Tournament: Seven teams, double elimination. May 20-23 at Barcroft Park, Washington DC.

BIG EAST CONFERENCE

Mailing Address: BIG EAST Conference, 655 3rd Avenue, 7th Floor, New York, NY 10017. **Telephone:** (212) 969-3181. **Fax:** (212) 969-2900. **E-Mail Address:** kquinn@bigeast.com. **Website:** www.bigeast.com.

Baseball Members (First Year): Butler (2014), Creighton (2014), Georgetown (1985), St. John's (1985), Seton Hall (1985), Villanova (1985), Xavier (2014).

Assistant Commissioner, Olympic Sports/Marketing Communications: Kristin Quinn.

2015 Tournament: Four teams, modified double-elimination. May 21-24 at TD Ameritrade Park, Omaha, Neb.

BIG SOUTH CONFERENCE

Mailing Address: 7233 Pineville-Matthews Rd., Suite 100, Charlotte, NC 28226. **Telephone:** (704) 341-7990. **Fax:** (704) 341-7991. **E-Mail Address:** brianv@bigsouth.org. **Website:** www.bigsouthsports.com.

Baseball Members (First Year): Campbell (2012), Charleston Southern (1983), Coastal Carolina (1983), Gardner-Webb (2009), High Point (1999), Liberty (1991), Longwood (2013), UNC Asheville (1985), Presbyterian (2009), Radford (1983), Winthrop (1983).

Assistant Director, Public Relations/Baseball Contact: Brian Verdi.

2015 Tournament: Eight teams, double-elimination. May 19-23, Boiling Springs, NC (Gardner-Webb University).

BIG TEN CONFERENCE

Mailing Address: 5440 Park Place, Rosemont, IL 60018. **Telephone:** (847) 696-1010. **Fax:** (847) 696-1110. **E-Mail Addresses:** kkane@bigten.org. **Website:** www.bigten.org.

Baseball Members (First Year): Illinois (1896), Indiana (1906), Iowa (1906), Maryland (1893), Michigan (1896), Michigan State (1950), Minnesota (1906), Nebraska (2012), Northwestern (1898), Ohio State (1913), Penn State (1992), Purdue (1906), Rutgers (1870).

2015 Tournament: Eight teams, double-elimination. May 20-24 at Target Field in Minneapolis, Minn.

BIG 12 CONFERENCE

Mailing Address: 400 E. John Carpenter Freeway, Irving, TX 75062. **Telephone:** (469) 524-1009. **E-Mail Address:** lrasmussen@big12sports.com. **Website:** www.big12sports.com.

Baseball Members (First Year): Baylor (1997), Kansas (1997), Kansas State (1997), Oklahoma (1997), Oklahoma State (1997), Texas Christian (2013), Texas (1997), Texas Tech (1997), West Virginia (2013).

Communications: Laura Rasmussen.

2015 Tournament: Double-elimination division play. May 20-24 at ONEOK Field, Tulsa, Okla.

BIG WEST CONFERENCE

Mailing Address: 2 Corporate Park, Suite 206, Irvine, CA 92606. **Telephone:** (949) 261-2525. **Fax:** (949) 261-2528. **E-Mail Address:** jstcyr@bigwest.org. **Website:**

www.bigwest.org.

Baseball Members (First Year): Cal Poly (1997), UC Davis (2008), UC Irvine (2002), UC Riverside (2002), UC Santa Barbara (1970), Cal State Fullerton (1975), Cal State Northridge (2001), Hawaii (2013), Long Beach State (1970).

Director, Communications: Julie St. Cyr.

2015 Tournament: None.

COLONIAL ATHLETIC ASSOCIATION

Mailing Address: 8625 Patterson Ave., Richmond, VA 23229. **Telephone:** (804) 754-1616. **Fax:** (804) 754-1973. **E-Mail Address:** rwashburn@caasports.com. **Website:** www.caasports.com.

Baseball Members (First Year): College of Charleston (2014), Delaware (2002), Elon (2015), Hofstra (2002), James Madison (1986), UNC Wilmington (1986), Northeastern (2006), Towson (2002), William & Mary (1986).

Associate Commissioner/Communications: Rob Washburn.

2015 Tournament: Six teams, double-elimination. May 20-23 at Charleston, S.C. (College of Charleston).

CONFERENCE USA

Mailing Address: 5201 N. O'Connor Blvd., Suite 300, Irving, TX 75039. **Telephone:** (214) 774-1300. **Fax:** (214) 496-0055. **E-Mail Address:** rdanderson@c-usa.org. **Website:** www.conferenceusa.com.

Baseball Members (First Year): Alabama-Birmingham (1996), Charlotte (2014), East Carolina (2002), Florida Atlantic (2014), Florida International (2014), Louisiana Tech (2014), Marshall (2006), Middle Tennessee State (2014), Old Dominion (2014), Rice (2006), Southern Mississippi (1996), Tulane (1996), Texas-San Antonio (2014).

Assistant Commissioner, Baseball Operations: Russell Anderson.

2015 Tournament: Eight teams, double-elimination. May 20-24 Pete Taylor Park at Hattiesburg, Miss. (Southern Miss).

HORIZON LEAGUE

Mailing Address: 201 S. Capitol Ave., Suite 500, Indianapolis, IN 46225. **Telephone:** (317) 237-5604. **Fax:** (317) 237-5620. **E-Mail Address:** bpotter@horizonleague. org. **Website:** www.horizonleague.org.

Baseball Members (First Year): Illinois-Chicago (1994), Oakland (2014), Valparaiso (2008), Wright State (1994), Wisconsin-Milwaukee (1994), Youngstown State (2002).

Assistant Commissioner, Messaging and Media: Bill Potter.

2015 Tournament: Six teams, modified double-elimination. May 20-23 at Oil City Stadium, Whiting, IN (Valparaiso).

IVY LEAGUE

Mailing Address: 228 Alexander Rd., Second Floor, Princeton, NJ 08544. **Telephone:** (609) 258-6426. **Fax:** (609) 258-1690. **E-Mail Address:** trevor@ivyleaguesports. com. **Website:** www.ivyleaguesports.com.

Baseball Members (First Year): Rolfe—Brown (1948), Dartmouth (1930), Harvard (1948), Yale (1930). Gehrig—Columbia (1930), Cornell (1930), Pennsylvania (1930), Princeton (1930).

Assistant Executive Director, Communications/ Championships: Trevor Rutledge-Leverenz.

2015 Tournament: Best-of-three series between division champions. May 2-3 at team with best Ivy League record.

METRO ATLANTIC ATHLETIC CONFERENCE

Mailing Address: 712 Amboy Ave., Edison, NJ 08837. **Telephone:** (732) 738-5455. **E-Mail Address:** sean.radu@ maac.org Website: www.maacsports.com.

Baseball Members (First Year): Canisius (1990), Fairfield (1982), Iona (1982), Manhattan (1982), Marist (1998), Monmouth (2014), Niagara (1990), Quinnipiac (2014), Rider (1998), Saint Peter's (1982), Siena (1990).

Assistant Commissioner, New Media: Lily Rodriguez.

Director, New Media (Baseball Contact): Sean Radu

2015 Tournament: Six teams, double-elimination. May 20-24 at Dutchess Stadium, Fishkill, N.Y.

MID-AMERICAN CONFERENCE

Mailing Address: 24 Public Square, 15th Floor, Cleveland, OH 44113. **Telephone:** (216) 566-4622. **Fax:** (216) 858-9622. **E-Mail Address:** jguy@mac-sports.com. **Website:** www.mac-sports.com.

Baseball Members (First Year): Akron (1992), Ball State (1973), Bowling Green State (1952), Buffalo (2001), Central Michigan (1971), Eastern Michigan (1971), Kent State (1951), Miami (1947), Northern Illinois (1997), Ohio (1946), Toledo (1950), Western Michigan (1947).

Director, Communications: Jeremy Guy.

2015 Tournament: Eight teams (regardless of division), double-elimination. May 20-24 at All Pro Freight Stadium (Avon, Ohio).

MID-EASTERN ATHLETIC CONFERENCE

Mailing Address: 2730 Ellsmere Ave., Norfolk, VA 23513. **Telephone:** (757) 951-2055. **Fax:** (757) 951-2077. **E-Mail Address:** brian.howard@themeac.com; porterp@ themeac.com. **Website:** www.meacsports.com.

Baseball Members (First Year): Bethune-Cookman (1979), Coppin State (1985), Delaware State (1970), Florida A&M (1979), Maryland Eastern Shore (1970), Norfolk State (1998), North Carolina A&T (1970), North Carolina Central (2012), Savannah State (2012).

Assistant Director, Media Relations/Baseball Contact: Brian Howard.

2015 Tournament: six-teams, double-elimination. May 13-16 at Perdue Stadium in Salisbury, Md.

MISSOURI VALLEY CONFERENCE

Mailing Address: 1818 Chouteau Ave., St. Louis, MO 63103. **Telephone:** (314) 444-4300. **Fax:** (314) 444-4333. **E-Mail Address:** kbriscoe@mvc.org. **Website:** www.mvc-sports.com.

Baseball Members (First Year): Bradley (1955), Dallas Baptist (2014), Evansville (1994), Illinois State (1980), Indiana State (1976), Missouri State (1990), Southern Illinois (1974), Wichita State (1945).

Assistant Commissioner, Communications: Kelli Briscoe.

2015 Tournament: Eight-team tournament with two four-team brackets mirroring the format of the College World Series, with the winners of each four-team bracket meeting in a single championship game. May 19-23 at Eck Stadium in Wichita, Kan.

MOUNTAIN WEST CONFERENCE

Mailing Address: 10807 New Allegiance Dr., Suite 250, Colorado Springs, CO 80921. **Telephone:** (719) 488-

4052. **Fax:** (719) 487-7241. **E-Mail Address:** jwillson@themw.com. **Website:** www.themw.com.

Baseball Members (First Year): Air Force (2000), Fresno State (2013), Nevada (2013), Nevada-Las Vegas (2000), New Mexico (2000), San Diego State (2000), San Jose State (2014).

Associate Director, Communications: Judy Willson.

2015 Tournament: Seven teams; play-in game, followed by six-team double-elimination. May 20-24 at Nevada.

NORTHEAST CONFERENCE

Mailing Address: 399 Campus Dr., Somerset, NJ 08873. **Telephone:** (732) 469-0440. **Fax:** (732) 469-0744. **E-Mail Address:** rventre@northeastconference.org. **Website:** www.northeastconference.org.

Baseball Members (First Year): Bryant (2010), Central Connecticut State (1999), Fairleigh Dickinson (1981), Long Island (1981), Mount St. Mary's (1989), Sacred Heart (2000), Wagner (1981).

Director, Communications/Social Media: Ralph Ventre.

2015 Tournament: Four teams, double-elimination. May 21-May 23 (location unavailable).

OHIO VALLEY CONFERENCE

Mailing Address: 215 Centerview Dr., Suite 115, Brentwood, TN 37027. **Telephone:** (615) 371-1698. **Fax:** (615) 891-1682. **E-Mail Address:** kschwartz@ovc.org. **Website:** www.ovcsports.com.

Baseball Members (First Year): Austin Peay State (1962), Belmont (2013), Eastern Illinois (1996), Eastern Kentucky (1948), Jacksonville State (2003), Morehead State (1948), Murray State (1948), Southeast Missouri State (1991), Southern Illinois Edwardsville (2012), Tennessee-Martin (1992), Tennessee Tech (1949).

Assistant Commissioner: Kyle Schwartz.

2015 Tournament: Six teams, double-elimination. May 20-24 at Jackson, Tenn.

PAC-12 CONFERENCE

Mailing Address: Pac-12 Conference 360 3rd Street, 3rd Floor San Francisco, CA 94107. **Telephone:** (415) 580-4200. **Fax:** (415)549-2828. **E-Mail Address:** jolivero@pac-12.org. **Website:** www.pac-12.com.

Baseball Members (First Year): Arizona (1979), Arizona State (1979), California (1916), UCLA (1928), Oregon (2009) Oregon State (1916), Southern California (1923), Stanford (1918), Utah (2012), Washington (1916), Washington State (1919).

Public Relations Contact: Jon Olivero

2015 Tournament: None.

PATRIOT LEAGUE

Mailing Address: 3773 Corporate Pkwy., Suite 190, Center Valley, PA 18034. **Telephone:** (610) 289-1950. **Fax:** (610) 289-1951. **E-Mail Address:** mdougherty@patriot-league.com. **Website:** www.patriotleague.org.

Baseball Members (First Year): Army (1993), Bucknell (1991), Holy Cross (1991), Lafayette (1991), Lehigh (1991), Navy (1993).

Assistant Executive Director, Communications: Matt Dougherty.

2015 Tournament: Four teams, May 9-10 and May 16-17 at higher seeds.

SOUTHEASTERN CONFERENCE

Mailing Address: 2201 Richard Arrington Blvd. N., Birmingham, AL 35203. **Telephone:** (205) 458-3000. **Fax:** (205) 458-3030. **E-Mail Address:** scartell@sec.org. **Website:** www.secsports.com.

Baseball Members (First Year): East—Florida (1933), Georgia (1933), Kentucky (1933), Missouri (2013), South Carolina (1992), Tennessee (1933), Vanderbilt (1933). West—Alabama (1933), Arkansas (1992), Auburn (1933), Louisiana State (1933), Mississippi (1933), Mississippi State (1933), Texas A&M (2013).

Director, Communications: Chuck Dunlap.

2015 Tournament: 12 teams, modified single/double-elimination. May 19-24 at Hoover, Ala.

SOUTHERN CONFERENCE

Mailing Address: 702 N. Pine St., Spartanburg, SC 29303. **Telephone:** (864) 591-5100. **Fax:** (864) 591-3448. **E-Mail Address:** pperry@socon.org. **Website:** www.soconsports.com.

Baseball Members (First Year): The Citadel (1937), ETSU (1979-2005, 2015), Furman (1937), Mercer (2015), UNCG (1998), Samford (2009), VMI (1925-2003, 2015), Western Carolina (1977), Wofford (1998).

Media Relations: Phil Perry.

2015 Tournament: Nine teams, single-game play-in for bottom two seeds, then double-elimination followed by a single-elimination championship game. May 19-24 at Joseph P. Riley, Jr. Park, Charleston, S.C.

SOUTHLAND CONFERENCE

Mailing Address: 2600 Network Blvd, Suite 150, Frisco, Texas 75034. **Telephone:** (972) 422-9500. **Fax:** (972) 422-9225. **E-Mail Address:** mcebold@southland. **Website:** southland.org. **Baseball Members (First Year):** Abilene Christian (2014), Central Arkansas (2007), Houston Baptist (2014), Incarnate Word (2014), Lamar (1999), McNeese State (1973), New Orleans (2014), Nicholls (1992), Northwestern State (1988), Sam Houston State (1988), Southeastern Louisiana (1998), Stephen F. Austin State (2006), Texas A&M-Corpus Christi (2007).

Baseball Contact/Assistant Director: Melissa Cebold.

2015 Tournament: Two four-team brackets, double-elimination. May 20-23 at Constellation Field, Sugar Land, Texas (Neutral Site).

SOUTHWESTERN ATHLETIC CONFERENCE

Mailing Address: 2101 6th Ave. North, Suite 700, Birmingham, AL 35203. **Telephone:** (205) 251-7573. **Fax:** (205) 297-9820. **E-Mail Address:** j.jones@swac.org. **Website:** www.swac.org.

Baseball Members (First Year): East Division—Alabama A&M (2000), Alabama State (1982), Alcorn State (1962), Jackson State (1958), Mississippi Valley State (1968). West Division—Arkansas-Pine Bluff (1999), Grambling State (1958), Prairie View A&M (1920), Southern (1934), Texas Southern (1954).

Director, Communications: Jennifer Jones.

2015 Tournament: Eight teams, double-elimination. May 13-17 at Wesley Barrow Stadium in New Orleans, La.

SUMMIT LEAGUE

Mailing Address: 340 W. Butterfield Rd., Suite 3D, Elmhurst, IL 60126. **Telephone:** (630) 516-0661. **Fax:** (630) 516-0673. **E-Mail Address:** mette@thesummitleague.org. **Website:** www.thesummitleague.org.

Baseball Members (First Year): IPFW (2008), Omaha

(2013), North Dakota State (2008), Oral Roberts (1998), South Dakota State (2008), Western Illinois (1984).
Associate Director, Communications (Baseball Contact): Greg Mette.
2015 Tournament: Four teams, double-elimination. May 20-23 at Sioux Falls, S.D. (South Dakota State).

SUN BELT CONFERENCE

Mailing Address: 1500 Sugar Bowl Dr., New Orleans, LA 70112. **Telephone:** (504) 556-0884. **Fax:** (504) 299-9068. **E-Mail Address:** nunez@sunbeltsports.org. **Website:** www.sunbeltsports.org.
Baseball Members (First Year): Appalachian State (2015), UALR (1991), Arkansas State (1991), Georgia Southern, (2015), Georgia State (2014), UL Lafayette (1991), UL Monroe (2007), South Alabama (1976), UT Arlington (2014), Texas State (2014), Troy (2006).
Assistant Director, Communications: Keith Nunez.
2015 Tournament: Eight teams, double-elimination. May 20-24 at Troy University (Riddle-Pace Field).

WESTERN ATHLETIC CONFERENCE

Mailing Address: 9250 East Costilla Ave., Suite 300, Englewood, CO 80112. Telephone: (303) 799-9221. **Fax:** (303) 799-3888. **E-Mail Address:** cthompson@wac.org. **Website:** www.wacsports.com.
Baseball Members (First Year): Cal State Bakersfield (2013), Chicago State (2014), Grand Canyon (2014), New Mexico State (2006), North Dakota (2014), Northern Colorado (2014), Sacramento State (2006), Seattle (2013), Texas-Pan American (2014), Utah Valley (2014).
Commissioner: Jeff Hurd. **Associate Commissioner:** Dave Chaffin. **Director, Media Relations:** Chris Thompson.
2015 Tournament: Six teams, double-elimination, May 20-24 at Hohokam Stadium, Mesa, Ariz.

WEST COAST CONFERENCE

Mailing Address: 1111 Bayhill Dr., Suite 405, San Bruno, CA 94066. **Telephone:** (650) 873-8622. **Fax:** (650) 873-7846. **E-Mail Addresses:** rmccrary@westcoast.org (primary), jtourial@westcoast.org (secondary). **Website:** www.wccsports.com.
Baseball Members (First Year): Brigham Young (2012), Gonzaga (1996), Loyola Marymount (1968), Pacific (2014), Pepperdine (1968), Portland (1996), Saint Mary's (1968), San Diego (1979), San Francisco (1968), Santa Clara (1968).
Senior Director, Communications: Ryan McCrary.
Associate Commissioner, Broadcast Administration/Strategic Communications: Jeff Tourial.
2015 Tournament: Four teams, May 21-23 at Banner Island Ballpark, Stockton, Calif.

NCAA DIVISION I TEAMS
* Denotes recruiting coordinator

AIR FORCE FALCONS

Conference: Mountain West
Mailing Address: 2169 Field House Drive, USAF Academy, CO 80840. **Website:** www.goairforcefalcons.com. **Twitter:** @AF_Baseball.
Head Coach: Mike Kazlausky (Maj. Retired).
Telephone: (719) 333-0835. **Baseball SID:** Nick Arseniak. **Telephone:** (719) 333-9251.
Assistant Coaches: Toby Bicknell. **Telephone:** (719) 333-7539.

Home Field: Falcon Field. **Seating Capacity:** 1,000. **Outfield Dimensions:** LF—340, CF—400, RF—315.

AKRON ZIPS

Conference: Mid-American
Mailing Address: University of Akron, Rhodes Arena, Suite 83, Akron, OH, 44325.
Website: www.gozips.com. **Twitter:** @ZipsBB.
Head Coach: Richard Rembielak. **Telephone:** 330-972-7290. **Baseball SID:** Melissa Powell. **Telephone:** (330) 972-6584.
Assistant Coaches: Kyle Smith, Fred Worth. **Telephone:** (330) 972-2393.
Home Field: Lee R. Jackson Field. **Seating Capacity:** 1,500. **Outfield Dimensions:** LF—330, CF—400, RF—330.

ALABAMA CRIMSON TIDE

Conference: Southeastern
Mailing Address: 1201 Coliseum Dr. Suite 205 Tuscaloosa, AL 35487. **Website:** www.rolltide.com. **Twitter:** @AlabamaBSB.
Head Coach: Mitch Gaspard. **Telephone:** (205) 348-4029. **Baseball SID:** David Kindred. **Telephone:** (205) 348-5258.
Assistant Coaches: *Dax Norris, Andy Phillips. **Telephone:** (205) 348-4029.
Home Field: Hoover Metropolitan Stadium. **Seating Capacity:** 10,800. **Outfield Dimensions:** LF—340, CF—405, RF—340.

ALABAMA A&M BULLDOGS

Conference: Southwestern Athletic
Mailing Address: 4900 Meridian Street. **Website:** www.aamusports.com. **Twitter:** @AAMU_Baseball
Head Coach: Mitch Hill. **Telephone:** (256) 372-4004. **Baseball SID:** Oralia Washington. **Telephone:** (256) 372-4550.
Assistant Coaches: LaDale Hayes. **Telephone:** (256) 372-4004.
Home Field: Bulldog Field. **Seating Capacity:** 500. **Outfield Dimension:** LF—375, CF—425, RF—420.

ALABAMA STATE HORNETS

Conference: Southwestern Athletic
Mailing Address: 915 S. Jackson St., Montgomery, AL 36104. **Website:** www.bamastatesports.com. **Twitter:** @ASUBaseball_
Head Coach: Mervyl Melendez. **Telephone:** (334) 229-5600. **Baseball SID:** Duane Lewis. **Telephone:** (334) 229-5230.
Assistant Coaches: Drew Clark, *Jose Vazquez. **Telephone:** (334) 229-5607.
Home Field: Wheeler-Watkins Complex. **Seating Capacity:** 500. **Outfield Dimension:** LF—330, CF—400, RF—330.

ALABAMA-BIRMINGHAM BLAZERS

Conference: Conference USA
Mailing Address: 1212 University Blvd., U236, Birmingham, AL 35294. **Website:** www.uabsports.com. **Twitter:** @UAB_Baseball
Head Coach: Brian Shoop. **Telephone:** (205) 934-5181. **Baseball SID:** Brandon Lee. **Telephone:** (205) 996-2576.
Assistant Coaches: Josh Hopper, *Perry Roth. **Telephone:** (205) 934-5182.

Home Field: Regions Field and Young Memorial Field. **Seating Capacity:** 9000/ 2000. **Outfield Dimensions:** LF—320, CF—400, RF—325.

ALBANY GREAT DANES

Conference: America East
Mailing Address: 1400 Washington Ave. PE Bldg. Ste. 123 Albany, NY 12222. **Website:** www.ualbanysports.com. **Twitter:** @DanesBaseball
Head Coach: Jon Mueller. **Telephone:** (518) 442-3014. **Baseball SID:** Lizzie Barlow. **Telephone:** (518) 442-3359.
Assistant Coaches: Jeff Kaier, *Drew Pearce. **Telephone:** (518) 442-3337.
Home Field: Varsity Field. **Seating Capacity:** NA. **Outfield Dimension:** LF—330, CF—400, RF—330.

APPALACHIAN STATE MOUNTAINEERS

Conference: Sun Belt
Mailing Address: PO Box 32025, Boone, NC 28608. **Website:** www.appstatesports.com. **Twitter:** @AppBaseball
Head Coach: Billy Jones. **Telephone:** (828) 262-6097. **Baseball SID:** Mike Flynn. **Telephone:** (828) 262-2845. **Fax:** (828) 262-6106.
Assistant Coaches: *Matt Payne, Michael Rogers. **Telephone:** (828) 265-8664.
Home Field: Beaver Field at Jim and Bettie Smith Stadium. **Seating Capacity:** 1,000. **Outfield Dimension:** LF—330, CF—400, RF—330.

ARIZONA WILDCATS

Conference: Pacific-12
Mailing Address: 1 National Championship Drive, Tucson, AZ 85721. **Website:** www.arizonaathletics.com. **Twitter:** @ArizonaBaseball
Head Coach: Andy Lopez. **Telephone:** (520) 621-4102. **Baseball SID:** Blair Willis. **Telephone:** (520) 621-0914.
Assistant Coaches: Josh Garcia, *Matt Siegel. **Telephone:** (520) 626-8859.
Home Field: Hi Corbett Field. **Seating Capacity:** 9,500. **Outfield Dimensions:** LF—366, CF—392, RF—349.

ARIZONA STATE SUN DEVILS

Conference: Pacific-12
Mailing Address: 500 East Veteran's Way, Tempe, AZ, 85287. **Website:** www.thesundevils.com. **Twitter:** @ASU_Baseball
Head Coach: Tracy Smith. **Telephone:** (480) 965-1904. **Baseball SID:** Thomas Lenneberg. **Telephone:** (480) 965-6594.
Assistant Coaches: *Ben Greenspan, Brandon Higelin. **Telephone:** (480) 727-6112.
Home Field: Phoenix Municipal Stadium. **Seating Capacity:** 8,775. **Outfield Dimensions:** LF—345, CF—410, RF—345.

ARKANSAS RAZORBACKS

Conference: Southeastern
Mailing Address: PO Box 7777, Fayetteville, AR 72702. **Website:** www.arkansasrazorbacks.com. **Twitter:** @RazorbackBSB
Head Coach: Dave Van Horn. **Telephone:** (479) 575-3655. **Baseball SID:** David Beall. **Telephone:** (479) 575-3114. **Fax:** (479) 575-7481.
Assistant Coaches: Dave Jorn, *Tony Vitello. **Telephone:** (479) 575-3552.

Home Field: Baum Stadium at George Cole Field. **Seating Capacity:** 10,737. **Outfield Dimensions:** LF—320, CF—400, RF—320.

ARKANSAS STATE RED WOLVES

Conference: Sun Belt
Mailing Address: PO Box 1000 State University, AR 72467. **Website:** www.astateredwolves.com. **Twitter:** @ASTATEBaseball
Head Coach: Tommy Raffo. **Telephone:** (870) 972-2700. **Baseball SID:** Chris Graddy. **Telephone:** (870) 972-2707.
Assistant Coaches: Tighe Dickinson, *Anthony Everman. **Telephone:** (870) 972-2700.
Home Field: Tomlinson Stadium/Kell Field. **Seating Capacity:** 1,200. **Outfield Dimension:** LF—335, CF—400, RF—335.

ARKANSAS-LITTLE ROCK TROJANS

Conference: Sun Belt
Mailing Address: 2801 S. University Ave., Little Rock, AR 72204. **Website:** www.ualrtrojans.com. **Twitter:** @UALRBaseball
Head Coach: Chris Curry. **Telephone:** (501) 663-8095. **Baseball SID:** Tyler Morrison/Patrick Newton. **Telephone:** (501) 569-3449/(501) 683-7003.
Assistant Coaches: *Roland Fanning, Russell Raley. **Telephone:** (501) 664-5443.
Home Field: Gary Hogan Field. **Seating Capacity:** 1,000. **Outfield Dimension:** LF—330, CF—400, RF—325.

ARKANSAS-PINE BLUFF GOLDEN LIONS

Conference: Southwestern Athletic
Mailing Address: 1200 N. University Dr. Pine Bluff, AR 71601. **Website:** www.uapblionsroar.com. **Twitter:** @UAPB_Baseball
Head Coach: Carlos James. **Telephone:** (870) 575-8995. **Baseball SID:** Cameo Stokes. **Telephone:** (870) 575-7949.
Assistant Coaches: Kirby Campbell, *Zach Clark. **Telephone:** (870) 575-8995.
Home Field: Torii Hunter Baseball Complex. **Seating Capacity:** 1,500. **Outfield Dimension:** LF—330, CF—400, RF—330.

ARMY BLACK KNIGHTS

Conference: Patriot
Mailing Address: 639 Howard Rd., West Point N.Y. 10996. **Website:** www.goarmysports.com. **Twitter:** @Army_Baseball
Head Coach: Matthew Reid. **Telephone:** (845) 938-3712. **Baseball SID:** Mark Mohrman. **Telephone:** (845) 938-6923.
Assistant Coaches: Tyler Cannon, *Anthony DeCicco. **Telephone:** (845) 938-5877.
Home Field: Doubleday Field. **Seating Capacity:** 1,000. **Outfield Dimension:** LF—325, CF—400, RF—325.

AUBURN TIGERS

Conference: Southeastern
Mailing Address: 351 S Donahue Dr., Auburn, AL 36849. **Website:** www.auburntigers.com. **Twitter:** @Auburn_Baseball
Head Coach: Sunny Golloway. **Telephone:** (334) 844-4922. **Baseball SID:** Taylor Bryan. **Telephone:** (334) 750-3862. **Fax:** (334) 844-9807.
Assistant Coaches: *Tom Holliday, Greg Norton.

Telephone: (334) 844-4990.
Home Field: Samford Stadium-Hitchcock Field at Plainsman Park. **Seating Capacity:** 4,096. **Outfield Dimension:** LF—315, CF—385, RF—331.

AUSTIN PEAY STATE GOVERNORS

Conference: Ohio Valley
Mailing Address: 601 College St. Clarksville, TN 37044. **Website:** www.letsgopeay.com. **Twitter:** @APSUBaseball
Head Coach: Gary McClure. **Telephone:** (931) 221-6266. **Baseball SID:** Cody Bush. **Telephone:** (931) 221-7561.
Assistant Coaches: *Derrick Dunbar, Chal Fanning. **Telephone:** (931) 221-6392.
Home Field: Raymond C Hand Park. **Seating Capacity:** 777. **Outfield Dimension:** LF—319, CF—392, RF—327.

BALL STATE CARDINALS

Conference: Mid-American
Mailing Address: 2000 University Avenue, Muncie, IN 47306. **Website:** www.ballstatesports.com. **Twitter:** @BallStateBB
Head Coach: Rich Maloney. **Telephone:** (765) 285-8911. **Baseball SID:** Joe Hernandez. **Telephone:** (765) 285-8242.
Assistant Coaches: *Scott French, Todd Linklater. **Telephone:** (765) 285-1425.
Home Field: Ball Diamond. **Seating Capacity:** 1,500. **Outfield Dimension:** LF—325, CF—395, RF—325.

BAYLOR BEARS

Conference: Big 12
Mailing Address: 1612 S. University Parks Dr., Waco, TX 76706. **Website:** www.baylorbears.com. **Twitter:** @BaylorBaseball
Head Coach: Steve Smith. **Telephone:** (254) 710-3097. **Baseball SID:** Zach Peters. **Telephone:** (254) 710-3784.
Assistant Coaches: Steve Johnigan, *Trevor Mote. **Telephone:** (254) 710-3044.
Home Field: Baylor Ballpark. **Seating Capacity:** 5,000. **Outfield Dimension:** LF—330, CF—400, RF—330.

BELMONT BRUINS

Conference: Ohio Valley
Mailing Address: 1900 Belmont Blvd. Nashville, TN 37212. **Website:** www.belmontbruins.com. **Twitter:** @BelmontBaseball
Head Coach: Dave Jarvis. **Telephone:** (615) 460-6166. **Baseball SID:** Liz Halvorson. **Telephone:** (615) 460-8023.
Assistant Coaches: Matt Barnett, *Aaron Smith. **Telephone:** (615) 460-5586.
Home Field: E.S. Rose Park. **Seating Capacity:** 800. **Outfield Dimension:** LF—330, CF—400, RF—330.

BETHUNE-COOKMAN WILDCATS

Conference: Mid-Eastern Athletic
Mailing Address: 640 Dr. Mary McLeod Bethune Blvd., Daytona Beach, FL 32214. **Website:** www.bccathletics.com. **Twitter:** @CookmanBaseball
Head Coach: Jason Beverlin. **Telephone:** (386) 481-2224. **Baseball SID:** Michael Stambaugh. **Telephone:** (386) 481-2278.
Assistant Coaches: Jason Bell, *Barrett Shaft. **Telephone:** (386) 481-2242.
Home Field: Jackie Robinson Ballpark. **Seating**

Capacity: 4,200. **Outfield Dimension:** LF—315, CF—400, RF—325.

BINGHAMTON BEARCATS

Conference: America East
Mailing Address: Binghamton University, Events Center Office No. 110, Binghamton, NY, 13902. **Website:** www.bubearcats.com. **Twitter:** @Binghamton_bsbl
Head Coach: Tim Sinicki. **Telephone:** (607) 777-2525.
Baseball SID: John Hartrick. **Telephone:** (607) 777-6800.
Assistant Coaches: *Ryan Hurba, Dan Jurik. **Telephone:** (607) 777-5808, (607) 777-4552.
Home Field: Bearcat Sports Complex. **Seating Capacity:** 500. **Outfield Dimension:** LF—325, CF—390, RF—325.

BOSTON COLLEGE EAGLES

Conference: Atlantic Coast
Mailing Address: 140 Commonwealth Ave., Chestnut Hill, MA 02467. **Website:** www.bceagles.com. **Twitter:** @BCBirdBall
Head Coach: Mike Gambino. **Telephone:** (617) 552-2674. **Baseball SID:** Zanna Ollove. **Telephone:** (617) 552-2004.
Assistant Coaches: *Jim Foster, Greg Sullivan. **Telephone:** (617) 552-3092.
Home Field: Pellagrini Diamond at Shea Field. **Seating Capacity:** 1,000. **Outfield Dimension:** LF—330, CF—400, RF—320.

BOWLING GREEN STATE FALCONS

Conference: Mid-American
Mailing Address: 1610 Stadium Drive, Bowling Green, Ohio 43403. **Website:** www.bgsufalcons.com. **Twitter:** @WEAREBGBaseball
Head Coach: Danny Schmitz. **Telephone:** (419) 372-7065. **Baseball SID:** Scott Swegan. **Telephone:** (419) 372-7105.
Assistant Coaches: *Rick Blanc, Ryan Shay. **Telephone:** (419) 372-7641.
Home Field: Warren E. Steller. **Seating Capacity:** 1,100. **Outfield Dimensions:** LF—345, CF—400, RF—345.

BRADLEY BRAVES

Conference: Missouri Valley
Mailing Address: 1501 W. Bradley Avenue, Peoria, IL 61625. **Website:** www.bradleybraves.com. **Twitter:** @BradleyBaseball
Head Coach: Elvis Dominguez. **Telephone:** (309) 677-2684. **Baseball SID:** Bobby Parker. **Telephone:** (309) 677-2624. **Fax:** (309) 677-2626.
Assistant Coaches: *Sean Lyons, Larry Scully. **Telephone:** (309) 677-4996.
Home Field: Dozer Park. **Seating Capacity:** 7,500. **Outfield Dimensions:** LF—310, CF—400, RF—310.

BRIGHAM YOUNG COUGARS

Conference: West Coast
Mailing Address: 111 Miller Park, BYU, Provo, UT 84602. **Website:** www.byucougars.com. **Twitter:** @BYUBaseball
Head Coach: Mike Littlewood. **Telephone:** (801) 422-5049. **Baseball SID:** Ralph Zobell. **Telephone:** (801) 422-9769.
Assistant Coaches: *Brent Haring, Trent Pratt. **Telephone:** (801) 422-5064.

Home Field: Larry H. Miller Field. **Seating Capacity:** 2,204. **Outfield Dimensions:** LF—345, CF—400, RF—345.

BROWN BEARS

Conference: Ivy
Mailing Address: 233 Hope Street Providence, RI 02912. **Website:** www.brownbears.com. **Twitter:** @BrownU_Baseball
Head Coach: Grant Achilles. **Telephone:** (401) 863-3090. **Baseball SID:** Eric Peterson. **Telephone:** (401) 863-7014.
Assistant Coaches: *Michael McCormack, William Murphy. **Telephone:** (401)-863-2032.
Home Field: Murray Stadium. **Seating Capacity:** 1,500. **Outfield Dimension:** LF—330, CF—415, RF—320.

BRYANT BULLDOGS

Conference: Northeast
Mailing Address: 1150 Douglas Pike, Smithfield RI 02917. **Website:** www.bryantbulldogs.com. **Twitter:** @_BryantBaseball
Head Coach: Steve Owens. **Telephone:** (401) 232-6967. **Baseball SID:** Tristan Hobbes. **Telephone:** (401) 232-6558 (ext. 2).
Assistant Coaches: *Ryan Fecteau, Kyle Pettoruto. **Telephone:** (401) 232-6967.
Home Field: Conaty Park. **Seating Capacity:** 500. **Outfield Dimension:** LF—330, CF—400, RF—330.

BUCKNELL BISON

Conference: Patriot
Mailing Address: One Dent Drive, Lewisburg, PA 17837. **Website:** www.bucknellbison.com. **Twitter:** @BucknellBall
Head Coach: Scott Heather. **Telephone:** (570) 577-3593. **Baseball SID:** Todd Merriett. **Telephone:** (570) 577-3488.
Assistant Coaches: *Jason Neitz, Ryan Wood. **Telephone:** (570) 577-1059.
Home Field: Depew Field. **Seating Capacity:** 500. **Outfield Dimensions:** LF—330, CF—400, RF—330.

BUFFALO BULLS

Conference: Mid-American
Mailing Address: 163 Alumni Arena. **Website:** www.ubbulls.com. **Twitter:** @UBBaseball
Head Coach: Ron Torgalski. **Telephone:** (716) 645-6834. **Baseball SID:** Louie Spina. **Telephone:** (716) 645-6837.
Assistant Coaches: Brad Cochrane, *Steve Ziroli. **Telephone:** (716) 645-6192, (716) 645-3437.
Home Field: Amherst Audubon Field. **Seating Capacity:** 200. **Outfield Dimension:** LF—320, CF—400, RF—320.

BUTLER BULLDOGS

Conference: Big East
Mailing Address: Butler University Athletics 510 W. 49th Street Indianapolis, IN 46208. **Website:** www.butler-sports.com. **Twitter:** @ButlerUBaseball
Head Coach: Steve Farley. **Telephone:** (317) 940-9721. **Baseball SID:** Kit Stetzel. **Telephone:** (317) 940-9994.
Assistant Coaches: Andy Judkins, *Miles Miller. **Telephone:** (317) 940-6536.
Home Field: Bulldog Park. **Seating Capacity:** 500. **Outfield Dimension:** LF—330, CF—400, RF—330.

CAL POLY MUSTANGS

Conference: Big West
Mailing Address: 1 Grand Avenue, San Luis Obispo, CA 93407. **Website:** www.gopoly.com. **Twitter:** @cal-poly_stangs
Head Coach: Larry Lee. **Telephone:** (805) 756-6367. **Baseball SID:** Eric Burdick. **Telephone:** (805) 756-6550.
Assistant Coaches: Thomas Eager, *Teddy Warrecker. **Telephone:** (805) 756-1201.
Home Field: Baggett Stadium. **Seating Capacity:** 1,734
Outfield Dimension: LF—335, CF—405, RF—335.

CAL STATE BAKERSFIELD ROADRUNNERS

Conference: Western Athletic
Mailing Address: 9001 Stockdale Highway, GYM 08, Bakersfield, CA 93311. **Website:** www.csub.edu. **Twitter:** @CSUBAthletics
Head Coach: Bill Kernen. **Telephone:** (661) 654-2678. **Baseball SID:** Matt Turk. **Telephone:** (661) 654-3071.
Assistant Coaches: Alex Hoover, *Bob Macaluso. **Telephone:** (661) 654-2678.
Home Field: Hardt Field. **Seating Capacity:** 2,000. **Outfield Dimension:** LF—327, CF—390, RF—327.

CAL STATE FULLERTON TITANS

Conference: Big West
Mailing Address: 800 N. State College Blvd., Fullerton, CA 92834. **Website:** www.fullertontitans.com. **Twitter:** @BaseballTitans
Head Coach: Rick Vanderhook. **Telephone:** (657) 278-3789. **Baseball SID:** Rafael Guerrero. **Telephone:** (657) 278-7547.
Assistant Coaches: Jason Dietrich, Chad Baum. **Telephone:** (657) 278-2492, (657) 278-5970.
Home Field: Goodwin Field. **Seating Capacity:** 3,500. **Outfield Dimension:** LF—330, CF—400, RF—330.

CAL STATE NORTHRIDGE MATADORS

Conference: Big West
Mailing Address: 18111 Nordhoff Street, Northridge, CA 91330. **Website:** www.gomatadors.com. **Twitter:** @CSUNBaseball
Head Coach: Greg Moore. **Telephone:** (818) 677-7055. **Baseball SID:** Kevin Strauss. **Telephone:** (818) 677-3860.
Assistant Coaches: Chris Hom, *Jordon Twohig. **Telephone:** (818) 677-3218.
Home Field: Matador Ballpark. **Seating Capacity:** 1,000. **Outfield Dimension:** LF—325, CF—395, RF—325.

CALIFORNIA GOLDEN BEARS

Conference: Pacific-12
Mailing Address: Berkeley, Calif. 94720. **Website:** www.calbears.com. **Twitter:** @Cal_Baseball
Head Coach: David Esquer. **Telephone:** (510) 643-6006. **Baseball SID:** Scott Ball. **Telephone:** (510) 643-1741.
Assistant Coaches: *Mike Neu, Brad Sanfilippo. **Telephone:** (510) 643-6006.
Home Field: Evans Diamond. **Seating Capacity:** 2,500. **Outfield Dimension:** LF—320, CF—395, RF—320.

CAMPBELL CAMELS

Conference: Big South
Mailing Address: PO Box 10 Buies Creek, NC 27506. **Website:** www.gocamels.com. **Twitter:** @

GoCampbellBSB
Head Coach: Justin Haire. **Telephone:** (910) 893-1338. **Baseball SID:** Jason Williams. **Telephone:** (910) 814-4367.
Assistant Coaches: *Chris Marx, Jeff Steele. **Telephone:** (910) 893-1354.
Home Field: Jim Perry Stadium. **Seating Capacity:** 1,500. **Outfield Dimension:** LF—337, CF—395, RF—328.

CANISIUS GOLDEN GRIFFINS

Conference: Metro Atlantic Athletic
Mailing Address: 2001 Main Street. **Website:** www.gogriffs.com. **Twitter:** @GriffsBaseball
Head Coach: Mike McRae. **Telephone:** (716) 888-8485. **Baseball SID:** Matt Lozar. **Telephone:** (716) 888-8266.
Assistant Coaches: *Matt Mazurek, Paul Panik. **Telephone:** (716) 888-8478.
Home Field: Demske Sports Complex. **Seating Capacity:** 1,000. **Outfield Dimension:** LF—325, CF—405, RF—325.

CENTRAL FLORIDA KNIGHTS

Conference: American Athletic
Mailing Address: 400 Central Florida Blvd., Orlando, FL 32816. **Website:** www.ucfathletics.com. **Twitter:** @UCF_Baseball
Head Coach: Terry Rooney. **Telephone:** (407) 823-0140. **Baseball SID:** Nate Blythe. **Telephone:** (407) 823-6489.
Assistant Coaches: Ryan Klosterman, *Kevin Schnall. **Telephone:** (407) 823-4320.
Home Field: Jay Bergman Field. **Seating Capacity:** 3,600. **Outfield Dimension:** LF—360, CF—390, RF—360.

CENTRAL MICHIGAN CHIPPEWAS

Conference: Mid-American
Mailing Address: Rose 120, Mt. Pleasant, MI 48859. **Website:** www.cmuchippewas.com. **Twitter:** @CMUBaseball
Head Coach: Steve Jaksa. **Telephone:** (989) 774-4291. **Baseball SID:** Andy Sneddon. **Telephone:** (989) 774-3277.
Assistant Coaches: *Jeff Opalewski, Doug Sanders. **Telephone:** (989) 774-2322.
Home Field: Theunissen Stadium. **Seating Capacity:** 2,400. **Outfield Dimension:** LF—330, CF—400, RF—330.

CHARLESTON SOUTHERN BUCCANEERS

Conference: Big South
Mailing Address: 9200 University Blvd, Charleston, SC, 29406. **Website:** www.csusports.com. **Twitter:** @CSUBucsBaseball
Head Coach: Stuart Lake. **Telephone:** (843) 863-7591. **Baseball SID:** Zeke Beam. **Telephone:** (843) 863-7687.
Assistant Coaches: Adam Ward. **Telephone:** (843) 863-7832.
Home Field: CSU Ballpark. **Seating Capacity:** 1,000. **Outfield Dimension:** LF—320, CF—400, RF—320.

CHARLOTTE 49ERS

Conference: Conference USA
Mailing Address: 9201 University City Blvd, Charlotte, NC 28223. **Website:** www.charlotte49ers.com. **Twitter:** @NinerBaseball
Head Coach: Loren Hibbs. **Telephone:** (704) 687-0726. **Baseball SID:** Sean Fox. **Telephone:** (704) 687-

1023. **Fax:** (704) 687-4918.
Assistant Coaches: *Brandon Hall, Bo Robinson. **Telephone:** (704) 687-0728.
Home Field: Robert and Mariam Hayes Stadium. **Seating Capacity:** 3,200. **Outfield Dimension:** LF—335, CF—390, RF—335.

CHICAGO STATE COUGARS

Conference: Western Athletic
Mailing Address: 9501 S. King Drive Chicago, IL 60628. **Website:** www.csu.edu. **Twitter:** @CSUBaseball
Head Coach: Steven Joslyn. **Telephone:** (773) 995-3637. **Baseball SID:** TBD. **Telephone:** (773) 995-2295. **Fax:** (773) 995-3656.
Assistant Coaches: *Raymond Napienetk, Daniel Pirillo. **Telephone:** (773) 995-3637.
Home Field: Cougar Stadium. **Seating Capacity:** 500. **Outfield Dimension:** LF—330, CF—390, RF—330.

CINCINNATI BEARCATS

Conference: American Athletic
Mailing Address: 2751 O'Varsity Way Suite 764, Cincinnati, OH 45221. **Website:** www.gobearcats.com. **Twitter:** @UCincyBaseball
Head Coach: Ty Neal. **Telephone:** (513) 556-1577. **Baseball SID:** Alex Lange. **Telephone:** (513) 556-5145.
Assistant Coaches: *Adam Bourassa, John Lackaff. **Telephone:** (513) 556-1577.
Home Field: Marge Schott Stadium. **Seating Capacity:** 3,085. **Outfield Dimension:** LF—325, CF—400, RF—325.

CITADEL BULLDOGS

Conference: Southern
Mailing Address: 171 Moultrie Street, Charleston, SC 29409. **Website:** www.citadelsports.com. **Twitter:** @CitadelBaseball
Head Coach: Fred Jordan. **Telephone:** (843) 953-5901. **Baseball SID:** Mike Hoffman. **Telephone:** (843) 953-5353.
Assistant Coaches: *David Beckley, Britt Reames. **Telephone:** (843) 953-7265.
Home Field: Riley Park. **Seating Capacity:** 6,000. **Outfield Dimension:** LF—305, CF—398, RF—337.

CLEMSON TIGERS

Conference: Atlantic Coast
Mailing Address: Jervey Athletic Center, 100 Perimeter Road, Clemson, SC, 29634. **Website:** www.clemsontigers.com. **Twitter:** @ClemsonBaseball
Head Coach: Jack Leggett. **Telephone:** (864) 656-1947. **Baseball SID:** Brian Hennessy. **Telephone:** (864) 656-1921.
Assistant Coaches: *Bradley LeCroy, Dan Pepicelli. **Telephone:** (864) 656-1948.
Home Field: Doug Kingsmore Stadium. **Seating Capacity:** 6,016. **Outfield Dimension:** LF—310, CF—390, RF—320.

COASTAL CAROLINA CHANTICLEERS

Conference: Big South
Mailing Address: 1 Landon Loop, Conway, SC. **Website:** www.goccusports.com. **Twitter:** @CoastalBaseball
Head Coach: Gary Gilmore. **Telephone:** (843) 349-2816. **Baseball SID:** Mike Cawood. **Telephone:** (843) 349-2822.
Assistant Coaches: *Joe Hastings, Drew Thomas.

Telephone: (843) 349-2849.
Home Field: Springs Brooks Stadium. **Seating Capacity:** 5,500. **Outfield Dimensions:** LF—320, CF—390, RF—315.

COLLEGE OF CHARLESTON COUGARS

Conference: Colonial Athletic
Mailing Address: 66 George Street, Charleston, SC 29424. **Website:** www.cofcsports.com. **Twitter:** @CofCBaseball
Head Coach: Monte Lee. **Telephone:** (843) 953-5916. **Baseball SID:** Nick Vlattas. **Telephone:** (843) 953-5465.
Assistant Coaches: Matt Heath, *Chris Morris. **Telephone:** (843) 953-6722.
Home Field: Patriots Point. **Seating Capacity:** 2,000. **Outfield Dimension:** LF—300, CF—400, RF—330.

COLUMBIA LIONS

Conference: Ivy
Mailing Address: 3030 Broadway, Mail Code 1930, New York, NY 10027. **Website:** www.gocolumbialions.com. **Twitter:** @CULionsBaseball
Head Coach: Brett Boretti. **Telephone:** (212) 854-8448. **Baseball SID:** Mike Kowalsky. **Telephone:** (212) 854-7064.
Assistant Coaches: Pete Maki. **Telephone:** (212) 854-7772.
Home Field: Robertson Field at Satow Stadium.

CONNECTICUT HUSKIES

Conference: American Athletic
Mailing Address: 2111 Hillside Road, Storrs, CT. **Website:** www.uconnhuskies.com. **Twitter:** @UConnBaseball
Head Coach: Jim Penders. **Telephone:** (860) 486-4089. **Baseball SID:** Bobby Mullen. **Telephone:** (860) 486-3531.
Assistant Coaches: *Jeffrey Hourigan, Joshua MacDonald. **Telephone:** (860) 486-5771.
Home Field: J.O. Christian Field. **Seating Capacity:** 2,000. **Outfield Dimension:** LF—340, CF—405, RF—340.

COPPIN STATE EAGLES

Conference: Mideastern
Mailing Address: 2500 W. North Ave., Baltimore, MD 21216. **Website:** www.coppinstatesports.com. **Twitter:** @CoppinBaseball
Head Coach: Sherman Reed. **Telephone:** (410) 951-3723. **Baseball SID:** Robert Knox. **Telephone:** (410) 951-3724.
Assistant Coaches: Gabe Acri. **Telephone:** (410) 951-6941.
Home Field: Joe Cannon Stadium. **Seating Capacity:** 2,000. **Outfield Dimension:** LF—325, CF—425, RF—325.

CORNELL BIG RED

Conference: Ivy
Mailing Address: Teagle Hall, Campus Rd. Ithaca, NY 14853. **Website:** www.cornellbigred.com. **Twitter:** @CornellBaseball
Head Coach: Bill Walkenbach. **Telephone:** (607) 255-3812. **Baseball SID:** Brandon Thomas. **Telephone:** (607) 255-5627. **Fax:** (607) 255-9791.
Assistant Coaches: Tom Ford, *Scott Marsh. **Telephone:** (607) 255-6604.
Home Field: Hoy Field. **Seating Capacity:** 1,000. **Outfield Dimension:** LF—315, CF—400, RF—325.

CREIGHTON BLUEJAYS

Conference: Big East
Mailing Address: 2500 California Plaza. **Website:** www.gocreighton.com. **Twitter:** @CU_Baseball
Head Coach: Ed Servais. **Telephone:** (402) 280-2483. **Baseball SID:** Glen Sisk. **Telephone:** (402) 280-2433.
Assistant Coaches: Brian Furlong, *Rich Wallace. **Telephone:** (402) 280-5545.
Home Field: TD Ameritrade Park Omaha. **Seating Capacity:** 24,000. **Outfield Dimension:** LF—335, CF—408, RF—335.

DALLAS BAPTIST PATRIOTS

Conference: Missouri Valley
Mailing Address: 3000 Mountain Creek Parkway Dallas, TX 75211. **Website:** www.dbu.edu. **Twitter:** @DBU_Baseball
Head Coach: Dan Heefner. **Telephone:** (214) 333-5324. **Baseball SID:** Reagan Ratcliff. **Telephone:** (214) 333-5942.
Assistant Coaches: *Dan Fitzgerald, Wes Johnson. **Telephone:** (214) 333-6987, (214) 333-6957.
Home Field: Horner Ballpark. **Seating Capacity:** 2,000. **Outfield Dimension:** LF—330, CF—390, RF—330.

DARTMOUTH BIG GREEN

Conference: Ivy
Mailing Address: 6083 Alumni Gym, Hanover, NH 03755. **Website:** www.dartmouthsports.com. **Twitter:** @BigGreenBaseball
Head Coach: Bob Whalen. **Telephone:** (603) 646-2477. **Baseball SID:** Rick Bender. **Telephone:** (603) 646-1030.
Assistant Coaches: *Jonathan Anderson, Evan Wells. **Telephone:** (603) 646-9775.
Home Field: Red Rolfe Field at Biondi Park. **Seating Capacity:** 2000. **Outfield Dimension:** LF—325, CF—403, RF—340.

DAVIDSON WILDCATS

Conference: Atlantic 10
Mailing Address: PO Box 7158, Davidson, NC 28035. **Website:** www.davidsonwildcats.com. **Twitter:** @dcbaseball_
Head Coach: Dick Cooke. **Telephone:** (704) 894-2368. **Baseball SID:** Mark Brumbaugh. **Telephone:** (704) 894-2931.
Assistant Coaches: *Rucker Taylor. **Telephone:** (704) 894-2772.
Home Field: Wilson Field. **Seating Capacity:** 700. **Outfield Dimension:** LF—320, CF—385, RF—330.

DAYTON FLYERS

Conference: Atlantic 10
Mailing Address: 300 College Ave., Dayton, OH 45469. **Website:** www.daytonflyers.com. **Twitter:** @DaytonBaseball
Head Coach: Tony Vittorio. **Telephone:** (937) 229-4456. **Baseball SID:** Ross Bagienski. **Telephone:** (937) 229-4431.
Assistant Coaches: Ryne Romick, *Matt Talarico. **Telephone:** .
Home Field: Time Warner Cable Stadium. **Seating Capacity:** 500.

DELAWARE FIGHTIN' BLUE HENS

Conference: Colonial Athletic
Mailing Address: 621 South College Ave., **Newark,
DE 19716. Website:** www.bluehens.com. **Twitter:** @
BlueHenBaseball
Head Coach: Jim Sherman. **Telephone:** (302) 831-
8596. **Baseball SID:** Joe Wirth. **Telephone:** (302) 831-
6519.
Assistant Coaches: Dan Hammer, *Brian Walker.
Telephone: (302) 831-2723.
Home Field: Bob Hannah Stadium. **Seating Capacity:**
2,000. **Outfield Dimension:** LF—320, CF—400, RF—330.

DELAWARE STATE HORNETS

Conference: Mid-Eastern Athletic
Mailing Address: 1200 North DuPont Hwy Dover,
DE 19901. **Website:** www.dsuhornets.com. **Twitter:** @
DelStBaseball
Head Coach: JP Blandin. **Telephone:** (302) 857-6035.
Baseball SID: Dennis Jones. **Telephone:** (302) 857-6068.
Assistant Coaches: Jordan Elliott, *Tom Riley.
Telephone: (302) 857-7815.
Home Field: Soldier Field. **Seating Capacity:** 500.
Outfield Dimension: LF—320, CF—380, RF—320.

DUKE BLUE DEVILS

Conference: Atlantic Coast
Mailing Address: 118 Cameron Indoor Stadium Box
90555 Durham, NC 27708. **Website:** www.goduke.com.
Twitter: @Duke_BASE
Head Coach: Chris Pollard. **Telephone:** (919) 668-
0255. **Baseball SID:** Ashley Wolf. **Telephone:** (919)
684-2489.
Assistant Coaches: *Josh Jordan, Andrew See.
Telephone: (919) 668-5735.
Home Field: Jack Coombs Field. **Seating Capacity:**
2,000. **Outfield Dimension:** LF—325, CF—400, RF—335.

EAST CAROLINA PIRATES

Conference: American Athletic.
Mailing Address: 102 Clark-Leclair Stadium,
Greenville, NC 27858. **Website:** www.ecupirates.com.
Twitter: @ECUBaseball
Head Coach: Cliff Godwin. **Telephone:** (252) 737-
1985. **Baseball SID:** Malcolm Gray. **Telephone:** (252)
737-4523.
Assistant Coaches: *Jeff Palumbo, Dan Roszel.
Telephone: (252) 737-1467.
Home Field: Lewis Field at Clark-Leclair Stadium.
Seating Capacity: 5,000. **Outfield Dimension:** LF—320,
CF—390, RF—320.

EAST TENNESSEE STATE BUCCANEERS

Conference: Southeastern
Mailing Address: PO Box 70707, Johnson City,
TN 37614. **Website:** www.etsubucs.com. **Twitter:** @
ETSU_Baseball
Head Coach: Tony Skole. **Telephone:** (423) 439-4496.
Baseball SID: Kevin Brown. **Telephone:** (423) 439-5263.
Assistant Coaches: Xan Barksdale, *Chris Gordon.
Telephone: (423) 439-5727.
Home Field: Thomas Stadium. **Seating Capacity:**
1,200. **Outfield Dimension:** LF—330, CF—400, RF—330.

EASTERN ILLINOIS PANTHERS

Conference: Ohio Valley

Mailing Address: 600 Lincoln Ave., Charleston, IL
61920. **Website:** www.eiupanthers.com. **Twitter:** @
EIU_Baseball
Head Coach: Jim Schmitz. **Telephone:** (217) 581-
2522. **Baseball SID:** Rich Moser. **Telephone:** (217) 581-
7480.
Assistant Coaches: Jason Anderson, Julio Godinez.
Telephone: (217) 581-7283, (217) 581-8510.
Home Field: Coaches Stadium. **Seating Capacity:**
500. **Outfield Dimension:** LF—340, CF—380, RF—340.

EASTERN KENTUCKY COLONELS

Conference: Ohio Valley
Mailing Address: 521 Lancaster Ave 115 AC. **Website:**
www.ekusports.com. **Twitter:** @EKUSports
Head Coach: Jason Stein. **Telephone:** (859) 622-2128.
Baseball SID: Kevin Britton. **Telephone:** (859) 622-2006.
Assistant Coaches: *John Peterson, Dan Scott.
Telephone: (859) 622-8295, (859) 622-4996.
Home Field: Turkey Hughes Field. **Seating Capacity:**
500. **Outfield Dimension:** LF—330, CF—415, RF—340.

EASTERN MICHIGAN EAGLES

Conference: Mid-American
Mailing Address: 206A Bowen Field House, Ypsilanti,
MI 48197. **Website:** www.emueagles.com. **Twitter:** @
EMU_Baseball
Head Coach: Mark Van Ameyde. **Telephone:** (734)
487-0315. **Baseball SID:** Adam Kuffner. **Telephone:** (734)
487-0317.
Assistant Coaches: Eric Roof, *Spencer Schmitz.
Telephone: (734) 487-1895.
Home Field: Oestrike Stadium. **Seating Capacity:**
1,200. **Outfield Dimension:** LF—340, CF—390, RF—325.

EVANSVILLE PURPLE ACES

Conference: Missouri Valley
Mailing Address: 1800 Lincoln Ave., Evansville, IN
47722. **Website:** www.gopurpleaces.com. **Twitter:** @
UEAthletics
Head Coach: Wes Carroll. **Telephone:** (812) 488-2059.
Baseball SID: Dustin Hall. **Telephone:** (812) 488-1152.
Assistant Coaches: Cody Fick, *Andy Pascoe.
Telephone: (812) 488-2764.
Home Field: Charles H. Braun Stadium. **Seating
Capacity:** 1,200. **Outfield Dimension:** LF—330, CF—400,
RF—330.

FAIRFIELD STAGS

Conference: MAAC
Mailing Address: 1073 North Benson Road, Fairfield,
CT 06824. **Website:** www.fairfieldstags.com. **Twitter:** @
FairfieldStags
Head Coach: Bill Currier. **Telephone:** (203) 254-4000
(ext. 2605). **Baseball SID:** Ivey Speight. **Telephone:** (203)
254-4000 (ext. **2878).**
Assistant Coaches: *Trevor Brown, Mike Cole.
Telephone: (203) 254-4000 (ext. 3178).
Home Field: Alumni Diamond. **Outfield Dimension:**
LF—330, CF—390, RF—330.

FAIRLEIGH DICKINSON KNIGHTS

Conference: Northeast
Mailing Address: 1000 River Road, Teaneck, NJ 07666.
Website: www.fduknights.com. **Twitter:** @FDUKnights
Head Coach: Gary Puccio. **Telephone:** (201) 692-2245.
Baseball SID: TBA. **Telephone:** (201) 692-2204.

Assistant Coaches: Ryan Kresky, *Ray Skjold. **Telephone:** (201) 692-2245.
Home Field: Naimoli Family Baseball Complex.
Seating Capacity: 515. **Outfield Dimension:** LF—320, CF—380, RF—320.

FLORIDA GATORS

Conference: Southeastern
Mailing Address: University Athletic Center, PO Box 14485, Gainesville, FL 32604-2485. **Website:** www.gatorzone.com. **Twitter:** @GatorzoneBB
Head Coach: Kevin O'Sullivan. **Telephone:** (352) 375-4683 (ext. 4457). **Baseball SID:** Buddy Munroe. **Telephone:** (352) 375-4683 (ext. 4457).
Assistant Coaches: *Craig Bell, Brad Weitzel. **Telephone:** (352) 375-4683 (ext. **4457).**
Home Field: Alfred A. McKethan Stadium at Perry Field. **Seating Capacity:** 5,500. **Outfield Dimension:** LF—326, CF—400, RF—321.

FLORIDA A&M RATTLERS

Conference: Mid-Eastern Athletic.
Mailing Address: 1800 Wahnish Way Tallahassee, FL 32307. **Website:** www.famuathletics.com. **Twitter:** @4FAMUBaseball
Head Coach: Jamey Shouppe. **Telephone:** (850) 599-1927. **Baseball SID:** Vaughn Wilson. **Telephone:** (850) 694-0277. **Fax:** N/A.
Assistant Coaches: Bryan Henry, *Bretton Richardson. **Telephone:** (850) 567-0981.
Home Field: Moore-Kittles Field. **Seating Capacity:** 500. **Outfield Dimension:** LF—330, CF—405, RF—330.

FLORIDA ATLANTIC OWLS

Conference: Conference USA
Mailing Address: 777 Glades Rd, Boca Raton, FL 33431. **Website:** www.fausports.com. **Twitter:** @FAU_Baseball
Head Coach: John McCormack. **Telephone:** (561) 297-1055. **Baseball SID:** Brandon Goodwin. **Telephone:** (561) 756-0653.
Assistant Coaches: Dickie Hart, *Jason Jackson. **Telephone:** (561) 297-1055.
Home Field: FAU Baseball Stadium. **Seating Capacity:** 2,000. **Outfield Dimension:** LF—330, CF—400, RF—330.

FLORIDA GULF COAST EAGLES

Conference: Atlantic Sun
Mailing Address: 10501 FGCU Blvd. S. Fort Myers, FL. 33965. **Website:** www.fgcuathletics.com. **Twitter:** @FGCU_Baseball
Head Coach: Dave Tollett. **Telephone:** (239) 590-7051. **Baseball SID:** Matt Moretti III. **Telephone:** (239) 590-1327.
Assistant Coaches: *Rusty McKee, Pete Woodworth. **Telephone:** (239) 590-7059.
Home Field: Swanson Stadium. **Seating Capacity:** 1,500. **Outfield Dimension:** LF—330, CF—400, RF—330.

FLORIDA INTERNATIONAL PANTHERS

Conference: Conference USA
Mailing Address: 11200 SW 8 St, Miami, FL 33199. **Website:** www.fiusports.com. **Twitter:** @FIUBaseball
Head Coach: Turtle Thomas. **Telephone:** (305) 348-3166. **Baseball SID:** Greg Kincaid. **Telephone:** (305) 348-1496.
Assistant Coaches: *Marc Kertenian, Sam Peraza.

Telephone: (305) 348-2145.
Home Field: Panthers Field. **Seating Capacity:** 3,000.
Outfield Dimension: LF—325, CF—400, RF—325.

FLORIDA STATE SEMINOLES

Conference: Atlantic Coast
Mailing Address: 403 Stadium Drive West, Room D0107 Tallahassee, FL 32306. **Website:** www.seminoles.com. **Twitter:** @FSU_Baseball
Head Coach: Mike Martin. **Telephone:** (850) 644-1073. **Baseball SID:** Jason Leturmy. **Telephone:** (850) 644-3920. **Fax:** (850) 644-3820.
Assistant Coaches: Mike Bell, *Mike Martin Jr. **Telephone:** (850) 644-1072.
Home Field: Mike Martin Field at Dick Howser Stadium. **Seating Capacity:** 6,700. **Outfield Dimension:** LF—340, CF—400, RF—320.

FORDHAM RAMS

Conference: Atlantic 10
Mailing Address: 441 East Fordham Road Bronx, NY 10458. **Website:** www.fordhamsports.com. **Twitter:** @FordhamBaseball
Head Coach: Kevin Leighton. **Telephone:** (718) 817-4292. **Baseball SID:** Scott Kwiatkowski. **Telephone:** (718) 817-4219. **Fax:** (718) 817-4244.
Assistant Coaches: Rob DiToma, *Jimmy Jackson. **Telephone:** (718) 817-4290.
Home Field: Houlihan Park. **Seating Capacity:** 1,000.
Outfield Dimension: LF—339, CF—400, RF—338.

FRESNO STATE BULLDOGS

Conference: Mountain West
Mailing Address: 1620 E Bulldog Lane. **Website:** www.gobulldogs.com. **Twitter:** @FresnoStateBSB
Head Coach: Mike Batesole. **Telephone:** (559) 278-2178. **Baseball SID:** Matt Burkholder. **Telephone:** (559) 278-2509 (ext. 6186).
Assistant Coaches: *Ryan Overland, Steve Rousey. **Telephone:** (559) 278-2178.
Home Field: Beiden Field. **Seating Capacity:** 5,300.
Outfield Dimension: LF—330, CF—400, RF—300.

FURMAN PALADINS

Conference: Southern
Mailing Address: 3300 Poinsett Highway Greenville, SC 29613. **Website:** www.furmanpaladins.com. **Twitter:** @FurmanBaseball
Head Coach: Ron Smith. **Telephone:** (864) 294-2146. **Baseball SID:** Hunter Reid. **Telephone:** (864) 294-2061.
Assistant Coaches: *Jeff Whitfield, Brett Harker. **Telephone:** (864) 294-3033, (864) 294-2243.
Home Field: Latham Baseball Stadium. **Seating Capacity:** 1,500. **Outfield Dimension:** LF—330, CF—395, RF—330.

GARDNER-WEBB RUNNIN' BULLDOGS

Conference: Big South
Mailing Address: PO Box 877 Boiling Springs, NC 28017. **Website:** www.gwusports.com. **Twitter:** @GWUSports
Head Coach: Rusty Stroupe. **Telephone:** (704) 406-4421. **Baseball SID:** Marc Rabb. **Telephone:** (704) 406-4355. **Fax:** (704) 406-4739.
Assistant Coaches: *Kent Cox, Ray Greene. **Telephone:** (704) 406-3557.
Home Field: John Henry Moss Stadium. **Seating**

Capacity: 1,000. **Outfield Dimension:** LF—330, CF—390, RF—330.

GEORGE MASON PATRIOTS

Conference: Atlantic 10
Mailing Address: 4400 University Dr., Fairfax, Va. 22030. **Website:** www.gomason.com. **Twitter:** @MasonBaseball
Head Coach: Bill Brown. **Telephone:** (703) 993-3282. **Baseball SID:** Greg Piduch. **Telephone:** (703) 993-3260.
Assistant Coaches: *Tag Montague, Brian Pugh. **Telephone:** (703) 993-3328.
Home Field: Raymond H. Hap Spuhler Field. **Seating Capacity:** 1,000. **Outfield Dimension:** LF—320, CF—400, RF—320.

GEORGE WASHINGTON COLONIALS

Conference: Atlantic 10
Mailing Address: Charles E. Smith Center, 600 22nd St. NW Washington, DC, 20052. **Website:** www.gwsports.com. **Twitter:** @GWBaseball1
Head Coach: Gregg Ritchie. **Telephone:** (202) 994-5933. **Baseball SID:** Dan DiVeglio. **Telephone:** (202) 994-0339.
Assistant Coaches: Dustin Johnson, *Dave Lorber. **Telephone:** (202) 994-5933.
Home Field: Tucker Field at Barcroft Park. **Seating Capacity:** 500. **Outfield Dimension:** LF—330, CF—380, RF—330.

GEORGETOWN HOYAS

Conference: Big East
Mailing Address: McDonough Arena, 3700 O St. NW, Washington, D.C. 20057. **Website:** www.guhoyas.com. **Twitter:** @GtownBaseball
Head Coach: Pete Wilk. **Telephone:** (202) 687-2462. **Baseball SID:** Brendan Thomas. **Telephone:** (202) 687-6783.
Assistant Coaches: Phil Disher, *Erik Supplee. **Telephone:** (202) 687-6406.
Home Field: Shirley Povich Field. **Seating Capacity:** 1,500. **Outfield Dimension:** LF—330, CF—375, RF—330.

GEORGIA BULLDOGS

Conference: Southeastern (East)
Mailing Address: PO Box 1472, Athens, GA 30602. **Website:** www.georgiadogs.com. **Twitter:** @BaseballUGA
Head Coach: Scott Stricklin. **Telephone:** (706) 542-7971. **Baseball SID:** Christopher Lakos. **Telephone:** (706) 542-7994.
Assistant Coaches: Fred Corral, *Scott Daeley. **Telephone:** (706) 542-8379.
Home Field: Foley Field. **Seating Capacity:** TBA. **Outfield Dimension:** LF—350, CF—404, RF—314.

GEORGIA SOUTHERN EAGLES

Conference: Sun Belt
Mailing Address: PO Box 8095, Statesboro, GA 30460. **Website:** www.georgiasoutherneagles.com. **Twitter:** @GSAthletics
Head Coach: Rodney Hennon. **Telephone:** (912) 478-7360. **Baseball SID:** Barrett Gilham. **Telephone:** (912) 478-5448.
Assistant Coaches: *B.J. Green, Chris Moore. **Telephone:** (912) 478-1331, (912) 478-5188.
Home Field: J.I. Clements Stadium. **Seating Capacity:** 3,000. **Outfield Dimension:** LF—325, CF—385,

RF—325.

GEORGIA STATE PANTHERS

Conference: Sun Belt
Mailing Address: PO Box 3875, Atlanta, GA 30302-3975. **Website:** www.georgiastatesports.com. **Twitter:** @GSUPanthers
Head Coach: Greg Frady. **Telephone:** (404) 413-4153. **Baseball SID:** Allison George. **Telephone:** (404) 413-4032.
Assistant Coaches: Willie Stewart, *Edwin Thompson. **Telephone:** (404) 413-4078.
Home Field: GSU Baseball Complex. **Seating Capacity:** 1,092. **Outfield Dimension:** LF—334, CF—385, RF—338.

GEORGIA TECH YELLOW JACKETS

Conference: Atlantic Coast
Mailing Address: 150 Bobby Dodd Way, NW, Atlanta, GA 30332. **Website:** www.ramblinwreck.com. **Twitter:** @GT_Baseball
Head Coach: Danny Hall. **Telephone:** (404) 894-5471. **Baseball SID:** Mike DeGeorge. **Telephone:** (404) 894-5467.
Assistant Coaches: Jason Howell, *Bryan Prince. **Telephone:** (404) 894-5081.
Home Field: Russ Chandler Stadium. **Seating Capacity:** 4,157. **Outfield Dimension:** LF—329, CF—390, RF—334.

GONZAGA BULLDOGS

Conference: West Coast
Mailing Address: 502 E. Boone, Spokane, WA 99258. **Website:** www.gozags.com. **Twitter:** @GonzagaBaseball
Head Coach: Mark Machtolf. **Telephone:** (509) 313-4209. **Baseball SID:** Kyle Scholzen. **Telephone:** (509) 313-4227.
Assistant Coaches: Steve Bennet, *Dan Evans. **Telephone:** (509) 313-4078.
Home Field: Patterson Baseball Complex and Washington Trust Field. **Seating Capacity:** 1,500. **Outfield Dimension:** LF—328, CF—398, RF—328.

GRAMBLING STATE TIGERS

Conference: Southwestern Athletic
Mailing Address: 403 Main St., PO Box 4252, Grambling, LA 71245. **Website:** www.gsutigers.com. **Twitter:** @GSU_Tigers
Head Coach: James Cooper. **Telephone:** (318) 274-6566. **Baseball SID:** Robert Vogel. **Telephone:** (318) 274-6562. **Fax:** N/A.
Assistant Coach: Davin Pierre. **Telephone:** (318) 274-2416.

GRAND CANYON ANTELOPES

Conference: Western Athletic
Mailing Address: 3300 W Camelback Road, Phoenix, AZ 85017. **Website:** gculopes.com. **Twitter:** @GCU_Lopes
Head Coach: Andy Stankiewicz. **Telephone:** (602) 639-6042. **Baseball SID:** Morgan Ballard. **Telephone:** (602) 639-7243.
Assistant Coaches: *Nathan Choate, Gregg Wallis. **Telephone:** (602) 639-7676.
Home Field: Brazell Stadium. **Seating Capacity:** 1,500. **Outfield Dimension:** LF—320, CF—385, RF—328.

HARTFORD HAWKS

Conference: America East
Mailing Address: 200 Bloomfield Ave, West Hartford, CT 06117. **Website:** www.hartfordhawks.com. **Twitter:** @HartfordHawks
Head Coach: Justin Blood. **Telephone:** (860) 768-5760. **Baseball SID:** Dan Ruede. **Telephone:** (860) 768-4501.
Assistant Coaches: Elliot Glynn, *Steve Malinowski. **Telephone:** (860) 768-4972.
Home Field: Fiondella Field. **Seating Capacity:** 1,500. **Outfield Dimension:** LF—325, CF—400, RF—325.

HAWAII RAINBOW WARRIORS

Conference: Big West
Mailing Address: 1337 Lower Campus Rd., Honolulu, HI 96822. **Website:** www.hawaiiathletics.com. **Twitter:** @HawaiiBaseball
Head Coach: Mike Trapasso. **Telephone:** (808) 956-6247. **Baseball SID:** John Barry. **Telephone:** (808) 956-7506.
Assistant Coaches: Carl Fraticelli, *Rusty McNamara. **Telephone:** (808) 956-6247.
Home Field: Les Murkami Stadium. **Seating Capacity:** 4,312. **Outfield Dimension:** LF—325, CF—385, RF—325.

HIGH POINT PANTHERS

Conference: Big South
Mailing Address: 833 Montlieu Avenue, High Point, NC 27262. **Website:** www.highpointpanthers.com. **Twitter:** @HPUBaseball
Head Coach: Craig Cozart. **Telephone:** (336) 841-9190. **Baseball SID:** Joe Arancio. **Telephone:** (336) 841-4638. **Fax:** (336) 841-9182.
Assistant Coaches: Jason Laws, *Kenny Smith. **Telephone:** (336) 841-4629.
Home Field: Williard Stadium. **Seating Capacity:** 500. **Outfield Dimension:** LF—325, CF—400, RF—330.

HOFSTRA PRIDE

Conference: Colonial Athletic
Mailing Address: 1000 Hempstead Turnpike, Hempstead, NY 11549. **Website:** www.gohofstra.com. **Twitter:** @HofstraBaseball
Head Coach: John Russo. **Telephone:** (516) 463-3759. **Baseball SID:** Len Skoros. **Telephone:** (516) 463-4602. **Fax:** (516) 463-5033.
Assistant Coaches: *Chris Johns, Jameel Ziadeh. **Telephone:** (516) 463-5923.
Home Field: University Field. **Seating Capacity:** 600. **Outfield Dimension:** LF—322, CF—382, RF—337.

HOLY CROSS CRUSADERS

Conference: Patriot
Mailing Address: One College Street Worcester, MA 01610. **Website:** www.goholycross.com. **Twitter:** @GoHolyCross
Head Coach: Greg DiCenzo. **Telephone:** (508) 793-2753. **Baseball SID:** Jim Sarkisian. **Telephone:** (508) 793-2583.
Assistant Coaches: Matt Antonelli, *Ron Rakowski. **Telephone:** (508) 793-2753.
Home Field: Fitton Field. **Seating Capacity:** 3,000. **Outfield Dimension:** LF—332, CF—385, RF—313.

HOUSTON COUGARS

Conference: American Athletic
Mailing Address: 3100 Cullen Blvd. Houston, Texas 77030. **Website:** www.uhcougars.com. **Twitter:** @UHCougarBB
Head Coach: Todd Whitting. **Telephone:** (713) 743-9396. **Baseball SID:** Allison McClain. **Telephone:** (713) 743-9406.
Assistant Coaches: Frank Anderson, *Trip Couch. **Telephone:** (713) 743-9396.
Home Field: Cougar Field. **Seating Capacity:** 3,500. **Outfield Dimension:** LF—330, CF—390, RF—330.

HOUSTON BAPTIST HUSKIES

Conference: Southland
Mailing Address: 7502 Fondren, Houston, TX 77074. **Website:** www.hbuhuskies.com. **Twitter:** @HBUHuskiesBSB
Head Coach: Jared Moon. **Telephone:** (281) 649-3332. **Baseball SID:** Russ Reneau. **Telephone:** (281) 649-3098.
Assistant Coaches: *Xavier Hernandez, Russell Stockton. **Telephone:** (281) 649-3264.
Home Field: Husky Field. **Seating Capacity:** 500. **Outfield Dimension:** LF—330, CF—400, RF—330.

ILLINOIS FIGHTING ILLINI

Conference: Big Ten
Mailing Address: 1700 S Fourth St, Champaign, IL 61820. **Website:** www.fightingillini.com. **Twitter:** @IlliniBaseball
Head Coach: Dan Hartleb. **Telephone:** (217) 244-8144. **Baseball SID:** Matt Wille. **Telephone:** (217) 300-9155.
Assistant Coaches: *Spencer Allen, Drew Dickinson. **Telephone:** (217) 244-5539.
Home Field: Illinois Field. **Seating Capacity:** 1,500. **Outfield Dimension:** LF—330, CF—400, RF—330.

ILLINOIS STATE REDBIRDS

Conference: Missouri Valley
Mailing Address: 207 Horton Field House. **Website:** www.goredbirds.com. **Twitter:** @REDBIRDBaseball
Head Coach: Bo Durkac. **Telephone:** (309) 438-4458. **Baseball SID:** Matt Wing. **Telephone:** (309) 438-3249.
Assistant Coaches: Michael Kellar, *Mike Stalowy. **Telephone:** (309) 438-5151.
Home Field: Duffy Bass Field. **Seating Capacity:** 1,500. **Outfield Dimension:** LF—330, CF—400, RF—330.

ILLINOIS-CHICAGO FLAMES

Conference: Horizon
Mailing Address: 839 West Roosevelt Rd, Chicago, IL 60608. **Website:** www.uicflames.com. **Twitter:** @UICBaseball
Head Coach: Mike Dee. **Telephone:** (312) 996-8645. **Baseball SID:** Mike Laninga. **Telephone:** (312) 996-5881. **Fax:** (312) 996-8349.
Assistant Coaches: *John Flood, Sean McDermott. **Telephone:** (312) 355-1757.
Home Field: Les Miller Field at Curtis Granderson Stadium. **Seating Capacity:** 1,800. **Outfield Dimension:** LF—320, CF—396, RF—324.

INCARNATE WORD CARDINALS

Conference: Southland
Mailing Address: 4301 Broadway, San Antonio, TX

78209. **Website:** www.cardinalathletics.com. **Twitter:** @UIWBaseball
Head Coach: Dan Heep. **Telephone:** (210) 829-3830.
Baseball SID: Shane Meling. **Telephone:** (210) 805-3071.
Fax: (210) 805-3574.
Assistant Coaches: Ryan Aguayo, *Chase Tidwell.
Telephone: (210) 829-3830.
Home Field: Sullivan Field. **Seating Capacity:** 1,000.
Outfield Dimension: LF—335, CF—405, RF—335.

INDIANA HOOSIERS

Conference: Big Ten
Mailing Address: Assembly Hall 1001 East 17th Street Bloomington, IN. **Website:** www.iuhoosiers.com. **Twitter:** @HoosierBaseball
Head Coach: Chris Lemonis. **Telephone:** (812) 855-8240. **Baseball SID:** Andrew Lentz. **Telephone:** (812) 855-4770.
Assistant Coaches: Kyle Bunn, *Kyle Cheesebrough.
Telephone: (812) 855-8240.
Home Field: Bart Kaufman Field. **Seating Capacity:** 2,500. **Outfield Dimension:** LF—330, CF—400, RF—330.

IOWA HAWKEYES

Conference: Big Ten
Mailing Address: N411 Carver-Hawkeye Arena, Iowa City, IA 52242. **Website:** www.hawkeyesports.com. **Twitter:** @UIBaseball
Head Coach: Rick Heller. **Telephone:** (319) 335-9743.
Baseball SID: James Allan. **Telephone:** (319) 335-9411.
Assistant Coaches: Scott Brickman, *Marty Sutherland. **Telephone:** (319) 335-9743.
Home Field: Duane Banks Field. **Seating Capacity:** 3,000. **Outfield Dimension:** LF—330, CF—400, RF—330.

IPFW MASTODONS

Conference: Summit
Mailing Address: 2101 E. Coliseum Blvd. Fort Wayne, IN 46805. **Website:** www.gomastodons.com. **Twitter:** @IPFWAthletics
Head Coach: Bobby Pierce. **Telephone:** (260) 481-5480. **Baseball SID:** Bill Salyer. **Telephone:** (260) 481-0729. **Fax:** (260) 481-0266.
Assistant Coaches: *Grant Birely, Scott Micinski.
Telephone: (260) 481-0710.
Home Field: Mastodon Park. **Seating Capacity:** 1,000.
Outfield Dimension: LF—330, CF—405, RF—330.

JACKSON STATE TIGERS

Conference: Southwestern Athletic
Mailing Address: 1400 John R. Lynch Street. **Website:** www.jsutigers.com. **Twitter:** @jsu_baseball
Head Coach: Omar Johnson. **Telephone:** (601) 979-3930. **Baseball SID:** Wesley Peterson. **Telephone:** (601) 979-5899.
Assistant Coaches: *Chris Crenshaw, Chris Stamps.
Telephone: (601) 979-3928.
Home Field: Robert "Bob" Braddy Field. **Seating Capacity:** 500. **Outfield Dimension:** LF—325, CF—401, RF—325.

JACKSONVILLE DOLPHINS

Conference: Atlantic Sun
Mailing Address: 2800 University Blvd. N, Jacksonville, FL 32211. **Website:** www.judolphins.com. **Twitter:** @JUBaseball
Head Coach: Tim Montez. **Telephone:** (904) 256-7414. **Baseball SID:** Ethan Kaufman. **Telephone:** (904) 256-7761.
Assistant Coaches: Chris Hayes, *Chuck Jeroloman.
Telephone: (904) 256-7476.
Home Field: John Sessions Stadium. **Seating Capacity:** 3,000. **Outfield Dimension:** LF—340, CF—405, RF—340.

JACKSONVILLE STATE GAMECOCKS

Conference: Ohio Valley
Mailing Address: 700 Pelham Road North, Jacksonville, AL 36265. **Website:** www.jsugamecock-sports.com. **Twitter:** @JSUBB
Head Coach: Jim Case. **Telephone:** (256) 782-5367.
Baseball SID: Greg Seitz. **Telephone:** (256) 782-5279.
Assistant Coaches: Mike Murphree, *Brandon Romans. **Telephone:** (256) 782-8141, (256) 782-5358.
Home Field: Rudy Abbott Field. **Seating Capacity:** 1,500. **Outfield Dimension:** LF—330, CF—400, RF—330.

JAMES MADISON DIAMOND DUKES

Conference: Colonial Athletic
Mailing Address: Memorial Hall, 395 S. High Street, Baseball Office, Harrisonburg, VA, 22807. **Website:** www.jmusports.com. **Twitter:** @JMUBaseball
Head Coach: Spanky McFarland. **Telephone:** (540) 568-3932. **Baseball SID:** Jason Krech. **Telephone:** (540) 568-6154.
Assistant Coaches: Brandon Cohen, *Ted White.
Telephone: (540) 568-5510.
Home Field: Eagle Field. **Seating Capacity:** 1,500.
Outfield Dimension: LF—330, CF—400, RF—320.

KANSAS JAYHAWKS

Conference: Big 12
Mailing Address: 1651 Naismith Drive Lawrence, KS 66045. **Website:** www.kuathletics.com. **Twitter:** @KUBaseball
Head Coach: Ritch Price. **Telephone:** (785) 864-4196.
Baseball SID: DJ Haurin. **Telephone:** (785) 864-3575.
Assistant Coaches: Ryan Graves, *Ritchie Price.
Telephone: (785) 864-7908.
Home Field: Hoglund Ballpark. **Seating Capacity:** 2,400. **Outfield Dimension:** LF—330, CF—400, RF—300.

KANSAS STATE WILDCATS

Conference: Big 12
Mailing Address: 1800 College Ave, Manhattan, KS 66503. **Website:** www.kstatesports.com. **Twitter:** @kstatesports
Head Coach: Brad Hill. **Telephone:** (785) 532-5723.
Baseball SID: Chris Kutz. **Telephone:** (785) 532-7976.
Assistant Coaches: *Josh Reynolds, Andy Sawyers.
Telephone: (785) 532-7714.
Home Field: Tointon Family Stadium. **Seating Capacity:** 2,331. **Outfield Dimension:** LF—340, CF—400, RF—325.

KENNESAW STATE OWLS

Conference: Atlantic Sun
Mailing Address: 590 Cobb Avenue MD #0201 Kennesaw, GA 30144. **Website:** www.ksuowls.com. **Twitter:** @KSUOwlsBaseball
Head Coach: Mike Sansing. **Telephone:** (470) 578-6264. **Baseball SID:** TBD. **Telephone:** (470) 578-2562.
Assistant Coaches: Kevin Erminio, *Derek Simmons.
Telephone: (470) 578-2099.

Home Field: Stillwell Stadium. **Seating Capacity:** 1200. **Outfield Dimension:** LF—331, CF—400, RF—370.

KENT STATE GOLDEN FLASHES

Conference: Mid-American
Mailing Address: 1025 Risman Dr. Kent, OH 44242. **Website:** www.kentstatesports.com. **Twitter:** @kentst-baseball
Head Coach: Jeff Duncan. **Telephone:** (330) 672-8432. **Baseball SID:** Mollie Radzinski. **Telephone:** (330) 672-8419.
Assistant Coaches: Mike Birkbeck, *Alex Marconi. **Telephone:** (330) 672-8433.
Home Field: Schoonover Stadium. **Seating Capacity:** 2,000. **Outfield Dimension:** LF—330, CF—405, RF—315.

KENTUCKY WILDCATS

Conference: Southeastern
Mailing Address: Lexington, KY. **Website:** www.ukathletics.com. **Twitter:** @UKBaseball
Head Coach: Gary Henderson. **Telephone:** (859) 257-8988. **Baseball SID:** Brent Ingram. **Telephone:** (859) 257-8504.
Assistant Coaches: *Brad Bohannon, Rick Eckstein. **Telephone:** (859) 257-8052.
Home Field: Cliff Hagan Stadium. **Seating Capacity:** 3000. **Outfield Dimension:** LF—340, CF—390, RF—310.

LA SALLE EXPLORERS

Conference: Atlantic 10
Mailing Address: 1900 W Olney Ave, Philadelphia, PA 19141. **Website:** www.goexplorers.com. **Twitter:** @GoExplorers
Head Coach: Mike Lake. **Telephone:** (215) 951-1995. **Baseball SID:** Mike Adleman. **Telephone:** (215) 991-2886.
Assistant Coaches: Scott Grimes, *Michael McCarry. **Telephone:** (215) 951-1995.
Home Field: Hank DeVincent Field. **Seating Capacity:** 1,000. **Outfield Dimension:** LF—305, CF—410, RF—321.

LAFAYETTE LEOPARDS

Conference: Patriot
Mailing Address: Kirby Sports Center, Pierce & Hamilton Streets, Easton, PA, 18042. **Website:** www.goleopards.com. **Twitter:** @LafayetteBsbl
Head Coach: Joe Kinney. **Telephone:** (610) 330-5476. **Baseball SID:** Brian Ludrof. **Telephone:** (610) 330-5003.
Assistant Coaches: *Tanner Biagini, Gregg Durrah. **Telephone:** (610) 330-5945.
Home Field: Kamine Stadium. **Seating Capacity:** 500. **Outfield Dimension:** LF—332, CF—403, RF—335.

LAMAR CARDINALS

Conference: Southland
Mailing Address: 211 Redbird Lane. **Website:** www.lamarcardinals.com. **Twitter:** @Lamar_Baseball
Head Coach: Jim Gilligan. **Telephone:** (409) 880-8315. **Baseball SID:** Matthew Fowler. **Telephone:** (409) 880-7845.
Assistant Coaches: Scott Hatten, *Jimmy Ricklefsen. **Telephone:** (409) 880-8135.
Home Field: Vincent-Beck Stadium. **Seating Capacity:** 3,500. **Outfield Dimension:** LF—325, CF—380, RF—325.

LEHIGH MOUNTAIN HAWKS

Conference: Patriot
Mailing Address: 641 Taylor St. Bethlehem, PA 18015. **Website:** www.lehighsports.com. **Twitter:** @LehighBaseball
Head Coach: Sean Leary. **Telephone:** (610) 758-4315. **Baseball SID:** Chelsea Vielhauer. **Telephone:** (610) 758-5101.
Assistant Coaches: *John Fugett, Lee Saverio. **Telephone:** (610) 758-4315.
Home Field: Goodman Campus Baseball Field. **Seating Capacity:** 500. **Outfield Dimension:** LF—320, CF—400, RF—320.

LIBERTY FLAMES

Conference: Big South
Mailing Address: 1971 University Blvd., Lynchburg, VA 24524. **Website:** www.libertyflames.com. **Twitter:** @libertybaseball
Head Coach: Jim Toman. **Telephone:** (434) 582-2305. **Baseball SID:** Ryan Bomberger. **Telephone:** (434) 582-2292.
Assistant Coaches: *Jason Murray, Garrett Quinn. **Telephone:** (434) 582-2119.
Home Field: Liberty Baseball Stadium. **Seating Capacity:** 2,500. **Outfield Dimension:** LF—325, CF—395, RF—325.

LIPSCOMB BISONS

Conference: Atlantic Sun
Mailing Address: One University Park Drive, Nashville, TN 37204. **Website:** www.lipscombsports.com. **Twitter:** @BisonBaseball
Head Coach: Jeff Forehand. **Telephone:** (615) 966-5716. **Baseball SID:** Kirk Downs. **Telephone:** (615) 966-5457.
Assistant Coaches: Paul Phillips, *Brian Ryman. **Telephone:** (615) 966-5149.
Home Field: Ken Dugan Field at Stephen L. Marsh Stadium. **Seating Capacity:** 1,500. **Outfield Dimension:** LF—330, CF—405, RF—330.

LONG BEACH STATE DIRTBAGS

Conference: Big West
Mailing Address: 1250 Bellflower Blvd. Long Beach, CA 90840. **Website:** www.longbeachstate.com. **Twitter:** @LBDirtbags
Head Coach: Troy Buckley. **Telephone:** (562) 985-8215. **Baseball SID:** Steven Olveda. **Telephone:** (562) 985-7797.
Assistant Coaches: Mike Steele, *Jesse Zepeda. **Telephone:** (562) 985-7548.
Home Field: Blair Field. **Seating Capacity:** 3,000. **Outfield Dimension:** LF—348, CF—400, RF—348.

LONG ISLAND-BROOKLYN BLACKBIRDS

Conference: Northeast
Mailing Address: 1 University Plaza Brooklyn,NY 11201. **Website:** www.liuathletics.com. **Twitter:** @liubrooklyn
Head Coach: Alex Trezza. **Telephone:** (718) 780-1538. **Baseball SID:** Case Snedecor. **Telephone:** (718) 488-1307.
Assistant Coaches: *Lou Bernardini, Matt Grosso. **Telephone:** (718) 488-3034.
Home Field: The Birdcage. **Seating Capacity:** 500. **Outfield Dimension:** LF—300, CF—401, RF—300.

LOUISIANA STATE TIGERS

Conference: Southeastern
Mailing Address: LSU Athletics Nicholson Dr. at N. Stadium Dr., Baton Rouge, LA 70803. **Website:** www.lsusports.net. **Twitter:** @LSUBaseball
Head Coach: Paul Mainieri. **Telephone:** (225) 578-4148. **Baseball SID:** Bill Franques. **Telephone:** (225) 578-8226.
Assistant Coaches: *Andy Cannizaro, Alan Dunn. **Telephone:** (225) 578-4148.
Home Field: Alex Box Stadium, Skip Bertman Field. **Seating Capacity:** 10,326. **Outfield Dimension:** LF—330, CF—405, RF—330.

LOUISIANA TECH BULLDOGS

Conference: Conference USA.
Mailing Address: Louisiana Tech Athletics, PO Box 3046, Ruston, LA 71272. **Website:** www.latechsports.com. **Twitter:** @LATechBSB
Head Coach: Greg Goff. **Telephone:** (318) 257-5318. **Baseball SID:** Anna Claire Thomas. **Telephone:** (318) 257-5314.
Assistant Coaches: Jake Wells, J.D. Hulse. **Telephone:** (318) 257-4789.
Home Field: J.C. Love Field. **Seating Capacity:** 2,000. **Outfield Dimension:** LF—315, CF—385, RF—325.

LOUISIANA-LAFAYETTE RAGIN' CAJUNS

Conference: Sun Belt
Mailing Address: 201 Reinhardt Drive, Lafayette, LA 70506. **Website:** www.ragincajuns.com. **Twitter:** @ULRaginCajuns
Head Coach: Tony Robichaux. **Telephone:** (337) 262-5189. **Baseball SID:** Jeff Schneider. **Telephone:** (337) 482-6332.
Assistant Coaches: *Anthony Babineaux, Jeremy Talbot. **Telephone:** (337) 262-5189.
Home Field: M.L. "Tigue" Moore Field. **Seating Capacity:** 3,755. **Outfield Dimension:** LF—330, CF—400, RF—330.

LOUISVILLE CARDINALS

Conference: Atlantic Coast
Mailing Address: Athletics Department, University of Louisville, Louisville, KY 40292. **Website:** www.gocards.com. **Twitter:** @UofLBaseball
Head Coach: Dan McDonnell. **Telephone:** (502) 852-0103. **Baseball SID:** Garett Wall. **Telephone:** (502) 852-3088.
Assistant Coaches: *Eric Snider, Roger Williams. **Telephone:** (502) 852-3929.
Home Field: Jim Patterson Stadium. **Seating Capacity:** 4,000. **Outfield Dimension:** LF—330, CF—402, RF—330.

LOYOLA MARYMOUNT LIONS

Conference: West Coast.
Mailing Address: 1 LMU Drive, Los Angeles, CA 90045. **Website:** www.lmulions.com. **Twitter:** @BaseballLMU
Head Coach: Jason Gill. **Telephone:** (310) 338-2949. **Baseball SID:** Tyler Geivett. **Telephone:** (310) 338-7638.
Assistant Coaches: Danny Ricabal, *Bryant Ward. **Telephone:** (310) 338-4511.
Home Field: Page Stadium. **Seating Capacity:** 600. **Outfield Dimension:** LF—326, CF—406, RF—321.

MAINE BLACK BEARS

Conference: America East
Mailing Address: 5747 Memorial Gym, Orono, ME 04469. **Website:** www.goblackbears.com. **Twitter:** @MaineBaseball
Head Coach: Steve Trimper. **Telephone:** (207) 581-1090. **Baseball SID:** Laura Reed. **Telephone:** (207) 581-3646.
Assistant Coaches: *Nick Derba, J.P. Pyne. **Telephone:** (207) 581-1096.
Home Field: Mahaney Diamond. **Seating Capacity:** 4,400. **Outfield Dimension:** LF—330, CF—400, RF—330.

MANHATTAN JASPERS

Conference: Metro Atlantic Athletic
Mailing Address: 4513 Manhattan College Parkway, Riverdale, NY 10471. **Website:** www.gojaspers.com. **Twitter:** @JaspersBaseball
Head Coach: Jim Duffy. **Telephone:** (718) 862-7821. **Baseball SID:** Kevin Ross. **Telephone:** (718) 862-7228.
Assistant Coaches: Justin Echevarria, *Rene Ruiz. **Telephone:** (718) 862-7218.
Home Field: Dutchess Stadium. **Seating Capacity:** 1,000. **Outfield Dimension:** LF—330, CF—400, RF—330.

MARSHALL THUNDERING HERD

Conference: Conference USA
Mailing Address: One John Marshall Way, Huntington, WV 25755. **Website:** www.herdzone.com. **Twitter:** @HerdBaseball
Head Coach: Jeff Waggoner. **Telephone:** (304) 696-6454. **Baseball SID:** Caitie Smith. **Telephone:** (304) 696-5276.
Assistant Coaches: *Tim Donnelly, Josh Newman. **Telephone:** (304) 696-7146.
Home Field: Appalachian Power Park. **Seating Capacity:** 4,500. **Outfield Dimension:** LF—330, CF—400, RF—320.

MARYLAND TERRAPINS

Conference: Big Ten
Mailing Address: XFINITY Center, Terrapin Trail, College Park, MD 20742. **Website:** www.umterps.com.
Head Coach: John Szefc. **Telephone:** (301) 314-1845. **Baseball SID:** Matt Bertram. **Telephone:** (301) 314-8093. **Twitter:** @UMTerpsBaseball
Assistant Coaches: Jim Belanger, *Rob Vaughn. **Telephone:** (301) 314-1286.
Home Field: Shipley Field at Bob "Turtle" Smith Stadium. **Seating Capacity:** 2500. **Outfield Dimension:** LF—320, CF—380, RF—325.

MARYLAND-BALTIMORE COUNTY RETRIEVERS

Conference: America East
Mailing Address: 1000 Hilltop Circle, Baltimore, MD 21250. **Website:** www.umbcretrievers.com. **Twitter:** @UMBCBaseball
Head Coach: Bob Mumma. **Telephone:** (410) 455-2239. **Baseball SID:** David Castellanos. **Telephone:** (410) 455-1530.
Assistant Coaches: *Liam Bowen, Larry Williams. **Telephone:** (410) 455-2239.
Home Field: Alumni Field. **Seating Capacity:** 1000. **Outfield Dimension:** LF—330, CF—360, RF—340.

MARYLAND-EASTERN SHORE HAWKS

Conference: Mid-Eastern Athletic
Mailing Address: 1 Backbone Road, Princess Anne, MD, 21853. **Website:** www.umeshawks.com. **Twitter:** @UMES_Baseball
Interim Head Coach: John O'Neil. **Telephone:** (410) 651-8158. **Baseball SID:** Matt McCann. **Telephone:** (410) 621-3358.
Assistant Coaches: Ted Aronow, Trevon Johnson. **Telephone:** (410) 651-8908.
Home Field: Hawks Stadium. **Seating Capacity:** 1,000. **Outfield Dimension:** LF—325, CF—400, RF—325.

MASSACHUSETTS MINUTEMEN

Conference: Atlantic 10
Mailing Address: 131 Commonwealth Ave., Amherst, MA 01003. **Website:** www.umassathletics.com. **Twitter:** @UMassBaseball
Head Coach: Mike Stone. **Telephone:** (860) 545-3120. **Baseball SID:** Jill Jakuba. **Telephone:** (413) 577-0053.
Assistant Coaches: Rich Graef, *Mike Sweeney. **Telephone:** (413) 545-3766.
Home Field: Earl Lorden Field. **Seating Capacity:** 1,400. **Outfield Dimension:** LF—330, CF—400, RF—330.

MCNEESE STATE COWBOYS

Conference: Southland
Mailing Address: 700 E. McNeese Street, Lake Charles, La. 70609. **Website:** www.mcneesesports.com. **Twitter:** @McNeeseBaseball
Head Coach: Justin Hill. **Telephone:** (337) 475-5484. **Baseball SID:** Hunter Bower. **Telephone:** (337) 475-5941.
Assistant Coaches: *Cory Barton, Roberto Vaz. **Telephone:** (337) 475-5904.
Home Field: Cowboy Diamond. **Seating Capacity:** 2,000. **Outfield Dimension:** LF—300, CF—400, RF—330.

MEMPHIS TIGERS

Conference: American Athletic.
Mailing Address: 570 Normal Room 207 Memphis TN 38152. **Website:** www.gotigersgo.com. **Twitter:** @MemphisBaseball
Head Coach: Daron Schoenrock. **Telephone:** (901) 678-4137. **Baseball SID:** Mark Taylor. **Telephone:** (901) 678-5108.
Assistant Coaches: *Clay Greene, Russ McNickle. **Telephone:** (901) 678-4139.
Home Field: Fed Ex Park. **Seating Capacity:** 1,500. **Outfield Dimension:** LF—318, CF—385, RF—319.

MERCER BEARS

Conference: Southern
Mailing Address: 1501 Mercer University Drive, Macon, GA 31207. **Website:** www.mercerbears.com. **Twitter:** @MercerBaseball
Head Coach: Craig Gibson. **Telephone:** (478) 301-2396. **Baseball SID:** Jordon Bruner. **Telephone:** (478) 301-5209.
Assistant Coaches: Ty Megahee, *Brent Shade. **Telephone:** (478) 301-2738.
Home Field: Claude Smith Field. **Seating Capacity:** 500. **Outfield Dimension:** LF—330, CF—400, RF—320.

MIAMI HURRICANES

Conference: Atlantic Coast
Mailing Address: 6201 San Amaro Drive, Coral Gables, FL 33146. **Website:** www.hurricanesports.com. **Twitter:** @CanesBaseball
Head Coach: Jim Morris. **Telephone:** (305) 284-4171. **Baseball SID:** Camron Ghorbi. **Telephone:** (305) 284-3230.
Assistant Coaches: J.D. Arteaga, *Gino DiMare. **Telephone:** (305) 284-4171.
Home Field: Alex Rodriguez Park at Mark Light Field. **Seating Capacity:** 4,999. **Outfield Dimension:** LF—330, CF—400, RF—330.

MIAMI (OHIO) REDHAWKS

Conference: Mid-American
Mailing Address: 120 Withrow Court, Oxford, OH 45056. **Website:** www.muredhawks.com. **Twitter:** @MiamiOHBaseball
Head Coach: Danny Hayden. **Telephone:** (513) 529-6631. **Baseball SID:** Chad Twaro. **Telephone:** (513) 529-1601.
Assistant Coaches: Matt Davis, *Jeremy Ison. **Telephone:** (513) 529-6746.
Home Field: Stanley G. McKie Field at Hayden Park. **Seating Capacity:** 1,500. **Outfield Dimension:** LF—332, CF—400, RF—343.

MICHIGAN WOLVERINES

Conference: Big Ten
Mailing Address: 1000 S. State St. Ann Arbor, MI 48109. **Website:** www.mgoblue.com. **Twitter:** @umich-baseball
Head Coach: Erik Bakich. **Telephone:** (734) 647-4550. **Baseball SID:** Kent Reichert. **Telephone:** (734) 647-1726.
Assistant Coaches: Sean Kenny, *Nick Schnabel. **Telephone:** (734) 647-4550.
Home Field: Wilpon Complex/Ray Fisher Stadium. **Seating Capacity:** 3,500. **Outfield Dimension:** LF—312, CF—395, RF—320.

MICHIGAN STATE SPARTANS

Conference: Big Ten
Mailing Address: 223 Kalamazoo St., East Lansing, MI 48824. **Website:** www.msuspartans.com. **Twitter:** @statebaseball
Head Coach: Jake Boss. **Telephone:** (517) 884-7365. **Baseball SID:** Jeff Barnes. **Telephone:** (517) 355-2271.
Assistant Coaches: Skylar Meade, *Graham Sikes. **Telephone:** (517) 355-3419.
Home Field: McLane Stadium at Kobs Field. **Seating Capacity:** 3,000. **Outfield Dimension:** LF—340, CF—402, RF—302.

MIDDLE TENNESSEE STATE BLUE RAIDERS

Conference: Conference USA
Mailing Address: 1500 Greenland Drive, Murfreesboro, TN 37132. **Website:** www.goblueraiders.com. **Twitter:** @MT_Baseball
Head Coach: Jim McGuire. **Telephone:** (615) 898-2961. **Baseball SID:** Tony Stinnett. **Telephone:** (615) 898-5270.
Assistant Coaches: JP Davis, *Scott Hall. **Telephone:** (615) 494-8796.
Home Field: Reese Smith Jr. Field. **Seating Capacity:** 2,100. **Outfield Dimension:** LF—330, CF—390, RF—330.

MINNESOTA GOLDEN GOPHERS

Conference: Big Ten
Mailing Address: Bierman Field Athletic Building, 516

15th Avenue SE, Minneapolis, MN 55455. **Website:** www.gophersports.com. **Twitter:** @GophersBaseball
Head Coach: John Anderson. **Telephone:** (612) 625-4057. **Baseball SID:** Justine Buerkle. **Telephone:** (612) 624-4345.
Assistant Coaches: *Rob Fornasiere, Scott Matyas, Todd Oakes. **Telephone:** (612) 625-3568.
Home Field: Siebert Field. **Seating Capacity:** 1,420. **Outfield Dimension:** LF—330, CF—390, RF—330.

MISSISSIPPI REBELS

Conference: Southeastern
Mailing Address: 400 University Place University, MS 38677. **Website:** www.olemisssports.com. **Twitter:** @OleMissBSB
Head Coach: Mike Bianco. **Telephone:** (662) 915-6643. **Baseball SID:** TBA. **Telephone:** (662) 915-7522.
Assistant Coaches: Mike Clement, *Carl Lafferty. **Telephone:** (662) 915-7556.
Home Field: Oxford University Stadium—Swayze Field. **Seating Capacity:** 10323. **Outfield Dimension:** LF—330, CF—390, RF—330.

MISSISSIPPI STATE BULLDOGS

Conference: Southeastern
Mailing Address: 288 Lakeview Dr. Bryan Building Attn: Media Relations Mississippi State, MS 39762. **Website:** www.mstateathletics.com. **Twitter:** @HailStateBB
Head Coach: John Cohen. **Telephone:** (662) 325-3597. **Baseball SID:** Kyle Niblett. **Telephone:** (662) 325-8040.
Assistant Coaches: *Nick Mingione, Butch Thompson. **Telephone:** (662) 325-3597.
Home Field: Dudy Noble Field at Polk-DeMent Stadium. **Seating Capacity:** 15,000. **Outfield Dimension:** LF—330, CF—390, RF—326.

MISSOURI TIGERS

Conference: Southeastern
Mailing Address: 100 MATC, Columbia, MO 65211. **Website:** www.mutigers.com. **Twitter:** @MizzouBaseball
Head Coach: Tim Jamieson. **Telephone:** (573) 882-1917. **Baseball SID:** Shawn Davis. **Telephone:** (573) 882-0711.
Assistant Coaches: *Kerrick Jackson, Hunter Mense. **Telephone:** (573) 882-8929.
Home Field: Simmons Field. **Seating Capacity:** 2,500. **Outfield Dimension:** LF—320, CF—400, RF—340.

MISSOURI STATE BEARS

Conference: Missouri Valley
Mailing Address: 901 S. National Ave, Springfield, MO 65897. **Website:** www.missouristatebears.com. **Twitter:** @MissouriStBears
Head Coach: Keith Guttin. **Telephone:** (417) 836-5242. **Baseball SID:** Eric Doennig. **Telephone:** (417) 836-4585.
Assistant Coaches: Paul Evans, *Nate Thompson. **Telephone:** (417) 836-5242.
Home Field: Hammons Field. **Seating Capacity:** 8,000. **Outfield Dimension:** LF—315, CF—400, RF—330.

MONMOUTH HAWKS

Conference: Metro Atlantic Athletic
Mailing Address: 400 Cedar Avenue, West Long Branch, NJ 07764. **Website:** monmouthhawks.com.

Twitter: @MUHawksBaseball
Head Coach: Dean Ehehalt. **Telephone:** (732) 263-5186. **Baseball SID:** Gary Kowal. **Telephone:** (732) 263-5557.
Assistant Coaches: George Brown, *Rick Oliveri. **Telephone:** (732) 263-5347.
Home Field: Monmouth University Baseball Field. **Seating Capacity:** 1,500. **Outfield Dimension:** LF—315, CF—390, RF—315.

MOREHEAD STATE EAGLES

Conference: Ohio Valley
Mailing Address: 195 AAC, Morehead, KY 40351. **Website:** www.msueagles.com. **Twitter:** @MSUAthletics
Head Coach: Mike McGuire. **Telephone:** (606) 783-2882. **Baseball SID:** Matt Schabert. **Telephone:** (606) 783-2556.
Assistant Coaches: *Adam Brown, Graham Johnson. **Telephone:** (606) 783-2881.
Home Field: Allen Field. **Seating Capacity:** 1,200. **Outfield Dimension:** LF—320, CF—380, RF—320.

MURRAY STATE RACERS

Conference: Ohio Valley
Mailing Address: 217 Stewart Stadium Murray, KY 42071. **Website:** www.goracers.com. **Twitter:** @MSURacers
Head Coach: Kevin Moulder. **Telephone:** (270) 809-4892. **Baseball SID:** Catherine Prince. **Telephone:** (270) 809-7051.
Assistant Coaches: Daniel Dulin, *Andy Morgan. **Telephone:** (270) 809-4192.
Home Field: Reagan Field. **Seating Capacity:** 800. **Outfield Dimension:** LF—330, CF—400, RF—330.

NAVY MIDSHIPMEN

Conference: Patriot
Mailing Address: 566 Brownson Rd. Annapolis, MD 21402. **Website:** www.navysports.com. **Twitter:** @NavyAthletics
Head Coach: Paul Kostacopoulos. **Telephone:** (410) 293-5571. **Baseball SID:** Alex Lumb. **Telephone:** (410) 293-8771.
Assistant Coaches: Bobby Applegate, *Jeff Kane. **Telephone:** (410) 293-5428.
Home Field: Terwilliger Brothers Field at Max Bishop Stadium. **Seating Capacity:** 1,500. **Outfield Dimension:** LF—322, CF—397, RF—304.

NEBRASKA CORNHUSKERS

Conference: Big Ten
Mailing Address: 403 Line Drive Circle, Suite B, PO Box 880160, Lincoln, NE 68588-0160. **Website:** www.huskers.com. **Twitter:** @Husker_Baseball
Head Coach: Darin Erstad. **Telephone:** (402) 472-9166. **Baseball SID:** Jeremy Foote. **Telephone:** (402) 472-7778.
Assistant Coaches: Mike Kirby, *Ted Silva. **Telephone:** (402) 472-1445.
Home Field: Hawks Field at Haymarket Park. **Seating Capacity:** 8,486. **Outfield Dimension:** LF—335, CF—395, RF—325.

NEBRASKA-OMAHA MAVERICKS

Conference: Summit
Mailing Address: Sapp Fieldhouse 109, Omaha, NE 68182. **Website:** www.omavs.com. **Twitter:** @

UNO_Baseball
Head Coach: Bob Herold. **Telephone:** (402) 554-3388.
Baseball SID: Bonnie Ryan. **Telephone:** (402) 554-3267.
Assistant Coaches: Chris Gadsden, Evan Porter.
Telephone: (402) 554-2141.
Home Field: Ballpark at Boys Town.

NEVADA WOLFPACK

Conference: Mountain West
Mailing Address: 1664 N. Virginia Street Reno, NV
89557. **Website:** www.nevadawolfpack.com. **Twitter:** @
NevadaBaseball
Head Coach: Jay Johnson. **Telephone:** (775) 682-
6978. **Baseball SID:** Brady Johnson. **Telephone:** (775)
682-6985.
Assistant Coaches: Dave Lawn, Marc Wanaka.
Telephone: (775) 682-6979.
Home Field: Peccole Park. **Seating Capacity:** 3000.
Outfield Dimension: LF—340, CF—401, RF—340.

NEW MEXICO LOBOS

Conference: Mountain West
Mailing Address: Maloof Administration Bldg.,
1 U. of New Mexico, MSC04 2680, Albuquerque,
NM 87131. **Website:** www.golobos.com. **Twitter:** @
UNMLoboBaseball
Head Coach: Ray Birmingham. **Telephone:** (505)
925-5721. **Baseball SID:** Terry Kelly. **Telephone:** (505)
925-5520.
Assistant Coaches: *Ken Jacome, Dan Spencer.
Telephone: (505) 925-5721.
Home Field: Lobo Field. **Seating Capacity:** 1,000.
Outfield Dimension: LF—350, CF—420, RF—350.

NEW YORK TECH BEARS

Conference: Independent
Mailing Address: Sports Complex, Northern Blvd., Old
Westbury, NY 11568. **Website:** www.nyit.edu. **Twitter:** @
NYITBaseball
Head Coach: Bob Malvagna. **Telephone:** (516) 686-
7513. **Baseball SID:** Sabrina Polidoro. **Telephone:** (516)
686-7504. **Fax:** (516) 686-1168.
Assistant Coaches: Steve Malvagna, *John Torres.
Telephone: (516) 686-1315.
Home Field: Angelo Lorenzo Memorial Field. **Seating
Capacity:** 500. **Outfield Dimension:** LF—315, CF—395,
RF—315.

NIAGARA PURPLE EAGLES

Conference: Metro Atlantic Athletic
Mailing Address: Upper Level Gallagher Center, PO
Box 2009 Niagara University, N.Y., **14109. Website:** www.
purpleeagles.com. **Twitter:** @NiagaraBASE
Head Coach: Rob McCoy. **Telephone:** (716) 286-7361.
Baseball SID: Bob Vail. **Telephone:** (716) 286-8586.
Assistant Coaches: Ronnie Bernick, *Matt Spatafora.
Telephone: (716) 286-8624.

NICHOLLS STATE COLONELS

Conference: Southland
Mailing Address: PO Box 2032; Thibodaux, LA;
70310. **Website:** www.geauxcolonels.com. **Twitter:** @
NichollsBasebal
Head Coach: Seth Thibodeaux. **Telephone:** (985) 449-
7149. **Baseball SID:** Zachary Carlton. **Telephone:** (985)
448-4282.
Assistant Coaches: Walter Jones, *Chris Prothro.

Telephone: (985) 448-4808.
Home Field: Ray E. Didier Field. **Seating Capacity:**
3,000. **Outfield Dimension:** LF—330, CF—400, RF—330.

NORFOLK STATE SPARTANS

Conference: Mid-Eastern Athletic
Mailing Address: 700 Park Ave., Norfolk, VA 23504.
Website: www.nsuspartans.com. **Twitter:** @NSUSpartans
Head Coach: Claudell Clark. **Telephone:** (757) 823-
8196. **Baseball SID:** Matt Michalec. **Telephone:** (757)
823-2628.
Assistant Coaches: Joey Seal. **Telephone:** (757) 823-
9533.
Home Field: Marty L. Miller Field. **Seating Capacity:**
1,500. **Outfield Dimension:** LF—330, CF—404, RF—318.

NORTH CAROLINA TAR HEELS

Conference: Atlantic Coast
Mailing Address: PO Box 2126, Chapel Hill, NC 27515.
Website: www.goheels.com. **Twitter:** @DiamondHeels
Head Coach: Mike Fox. **Telephone:** (919) 962-3865.
Baseball SID: Bobby Hundley. **Telephone:** (919) 843-
5678.
Assistant Coaches: Scott Forbes, *Scott Jackson.
Telephone: (919) 962-5451.
Home Field: Boshamer Stadium. **Seating Capacity:**
5,000. **Outfield Dimension:** LF—335, CF—400, RF—340.

NORTH CAROLINA A&T AGGIES

Conference: Mid-Eastern Athletic
Mailing Address: 1601 E. Market Street, Greensboro,
NC 27411. **Website:** www.ncataggies.com. **Twitter:** @
NCATAGGIES
Head Coach: Ben Hall. **Telephone:** (336) 285-4272.
Baseball SID: Brian Holloway. **Telephone:** (336) 285-3608.
Assistant Coaches: *Tyrone Dawson, Cory Lima.
Telephone: (336) 285-3620.
Home Field: War Memorial Stadium. **Seating
Capacity:** 2,000. **Outfield Dimension:** LF—370, CF—401,
RF—336.

NORTH CAROLINA CENTRAL EAGLES

Conference: Mid-Eastern Athletic
Mailing Address: 1801 Fayetteville Street,
McDouagld-McLendon Gym, Room 116, Durham, NC
27707. **Website:** www.nccueaglepride.com. **Twitter:** @
NCCUBaseball
Head Coach: Jim Koerner. **Telephone:** (919) 530-6723.
Baseball SID: Chris Hooks. **Telephone:** (919) 530-6017.
Assistant Coaches: *Tyler Hanson, Joe Witkowski.
Telephone: (919) 530-5268, (919) 530-5439.
Home Field: Durham Athletic Park. **Seating Capacity:**
2,000. **Outfield Dimension:** LF—330, CF—395, RF—290.

NORTH CAROLINA STATE WOLFPACK

Conference: Atlantic Coast
Mailing Address: 1081 Varsity Drive, Raleigh,
NC 27695. **Website:** www.gopack.com. **Twitter:** @
NCStateBaseball
Head Coach: Elliott Avent. **Telephone:** (919) 515-
3613. **Baseball SID:** Cavan Fosnes. **Telephone:** (919)
513-8195.
Assistant Coaches: Scott Foxhall, *Chris Hart.
Telephone: (919) 513-3613.
Home Field: Doak Field at Dail Park. **Seating
Capacity:** 3,100. **Outfield Dimension:** LF—325, CF—400,
RF—330.

NORTH DAKOTA FIGHTING SIOUX

Conference: Western Athletic
Mailing Address: 2751 2nd Ave N Stop 9013 Grand Forks, ND 58202. **Website:** www.fightingsioux.com. **Twitter:** @UND_Baseball
Head Coach: Jeff Dodson. **Telephone:** (701) 777-4038. **Baseball SID:** Mitch Wigness. **Telephone:** (701) 777-4210. **Fax:** (701) 777-2285.
Assistant Coaches: *Brian DeVillers, JC Field. **Telephone:** (701) 777-2352.
Home Field: Kraft Field. **Seating Capacity:** 2,000. **Outfield Dimension:** LF—330, CF—410, RF—330.

NORTH DAKOTA STATE BISON

Conference: Summit
Mailing Address: 1301 39th St N. Fargo, ND 58102. **Website:** www.gobison.com. **Twitter:** @NDSUBaseball
Head Coach: Tod Brown. **Telephone:** (701) 231-8853. **Baseball SID:** Ryan Anderson. **Telephone:** (701) 231-5591.
Assistant Coaches: Tyler Oakes, *David Pearson. **Telephone:** (701) 231-7817.
Home Field: Newman Outdoor Field. **Seating Capacity:** 4,419. **Outfield Dimension:** LF—318, CF—408, RF—314.

NORTH FLORIDA OSPREYS

Conference: Atlantic Sun
Mailing Address: 1 UNF Drive Jacksonville, FL 32224. **Website:** www.unfospreys.com. **Twitter:** @OspreyBSB
Head Coach: Smoke Laval. **Telephone:** (904) 620-1556. **Baseball SID:** Scott Fitzgerald. **Telephone:** (904) 620-2586.
Assistant Coaches: Andrew Hannon, *Judd Loveland. **Telephone:** (904) 620-2586.
Home Field: Harmon Stadium. **Seating Capacity:** 1,000. **Outfield Dimension:** LF—325, CF—400, RF—325.

NORTHEASTERN HUSKIES

Conference: Colonial Athletic
Mailing Address: 360 Huntington Ave, 219 Cabot Center, Boston, MA 02115. **Website:** www.gonu.com. **Twitter:** @GoNUBaseball
Head Coach: Mike Glavine. **Telephone:** (617) 373-3657. **Baseball SID:** Mike Skovan. **Telephone:** (617) 373-2691.
Assistant Coaches: *Kevin Cobb, Jeff Vigurs. **Telephone:** (617) 373-3657.
Home Field: Friedman Diamond. **Seating Capacity:** 2,000. **Outfield Dimension:** LF—326, CF—415, RF—375.

NORTHERN COLORADO BEARS

Conference: Western Athletic
Mailing Address: 270D Butler-Hancock Athletic Center, Greeley, CO 80639. **Website:** www.wacsports.com. **Twitter:** @NCBearsBaseball
Head Coach: Carl Iwasaki. **Telephone:** (970) 351-1714. **Baseball SID:** Kobee Stalder. **Telephone:** (970) 351-1065.
Assistant Coaches: Patrick Perry, *RD Spiehs. **Telephone:** (970) 351-1203.
Home Field: Jackson Field. **Seating Capacity:** 1,500. **Outfield Dimension:** LF—345, CF—407, RF—356.

NORTHERN ILLINOIS HUSKIES

Conference: Mid-American
Mailing Address: 1525 W Lincoln Hwy, DeKalb, IL 60115. **Website:** www.niuhuskies.com. **Twitter:** @NIU_Baseball
Head Coach: Mike Kunigonis. **Telephone:** (815) 753-2225. **Baseball SID:** Matt Scheerer. **Telephone:** (815) 753-1708.
Assistant Coaches: Andrew Maki, Luke Stewart. **Telephone:** (815) 753-0147.
Home Field: Ralph McKinzie Field. **Seating Capacity:** 2,000. **Outfield Dimension:** LF—312, CF—395, RF—322.

NORTHERN KENTUCKY NORSE

Conference: Atlantic Sun
Mailing Address: 133 The Bank of Kentucky Cetner, 500 Nunn Drive, Highland Heights, KY 41099. **Website:** www.nkunorse.com. **Twitter:** @NKUNorseBSB
Head Coach: Todd Asalon. **Telephone:** (859) 572-6474. **Baseball SID:** Kelli Marksbury. **Telephone:** (859) 572-7850.
Assistant Coaches: Dizzy Peyton, Brad Gschwind. **Telephone:** (859) 572-5940, (859) 572-1525.
Home Field: Friendship Field. **Seating Capacity:** 500. **Outfield Dimension:** LF—325, CF—365, RF—325.

NORTHWESTERN WILDCATS

Conference: Big Ten
Mailing Address: 1501 Central St. Evanston, IL 60208. **Website:** www.nusports.com. **Twitter:** @NUCatsBaseball
Head Coach: Paul Stevens. **Telephone:** (847) 491-4652. **Baseball SID:** Dan Yopchick. **Telephone:** (847) 467-3418.
Assistant Coaches: *Jon Mikrut, Tim Stoddard. **Telephone:** (847) 491-4651.
Home Field: Rocky Miller Park. **Seating Capacity:** 1,000. **Outfield Dimension:** LF—350, CF—400, RF—350.

NORTHWESTERN STATE DEMONS

Conference: Southland
Mailing Address: 468 Caspari St. Natchitoches, LA 71497. **Website:** www.nsudemons.com. **Twitter:** @NSUDemonsBsB
Head Coach: Lane Burroughs. **Telephone:** (318) 357-4139. **Baseball SID:** Jason Pugh. **Telephone:** (318) 357-6469.
Assistant Coaches: *Bobby Barbier, GT McCullough. **Telephone:** (318) 357-4134.
Home Field: Brown-Stroud Field. **Seating Capacity:** 1,200. **Outfield Dimension:** LF—325, CF—405, RF—325.

NOTRE DAME FIGHTING IRISH

Conference: Atlantic Coast
Mailing Address: University of Notre Dame, C113 Joyce Center, Notre Dame, IN 46556. **Website:** www.und.com. **Twitter:** @NDBaseball
Head Coach: Mik Aoki. **Telephone:** (574) 631-8466. **Baseball SID:** Russell Dorn. **Telephone:** (574) 631-4780.
Assistant Coaches: Chuck Ristano, *Jesse Woods. **Telephone:** (574) 631-6366.
Home Field: Jake Kline Field at Frank Eck Stadium. **Seating Capacity:** 2,500. **Outfield Dimension:** LF—330, CF—400, RF—330.

OAKLAND GOLDEN GRIZZLIES

Conference: Horizon
Mailing Address: 2200 N. Squirrel Athletics Center, Rochester, MI 48309. **Website:** www.ougrizzlies.com. **Twitter:** @GoldenGrizzlies
Head Coach: John Musachio. **Telephone:** (248) 370-4059. **Baseball SID:** Dan Gliot. **Telephone:** (248) 370-3201.
Assistant Coaches: Jacke Healey. **Telephone:** (248) 370-4228.
Home Field: Oakland Baseball Field. **Seating Capacity:** 500. **Outfield Dimension:** LF—333, CF—380, RF—320.

OHIO STATE BUCKEYES

Conference: Big Ten
Mailing Address: 250 Bill Davis Stadium, 650 Borror Drive, Columbus, OH 43210. **Website:** www.ohiostate-buckeyes.com. **Twitter:** @OhioState_BASE
Head Coach: Greg Beals. **Telephone:** (614) 292-1075. **Baseball SID:** Alex Morando. **Telephone:** (614) 292-1389. **Fax:** (614) 688-8707.
Assistant Coaches: *Chris Holick, Mike Stafford. **Telephone:** (614) 292-1075.
Home Field: Bill Davis Stadium. **Seating Capacity:** 4,450. **Outfield Dimension:** LF—330, CF—400, RF—330.

OKLAHOMA SOONERS

Conference: Big 12
Mailing Address: 180 W. Brooks St. Norman, OK 73019. **Website:** www.soonersports.com. **Twitter:** @OU_Baseball
Head Coach: Pete Hughes. **Telephone:** (405) 325-8354. **Baseball SID:** Brendan Flynn. **Telephone:** (405) 325-6449.
Assistant Coaches: Mike Anderson, *Ryan Connolly. **Telephone:** (405) 325-8354.
Home Field: L. Dale Mitchell Park. **Seating Capacity:** 3,180. **Outfield Dimension:** LF—335, CF—411, RF—335.

OKLAHOMA STATE COWBOYS

Conference: Big 12
Mailing Address: 220 Athletics Center Stillwater, OK 74078. **Website:** www.okstate.com. **Twitter:** @OSUBaseball
Head Coach: Josh Holliday. **Telephone:** (405) 744-7141. **Baseball SID:** Wade McWhorter. **Telephone:** (405) 744-7853. **Fax:** (405) 744-7754.
Assistant Coaches: *Marty Lees, Rob Walton. **Telephone:** (405) 744-7141.
Home Field: Allie P. Reynolds Stadium. **Seating Capacity:** 4,000. **Outfield Dimension:** LF—330, CF—398, RF—330.

OLD DOMINION MONARCHS

Conference: Conference USA
Mailing Address: ODU Baseball, Jim Jarrett Athletic Admin. Building, Norfolk, VA 23529. **Website:** www.odusports.com. **Twitter:** @ODUBaseball
Head Coach: Chris Finwood. **Telephone:** (757) 683-4230. **Baseball SID:** Carol Hudson, Jr. **Telephone:** (757) 683-3395.
Assistant Coaches: Tim LaVigne, *Karl Nonemaker. **Telephone:** (757) 683-4230.
Home Field: Bud Metheny Baseball Complex. **Seating Capacity:** 2,500. **Outfield Dimension:** LF—325, CF—390, RF—325.

ORAL ROBERTS GOLDEN EAGLES

Conference: Summit
Mailing Address: 7777 S. Lewis Ave., Tulsa, OK 74147. **Website:** www.oruathletics.com. **Twitter:** @ORUBaseball
Head Coach: Ryan Folmar. **Telephone:** (918) 495-7639. **Baseball SID:** Eric Scott. **Telephone:** (918) 495-6646.
Assistant Coaches: *Ryan Neill, Sean Snedeker. **Telephone:** (918) 495-7205.
Home Field: J.L. Johnson Stadium. **Seating Capacity:** 2,418. **Outfield Dimension:** LF—330, CF—400, RF—330.

OREGON DUCKS

Conference: Pacific-12
Mailing Address: Len Casanova Center, 2727 Leo Harris Parkway, Eugene, OR 97401. **Website:** www.goducks.com. **Twitter:** @OregonBaseball
Head Coach: George Horton. **Telephone:** (541) 646-5235. **Baseball SID:** Todd Miles. **Telephone:** (541) 346-0962.
Assistant Coaches: Jay Uhlman, *Mark Wasikowski. **Telephone:** (541) 346-5261.
Home Field: PK Park. **Seating Capacity:** 4,000. **Outfield Dimension:** LF—335, CF—400, RF—325.

OREGON STATE BEAVERS

Conference: Pacific-12
Mailing Address: 115 Gill Coliseum. **Website:** www.osubeavers.com. **Twitter:** @Beaver_Baseball
Head Coach: Pat Casey. **Telephone:** (541) 737-0598. **Baseball SID:** Hank Hager. **Telephone:** (541) 737-7472.
Assistant Coaches: *Pat Bailey. **Telephone:** (541) 737-7484.
Home Field: Goss Stadium and Coleman Field. **Seating Capacity:** 3,248. **Outfield Dimension:** LF—330, CF—400, RF—300.

PACIFIC TIGERS

Conference: West Coast
Mailing Address: 3601 Pacific Ave., Stockton, CA 95211. **Website:** www.pacifictigers.com. **Twitter:** @PacificBaseball
Head Coach: Ed Sprague. **Telephone:** (209) 946-2386. **Baseball SID:** Ben Laskey. **Telephone:** (209) 946-2703. **Fax:** (209) 946-2731.
Assistant Coaches: Joey Centanni, *Mike McCormick. **Telephone:** (209) 946-2613.
Home Field: Klein Family Field. **Seating Capacity:** 2,000. **Outfield Dimension:** LF—317, CF—405, RF—325.

PENN STATE NITTANY LIONS

Conference: Big Ten
Mailing Address: Medlar Field at Lubrano Park, Suite 230, University Park, PA 16802. **Website:** www.gopsusports.com. **Twitter:** @PennStateBASE
Head Coach: Rob Cooper. **Telephone:** (814) 863-0230. **Baseball SID:** Mark Brumbaugh. **Telephone:** (814) 863-1377.
Assistant Coaches: *Brian Anderson, Ross Oeder. **Telephone:** (814) 865-8606.
Home Field: Medlar Field at Lubrano Park. **Seating Capacity:** 5,780. **Outfield Dimension:** LF—325, CF—399, RF—320.

PENNSYLVANIA QUAKERS

Conference: Ivy
Mailing Address: James D. Dunning Coaches Center 235 South 33rd St. Philadelphia, Pa. 19104-6322. **Website:** www.pennathletics.com. **Twitter:** @PennBaseball
Head Coach: John Yurkow. **Telephone:** (215) 898-6282. **Baseball SID:** Paul Seiter. **Telephone:** (215) 898-1748.
Assistant Coaches: *Mike Santello, Josh Schwartz. **Telephone:** (215) 746-2325.
Home Field: Meiklejohn Stadium. **Seating Capacity:** 850. **Outfield Dimension:** LF—330, CF—380, RF—330.

PEPPERDINE WAVES

Conference: West Coast
Mailing Address: 24255 Pacific Coast Highway, Malibu, CA 90263. **Website:** www.pepperdinesports.com. **Twitter:** @PeppBaseball
Head Coach: Steve Rodriguez. **Telephone:** (310) 506-4371. **Baseball SID:** Jacob Breems. **Telephone:** (310) 506-4333. **Fax:** (310) 506-7459.
Assistant Coaches: Rick Hirtensteiner, *Jon Strauss. **Telephone:** (310) 506-4404.
Home Field: Eddy D. **Field Stadium. Seating Capacity:** 1,800. **Outfield Dimension:** LF—330, CF—390, RF—330.

PITTSBURGH PANTHERS

Conference: Big East
Mailing Address: Dept. of Athletics, PO Box 7436, Pittsburgh, PA 15213. **Website:** www.pittsburghpanthers.com. **Twitter:** @PITTBASEBALL
Head Coach: Joe Jordano. **Telephone:** (412) 648-8208. **Baseball SID:** Barbara Osman. **Telephone:** (412) 383-9078.
Assistant Coaches: Jerry Oakes, Bryan Peters. **Telephone:** (412) 680-8877, (412) 648-8238.
Home Field: Charles L. Cost Field. **Seating Capacity:** 900. **Outfield Dimension:** LF—330, CF—405, RF—330.

PORTLAND PILOTS

Conference: West Coast
Mailing Address: 5000 North Willamette Blvd Portland OR 97203. **Website:** www.portlandpilots.com. **Twitter:** @UPPilotBaseball
Head Coach: Chris Sperry. **Telephone:** (503) 943-7707. **Baseball SID:** Adam Linnman. **Telephone:** (503) 943-8439.
Assistant Coaches: Tucker Brack, *Larry Casian. **Telephone:** (503) 943-7745, (503) 943-7732.
Home Field: Joe Etzel Field. **Outfield Dimension:** LF—325, CF—388, RF—325.

PRESBYTERIAN BLUE HOSE

Conference: Big South
Mailing Address: 105 Ashland Ave, Clinton, SC 29325. **Website:** www.gobluehose.com. **Twitter:** @PCHoseBaseball
Head Coach: Elton Pollock. **Telephone:** (864) 833-7133. **Baseball SID:** Ryan Real. **Telephone:** (864) 833-7095.
Assistant Coaches: Mark Crocco, Jamie Serber. **Telephone:** (864) 833-7134, (336) 407-2712.
Home Field: PC Baseball Complex. **Seating Capacity:** 500. **Outfield Dimension:** LF—325, CF—400, RF—325.

PRINCETON TIGERS

Conference: Ivy
Mailing Address: Nassau Street, Princeton University, Princeton, NJ 08544. **Website:** www.goprincetontigers.com. **Twitter:** @PUTigerBaseball
Head Coach: Scott Bradley. **Telephone:** (609) 258-5059. **Baseball SID:** Ben Badua. **Telephone:** (609) 258-2630.
Assistant Coaches: Lloyd Brewer, Mike Russo. **Telephone:** (609) 258-5684.
Home Field: Clarke Field. **Seating Capacity:** 1,000. **Outfield Dimension:** LF—335, CF—400, RF—320.

PURDUE BOILERMAKERS

Conference: Big Ten
Mailing Address: Mackey Arena, 900 John Wooden Drive, West Lafayette, IN 47907. **Website:** www.purduesports.com. **Twitter:** @PurdueBaseball
Head Coach: Doug Schreiber. **Telephone:** (765) 494-3998. **Baseball SID:** Ben Turner. **Telephone:** (765) 494-3198. **Fax:** (765) 494-5447.
Assistant Coaches: Wally Crancer, *Tristan McIntyre. **Telephone:** (765) 496-9360.
Home Field: Alexander Field. **Seating Capacity:** 2,000. **Outfield Dimension:** LF—340, CF—408, RF—330.

QUINNIPIAC BOBCATS

Conference: Metro Atlantic
Mailing Address: 275 Mount Carmel Ave., Hamden, CT 06518. **Website:** www.quinnipiacbobcats.com. **Twitter:** @QUAthletics
Head Coach: John Delaney. **Telephone:** (203) 582-6546. **Baseball SID:** Kevin Noonan. **Telephone:** (203) 582-5387.
Assistant Coaches: *Pat Egan, Kyle Nisson. **Telephone:** (203) 582-6571.
Home Field: Bobcat Field. **Seating Capacity:** 1,000. **Outfield Dimension:** LF—330, CF—400, RF—320.

RADFORD HIGHLANDERS

Conference: Big South
Mailing Address: 101 University Drive Radford, VA 24141. **Website:** www.ruhighlanders.com. **Twitter:** @RadfordBaseball
Head Coach: Joe Raccuia. **Telephone:** (540) 831-5881. **Baseball SID:** Tom Galbraith. **Telephone:** (540) 831-5726.
Assistant Coaches: *Alex Guerra, Mark McQueen. **Telephone:** (540) 831-6513.
Home Field: Radford Baseball Stadium. **Seating Capacity:** 1,000. **Outfield Dimension:** LF—330, CF—400, RF—330.

RHODE ISLAND RAMS

Conference: Atlantic 10
Mailing Address: 3 Keaney Rd. Suite One. Kingston, RI 02881. **Website:** www.gorhody.com. **Twitter:** @RhodyBaseball
Head Coach: Raphael Cerrato. **Telephone:** (401) 874-4550. **Baseball SID:** Jodi Pontriand. **Telephone:** (401) 874-5356.
Assistant Coaches: Casey Buckley, *Jim Martin, Sean O'Brien. **Telephone:** (401) 874-4888.
Home Field: Bill Beck Field. **Seating Capacity:** 500. **Outfield Dimension:** LF—330, CF—400, RF—330.

RICE OWLS

Conference: Conference USA
Mailing Address: PO Box 1892; MS 548; Houston, Texas 77251-1892. **Website:** www.riceowls.com. **Twitter:** @RiceOwlsBSB
Head Coach: Wayne Graham. **Telephone:** (713) 348-8864. **Baseball SID:** John Sullivan. **Telephone:** (713) 348-5636.
Assistant Coaches: *Patrick Hallmark, Clay Van Hook. **Telephone:** (713) 348-8859.
Home Field: Reckling Park. **Seating Capacity:** 6,193.
Outfield Dimension: LF—330, CF—400, RF—330.

RICHMOND SPIDERS

Conference: Atlantic 10
Mailing Address: 28 Westhampton Way, Richmond, VA 23173. **Website:** www.richmondspiders.com. **Twitter:** @SpiderBaseball
Head Coach: Tracy Woodson. **Telephone:** (804) 289-8391. **Baseball SID:** Scott Burns. **Telephone:** (804) 287-6313.
Assistant Coaches: Josh Davis, *Matt Tyner. **Telephone:** (804) 289-8391.
Home Field: Pitt Field. **Seating Capacity:** 600.
Outfield Dimension: LF—328, CF—390, RF—328.

RIDER BRONCS

Conference: Metro Atlantic Athletic
Mailing Address: 2083 Lawrenceville Rd, Lawrenceville, NJ 08648. **Website:** www.gobroncs.com. **Twitter:** @RIDERATHLETICS
Head Coach: Barry Davis. **Telephone:** (609) 896-5055. **Baseball SID:** Bud Focht. **Telephone:** (609) 896-7264.
Assistant Coaches: Lou Proletti, Jaime Steward. **Telephone:** (609) 896-5703.
Home Field: Sonny Pittaro Field. **Seating Capacity:** 1,000. **Outfield Dimension:** LF—330, CF—405, RF—330.

RUTGERS SCARLET KNIGHTS

Conference: Big Ten
Mailing Address: 83 Rockafeller Road, Piscataway, NJ 08854. **Website:** www.scarletknights.com. **Twitter:** @BaseballRU
Head Coach: Joe Litterio. **Telephone:** (732) 445-7834. **Baseball SID:** Jimmy Gill. **Telephone:** (732) 445-8103.
Assistant Coaches: Casey Gaynor, *Tim Reilly. **Telephone:** (732) 445-7834.
Home Field: Bainton Field. **Seating Capacity:** 1,500.
Outfield Dimension: LF—330, CF—410, RF—320.

SACRAMENTO STATE HORNETS

Conference: Western Athletic
Mailing Address: 6000 J Street, Sacramento, CA, 95819-6099. **Website:** www.hornetsports.com. **Twitter:** @SacStBaseball
Head Coach: Reggie Christiansen. **Telephone:** (916) 278-4036. **Baseball SID:** Andrew Tomsky. **Telephone:** (916) 278-6896.
Assistant Coaches: *Jake Angier, Steve Holm. **Telephone:** (916) 278-2018.
Home Field: John Smith Field. **Seating Capacity:** 1,200. **Outfield Dimension:** LF—333, CF—400, RF—333.

SACRED HEART PIONEERS

Conference: Northeast
Mailing Address: 5151 Park Avenue, Farifield, CT.

06825. **Website:** www.sacredheartpioneers.com. **Twitter:** @SHUBigRed
Head Coach: Nick Giaquinto. **Telephone:** (203) 365-7632. **Baseball SID:** Zachary Durham. **Telephone:** (203) 365-4813.
Assistant Coaches: Wayne Mazzoni, *Nick Restaino. **Telephone:** (203) 365-4469.
Home Field: Ballpark at Harbor Yard. **Seating Capacity:** 5,300. **Outfield Dimension:** LF—325, CF—405, RF—325.

SAINT LOUIS BILLIKENS

Conference: Atlantic 10
Mailing Address: 3330 Laclede, St. Louis, MO 63103.
Website: www.slubillikens.com. **Twitter:** @SLUBaseball
Head Coach: Darin Hendrickson. **Telephone:** (314) 977-3172. **Baseball SID:** Jake Gossage. **Telephone:** (314) 977-2524.
Assistant Coaches: *Will Bradley, Connor Gandossy. **Telephone:** (314) 977-3,260.
Home Field: Billiken Sports Center. **Seating Capacity:** 500. **Outfield Dimension:** LF—330, CF—403, RF—330.

SAM HOUSTON STATE BEARKATS

Conference: Southland
Mailing Address: 620 Bowers Blvd Box 2268 Huntsville, TX 77340. **Website:** www.gobearkats.com. **Twitter:** @SHSU_Baseball
Head Coach: Matt Deggs. **Telephone:** (936) 294-1731. **Baseball SID:** Kevin Rodriguez. **Telephone:** (936) 294-3533.
Assistant Coaches: *Lance Harvell, Jay Sirianni. **Telephone:** (936) 294-2580.
Home Field: Don Sanders Stadium. **Seating Capacity:** 1,163. **Outfield Dimension:** LF—330, CF—400, RF—330.

SAMFORD BULLDOGS

Conference: Southern
Mailing Address: 800 Lakeshore Dr., Birmingham, AL 35229. **Website:** www.samfordsports.com. **Twitter:** @samfordbaseball
Head Coach: Casey Dunn. **Telephone:** (205) 726-2134. **Baseball SID:** Joey Mullins. **Telephone:** (205) 726-2799.
Assistant Coaches: Tony David, *Tyler Shrout. **Telephone:** (205) 726-4294, (205) 726-4095.

SAN DIEGO TOREROS

Conference: West Coast
Mailing Address: 5998 Alcala Park, San Diego, CA 92110. **Website:** www.usdtoreros.com. **Twitter:** @USDBaseball
Head Coach: Rich Hill. **Telephone:** (619) 260-5953. **Baseball SID:** Brad Marcelino. **Telephone:** (619) 260-7486.
Assistant Coaches: *Tyler Kincaid, Ramon Orozco. **Telephone:** (619) 260-7486.
Home Field: Fowler Park. **Seating Capacity:** 3,000. **Outfield Dimension:** LF—312, CF—395, RF—329.

SAN DIEGO STATE AZTECS

Conference: Mountain West
Mailing Address: 5500 Campanile Rd San Diego, CA 92182. **Website:** www.goaztecs.com. **Twitter:** @SDSUBaseball
Head Coach: Mark Martinez. **Telephone:** (619) 594-1818. **Baseball SID:** Dave Kuhn. **Telephone:** (619)

594-5242.
Assistant Coaches: *Joe Oliveira, John Pawlowski.
Telephone: (619) 594-6582.
Home Field: Tony Gwynn Stadium. **Seating Capacity:** 3,500. **Outfield Dimension:** LF—340, CF—405, RF—340.

SAN FRANCISCO DONS

Conference: West Coast
Mailing Address: 2130 Fulton St. San Francisco, CA 94117. **Website:** www.usfdons.com. **Twitter:** @SFDonsBaseball
Head Coach: Nino Giarratano. **Telephone:** (415) 422-2934. **Baseball SID:** Zack Farmer. **Telephone:** (415) 422-3222.
Assistant Coaches: Seth Etherton, *Troy Nakamura.
Telephone: (415) 422-2393.
Home Field: Benedetti Diamond. **Seating Capacity:** 1,000. **Outfield Dimension:** LF—315, CF—415, RF—321.

SAN JOSE STATE SPARTANS

Conference: Mountain West
Mailing Address: 1 Washington Square San Jose, CA. **95192. Website:** www.sjsuspartans.com. **Twitter:** @SJSUBaseball
Head Coach: Dave Nakama. **Telephone:** (408) 924-1255. **Baseball SID:** Nathan Edwards. **Telephone:** (408) 924-1229.
Assistant Coaches: Tom Kunis, Nicholas Enriquez.
Telephone: (408) 924-1467, (408) 924-1262.
Home Field: San Jose Municipal Stadium. **Seating Capacity:** 5,200. **Outfield Dimension:** LF—330, CF—405, RF—320.

SANTA CLARA BRONCOS

Conference: West Coast
Mailing Address: 500 El Camino Real, Santa Clara, CA 95053. **Website:** www.santaclarabroncos.com. **Twitter:** @SCU_Baseball
Head Coach: Dan O'Brien. **Telephone:** (408) 554-4882.
Baseball SID: David Gentile. **Telephone:** (408) 554-4661.
Assistant Coaches: Keith Beauregard, *Gabe Ribas.
Telephone: (408) 554-4151.
Home Field: Stephen Schott Stadium. **Seating Capacity:** 1,500. **Outfield Dimension:** LF—340, CF—402, RF—335.

SAVANNAH STATE TIGERS

Conference: Mid-Eastern Athletic
Mailing Address: 3219 College Street, PO Box 20271, Savannah, GA 31404. **Website:** www.ssuathletics.com. **Twitter:** @SavStateTigers
Head Coach: Carlton Hardy. **Telephone:** (912) 358-3082. **Baseball SID:** Opio Mashariki. **Telephone:** (912) 358-3430.
Assistant Coaches: *Carlton Hardy, Anthony Macon.
Telephone: (912) 358-3082.
Home Field: Tiger Field. **Seating Capacity:** 800.
Outfield Dimension: LF—330, CF—400, RF—330.

SEATTLE REDHAWKS

Conference: Western Athletic
Mailing Address: 901 12th Avenue, Seattle, WA 98122. **Website:** www.goseattleu.com. **Twitter:** @SU_Baseball
Head Coach: Donny Harrel. **Telephone:** (206) 398-4399. **Baseball SID:** Jason Behenna. **Telephone:** (206) 296-5915.

Assistant Coaches: *Elliott Cribby, Mike Nadeau.
Telephone: (206) 398-4397.
Home Field: Bannerwood Park. **Seating Capacity:** 1,500. **Outfield Dimension:** LF—325, CF—400, RF—325.

SETON HALL PIRATES

Conference: Big East
Mailing Address: 400 South Orange Ave., South Orange, NJ 07079. **Website:** www.shupirates.com. **Twitter:** @SHUBaseball
Head Coach: Rob Sheppard. **Telephone:** (973) 761-9557. **Baseball SID:** Matt Sweeney. **Telephone:** (973) 761-9493.
Assistant Coaches: *Phil Cundari, Mark Pappas.
Telephone: (973) 761-9557.
Home Field: Owen T. **Carroll Field. Seating Capacity:** 2,000. **Outfield Dimension:** LF—315, CF—400, RF—325.

SIENA SAINTS

Conference: Metro Atlantic
Mailing Address: 515 Loudon Rd., Loudonville, NY 12211. **Website:** www.sienasaints.com. **Twitter:** @SienaBaseball
Head Coach: Tony Rossi. **Telephone:** (518) 786-5044.
Baseball SID: Jason Rich. **Telephone:** (518) 783-2411.
Fax: (518) 783-2992.
Assistant Coaches: Pat Carroll, *Brian McCullough.
Telephone: (518) 782-6875.
Home Field: Siena Field. **Seating Capacity:** 500.
Outfield Dimension: LF—300, CF—400, RF—325.

SOUTH ALABAMA JAGUARS

Conference: Sun Belt
Mailing Address: 1209 MC, Mobile, AL 36688.
Website: www.usajaguars.com. **Twitter:** @SouthALBaseball
Head Coach: Mark Calvi. **Telephone:** (251) 414-8243.
Baseball SID: Charlie Nichols. **Telephone:** (251) 414-8017. **Fax:** (251) 460-7297.
Assistant Coaches: Bob Keller, *Jerry Zulli.
Telephone: (251) 414-8209.
Home Field: Stanky Field. **Seating Capacity:** 3,775.
Outfield Dimension: LF—330, CF—400, RF—330.

SOUTH CAROLINA GAMECOCKS

Conference: Southeastern
Mailing Address: 431 Williams St; Columbia, SC 29201. **Website:** www.gamecocksonline.com. **Twitter:** @GamecockBasebll
Head Coach: Chad Holbrook. **Telephone:** (803) 777-0116. **Baseball SID:** Andrew Kitick. **Telephone:** (803) 777-5257.
Assistant Coaches: *Sammy Esposito, Jerry Meyers.
Telephone: (803) 777-7913.
Home Field: Carolina Stadium. **Seating Capacity:** 8,242. **Outfield Dimension:** LF—325, CF—400, RF—325.

SOUTH CAROLINA-UPSTATE SPARTANS

Conference: Atlantic Sun
Mailing Address: 800 University Way, Spartanburg, SC 29303. **Website:** www.upstatespartans.com. **Twitter:** @UPSTBSB
Head Coach: Matt Fincher. **Telephone:** (864) 503-5135. **Baseball SID:** Jay D'Abramo. **Telephone:** (864) 503-5166.
Assistant Coaches: *Ethan Guevin, Jordan Stampler.
Telephone: (864) 503-5164.

Home Field: Cleveland S. Harley Baseball Park.
Seating Capacity: 500. **Outfield Dimension:** LF—335, CF—402, RF—335.

SOUTH DAKOTA STATE JACKRABBITS

Conference: Summit
Mailing Address: HPER Center Brookings, SD 57007.
Website: www.gojacks.com. **Twitter:** @GoJacksSDSU
Head Coach: David Schrage. **Telephone:** (605) 688-5027. **Baseball SID:** Jason Hove. **Telephone:** (605) 688-4623.
Assistant Coaches: *Brian Grunzke, Ben Norton. **Telephone:** (605) 688-5778.
Home Field: Erv Heuther Field. **Seating Capacity:** 1,000. **Outfield Dimension:** LF—325, CF—390, RF—320.

SOUTH FLORIDA BULLS

Conference: American Athletic
Mailing Address: 4202 E Fowler Ave, Tampa, FL 33620. **Website:** www.gousfbulls.com. **Twitter:** @USFBaseball
Head Coach: Mark Kingston. **Telephone:** (813) 974-2504. **Baseball SID:** Lindsey Morrison. **Telephone:** (813) 974-4029.
Assistant Coaches: *Mike Current, Billy Mohl. **Telephone:** (813) 974-2507.
Home Field: USF Baseball Stadium. **Seating Capacity:** 3211. **Outfield Dimension:** LF—325, CF—400, RF—330

SOUTHEAST MISSOURI STATE REDHAWKS

Conference: Ohio Valley
Mailing Address: One University Plaza Cape Girardeau, MO 63701. **Website:** www.gosoutheast.com. **Twitter:** @SEMOBaseball
Head Coach: Steve Bieser. **Telephone:** (573) 986-6002. **Baseball SID:** Sean Stevenson. **Telephone:** (573) 651-2294.
Assistant Coaches: Dillon Lawson, *Lance Rhodes. **Telephone:** (573) 986-6002.
Home Field: Capaha Park. **Seating Capacity:** 1,000. **Outfield Dimension:** LF—330, CF—400, RF—330.

SOUTHEASTERN LOUISIANA LIONS

Conference: Southland
Mailing Address: 800 Galloway Drive. **Website:** www.lionsports.net. **Twitter:** @sluathletics
Head Coach: Matt Riser. **Telephone:** (985) 549-3566.
Baseball SID: Damon Sunder. **Telephone:** (985) 549-5189. **Fax:** (985) 549-3495.
Assistant Coaches: Daniel Latham, *Zack Zulli. **Telephone:** (985) 549-2896.
Home Field: Pat Kenelly Diamond at Alumni Field. **Seating Capacity:** 2,500. **Outfield Dimension:** LF—330, CF—400, RF—330.

SOUTHERN CALIFORNIA TROJANS

Conference: Pacific-12
Mailing Address: 1021 Childs Way, Los Angeles, CA 90089. **Website:** www.usctrojans.com. **Twitter:** @USC_Baseball
Head Coach: Dan Hubbs. **Telephone:** (213) 740-5762.
Baseball SID: Rachel Caton. **Telephone:** (213) 740-3809.
Assistant Coaches: *Gabe Alvarez, Matt Curtis. **Telephone:** (213) 740-8447.
Home Field: Dedeaux Field. **Seating Capacity:** 2,500. **Outfield Dimension:** LF—335, CF—395, RF—335.

SOUTHERN ILLINOIS SALUKIS

Conference: Missouri Valley
Mailing Address: 425 Saluki Drive Carbondale, IL 62901. **Website:** www.siusalukis.com. **Twitter:** @SIU_Baseball
Head Coach: Ken Henderson. **Telephone:** (618) 453-3794. **Baseball SID:** Ricardo Cruz. **Telephone:** (618) 453-7236.
Assistant Coaches: *PJ Finigan, Ryan Strain. **Telephone:** (618) 453-7646.
Home Field: Itchy Jones Stadium. **Seating Capacity:** 1,000. **Outfield Dimension:** LF—330, CF—390, RF—330.

SOUTHERN ILLINOIS-EDWARDSVILLE COUGARS

Conference: Ohio Valley
Mailing Address: 1 University Drive Edwardsville, IL 62026. **Website:** www.siuecougars.com. **Twitter:** @SIUEBaseball
Head Coach: Tony Stoecklin. **Telephone:** (618) 650-2032. **Baseball SID:** Eric Hess. **Telephone:** (618) 650-3608. **Fax:** (618) 650-3369.
Assistant Coaches: *Danny Jackson, Brandon McCall. **Telephone:** (618) 650-2032.
Home Field: Roy E. Lee Field at Simmons Complex. **Seating Capacity:** 1,000. **Outfield Dimension:** LF—330, CF—390, RF—330.

SOUTHERN MISSISSIPPI GOLDEN EAGLES

Conference: Conference USA
Mailing Address: 118 College Dr. No. 5017, Hattiesburg, MS 39406. **Website:** www.southernmiss.com. **Twitter:** @USMGoldenEagles
Head Coach: Scott Berry. **Telephone:** (601) 266-6542.
Baseball SID: Jack Duggan. **Telephone:** (601) 266-4503.
Assistant Coaches: *Chad Caillet, Michael Federico. **Telephone:** (601) 266-6542.
Home Field: Pete Taylor Park. **Seating Capacity:** 6,600. **Outfield Dimension:** LF—340, CF—400, RF—340.

ST. BONAVENTURE BONNIES

Conference: Atlantic 10
Mailing Address: PO Box G, Reilly Center, St. Bonaventure, NY 14778. **Website:** gobonnies.sbu.edu. **Twitter:** @BonniesBaseball
Head Coach: Larry Sudbrook. **Telephone:** (716) 375-2641. **Baseball SID:** Corey Dieteman. **Telephone:** (716) 375-4019.
Assistant Coaches: BJ Salerno, Eddie Gray. **Telephone:** (716) 375-2699.
Home Field: Fred Handler Park at McGraw Jennings Field. **Seating Capacity:** 500. **Outfield Dimension:** LF—330, CF—403, RF—330.

ST. JOHN'S RED STORM

Conference: Big East
Mailing Address: 8000 Utopia Parkway Queens, N.Y. 11439. **Website:** www.redstormsports.com. **Twitter:** @StJohnsBaseball
Head Coach: Ed Blankmeyer. **Telephone:** (718) 990-6148. **Baseball SID:** Tim Brown. **Telephone:** (718) 990-1521.
Assistant Coaches: *Mike Hampton, Corey Muscara. **Telephone:** (718) 990-7523.
Home Field: Jack Kaiser Stadium. **Seating Capacity:** 3500. **Outfield Dimension:** LF—325, CF—400, RF—325.

ST. JOSEPH'S HAWKS

Conference: Atlantic 10
Mailing Address: 5600 City Avenue, Philadelphia, Pa., **19131. Website:** www.sjuhawks.com. **Twitter:** @SJUHawks_Base
Head Coach: Fritz Hamburg. **Telephone:** (610) 660-1718. **Baseball SID:** Joe Greenwich. **Telephone:** (610) 660-1738.
Assistant Coaches: Matt Allison, *Ryan Wheeler. **Telephone:** (610) 660-2592.
Home Field: John W. Smithson Field. **Seating Capacity:** 400. **Outfield Dimension:** LF—327, CF—400, RF—331.

ST. MARY'S GAELS

Conference: West Coast
Mailing Address: 1928 Saint Mary's Road, Moraga, CA 94556. **Website:** www.smcgaels.com. **Twitter:** @SMGaelsBaseball
Head Coach: Eric Valenzuela. **Telephone:** (925) 631-4637. **Baseball SID:** Ben Enos. **Telephone:** (925) 631-4950.
Assistant Coaches: Matt Fonteno, *Mark Viramontes. **Telephone:** (925) 631-8141.
Home Field: Louis Guisto Field. **Seating Capacity:** 1,000. **Outfield Dimension:** LF—330, CF—400, RF—330.

ST. PETER'S PEACOCKS

Conference: Metro Atlantic
Mailing Address: 2641 Kennedy Blvd, Jersey City, NJ 07306. **Website:** www.saintpeterspeacocks.com. **Twitter:** @PeacockNation
Head Coach: TJ Baxter. **Telephone:** (201) 761-7319. **Baseball SID:** Dave Musil Jr. **Telephone:** (201) 761-7316.
Assistant Coaches: Matt Owens, Ed Moskal. **Telephone:** (201) 761-7319, (201) 761-6362.
Home Field: Jaroshack Field. **Outfield Dimension:** LF—318, CF—405, RF—310.

STANFORD CARDINAL

Conference: Pacific-12
Mailing Address: Arrillaga Family Sports Center, 641 E. Campus Dr., Stanford, CA 94305-6150. **Website:** www.gostanford.com. **Twitter:** @StanfordBSB
Head Coach: Mark Marquess. **Telephone:** (309) 723-4528. **Baseball SID:** Brett Moore. **Telephone:** (309) 212-6367.
Assistant Coaches: *Rusty Filter, Brock Ungricht. **Telephone:** (309) 725-2373, (309) 723-9258.
Home Field: Klein Field at Sunken Diamond. **Seating Capacity:** 4,000. **Outfield Dimension:** LF—335, CF—400, RF—335.

STETSON HATTERS

Conference: Atlantic Sun
Mailing Address: Unit 8359, 421 N. Woodland Blvd., DeLand, FL 32723. **Website:** www.gohatters.com. **Twitter:** @StetsonBaseball
Head Coach: Pete Dunn. **Telephone:** (386) 822-8106. **Baseball SID:** Cris Belvin. **Telephone:** (386) 822-8937.
Assistant Coaches: Mark Leavitt, Chris Roberts. **Telephone:** (386) 822-8122, (386) 822-8733.
Home Field: Melching Field at Conrad Park. **Seating Capacity:** 2,500. **Outfield Dimension:** LF—335, CF—403, RF—335.

STONY BROOK SEAWOLVES

Conference: America East
Mailing Address: University Indoor Sports Complex, Stony Brook, N.Y. 11794-3500. **Website:** www.stonybrookathletics.com. **Twitter:** @StonyBrookBASE
Head Coach: Matt Senk. **Telephone:** (631) 632-9226. **Baseball SID:** Taylor Powers. **Telephone:** (631) 632-4338.
Assistant Coaches: Mike Marron, *Joe Pennucci. **Telephone:** (631) 632-4755.
Home Field: Joe Nathan Field. **Seating Capacity:** 1,000. **Outfield Dimension:** LF—330, CF—390, RF—330.

TENNESSEE VOLUNTEERS

Conference: Southeastern
Mailing Address: 1551 Lake Loudon Blvd., Knoxville, TN 37996. **Website:** www.utsports.com. **Twitter:** @Vol_Baseball
Head Coach: Dave Serrano. **Telephone:** (865) 974-2057. **Baseball SID:** MJ Burns. **Telephone:** (865) 974-8876.
Assistant Coaches: Greg Bergeron, *Aric Thomas. **Telephone:** (865) 974-2057.
Home Field: Lindsey Nelson Stadium. **Seating Capacity:** 4,283. **Outfield Dimension:** LF—320, CF—390, RF—320.

TENNESSEE TECH GOLDEN EAGLES

Conference: Ohio Valley
Mailing Address: 1100 McGeen Blvd., Box 5057, Cookeville, TN 38505. **Website:** www.ttusports.com. **Twitter:** @TTUGoldenEagles
Head Coach: Matt Bragga. **Telephone:** (931) 372-3925. **Baseball SID:** Mike Lehman. **Telephone:** (931) 372-6139.
Assistant Coaches: *Justin Holmes, Derek Weldon. **Telephone:** (931) 372-6546.
Home Field: Quillen Field. **Seating Capacity:** 1,500. **Outfield Dimension:** LF—320, CF—405, RF—330.

TENNESSEE-MARTIN SKYHAWKS

Conference: Ohio Valley
Mailing Address: 1022 Elam Center, Martin TN 38238. **Website:** www.utmsports.com. **Twitter:** @UTMBaseball
Head Coach: Rick Robinson. **Telephone:** (731) 881-7337. **Baseball SID:** Ryne Rickman. **Telephone:** (731) 881-7632.
Assistant Coaches: Seth Cutler-Voltz, *Rick Guarno. **Telephone:** (731) 881-3691.
Home Field: Skyhawk Field. **Seating Capacity:** 500. **Outfield Dimension:** LF—330, CF—385, RF—330.

TEXAS LONGHORNS

Conference: Big 12
Mailing Address: 2139 San Jacinto Blvd, RMRZ B.206, Austin, TX 78712. **Website:** www.texassports.com. **Twitter:** @Texas_Baseball
Head Coach: Augie Garrido. **Telephone:** (512) 471-5732. **Baseball SID:** Justin Moore. **Telephone:** (512) 232-9438.
Assistant Coaches: Skip Johnson, *Tommy Nicholson. **Telephone:** (512) 471-5732.
Home Field: UFCU Disch-Falk Field. **Seating Capacity:** 7,373. **Outfield Dimension:** LF—340, CF—400, RF—325.

TEXAS A&M AGGIES

Conference: Southeastern
Mailing Address: 756 Houston Street, College Station, TX 77843-1228. **Website:** www.12thman.com. **Twitter:** @Aggie_Baseball
Head Coach: Rob Childress. **Telephone:** (979) 845-4810. **Baseball SID:** Thomas Dick. **Telephone:** (979) 862-5486.
Assistant Coaches: Will Bolt, *Justin Seely. **Telephone:** (979) 845-4810.
Home Field: Olsen Field at Blue Bell Park. **Seating Capacity:** 6100. **Outfield Dimension:** LF—330, CF—400, RF—330.

TEXAS A&M-CORPUS CHRISTI ISLANDERS

Conference: Southland
Mailing Address: 6300 Ocean Drive, Unit 5719, Corpus Christi, TX 78412. **Website:** www.goislanders.com. **Twitter:** @IslandersBSB
Head Coach: Scott Malone. **Telephone:** (361) 825-3413. **Baseball SID:** Tim McCaughan. **Telephone:** (361) 825-3411.
Assistant Coaches: *Brett Gips, Marty Smith. **Telephone:** (361) 825-3720.
Home Field: Chapman Field. **Seating Capacity:** 2,000. **Outfield Dimension:** LF—325, CF—399, RF—325.

TEXAS CHRISTIAN HORNED FROGS

Conference: Big 12
Mailing Address: 2900 Stadium Dr., Fort Worth, TX 76129. **Website:** www.gofrogs.com. **Twitter:** @TCU_Baseball
Head Coach: Jim Schlossnagle. **Telephone:** (817) 257-5354. **Baseball SID:** Brandie Davidson. **Telephone:** (817) 257-7479.
Assistant Coaches: Bill Mosiello, *Kirk Saarloos. **Telephone:** (817) 257-5588.
Home Field: Lupton Stadium at Williams-Reilly Field. **Seating Capacity:** 4,500. **Outfield Dimension:** LF—330, CF—395, RF—330.

TEXAS STATE BOBCATS

Conference: Sun Belt
Mailing Address: Casey Athletic Administration Complex, 601 University Drive, San Marcos, TX 78666. **Website:** www.txstatebobcats.com. **Twitter:** @TxStateBaseball
Head Coach: Ty Harrington. **Telephone:** (512) 245-3383. **Baseball SID:** Joshua Flanagan. **Telephone:** (512) 245-4387. **Fax:** (512) 245-8387.
Assistant Coaches: *Jeremy Fikac, Mike Silva. **Telephone:** (512) 245-3383.
Home Field: Bobcat Ballpark. **Seating Capacity:** 2500. **Outfield Dimension:** LF—330, CF—405, RF—330.

TEXAS-ARLINGTON MAVERICKS

Conference: Sun Belt
Mailing Address: 1309 W. Mitchell St. Arlington, TX 76019. **Website:** www.utamavs.com. **Twitter:** @UTAMAVS
Head Coach: Darin Thomas. **Telephone:** (817) 272-2542. **Baseball SID:** Paul Watley. **Telephone:** (817) 272-9768.
Assistant Coaches: *Fuller Smith, John Wente. **Telephone:** (817) 272-0111.
Home Field: Clay Gould Ballpark. **Seating Capacity:** 1,600. **Outfield Dimension:** LF—330, CF—400, RF—330.

TEXAS-SAN ANTONIO ROADRUNNERS

Conference: Conference USA
Mailing Address: One UTSA Circle San Antonio, Texas 78249. **Website:** www.goutsa.com. **Twitter:** @UTSABSB
Head Coach: Jason Marshall. **Telephone:** (210) 458-4811. **Baseball SID:** Zena Rex. **Telephone:** (956) 739-4878.
Assistant Coaches: Jim Blair, Brett Lawler. **Telephone:** (210) 458-4811, (210) 458-4195.
Home Field: Roadrunner Field. **Seating Capacity:** 800. **Outfield Dimension:** LF—335, CF—405, RF—340.

TOLEDO ROCKETS

Conference: Mid-American
Mailing Address: 2801 W. Bancroft St., MS-408, Toledo, OH 43606. **Website:** www.utrockets.com. **Twitter:** @ToledoBaseball
Head Coach: Cory Mee. **Telephone:** (419) 530-6263. **Baseball SID:** Brian DeBenedictis. **Telephone:** (419) 530-4919.
Assistant Coaches: *Josh Bradford, Nick McIntyre. **Telephone:** (419) 530-3097.
Home Field: Scott Park. **Seating Capacity:** 1,000. **Outfield Dimension:** LF—330, CF—400, RF—300.

TOWSON TIGERS

Conference: Colonial Athletic
Mailing Address: 8000 York Rd Towson, MD 21252. **Website:** www.towsontigers.com. **Twitter:** @Towson_BASE
Head Coach: Mike Gottlieb. **Telephone:** (410) 704-3775. **Baseball SID:** John Brush. **Telephone:** (410) 704-3102.
Assistant Coaches: Jon Karsos, *Scott Roane. **Telephone:** (410) 704-4587.
Home Field: Scheurholz Park. **Seating Capacity:** 1,000. **Outfield Dimension:** LF—312, CF—424, RF—301.

TROY TROJANS

Conference: Sun Belt
Mailing Address: 5000 Veterans Stadium Drive, Troy, AL, 36082. **Website:** www.troytrojans.com. **Twitter:** @TroyTrojansBSB
Head Coach: Bobby Pierce. **Telephone:** (334) 670-5945. **Baseball SID:** Wes Johnson. **Telephone:** (334) 670-5655.
Assistant Coaches: Brad Phillips, *Mark Smartt. **Telephone:** (334) 670-3333, (334) 670-5705.
Home Field: Riddle-Pace Field. **Seating Capacity:** 2,000. **Outfield Dimension:** LF—340, CF—400, RF—310.

TULANE GREEN WAVE

Conference: American Athletic.
Mailing Address: James W. Wilson, Jr. Center, Ben Weiner Drive, New Orleans, La. 70118. **Website:** www.tulanegreenwave.com. **Twitter:** @GreenWaveBSB
Head Coach: David Pierce. **Telephone:** (504) 862-9238. **Baseball SID:** Curtis Akey. **Telephone:** (504) 314-7271.
Assistant Coaches: *Sean Allen, Philip Miller. **Telephone:** (504) 314-7202.
Home Field: Greer Field at Turchin Stadium. **Seating Capacity:** 5,000. **Outfield Dimension:** LF—325, CF—400, RF—325.

C DAVIS AGGIES

Conference: Big West
Mailing Address: One Shields Ave, Davis, CA, 95616. **Website:** www.ucdavisaggies.com. **Twitter:** @UCDavisBaseball
Head Coach: Matt Vaughn. **Telephone:** (530) 752-7513. **Baseball SID:** Jason Spencer. **Telephone:** (530) 752-2663.
Assistant Coaches: Brett Lindgren, Tony Schifano. **Telephone:** (530) 752-7513.
Home Field: Dobbins Stadium. **Seating Capacity:** 3,500. **Outfield Dimension:** LF—310, CF—410, RF—310.

UC IRVINE Anteaters
Conference: Big West
Mailing Address: Intercollegiate Athletics Building, Irvine CA 92697. **Website:** www.ucirvinesports.com. **Twitter:** @UCIbsb
Head Coach: Mike Gillespie. **Telephone:** (949) 827-4292. **Baseball SID:** Fumi Kimura. **Telephone:** (949) 824-9474.
Assistant Coaches: Daniel Bibona, *Ben Orloff. **Telephone:** (949) 824-1154.
Home Field: Anteater Ballpark. **Seating Capacity:** 3,200. **Outfield Dimension:** LF—335, CF—405, RF—335.

UC RIVERSIDE HIGHLANDERS

Conference: Big West
Mailing Address: 900 University Ave., Riverside CA 92521. **Website:** www.gohighlanders.com. **Twitter:** @UCR_Baseball
Head Coach: Troy Percival. **Telephone:** (951) 827-5441. **Baseball SID:** John Maxwell. **Telephone:** (951) 827-5438.
Assistant Coaches: *Bryson LeBlanc, Curtis Smith. **Telephone:** (951) 827-5441.
Home Field: Riverside Sports Complex. **Seating Capacity:** 2,227. **Outfield Dimension:** LF—330, CF—405, RF—330.

UC SANTA BARBARA GAUCHOS

Conference: Big West
Mailing Address: UCSB Intercollegiate Athletics Department ICA Building Santa Barbara, CA 93106-5200. **Website:** www.ucsbgauchos.com. **Twitter:** @UCSB_Baseball
Head Coach: Andrew Checketts. **Telephone:** (805) 893-3690. **Baseball SID:** Andrew Wagner. **Telephone:** (805) 893-8603.
Assistant Coaches: *Eddie Cornejo, Neil Walton. **Telephone:** (805) 893-2021.
Home Field: Caesar Uyesaka Stadium. **Seating Capacity:** 1,000. **Outfield Dimension:** LF—335, CF—385, RF—335.

UCLA BRUINS

Conference: Pacific-12
Mailing Address: 325 Westwood Plaza, Los Angeles, CA 90095. **Website:** www.uclabruins.com. **Twitter:** @UCLABaseball
Head Coach: John Savage. **Telephone:** (310) 794-2470. **Baseball SID:** Evan Kaplan. **Telephone:** (310) 206-7873.
Assistant Coaches: *TJ Bruce, Rex Peters. **Telephone:** (310) 794-8210.
Home Field: Jackie Robinson Stadium. **Seating Capacity:** 1,820. **Outfield Dimension:** LF—330, CF—395, RF—330.

UNC ASHEVILLE BULLDOGS

Conference: Big South
Mailing Address: One University Heights, Asheville, NC 28804. **Website:** www.uncabulldogs.com. **Twitter:** @AshevilleDogs
Head Coach: Scott Friedholm. **Telephone:** (828) 251-6920. **Baseball SID:** Mike Gore. **Telephone:** (828) 251-6923.
Assistant Coaches: Chris Bresnahan, *Jonathan Johnston. **Telephone:** (828) 250-2309.
Home Field: Greenwood Field. **Seating Capacity:** 500. **Outfield Dimension:** LF—335, CF—405, RF—332.

UNC GREENSBORO SPARTANS

Conference: Southern
Mailing Address: 1408 Walker Ave., Greensboro, NC 27412. **Website:** www.uncgspartans.com. **Twitter:** @UNCGBaseball
Head Coach: Link Jarrett. **Telephone:** (336) 334-3247. **Baseball SID:** Chip Welch. **Telephone:** (336) 334-5615. **Fax:** (336) 334-4063.
Assistant Coaches: *Matt Boykin, Jerry Edwards. **Telephone:** (336) 334-3247.
Home Field: UNCG Baseball Stadium. **Seating Capacity:** 3,500. **Outfield Dimension:** LF—340, CF—405, RF—340.

UNC WILMINGTON SEAHAWKS

Conference: Colonial Athletic
Mailing Address: 601 South College Road, Wilmington, NC 28403. **Website:** www.uncwsports.com. **Twitter:** @UNCWBaseball
Head Coach: Mark Scalf. **Telephone:** (910) 962-3570. **Baseball SID:** Tom Riordan. **Telephone:** (910) 962-4099.
Assistant Coaches: *Randy Hood, Matt Williams. **Telephone:** (910) 962-7471.
Home Field: Brooks Field. **Seating Capacity:** 3500. **Outfield Dimension:** LF—340, CF—380, RF—340.

UNLV REBELS

Conference: Mountain West
Mailing Address: 4505 S Maryland Pkwy, Las Vegas, NV 89154. **Website:** www.unlvrebels.com. **Twitter:** @UNLVBaseball
Head Coach: Tim Chambers. **Telephone:** (702) 895-3499. **Baseball SID:** Sage Sammons. **Telephone:** (702) 895-3764.
Assistant Coaches: Kevin Higgins, *Stan Stolte. **Telephone:** (702) 895-3802.
Home Field: Roger Barnson Field at Earl E. Wilson Stadium. **Seating Capacity:** 3000. **Outfield Dimension:** LF—335, CF—400, RF—335.

UTAH UTES

Conference: Pacific-12
Mailing Address: 1825 E. South Campus Dr., Salt Lake City, UT 84112. **Website:** www.utahutes.com. **Twitter:** @utahbaseball
Head Coach: Bill Kinneberg. **Telephone:** (801) 581-3526. **Baseball SID:** Brooke Frederickson. **Telephone:** (801) 581-8302.
Assistant Coaches: *Mike Crawford, Jason Hawkins. **Telephone:** (801) 581-4974.
Home Field: Smith's Ballpark. **Seating Capacity:** 15,500. **Outfield Dimension:** LF—345, CF—420, RF—315.

UTAH VALLEY WOLVERINES

Conference: Western Athletic
Mailing Address: MS 104, 800 W. University Parkway, Orem, Utah 84058. **Website:** www.wolverinegreen.com. **Twitter:** @UVUBaseball
Head Coach: Eric Madsen. **Telephone:** (801) 863-6509. **Baseball SID:** Clint Burgi. **Telephone:** (801) 863-8644.
Assistant Coaches: Dave Carter, *Cooper Fouts. **Telephone:** (801) 863-8647.
Home Field: Brent Brown Ballpark. **Seating Capacity:** 5,000. **Outfield Dimension:** LF—312, CF—408, RF—315.

VALPARAISO CRUSADERS

Conference: Horizon
Mailing Address: 1009 Union St., Valparaiso, IN 46383. **Website:** www.valpoathletics.com. **Twitter:** @ValpoBaseball1
Head Coach: Brian Schmack. **Telephone:** (219) 464-6117. **Baseball SID:** Brad Collignon. **Telephone:** (219) 464-5396.
Assistant Coaches: Adam White, *Ben Wolgamot. **Telephone:** (219) 465-7961.
Home Field: Emory G. Bauer Field. **Seating Capacity:** 500. **Outfield Dimension:** LF—330, CF—400, RF—330.

VANDERBILT COMMODORES

Conference: Southeastern
Mailing Address: 2601 Jess Neely Dr., Nashville TN 37212. **Website:** www.vucommodores.com. **Twitter:** @VandyBaseball
Head Coach: Tim Corbin. **Telephone:** (615) 322-3716. **Baseball SID:** Kyle Parkinson. **Telephone:** (615) 343-0020.
Assistant Coaches: Scott Brown, *Travis Jewett. **Telephone:** (615) 322-3716.
Home Field: Hawkins Field. **Seating Capacity:** 3,626. **Outfield Dimension:** LF—310, CF—400, RF—335.

VILLANOVA WILDCATS

Conference: Big East
Mailing Address: Jake Nevin Field House, 800 East Lancaster Ave, Villanova, PA 19085. **Website:** www.villanova.com. **Twitter:** @VUBaseball
Head Coach: Joe Godri. **Telephone:** (610) 519-4529. **Baseball SID:** David Berman. **Telephone:** (610) 519-4122.
Assistant Coaches: Chris Collazo, *Kevin Mulvey. **Telephone:** (610) 519-5520.
Home Field: Villanova Ballpark at Plymouth Meeting. **Seating Capacity:** 750. **Outfield Dimension:** LF—330, CF—400, RF—330.

VIRGINIA CAVALIERS

Conference: Atlantic Coast
Mailing Address: PO Box 400853, Charlottesvllle, VA 22904. **Website:** www.virginiasports.com. **Twitter:** @UVABaseball
Head Coach: Brian O'Connor. **Telephone:** (434) 982-4932. **Baseball SID:** Andy Fledderjohann. **Telephone:** (434) 982-5131.
Assistant Coaches: Karl Kuhn, *Kevin McMullan. **Telephone:** (434) 982-5776.
Home Field: Davenport Field. **Seating Capacity:** 5025. **Outfield Dimension:** LF—332, CF—404, RF—332.

VIRGINIA COMMONWEALTH RAMS

Conference: Atlantic 10
Mailing Address: 821 W Franklin St, Richmond, VA 23284. **Website:** www.vcuathletics.com. **Twitter:** @VCUBaseball
Head Coach: Shawn Stiffler. **Telephone:** (804) 828-4822. **Baseball SID:** Chris Cullum. **Telephone:** (804) 828-3440.
Assistant Coaches: *Steve Hay, Kurt Elbin. **Telephone:** (804) 828-4820, (804) 828-4821.
Home Field: The Diamond. **Seating Capacity:** 12,134. **Outfield Dimension:** LF—330, CF—402, RF—330.

VIRGINIA MILITARY INSTITUTE KEYDETS

Conference: Southern
Mailing Address: Cameron Hall, Lexington, VA 24450. **Website:** vmikeydets.com. **Twitter:** @VMIAthletics
Head Coach: Jonathan Hadra. **Telephone:** (540) 464-7601. **Baseball SID:** Brad Salois. **Telephone:** (540) 464-7015.
Assistant Coaches: Travis Beazley, *Casey Dykes. **Telephone:** (540) 464-7605.
Home Field: Gray-Minor Stadium. **Seating Capacity:** 1,400. **Outfield Dimension:** LF—330, CF—395, RF—330.

VIRGINIA TECH HOKIES

Conference: Atlantic Coast
Mailing Address: 460 Jamerson Athletic Center, Blacksburg, Va. **24061. Website:** www.hokiesports.com. **Twitter:** @VT_Baseball
Head Coach: Patrick Mason. **Telephone:** (540) 231-3671. **Baseball SID:** Marc Mullen. **Telephone:** (540) 231-1894.
Assistant Coaches: Ryan Connolly, Robert Woodard. **Telephone:** (540) 231-0398.
Home Field: English Field. **Seating Capacity:** 4,000. **Outfield Dimension:** LF—330, CF—400, RF—330.

WAGNER SEAHAWKS

Conference: Northeast
Mailing Address: Spiro Sports Center, 1 Campus Rd., Staten Island, NY 10301. **Website:** www.wagnerathletics.com. **Twitter:** @WagBaseball
Head Coach: Jim Carone. **Telephone:** (718) 390-3154. **Baseball SID:** John Beisser. **Telephone:** (718) 390-3227.
Assistant Coaches: Josh Horton, Eddie Brown. **Telephone:** (718) 420-4081, (718) 420-4121.
Home Field: Richmond County Bank Ballpark. **Seating Capacity:** 7,171. **Outfield Dimension:** LF—320, CF—390, RF—318.

WAKE FOREST DEMON DEACONS

Conference: Atlantic Coast
Mailing Address: 1834 Wake Forest Dr., Winston-Salem, NC 27103. **Website:** www.wakeforestsports.com. **Twitter:** @WakeBaseball
Head Coach: Tom Walter. **Telephone:** (336) 758-5570. **Baseball SID:** Nick Sebesta. **Telephone:** (336) 758-5842.
Assistant Coaches: Matt Hobbs, Bill Cilento. **Telephone:** (336) 758-4208, (336) 758-5645.
Home Field: Gene Hooks Field at Wake Forest Baseball Park. **Seating Capacity:** 6,000. **Outfield Dimension:** LF—325, CF—400, RF—315.

WASHINGTON HUSKIES

Conference: Pacific-12
Mailing Address: Wayne Gittinger Team Building, 4000 Walla Walla Rd. NE, Seattle, WA 98195. **Website:** www.gohuskies.com. **Twitter:** @UW_Baseball
Head Coach: Lindsay Meggs. **Telephone:** (206) 616-4335. **Baseball SID:** Brian Tom. **Telephone:** (206) 897-1742.
Assistant Coaches: Donegal Fergus, *Jason Kelly. **Telephone:** (206) 685-7016.
Home Field: Husky Ballpark. **Seating Capacity:** 2,200. **Outfield Dimension:** LF—327, CF—395, RF—317.

WASHINGTON STATE COUGARS

Conference: Pacific-12
Mailing Address: 195 Bohler Athletic Complex, Pullman, WA 99164. **Website:** www.wsucougars.com. **Twitter:** @Cougbaseball
Head Coach: Donnie Marbut. **Telephone:** (509) 335-0332. **Baseball SID:** Craig Lawson. **Telephone:** (509) 335-0265.
Assistant Coaches: *Joe Ross, Gregg Swenson. **Telephone:** (509) 335-0216, (509) 335-0211.
Home Field: Bailey-Brayton Field. **Seating Capacity:** 3,500. **Outfield Dimension:** LF—330, CF—400, RF—330.

WEST VIRGINIA MOUNTAINEERS

Conference: Big 12
Mailing Address: PO Box 0877, Morgantown WV, 26507. **Website:** www.wvusports.com. **Twitter:** @WVU_Baseball
Head Coach: Randy Mazey. **Telephone:** (336) 293-2300. **Baseball SID:** Grant Dovey. **Telephone:** (336) 293-2821.
Assistant Coaches: Derek Matlock, Steven Trout. **Telephone:** (336) 293-9880, (336) 293-0067.
Home Field: Hawley Field. **Seating Capacity:** 1,500. **Outfield Dimension:** LF—325, CF—390, RF—325.

WESTERN CAROLINA CATAMOUNTS

Conference: Southern
Mailing Address: 92 Catamount Rd., Cullowhee, NC 28723. **Website:** www.catamountsports.com. **Twitter:** @Catamounts
Head Coach: Bobby Moranda. **Telephone:** (828) 227-2021. **Baseball SID:** Daniel Hooker. **Telephone:** (828) 227-2339.
Assistant Coaches: Alan Beck, Bruce Johnson. **Telephone:** (828) 227-2510, (828) 227-2022.
Home Field: Hennon Stadium. **Seating Capacity:** 1,500. **Outfield Dimension:** LF—325, CF—395, RF—325.

WESTERN ILLINOIS LEATHERNECKS

Conference: Summit
Mailing Address: Western Hall 209, 1 University Cir Macomb, IL 61455. **Website:** www.wiuathletics.com. **Twitter:** @WIU_Baseball
Head Coach: Ryan Brownlee. **Telephone:** (309) 298-1521. **Baseball SID:** Sam Boender. **Telephone:** (309) 298-1133.
Assistant Coaches: *Shane Davis, Matt Igara. **Telephone:** (309) 298-1521.
Home Field: Alfred D Boyer Stadium. **Seating Capacity:** 500. **Outfield Dimension:** LF—330, CF—400, RF—330.

WESTERN KENTUCKY HILLTOPPERS

Conference: Conference USA
Mailing Address: 1605 Avenue of Champions Bowling Green, KY 42101. **Website:** wkusports.com. **Twitter:** @WKUBaseball
Head Coach: Matt Myers. **Telephone:** (270) 745-2277. **Baseball SID:** Jeremy Brown. **Telephone:** (270) 745-5388.
Assistant Coaches: *Blake Allen, Brendan Dougherty. **Telephone:** (270) 745-2274.
Home Field: Nick Denes Field. **Seating Capacity:** 1,500. **Outfield Dimension:** LF—330, CF—400, RF—330.

WESTERN MICHIGAN BRONCOS

Conference: Mid-American
Mailing Address: 1903 W. Michigan Ave. Kalamazoo, MI 49008-5406. **Website:** www.wmubroncos.com. **Twitter:** @WMUBaseball
Head Coach: Billy Gernon. **Telephone:** (269) 276-3205. **Baseball SID:** Kristin Keirns. **Telephone:** (269) 387-4123.
Assistant Coaches: Blaine McFerrin, *Adam Piotrowicz. **Telephone:** (269) 276-3208.
Home Field: Robert J. Bobb Stadium at Hyames Field. **Seating Capacity:** 1,500. **Outfield Dimension:** LF—310, CF—395, RF—335.

WICHITA STATE SHOCKERS

Conference: Missouri Valley
Mailing Address: 1845 Fairmount, Box 18, Wichita, KS 67260-0018. **Website:** www.goshockers.com. **Twitter:** @GoShockers
Head Coach: Todd Butler. **Telephone:** (316) 978-3636. **Baseball SID:** Tami Cutler. **Telephone:** (316) 978-5559.
Assistant Coaches: Brent Kemnitz, *Brian Walker. **Telephone:** (316) 978-5302.
Home Field: Eck Stadium. **Seating Capacity:** 7,851. **Outfield Dimension:** LF—330, CF—390, RF—330.

WILLIAM & MARY TRIBE

Conference: Colonial Athletic
Mailing Address: 751 Ukrop Way, Williamsburg, VA 23185. **Website:** www.tribeathletics.com. **Twitter:** @WMTribeBaseball
Head Coach: Brian Murphy. **Telephone:** (757) 221-3492. **Baseball SID:** Andrew Phillips. **Telephone:** (757) 221-3344.
Assistant Coaches: *Brian Casey, Andrew Kiriakedes. **Telephone:** (757) 221-3399.
Home Field: Plumeri Park. **Seating Capacity:** 1,100. **Outfield Dimension:** LF—325, CF—400, RF—325.

WINTHROP EAGLES

Conference: Big South
Mailing Address: Winthrop Coliseum, 1162 Eden Terrace Drive, Rock Hill, SC 29733. **Website:** www.winthropeagles.com. **Twitter:** @WUEagles
Head Coach: Tom Riginos. **Telephone:** (803) 323-6235. **Baseball SID:** Jack Frost. **Telephone:** (803) 323-2433.
Assistant Coaches: Clint Chrysler, Rich Witten. **Telephone:** (859) 319-1398.
Home Field: Winthrop Ballpark. **Seating Capacity:** 2,000. **Outfield Dimension:** LF—325, CF—390, RF—325.

WISCONSIN-MILWAUKEE PANTHERS

Conference: Horizon
Mailing Address: 3409 N. Downer Ave., Milwaukee, WI 53211. **Website:** www.uwmpanthers.com. **Twitter:** @MKE_Baseball
Head Coach: Scott Doffek. **Telephone:** (414) 229-5670. **Baseball SID:** Chris Zills. **Telephone:** (414) 229-4593.
Assistant Coaches: Cory Bigler, *Cole Kraft. **Telephone:** (414) 229-2433, (414) 229-7140.
Home Field: Henry Aaron Field. **Outfield Dimension:** LF—320, CF—390, RF—320.

WOFFORD TERRIERS

Conference: Southern
Mailing Address: Wofford College Athletics, 429 North Church Street, Spartanburg, SC 29303. **Website:** www.woffordterriers.com. **Twitter:** @WoffordBaseball
Head Coach: Todd Interdonato. **Telephone:** (864) 597-4497. **Baseball SID:** Brent Williamson. **Telephone:** (864) 597-4497.
Assistant Coaches: Jason Burke, JJ Edwards. **Telephone:** (864) 597-4126, (864) 597-4499.
Home Field: Russell King Field. **Seating Capacity:** 1,600. **Outfield Dimension:** LF—325, CF—395, RF—325.

WRIGHT STATE RAIDERS

Conference: Horizon
Mailing Address: 3640 Colonel Glenn Highway, Dayton, OH 45435 Website: www.wsuraiders.com. **Twitter:** @WSURaiders
Head Coach: Greg Lovelady. **Telephone:** (937) 775-3668. **Baseball SID:** Matt Zircher. **Telephone:** (937) 775-2831.
Assistant Coaches: *Jeff Mercer, Justin Parker. **Telephone:** (937) 775-4188.
Home Field: Nischwitz Stadium. **Seating Capacity:** 750. **Outfield Dimension:** LF—330, CF—400, RF—330.

XAVIER MUSKETEERS

Conference: Big East
Mailing Address: 3800 Victory Parkway, Cincinnati, OH 45207. **Website:** www.goxavier.com. **Twitter:** @XavierBASE
Head Coach: Scott Googins. **Telephone:** (513) 745-2891. **Baseball SID:** Brendan Bergen. **Telephone:** (513) 745-3388.
Assistant Coaches: Billy O'Conner, *Nick Otte. **Telephone:** (513) 745-2890.
Home Field: Hayden Field. **Seating Capacity:** 500. **Outfield Dimension:** LF—310, CF—380, RF—310.

YALE BULLDOGS

Conference: Ivy.
Mailing Address: PO Box 208216, New Haven, CT 06520. **Website:** www.yalebulldogs.com. **Twitter:** @YaleBaseball
Head Coach: John Stuper. **Telephone:** (203) 432-1466. **Baseball SID:** Steve Lewis. **Telephone:** (203) 232-3454.
Assistant Coaches: Tucker Frawley, Ray Guarino. **Telephone:** (203) 432-1467.
Home Field: Yale Field. **Seating Capacity:** 6,000.

YOUNGSTOWN STATE PENGUINS

Conference: Horizon
Mailing Address: 1 University Plaza Youngstown, OH 44555. **Website:** www.ysusports.com. **Twitter:** @YSUBaseball
Head Coach: Steve Gillispie. **Telephone:** (256) 239-1960. **Baseball SID:** John Vogel. **Telephone:** (330) 941-1480.
Assistant Coaches: *Jason Neal, Kevin Smallcomb. **Telephone:** N/A.
Home Field: Eastwood Field. **Seating Capacity:** 6,000. **Outfield Dimension:** LF—335, CF—400, RF—335.

AMATEUR
& YOUTH

INTERNATIONAL ORGANIZATIONS

INTERNATIONAL BASEBALL FEDERATION

Headquarters: Maison du Sport International—54, Avenue de Rhodanie, 1007 Lausanne, Switzerland. **Telephone:** (+41-21) 318-82-40. **Fax:** (41-21) 318-82-41. **Website:** www.ibaf.org. **E-Mail:** office@ibaf.org. **Year Founded:** 1938.
President: Riccardo Fraccari.
1st Vice President: Alonso Perez Gonzalez. **2nd Vice President:** Tom Peng. **3rd Vice President:** Antonio Castro. **Secretary General:** Israel Roldan. **Treasurer:** Angelo Vicini. **Members at Large:** Masaaki Nagino, Paul Seiler, Luis Melero. **Continental VP, Africa:** Sabeur Jlajla. **Continental VP, Americas:** Jorge Otsuka. **Continental VP, Asia:** Byung-Suk Lee. **Continental VP, Europe:** Jan Esselman. **Continental VP, Oceania:** Ron Finlay. **Executive Director:** Michael Schmidt.
Assistant to the President: Victor Isola. **Marketing/Tournament Manager:** Masaru Yokoo. **Public Relations Officer:** Oscar Lopez. **National Federation Relations:** Francesca Fabretto. **Antidoping Officer:** Victor Isola. **Administration/Finance:** Sandrine Pennone.

CONTINENTAL ASSOCIATIONS

CONFEDERATION PAN AMERICANA DE BEISBOL (COPABE)

Mailing Address: Calle 3, Francisco Filos, Vista Hermosa, Edificio 74, Planta Baja Local No. 1, Panama City, Panama. **Telephone:** (507) 229-8684. **Fax:** Unavailable. **Website:** www.copabe.net. **E-Mail:** copabe@sinfo.net. **Chairman:** Eduardo De Bello (Panama). **Secretary General:** Hector Pereyra (Dominican Republic).

AFRICA BASEBALL SOFTBALL ASSOCIATION (ABSA)

Office Address: Paiko Road, Chanchaga, Minna, Niger State, Nigeria.
Mailing Address: P.M.B. 150, Minna, Niger State, Nigeria.
Telephone: (234) 8037188491. **E-mail:** absasecretariat@yahoo.com
President: Sabeur Jlajla. **Vice President Baseball:** Etienne N'Guessan. **Vice President Softball:** Fridah Shiroya. **Secretary General:** Ibrahim N'Diaye. **Treasurer:** Moira Dempsey. **Executive Director:** Lieutenant Colonel (rtd) Friday Ichide. **Deputy Executive Director:** Francoise Kameni-Lele.

BASEBALL FEDERATION OF ASIA

Mailing Address: 4F., No. 238, Sec. 2 Jianguo. N. Rd., Zhongshan District, Taipei City 104, Taiwan, R.O.C. **Telephone:** 886-2-2516-1483. **E-Mail Address:** hfa@baseballasia.org
President: Tom Peng. **Vice Presidents:** Suzuki Yoshinobu, Kim Jong-Up, Shen Wei (China). **Secretary General:** Hua-Wei Lin. **Executive Director, West Asia:** Syed Khawar Shah. **Members At Large:** Allan Mak, Tom Navasero, Vutichai Udomkarnjananan.

EUROPEAN BASEBALL CONFEDERATION

Mailing Address: Savska cesta 137, 10 000 Zagreb, Croatia. **Telephone/Fax:** +385 1 561 5227. **E-Mail Address:** office@baseballeurope.com. **Website:** baseballeurope.com.
President: Jan Esselman (Netherlands). **1st Vice President:** Peter Kurz (Israel). **2nd Vice President:** Jürgen Elsishans (Germany). **3rd Vice President:** Petr Ditrich (Czech Republic). **Secretary General:** Krunoslav Karin (Croatia) Treasurer: Rene Laforce (Belgium). **Vocals:** Mick Manning (Ireland), Mats Fransson (Sweden), Monique Schmitt (Switzerland), Valentinas Bubulis (Lithuania).

BASEBALL CONFEDERATION OF OCEANIA

Mailing Address: 48 Partridge Way, Mooroolbark, Victoria 3138, Australia. **Telephone:** 613 9727 1779. **Fax:** 613 9727 5959. **E-Mail Address:** bcosecgeneral@baseballoceania.com. **Website:** www.baseballoceania.com.
President: Bob Steffy (Guam). **1st Vice President:** Laurent Cassier (New Caledonia). **2nd Vice President:** Victor Langkilde (American Samoa). **Secretary General:** Chet Gray (Australia). **Executive Committee:** Rose Igitol (CNMI), Temmy Shmull (Palau), Innoke Niubalavu (Fiji).

INTERNATIONAL GOODWILL SERIES, INC.

Mailing Address: 982 Slate Drive, Santa Rosa, CA 95405. **Telephone:** (707) 538-0777. **E-Mail Address:** rwilliams@goodwillseries.org. **Website:** www.goodwillseries.org.
President, Goodwill Series, Inc.: Bob Williams.

INTERNATIONAL SPORTS GROUP

Mailing Address: 3135 South Vermont Ave., Milwaukee, WI 53207. **Telephone:** (541) 882-4293. **E-Mail Address:** isgbaseball14@gmail.com. **Website:** www.isgbaseball.com.
President: Tom O'Connell. **Vice President:** Peter Caliendo.
Secretary/Treasurer: Randy Town. **Board Members:** Jim Jones, Rick Steen, Bill Mathews, Pat Doyle. **Founder/Senior Consultant:** Bill Arce.

NATIONAL ORGANIZATIONS

USA BASEBALL

Mailing Address, Corporate Headquarters: 403 Blackwell St., Durham, NC 27701. **Telephone:** (919) 474-8721. **Fax:** (919) 474-8822. **Email Address:** info@usabaseball.com. **Website:** www.usabaseball.com.
President: Mike Gaski. **Treasurer:** Jason Dobis. **Board of Directors:** Jenny Dalton-Hill, John McHale, Jr. (Major League Baseball), Wes Skelton (Dixie Baseball), Steve Keener (Little League), Steve Tellefsen (Babe Ruth), Damani Leech (NCAA); John Gall (Recent Athlete), George Grande (At Large).
Executive Director/Chief Executive Officer: Paul Seiler. **Director, National Team Development Programs/Women's National Team:** Ashley Bratcher. **General Manager, National Teams:** Eric Campbell. **Chief Financial Officer:** Ray Darwin. **Director, Travel Services:** Jocelyn Fern. **Assistant Director, Operations:** Tom Gottlieb. **Director, Digital/Social Media:** Kevin Jones. **Assistant Director, Accounting/Finance:** Cicely

Lopez. **Chief Operating Officer:** David Perkins. **Director, Development:** Rick Riccobono. **Director, Community Relations:** Lindsay Robertson. **Director, 18U National Team/Alumni:** Brant Ust.

National Members: Amateur Athletic Union (AAU), American Amateur Baseball Congress (AABC), American Baseball Coaches Association (ABCA), American Legion Baseball, Babe Ruth Baseball, Dixie Baseball, Little LeagueBaseball, National Amateur Baseball Federation (NABF), National Association of Intercollegiate Athletics (NAIA), National Baseball Congress (NBC), National Collegiate Athletic Association (NCAA), National Federation of State High School Athletic Associations, National High School Baseball Coaches Association (BCA), National Junior College Athletic Association (NJCAA), Police Athletic League (PAL), PONY Baseball, T-Ball USA, United States Specialty Sports Association (USSSA), YMCAs of the USA.

Events: www.usabaseball.com/events/schedule.jsp.

BASEBALL CANADA

Mailing Address: 2212 Gladwin Cres., Suite A7, Ottawa, Ontario K1B 5N1. **Telephone:** (613) 748-5606. **Fax:** (613) 748-5767. **Email Address:** info@baseball.ca. **Website:** www.baseball.ca.

Director General: Jim Baba. **Head Coach/Director, National Teams:** Greg Hamilton. **Manager, Baseball Operations:** Andre Lachance. **Program Coordinator:** Kelsey McIntosh. **Manager, Media/Public Relations:** Adam Morissette. **Administrative Coordinator:** Denise Thomas. **Administrative Assistant:** Penny Baba.

NATIONAL BASEBALL CONGRESS

Mailing Address: 300 S. Sycamore, Wichita, KS 67213. **Telephone:** (316) 264-6887. **Fax:** (316) 264-2129. **Website:** www.nbcbaseball.com.

Year Founded: 1931.

General Manager: Josh Robertson. **Tournament Director:** Casey Walkup.

ATHLETES IN ACTION

Mailing Address: 651 Taylor Dr., Xenia, OH 45385. **Telephone:** (937) 352-1000. **Fax:** (937) 352-1245. **Email Address:** baseball@athletesinaction.org. **Website:** www. aiabaseball.org.

Director, AIA Baseball: Chris Beck. **General Manager, Alaska:** Chris Beck. **General Manager, Great Lakes:** John Henschen. **General Manager, New York Collegiate League:** Chris Rainwater. **International Teams Director:** John McLaughlin. **Youth Baseball Director:** Matt Richter.

SUMMER COLLEGE LEAGUES

NATIONAL ALLIANCE OF COLLEGE SUMMER BASEBALL

Telephone: (321) 206-9714 **E-Mail Address:** RSitz@ FloridaLeague.com **Website:** www.nacsb.org

Executive Director: Rob Sitz (Florida League). **Assistant Executive Director:** Bobby Bennett (Sunbelt Baseball League), Jeff Carter (Southern Collegiate Baseball League) **Treasurer:** Larry Tremitiere (Southern Collegiate Baseball League). **Director, Public Relations/ Secretary:** Stefano Foggi (Florida Collegiate Summer League). **Compliance Officer:** Paul Galop (Cape Cod Baseball League).

Member Leagues: Atlantic Collegiate Baseball League, Cal Ripken Collegiate Baseball League, Cape Cod Baseball League, Florida Collegiate Summer League, Great Lakes Summer Collegiate League, New England Collegiate Baseball League, New York Collegiate Baseball League, Southern Collegiate Baseball League, Sunbelt Baseball League, Valley Baseball League, Hamptons Collegiate Baseball League.

ALASKA BASEBALL LEAGUE

Mailing Address: 651 Taylor Drive, Xenia, OH 45385. **Telephone:** (907) 283-6186. **Fax:** (907) 746-5068. **E-Mail Address:** mikebaxter@acsalaska.net.

Year Founded: 1974 (reunited, 1998).

President/Secretary: Chris Beck (Chugiak-Eagle River Chinooks). **1st VP, Marketing/Umpire Payroll:** Pete Christopher (Mat-Su Miners). **2nd VP, Rules:** Mike Hinshaw (Anchorage Glacier Pilots). **3rd VP, Scheduling:** Todd Dennis (Fairbanks Alaska Goldplanners). **4th VP, Umpires:** Shawn Maltby (Anchorage Bucs). **5th VP, By-Laws:** Mike Baxter (Peninsula Oilers). **League Spokesperson:** Mike Baxter.

Regular Season: 41 league games and approximately 5 non-league games. **2015 Opening Date:** June 12.

Closing Date: August 4..

Playoff Format: Regular season league champion qualifies for National Baseball Congress World Series if desired. Also, a round robin end-of-season tournament with a best of three final determines playoff champion.

Roster Limit: 26 plus exemption for Alaska residents. **Player Eligibility:** Open except drafted college seniors.

ANCHORAGE BUCS

Mailing Address: PO Box 240061, Anchorage, AK 99524-0061. **Telephone:** (907) 561-2827. **Fax:** (907) 561-2920. **E-Mail Address:** gm@anchoragebucs.com. **Website:** anchoragebucs.com. **General Manager:** Shawn Maltby. **Head Coach:** Mike Grahovac (Concordia Irvine, Calif.). **Field:** Mulcahy Field—Turf infield, grass outfield, lights.

ANCHORAGE GLACIER PILOTS

Mailing Address: 435 West 10th Avenue, Suite A, Anchorage, AK 99501. **Telephone:** (907) 274-3627. **Fax:** (907) 274-3628. **E-Mail Address:** gpilots@alaska.net. **Website:** glacierpilots.com. **General Manager:** Mike Hinshaw. **Head Coach:** Darren Westergard (Everett CC, Wash.). **Field:** Mulcahy Field—turf infield, grass outfield, lights.

CHUGIAK-EAGLE RIVER CHINOOKS

Mailing Address: 651 Taylor Dr, Xenia, OH 45385. **Telephone:** (937) 352-1237. **Fax:** (937) 352-1245. **E-Mail Address:** chris.beck@athletesinaction.org. **Website:** www.aiabaseball.org. **Additional Website:** www.cerchinooks.com. **General Manager:** Chris Beck. **Head Coach:** Jon Groth (Tyler, Texas, CC). **Field:** Loretta French Field—grass, no lights.

FAIRBANKS ALASKA GOLDPANNERS

Mailing Address: 1747 Crosson Ave., Fairbanks, AK, 99707. **Telephone:** (907) 451-0095, (619) 561-4581. **Fax:** (907) 456-6429, (619) 561-4581. **E-Mail Address:** todd@goldpanners.com. **Website:** goldpanners.com. **General Manager:** Todd Dennis. **Head Coach:** Jeff Stephens (Sierra CC, Calif.). **Field:** Growden Memorial Park—turf infield, grass outfield, lights.

MAT-SU MINERS

Mailing Address: PO Box 2690, Palmer, AK 99645-2690. **Telephone:** (907) 746-4914; (907) 745-6401. **Fax:** (907) 746-5068. **E-Mail Address:** generalmanager@matsuminers.org. **Website:** matsuminers.org. **General Manager:** Pete Christopher. **Assistant GM:** Bob Plumley. **Head Coach:** Ben Taylor (Chandler-Gilbert, CC). **Field:** Hermon Brothers Field—grass, no lights.

PENINSULA OILERS

Mailing Address: 601 S Main St, Kenai, AK 99611. **Telephone:** (907) 283-7133. **Fax:** (907) 283-3390. **E-Mail Address:** gm@oilersbaseball.com. **Website:** oilersbaseball.com. **General Manager:** Mike Baxter. **Head Coach:** TBA **Field:** Coral Seymour Memorial Park—grass, no lights.

ALL AMERICAN COLLEGIATE BASEBALL LEAGUE

Mailing Address: 8442 Sandowne Ln, Huntersville NC 28078. **Website:** www.allamericanleague.com. **VP/CFO:** Joseph Finch. **Telephone:** 304-685-3532. **Commissioner:** Paul Busa. **Telephone:** 617-543-4247. **Email Address:** coachbusa@gmail.com.

Founded: 2013.

Teams: Mooresville All Americans (Mooresville, NC), Carolina Freedom (Morganton, NC), North Carolina Liberty (Salisbury, NC), Rowan Patriots (Spencer, NC), Stanly Pioneers (Oakboro, NC), Mt Pleasant Militia (Mt Pleasant, NC), Caldwell Warriors (Lenoir, NC).

ATLANTIC COLLEGIATE BASEBALL LEAGUE

Mailing Address: 1760 Joanne Drive, Quakertown, PA 18951. **Telephone:** (215) 536-5777. **Fax:** (215) 536-5777. **E-Mail:** tbonekemper@verizon.net. **Website:** www.acbl-online.com.

Year Founded: 1967.

Commissioner: Ralph Addonizio. **President/Acting Secretary:** Tom Bonekemper. **Assistant Commissioner:** Doug Cinella. **Vice Presidents:** Brian Casey, Ben Smookler. **Treasurer:** Bob Hoffman.

Regular Season: 40 games. **2015 Opening Date:** May 30. **Closing Date:** August 9. **All-Star Game:** Unavailable. **Roster Limit:** 25.

ALLENTOWN RAILERS

Mailing Address: Suite 202, 1801 Union Blvd, Allentown, PA 18109. **E-Mail Address:** ddando@lehigh-valleybaseballacademy.com. **Field Manager:** Dylan Dando.

JERSEY PILOTS

Mailing Address: 401 Timber Dr, Berkeley Heights, NJ 07922. **Telephone:** (908) 464-8042. **E-Mail Address:**

bensmookler@aol.com. **President/General Manager:** Ben Smookler. **Field Manager:** Aaron Kalb.

LEHIGH VALLEY CATZ

Mailing Address: 103 Logan Dr, Easton, PA 18045. **Telephone:** (610) 533-9349. **Website:** www.lvcatz.com. **General Manager:** Adrian Yaguez. **Field Manager:** Jake McGeary.

NORTH JERSEY EAGLES

Mailing Address: 107 Pleasant Avenue, Upper Saddle River, NJ 07458. **General Manager:** Brian Casey. **Field Manager:** Doug Cinnella.

QUAKERTOWN BLAZERS

Telephone: (215) 679-5072. **E-Mail Address:** quakertownblazers@outlook.com. **Website:** www.quakertownblazers.com. **General Manager:** Pat O'Connell. **Field Manager:** Matt Hollod.

SOUTH JERSEY GIANTS

Website: www.southjerseygiants.com. **Field Manager:** Greg Manco (gmanco@sju.edu).

STATEN ISLAND TIDE

Website: www.statenislandtide.com. **General Manager/Field Manager:** Tommy Weber.

TRENTON GENERALS

E-Mail Address: gally22@aol.com. **General Manager:** Dave Gallagher. **Field Manager:** Jim Maher.

CALIFORNIA COLLEGIATE LEAGUE

Mailing Address: 806 W Pedregosa St, Santa Barbara, CA 93101. **Telephone:** (805) 680-1047. **Fax:** (805) 684-8596. **Email Address:** burns@calsummerball.com. **Website:** www.calsummerball.com.

Founded: 1993.

Commissioner: Pat Burns.

Division Structure: North Division—Menlo Park Legends, Neptune Beach Pearl, Walnut Creek Crawdads. Central—Conejo Oaks, San Luis Obispo Blues, Santa Barbara Foresters, Santa Paula Halos. South—Academy Barons, Los Angeles Brewers, Southern California Catch, South Coast Saints.

Regular Season: 36 games (24 divisional games, 12 inter-divisional games). **2014 Opening Date:** June 1. **Closing Date:** July 31. **Playoff Format:** Divisional champions and wild card team play double-elimination championship tournament. **Roster Limit:** 33.

ACADEMY BARONS

Address: 901 E. **Artesia Blvd, Compton, CA 90221.** **Telephone:** (310) 635-2967. **Website:** www.academybarons.org. **Email Address:** don.buford@mlb.com. **Director:** Don Buford. **Field Manager:** Kenny Landreaux.

CONEJO OAKS

Address: 1710 N. Moorpark Rd., #106, Thousand Oaks, CA 91360. **Telephone:** (805) 797-7889. **Fax:** (805) 529-9862. **Email Address:** oaksbaseball@roadrunner.com. **Website:** www.oaksbaseball.org. **General Managers:**

Randy Riley, Verne Merrill. **Field Manager:** David Soilz.
LOS ANGELES BREWERS
   Address: 2312 Park Ave., #413, Tustin CA 92626.
Telephone: (323) 379-4833. **Email Address:** jwicks@
labrewersbaseball.com. **Website:** www.labrewersbase-
ball.com. **General Manager:** Jameson Wicks. **Field
Manager:** Larry Mahoney.

MENLO PARK LEGENDS

   Address: PO Box 280, Menlo Park, CA 94026-0280.
Telephone: (650) 387-4427. **Email Address:** david@men-
loparklegends.com. **Website:** www.menloparklegends.
com. **General Manager:** David Klein. **Field Manager:**
Dustin Woodward.

NEPTUNE BEACH PEARL

   Address: PO Box 2602, Alameda, CA 94501.
Telephone: (510) 590-3139. **Email Address:** info@nep-
tunebeachpearl.com. **Website:** www.neptunebeachpearl.
com. **General Manager:** Dustin Chavez. **Field Manager:**
Brant Cummings.

SAN LUIS OBISPO BLUES

   Address: 241-B Prado Rd., San Luis Obispo, CA 93401.
Telephone: (805) 704-4388. **Fax:** (805) 528-1146. **Email
Address:** chal@bluesbaseball.com. **Website:** www.blues-
baseball.com. **General Manager:** Adam Stowe. **Field
Manager:** Jamie Clark.

SANTA BARBARA FORESTERS

   Address: 4299 Carpinteria Ave., Suite 201, Carpinteria,
CA 93013. **Telephone:** (805) 684-0657. **Email Address:**
pintard@earthlink.net **Website:** www.sbforesters.org.
General Manager/Field Manager: Bill Pintard.

SANTA PAULA HALOS

   Address: 722 W Santa Paula St., Santa Paula, CA
93060. **Telephone:** (805) 207-3565. **Email Address:** c_t_
gomez@hotmail.com. **Website:** www.santapaulahalos.
com. **General Manager:** Chris Gomez. **Field Manager:**
Jimmy Walker.

SOUTH COAST SAINTS

   Address: 444 Alaska Ave., Torrance, CA 90503.
Telephone: (310) 606-9390. **Email Address:** sua.mur-
phy@gmail.com. **Website:** N/A. **General Manager/Field
Manager:** Murphy Sua.

SOUTHERN CALIFORNIA CATCH

   Address: 14830 Grayville Drive, La Mirada, CA 90638.
Telephone: (562) 686-8262. **Email Address:** borr@fca.
org. **Website:** www.socalcatch.com. **General Manager:**
Ben Orr. **Field Manager:** Justin Duarte.

WALNUT CREEK CRAWDADS

   Address: 1630 Challenge Dr., Concord, CA 94520.
Telephone: (925) 354-7315.
   Email Address: phewitt@walnutcreekcrawdads.com.
Website: www.walnutcreekcrawdads.com. **General
Manager:** Paul Hewitt. **Field Manager:** Jordan Bautista.

CAL RIPKEN COLLEGIATE LEAGUE

   Address: 4006 Broadstone St, Frederick, MD 21704.
Telephone: 301-693-2577. **E-Mail:** jwoodward@calrip-
kenleague.org or brifkin@calripkenleague.org. **Website:**
www.calripkenleague.org.
   Year Founded: 2005.
   Commissioner: Jason Woodward. **League President:**
Brad Rifkin. **Deputy Commissioner:** Jerry Wargo.
   Regular Season: 40 games. **2015 Opening Date:**
June 2. **Closing Date:** July 25. **All-Star Game:** July 15.
Playoff Format: Top two teams from each division plus
two remaining teams with best records qualify. Teams
play best of three series, winners advance to best of
three series for league championship. **Roster Limit:** 30
(college-eligible players 22 and under).

ALEXANDRIA ACES

   Address: 600 14th Street NW, Suite 400, Washington,
DC 20005. **Telephone:** (202) 255-1683. **E-Mail:** ddinan@
ralaw.com. **Website:** www.alexandriaaces.org. **Chairman/
CEO:** Donald Dinan. **VP Operations/GM:** Don Kaniewski.
Head Coach: David DeSilva. **Ballpark:** Frank Mann Field
at Four Mile Run Park.

BALTIMORE DODGERS

   Address: 131 Sunnydale Way, Reisterstown, MD
21136. **Telephone:** (443) 834-3500. **Email:** juan.waters@
verizon.net. **Website:** www.baltimoredodgers.org.
President: Juan Waters. **Head Coach:** Derek Brown.
Ballpark: Joe Cannon Stadium at Harmans Park.

BALTIMORE REDBIRDS

   Address: 2208 Pine Hill Farms Lane, Cockeysville, MD
21030. **Telephone:** (410) 802-2220. **Fax:** (410) 785-6138.
E-Mail: johntcarey@hotmail.com. **Website:** www.balti-
moreredbirds.org. **President:** John Carey. **Head Coach:**
Larry Sheets. **Ballpark:** Carlo Crispino Stadium at Calvert
Hall High School.

BETHESDA BIG TRAIN

   Address: 5420 Butler Road, Bethesda, MD 20816.
Telephone: 301-365-1076. **Fax:** 301- 229-8362. **E-Mail:**
faninfo@bigtrain.org. **Website:** www.bigtrain.org.
General Manager: Eddie Herndon. **Head Coach:** Sal
Colangelo. **Ballpark:** Shirley Povich Field.

D.C. GRAYS

   Address: 900 19th Street NW, 8th floor, Washington,
DC 20006. **Telephone:** (202) 327-8116. **Fax:** (202) 327-
8101. **Website:** www.dcgrays.com. **E-Mail Address:**
barbera@acg-consultants.com. **President/Chairman:**
Michael Barbera. **General Manager:** Antonio Scott. **Head
Coach:** Reggie Terry. **Ballpark:** Washington Nationals
Youth Academy.

GAITHERSBURG GIANTS

   Address: 10 Brookes Avenue, Gaithersburg, MD
20877. **Telephone:** (240) 888-6810. **Fax:** (301) 355-5006.
E-Mail: alriley13@gmail.com. **Website:** www.gaithers-
burggiants.org. **General Manager:** Alfie Riley. **Head
Coach:** Jeff Rabberman. **Ballpark:** Criswell Automotive
Field at Kelley Park.

FCA HERNDON BRAVES

Address: 1305 Kelly Court, Herndon, VA 20170-2605. **Telephone:** (702) 909-2750. **Fax:** (703) 783-1319. **E-Mail:** fcaherndonbraves@yahoo.com. **Website:** www.herndon-braves.com. **President/General Manager:** Todd Burger. **Head Coach:** Justin Janis. **Ballpark:** Alan McCullock Field at Herndon High School.

ROCKVILLE EXPRESS

Address: PO Box 10188, Rockville, MD 20849. **Telephone:** 301-367-9435. **E-Mail:** info@rockvilleexpress.org. **Website:** www.rockvilleexpress.org. **President/GM:** Jim Kazunas. **Email:** jameskazunas@rockvilleexpress.org. **Head Coach:** Rick Price. **Ballpark:** Knights Field at Montgomery College-Rockville.

SILVER SPRING-TAKOMA T-BOLTS

Address: 906 Glaizewood Court, Takoma Park, MD 20912. **Telephone:** (301) 270-0794. **E-Mail:** tboltsbaseball@gmail.com. **Website:** www.tbolts.org. **General Manager:** David Stinson. **Head Coach:** Doug Remer. **Ballpark:** Blair Stadium at Montgomery Blair High School.

VIENNA RIVER DOGS

Address: 12703 Hitchcock Ct, Reston, VA 20191. **Telephone:** (703) 615-4396. **Fax:** (703) 904-1723. **E-Mail Address:** tickets@brucehallsports.com. **Website:** www.viennariverdogs.org. **President/General Manager/Head Coach:** Bruce Hall. **Ballpark:** James Madison High School.

CAPE COD LEAGUE

Mailing Address: PO Box 266, Harwich Port, MA 02646. **Telephone:** (508) 404-8597. **E-Mail:** info@capecodbaseball.org. **Website:** www.capecodbaseball.org.

Year Founded: 1885.

Commissioner: Paul Galop. **President:** Judy Walden Scarafile. **Treasurer/Webmaster:** Steven Wilson. **Secretary:** Kim Wolfe. **Senior Vice President:** Jim Higgins. **VP/Deputy Commissioner:** Bill Bussiere. **VP:** Peter Ford. **Senior Deputy Commissioner/Director of Officiating:** Sol Yas. **Deputy Commissioner, West:** Mike Carrier. **Deputy Commissioner, East:** Peter Hall. **Deputy Commissioner Emeritus:** Dick Sullivan.

Director, Public Relations/Broadcasting: John Garner Jr. **Director, Communications:** Jim McGonigle. **Director, Publications:** Lou Barnicle. **Director, Memorabilia:** Dan Dunn. **Editor, Publications:** Rich Plante. **Assistant to the Officers:** Bill Watson. **Assistants, Marketing:** Melissa Ellis, Sue Pina. **Director, Social Media:** Ashley Crosby. **Coordinator, Special Events/Projects:** Joe Sherman. **Website Editor:** Victoria Martin.

Division Structure: East—Brewster, Chatham, Harwich, Orleans, Yarmouth-Dennis. West—Bourne, Cotuit, Falmouth, Hyannis, Wareham. **Regular Season:** 44 games. **2015 Opening Date:** June 9. **Closing Date:** August 11. **All-Star Game:** July 25. **Playoff Format:** Top four teams in each division qualify for three rounds of best-of-three series.

Roster Limit: 30 (college-eligible players only).

BOURNE BRAVES

Mailing Address: PO Box 895, Monument Beach, MA 02553. **Telephone:** (508) 345-1013. **E-Mail Address:** bournebravesgm@hotmail.com. **Website:** www.bour-nebraves.org. **President:** Nicole Norkevicius. **General Manager:** Chuck Sturtevant. **Head Coach:** Harvey Shapiro.

BREWSTER WHITECAPS

Mailing Address: PO Box 2349, Brewster, MA 02631. **Telephone:** (508) 896-8500, ext. **147. Fax:** (508) 896-9845. **E-Mail Address:** cagradone@comcast.net. **Website:** www.brewsterwhitecaps.com. **President:** Claire Gradone. **General Manager:** Ned Monthie. **Head Coach:** Jamie Shevchick.

CHATHAM ANGLERS

Mailing Address: PO Box 428, Chatham, MA 02633. **Telephone:** (508) 241-8382. **Fax:** (508) 430-8382. **Website:** www.chathamas.com. **President:** Steve West. **General Manager:** Mike Geylin. **Head Coach:** John Schiffner.

COTUIT KETTLEERS

Mailing Address: PO Box 411, Cotuit, MA 02635. **Telephone:** (508) 428-3358. **Fax:** (508) 420-5584. **E-Mail Address:** info@kettleers.org. **Website:** www.kettleers.org. **President:** Paul Logan. **General Manager:** Bruce Murphy. **Head Coach:** Mike Roberts.

FALMOUTH COMMODORES

Mailing Address: PO Box 808 Falmouth, MA 02541. **Telephone:** (508) 472-7922. **Fax:** (508) 862-6011. **Website:** www.falcommodores.org. **President:** Steve Kostas. **General Manager:** Eric Zmuda. **Head Coach:** Jeff Trundy.

HARWICH MARINERS

Mailing Address: PO Box 201, Harwich Port, MA 02646. **Telephone:** (508) 432-2000. **Fax:** (508) 432-5357. **E-Mail Address:** mehendy@comcast.net. **Website:** www.harwichmariners.org. **President:** Mary Henderson. **General Manager:** Ben Layton. **Head Coach:** Steve Englert.

HYANNIS HARBOR HAWKS

Mailing Address: PO Box 852, Hyannis, MA 02601. **Telephone:** (508) 364-3164. **Fax:** (508) 534-1270. **E-Mail Address:** bbussiere@harborhawks.org. **Website:** www.harborhawks.org. **President:** Brad Pfeifer. **General Manager:** Tino DiGiovanni. **Head Coach:** Chad Gassman.

ORLEANS FIREBIRDS

Mailing Address: PO Box 504, Orleans, MA 02653. **Telephone:** (508) 255-0793. **Fax:** (508) 255-2237. **Website:** www.orleansfirebirds.com. **President:** Gene Hormsby. **General Manager:** Sue Horton. **Head Coach:** Kelly Nicholson.

WAREHAM GATEMEN

Mailing Address: PO Box 287, Wareham, MA 02571. **Telephone:** (508) 748-0287. **Fax:** (508) 880-2602. **E-Mail Address:** sheri.gay4gatemen@comcast.net. **Website:** www.gatemen.org. **President/General Manager:** Andrew Lang. **Head Coach:** Cooper Farris.

YARMOUTH-DENNIS RED SOX

Mailing Address: PO Box 814, South Yarmouth, MA 02664. **Telephone:** (508) 394-9387. **Fax:** (508) 398-2239. **E-Mail Address:** jimmartin321@yahoo.com. **Website:** www.ydredsox.org. **President/General Manager:** Steve Faucher. **Head Coach:** Scott Pickler.

CENTENNIAL STATE LEAGUE

Mailing Address: 543 Saturn Drive, Fort Collins, CO 80525. **Telephone:** (970) 225-9564. **Commissioner:** Kurt Colicchio. **Director of Umpires:** Gary Weibert.

Regular Season: 38 games (June 4-July 15). **Playoff Format:** Second-place team plays best of three series against first-place team for league championship. **All-Star Game:** None. **Roster limit:** 23 active (college-eligible players only).

Participating teams: Fort Collins Foxes, Loveland Blue Jays, Windsor Beavers.

CENTRAL VALLEY COLLEGIATE LEAGUE

Mailing Address: P.O. Box 561, Fowler, CA 93625. **E-mail:** jcederquist@aol.com. **Website:** www.cvclbaseball.webs.com. **Twitter:** @CVCL1.

Year Founded: 2013. **President:** Jamie Cederquist. **Vice-President:** Jon Scott. **Regular Season:** 30 games. **2015 Opening Date:** June 2. **Closing Date:** July 26. **All-Star Game:** July 15, Kingsburg, Calif. **Roster Limit:** 35 (college-eligible players only).

BAKERSFIELD BRAVES

Mailing Address: PO Box 20760, Bakersfield, CA, 93390. **Website:** eteamz.com/bakersfieldbraves. **Field Manager:** Bobby Maitia.

CALIFORNIA EXPOS

Mailing Address: P.O. Box 561, Fowler, CA 93625. **E-mail:** exposcv@aol.com. **Website:** www.california-expos.webs.com. **Twitter:** @cvexpos. **Field Manager:** Thomas Raymundo.

CALIFORNIA PILOTS

Mailing Address: PO Box 561 Fowler, CA 93625. **E-mail:** valleystormbaseball@aol.com. **Website:** valleystormbaseball.webs.com. **Twitter:** @calistorm1. **Field Manager:** Kolton Carbal

LIGHTNING BASEBALL

Mailing Address: Visalia, CA. **E-mail:** d.dominguez@att.net. **Website:** Unavailable. **General Manager:** Dereck Dominguez. **Field Manager:** Dereck Dominguez.

MERCED VOLUNTEERS

Mailing Address: 472 Grogan Avenue Merced, CA 95341 **E-mail:** rollo@allprojanitorialservices.com **Field Manager:** Rollo Adams

SOUTH COUNTY VIPERS

Mailing Address: P.O. Box 144, Kingsburg, CA 93631. **E-mail:** j_scot25@hotmail.com. **Website:** www.cvipers.webs.com. **Twitter:** @SouthcountryV. **Field Manager:** Jon Scott.

COASTAL PLAIN LEAGUE

Mailing Address: 102 Hyannis Drive, Holly Springs, NC 27540. **Telephone:** (919) 852-1960. **Fax:** (919) 516-0852. **Email Address:** justins@coastalplain.com. **Website:** www.coastalplain.com.

Year Founded: 1997.

Chairman/CEO: Jerry Petitt. **President:** Pete Bock. **Commissioner:** Justin Sellers. **Director, On-Field Operations:** Jeff Bock.

Division Structure: East—Edenton, Fayetteville, Holly Springs, Morehead City, Peninsula, Petersburg, Wilmington, Wilson. West—Asheboro, Florence, Forest City, Gastonia, High Point-Thomaville, Lexington, Martinsville. **Regular Season:** 56 games (split schedule). **2015 Opening Date:** May 26. **Closing Date:** August 15. **All-Star Game:** July 13. **Playoff Format:** Three rounds of best of three series.

Roster Limit: 30 (college-eligible players only).

ASHEBORO COPPERHEADS

Mailing Address: PO Box 4006, Asheboro, NC 27204. **Telephone:** (336) 460-7018. **Fax:** (336) 629-2651. **E-Mail Address:** info@teamcopperhead.com. **Website:** www.teamcopperhead.com. **Owners:** Ronnie Pugh, Steve Pugh, Doug Pugh, Mike Pugh. **General Manager:** David Camp. **Head Coach:** Keith Ritsche (Winston-Salem State)..

EDENTON STEAMERS

Mailing Address: PO Box 86, Edenton, NC 27932. **Telephone:** (252) 482-4080. **Fax:** (252) 482-1717. **E-Mail Address:** edentonsteamers@hotmail.com. **Website:** www.edentonsteamers.com. **Owner:** Edenton Steamers Inc. **President:** Wallace Evans. **General Manager:** Tyler Russell. **Head Coach:** Bryan Hill (Chowan University).

FAYETTEVILLE SWAMPDOGS

Mailing Address: PO Box 64691, Fayetteville, NC 28306.**Telephone:** (910) 426-5900. **Fax:** (910) 426-3544. **E-Mail Address:** info@goswampdogs.com. **Website:** www.goswampdogs.com. **Owners:** Lew Handelsman. **General Manager:** Jeremy Aagard. **Head Coach:** Zach Brown

FLORENCE REDWOLVES

Mailing Address: PO Box 809, Florence, SC 29503. **Telephone:** (843) 629-0700. **Fax:** (843) 629-0703. **E-Mail Address:** barbara@florenceredwolves.com. **Website:** www.florenceredwolves.com. **Owners:** Kevin Barth, Donna Barth. **General Manager:** Barbara Osborne. Head Coach: Blake Maxwell.

FOREST CITY OWLS

Mailing Address: PO Box 1062, Forest City, NC 28043. **Telephone:** (828) 245-0000. **Fax:** (828) 245-6666. **E-Mail Address:** info@forestcitybaseball.com. **Website:** www.forestcitybaseball.com. **Owner/President:** Ken Silver. **Managing Partner:** Jesse Cole. **General Manager:** Kiva Fuller. **Head Coach:** JT Maguire (Wofford College).

GASTONIA GRIZZLIES

Mailing Address: PO Box 177, Gastonia, NC 28053. **Telephone:** (704) 866-8622. **Fax:** (704) 864-6122. **E-Mail Address:** jesse@gastoniagrizzlies.com. **Website:** www.gastoniagrizzlies.com. **Owner:** Jesse Cole. **Assistant**

General Manager: David McDonald. Head Coach: Evan Wise (Lenoir-Rhyne).

HIGH POINT-THOMASVILLE HI-TOMS

Mailing Address: PO Box 3035, Thomasville, NC 27361. Telephone: (336) 472-8667. Fax: (336) 472-7198. E-Mail Address: info@hitoms.com. Website: www.hitoms.com. Owner: Richard Holland. President: Greg Suire. General Manager: Brian Roundtree.

HOLLY SPRINGS SALAMANDERS

Mailing Address: PO Box 1208, Holly Springs, NC 27540. Telephone: 919-249-7322. Email Address: tommya@salamandersbaseball.com. Website: www.salamandersbaseball.com. Owner: Jerry Petitt and Pete Bock. General Manager: Tommy Atkinson. Head Coach: Andrew Ciencin.

LEXINGTON COUNTY BLOWFISH

Mailing Address: PO Box 2018, Lexington, SC. Telephone: (803) 254-3474. Fax: (803) 254-4482. E-Mail Address: info@blowfishbaseball.com. Website: www.blowfishbaseball.com. Owner: HWS Baseball V (Michael Savit, Bill Shanahan). General Manager: Kelly Evans Head Coach: Jonathan Johnson

MARTINSVILLE MUSTANGS

Mailing Address: PO Box 1112, Martinsville, VA 24114. Telephone: (276) 403-5250. Fax: (276) 403-5387. E-Mail Address: shea@martinsvillemustangs.com. Website: www.martinsvillemustangs.com. Owner: City of Martinsville. General Manager: Shea Maple. Head Coach: Sean West.

MOREHEAD CITY MARLINS

Mailing Address: 1921 Oglesby Road, Morehead City, NC 28557. Telephone: (252) 269-9767. Fax: (252) 727-9402. E-Mail Address: croth@mhcmarlins.com. Website: www.mhcmarlins.com. President: Buddy Bengel. General Manager: Catherine Roth. Head Coach: Jason Wood.

PENINSULA PILOTS

Mailing Address: PO Box 7376, Hampton, VA 23666. Telephone: (757) 245-2222. Fax: (757) 245-8030. E-Mail Address: jeffscott@peninsulapilots.com. Website: www.peninsulapilots.com. Owner: Henry Morgan. General Manager: Jeffrey Scott. Head Coach/Vice President: Hank Morgan.

PETERSBURG GENERALS

Mailing Address: 1981 Midway Ave, Petersburg, VA 23803. Telephone: (804) 722-0141. Fax: (804) 733-7370. E-Mail Address: rmassenburg@petersburg-va.org. Website: www.petersburggenerals.com. Owner: City of Petersburg. General Manager: Ryan Massenburg. Head Coach: Matt Laney (Lander).

WILMINGTON SHARKS

Mailing Address: PO Box 15233, Wilmington, NC 28412. Telephone: (910) 343-5261. Fax: (910) 343-8932. E-Mail Address: info@wilmingtonsharks.com. Website: www.wilmingtonsharks.com. Owners: Smith

Family Baseball Wilmington, LLC. General Manager: Pat Hutchins. Head Coach: Parker Bangs.

WILSON TOBS

Mailing Address: PO Box 633, Wilson, NC 27894. Telephone: (252) 291-8627. Fax: (252) 291-1224. E-Mail Address: wilsontobs@gmail.com. Website: www.wilsontobs.com. Owner: Richard Holland. President: Greg Suire. General Manager: Thomas Webb. Head Coach: Bryant Gaines (North Carolina).

FLORIDA COLLEGIATE SUMMER LEAGUE

Mailing Address: 2410 N Rio Grande Ave, Orlando, FL 32804. Telephone: (321) 206-9174. Fax: (407) 574-7926. E-Mail Address: info@floridaleague.com. Website: www.floridaleague.com.

Year Founded: 2004.
President: Rob Sitz. Vice President: Stefano Foggi. League Operations Director: Phil Chinnery.
Regular Season: 45 games. 2015 Opening Date: June 4. Closing Date: August 9. All-Star Game: July 7. Playoff Format: Five teams qualify; No. 4 and No. 5 seeds meet in one-game playoff. Remaining four teams play best of three series. Winners play one game for league championship.
Roster Limit: 28 (college-eligible players only).

ALTAMONTE SPRINGS BOOM

Operated by the league office. Email Address: altamonte@floridaleague.com. Head Coach: Kevin Davidson. General Manager: Dave Nathanson

DELAND SUNS

Operated by the league office. E-Mail Address: delandsuns@floridaleague.com. Head Coach: Rick Hall. General Manager: Theresa Brooks

LEESBURG LIGHTNING

Mailing Address: 318 South 2nd St, Leesburg, FL 34748. Telephone: (352) 728-9885. E-Mail Address: leesburglightning@floridaleague.com. Head Coach: Rich Billings. General Manager: Unavailable.

SANFORD RIVER RATS

Operated by the league office. E-Mail Address: sanfordriverrats@floridaleague.com. Head Coach: Ken Kelly. General Manager: Ken Kelly. Assistant GM: Phil Chinnery.

WINTER GARDEN SQUEEZE

Operated by the league office. Email Address: info@floridaleague.com. Head Coach: Ruben Felix. General Manager: Adam Bates.

WINTER PARK DIAMOND DAWGS

Operated by the league office. E-Mail Address: winterparkdiamonddawgs@floridaleague.com. Head Coach: Scotty Makarewicz. General Manager: Unavailable.

FUTURES COLLEGIATE LEAGUE OF NEW ENGLAND

Mailing Address: 46 Chestnut Hill Rd, Chelmsford, MA 01824. **Telephone:** (617) 593-2112. **E-Mail Address:** futuresleague@yahoo.com. **Website:** www.thefutures-league.com.

Year Founded: 2010.

Commissioner: Chris Hall.

Teams (Contact): Bristol Blues (Rick Muntean: rmuntean717@gmail.com): Brockton Rox (Mike Canina: mcanina@brocktonrox.com); Martha's Vineyard Sharks (Nelson Giannakopoulos: nelson.giannakopoulos@mvsharks.com); Nashua Silver Knights (Ronnie Wallace: ronnie@nashuasilverknights.com); North Shore Navigators (Bill Terlecky: navigatorsgm@gmail.com,); Pittsfield Suns (Kevin McGuire: kevin@pittsfieldsuns.com); Seacoast Mavericks (Dave Hoyt, owner: dave@usamavs.com, or Jarrett Daniel, general manager: jdaniel@seacoastmavericks.com); Torrington Titans (Alan Seraita: adshalls@aol.com); Wachusett Dirt Dawgs (John Morrison: lefty@dirtdawgsball.com); Worcester Bravehearts (Dave Peterson: dave@worcesterbravehearts.com).

Regular Season: 56 games; 28 home, 28 away.

Playoff Format: Eight teams qualify. First two rounds are single games, followed by a best of three series to determine league champion.

Roster Limit: 30. Half must be from New England or play collegiately at a New England college.

GREAT LAKES SUMMER COLLEGIATE LEAGUE

Mailing Address: 133 W Winter St, Delaware, OH 43015. **Telephone:** (740) 368-3527. **Fax:** (740) 368-3999. **Website:** www.greatlakesleague.org.

Year Founded: 1986.

President/Commissioner: Deron Brown.

Regular Season: 40 games. **Playoff Format:** Top six teams meet in playoffs.

Roster Limit: 30 (college-eligible players only).

Teams: Cincinnati Steam, Grand Lake Mariners, Hamilton Joes, Lake Erie Monarchs, Xenia Scouts, Licking County Setllers, Lima Locos, Southern Ohio Copperheads, Lexington Hustlers, Galion Graders, Lorain County Ironmen, North Ohio Baseball Club.

JAYHAWK LEAGUE

Mailing Address: 865 Fabrique, Wichita, KS 67218. **Telephone:** (316) 942-6333. **Fax:** (316) 942-2009. **Website:** www.jayhawkbaseballleague.org. **Year Founded:** 1976.

Commissioner: Phil Stephenson. **President:** J.D. Schneider. **Vice President:** Frank Leo. **Public Relations/Statistician:** Gary Karr. **Secretary:** Cheryl Kastner.

Regular Season: 36 games. **Playoff Format:** Top three teams qualify for National Baseball Congress World Series. **Roster Limit:** Unlimited until July 1; 28 at July 1

Teams: Bethany Bulls, Derby Twins, Dodge City A's, El Dorado Broncos, Hays Larks, Haysville Aviators, Liberal Bee Jays, Wellington Heat.

MIDWEST COLLEGIATE LEAGUE

Mailing Address: PO Box 172, Flossmoor, IL 60422. **E-Mail Address:** commissioner@midwestcollegiateleague.com. **Website:** www.midwestcollegiateleague.com.

Year Founded: 2010.

President/Commissioner: Don Popravak.

Regular Season: 42 games. **2015 Opening Date:** May 27. **Closing Date:** Aug. 9. **All-Star Game:** July 8. **Playoff**

Format: Top four teams meet in best of three series. Winners meet in best of three championship series.

Roster Limit: 28.

CHICAGO SOUTHLAND VIKINGS

Mailing Address: PO Box 172, Flossmoor, IL 60422. **Telephone:** (312) 420-1268. **E-Mail Address:** don@southlandvidings.com. **Website:** www.southlandvikings.com. **General Manager:** Don Popravak. **Head Coach:** Chris Cunningham.

DUPAGE COUNTY HOUNDS

Mailing Address: 1450 S New Wilke Rd, Suite 205, Arlington Heights, IL 60005.. **Telephone:** (815) 704-3839. **E-Mail Address:** tickets@dupagehounds.com. **Website:** www.DuPageHounds.com. **General Managers:** Joe Stefani, Josh VanSwol. **Head Coach:** Sean Osborne.

LEXINGTON SNIPES

Mailing Address: 216 Prairie Ridge Drive, Lexington, IL 61753. **Telephone:** (309) 287-1668. **E-Mail Address:** billyd_73@yahoo.com. **Website:** www.lexingtonsnipes.com. **General Manager/Head Coach:** Billy Dubois.

MICHIGAN CITY LAKERS

Mailing Address: 215 Douglas Ave Michigan City, IN 46360. **Telephone:** 219-898-0191. **E-Mail Address:** tim@voodooride.com. **Website:** www.citylakersbaseball.org **General Manager/Head Coach:** Tim "TJ" Jahnz.

NORTHWEST INDIANA OILMEN

Mailing Address: 1500 119th Street, Whiting, IN 46394. **Telephone:** (219) 659-1000. **E-Mail Address:** info@nwioilmen.com. **Website:** www.nwioilmen.com. **General Manager:** Chris Doherty. **Head Coach:** Adam Enright.

JOLIET ADMIRALS

Mailing Address: 1450 S New Wilke Rd, Suite 205, Arlington Heights, IL 60005. **Telephone:** 815-704-3839. **Email Address:** joe@dupagehounds.com. **Website:** Unavailable. **General Manager:** Joe Stefani. **Head Coach:** Tom Barry.

M.I.N.K. LEAGUE

(Missouri, Iowa, Nebraska, Kansas)

Mailing Address: PO Box 601, Nevada, MO 64772. **Telephone:** (417) 667-6159. **Fax:** (417) 667-4210. **E-mail Address:** jpost@morrisonpost.com. **Website:** www.minkleaguebaseball.com.

Year Founded: 1995.

Commissioner: Bob Steinkamp. **President:** Jeff Post. **Vice President:** Jud Kindle. **Secretary:** Edwina Rains.

Regular Season: 44 games. **Playoff Format:** Division winners play best of three series for league championship. Top team in each division also qualifies for National Baseball Congress World Series. **All-Star Game:** July 7 at Phil Welch Stadium.

Roster Limit: 30.

CHILLICOTHE MUDCATS

Mailing Address: 426 E Jackson, Chillicothe, MO 64601. **Telephone:** (660) 247-1504. **Fax:** (660) 646-6933.

E-Mail Address: doughty@greenhills.net. Website: www.chillicothemudcats.com. General Manager: Doug Doughty. Head Coach: Eric Peterson.

CLARINDA A'S

Mailing Address: 225 East Lincoln, Clarinda, IA 51632. Telephone: (712) 542-4272. E-Mail Address: m.everly@mchsi.com. Website: www.clarindaiowa-as-baseball.org. General Manager: Merle Eberly. Head Coach: Ryan Eberly.

JOPLIN OUTLAWS

Mailing Address: 5860 North Pearl, Joplin, MO 64801. Telephone: (417) 825-4218. E-Mail Address: merains@mchsi.com. Website: www.joplinoutlaws.com. President/General Manager: Mark Rains. Head Coach: Rob Vessell.

NEVADA GRIFFONS

Mailing Address: PO Box 601, Nevada, MO 64772. Telephone: (417) 667-6159. E-Mail Address: jpost@morrisonpost.com. Website: www.nevadagriffons.org. President: Bob Hawks. General Manager: Jeff Post. Head Coach: Ryan Mansfield.

OMAHA DIAMOND SPIRIT

Mailing Address: 4618 N 135th Ave, Omaha, NE 68164. Telephone: (402) 679-0206. E-Mail Address: arden@omahadiamondspirit.com. Website: www.omahadiamondspirit.com. General Manager: Arden Rakosky. Head Coach: Adam Steyer.

OZARK GENERALS

Mailing Address: 1336 W Farm Road 182, Springfield, MO 65810. Telephone: (417) 832-8830. Fax: (417) 877-4625. E-Mail Address:rda160@yahoo.com. Website: www.generalsbaseballclub.com. General Manager/Head Coach: Rusty Aton.

ST. JOSEPH MUSTANGS

Mailing Address: 2600 SW Parkway, St. Joseph, MO 64503. Telephone: (816) 279-7856. Fax: (816) 749-4082. E-Mail Address:rmuntean717@gmail.com. Website: www.stjoemustangs.com. President: Dan Gerson. General Manager: Rick Muntean. Manager/Director, Player Personnel: Matt Johnson.

SEDALIA BOMBERS

Mailing Address: 2205 S Grand, Sedalia, MO 65301. Telephone: (660) 287-4722. E-Mail Address: jkindle@knobnoster.k12.mo.us. Website: www.sedaliabombers.com. President/General Manager/Head Coach: Jud Kindle. Vice President: Ross Dey.

NEW ENGLAND COLLEGIATE LEAGUE

Mailing Address: 122 Mass Moca Way, North Adams, MA 01247. Telephone: (413) 652-1031. Fax: (413) 473-0012. E-Mail Address: smcgrath@necbl.com. Website: www.necbl.com.
Year founded: 1993.
President: John DeRosa. Commissioner: Sean McGrath. Deputy Commissioner: Gregg Hunt. Secretary: Max Pinto. Treasurer: Brigid Schaffer.

Regular Season: 42 games. 2015 Opening Date: June 4. Closing Date: Aug. 11. All-Star Game: July 19 in Sanford, ME.
Roster Limit: 30 (college-eligible players only).

DANBURY WESTERNERS

Mailing Address: 9 Pleasant View, New Milford, CT 06776. Telephone: (203) 502-9167. E-Mail Address: jspitser@msn.com. Website: www.danburywesterners.com. President: Paul Schaffer. General Manager: Jon Pitser. Field Manager: Ryan Smythe.

VALLEY BLUE SOX

Mailing Address: 100 Congress St, Springfield, MA 01104. Telephone: 860-305-1684. E-Mail Address: hunter@valleybluesox.com. Website: www.valleybluesox.com. President: Clark Eckhoff. General Manager: Hunter Golden. Field Manager: Unavailable.

KEENE SWAMP BATS

Mailing Address: PO Box 160, Keene, NH 13431. Telephone: (603) 357-5464. Fax: (603) 357-5090. E-Mail Address: kwatterson@ne.rr.com. Website: www.swampbats.com. President: Kevin Watterson. VP/General Manager: Dan Moylan.

LACONIA MUSKRATS

Mailing Address: 134 Stevens Rd, Lebanon, NH 03766. Telephone: (864) 380-2873. E-Mail Address: noah@laconiamuskrats.com. Website: www.laconiamuskrats.com. President: Jonathan Crane. General Manager: Noah Crane. Field Manager: Nick Cenatiempo.

MYSTIC SCHOONERS

Mailing Address: PO Box 432, Mystic, CT 06355. Telephone: (860) 608-3287. E-Mail Address: dlong@mysticbaseball.org. Website: www.mysticbaseball.org. Executive Director: Don Benoit. General Manager: Dennis Long. Field Manager: Phil Orbe.

NEW BEDFORD BAY SOX

Mailing Address: 427 John St, New Bedford, MA 02740. Telephone: 802-578-9935. E-Mail Address: poconnor@nbbaysox.com. Website: www.nbbaysox.com. President: Pat O'Connor. General Manager: Rick Avila. Field Manager: TBD

NEWPORT GULLS

Mailing Address: PO Box 777, Newport, RI 02840. Telephone: (401) 845-6832. E-Mail Address: gm@newportgulls.com. Website: www.newportgulls.com. President/General Manager: Chuck Paiva. Field Manager: Mike Coombs.

NORTH ADAMS STEEPLECATS

Mailing Address: PO Box 540, North Adams, MA 01247. Telephone: 615-925-9577. E-Mail Address: nasteeplecatsgm@gmail.com. Website: www.steeplecats.com. President: Dan Bosley. General Manager: Jonah Bayliss. Field Manager: TBD.

CEAN STATE WAVES

Mailing Address: 1174 Kingstown Rd, Wakefield, RI 02879. **Telephone:** (401) 360-2977. **E-Mail Address:** matt@oceanstatewaves.com. **Website:** www. oceanstatewaves.com. **President:** Jeff Sweenor. **General Manager:** Matt Finlayson. **Field Manager:** Eric Cirella.

PLYMOUTH PILGRIMS

Mailing Address: 134 Court Street, Plymouth, MA 02360. **Telephone:** (508) 566-4192. **Fax:** (508) 566-4192. **E-Mail Address:** chris@pilgrimsbaseball.com.
Website: www.pilgrimsbaseball.com. **President:** Dave Dittmann. **General Manager:** Bob Kruse. **Field Manager:** Greg Zackrison.

SANFORD MAINERS

Mailing Address: PO Box 26, 4 Washington St, Sanford, ME 04073. **Telephone:** (207) 324-0010. **Fax:** (207) 324-2227. **E-Mail Address:** jwebb@nicholswebb. com. **Website:** www.sanfordmainers.com. **CEO:** Steve Cabana. **General Manager:** John Webb. **Field Manager:** Aaron Izaryk.

VERMONT MOUNTAINEERS

Mailing Address: PO Box 57, East Montpelier, VT 05651. **Telephone:** (802) 223-5224. **E-Mail Address:** gmvtm@comcast.net. **Website:** www.thevermontmountaineers.com. **General Manager:** Brian Gallagher. **Field Manager:** Joe Brown.

NEW YORK COLLEGIATE BASEBALL LEAGUE

Mailing Address: 398 East Dyke St. Wellsville, NY 14895. **Telephone:** (585) 455-2345 **E-Mail Address:** jdennste@gmail.com. **Website:** www.nycbl.com.
Year founded: 1978.
President: Steve Pindar. **Commissioner:** Jake Dennstedt. **Vice President:** Cal Kern. **Treasurer:** Dan Russo. **Secretary:** Paul Welker. **Franchise Development:** Cal Kern.
Franchises: Cortland Crush, Genesee Rapids, Geneva Red Wings, Geneva Twins, Hornell Dodgers, Niagara Power, Olean Oilers, Oneonta Outlaws, Rochester Ridgemen, Sherrill Silversmiths, Syracuse Junior Chiefs, Syracuse Salt Cats, Wellsville Nitros.
2015 Opening Date: May 30th. **Season Ends:** July 25. **All-Star Game/Scout Day:** July 16 at Damaschke Field, Oneonta, NY. **Playoff Format:** Eight teams qualify and play three rounds of best of three series.
Roster Limit: Unlimited (college-eligible players only).

CORTLAND CRUSH

Mailing Address: 2745 Summer Ridge Rd, LaFayette, NY 13084. **Telephone:** 315-391-8167. **Email Address:** wmmac4@aol.com. **Website:** www.cortlandcrush. com. **President:** Bill McConnell. **Field Manager:** Bill McConnell.

GENESEE RAPIDS

Mailing Address: 9726 Rt. 19 Houghton, NY 14474. **Telephone:** 716-969-0688. **Email Address:** rkerr@ frontiernet.net. **President:** Ralph Kerr. **Field Manager:** Unavailable.

GENEVA RED WINGS

Mailing Address: PO BOX 17624, Rochester, NY 14617. **Telephone:** 585-342-5750. **Fax:** 585-342-5155. **E-Mail Address:** gwings@rochester.rr.com. **Website:** genevaredwings.com. **President:** David Herbst. **Executive GM:** John Oughterson.

GENEVA TWINS

Mailing Address: PO BOX 17624, Rochester, NY 14617. **Telephone:** 585-342-5750. **Fax:** 585-342-5155. **E-Mail Address:** gwings@rochester.rr.com. **Website:** genevaredwings.com. **President:** David Herbst. **Executive GM:** John Oughterson.

HORNELL DODGERS

Mailing Address: PO Box 235, Hornell, NY 14843. **Telephone:** (607) 661-4173. **Fax:** (607) 661-4173. **E-Mail Address:** gm@hornelldodgers.com. **Website:** www.hornelldodgers.com. **General Manager:** Paul Welker. **Field Manager:** Unavailable.

NIAGARA POWER

Mailing Address: 2905 Staley Road, Grand Island, NY 14072. **Telephone:** (716) 773-1748. **Fax:** (716) 773-1748. **E-Mail Address:** ckern@fca.org **Website:** www. niagarapower.org. **General Manager:** Cal Kern. **Field Manager:** Josh Rebandt.

OLEAN OILERS

Mailing Address: 126 N 10th, Olean, NY 14760. **Telephone:** 716-378-0641. **E-Mail Addresses:** baseball@ oleanoilers.com, Bellr41@yahoo.com. **General Manager:** Bobby Bell. **Field Manager:** Bobby Bell.

ONEONTA OUTLAWS

Mailing Address: PO Box 608, Oneonta, NY 13820. **Telephone:** (607) 432-6326. **Fax:** (607) 432-1965. **E-Mail Address:** stevepindar@oneontaoutlaws.com. **Website:** www.oneontaoutlaws.com. **General Manager:** Steve Pindar. **Field Manager:** Joe Hughes.

ROCHESTER RIDGEMEN

Mailing Address: 651 Taylor Dr, Xenia, OH 45385. **Telephone:** (937) 352-1225. **E-Mail Addresses:** baseball@athletesinaction.org, chris.rainwater@athletesinaction.org. **Website:** www.aiabaseball.org. **General Manager:** Chris Rainwater. **Field Manager:** Unavailable.

SHERRILL SILVERSMITHS

Mailing Address: PO Box 111, Sherrill, NY 13440. **Telephone:** (315) 264-4334. **E-Mail Address:** sherrillsilversmiths@hotmail.com. **Website:** www.leaguelineup.com/silversmiths. **General Manager:** Matthew Rafte. **Field Manager:** Unavailable.

SYRACUSE JR CHIEFS

Mailing Address: 227 Walters Dr, Liverpool, NY 13088. **Telephone:** (315) 263-3777. **E-Mail Address:** perfect. practice@yahoo.com. **General Manager:** Mike DiPaulo. **Field Manager:** Unavailable.

SYRACUSE SALT CATS

Mailing Address: 208 Lakeland Ave, Syracuse, NY 13209. **Telephone:** (315) 727-9220. **Fax:** (315) 488-1750. **E-Mail Address:** mmarti6044@yahoo.com. **Website:** www.leaguelineup.com/saltcats. **General Manager:** Manny Martinez. **Field Manager:** Mike Martinez.

WELLSVILLE NITROS

Mailing Address: 2848 O'Donnell Rd, Wellsville, NY 14895. **Telephone:** 585-596-9523. **Fax:** 585-593-5260. **E-Mail Address:** ackley8122@roadrunner.com. **Website:** www.nitros baseball.com. **General Manager:** Steven J. Ackley. **Assistant Manager:** Shelley Butler.

NORTHWOODS LEAGUE

Office Address: 2900 4th St SW, Rochester, MN 55902. **Telephone:** (507) 536-4579. **Fax:** (507) 536-4597. **E-Mail Address:** info@northwoodsleague.com. **Website:** www.northwoodsleague.com.

Year Founded: 1994.

President: Dick Radatz Jr. **Vice President, Business Development:** Matt Bomberg. **Vice President, Operations:** Glen Showalter. **Vice President, Technology Development:** Gary Hoover

Division Structure: North—Alexandria, Duluth, Eau Claire, Mankato, Rochester, St. Cloud, Thunder Bay, Waterloo, Willmar. South—Battle Creek, Green Bay, Kalamazoo, Kenosha, La Crosse, Lakeshore, Madison, Wisconsin, Wisconsin Rapids.

Regular Season: 70 games (split schedule).

2015 Opening Date: May 26. **Closing Date:** August 9. **All-Star Game:** July 21at Wisconsin Rapids. **Playoff Format:** First-half and second-half division winners meet in best of three series. Winners meet in best of three series for league championship.

Roster Limit: 30 (college-eligible players only).

ALEXANDRIA BLUE ANCHORS

Mailing Address: PO Box 517, Alexandria, MN 56308. **Telephone:** 320-492-9025. **E-Mail Address:** info@northwoodsleague.com. **Website:** www.blueanchors.com. **General Manager:** Scott Allen. **Field Manager:** Al Newman. **Field:** Knute Nelson Memorial Stadium.

BATTLE CREEK BOMBERS

Mailing Address: 189 Bridge Street, Battle Creek, MI 49017. **Telephone:** (269) 962-0735. **Fax:** (269) 962-0741. **Email Address:** info@battlecreekbombers.com. **Website:** www.battlecreekbombers.com. **General Manager:** Tony Iovieno. **Field Manager:** Robbie Robinson **Field:** C.O. Brown Stadium.

DULUTH HUSKIES

Mailing Address: PO Box 16231, Duluth, MN 55816. **Telephone:** (218) 786-9909. **Fax:** (218) 786-9001. **E-Mail Address:** huskies@duluthhuskies.com. **Website:** www.duluthhuskies.com. **Owners:** Andy Karon, Michael Rosenzweig. **General Manager:** Craig Smith. **Field Manager:** Daniel Hersey. **Field:** Wade Stadium.

EAU CLAIRE EXPRESS

Mailing Address: 108 E Grand Ave, Eau Claire, WI 54701. **Telephone:** (715) 839-7788. **Fax:** (715) 839-7676. **E-Mail Address:** info@eauclaireexpress.com. **Website:** www.eauclaireexpress.com. **Owner:** Bill Rowlett. **General Manager:** Andy Neborak. **Director of Operations/Field Manager:** Dale Varsho. **Field:** Carson Park.

GREEN BAY BULLFROGS

Mailing Address: 1306 Main Street, Green Bay, WI 54302. **Telephone:** (920) 497-7225. **Fax:** (920) 437-3551. **Email Address:** info@greenbaybullfrogs.com. **Website:** www.greenbaybullfrogs.com. **General Manager:** Liz Kern.**Field Manager:** Darrell Handelsman. **Field:** Joannes Stadium.

KALAMAZOO GROWLERS

Mailing Address: 251 Mills St, Kalamazoo, MI 49048. **Telephone:** 555-555-1212. **Website:** www.kzoobaseball.com. **General Manager:** Brian Colopy. **Field Manager:** Travis Wade. **Field:** Homer Stryker Field.

KENOSHA KINGFISH

Mailing Address: 7817 Sheridan Rd, Kenosha, WI 53143. **Telephone:** 262-653-0900. **Website:** www.kingfishbaseball.com. **General Manager:** Jake McGhee. **Field Manager:** Duffy Dyer. **Field:** Simmons Field.

LA CROSSE LOGGERS

Mailing Address: 1223 Caledonia St, La Crosse, WI 54603. **Telephone:** (608) 796-9553. **Fax:** (608) 796-9032. **E-Mail Address:** info@lacrosseloggers.com. **Website:** www.lacrosseloggers.com. **Owner:** Dan Kapanke. **General Manager:** Chris Goodell. **Assistant General Manager:** Ben Kapanke. **Field Manager:** Bill Sandillo. **Field:** Copeland Park.

LAKESHORE CHINOOKS

Mailing Address: 995 Badger Circle, Grafton, WI 53024. **Telephone:** (262) 618-4659. **Fax:** (262) 618-4362. **E-Mail Address:** info@lakeshorechinooks.com. **Website:** www.lakeshorechinooks.com. **Owner:** Jim Kacmarcik. **General Manager:** Dean Rennicke. **Assistant GM:** Chad Bauer. **Field Manager:** Eddy Morgan. **Field:** Kapco Park.

MADISON MALLARDS

Mailing Address: 2920 N Sherman Ave, Madison, WI 53704. **Telephone:** (608) 246-4277. **Fax:** (608) 246-4163. **E-Mail Address:** conor@mallardsbaseball.com. **Website:** www.mallardsbaseball.com. **Owner:** Steve Schmitt. **President:** Vern Stenman. **General Manager:** Tyler Isham. **Field Manager:** Donnie Scott. **Field:** Warner Park.

MANKATO MOONDOGS

Mailing Address: 1221 Caledonia Street, Mankato, MN 56001. **Telephone:** (507) 625-7047. **Fax:** (507) 625-7059. **E-Mail Address:** office@mankatomoondogs.com. **Website:** www.mankatomoondogs.com. **Owner:** Mark Ogren. **Vice President:** Kyle Mrozek. **General Manager:** Greg Weis. **Field Manager:** Mike Orchard. **Field:** Franklin Rogers Park.

ROCHESTER HONKERS

Mailing Address: 307 E Center St, Rochester, MN 55904. **Telephone:** (507) 289-1170. **Fax:** (507) 289-1866. **E-Mail Address:** honkers@rochesterhonkers.com. **Website:** www.rochesterhonkers.com. **Owner/**

General Manager: Dan Litzinger. Field Manager: Trevor Hairgrove. Field: Mayo Field.

ST. CLOUD ROX

Mailing Address: 5001 8th St N, St. **Cloud, MN 56303. Telephone:** (320) 240-9798. **Fax:** (320) 255-5228. **E-Mail Address:** info@stcloudrox.com. **Website:** www. stcloudrox.com. **President:** Gary Posch. **Vice President:** Scott Schreiner. **Field Manager:** Augie Rodriguez. **Field:** Joe Faber Field.

THUNDER BAY BORDER CATS

Mailing Address: PO Box 29105, Thunder Bay, ON P7B 6P9. **Telephone:** (807) 766-2287. **Fax:** (807) 345-8299. **E-Mail Address:** baseball@tbaytel.net. **Website:** www. bordercatsbaseball.com. **President/General Manager:** Brad Jorgenson. **Field Manager:** Danny Benedetti. **Field:** Port Arthur Stadium.

WATERLOO BUCKS

Mailing Address: PO Box 4124, Waterloo, IA 50704. **Telephone:** (319) 232-0500. **Fax:** (319) 232-0700. **E-Mail Address:** waterloobucks@waterloobucks.com. **Website:** www.waterloobucks.com. **General Manager:** Dan Corbin. **Field Manager:** Tony Manville. **Field:** Riverfront Stadium.

WILLMAR STINGERS

Mailing Address: PO Box 201, Willmar, MN, 56201. **Telephone:** (320) 222-2010. **E-Mail Address:** ryan@ willmarstingers.com. **Website:** www.willmarstingers.com. **Owners:** Marc Jerzak, Ryan Voz. **General Manager:** Nick McCallum. **Field Manager:** Drew Saberhagen. **Field:** Bill Tauton Stadium.

WISCONSIN RAPIDS RAFTERS

Mailing Address: 521 Lincoln St, Wisconsin Rapids, WI 54494. **Telephone:** (715) 424-5400. **E-Mail Address:** info@raftersbaseball.com. **Website:** www.raftersbaseball.com. **Owner/President:** Vern Stenman. **General Manager:** John Fanta. **Field Manager:** Craigh Noto. **Field:** Witter Field.

WISCONSIN WOODCHUCKS

Mailing Address: PO Box 6157, Wausau, WI 54402. **Telephone:** (715) 845-5055. **Fax:** (715) 845-5015. **E-Mail Address:** info@woodchucks.com. **Website:** www. woodchucks.com. **Owner:** Mark Macdonald. **General Manager:** Ryan Treu. **Field:** Athletic Park.

PACIFIC INTERNATIONAL LEAGUE

Mailing Address: 4400 26th Ave W, Seattle, WA 98199. **Telephone:** (206) 623-8844. **Fax:** (206) 623-8361. **E-Mail Address:** spotter@potterprinting.com. **Website:** www. pacificinternationalleague.com.

Year Founded: 1992.

President: Barry Aden. **Vice President:** Martin Lawrence. **Commissioner:** Brian Gooch. **Secretary:** Steve Potter. **Treasurer:** Mark Dow. **Member Clubs:** Northwest Honkers, Everett Merchants, Kamloops Sundevils, Seattle Studs, Trail Orioles (BC), Burnaby Collegiate Bulldogs (BC), Highline Bears, Snoqualmie Valley Hurricanes.

Regular Season: 20 league games. **2015 Opening Date:** Unavailable. **Playoff Format:** Top team is invited

to National Baseball Congress World Series. **Roster Limit:** 30; 25 eligible for games (players must be at least 18 years old).

PERFECT GAME COLLEGIATE BASEBALL LEAGUE

Mailing Address: 8 Michaels Lane, Old Brookville, NY 11545. **Telephone:** (516) 521-0206. **Fax:** (516) 801-0818. **E-Mail Address:** valkun@aol.com. **Website:** www.pgcbl. org. **Year Founded:** 2010.

President: Jeffrey Kunion. **Assistant to the President:** Justin Mattingly. **Executive Committee:** Tom Hickey (Cooperstown Hawkeyes), Bob Ohmann (Newark Pilots), Paul Samulski (Albany Dutchmen).

Teams: East—Albany Dutchmen, Amsterdam Mohawks, Glens Falls Dragons, Mohawk Valley DiamondDawgs, Saugerties Stallions. West—Adirondack Trail Blazers, Elmira Pioneers, Newark Pilots, Utica Brewers, Victor.

Regular Season: 50. **2015 Opening Date:** June 2. **Closing Date:** July 30. **All-Star Game:** July 20. **Playoff Format:** Top three teams in each division qualify; second- and third-place finishers have one-game playoff; next two series are best of three. **Roster Limit:** 30 (maximum of two graduated high school players per team).

PROSPECT LEAGUE

Mailing Address: 59 N. Paint St., Chillicothe, OH 45601. **Telephone:** (815) 980-9045. **Fax:** (480) 247-5068. **E-Mail Address:** commissioner@prospectleague.com. **Website:** www.prospectleague.com.

Year Founded: 1963 as Central Illinois Collegiate League; known as Prospect League since 2009.

Commissioner: Bryan Wickline.

Regular Season: 60 games. **2015 Opening Date:** May 27. **Closing Date:** August 6. **Championship Series:** Aug 11-14. **Roster Limit:** 28.

BUTLER BLUESOX

Mailing Address: 6 West Diamond Street, Butler, PA 16001. **Telephone:** (724) 282-2222 or (724) 256-9994. **Fax:** (724) 282-6565. **E-Mail Address:** frontoffice@butlerbluesox.net. **Website:** www.butlerbluesox.com. **League President:** Wink Robinson. **General Manager:** Matt Cunningham. **Field Manager:** Jason Radwan.

CHAMPION CITY KINGS

Mailing Address: 1301 Mitchell Blvd., Springfield, OH 45503. **Telephone:** (937) 342-0320. **Fax:** (937) 342-0320. **E-Mail Address:** rwhite@championcitykings. com. **Website:** www.championcitykings.com. **League Director:** Ronald Heineman. **Field Manager:** Chris Perkovich.

CHILLICOTHE PAINTS

Mailing Address: 59 North Paint Street, Chillicothe, OH 45601. **Telephone:** (740) 773-8326. **Fax:** (740) 773-8338. **E-Mail Address:** paints@bright.net. **Website:** www. chillicothepaints.com. **League Director:** Shirley Bandy. **Field Manager:** Greg Cypret.

DANVILLE DANS

Mailing Address: 4 Maywood, Danville, IL 61832. **Telephone:** (217) 918-3401. **Fax:** (217) 446-9995. **E-Mail Address:** danvilledans@comcast.net. **Website:** www.

danvilledans.com. **League Director:** Jeanie Cooke. **Co-General Managers:** Jeanie Cooke, Rick Kurth. **Field Manager:** Eric Coleman.

HANNIBAL CAVEMEN

Mailing Address: 403 Warren Barrett Drive, Hannibal, MO 63401. **Telephone:** (573) 221-1010. **Fax:** (573) 221-5269. **E-Mail Address:** greg@hannibalbaseball.com. **Website:** www.hannibalcavemen.com. **President:** Robert Hemond. **League Director/General Manager:** Greg McVey. **Field Manager:** Greg McVey.

JAMESTOWN JAMMERS

Mailing Address: 485 E. Falconer St., Jamestown, NY 17401. **Telephone:** (414) 224-9283). **Fax:** (414) 224-9290. **E-Mail Address:** info@jamestownbaseball.com. **Website:** www.jamestownbaseball.com. **League Director/General Manager:** Dan Kuenzi. **Field Manager:** TBA

KOKOMO JACKRABBITS

Mailing Address: 319 S Union St, Kokomo, IN 46901. **Telephone:** (800) 525-0133. **Fax:** (414) 224-9290. **E-Mail Address:** no-reply@mkesports.com. **Website:** www.kokomojackrabbits.com. **League Director:** Mike Zimmerman. **Field Manager:** Greg Van Horn.

QUINCY GEMS

Mailing Address: 1400 N. 30th St., Suite 1, Quincy, IL 62301. **Telephone:** (217) 214-7436. **Fax:** (217) 214-7436. **E-Mail Address:** quincygems@yahoo.com. **Website:** www.quincygems.com. **League Director:** Terry Martin. **General Manager:** Chris Martin. **Field Manager:** Chris Martin.

RICHMOND RIVERRATS

Mailing Address: 201 NW 13th Street, Richmond, IN 47374. **Telephone:** (765) 935-7287. **Fax:** (765) 935-7529. **E-Mail Address:** dbeaman@richmondriverrats.com. **Website:** www.richmondriverrats.com. **League Director:** Duke Ward. **General Manager:** Deanna Beaman. **Field Manager:** Tyler Lairson.

SPRINGFIELD SLIDERS

Mailing Address: 1415 North Grand Avenue East, Suite B, Springfield, IL 62702. **Telephone:** (217) 679-3511. **Fax:** (217) 679-3512. **E-Mail Address:** slidersfun@springfieldsliders.com. **Website:** www.springfieldsliders.com. **League Director:** Shane Martin. **General Manager:** Bill Hill. **Field Manager:** Casey Dill.

TERRE HAUTE REX

Mailing Address: 111 North 3rd St, Terre Haute, IN 47807. **Telephone:** (812) 478-3817. **Fax:** (812) 232-5353. **E-mail Address:** frontoffice@rexbaseball.com. **Website:** www.rexbaseball.com. **League Director/General Manager:** Bruce Rosselli. **Field Manager:** Bobby Segal.

WEST VIRGINIA MINERS

Mailing Address: 476 Ragland Road, Suite 2, Beckley, WV 25801. **Telephone:** (304) 252-7233. **Fax:** (304) 253-1998. **E-mail Address:** wvminers@wvminersbaseball.com. **Website:** www.wvminersbaseball.com. **President:** Doug Epling. **League Director/General Manager:** Tim Epling. **Field Manager:** Tim Epling.

SOUTHERN COLLEGIATE BASEBALL LEAGUE

Mailing Address: 9723 Northcross Center Court, Huntersville, NC 28078. **Telephone:** (704) 635-7126. **Cell:** (704) 621-0940. **Fax:** (704) 234-8448. **E-Mail Address:** SCBLCommissioner@aol.com. **Website:** www.scbl.org. **Year Founded:** 1999.
Commissioner: Bill Capps. **President:** Jeff Carter. **Executive Vice President:** Brian Swords. **VP/Secretary:** Brian Suarez. **Treasurer:** Brenda Templin. **League Historian:** Larry Tremitiere. **Umpire in Chief:** Gary Swanson.
Regular Season: 42 games. **Playoff Format:** Six-team single-elimination tournament with best of three championship series between final two teams.
Roster Limit: 30 (College-eligible players only).concord weavers
Mailing Address: 8875 Bowman Barrier Rd, Mr Pleasant, NC 28124. **Telephone:** (704) 305-3649. **Email Address:** eastcoastbats@gmail.com. **General Manager:** Derek Shoe. **Head Coach:** Brandon Taylor.

LAKE NORMAN COPPERHEADS

Mailing Address: PO Box 9723, Northcross Center Court, Huntersville, NC 28078. **Telephone:** (704) 892-1041, (704) 564-9211. **E-Mail Address:** eastcoastbats@gmail.com. **Website:** www.copperheadsports.org. **General Manager:** Derek Shoe. **Head Coach:** Jeremy Johnson.

PIEDMONT PRIDE

Mailing Address: 452 Lakeshore Parkway, Ste 205, Rock Hill, SC 29730. **Telephone:** (803) 412-7982. **E-Mail Address:** jhudak@fca.org. **General Manager:** Joe Hudak. **Head Coach:** Joe Hudak.

SBA BONES

Mailing Address: 12857 East Independence Blvd, Ste. J, Matthews, NC 28173. **Telephone:** (704) 641-1035. **E-Mail Address:** jowens@showcasebaseball.org. **General Manager:** John Owens. **Head Coach:** TBA.

STATESVILLE OWLS

Mailing Address: PO Box 17637, Asheville, NC 28816. **Telephone:** (828) 320-5100. **Email Address:** brian.suarez@statesvilleowls.com. **General Manager:** Brian Suarez. **Head Coach:** TBA.

UNION COUNTY VIPERS

Mailing Address: 10800 Sikes Place, Ste 205, Charlotte, NC 28227. **Telephone:** (704) 578-3468. **E-Mail Address:** mpolito@tprsolutions.com. **General Manager:** Mike Polito. **Assistant GM:** Keith Bray. **Head Coach:** Aaron Bray.

SUNBELT BASEBALL LEAGUE

Mailing Address: 3022 Liberty Way, Atlanta, GA 30318. **Telephone:** (770) 490-7912. **E-mail Address:** info@sunbeltleague.com. **Website:** www.sunbeltleague.com. **Year Founded:** 2006.
Commissioner: Bobby Bennett. **Email:** bobbybennett27@me.com. **Executive Director:** Marty Kelly. **Director of Player Development:** Todd Pratt. **Director, Operations:** Karl Garcia. **Regular Season:** 28 games.

Playoff Format: division championship series and league championship series, best of 3. **Roster Limit:** 30 (college-eligible players 22 and under).

Teams: Atlanta Crackers, Brookhaven Bucks, Douglasville Bulls, East Cobb Patriots, Gwinnett Tides,

TEXAS COLLEGIATE LEAGUE

Mailing Address: 735 Plaza Blvd, Suite 200, Coppell, TX 75019. **Telephone:** (979) 985-5198. **Fax:** (979) 779-2398. **E-Mail Address:** info@tclbaseball.com. **Website:** www.texascollegiateleague.com.
Year Founded: 2004.
President: Uri Geva.
Regular Season: 60 games (split schedule). **Playoff Format:** First- and second-half champions qualify, with two wild card teams. Winners of one-game divisional round meet in best of three championship series.
Roster Limit: 30 (College-eligible players only)

ACADIANA CANE CUTTERS

Telephone: (337) 451-6582. **Fax:** (440) 425-8592. **E-Mail Address:** info@canecuttersbaseball.com. **Website:** www.canecuttersbaseball.com. **Owners:** Richard Chalmers, Sandi Chalmers. **General Manager:** Jacob Andrews. **Head Coach:** Lonny Landry.

BRAZOS VALLEY BOMBERS

Mailing Address: 405 Mitchell St, Bryan, TX 77801. **Telephone:** (979) 799-7529. **Fax:** (440) 425-8592. **E-Mail Address:** info@bvbombers.com. **Website:** www.bvbombers.com. **Owners:** Uri Geva, Chris Clark. **General Manager:** Chris Clark. **Head Coach:** Curt Dixon.

EAST TEXAS PUMP JACKS

Mailing Address: PO Box 2369, Kilgore, TX 75663. **Telephone:** (903) 218-4638. **Fax:** (866) 511-5449. **E-mail Address:** info@pumpjacksbaseball.com. **Website:** www.pumpjacksbaseball.com. **Owners:** Alan Poff, Brett Cox, Mike Lieberman. **General Manager:** Mike Lieberman. **Head Coach:** Mark Kertenian.

TEXAS MARSHALS

Mailing Address: 7920 Beltline Rd, Suite 1005 Dallas, TX 75254. **Telephone:** (214) 578-4388. **E-Mail Address:** info@texasmarshals.com. **Website:** www.texasmarshals.com. **Owner:** Marc Landry. **General Manager:** Kendrick Moore. **Head Coach:** Dax Powell.

WOODLANDS STRYKERS

Mailing Address: 25009 OakHurst Dr, Spring, TX 77386. **Telephone:** (720) 205-5709. **Fax:** (281) 465-0748. **Owner/General Manager:** Ramiro Lozano. **Head Coach:** John Villarreal.

VICTORIA GENERALS

Mailing Address: 1307 E Airline Road, Suite H, Victoria, TX 77901. **Telephone:** (361) 485-9522. **Fax:** (361) 485-0936. **E-Mail Address:** info@baseballinvictoria.com, tkyoung@victoriagenerals.com. **Website:** www.victoriagenerals.com. **President:** Tracy Young. **VP/General Manager:** Blake Koch. **Head Coach:** Jonathan Burns.

VALLEY BASEBALL LEAGUE

Mailing Address: Valley Baseball League, 3006

Preston Lake Boulevard, Harrisonburg, VA 22801. **Telephone:** (540) 810-9194. **Fax:** (540) 434-5083. **E-Mail Addresses:** don@lemish.com & baseball@shentel.net. **Website:** www.valleyleaguebaseball.com.
Year Founded: 1897.
President: Donald L. Lemish. **Assistant to the President:** Don Harper. **Executive Vice President:** Bruce Alger. **Media Relations Director:** Lauren Jefferson. **Secretary:** Stacy Locke. **Treasurer:** Ed Yoder.
Regular Season: 42 games. **2015 Opening Date:** June 5. **Closing Date:** August 9. **All-Star Game:** North vs South, July 12 at Harrisonburg. **Playoff Format:** Eight teams qualify; play three rounds of best of three series.
Roster Limit: 28 (college eligible players only)

COVINGTON LUMBERJACKS

Mailing Address: PO Box 30, Covington, VA 24426. **Telephone:** (540) 969-9923, (540) 962-1155. **Fax:** (540) 962-7153. **E-Mail Address:** covingtonlumberjacks@valley-leaguebaseball.com. **Website:** www.lumberjacksbaseball.com. **President:** Dizzy Garten. **Head Coach:** Dan Scott.

ALDIE SENATORS

Mailing Address: 42020 Village Center Plaza, Suite 120-50, Stoneridge, VA 20105. **Telephone:** (703) 542-2110, (703) 989-5009. **Fax:** (703)327-7435. **E-Mail Address:** haymarketsenators@valleyleaguebaseball.com. **Website:** www.haymarketbaseball.com. **President:** Scott Newell. **General Manager:** BernieSchaffler. **Head Coach:** Justin Aspegren.

CHARLES TOWN (WV) CANNONS

Mailing Address: 2862 Northwestern Pike, Capon Bridge, WV 26711. **Telephone:** (540) 743-3338, (540) 843-4472. **Fax:** (304) 856-1619. **E-Mail Address:** bigdaddy432@verizon.net. **Website:** www.charlestowncannons.com. **President:** Brett Fuller. **Recruiting Coordinator:** Brett Fuller. **General Manager:** Steve Sabins.

CHARLOTTESVILLE TOM SOX

Mailing Address: P. O. Box 166, Ivy, Virginia 22945-0166..**Telephone:** (703)282-4425. **E-Mail:** contact@tom-sox.com. **Website:** www.TomSox.com. **President:** Greg Allen. **General Manager:** Joe Koshansky.

FRONT ROYAL CARDINALS

Mailing Address: 382 Morgans Ridge Road, Front Royal, VA 22630. **Telephone:** (703) 244-6662, (540) 905-0152. **E-Mail Address:** DonnaSettle@centurylink.net frontroyalcardinals@valleyleaguebaseball.com. **Website:** www.valleyleaguebaseball.com. **President:** Donna Settle. **Head Coach:** Jake Weghorst.

HARRISONBURG TURKS

Mailing Address: 1489 S Main St, Harrisonburg, VA 22801. **Telephone:** (540) 434-5919. **Fax:** (540) 434-5919. **E-Mail Address:** turksbaseball@hotmail.com. **Website:** www.harrisonburgturks.com. **Operations Manager:** Teresa Wease. **General Manager/Head Coach:** Bob Wease.

NEW MARKET REBELS

Mailing Address: PO Box 902, New Market, VA 22844. **Telephone:** (304) 856-1623. **Fax:** (540) 740-9486. **E-Mail Address:** nmrebels@shentel.net. **Website:** www.rebels-

baseball.biz. **President/General Manager:** Bruce Alger. **Head Coach:** C.J. Rhodes.

STAUNTON BRAVES

Mailing Address: 14 Shannon Place, Staunton, VA 24401.Telephone: (540) 886-0987, (540) 885-1645. **Fax:** (540) 886-0905. **E-Mail Address:** sbraves@hotmail.com. **Website:** www.stauntonbravesbaseball.com. **General Manager:** Steve Cox. **Head Coach:** George Laase.

STRASBURG EXPRESS

Mailing Address: PO Box 417, Strasburg, VA 22657. **Telephone:** (540) 325-5677, (540) 459-4041. **Fax:** (540) 459-3398. **E-Mail Address:** neallaw@shentel.net. **Website:** www.strasburgexpress.com. **General manager:** Jay Neal. **Head coach:** Butch Barnes.

WAYNESBORO GENERALS

Mailing Address: 435 Essex Ave., Suite 105, Waynesboro VA 22980. **Telephone:** (540) 932-2300. **Fax:** (540) 932-2322. **E-Mail Address:** waynesborogenerals@valleyleaguebaseball.com. **Website:** www.waynesborogenerals.com. **Chairman:** David T Gauldin II. **Head Coach:** Mike Bocock.

WINCHESTER ROYALS

Mailing Address: PO Box 2485, Winchester, VA 22604. **Telephone:** (540) 539-8888, (540) 664-3978. **Fax:** (540) 662-1434. **E-Mail Addresses:** winchesterroyals@valleyleaguebaseball.com, jimphill@shentel.net.Website: www.winchesterroyals.com. **President:** Todd Thompson. **Operations Director:** Jimmie Shipp. **Coach:** Kyle Phelps

WOODSTOCK RIVER BANDITS

Mailing Address: P.O. Box 227, Woodstock, VA 22664. **Telephone:** (540) 481-0525. **Fax:** (540) 459-8227. **E-Mail Address:** woodstockriverbandits@valleyleaguebaseball.com. **Website:** www.woodstockriverbandits.org. **General Manager:** R.W. Bowman Jr. **Head Coach:** Phil Betterly.

WEST COAST LEAGUE

Mailing Address: PO Box 20790, Keizer, OR 97307. **Telephone:** (503) 390-2543. **E-Mail Address:** dkoho@westcoastleague.com. **Website:** www.westcoastleague.com.

Year Founded: 2005.
President: Dennis Koho. **Vice President:** Eddie Poplawski. **Secretary:** Jerry Walker. **Treasurer:** Tony Bonacci. **Supervisor, Umpires:** Tom Hiler.
Division Structure: South— Bend Elks, Corvallis Knights, Klamath Falls Gems, Medford Rogues. West—Bellingham Bells, Cowlitz Blackbears, Kitsap Bluejackets,Victoria Harbourcats. East—Kelowna Falcons, Walla Walla Sweets, Wenatchee Applesox, Yakima Valley Pippins.
Regular Season: 54 games. **2015 Opening Date:** June 5. **Closing Date:** August 9. **Playoff Format:** Four-team tournament.
Roster Limit: 25 (college-eligible players only).

BELLINGHAM BELLS

Mailing Address: 1221 Potter Street, Bellingham, WA 98229. **Telephone:** (360) 746-0406. **E-Mail Address:** info@bellinghambells.com. **Website:** www.bellinghambells.com. **Owner:** Eddie Poplawski. **General Manager:** Nick Caples. **Head Coach:** Jeff James.

BEND ELKS

Mailing Address: 70 SW Century Dr Suite 100-373 Bend, Oregon 97702. **Telephone:** (541) 312-9259. **E-Mail Address:** kelsie@bendelks.com. **Website:** www.bendelks.com. **Owners:** John and Tami Marick. **General Manager:** Casey Powell.

CORVALLIS KNIGHTS

Mailing Address: PO Box 1356, Corvallis, OR 97339. **Telephone:** (541) 752-5656. **E-Mail Address:** dan.segel@corvallisknights.com. **Website:** www.corvallisknights.com. **President:** Dan Segel. **General Manager:** Bre Miller. **Head Coach:** Brooke Knight.

COWLITZ BLACK BEARS

Mailing Address: PO Box 1255, Longview, WA 98632. **Telephone:** (360) 703-3195. **E-Mail Address:** gwilsonagm@gmail.com. **Website:** www.cowlitzblackbears.com. **Owner/ General Manager:** Tony Bonacci. **Head Coach:** Grady Tweit.

KELOWNA FALCONS

Mailing Address: 201-1014 Glenmore Dr, Kelowna, BC, V1Y 4P2. **Telephone:** (250) 763-4100. **E-Mail Address:** mark@kelownafalcons.com. **Website:** www.kelownafalcons.com. **Owner:** Dan Nonis. **General Manager:** Mark Nonis. **Head Coach:** Geoff White.

KITSAP BLUEJACKETS

Mailing Address: PO Box 68, Silverdale, WA 98383. **Telephone:** (360) 692-5566.
E-Mail Address: rsmith@kitsapbluejackets.com. **Website:** www.kitsapbluejackets.com. **Managing Partner/General Manager:** Rick Smith. **Head Coach:** Ryan Parker.

KLAMATH FALLS GEMS

Mailing Address: 2001 Crest Street, Klamath Falls, Oregon 97603. **Telephone:** (541) 883-4367. **E-Mail Address:** grant@klamathfallsgems.com. **Website:** www.klamathfallsgems.com. **Owners:** Jerry and Lisa Walker. **General Manager:** Grant Wilson. **Head Coach:** Mitch Karraker.

MEDFORD ROGUES

Mailing Address: PO Box 699, Medford, Oregon 97501. **Telephone:** (541) 973-2883. **E-Mail Address:** ian@medfordrogues.com. **Website:** www.medfordrogues.com. **Owner:** CSH International. **General Manager:** Ian Church. **Head Coach:** Josh Hogan.

VICTORIA HARBOURCATS

Mailing Address: 1014 Caledonia Avenue, Victoria, BC, V8T 1G1. **Telephone:** (250) 216-0006. **E-Mail Address:** jim@harbourcats.com. **Website:** www.harbourcats.com. **Owner:** John McLean. **General Manager:** Jim Swanson. **Head Coach:** Graig Merritt.

WALLA WALLA SWEETS

Mailing Address: 109 E Main Street, Walla Walla, WA 99362. **Telephone:** (509) 522-2255. **E-Mail Address:** info@wallawallasweets.com. **Website:** www.wallawallabaseball.com. **Owner:** Pacific Baseball Ventures, LLC. **General Manager:** Katie Biagi. **Head Coach:** Frank Mutz.

WENATCHEE APPLESOX

Mailing Address: PO Box 5100, Wenatchee, WA 98807. **Telephone:** (509) 665-6900. **E-Mail Address:** sales@applesox.com. **Website:** www.applesox.com. **Owner/General Manager:** Jim Corcoran. **Head Coach:** A.J. Proszek.

YAKIMA VALLEY PIPPINS

Mailing Address: 1301, S. Fair Avenue, Shattuck Bldg., Yakima, WA 98908. **Telephone:** (509) 575-4487. **E-Mail Address:** info@pippinsbaseball.com. **Website:** www.pippinsbaseball.com. **Ownership Group:** Theresa Gillespie, Greg Shaw, Jeff Cirillo, John Stanton, Mikal Thomasen, Peter van Oppen, Zachary Fraser. **Head Coach:** Marcus McKimmy.

HIGH SCHOOL BASEBALL

NATIONAL FEDERATION OF STATE HIGH SCHOOL ASSOCIATIONS

Mailing Address: PO Box 690, Indianapolis, IN 46206. **Telephone:** (317) 972-6900. **Fax:** (317) 822-5700. **E-Mail Address:** baseball@nfhs.org. **Website:** www.nfhs.org.

Executive Director: Bob Gardner. **Chief Operating Officer:** James Tenopir. **Director of Sports, Sanctioning and Student Services:** Elliot Hopkins. **Director, Publications/Communications:** Bruce Howard.

NATIONAL HIGH SCHOOL BASEBALL COACHES ASSOCIATION

Mailing Address: PO Box 12843, Tempe, AZ 85284. **Telephone:** (602) 615-0571. **Fax:** (480) 838-7133. **E-Mail Address:** rdavini@cox.net. **Website:** www.baseballcoach-es.org. **Executive Director:** Ron Davini.

Executive Secretary: Robert Colburn (St. Andrews's School, New Castle, Del.). **President:** Tim Saunders (Dublin Coffman HS, Dublin, Ohio). **First Vice President:** Steve Vickery (El Capitan HS, Lakeside, Calif.). **Second Vice President:** Mel Gardner (Delaware BCA, New Castle, Del.).

2015 National Convention: Dec. 3-6 at St. Louis.

NATIONAL TOURNAMENTS

IN-SEASON

HORIZON NATIONAL INVITATIONAL

Mailing Address: Horizon High School, 5653 Sandra Terrace, Scottsdale, AZ 85254. **Telephone:** 602-291-1952. **E-mail:** huskycoach1@yahoo.com. **Website:** www.horizonbaseball.com.

Tournament Director: Eric Kibler.
2015 Tournament: March 24-27.

INTERNATIONAL PAPER CLASSIC

Mailing Address: 4775 Johnson Rd., Georgetown, SC 29440. **Telephone:** (843) 527-9606. **Fax:** (843) 546-8521. **Website:** www.ipclassic.com.

Tournament Director: Alicia Johnson.
2015 Tournament: March 5-8 (eight teams).

LIONS INVITATIONAL

Mailing Address: 8281 Walker Street, La Palma, CA 90623. **Telephone:** (714) 220-4101x502. **Fax:** (714) 995-1833. **Email:** Pascal_C@AUHSD.US. **Website:** www.anaheimlionstourney.com.

Tournament Director: Chris Pascal.
2015 Tournament: March 28-April 1 (78 teams).

NATIONAL CLASSIC BASEBALL TOURNAMENT

Mailing Address: PO Box 338, Placentia, CA 92870. **Telephone:** (714) 993-2838. **Fax:** (714) 993-5350. **E-Mail**

Address: placentiamustang@aol.com. **Website:** www.national-classic.com.

Tournament Director: Marcus Jones.
2015 Tournament: April 6-10 (16 teams).

USA BASEBALL NATIONAL HIGH SCHOOL INVITATIONAL

Mailing Address: 403 Blackwell St., Durham, NC 27701. **Telephone:** (919) 474-8721. **Fax:** (919) 474-8822. **Email:** markdvoroznak@usabaseball.com. **Website:** www.usabaseball.com.

Tournament Director: Mark Dvoroznak.
2015 Tournament: March 25-28 at USA Baseball National Training Complex, Cary, NC (16 teams).

USA CLASSIC NATIONAL HIGH SCHOOL INVITATIONAL

Mailing Address: PO Box 247, Millington, TN 38043. **Telephone:** (901) 873-5880. **Fax:** (901) 873-5885. **Email:** jwaits@cityofmillington.org. **Website:** www.millingtontn.gov.

Tournament Organizers: Jeff Waits, Johnny Ray.
2015 Tournament: Unavailable.

POSTSEASON

SUNBELT BASEBALL CLASSIC SERIES

Mailing Address: 505 North Blvd., Edmond, OK 73034. **Telephone:** (405) 348-3839. **Fax:** (405) 340-7538. **Email:** lyngor@aol.com. **Website:** www.sunbeltclassicbaseball.com.

Chairman: John Schwartz.
2015 Senior Series: Unavailable.
2015 Junior Series: Unavailable.
2015 Sophomore Series: Unavailable.

ALL-STAR GAMES/AWARDS

PERFECT GAME ALL-AMERICAN CLASSIC

Mailing Address: 850 Twixt Town Rd. NE Cedar Rapids, IA 52402. **Telephone:** (319) 298-2923. **Fax (319) 298-2924. Event Organizer:** Blue Ridge Sports & Entertainment. **Vice President, Events:** Lou Lacy.

2015 Game: Aug. 16 at Petco Park, San Diego.

UNDER ARMOUR ALL-AMERICA GAME, POWERED BY BASEBALL FACTORY

Mailing Address: 9212 Berger Rd., Suite 200, Columbia, MD 21046. **Telephone:** (410) 715-5080. **Email Address:** jason@factoryathletics.com. **Website:** baseballfactory.com/AllAmerica. **Event Organizers:** Baseball Factory, Team One Baseball.

2015 Game: Aug 15 at Wrigley Field, Chicago.

GATORADE CIRCLE OF CHAMPIONS (National HS Player of the Year Award)

Mailing Address: The Gatorade Company, 321 N. Clark St., Suite 24-3, Chicago, IL, 60610. **Telephone:** 312-821-1000. **Website:** www.gatorade.com.

SHOWCASE EVENTS

AREA CODE BASEBALL GAMES PRESENTED BY NEW BALANCE

Mailing Address: 23954 Madison Street, Torrance, CA 90505. **Telephone:** 310-791-1142 x 4426. **Website:** AreaCodeBaseball.com

Event Organizer: Kirsten Leetch.

2015 Area Code Games: Aug 4-11 at Blair Field in Long Beach, Calif.

ARIZONA FALL CLASSIC

Mailing Address: 6102 W. Maui Lane, Glendale, AZ 85306. **Telephone:** (602) 978-2929. **Fax:** (602) 439-4494. **Email Address:** azbaseballted@msn.com.

Website: www.azfallclassic.com.
Directors: Ted Heid, Tracy Heid.

2015 EVENTS

Four Corner Classic . . . . Peoria, AZ, May 28-31
Classic Qualifier . . . . Peoria, AZ, June 12-14
Arizona Summer Classic, ... Peoria, AZ, July 16-19
Arizona Summer Classic (16U), ... July 23-26
AZ Sophomore Fall Classic. . . . . , Oct. 1-4
AZ Senior Fall Classic (HS seniors), Peoria, AZ. . . Oct. 7-11
Senior All Academic Tryout & Game. . . . . Oct. 8
AZ Junior Fall Classic (HS juniors), Peoria, AZ . . Oct. 15-18
Junior All Academic Tryout & Game. . . . . Oct. 15
Mizuno Universal Classic, Peoria, AZ . . . . Oct. 22-25

BASEBALL FACTORY

Office Address: 9212 Berger Rd., Suite 200, Columbia, MD 21046. **Telephone:** (800) 641-4487, (410) 715-5080. **Fax:** (410) 715-1975. **Email Address:** info@baseballfactory.com. **Website:** www.baseballfactory.com.
Chief Executive OfficerFounder: Steve Sclafani. **President:** Rob Naddelman. **CFO:** Gene Mattingly. **CRO:** Marty Conway. **Executive VPChairman, Under Armour All-America Game Selection Committee:** Steve Bernhardt. **Senior VP, Marketing/Brand:** Jason Budden. **Senior VP, Baseball Operations:** Jim Gemler. **Senior VP, Player Development:** Dan Forester. **VP, Creative:** Matt Kirby. **VP, Business Development:** Jeff Brazier. **Senior Director, Player Development/Scouting:** Andy Ferguson. **Senior Director, College Recruiting:** Dan Mooney. **Senior Director, Event Marketing/ Partnerships:** Dave Lax. **Senior Multimedia Producer:** Brian Johnson. **Senior Director, Youth Baseball:** Joe Lake. **Senior Director, Web Development:** Wei Xue. **Executive Player Development Coordinator:** Steve Nagler. **Senior Player Development Coordinators:** Adam Darvick, Dave Packer, John Perko. **Regional Player Development Coordinators:** Ed Bach, Will Bach, Drew Baldwin, Chris Brown, Nick Criscuolo, Josh Hippensteel, Rob Onolfi, Julia Rice, Matt Richter, Ryan Schweikert, Shauna Scott, Jesse Tome, Patrick Wuebben. **Director of Factory Development Institute Operations:** Mark Lemon. **Director, PVP Program/ National Tryouts:** Scott Ritter. **Director, Social Media:** Becky Oldham. **Director, College Recruiting Operations:** Dan Rollins. **Director, Youth Baseball Operations:** Ryan Liddle. **Director, Retail/Team Sales:** Adam Beaver. **Director, Development, Factory Athletics Foundation:** Anita Broccolino.
Under Armour All-America Pre-Season Tournament: Jan. 16-18, Mesa, Ariz. (Cubs Park).
Under Armour All-America Game: Aug. 15 Chicago (Wrigley Field)
2015 Under Armour Baseball Factory National Tryouts/College Recruiting Program: Year round at various locations across the country. Open to high school players, ages 14–18, with a separate division for pre-high school players, ages 12–14. **Full schedule:** www.baseballfactory.com/tryouts.

BOBBY VALENTINE ALL-AMERICAN CAMPS

Address: 52 Mason Street, Greenwich, CT 06830. **Telephone:** (203) 517-1277. **Fax:** (203) 517-1377. **Website:** www.allamericanfoundation.com

EAST COAST PROFESSIONAL SHOWCASE

Website: www.eastcoastproshowcase.com.

Tournament Directors: John Castleberry, Howard McCullough.
2015 Showcase: July 27-30, Tampa.

IMPACT BASEBALL

Mailing Address: P.O. Box 47, Sedalia, NC 27342. **Email Address:** andypartin@aol.com. **Website:** impactbaseball.com. **Founder/CEO:** Andy Partin.
2015 Events: Various dates, May-Aug. 2015.

NORTHWEST CHAMPIONSHIPS

Mailing Address: 9849 Fox Street, Aumsville, OR 97325. **Telephone:** (503) 302-7117. **Email Address:** warner@baseballnorthwest.com. **Website:** www.baseballnorthwest.com. **Tournament Organizer:** Josh Warner.
2015 Events: Aug. 12-23 at Centralia, Wash.

PERFECT GAME USA

Mailing Address: 850 Twixt Town Rd. NE Cedar Rapids, IA 52402. **Telephone:** (319) 298-2923. **Fax:** (319) 298-2924. **Email Address:** jerry@perfectgame.org. **Website:** www.perfectgameusa.com.
President/Director: Jerry Ford. **Vice Presidents:** Andy Ford, Jason Gerst, Tyson Kimm, Steve Griffin. **VP, Business Development:** Brad Clement. **VP, Tournaments:** Taylor McCollough. **International Scouting Director:** Kentaro Yasutake. **National Showcase Director:** Jim Arp. **National Scouting Director:** Greg Sabers. **National Tournament Director:** Matthew Bliven. **National BCS Director:** Justin Amidon. **Spring Swing Director:** Kevin Herlihy. **National Youth Director:** Scott Weiss. **Super25 Director:** Drake Browne. **Director, PGCrosschecker:** Allan Simpson. **College Baseball Content:** Frankie Piliere, Jheremy Brown. **Iowa League Director:** Steve James. **Scouting Coordinators:** Kirk Gardner, Jason Piddington, Brian Sakowski, Matt Huck. **Tournament Directors:** Ken Gardner, Michael Palazzone, Justin Hlubek, Mark Mathison, Breanne Schoby, Austin Bynum. **National Spokesman:** Daron Sutton. **All American Spokesman:** Trevor Hoffman.
2015 Showcase/Tournament Events: Sites across the United States, Jan. 3-Aug. 30.

PROFESSIONAL BASEBALL INSTRUCTION—BATTERY INVITATIONAL

(for top high school pitchers and catchers)
Mailing Address: 107 Pleasant Avenue, Upper Saddle River N.J. 07458. **Telephone:** (800) 282-4638. **Fax:** (201) 760-8820. **Email Address:** info@baseballclinics.com. **Website:** www.baseballclinics.com/battery-invitational/.
President: Doug Cinnella.
Senior Staff Administrator: Greg Cinnella. **General Manager/PR/Marketing:** Jim Monaghan.
Event Date: November 7.

SELECTFEST BASEBALL

Mailing Address: P.O. Box 852, Morris Plains, NJ 07950. **Email Address:** selectfest@optonline.net. **Website:** www.selectfestbaseball.org. **Camp Directors:** Bruce Shatel, Robert Maida.
2015 Showcase: June 26-28.

TEAM ONE BASEBALL (A DIVISION OF BASEBALL FACTORY)

Office Address: 1000 Bristol Street North, Box 17285, Newport Beach, CA 92660. **Telephone:** (800) 621-5452.

Fax: (949) 209-1829. **Email Address:** jroswell@teamone-baseball.com. **Website:** www.teamonebaseball.com.
Senior Director: Justin Roswell. **Executive VP:** Steve Bernhardt. **Senior VP, Baseball Operations:** Jim Gemler. **VP, Player Development:** Dan Forester.
2015 Under Armour Showcases: Team One National East: July 10-11 in Peachtree City, GA (The Chuck at Homeplate); **Team One National West:** July 20–21 in Azusa, CA (Azusa Pacific University); **Team One Futures Series East:** September 19 in Jupiter, FL (Roger Dean Stadium); **Team One Futures Series West:** Fall 2015 in Azusa, CA (Azusa Pacific University); **Team One Futures Series South:** Fall 2015 in Peachtree City, GA (The Chuck at Homeplate); **Team One Futures Series Texas:** November 7 in Plano, TX (John Paul II High School).
2015 Under Armour Tournaments: Under Armour Memorial Day Classic: May 22-25 in Jupiter, FL (Roger Dean Sports Complex), **Under Armour Southeast Championships:** June 6–9 in Jupiter, FL (Roger Dean Sports Complex), **Under Armour Firecracker Classic:** June 29–July 3 in Jupiter, FL (Roger Dean Sports Complex), **Under Armour Southwest Championships 16U:** July 24-28 in Azusa, CA (Azusa Pacific University/Univ. of La Verne/Citrus College). **Under Armour Southwest Championships 17U:** July 31–Aug. 4 in Azusa, CA (Azusa Pacific University/Univ. of La Verne/Citrus College). **Under Armour Fall Classic:** Sept. 19–21 in Jupiter, FL (Roger Dean Sports Complex), **Under Armour Invitational:** Oct. 17–18 in St. Petersburg, FL (Walter Fuller Complex), **Under Armour SoCal Underclass Classic:** Oct. 23–25 in Azusa, CA (Azusa Pacific University/Univ. of La Verne/Citrus College), **Under Armour SoCal Upperclass Classic:** Oct. 30–Nov. 1 in Azusa, CA (Azusa Pacific University/Univ. of La Verne/Citrus College).

TOP 96 COLLEGE COACHES CLINICS
Mailing Address: 6 Foley Dr. Southboro, MA 01772. **Telephone:** 508-481-5935.
Email Address: doug.henson@top96.com. **Website:** www.top96.com. **Directors:** Doug Henson, Dave Callum.

YOUTH BASEBALL

ALL AMERICAN AMATEUR BASEBALL ASSOCIATION
Mailing Address: 331 Parkway Dr., Zanesville, OH 43701. **Telephone:** (740) 453-8531. **Email Address:** clw@aol.com. **Website:** www.aaaba.us.
Year Founded: 1944.
President: George Arcurio, III. **Executive Director/Secretary:** Bob Wolfe.
2015 Events: AAABA Regional Tournaments—July 24-28; National Tournament—Aug. 3-9.

AMATEUR ATHLETIC UNION OF THE UNITED STATES, INC.
Mailing Address: P.O. Box 22409, Lake Buena Vista, FL 32830. **Telephone:** (407) 828-3459. **Fax:** (407) 934-7242. **Email Address:** debra@aausports.org. **Website:** www.aaubaseball.org.
Year Founded: 1982. **Sports Manager, Baseball:** Debra Horn.

AMERICAN AMATEUR BASEBALL CONGRESS
National Headquarters: 100 West Broadway, Farmington, NM 87401. **Telephone:** (505) 327-3120. **Fax:** (505) 327-3132. **Email Address:** aabc@aabc.us. **Website:** www.aabc.us.
Year Founded: 1935.
President: Richard Neely.

AMERICAN AMATEUR YOUTH BASEBALL ALLIANCE
Mailing Address: 3851 Iris Lane, Bonne Terre, MO 63628. **Telephone:** (636) 332-2803. **Email Address:** clwjr28@aol.com. **Website:** www.aayba.com.
President, Baseball Operations: Carroll Wood. **President, Business Operations:** Greg Moore.

AMERICAN LEGION BASEBALL
National Headquarters: American Legion Baseball, 700 N Pennsylvania St., Indianapolis, IN 46204. **Telephone:** (317) 630-1213. **Fax:** (317) 630-1369. **Email Address:** baseball@legion.org. **Website:** www.legion.org/baseball.
Year Founded: 1925.
Program Coordinator: Mike Buss.
2015 World Series (19 and under): Aug. 13-18 at Keeter Stadium, Shelby, N.C. **2015 Regional Tournaments (Aug. 5-9):** Northeast—Bristol, Conn.; Mid-Atlantic—Leesburg, Va.; Southeast—Asheboro, N.C.; Mid-South—North Conway, Ark.; Great Lakes—Alton, Ill.; Central Plains—Bismarck, N.D.; Northwest—Cheyenne, Wyo.; West—Boulder, Col.

BABE RUTH BASEBALL
International Headquarters: 1770 Brunswick Pike, P.O. Box 5000, Trenton, NJ 08638. **Telephone:** (609) 695-1434. **Fax:** (609) 695-2505. **Email Address:** info@baberuthleague.org. **Website:** www.baberuthleague.org.
Year Founded: 1951.
President/Chief Executive Officer: Steven Tellefsen.

CONTINENTAL AMATEUR BASEBALL ASSOCIATION
Mailing Address: P.O. Box 1684 Mt. Pleasant, SC 29465. **Telephone:** (843) 860-1568. **Fax:** (843) 856-7791. **Email Address:** Diamonddevils.org. **Website:** www.cababaseball.com.
Year Founded: 1984.
Chief Executive Officer: Larry Redwine. **President/COO:** John Rhodes. **Executive Vice President:** Fran Pell.

DIXIE YOUTH BASEBALL
Mailing Address: P.O. Box 877, Marshall, TX 75671. **Telephone:** (903) 927-2255. **Fax:** (903) 927-1846. **Email Address:** dyb@dixie.org. **Website:** www.dixie.org.
Year Founded: 1955.
Commissioner: Wes Skelton.

DIXIE BOYS BASEBALL
Mailing Address: P.O. Box 8263, Dothan, Alabama 36304. **Telephone:** (334) 793-3331. **Email Address:** jjones29@sw.rr.com. **Website:** http://baseball.dixie.org.
Commissioner/Chief Executive Officer: Sandy Jones.

DIZZY DEAN BASEBALL

Mailing Address: P.O. Box 856, Hernando, MS 38632. **Telephone:** (662) 429-4365, (423) 596-1353. **Email Address:** DPhil10513@aol.com, jimmywahl@bellsouth.net, Bdunn39270@comcast.net, hsuggsdizzydean@aol.com. **Website:** www.dizzydeanbbinc.org.

Year Founded: 1962.

Commissioner: Danny Phillips. **President:** Jimmy Wahl. **VP:** Bobby Dunn. **Secretary:** Donnie Stone. **Treasurer:** Houston Suggs.

HAP DUMONT YOUTH BASEBALL (A DIVISION OF THE NATIONAL BASEBALL CONGRESS)

Email Address: bruce@prattrecreation.com, gbclev@hapdumontbaseball.com. **Website:** www.hapdumont-baseball.com.

Year Founded: 1974.

President: Bruce Pinkall

LITTLE LEAGUE BASEBALL

International Headquarters: 539 US Route 15 Hwy, P.O. Box 3485, Williamsport, PA 17701-0485. **Telephone:** (570) 326-1921. **Fax:** (570) 326-1074. **Website:** www.littleleague.org.

Year Founded: 1939.

Chairman: Dr. Davie Jane Gilmour. **President/Chief Executive Officer:** Stephen D. Keener. **Chief Financial Officer:** David Houseknecht. **Vice President, Operations:** Patrick Wilson. **Treasurer:** Melissa Singer. **Senior Communications Executive:** Wayne Henninger.

NATIONS BASEBALL- ARIZONA

Mailing Address: 5160 W Glenview Pl, Chandler, AZ 85226. **Telephone:** (602) 793-8940. **Website:** Nationsbaseballaz.com. **E-Mail:** Nationsbaseballarizona@gmail.com.

NATIONAL AMATEUR BASEBALL FEDERATION

Mailing Address: P.O. Box 705, Bowie, MD 20718. **Telephone:** (410) 721-4727. **Fax:** (410) 721-4940. **Email Address:** nabf1914@aol.com. **Website:** www.nabf.com.

Year Founded: 1914.

Executive Director: Charles Blackburn.

NATIONAL ASSOCIATION OF POLICE ATHLETIC LEAGUES

Mailing Address: 1662 N. US Highway 1 Suite C, Jupiter, FL 33469. **Telephone:** (561) 745-5535. **Fax:** (561) 745-3147. **Email Address:** copnkid@nationalpal.org. **Website:** www.nationalpal.org.

Year Founded: 1914.

President: Christopher Hill.

PONY BASEBALL AND SOFTBALL

International Headquarters: P.O. Box 225, Washington, PA 15301. **Telephone:** (724) 225-1060. **Fax:** (724) 225-9852. **Email Address:** info@pony.org.

Website: www.pony.org.

Year Founded: 1951.

President: Abraham Key.

REVIVING BASEBALL IN INNER CITIES

Mailing Address: 245 Park Ave., New York, NY **10167.** **Telephone:** (212) 931-7800. **Fax:** (212) 949-5695. **Year Founded:** 1989. **Senior Director, Reviving Baseball in Inner Cities:** David James (David.James@mlb.com). **Vice President, Community Affairs:** Thomas C. **Brasuell.** **Email:** rbi@mlb.com. **Website:** www.mlb.com/rbi.

SUPER SERIES BASEBALL OF AMERICA

National Headquarters: 3449 East Kael St., Mesa, AZ 85213-1773. **Telephone:** (480) 664-2998. **Fax:** (480) 664-2997. **Email Address:** info@superseriesbaseball.com. **Website:** www.superseriesbaseball.com.

President: Mark Mathew.

TRIPLE CROWN SPORTS

Mailing Address: 3930 Automation Way, Fort Collins, CO 80525. **Telephone:** (970) 223-6644. **Fax:** (970) 223-3636. **Websites:** www.triplecrownsports.com. **Email:** joseph@triplecrownsports.com.

Director, Baseball Operations: Joe Santilli.

U.S. AMATEUR BASEBALL FEDERATION

Mailing Address: 301 Winters Ct., San Marcos, CA 92069. **Telephone:** (760) 580-9934. **Fax:** (760) 798-9379. **Email Address:** usabf@cox.net. **Website:** www.usabf.com.

Year Founded: 1997.

Senior Chief Executive Officer/President: Jay Gracio.

UNITED STATES SPECIALTY SPORTS ASSOCIATION

Executive Vice President, Baseball: Don DeDonatis III, 33600 Mound Rd., Sterling Heights, MI 48310. **Telephone:** (810) 397-6410. **Email Address:** michusssa@aol.com.

Executive VP, Baseball Operations: Rick Fortuna, 6324 N. Chatham Ave., #136, Kansas City, MO 64151. **Telephone:** (816) 587-4545. **Email Address:** rick@kcsports.org. **Website:** www.usssabaseball.org. **Year Founded:** 1965/Baseball 1996.

WORLD WOOD BAT ASSOCIATION (A DIVISION OF PERFECT GAME USA)

Mailing Address: 850 Twixt Town Rd., Cedar Rapids, IA 52402. **Telephone:** (319) 298-2923. **Fax:** (319) 298-2924. **Email Address:** taylor@perfectgame.org. **Website:** www.perfectgame.org.

Year Founded: 1997.

President: Jerry Ford. **National Director:** Taylor McCollough. **Scouting Director:** Greg Sabers.

BASEBALL USA

Mailing Address: 2626 West Sam Houston Pkwy. N., Houston, TX 77043. **Telephone:** (713) 690-5564. **Email Address:** info@baseballusa.com. **Website:** www.baseballusa.com.

Tournament Director: Steve Olson

CALIFORNIA COMPETITIVE YOUTH BASEBALL

Mailing Address: P.O. Box 338, Placentia, CA 92870.
Telephone: (714) 993-2838. **Email Address:** ccybnet@
aol.com. **Website:** www.ccyb.net.
　Tournament Director: Todd Rogers.

COCOA EXPO SPORTS CENTER

Mailing Address: 500 Friday Road, Cocoa, FL 32926.
Telephone: (321) 639-3976. **Fax:** (407) 390-9435.
Email Address: brad@cocoaexpo.com. **Website:** www.
cocoaexpo.com.
　Athletic Director: Brad Traina.
　Activities: Spring training program, spring & fall
leagues, instructional camps, team training camps, youth
tournaments.

COOPERSTOWN BASEBALL WORLD

Mailing Address: P.O. Box 646, Allenwood, NJ 08720.
Telephone: (888) CBW-8750. **Fax:** (888) CBW-8720.
Email: cbw@cooperstownbaseballworld.com. **Website:**
www.cooperstownbaseballworld.com.
　Complex Address: Cooperstown Baseball World,
SUNY-Oneonta, Ravine Parkway, Oneonta, NY 13820.
　President: Debra Sirianni.
　2015 Tournaments (15 Teams Per Week): Open to
12U, 13U, 14U, 15U, 16U

COOPERSTOWN DREAMS PARK

Mailing Address: 330 S. Main St., Salisbury, NC 28144.
Telephone: (704) 630-0050. **Fax:** (704) 630-0737. **Email
Address:** info@cooperstowndreamspark.com. **Website:**
www.cooperstowndreamspark.com.
　Complex Address: 4550 State Highway 28, Milford,
NY 13807.
　Chief Executive Officer: Louis Presutti. **Director,
Baseball Operations:** Geoff Davis.
　2015 Tournaments: June 6-Aug. 29.

COOPERSTOWN ALL STAR VILLAGE

Mailing Address: P.O. Box 670, Cooperstown, NY
13326. **Telephone:** (800) 327-6790. **Fax:** (607) 432-1076.
Email Address: info@cooperstownallstarvillage.com.
Website: www.cooperstownallstarvillage.com.
　Team Registrations: Jim Rudloff. **Hotel Room
Reservations:** Becky Talbot. **Presidents:** Martin and
Brenda Patton.

ESPN WIDE WORLD OF SPORTS

Mailing Address: P.O. Box 470847, Celebration, FL
34747. **Telephone:** (407) 938-3802. **Fax:** (407) 938-3442.
Email address: wdw.sports.baseball@disneysports.com.
Website: www.disneybaseball.com.
　Manager, Sports Events: Aaron Hudson. **Senior
Sports Manager:** Kyle Cantrell. **Tournament Director:**
Al Schlazer.

KC SPORTS TOURNAMENTS

Mailing Address: KC Sports, 6324 N. Chatham Ave.,
No. 136, Kansas City, MO 64151.
　Telephone: (816) 587-4545. **Fax:** (816) 587-4549.
　Email Address: info@kcsports.org.
　Website: www.kcsports.org.
　Activities: USSSA Youth tournaments (ages 6-18).

INSTRUCTIONAL SCHOOLS/ PRIVATE CAMPS

ACADEMY OF PRO PLAYERS

Mailing Address: 140 5th Avenue, Hawthorne,
NJ 07506. **Telephone:** (973) 304-1470. **Fax:** (973)
636-6375. **Email Address:** taylor@akademapro.com.
Website: www.academypro.com. **Camp Director:** Taylor
Bargiacchi.

ALL-STAR BASEBALL ACADEMY

Mailing Addresses: 223 Wilmington Pike, Suite 301
Chadds Ford, PA 19317. **Telephone:** (484) 770-8350. **Fax:**
(484)-770-8336 . **Email Address:** basba@allstarbaseball-
academy.com. **Website:** www.allstarbaseballacademy.
com. **President/CEO :** Jim Freeman. **Executive Director:**
Mike Manning.

AMERICAN BASEBALL FOUNDATION

Mailing Address: 2660 10th Ave. South, Suite 620,
Birmingham, AL 35205. **Telephone:** (205) 558-4235. **Fax:**
(205) 918-0800. **Email Address:** abf@asmi.org. **Website:**
http://americanbaseballfoundation.com/. **Executive
Director:** David Osinski.

AMERICA'S BASEBALL CAMPS

Mailing Address: 3020 ISSQ Pine Lake Road #12,
Sammamish, WA 98075. **Telephone:** (800) 222-8152. **Fax:**
(888) 751-8989. **Email Address:** info@baseballcamps.
com. **Website:** www.baseballcamps.com.

CHAMPIONS BASEBALL ACADEMY

Mailing Address: 5994 Linneman Street Cincinnati,
OH 45230. **Telephone:** (513) 831-8873. **Fax:** (513) 247-
0040. **Email Address:** championsbaseball@ymail.com.
Website: www.championsbaseball.net. **Director:** Mike
Bricker.

DOYLE BASEBALL ACADEMY

Mailing Address: P.O. Box 9156, Winter Haven, FL
33883. **Telephone:** (863) 439-1000. **Fax:** (863) 294-8607.
Email Address: info@doylebaseball.com.
Website: www.doylebaseball.com. **President:** Denny
Doyle. **CEO/CFO:** Blake Doyle.

ELEV8 SPORTS INSTITUTE

Mailing Address: 490 Dotterel Road, Delray Beach,
FL 33444. **Telephone:** (800) 970-5896. **Fax:** (561) 278-
6679. **Email Address:** info@elev8si.com. **Website:** http://
elev8sportsinstitute.com/

FROZEN ROPES TRAINING CENTERS

Mailing Address: 24 Old Black Meadow Rd., Chester,
NY 10918. **Telephone:** (845) 469-7331. **Fax:** (845) 469-
6742. **Email Address:** info@frozenropes.com. **Website:**
www.frozenropes.com.

IMG ACADEMY

Mailing Address: IMG Academy, 5500 34th St. W.,
Bradenton, FL 34210. **Telephone:** 941-739-7480. **Fax:**
941-739-7484. **Email Address:** acad_baseball@img.com.
Website: www.imgacademy.com.

MARK CRESSE BASEBALL SCHOOL

Mailing Address: P.O. Box 1596 Newport Beach, CA 92659. **Telephone:** (714) 892-6145. **Fax:** (714) 890-7017. **Email Address:** info@markcresse.com. **Website:** www.markcresse.com.
Owner/Founder: Mark Cresse.

US SPORTS CAMPS/NIKE BASEBALL CAMPS

Mailing Address: 1010 B Street Suite 450, San Rafael, CA 94901. **Telephone:** (415) 479-6060. **Fax:** (415) 479-6061. **Email Address:** baseball@ussportscamps.com. **Website:** www.ussportscamps.com/baseball/.

MOUNTAIN WEST BASEBALL ACADEMY

Mailing Address: 389 West 10000 South, South Jordan, UT 84095. **Telephone:** (801) 561-1700. **Fax:** (801) 561-1762. **Email Address:** kent@utahbaseballacademy.com. **Website:** www.mountainwestbaseball.com. **Director:** Bob Keyes

NORTH CAROLINA BASEBALL ACADEMY

Mailing Address: 1137 Pleasant Ridge Road, Greensboro, NC 27409. **Telephone:** (336) 931-1118. **Email Address:** info@ncbaseball.com. **Website:** www.ncbaseball.com.
Owner/Director: Scott Bankhead.

PENNSYLVANIA DIAMOND BUCKS

Mailing Address: 2320 Whitetail Court, Hellertown, PA 18055. **Telephone:** (610) 838-1219, (610) 442-6998. **Email Address:** janciganick@yahoo.com. **Camp Director:** Jan Ciganick. **Head of Instruction:** Chuck Ciganick.

PROFESSIONAL BASEBALL INSTRUCTION

Mailing Address: 107 Pleasant Ave., Upper Saddle River, NJ 07458. **Telephone:** (800) 282-4638 (NY/NJ), (877) 448-2220 (rest of U.S.). **Fax:** (201) 760-8820. **Email Address:** info@baseballclinics.com. **Website:** http://www.baseballclinics.com. **President:** Doug Cinnella.

RIPKEN BASEBALL CAMPS

Mailing Address: 1427 Clarkview Rd., Suite 100, Baltimore, MD 21209. **Telephone:** (410) 297-9292. **Fax:** (410) 823-0850. **Email Address:** information@ripken-baseball.com. **Website:** www.ripkenbaseball.com.

SHO-ME BASEBALL CAMP

Mailing Address: P.O. Box 2270, Branson West, MO 65737. **Telephone:** (417) 338-5838. **Fax:** (417) 338-2610. **Email Address:** info@shomebaseball.com. **Website:** www.shomebaseball.com.

COLLEGE CAMPS

Almost all of the elite college baseball programs have summer/holiday instructional camps. Please consult the college section for listings.

SENIOR BASEBALL

MEN'S SENIOR BASEBALL LEAGUE

(25 and Over, 35 and Over, 45 and Over, 55 and Over)
Mailing Address: One Huntington Quadrangle, Suite 3N07, Melville, NY 11747. **Telephone:** (631) 753-6725. **Fax:** (631) 753-4031.
President: Steve Sigler. **Vice President:** Gary D'Ambrisi.
E-Mail Address: info@msblnational.com.
Website: www.msblnational.com.

MEN'S ADULT BASEBALL LEAGUE

(18 and Over)
Mailing Address: One Huntington Quadrangle, Suite 3N07, Melville, NY 11747. **Telephone:** (631) 753-6725. **Fax:** (631) 753-4031.
E-Mail Address: info@msblnational.com. **Website:** www.msblnational.com.
President: Steve Sigler. **Vice President:** Gary D'Ambrisi.

NATIONAL ADULT BASEBALL ASSOCIATION

Mailing Address: 5944 S. Kipling St., Suite 200, Littleton, CO 80127. **Telephone:** (800) 621-6479. **Fax:** (303) 639-6605. **E-Mail:** nabanational@aol.com. **Website:** www.dugout.org.
President: Shane Fugita.

NATIONAL AMATEUR BASEBALL FEDERATION

Mailing Address: P.O. Box 705, Bowie, MD 20718. **Telephone:** (410) 721-4727. **Fax:** (410) 721-4940.
Email Address: nabf1914@aol.com.
Website: www.nabf.com.
Year Founded: 1914.
Executive Director: Charles Blackburn.

ROY HOBBS BASEBALL

Open (18-over), Veterans (35-over), Masters (45-over), Legends (53-over); Classics (60-over), Vintage (65-over), Timeless (70-over), Forever Young (75-over), Women's open.
Mailing Address: 2048 Akron Peninsula Rd., Akron, OH 44313. **Telephone:** (330) 923-3400. **Fax:** (330) 923-1967. **E-Mail Address:** rhbb@royhobbs.com. **Website:** www.royhobbs.com.
CEO: Tom Giffen. **President:** Rob Giffen..

DIRECTORIES

- **AGENT**
- **SERVICE**

AGENT DIRECTORY

ACES, INC.
188 Montague Street
Brooklyn, NY 11201
Phone: (718) 237-2900
Fax: (718) 522-3906
www.acesincbaseball.com
ACES@acesinc1.com
Seth Levinson, Esq; Sam Levinson;
Keith Miller; Peter Pedalino, Esq;
Mike Zimmerman; Jamie Appel;
Brandon O'Hearn; Josh Yates;
Eric McQueen; Josh Borkin, Esq;
Anthony Lovende, Esq

JACKSON MANAGEMENT GROUP, LLC
132 North Old Woodward Ave.
Birmingham, MI 48009
Phone: (248) 594-1070
Fax: (248) 281-5150
www.jackson-management.com
baseball@jackson-management.com
Storm T. Kirschenbaum, Esq; Hector
Faneytt; Michael Bonanno; Jack Fang

KPT SPORTS
200 Central Avenue
24th Floor
St. Petersburg, FL 33701
Phone: (727) 898-5786
Fax: (727) 821-1211
KPTsports.com
info@KPTsports.com
Ed Kravitz, Esq.; Aaron Ledesma;
Travis Phelps

THE L. WARNER COMPANIES, INC
9690 Deereco Rd., Ste. 650
Timonium, MD 21093
Phone: (410) 252-0808
Fax: (443) 281-5554
www.lwarner.com/baseball
roliver@lwarner.com
Lee Warner, Chairman and CEO;
Rick Oliver, President

THE LEGACY AGENCY
1500 Broadway, Suite 2501
New York, NY 10036
Phone: (212) 334-6880
Fax: (212) 334-6895
www.legacy-agency.com
info@legacy-agency.com
Peter E. Greenberg, Esq;
Edward L. Greenberg; Chris Leible; Eric Izen

THE LEGACY AGENCY
500 Newport Center Dr., Ste 800
Newport Beach, CA 92660
Phone: (949) 720-8700
Fax: (949) 720-1331
www.legacy-agency.com
info@legacy-agency.com
Greg Genske; Brian Peters; Brodie Scoffield;
RJ Hernandez; Kenny Felder;
Joe Brennan;Joe Mizzo; Hiram Bocachica;
Mike Maulini

ONYX SPORTS MANAGEMENT
60 E. Rio Salado Pkwy., Suite 900
Tempe, AZ 85281
Phone: (480) 643-9112; (480) 213-2421
Fax: (480) 696-5474
www.onyxsm.com
jcook@onyxsm.com; zprice@onyxsm.com
Jesse Cook, Esq; Zach Price, Esq

PRO STAR MANAGEMENT, INC,
1600 Scripps Center, 312 Walnut Street
Cincinnati, OH 45202
Phone: (513) 762-7676
Fax: (513) 721-4628
www.prostarmanagement.com
prostar@fuse.net
Joe Bick, President;
Brett Bick, Executive Vice President;
Jeff Gatch, Recruiting Coordinator

SOSNICK COBBE SPORTS
712 Bancroft Rd., #510
Walnut Creek, CA 94598
Phone: (925) 890-5283
Fax: (925) 476-0130
www.sosnickcobbesports.com
Mattsoz@aol.com
PaulCobbe@me.com
Matt Sosnick; Paul Cobbe; Adam Karon;
Matt Hofer; Jonathan Pridie;
Tripper Johnson; John Furmaniak

VERRILL DANA SPORTS LAW GROUP
One Portland Square
Portland, ME 04101
Phone: (207) 774-4000
Fax: (207) 774-7499
www.verrilldana.com
dabramson@verrilldana.com
David S. Abramson, Esq

SERVICE DIRECTORY

ACCESSORIES

WILSON SPORTING GOODS
8750 West Bryn Mawr Ave.
13th Floor
Chicago, IL 60631
Phone: (800) 333-8326
Fax: (773) 714-4565
www.wilson.com
askwilson@wilson.com

APPAREL

B45 – THE ORIGINAL YELLOW BIRCH BAT COMPANY
281 Rue Edward-Assh
Ste-Catherine-de-la-Cartier, QC
G3N 1A3
Phone: (888) 669-0145
Fax: (418) 875-3535
www.b45online.com
info@b45online.com
MLB/Pro Contact: Rick Kramer
(301) 346-1046 rkramer@b45online.com

DEMARINI
6435 NW Croeni Rd.
Hillsboro, OR 97124
Phone: (800) 937-BATS (2287)
Fax: (503) 531-5506
www.demarini.com

MINOR LEAGUES, MAJOR DREAMS
P.O. Box 6098
Anaheim, CA 92816
Phone: (800) 345-2421
Fax: (714) 939-0655
www.minorleagues.com
mlmd@minorleagues.com

BAGS

DEMARINI
6435 NW Croeni Rd.
Hillsboro, OR 97124
Phone: (800) 937-BATS (2287)
Fax: (503) 531-5506
www.demarini.com

DIAMOND BASEBALL
1880 E. St. Andrew Place
Santa Ana, CA 92705
Phone: (714) 415-7600
Fax: (714) 415-7601
www.diamond-sports.com
info@diamond-sports.com

GERRY COSBY AND COMPANY
11 Pennsylvania Plaza
New York, NY 10001
Phone: (877) 563-6464
Fax: (212) 967-0876
www.cosbysports.com
gcsmsg@cosbysport.com

LOUISVILLE SLUGGER
800 W. Main St.
Louisville, KY 40202
Phone: (800) 282-2287
Fax: (502) 585-1179
www.slugger.com
customer.service@slugger.com

WILSON SPORTING GOODS
8750 West Bryn Mawr Ave.
13th Floor
Chicago, IL 60631
Phone: (800) 333-8326
Fax: (773) 714-4565
www.wilson.com
askwilson@wilson.com

BASEBALLS

DIAMOND BASEBALL
1880 E. St. Andrew Place
Santa Ana, CA 92705
Phone: (714) 415-7600
Fax: (714) 415-7601
www.diamond-sports.com
info@diamond-sports.com

WILSON SPORTING GOODS
8750 West Bryn Mawr Ave.
13th Floor
Chicago, IL 60631
Phone: (773) 333-8326
Fax: (773) 714-4565
www.wilson.com
askwilson@wilson.com

BASES

BEAM CLAY
One Kelsey Park
Great Meadows, NJ 7838
Phone: (800) 247-BEAM (2326)
Fax: (908) 637-8421
www.beamclay.com
sales@beamclay.com

See our ad on the the inside back cover!

BATS

B45 – THE ORIGINAL YELLOW BIRCH BAT COMPANY
281 Rue Edward-Assh
Ste-Catherine-de-la-Cartier, QC G3N 1A3
Phone: (888) 669-0145
Fax: (418) 875-3535
www.b45online.com
info@b45online.com
MLB/Pro Contact: Rick Kramer
(301) 346-1046 rkramer@b45online.com

BWP BATS
80 Womeldorf Lane
Brookville, PA 15825
Phone: (814) 849-0089
Fax: (814) 849-8584
www.shopbwp.com
josh@bwpbats.com

DEMARINI
6435 NW Croeni Rd.
Hillsboro, OR 97124
Phone: (800) 937-BATS (2287)
Fax: (503) 531-5506
www.demarini.com

DINGER BATS
109 S. Kimbro St.
Ridgway, IL 62979
Phone: (618) 272-7250
Fax: (618) 272-7253
www.dingerbats.com
info@dingerbats.com

LOUISVILLE SLUGGER
800 W. Main St.
Louisville, KY 40202
Phone: (800) 282-2287
Fax: (502) 585-1179
www.slugger.com
customer.service@slugger.com

OLD HICKORY BAT COMPANY
P.O Box 588
White House, TN 37188
Phone: (615) 285-0588
Fax: (615) 285-0512
www.oldhickorybats.com
mail@oldhickorybats.com

VIPER BATS
4807 Ivan Lane
Sedro Woolley, WA 98284
Phone: (360) 630-5168
Fax: (360) 205-7488
www.viperbats.com
sales@viperbats.com

BATTING CAGES

BEAM CLAY
One Kelsey Park
Great Meadows, NJ 7838
Phone: (800) 247-BEAM (2326)
Fax: (908) 637-8421
www.beamclay.com
sales@beamclay.com

See our ad on the the inside back cover!

C&H BASEBALL, INC
10615 Technology Terrace, #100
Bradenton, FL 34211
Phone: (800) 248-5192
Fax: (941) 727-0588
www.chbaseball.com
info@chbaseball.com

MASTER PITCHING MACHINE, INC.
4200 NE Birmingham Rd.
Kansas City, MO 64117
Phone: (800) 878-8228
Fax: (816) 452-7581
www.masterpitch.com
joeg@masterpitch.com

NATIONAL SPORTS PRODUCTS
3441 S 11th Ave.
Eldridge, IA 52748
Phone: (800) 478-6497
Fax: (800) 443-8407
www.nationalsportsproducts.com
sales@nationalsportsproducts.com

WEST COAST NETTING
5075 Flightline Dr.
Kingman, AZ 86401
Phone: (928) 692-1144
Fax: (928) 692-1501
www.westcoastnetting.com
juhles@westcoastnetting.com

BATTING GLOVES

DEMARINI
6435 NW Croeni Rd.
Hillsboro, OR 97124
Phone: (800) 937-BATS (2287)
Fax: (503) 531-5506
www.demarini.com

CAPS/HEADWEAR

MINOR LEAGUES, MAJOR DREAMS
P.O. Box 6098
Anaheim, CA 92816
Phone: (800) 345-2421
Fax: (714) 939-0655
www.minorleagues.com
mlmd@minorleagues.com

OC SPORTS
1201 Melissa Drive
Bentonville, AR 72712
Phone: (866) 776-6774
Fax: (866) 776-1010
www.ocsports.com
customsports@ocsports.com

CONCESSION OPERATIONS

STADIUM1 SOFTWARE, LLC.
13479 Polo Trace Drive
Delray Beach, FL 33446
Phone: (561) 779-4040
Fax: (561) 498-8358
www.stadium1.com
tim.mcdulin@stadium1.com

THUNDERBIRD MARKETING
4938 E Kemper Rd.
Cincinnati, OH 45241
Phone: (513) 399-4816
Fax: (513) 530-9546
www.unclejohnsburgerdog.com;
www.gorocktops.com
bob.thunderbird@fuse.net

EMBROIDERED PATCHES

THE EMBLEM SOURCE
4575 Westgrove #500
Addison, TX 75001
Phone: (972) 248-1909
Fax: (972) 248-1615
www.theemblemsource.com
larry@theemblemsource.com

ENTERTAINMENT

BUCKET RUCKUS
P.O. Box 36061
Louisville, KY 40233
Phone: (502) 458-4020
Fax: (502) 458-0867
www.theskillvillegroup.com/
bucket_ruckus.html
info@theskillvillegroup.com

SCOLLON PRODUCTIONS
P.O. Box 486
White Rock, SC 29177
Phone: (803) 345-3922 x43
Fax: (803) 345-9313
www.scollon.com
rbrian@scollon.com

THE SKILLVILLE GROUP – ZOOPERSTARS!
P.O. Box 36061
Louisville, KY 40233
Phone: (502) 458-4020
Fax: (502) 458-0867
www.theskillvillegroup.com
info@theskillvillegroup.com

FIELD COVERS/TARPS

BEAM CLAY
One Kelsey Park
Great Meadows, NJ 7838
Phone: (800) 247-BEAM (2326)
Fax: (908) 637-8421
www.beamclay.com
sales@beamclay.com

See our ad on the the inside back cover!

COVERMASTER, INC.
100 Westmore Dr. 11-D
Rexdale, ON
M9V 5C3
Phone: (800) 387-5808
Fax: (416) 742-6837
www.covermaster.com
info@covermaster.com

C&H BASEBALL, INC
10615 Technology Terrace, #100
Bradenton, FL 34211
Phone: (800) 248-5192
Fax: (941) 727-0588
www.chbaseball.com
info@chbaseball.com

SOUTHERN ATHLETIC FIELDS, INC.
1309 Mainsail Dr.
Columbia, TN 38401
Phone: (800) 837-8062
Fax: (931) 380-0145
www.safdirt.com
saf@safdirt.com

FIELD EQUIPMENT

DIAMOND BASEBALL
1880 E. St. Andrew Place
Santa Ana, CA 92705
Phone: (714) 415-7600
Fax: (714) 415-7601
www.diamond-sports.com
info@diamond-sports.com

FIELD WALL PADDING

BEAM CLAY
One Kelsey Park
Great Meadows, NJ 7838
Phone: (800) 247-BEAM (2326)
Fax: (908) 637-8421
www.beamclay.com
sales@beamclay.com

See our ad on the the inside back cover!

COVERMASTER, INC.
100 Westmore Dr. 11-D
Rexdale, ON
M9V 5C3
Phone: (800) 387-5808
Fax: (416) 742-6837
www.covermaster.com
info@covermaster.com

C&H BASEBALL, INC
10615 Technology Terrace, #100
Bradenton, FL 34211
Phone: (800) 248-5192
Fax: (941) 727-0588
www.chbaseball.com
info@chbaseball.com

NATIONAL SPORTS PRODUCTS
3441 S 11th Ave.
Eldridge, IA 52748
Phone: (800) 478-6497
Fax: (800) 443-8407
www.nationalsportsproducts.com
sales@nationalsportsproducts.com

WEST COAST NETTING
5075 Flightline Dr.
Kingman, AZ 86401
Phone: (928) 692-1144
Fax: (928) 692-1501
www.westcoastnetting.com
juhles@westcoastnetting.com

FIREWORKS

PYROTECNICO
P.O. Box 149
New Castle, PA 16103
Phone: (800) 854-4705
Fax: (724) 652-1288
www.pyrotecnico.com
info@pyrotecnico.com

FOOD SERVICE

STADIUM1 SOFTWARE, LLC.
13479 Polo Trace Drive
Delray Beach, FL 33446
Phone: (561) 779-4040
Fax: (561) 498-8358
www.stadium1.com
tim.mcdulin@stadium1.com

THUNDERBIRD MARKETING
4938 E Kemper Rd.
Cincinnati, OH 45241
Phone: (513) 399-4816
Fax: (513) 530-9546
www.unclejohnsburgerdog.com;
www.gorocktops.com
bob.thunderbird@fuse.net

GLOVES

B45 – THE ORIGINAL YELLOW BIRCH BAT COMPANY
281 Rue Edward-Assh
Ste-Catherine-de-la-Cartier, QC
G3N 1A3
Phone: (888) 669-0145
Fax: (418) 875-3535
www.b45online.com
info@b45online.com
MLB/Pro Contact: Rick Kramer
(301) 346-1046 rkramer@b45online.com

FRANK'S SPORT SHOP
430 E. Tremont Ave.
Bronx, NY 10457
Phone: (718) 299-5223 / (212) 945-0020
Fax: (718) 583-1653
www.frankssportshop.com

See our ad on the insert!

LOUISVILLE SLUGGER
800 W. Main St.
Louisville, KY 40202
Phone: (800) 282-2287
Fax: (502) 585-1179
www.slugger.com
customer.service@slugger.com

OLD HICKORY BAT COMPANY
P.O Box 588
White House, TN 37188
Phone: (615) 285-0588
Fax: (615) 285-0512
www.oldhickorybats.com
mail@oldhickorybats.com

WILSON SPORTING GOODS
8750 West Bryn Mawr Ave.
13th Floor
Chicago, IL 60631
Phone: (800) 333-8326
Fax: (773) 714-4565
www.wilson.com
askwilson@wilson.com

INSURANCE

K&K INSURANCE
1712 Magnavox Way
Fort Wayne, IN 46804
Phone: (800) 441-3994
Fax: (260) 459-5120
www.kandkinsurance.com
kk-sports@kandkinsurance.com

See our ad on the inside front cover!

MASCOTS

SCOLLON PRODUCTIONS
P.O. Box 486
White Rock, SC 29177
Phone: (803) 345-3922 x43
Fax: (803) 345-9313
www.scollon.com
rbrian@scollon.com

MOUND/PLATE CLAY

SOUTHERN ATHLETIC FIELDS, INC.
1309 Mainsail Dr.
Columbia, TN 38401
Phone: (800) 837-8062
Fax: (931) 380-0145
www.safdirt.com
saf@safdirt.com

MUSIC/SOUND EFFECTS

SOUND DIRECTOR, INC.
2918 SW Royal Way
Gresham, OR 97080
Phone: (503) 665-6869
Fax: (503) 914-1812
www.sounddirector.com
jj@sounddirector.com

NETTING/POSTS

BEAM CLAY
One Kelsey Park
Great Meadows, NJ 7838
Phone: (800) 247-BEAM (2326)
Fax: (908) 637-8421
www.beamclay.com
sales@beamclay.com

See our ad on the the inside back cover!

C&H BASEBALL, INC
10615 Technology Terrace, #100
Bradenton, FL 34211
Phone: (800) 248-5192
Fax: (941) 727-0588
www.chbaseball.com
info@chbaseball.com

NATIONAL SPORTS PRODUCTS
3441 S 11th Ave.
Eldridge, IA 52748
Phone: (800) 478-6497
Fax: (800) 443-8407
www.nationalsportsproducts.com
sales@nationalsportsproducts.com

WEST COAST NETTING
5075 Flightline Dr.
Kingman, AZ 86401
Phone: (928) 692-1144
Fax: (928) 692-1501
www.westcoastnetting.com
juhles@westcoastnetting.com

PITCHING MACHINES

ATHLETIC TRAINING EQUIPMENT COMPANY – ATEC
655 Spice Island Dr.
Sparks, NV 89431
Phone: (800) 998-ATEC (2832)
Fax: (800)-959-ATEC (2832)
www.atecsports.com
askATEC@wilson.com

C&H BASEBALL, INC
10615 Technology Terrace, #100
Bradenton, FL 34211
Phone: (800) 248-5192
Fax: (941) 727-0588
www.chbaseball.com
info@chbaseball.com

MASTER PITCHING MACHINE, INC.
4200 NE Birmingham Rd.
Kansas City, MO 64117
Phone: (800) 878-8228
Fax: (816) 452-7581
www.masterpitch.com
joeg@masterpitch.com

SPORTS TUTOR, INC
3300 Winona Ave.
Burbank, CA 91504
Phone: (818) 972-2772
Fax: (818) 972-9651
www.sportsmachines.com
customerservice@sportstutorinc.com

PLAYING FIELD PRODUCTS

APPLIED CONCEPTS
2609 Technology Dr.
Plano, TX 75074
Phone: 1 (888) STALKER
Fax: (972) 398-3781
www.stalkerradar.com
sales@stalkerradar.com

See our ad on page 2!

BEAM CLAY
One Kelsey Park
Great Meadows, NJ 7838
Phone: (800) 247-BEAM (2326)
Fax: (908) 637-8421
www.beamclay.com
sales@beamclay.com

See our ad on the the inside back cover!

C&H BASEBALL, INC
10615 Technology Terrace, #100
Bradenton, FL 34211
Phone: (800) 248-5192
Fax: (941) 727-0588
www.chbaseball.com
info@chbaseball.com

SOUTHERN ATHLETIC FIELDS, INC.
1309 Mainsail Dr.
Columbia, TN 38401
Phone: (800) 837-8062
Fax: (931) 380-0145
www.safdirt.com
saf@safdirt.com

POINT OF SALE ITEMS

STADIUM1 SOFTWARE, LLC.
13479 Polo Trace Drive
Delray Beach, FL 33446
Phone: (561) 779-4040
Fax: (561) 498-8358
www.stadium1.com
tim.mcdulin@stadium1.com

PRINTING

WORLDWIDE TICKETCRAFT
3606 Quantum Blvd.
Boynton Beach, FL 33426
Phone: (877) 426-5754
Fax: (954) 426-5761
www.worldwideticketcraft.com
brian@wwticket.com

PROTECTIVE EQUIPMENT

BEAM CLAY
One Kelsey Park
Great Meadows, NJ 7838
Phone: (800) 247-BEAM (2326)
Fax: (908) 637-8421
www.beamclay.com
sales@beamclay.com

See our ad on the the inside back cover!

C&H BASEBALL, INC
10615 Technology Terrace, #100
Bradenton, FL 34211
Phone: (800) 248-5192
Fax: (941) 727-0588
www.chbaseball.com
info@chbaseball.com

DIAMOND BASEBALL
1880 E. St. Andrew Place
Santa Ana, CA 92705
Phone: (714) 415-7600
Fax: (714) 415-7601
www.diamond-sports.com
info@diamond-sports.com

WILSON SPORTING GOODS
8750 West Bryn Mawr Ave.
13th Floor
Chicago, IL 60631
Phone: (800) 333-8326
Fax: (773) 714-4565
www.wilson.com
askwilson@wilson.com

WEST COAST NETTING
5075 Flightline Dr.
Kingman, AZ 86401
Phone: (928) 692-1144
Fax: (928) 692-1501
www.westcoastnetting.com
juhles@westcoastnetting.com

RADAR EQUIPMENT

APPLIED CONCEPTS
2609 Technology Dr.
Plano, TX 75074
Phone: 1 (888) STALKER
Fax: (972) 398-3781
www.stalkerradar.com
sales@stalkerradar.com

See our ad on page 2!

SHOES

FRANK'S SPORT SHOP
430 E. Tremont Ave.
Bronx, NY 10457
Phone: (718) 299-5223 / (212) 945-0020
Fax: (718) 583-1653
www.frankssportshop.com

See our ad on the insert!

SPECIAL EFFECTS/LASERS

PYROTECNICO
P.O. Box 149
New Castle, PA 16103
Phone: (800) 854-4705
Fax: (724) 652-1288
www.pyrotecnico.com
info@pyrotecnico.com

TICKETS

WORLDWIDE TICKETCRAFT
3606 Quantum Blvd.
Boynton Beach, FL 33426
Phone: (877) 426-5754
Fax: (954) 426-5761
www.worldwideticketcraft.com
brian@wwticket.com

TRAINING EQUIPMENT

ATHLETIC TRAINING EQUIPMENT COMPANY – ATEC
655 Spice Island Dr.
Sparks, NV 89431
Phone: (800) 998-ATEC (2832)
Fax: (800)-959-ATEC (2832)
www.atecsports.com
askATEC@wilson.com

LOUISVILLE SLUGGER
800 W. Main St.
Louisville, KY 40202
Phone: (800) 282-2287
Fax: (502) 585-1179
www.slugger.com
customer.service@slugger.com

TRAVEL

SPORTS TRAVEL AND TOURS
P.O. Box 50
60 Main Street
Hatfield, MA 01038
Phone: (800) 662-4424
Fax: (413) 247-5700
www.sportstravelandtours.com

UNIFORMS

B45 – THE ORIGINAL YELLOW BIRCH BAT COMPANY
281 Rue Edward-Assh
Ste-Catherine-de-la-Cartier, QC
G3N 1A3
Phone: (888) 669-0145
Fax: (418) 875-3535
www.b45online.com
info@b45online.com
MLB/Pro Contact: Rick Kramer 301-346-1046 rkramer@b45online.com

WILSON SPORTING GOODS
8750 West Bryn Mawr Ave.
13th Floor
Chicago, IL 60631
Phone: (800) 333-8326
Fax: (773) 714-4565
www.wilson.com
askwilson@wilson.com

WINDSCREENS

BEAM CLAY
One Kelsey Park
Great Meadows, NJ 7838
Phone: (800) 247-BEAM (2326)
Fax: (908) 637-8421
www.beamclay.com
sales@beamclay.com

See our ad on the the inside back cover!

COVERMASTER, INC.
100 Westmore Dr. 11-D
Rexdale, ON
M9V 5C3
Phone: (800) 387-5808
Fax: (416) 742-6837
www.covermaster.com
info@covermaster.com

C&H BASEBALL, INC
10615 Technology Terrace, #100
Bradenton, FL 34211
Phone: (800) 248-5192
Fax: (941) 727-0588
www.chbaseball.com
info@chbaseball.com

NATIONAL SPORTS PRODUCTS
3441 S 11th Ave.
Eldridge, IA 52748
Phone: (800) 478-6497
Fax: (800) 443-8407
www.nationalsportsproducts.com
sales@nationalsportsproducts.com

SOUTHERN ATHLETIC FIELDS, INC.
1309 Mainsail Dr.
Columbia, TN 38401
Phone: (800) 837-8062
Fax: (931) 380-0145
www.safdirt.com
saf@safdirt.com

WEST COAST NETTING
5075 Flightline Dr.
Kingman, AZ 86401
Phone: (928) 692-1144
Fax: (928) 692-1501
www.westcoastnetting.com
juhles@westcoastnetting.com

YOUR NAME HERE. Make sure the baseball community can find you in 2016
Call 919-213-7924 or e-mail advertising@baseballamerica.com

INDEX

MAJOR LEAGUE TEAMS

MINOR LEAGUE TEAMS

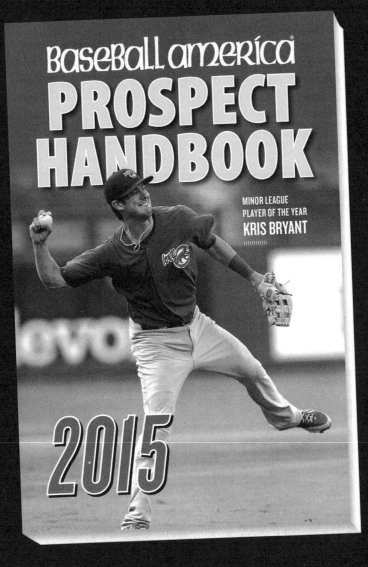